Financial Accounting

Written in a very friendly, easy-to-read style, this excellent ..ancial accounting text will suit beginners as well as more experienced learners. Comprehensive and up-to-date, it enables readers to explore different angles of financial reporting. It makes good use of a number of relevant contemporary examples, which helps with maintaining student motivation.

Petros Vourvachis, *Lecturer in Financial Accounting, Loughborough University, UK*

Financial accounting is the branch of accounting thought and practice concerned with preparing and providing information for external users of financial statements. This textbook helps students to understand the underlying concepts that underpin the theory of financial accounting in the solution of accounting problems.

This international edition includes learning-path tools at the beginning of each chapter, extracts from the financial statements of listed companies, definitions of key terms and exam examples. Unlike other textbooks, *Financial Accounting* provides analysis of why accountants do what they do and not just how. With such a wealth of accounting models and diagrams intertwined with this analysis, this book guides the reader through all the concepts and practicalities of financial accounting.

This book is an essential guide for students new to accountancy and finance and an equally useful tool for more experienced students and researchers.

David Kolitz is Senior Lecturer in Accounting at the University of Exeter, UK.

A companion website for this book is available at www.routledge.com/cw/kolitz

Financial Accounting

A concepts-based introduction

David Kolitz

LONDON AND NEW YORK

First published 2017
by Routledge
2 Park Square, Milton Park, Abingdon, Oxon OX14 4RN

and by Routledge
711 Third Avenue, New York, NY 10017

Routledge is an imprint of the Taylor & Francis Group, an informa business

British Library Cataloguing in Publication Data
A catalogue record for this book is available from the British Library

Library of Congress Cataloging in Publication Data
Names: Kolitz, David L., author.
Title: Financial accounting: a concepts-based introduction/David Kolitz.
Description: Abingdon, Oxon; New York, NY: Routledge, 2017.
Identifiers: LCCN 2016024035 | ISBN 9781138844964 (hardback) | ISBN 9781138844971 (pbk.) | ISBN 9781315728445 (ebook)
Subjects: LCSH: Accounting.
Classification: LCC HF5635.K792 2017 | DDC 657–dc23
LC record available at https://lccn.loc.gov/2016024035

ISBN: (hbk) 978-1-138-84496-4
ISBN: (pbk) 978-1-138-84497-1
ISBN: (ebk) 978-1-315-72844-5

Typeset in Bembo
by Sunrise Setting Ltd, Brixham, UK

Printed and bound in the United States of America by
Edwards Brothers Malloy on sustainably sourced paper

To Maeve

Contents

Preface

Pedagogical philosophy

The literature refers to the procedural and conceptual approaches in the teaching of an introductory accounting course. The procedural course is usually described as being concerned mainly with the techniques of double-entry bookkeeping, while the conceptual approach in its pure form moves away from the techniques of accounting for transactions and uses a decision-making approach as the foundation for explaining the need and role of accounting in society.

It is submitted that the procedural approach places too much emphasis on how to perform various techniques rather than why these techniques are performed. It is proposed that this may not develop the student's ability to apply the techniques to practical situations. On the other hand, the application of the pure conceptual approach places little emphasis on the techniques of double-entry bookkeeping.

The *concepts* model integrates the conceptual and procedural approaches to the teaching of introductory accounting by teaching students to understand the *why* of accounting before considering the *how* of accounting. This impacts on both the order of the teaching of topics and the way in which the various topics are taught.

Features

The requirements and terminology of the latest IAS 1 have been incorporated throughout the book. The statement of profit or loss is introduced and used throughout, except where there are items of comprehensive income, where a statement of comprehensive income is used. The statement of financial position is used throughout instead of the balance sheet.

The text takes account of the latest amendments in the *Conceptual Framework* project as well as the latest relevant International Financial Reporting Standards.

Learning path tools are included at the beginning of each chapter. These include a *Business focus* section, where a real life scenario is discussed in the context of the chapter contents, as well as a *Dashboard*, which guides the student on how to study the particular chapter. Other features include the *Key definitions*, highlighted in each chapter, and the *Pause and reflect* scenarios. The former give students a focus when reading the text and are useful for revision purposes. The latter are short scenarios, both narrative and numerical, designed to confirm understanding, illustrate a specific point or make the reader think about the meaning and implication of the preceding paragraphs.

The transactions in the *Smart Concepts* case study (that runs from Chapters 2 to 7) are grouped into distinct sets to make the case study manageable and understandable to students. In addition, there is an innovative way of explaining and linking each transaction to the conceptual underpinning: the accounting equation and the double-entry system.

All journal entry account names have a suffix, A (asset), L (liability), I (income), E (expense) and OE (owner's equity). This helps students to understand journal entries and constantly relate back to the conceptual underpinnings. Although 'bank' could be an asset or liability, it is designated throughout the book as an asset.

Within each chapter, there are extracts from published financial statements of listed companies, together with a short discussion inviting students to consider the *Concepts in context*. The discussion shows students the practical relevance of what they have read in the chapter.

All examples have explanations so that students can see the 'why' as well as the 'how'.

Outline

In Part I, *A conceptual overview*, the entity concept (separation of the business entity and the owner from an accounting perspective) is emphasised as being essential to the understanding of how transactions affect owner's equity. The *Conceptual Framework* definitions of the elements of the financial statements (assets, liabilities, equity, income and expenses) are introduced and form the basis of analysing transactions. The *accrual basis* of accounting is described in detail and is used as the basis to explain how a statement of profit or loss and a statement of financial position are prepared. Complete, albeit simple, financial statements are drawn up based on the conceptual introduction without any reference to debits and credits or the double-entry bookkeeping system.

The accounting equation in the form of 'assets = liabilities + owner's equity' is introduced next, and transactions are analysed by examining the effect that the transaction has on the assets, liabilities or owner's equity. If the transaction affects owner's equity, it is analysed further into income, expense or other items affecting owner's equity (contributions by the owner or distributions to the owner). Emphasis is placed on an appreciation of the impact of transactions on owner's equity. The change in owner's equity is analysed, and after reversing the effect of investments and distributions, the profit for the period can be established. The statement of profit or loss is drawn up by extracting the income and expense items from the analysis of owner's equity and the statement of financial position is drawn up by including the balances on each asset, liability and the owner's equity column from the accounting equation. There is still no reference at this stage to debit or credit rules and the double-entry system.

Part II, *The accounting process*, introduces double-entry bookkeeping as a direct outgrowth of the *Conceptual Framework* and the accounting equation. Debits and credits are taught as a form of recording changes in the components of the accounting equation, and extensive emphasis is placed on understanding debits and credits in the context of the *Conceptual Framework* and the accounting equation before teaching the procedural aspects of recording transactions in a journal and posting to a ledger.

Adjusting entries are introduced conceptually as part of the accrual basis of accounting, and the statement of profit or loss and statement of financial position effects of adjusting entries are taught by reference to the *Conceptual Framework* definitions.

The accounting equation worksheet is used to explain further the impact of adjusting entries on the statement of profit or loss and statement of financial position, before finally considering the debits and credits involved.

Closing entries are then taught as a procedural exercise after the preparation of the financial statements.

A unique feature of this book is the use of a common example to explain the accounting process throughout Chapters 2 to 7. The transactions of a computer retailer, Simon Smart, who operates under the name of Smart Concepts, are used. Using the concepts model, students learn how to analyse transactions and prepare a statement of profit or loss, statement of financial position and statement of changes in equity in Chapter 2, using the principles of the *Conceptual Framework* only. The same transactions are analysed in Chapter 3 using an accounting equation worksheet and students recognise that the financial statements prepared are the same as in Chapter 2. In Chapter 4, the same transactions are processed again, this time through a bookkeeping system where the transactions are entered in a journal and posted to a ledger, and a trial balance is extracted. The resultant financial statements are identical to those prepared using the principles of the *Conceptual Framework* in Chapter 2 and the accounting equation in Chapter 3. When considering the adjusting entries in Chapter 5, students understand the reasons for the adjustments having been exposed to these transactions on a conceptual level in earlier chapters.

Part III, *The accounting process expanded*, deals with further relevant and practical issues not covered in Part II, including the specific issues relating to the purchase and sale of inventory as well as additional procedural aspects concerning the use of cash, sales and purchases journals.

Part IV, *Recognition and measurement of the elements of the financial statements*, includes sections on property, plant and equipment and depreciation; inventory and cost of sales; accounts receivable and bad debts; cash and bank; current liabilities as well as non-current liabilities, and owner's equity. Emphasis in teaching is on the *Conceptual Framework* definitions of assets and liabilities and on the impact of relevant transactions on the accounting equation.

Part V, *Entity forms*, deals with partnerships and companies. The emphasis is placed here on how profit is distributed to the owners in the various entity forms and on the composition of owner's equity in each entity form.

Part VI deals with various topics often found in an introductory accounting course, such as statements of cash flow, analysis of financial statements, accounting for non-business entities and incomplete records.

Icons used in text

The following is a list of the icons used throughout the text to assist in teaching, learning and understanding:

Key definitions. This enables the reader to focus on important definitions when reading the text and is useful for revision purposes.

Pause and reflect. These are short scenarios, both narrative and numerical, designed to confirm understanding, illustrate a specific point or make the reader think about the meaning and implication of the preceding paragraphs.

Concepts in context. Extracts from published financial statements of listed companies highlighting the practical relevance of what has been read in the chapter.

This indicates an example.

This indicates a solution.

This indicates an explanation.

Supplements

Lecturers' support material includes PowerPoint slides as well as notes for each chapter. The teaching notes provide guidance on the concepts-based approach and are also useful to assist lecturers in the presentation of each topic. There are over 300 slides that closely follow the order of each chapter and include selected diagrams from the book as well as solutions to the main examples. These are made available to prescribing institutions.

For each chapter, a selection of multiple choice questions, shorter exercises and longer problems are available on-line.

PART I

A conceptual overview

1 The accounting environment

Business focus

In a speech delivered in Japan in November 2014, the chairman of the IFRS Foundation trustees, Michel Prada, said that the IFRS Foundation and the International Accounting Standards Board (IASB) had evolved into a global accounting standard setter. International Financial Reporting Standards (IFRS) are the predominant basis on which companies' financial statements are prepared because 'investors have a clear bias for the familiar' and that IFRS have become the means to provide that familiarity to international investors.

He said that companies or jurisdictions that decide not to apply IFRS would need to be aware of becoming increasingly isolated and that the 'costs of being outside the familiarity of the IFRS system' would rise in the future.

He commented that the option of voluntary adoption of IFRS was being watched carefully by jurisdictions around the world as it would allow larger, multinational companies to benefit from IFRS without obliging smaller domestic companies to adopt IFRS. However, he was hesitant when it came to modified IFRS as he believed that investor familiarity can only come from the full use of IFRS.

You will be introduced to the role of the IASB and IFRS in this chapter and learn about some of the IFRS in later chapters.

In this chapter

While you may not be certain about your future career, what is certain is that accounting will play an important role in your life. Even the most seemingly simple tasks like managing your bank account, reading your own payslip or buying a car are going to require some level of financial literacy. It should therefore come as no surprise that, directly or indirectly, you are going to be exposed to financial information as part of day-to-day business activities, and you need to be in a position to interpret that information correctly.

This chapter introduces you to accounting and allows you to become familiar with some basic concepts of business as well as accounting terminology before moving on to the rest of the book.

Dashboard

- Look at the *Learning outcomes* so that you know what you should be able to do after studying this chapter.
- Read the *Business focus* to place this chapter's contents in a real-world context.
- Preview *In this chapter* to focus your mind on its contents.
- Read the *text* in detail.
- Apply your mind to the *Pause and reflect* scenarios.

You will be introduced to a lot of new words and terms in this chapter, and you are advised to pay attention to their meaning, as you will encounter them frequently throughout the book.

Learning outcomes

After studying this chapter, you should be able to do the following:

1. Describe how a business works.
2. Describe the value of information in the commercial decision-making process.
3. Recall the various forms of ownership of business entities and the different types of business.
4. Describe the role of financial information in the accounting information system.
5. Recall and explain the objective of financial reporting, and describe how it relates to the users of financial information and the qualitative characteristics.
6. Discuss the role of accounting standards and the IASB.
7. Identify the four main fields of accounting activity.
8. Explain the importance of internal control in a business entity.

The accounting environment

1.1 How a business works

Accounting is often described as the language of business. Before beginning your journey of learning accounting, it is important for you to have a basic understanding of how a business works and an introduction to some of the terminology of accounting and business.

Owners of a business, known as ***investors***, contribute funding to the business, known as ***equity***. Further funding is obtained by borrowing from ***lenders***, referred to as ***liabilities***. The funds are used to buy ***assets***, often referred to as the *resources* of the business. Typical examples include property, plant and equipment, goods for resale to customers (known as inventory) and the remaining cash in the bank. Management of the business uses the resources to earn ***income***. During this process, ***expenses*** are incurred. The difference between income and expenses is known as the ***profit***, which reverts to the investors as an increase in equity.

This, in a nutshell, is how a business works. It is obviously simplified in an attempt to convey the essence in one understandable paragraph. All of the terms highlighted here will be explained and further developed as you read this chapter and other chapters in the book. To help you see this in context, Diagram 1.1 illustrates this process.

1.2 Decision making and information

In general, accounting is concerned with the identifying, recording and reporting of ***financial information*** needed to make economic decisions.

A decision is a choice between two or more alternatives and can be rational only when sufficient information is available. Every individual or group in society makes decisions about the future. Students make decisions about which university to attend, what courses to study and whether to apply for a bank loan. A bank manager decides whether to advance funds to a student or any other individual or *entity* applying for a loan. The management of a *business entity* decides how to finance operations of the entity, in other words whether

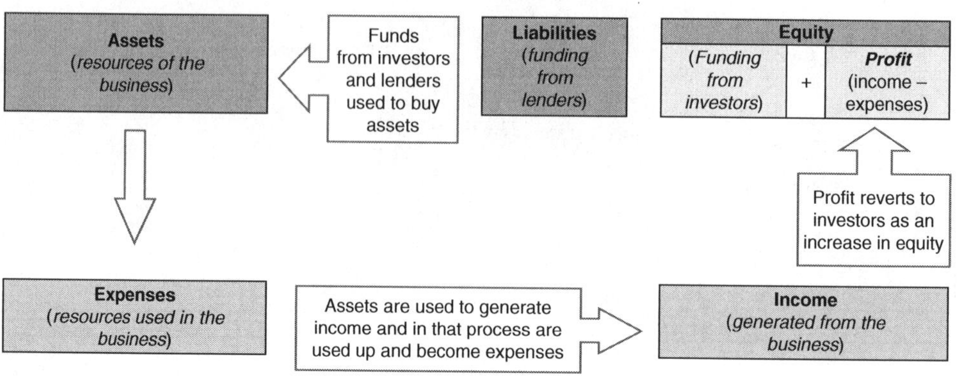

Diagram 1.1 How a business works

to borrow funds from a lender such as a financial institution or to obtain them from the owners. Individuals or organisations with cash available decide on the type of investment they wish to make.

You will frequently come across the term 'entity' in this book. An ***entity*** could be any individual, business or organisation with its own identity. The focus of this book is on a ***business entity***, often referred to as a ***reporting entity***, in the context of providing financial information. A separate chapter in Part VI (Chapter 20) is devoted to non-business entities.

A **business entity** is an organisation that uses economic resources for the primary goal of maximising profit. A **non-business entity** is concerned with providing a service to members.

Accounting contributes to these decisions by identifying what information will assist the various decision makers, how it should be recognised and measured, and how it should be communicated to them. Accounting provides information about an entity to ***users*** for decision-making purposes.

Users of financial information may be broadly categorised as ***primary users*** or as ***management***. Primary users are sometimes referred to as *external users* and management is sometimes referred to as *internal users*.

- Primary users, for example investors or lenders, are not involved in the management of an entity's activities but require financial information about the entity for decision making. They lack the ability to prescribe all the financial information they need from an entity and therefore must rely on information provided in financial reports.
- Management, who is responsible for the entity's activities, is also interested in financial information about the entity. Management, however, does have access to detailed information relating to the entity and is responsible for preparing financial information for the primary users. Management therefore does not need to rely only on the information provided in financial reports.

The relationship between internal and external users and their information needs is shown in Diagram 1.2. A more detailed discussion of users is provided in Section 1.5.1.

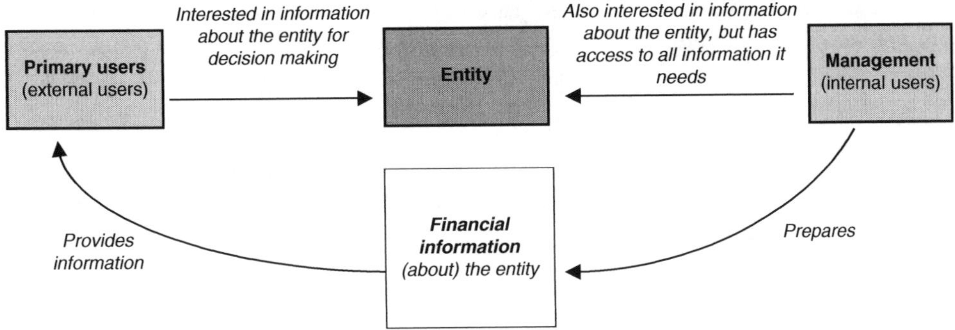

Diagram 1.2 Users and their information needs

Accounting thought and practice can be classified according to the user group to whom it is directed.

- ***Financial accounting*** is concerned with providing useful information about business entities for primary users.
- ***Management accounting*** is concerned with providing useful information related to the deployment of resources and the exploitation of opportunities for management.

The emphasis in this text is on financial accounting for primary users.

1.3 Introduction to business entities

Entrepreneurs are individuals who provide goods or services in response to demand from potential customers. They use their entrepreneurial skill together with the other factors of production (resources, labour and capital) to produce goods or services. They also take the risk that the income generated from the goods or services may or may not exceed the expenses incurred. In the business world, there are many different forms of ownership of a business entity and many different types of business entity. No matter what the form or type of business entity, accounting information is required for the successful running of the business and the making of decisions.

1.3.1 Forms of business ownership

Three forms of business ownership are found in practice:

- a sole proprietorship
- a partnership
- a company.

Entrepreneurs wishing to form a business entity consider a number of factors in deciding which of the forms to choose. These factors include the number of owners, access to funding and tax considerations, and whether to operate as an ***unincorporated*** or ***incorporated*** entity.

As you will see in the following paragraphs, a sole proprietorship and a partnership are *unincorporated* entities, whereas a company is an *incorporated* entity. The reason for this distinction lies in the legal form of the entity associated with each type of entity.

A sole proprietorship and a partnership are not formed or incorporated as legal entities through legislation and are thus known as unincorporated entities. On the other hand, a company is formed or incorporated as a separate legal entity from the owners and is thus known as an incorporated entity.

The sole proprietorship is used as the entity form in Parts 1 to 4 of this book. There are separate chapters dedicated to partnerships (Chapter 16) and companies (Chapter 17) in Part V. Each of the three entity forms are described briefly in the paragraphs that follow.

Sole proprietorship

This type of business entity is owned by one person. For small entities, this is a popular form of ownership since there are *no formal procedures* required to set up the entity. Expansion in the sole proprietorship is limited by the funding available to the owner.

The sole proprietorship or sole trader, as it is often referred to, is *not a separate legal entity* from its owner. It cannot be involved in any legal relationship or activity except in the name of the owner. The owner thus benefits from all profits earned through the business entity, but is also held personally liable for any debts that the business incurs.

For normal tax purposes, the sole proprietor is *not a separate taxable entity*, and therefore the owner is taxed on the activities of the business entity in his or her personal capacity.

Partnership

A partnership is widely used for comparatively small business entities that wish to take advantage of combined financial capital, managerial talent and experience. This form of entity is also frequently found amongst the professions, such as doctors, dentists, lawyers and accountants. However, some of the large audit, tax and advisory practices have chosen to incorporate.

A partnership is also not a legal entity that is separate from its owners and it has no separate legal standing from the members who constitute it. The individual partners are the joint owners of the assets and are jointly and severally liable for the liabilities of the partnership. In other words, each partner could incur unlimited liability for all the debts and obligations of the partnership.

A partnership is also *not a separate taxable entity*. The profits are taxed in the hands of the individual partners.

Company

As an *incorporated* entity, a company is a legal entity distinct from the persons who own it. The owners, known as ***shareholders***, own the company through ownership of the shares issued by it. They do not personally own its assets. They have no direct claim on the profit of the company, which becomes due to them only if it is distributed by way of dividends. As the shareholders and the company are separate legal persons, they enjoy what is known as ***limited liability***; in other words, the obligation of shareholders is limited to their investment in the shares of the company. A company, being a separate legal entity, is liable for the payment of tax on its profits.

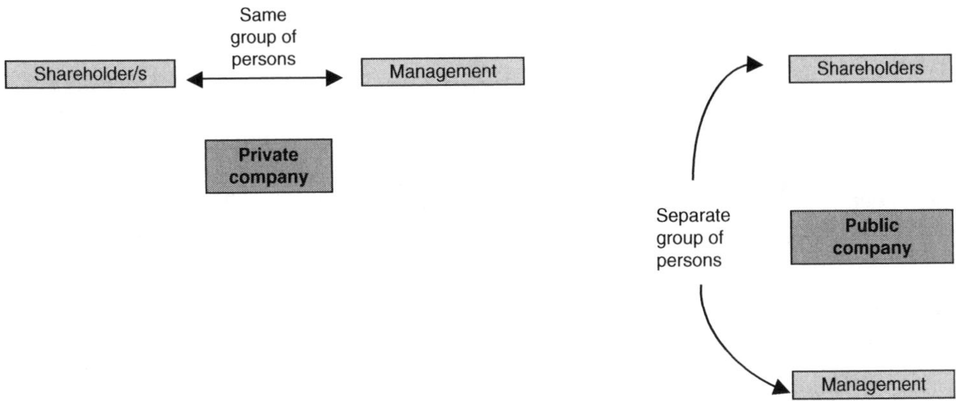

Diagram 1.3 Relationship between shareholders and management

There are four types of company that can be formed under the UK Companies Act 2006: companies whose liability is limited by shares (known as limited companies), companies with unlimited liability, companies whose liability is limited by guarantee and companies limited by shares and guarantee. There is a detailed discussion on the different types of companies in Chapter 17, *Companies*.

The focus here is on comparing the two types of limited companies, namely a private company and a public limited company, for the purpose of comparing the relationship between shareholders and management.

A **private company** may be formed and managed by just one person, who is the sole shareholder or director. There may be more than one shareholder or director, but a private company is typically used by small or micro businesses that wish to incorporate. The owner or owners and management are usually the same group of persons, similar to a sole proprietorship or partnership.

In the UK, the name of a private company must end with 'limited' or 'Ltd'.

A **public company** is typically used for larger business entities and is often listed on a stock exchange. Most listed public companies have hundreds, if not thousands, of shareholders and a large board of directors.

The shareholders are the owners of the company, and management, in the form of the board of directors, manages the company on their behalf. In comparison to a private company, shareholders and management are thus typically different groups of persons.

In the UK, the name of a public company must end with 'public limited company' or 'plc'. The relationship between shareholders and management in a private company compared to a public company is shown in Diagram 1.3.

1.3.2 Types of business entities

Business entities engage in different business activities. From an accounting point of view, it is important to understand the different activities that these businesses enter into in order to account for those activities.

Table 1.1 summarises the main types of business, illustrating for each type of business the activity performed, the nature of the income earned and an example of that type of business.

Table 1.1 Types of business entities

Type of business	*Activity*	*Income*	*Example*
Service entity	Provides a service to clients	Fees	Lawyers, accountants
Merchandising entity or retailer	Buys and sells goods to the public	Sales	Supermarket
Wholesaler	Buys and sells goods to the retailer	Sales	The fresh produce market
Manufacturer	Manufactures goods for resale	Sales	Car manufacturer
Agent	Performs services on behalf of someone else	Commission	Estate agent
Financial institution	Advances funds to individuals and business entities, and accepts funds for investment	Fees, interest	Bank

1.4 The nature of accounting

1.4.1 The accounting information system

Accounting is an information system which **selects data**, **processes that data** and **produces information** about an economic entity. Information is central to the operation of effective capital markets. Accounting, and more specifically financial accounting, has the unique role of reducing the risks and uncertainties that investors and lenders must deal with by providing useful information about the reporting entity. The input, processing and output of the system are governed by accounting principles, theory and concepts.

The accounting process begins by **selecting data** which has an economic impact upon the reporting entity. This can take the form of the receipt of cash, the payment of cash, and the purchase or sale of goods and services.

The **data is processed** in the accounting records. This activity is referred to as *bookkeeping*. Bookkeeping must not be confused with accounting, as in fact accounting involves much more than bookkeeping. Bookkeeping is that part of accounting that records transactions and other events, traditionally by entering the transactions into a book of original entry referred to as a *journal* and from there transferring the details into a list of accounts called a *ledger*. This will be described in Chapter 4, *Recording external transactions*. However, before looking at the bookkeeping procedures to process data, Chapter 2, *Fundamental accounting concepts*, will introduce the concepts and definitions which underpin the preparation of financial information. You will be shown how to process data on a conceptual level. In Chapter 3, *The accounting equation* and the analysis of transactions, you will be introduced to the concept of the accounting equation and be shown how to process data using the accounting equation.

Finally, **information** is produced in the form of the ***financial statements***. You will come across financial statements throughout this book, starting with Chapters 2, 3 and 4 where financial statements (as the information output of the accounting information system) are produced following the selection and processing of the data. A more detailed discussion on the financial statements is provided in Chapter 6, *Preparation and presentation of financial statements*. You will learn in all of these chapters that a basic set of financial statements comprises a *statement of profit or loss*, a *statement of financial position* and a *statement of changes in equity*. In addition, a statement of cash flows is also prepared and this is described in detail in Chapter 18, *Statement of cash flows*.

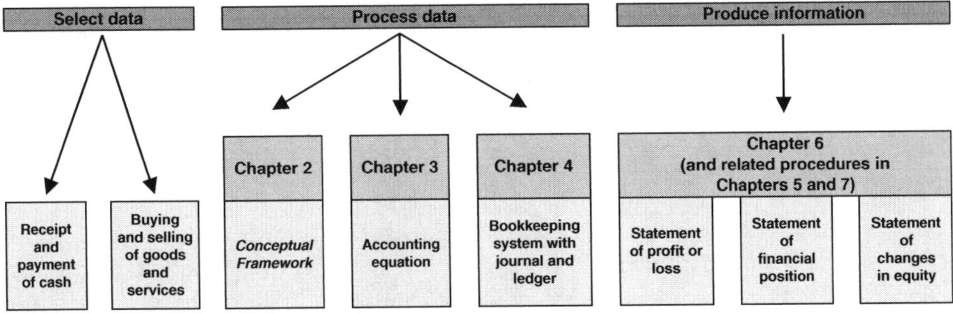

Diagram 1.4 The accounting information system

The accounting information system and how it relates to the structure of Parts I and II of this book, can be represented as shown in Diagram 1.4.

1.4.2 Financial reporting and financial statements

We will now briefly introduce the ***financial statements*** and discuss them in the context of wider ***financial reporting***.

Consider an investor who wishes to buy shares in a company listed on a stock exchange. There are many well-known stock exchanges around the world, including the New York Stock Exchange and the NASDAQ in the United States, the London Stock Exchange in the United Kingdom, the Deutsche Bourse in Germany and the JSE in South Africa.

The investor requires information about the entity's ***resources*** and ***claims against the entity*** as well as information about the entity's performance and cash flows. You read in Section 1.1 that the resources of an entity include items such as property, plant and equipment, inventory and cash in the bank. The claims against the entity are claims by the *lenders* and *investors*. The lenders have a claim against the entity for the funds loaned by them, usually referred to as borrowings or loans. In addition, the investors have a claim against the entity for the funds invested by them and for the profits earned. Refer back to Diagram 1.1 to see this.

The performance is represented by the *profit*, which is the income earned less the expenses incurred.

 **Pause and reflect...**

Can you understand why the investors have a claim against the entity? After all, are they not the owners?

Response

Investors are the owners of an entity. Remember, however, that an entity is any individual business or organisation with its own identity. The investors therefore are a *separate* entity to the business entity. Financial information relating to a business entity is produced from the *perspective of the business entity*. This is a very important concept and will be further developed in Chapter 2.

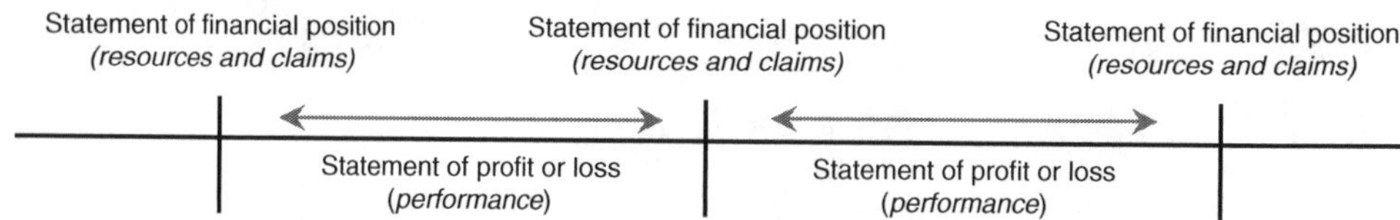

Diagram 1.5 Relationship between financial position and performance

A detailed discussion about the determination of the financial position and performance is provided in Chapter 2. For the moment, you should understand that the ***statement of financial position*** is a representation of the financial position (*resources of the entity* and *claims against the entity*) at a particular point in time and that the ***statement of profit or loss*** is a measure of the *performance* of an entity over a period of time.

This can be represented as shown in Diagram 1.5.

Remember that management prepares ***financial information*** for the primary users, investors and lenders. Much of this information is contained in the company's ***annual report***, which is a document produced by management for external users. The annual report of a listed company typically contains many parts, including financial and non-financial information. The ***financial statements*** form part of the wider annual report. Although annual reports are still printed and distributed, all listed companies have their annual reports available online.

Concepts in context

SABMiller plc
SUMMARISED CONTENTS OF ANNUAL REPORT, 2014

	Pages
Strategic report	1–45
Governance	49–60
Financial statements	91–175
Shareholder information	176–177

Summarised extract from balance sheet at 31 March 2014	**US$m**
ASSETS	
Non-current assets	
Goodwill	18 497
Intangible assets	8 532
Property, plant and equipment	9 065
Other non-current assets (combined for this summarised extract)	12 272
	48 366
Current assets	
Inventories	1 168
Trade and other receivables	1 821
Cash and cash equivalents	2 081
Other current assets (combined for this summarised extract)	315
	5 385
Total assets	**53 751**

LIABILITIES	
Non-current liabilities	
Borrowings	(12 528)
Other non-current liabilities (combined for this summarised extract)	(3 741)
	(16 269)
Current liabilities	
Borrowings	(4 519)
Trade and other payables	(3 847)
Current tax liabilities	(1 106)
Other current liabilities (combined for this summarised extract)	(528)
	(10 000)
Total liabilities	**26 269**
Net assets	**27 482**
Total equity	**27 482**

What concepts in context do you see here?

The annual report of SABMiller runs to 177 pages. The financial statements comprise only 85 pages of the annual report, with other information such as the strategic report and governance comprising the rest.

The balance sheet (another term for statement of financial position) is found within the financial statements. There are some terms that you may be unfamiliar with (such as 'non-current' and 'current', 'goodwill' and 'intangible assets') – do not worry about these now as you will come across them as you progress through the book.

Looking at the assets, you will see some of the items that we have already mentioned such as property, plant and equipment, inventories and cash. The total assets of $53 751 million are the resources of the entity, SABMiller.

Remember, we said that the lenders (as shown by the *liabilities*) and the investors (as shown by *equity*) represent claims against the entity. For liabilities, you will see the borrowings as a term we have already mentioned, which are funds loaned to the entity by lenders. Notice how SABMiller shows its liabilities as a negative (indicated by brackets). This indicates that the total liabilities of $26 269 million represent a claim against the entity.

The total equity of $27 482 million is the investors' claim against the entity, often referred to as the owners' interest in the entity.

(The relationship between assets, liabilities and equity is discussed in detail in Chapter 3).

SABMiller plc is a South African multinational brewing and beverage company headquartered in London, England. It has a primary listing on the London Stock Exchange and a secondary listing on the Johannesburg Stock Exchange. It is the world's second-largest brewer measured by revenues and is also a major bottler of Coca-Cola.

Source: www.sabmiller.com/docs/default-source/investor-documents/reports/2014/financial-reports/annual-report-2014-(interactive).pdf?sfvrsn=6.

1.5 The *Conceptual Framework* and the objective of financial reporting

An important document for any student of accountancy is *The Conceptual Framework for Financial Reporting*. It is issued by the IASB and is a framework which sets out the concepts that underlie the preparation and presentation of financial statements. It will be referred to in this book as the *Conceptual Framework*.

The IASB is an independent private-sector body that develops and approves standards, known as ***International Financial Reporting Standards (IFRS)***. Accounting standards are authoritative documents for financial reporting and specify how transactions and other events are to be recognised, measured and disclosed in financial statements.

The role of the IASB is described in more detail in Section 1.6.2.

The objective of ***general purpose financial reporting*** forms the basis of the *Conceptual Framework*, with other aspects of the *Framework flowing from it*.

The objective of general purpose financial reporting is to provide financial information about the reporting entity that is useful to existing and potential investors, lenders and other creditors in making decisions about providing resources to the entity.

Pause and reflect. . .

What is the significance of the words 'general purpose' and 'financial reporting' in the above definition?

Response

Financial reporting has to meet the needs of a variety of users and is therefore referred to as 'general purpose'. Financial statements, as you saw in the previous section, are a central part of 'financial reporting', but the scope of financial reporting is wider.

This is the starting point of the *Conceptual Framework*, addressing the question of why financial statements are prepared – to provide ***useful information*** to identified ***users*** (investors, lenders and other creditors) for decision-making purposes. These include decisions taken by investors (to buy shares in the entity), lenders (to loan funds to the entity) and creditors (to supply goods and services to the entity).

This leads to the *Conceptual Framework* addressing users and their information needs as well as what is meant by useful information.

1.5.1 Users and their information needs

The information flow between management and primary users was described briefly in Section 1.2 of this chapter. You learnt there that management, who has access to detailed information relating to the entity, provides financial information to primary users who need this information for decision making.

Pause and reflect...

Think of an existing or potential investor in a company. What information would be useful for making a decision to buy, sell or hold shares, and how would this information be obtained?

Response

An existing or potential investor requires information about the expected returns from an investment, for example dividends and market price increases. Information about returns depends on their assessment of the amount, timing and uncertainty of future cash flows to the entity. In turn, an assessment of future cash flows requires information about the resources of an entity, the claims against the entity and its performance.

Investors lack the ability to prescribe all the financial information they need from an entity and therefore must rely, at least partly, on the information provided in financial reports.

Let us now examine the information needs of the users of financial information. As already described in Section 1.2, users of financial information may be broadly categorised as *primary users* or as *management.*

Primary users

The ***primary users*** are identified as the *investors, lenders* and *other creditors*. This is because they cannot require a reporting entity to provide information to meet their specific needs and therefore must rely on general purpose financial reports.

Investors are those with an ownership interest in the entity, typically through the holding of shares. Equity investors generally invest economic resources in the form of cash in an entity with the expectation of receiving a return *on*, as well as a return *of*, the cash provided. In other words, they expect to receive more cash than they provided in the form of cash distributions, known as dividends and increases in the prices of shares. Equity investors are therefore directly interested in the amount, timing and uncertainty of an entity's future cash flows and also in how the perception of an entity's ability to generate those cash flows affects the prices of their shares. Equity investors often have the right to vote on management actions and therefore are interested in how well the directors and managers of the entity have discharged their responsibility to make efficient and profitable use of the assets entrusted to them.

Lenders are those with a financial but not an ownership interest in the business. They provide funding to an entity by lending it economic resources in the form of cash.

Lenders generally expect to receive a return in the form of interest and repayments of borrowings. Like investors, lenders are interested in the amount, timing and uncertainty of an entity's future cash flows. Significant lenders also may have the right to influence or approve some management actions and therefore also may be interested in how well management has discharged its responsibilities.

Other creditors also have a financial but not an ownership interest in the business. They provide resources as a consequence of their relationship with an entity, even though the relationship is not primarily that of an investor or lender. For example, *employees* provide human capital in exchange for a salary or other compensation, some of which may be deferred for many years. *Suppliers* may extend credit to facilitate a sale. *Customers* may prepay for goods or services to be provided by the entity.

The *Conceptual Framework* acknowledges that other parties such as regulators and members of the public (other than investors, lenders and other creditors) may find general purpose financial reports useful. However, those reports are not directed at these groups. Regulators, such as the taxation authority, have the power to demand information they need.

Management

The board of directors and managers of an entity, often referred to simply as management, are also interested in financial information about the entity. Management is responsible for preparing financial reports rather than being a recipient of them.

1.5.2 Qualitative characteristics of financial statements

You have already learnt that the objective of general purpose financial reporting is to provide financial information about the reporting entity to users of the financial statements, which is useful in making decisions about providing resources to the entity. In order to be useful to users, information needs to possess certain attributes. ***Qualitative characteristics*** are the attributes that make the information provided in financial statements useful to users.

The *Conceptual Framework* distinguishes between two types of qualitative characteristics that are necessary to provide useful information (Diagram 1.6):

- fundamental qualitative characteristics
- enhancing qualitative characteristics.

Fundamental qualitative characteristics

The fundamental characteristics are **relevance** and **faithful representation** (Diagram 1.7).

Relevant financial information is capable of making a difference to the decisions made by users. In order to make a difference, financial information has to have *predictive* or

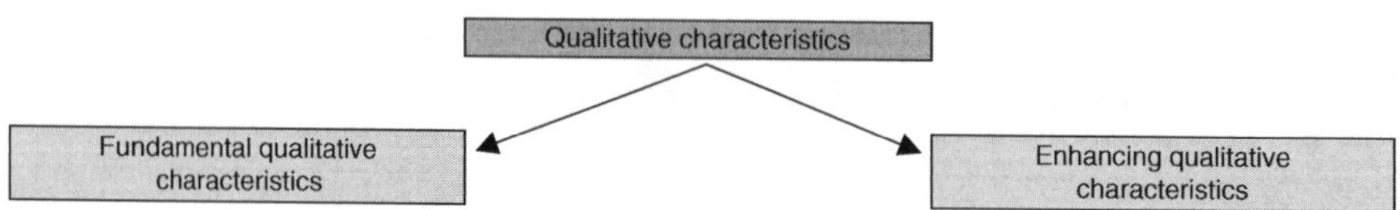

Diagram 1.6 Fundamental and enhancing qualitative characteristics

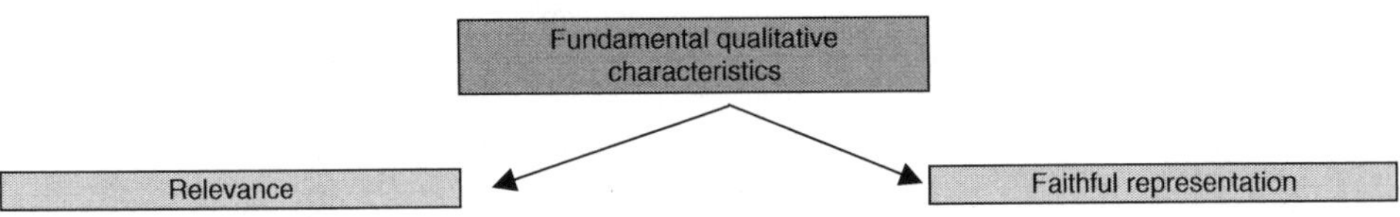

Diagram 1.7 Fundamental qualitative characteristics

confirmatory value, or both. Predictive value helps users in predicting or anticipating future outcomes. Confirmatory value enables users to check and confirm predictions or evaluations.

Materiality is also included as an element of relevance. Information is material if is significant enough to influence the decisions of users. An item can be material in either *nature* or *amount* (or both), but materiality is an entity-specific aspect of relevance. In other words, it needs to be considered in relation to a specific entity. What is material to one entity may not be material to another.

Faithful representation of economic transactions requires the information to be *complete*, *neutral* and *free from error*. Completeness implies adequate or full disclosure of information, neutrality means fairness and freedom from bias, and free from error requires no inaccuracies or omissions.

It is obviously almost impossible to achieve perfectly faithful representation because of inherent uncertainties, estimates and assumptions, but the aim is to maximise these qualities.

Faithful representation, however, is achieved if there are no errors or omissions in the selection and description of economic transactions.

 **Pause and reflect...**

As part of a scheme to encourage economic development in a rural area, the government sells land to an entity for C1 000 when the market value is C50 000. At what amount should the entity record this land in its financial statements?

Response

Recording the land at a cost of C1 000 would be a faithful representation of the transaction, but would not be very useful to users. The information could be made more useful by using the C50 000 market value as more relevant information.

Enhancing qualitative characteristics

The enhancing characteristics are **comparability**, **verifiability, timeliness** and **understandability**, and are intended to enhance both relevant and faithfully represented financial information (Diagram 1.8).

- **Comparability** allows users to identify similarities and differences between financial statement items, both between different periods of one entity and across different entities. The application of methods of accounting in a consistent manner helps to achieve comparability.

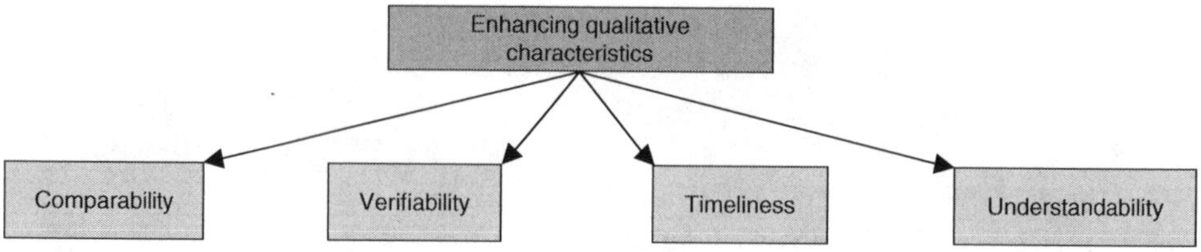

Enhancing qualitative characteristics → Comparability; Verifiability; Timeliness; Understandability

Diagram 1.8 Enhancing qualitative characteristics

- **Verifiability** helps to assure users that information represents faithfully what it purports to represent. Financial information is supported by evidence, and independent individuals can check them to see whether such information is faithfully represented. In other words, information is verifiable if it can be audited.
- **Timeliness** means providing information to decision makers in time to be capable of influencing their decisions. Delays in publishing financial information reduce the usefulness of the information.
- **Understandability** requires financial information to be comprehensible to users with a reasonable knowledge of business and economics. To be understandable, information should be presented clearly and concisely. However, it is not appropriate to exclude complex items just to make financial reports simple and understandable.

Constraints on useful financial reporting

Cost is identified as a pervasive constraint to financial reporting, as it is important that the benefits of financial reporting exceed the cost of preparation.

The qualitative characteristics are summarised in Diagram 1.9.

1.6 Accounting standards

1.6.1 Background

You have seen a number of times in this chapter that the objective of general purpose financial reporting is to provide financial information about the reporting entity that is useful to users in making decisions. You also know that the information needs to have certain ***qualitative characteristics*** in order to be useful to users.

Accounting standards have evolved over a number of years in an attempt to establish practices and principles for the communication of information to users. More specifically, accounting standards govern how the financial data of a business entity is recognised, measured and reported. Without accounting standards, business entities could present accounting information in a variety of ways. This would seriously hinder the ability of users to make comparisons between different entities and of the same entity over a period of time.

Accounting standards are often referred to as ***generally accepted accounting practice*** or ***generally accepted accounting principles***, both abbreviated as ***GAAP***. Most countries around the world developed their own national GAAP over a period stretching from the 1940s to the 1970s. Some countries today still use their own national GAAP. Increased globalisation and the need for international standards led to the formation of the

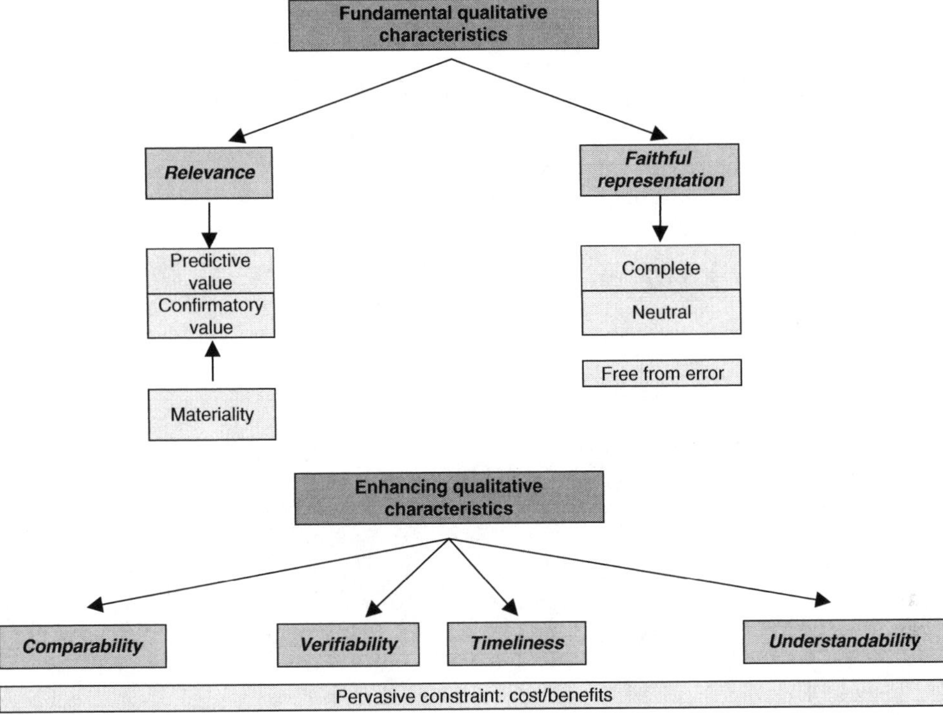

Diagram 1.9 Qualitative characteristics

International Accounting Standards Committee (IASC) in 1973 and its successor body, the IASB in 2001.

1.6.2 The IASB and IFRS

Internationally, the IASB publishes its standards as a series of pronouncements known as IFRS.

For a number of years, particularly since the early 2000s, the IASB has embarked on a process of encouraging countries and jurisdictions around the world to harmonise their *national* GAAP to IFRS, in other words to a *global* GAAP.

1.6.3 Use of IFRS around the world

The IASB has no authority to enforce the use of IFRS in any country or jurisdiction around the world. However, a country's specific *national* legislation may *require* compliance with IFRS. On the other hand, the national legislation of some countries *neither requires nor disallows* compliance. There are also some countries whose national legislation *disallows* compliance.

Over 100 countries and jurisdictions already *require* the use of IFRS, including the United Kingdom, Australia, New Zealand, Canada, South Africa, Hong Kong, Israel and member states of the European Union, to name but a few.

Other jurisdictions *permit* but do not *require* the use of IFRS, including India, Japan and Switzerland. Japan, for example, is considering the introduction of Japanese

Modified International Standards (JMIS) and many listed Swiss companies choose to report using IFRS.

The notable exceptions where IFRS are not required include the United States and Russia. The United States *permits* the use of IFRS by foreign companies whose shares are listed on the New York Stock Exchange or NASDAQ, but does not permit the use of IFRS for listed domestic companies. US GAAP is used instead.

Countries such as South Africa, Australia and New Zealand have adopted IFRS *word for word* as their own national GAAP. Others have adopted IFRS but with certain *modifications* that they consider necessary due to reasons that are peculiar to that jurisdiction and which they thus believe have not been dealt with in IFRS.

 **Pause and reflect...**

Why would a country comply with IFRS?

Response

Where the *national* legislation requires compliance, preparers of financial information have no choice but to comply. However, in situations where compliance is neither required nor disallowed, compliance with IFRS gives credibility to the financial statements and makes them understandable to investors from around the world, thus encouraging foreign investment.

1.6.4 Structure of IFRS

IFRS refer to the entire body of IASB pronouncements. IFRS manifest themselves as a numbered series of pronouncements labelled International Accounting Standards (IAS), issued by its predecessor (IASC), as well as a new, numbered series of pronouncements, which are labelled IFRS (Diagram 1.10). All references in this book are to the relevant IAS or IFRS.

1.6.5 Development of IFRS

IFRS are developed through a formal system of due process and international consultation that involves accountants, analysts, the business community, stock exchanges, regulatory authorities, academics and interested parties around the world.

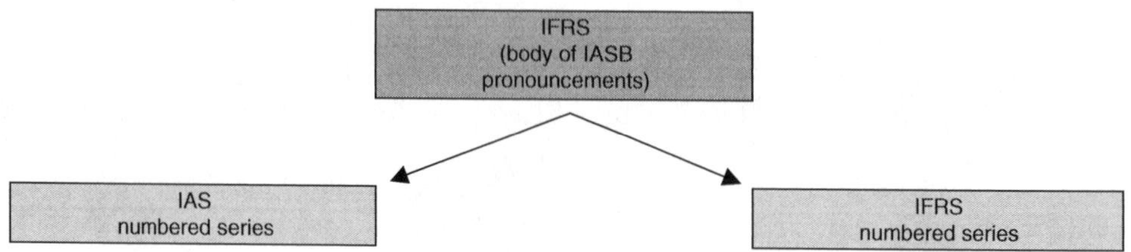

Diagram 1.10 IFRS and the distinction between IAS and IFRS

1.7 Fields of accounting activity

Accountants perform work in four main areas. These fields of activity are financial accounting, management accounting, auditing and taxation.

1.7.1 Financial accounting

Financial accounting provides information to users who are not involved in the daily operations of the entity. These would include all the primary and other users described above. The information is distributed through the financial statements. Such financial statements are prepared and presented at least annually and are directed towards the common information needs of a wide range of users.

Financial statements form part of the process of financial reporting. As already mentioned, a basic set of financial statements normally includes a statement of financial position, a statement of profit or loss and a statement of changes in equity. These will be described in Chapter 2.

1.7.2 Management accounting

Management accounting provides information to the management of an entity. Management accounting statements include much of the same information that is reported in financial accounting. However, management accounting goes further and includes a great deal of information that is not reported outside the company.

As mentioned above, management is also interested in the information contained in the financial statements, even though it has access to additional management and financial information that help it carry out its planning, decision-making and control responsibilities.

1.7.3 Auditing

It is the responsibility of the board of directors to have financial statements prepared which fairly present the company's financial position, performance and cash flows. The role of the auditor is to express an opinion on the fair presentation of the information and whether or not it has been prepared in accordance with IFRS.

An audit is carried out by a firm of independent auditors and, as such, adds credibility to the financial statements.

1.7.4 Taxation

Accountants who are specialists in taxation assist their clients in planning their affairs in order to minimise taxes payable. The taxes may include any of the following, depending on the nature of the transaction: income tax, corporation/company tax, donations tax, estate duty/inheritance tax, VAT and transfer duty.

Tax specialists may also assist clients with the rendering of tax returns, the checking of assessments, objections to assessments with which the client disagrees, and generally assisting with any tax-related problems which might arise.

1.8 Internal control

A sound system of internal control is important to ensure that the business organisation is effectively and efficiently run, that the assets are safeguarded and that the financial statements faithfully present the information which they purport to present. A system of internal control ensures that:

- the information the directors need to make decisions is available
- the delegated authorities are properly exercised
- the data needed for the control of costs is accurate and complete
- the data needed for the preparation of financial statements is accurate and complete.

The internal control system is integral to ongoing business operations and is as important to the continuation of the business as are market opportunities and cash flows.

Bibliography

AccountingVerse. www.accountingverse.com (Accessed 29 June 2016).

Arnold, J; Hope, T; Southworth, A and Kirkham, L. 1994. *Financial Accounting*. London: Prentice Hall Inc. (UK) Limited.

Business owl. www.businessowl.co.za (Accessed 14 November 2014).

IFRS Application around the World. www.ifrs.org/Use-around-the-world/Pages/Jurisdiction-profiles.aspx (Accessed 29 June 2016).

Prada, M. *Japan and Global Standards*. www.ifrs.org/Alerts/Conference/Documents/2014/Speech-Michel-Prada-Tokyo-November-2014.pdf (Accessed 17 November 2014).

2 Fundamental accounting concepts

Business focus

The *Conceptual Framework*: a student's best friend

IFRS apply a conceptual framework for accounting for transactions. The aim is not to provide an all-inclusive set of rules, but to rely on a model which describes key principles that ought to inform the development of suitable accounting policies. However, increasing commercial complexity coupled with political interest and pressure to improve accounting standards after a series of highly publicised corporate scandals has led to an increasing rules-based approach by our standard setter. The result is that what we presently refer to colloquially as 'IFRS' actually includes 16 IFRSs, 29 IASs and numerous interpretations equating to well over 3 000 pages of text. Before starting to complain about the time that it is going to take to become familiar with each of these, think about your American counterparts. US GAAP – which attempts to codify the accounting for transactions using a prescriptive approach – is possibly ten times the volume of IFRS! In other words, the alternative to reading through this chapter and related references would be to study roughly 27 000 pages of US GAAP. At an average of 2 minutes per page (and assuming an effective 8 hours of reading per day), that would equate to 900 hours, 112 days or a third of a year just spent reading accounting standards.

In this chapter

When preparing financial statements, from whose perspective are they prepared – the business entity or the owner/s? How do we identify the resources and obligations of a business entity as well as the income earned and expenses incurred? And how do we measure performance – by cash flows or some other measure? These questions relate to the three fundamental accounting concepts that form the basis of your concepts-based introduction to financial accounting. This chapter will introduce you to these concepts – the entity concept, the definitions of the elements of financial statements and the accrual basis of accounting, along with some other fundamental accounting concepts.

Dashboard

- Look at the *Learning outcomes* so that you know what you should be able to do after studying this chapter.
- Read the *Business focus* to place this chapter's contents in a real-world context.

- Preview *In this chapter* to focus your mind on the contents of the chapter.
- Read the *text* in detail.
  - Pay attention to the *definitions*, and apply your mind to the *Pause and reflect* scenarios.
  - There are three key concepts for you to understand when reading this chapter – the entity concept (in Section 2.3), the definitions of the elements of the financial statements (in Section 2.5) and the accrual basis of accounting (in Section 2.6).
  - The case study in Section 2.7 enables you to apply your understanding of the above concepts and to prepare a set of financial statements. This case study is used throughout Chapters 2 to 7. The transactions in the case study are grouped in sections for ease of learning, and each transaction has a detailed explanation. Work through the transactions in each section and make sure that you understand the explanations.
- Prepare solutions to the other examples as you read through the chapter.
- Prepare a solution to the *Revision example* at the end of the chapter without reference to the suggested one. Compare your solution to the suggested solution provided.

Learning outcomes

After studying this chapter, you should be able to do the following:

1 Describe the nature and purpose of the *Conceptual Framework*.
2 Explain the relevance of cash in the decision-making process.
3 Define, recall and apply the entity concept.
4 Explain the objective of general purpose financial reporting.
5 Identify the financial statements and define, recall and apply the definitions of their elements.
6 Define and apply the accrual basis of accounting.
7 Analyse a set of typical business transactions using the *Conceptual Framework*, and prepare a set of financial statements.
8 Explain the differences between a statement of cash flows prepared using the cash basis of accounting and a statement of profit or loss prepared using the accrual basis of accounting.

Fundamental accounting concepts

2.1 What is the *Conceptual Framework*?

The *Conceptual Framework for Financial Reporting* (known as the *Conceptual Framework*) is a document issued by the IASB. It describes the basic concepts that underlie the preparation and presentation of financial statements for external users. It also serves as a guide to the IASB in developing future standards and as a guide to resolving accounting issues that are not addressed directly in existing standards.

It is important to note that the *Conceptual Framework* is not an accounting standard, and where there is perceived to be a conflict between the *Conceptual Framework* and the specific provisions of an accounting standard, the accounting standard prevails.

2.1.1 Concepts included in the Conceptual Framework

Understanding the concepts addressed in the *Conceptual Framework* forms the basis for correctly applying the standards.

Table 2.1 summarises the concepts included in the *Conceptual Framework* and where they are covered in this book.

2.1.2 Purpose of the Conceptual Framework

The purpose of the *Conceptual Framework* is to set out the various concepts that underpin financial reporting. These concepts assist:

- the IASB in the development of coherent and consistent accounting standards;
- the various national standard setters to develop national standards;

Table 2.1 Concepts included in the *Conceptual Framework*

Concepts included in the Conceptual Framework	*Chapter in this book*
Objective of general purpose financial reporting	Covered in Chapter 1, *The accounting environment* (Section 1.5) and in this chapter (Section 2.4)
Qualitative characteristics of useful financial statements	Covered in Chapter 1, *The accounting environment* (Section 1.5.2)
Underlying assumptions inherent in a set of financial statements	Covered in Chapter 6, *Preparation and presentation of financial statements* (Section 6.3)
Elements of the financial statements	Covered in this chapter (Section 2.5)
Recognition criteria to be met before the element may be recognised	Covered in Chapter 6, *Preparation and presentation of financial statements* (Section 6.4)
Measurement bases that may be used when measuring the elements	Covered briefly in this chapter (Section 2.5) and referred to in later chapters
Concepts of capital and capital maintenance	Beyond the scope of this book

- preparers of financial statements in applying standards or in creating their own policies where existing IFRSs do not provide guidance or do not cater for the topic;
- auditors when assessing whether financial statements comply with IFRS;
- users in interpreting financial statements that comply with IFRS;
- other parties interested in how the IASB develops IFRS.

2.2 Information for decision making

2.2.1 Forecasting cash flows

In Section 1.4.1 of Chapter 1, *The accounting environment*, you were briefly introduced to the information output of the accounting information system. You learnt that information about the financial position is primarily provided in a ***statement of financial position***, while information on financial performance is primarily provided in a ***statement of profit or loss***.

The statement of financial position represents, as its name implies, the financial position of an entity *at a specific point in time*, while the statement of profit or loss reflects the financial performance of an entity *over a period of time*. Both the statements will be discussed in more detail later in this chapter. Further, and as mentioned in Chapter 1, we are using the term 'statement of profit or loss' to depict the financial performance in Chapters 1 to 5 of this book. In Chapter 6, *Preparation and presentation of financial statements*, we will introduce the concept of other comprehensive income, and elaborate further on the presentation of financial performance including the 'statement of profit or loss and other comprehensive income' and the alternative separate 'statement of profit or loss' and 'statement of comprehensive income'.

You learnt about ***external*** and ***internal users*** of financial statements in Chapter 1. External users, such as investors and lenders, need to predict the entity's *future* performance and future cash flows. Cash flows in and out of a business entity are fundamental to its operations. If the business does not generate enough cash, it may be unable to distribute cash to its owners. Cash is needed to pay interest on borrowings, to pay suppliers and also to repay amounts borrowed. When the owner decides to sell part or all of his or her ownership interest, potential investors will look to future cash flow in valuing the business.

Future cash flows are therefore important information to users of financial statements. This leads us to ask how users can obtain this information. Management, as an internal user, has this information, but is reluctant to provide forecasts of future cash flows for strategic reasons and because they might prove to be inaccurate. External users do not have access to the data needed to generate cash forecasts.

As a result, external users need to analyse and interpret the information about the *current* financial position and *past* performance presented in the statement of financial position and statement of profit or loss in order to assess the entity's *future* financial position and performance. By so doing, we assume the continuity of business activities. Although many aspects change over time, other important aspects remain constant.

One possible way of providing information to users for decision-making purposes is the ***cash basis*** of accounting. The next section examines this, followed by a discussion of the ***accrual basis*** in the sections that follow. We will then consider which basis provides the best information for external users' decision-making purposes.

2.2.2 Cash basis of accounting

The cash basis of accounting measures performance by subtracting cash outflows from cash inflows to arrive at a net cash flow for the period. Cash flows can be analysed into three categories, namely cash flows from operating, investing and financing activities. Operating activities are the primary revenue-producing activities of the entity, including cash received from the sale of goods and services, as well as cash paid to suppliers for the purchase of goods and services. Investing activities incorporate the acquisition and disposal of long-term assets; in other words, cash flows relating to resources used to generate future profits and cash flows. Financing activities, on the other hand, relate to cash flows involving owners and lenders.

You will learn more about cash flows relating to operating, investing and financing activities much later in this book (Chapter 18, *Statement of cash flows*), but it is useful to have a basic appreciation of these terms as we discuss the cash basis of accounting.

Example: Cash inflows and outflows

This example introduces you to the activities of Simon Smart, a computer retailer, operating under the name of Smart Concepts. The example will be used throughout Parts I and II of this book to introduce the conceptual aspects of accounting and to explain the accounting process. The following is a record of the transactions of the business for the three-month period from 1 January to 31 March 20X5.

External transactions

Starting the business

1 On 2 January, Simon Smart started a business as a computer retailer. He drew C950 000 from a savings account and opened a bank account in the name of Smart Concepts into which he paid C950 000.
2 On 2 January, Smart Concepts negotiated a loan from Techno Bank for an amount of C600 000. The loan is repayable in four equal annual instalments, beginning on 31 December 20X5. The interest rate is 12 per cent per annum, payable quarterly in arrears.
3 On 2 January, Simon located premises from which to operate in Hyde Park. The monthly rent for the premises is C12 000. Smart Concepts paid four months' rent in advance on 2 January.

4 On 2 January, Simon transferred C120 000 from the bank account into a fixed deposit account earning interest at 5 per cent per annum.
5 On 2 January, Smart Concepts purchased furniture and fittings for C240 000. This was paid for from funds in the bank account. The expected useful life of the furniture and fittings is five years.
6 On 5 January, Smart Concepts purchased supplies of stationery for C5 000 as well as supplies of computer parts for C12 000. All of these were paid for in cash.
7 On 7 January, Smart Concepts opened an account with Computer World, the supplier of its inventory.

Trading and operating transactions for January

8 On 10 January, Smart Concepts purchased inventory of 60 computers from Computer World at a cost of C10 000 each. The total amount owing is to be paid by 25 March.
9 On 12 January, Smart Concepts paid a service provider C750 for internet access.
10 On 25 January, Smart Concepts sold 15 computers on credit to a customer for C12 500 each. An amount of C125 000 is due by 15 March and the balance by 15 April.

Trading and operating transactions for February

11 On 1 February, Smart Concepts employed a computer technician at a salary of C8 000 per month.
12 On 8 February, Smart Concepts paid C7 000 for an advertisement in a newspaper, advertising the computers available for sale.
13 On 12 February, Smart Concepts sold 30 computers to customers for C12 500 each. The customers paid cash for them.
14 On 25 February, Smart Concepts received cash of C48 000 in respect of technical support contracts taken out by customers. The contracts are for a two-year period.
15 On 28 February, Smart Concepts paid the computer technician his salary for February.

Trading and operating transactions for March

16 On 4 March, Smart Concepts purchased inventory of a further 75 computers from Computer World at a cost of C10 000 each. The total amount owing is to be paid by 25 May.
17 On 5 March, Smart Concepts paid a service provider C750 for internet access.
18 On 15 March, Smart Concepts received C125 000 from the customer in transaction 10.
19 On 25 March, Smart Concepts paid Computer World an amount of C600 000.
20 On 29 March, Smart Concepts sold 30 computers on credit to customers for C12 500 each. The full amount owing is due by 30 April.
21 On 30 March, Smart Concepts paid the computer technician his salary for March.

Rewarding the providers of finance

22 On 30 March, Smart Concepts paid the interest on the loan from Techno Bank for the three-month period.
23 On 30 March, Simon authorised a distribution to himself of C60 000 for personal use.

You are required to:

Prepare a statement of cash inflows and outflows for Smart Concepts for the three-month period ended 31 March 20X5.

Solution: Cash inflows and outflows

SMART CONCEPTS
STATEMENT OF CASH INFLOWS AND OUTFLOWS
FOR THE PERIOD ENDED 31 MARCH 20X5

		C
Cash inflows		2 098 000
Contribution from owner		950 000
Borrowings		600 000
Sales	*(375 000 + 125 000)*	500 000
Service fees		48 000
Cash outflows		(1 127 500)
Rent	*(12 000 × 4)*	48 000
Fixed deposit investment		120 000
Furniture and fittings		240 000
Computer parts & stationery supplies	*(5 000 + 12 000)*	17 000
Internet	*(750 + 750)*	1 500
Advertising		7 000
Salaries	*(8 000 + 8 000)*	16 000
Inventory	*(10 000 × 60)*	600 000
Interest	*(600 000 × 12% × 3/12)*	18 000
Distribution		60 000
Net cash inflow		970 500

Each transaction needs to be examined in order to determine whether cash has been received or paid. If a transaction involves an inflow or outflow of cash, the amount is included with an appropriate description on the statement of cash inflows and outflows.

Transactions 1 and 2 involve the receipt of cash from *financing* activities. The C950 000 contribution from the owner and the C600 000 loan from the bank are shown as cash inflows.

Transactions 13, 14 and 18 involve the receipt of cash from operating activities. Both transaction 13, a sale of computers for cash, and transaction 14, where customers pay C48 000 in respect of technical support contracts relating to the next two years, result in a cash inflow on the cash basis of accounting. Transaction 18 records the receipt of cash amounting to C125 000 from a customer for the computers sold on credit in transaction 10, where no cash inflow was recorded.

Transactions 3, 6, 9, 12, 15, 17, 19, 21 and 22 comprise an outflow of cash from *operating* activities. In transaction 3, the full C48 000 rent paid for four months is shown as a cash outflow. The C17 000 paid for supplies and parts in transaction 6 is shown as a cash outflow, as opposed to the cost of inventory purchased of C600 000 in transaction 8 and C750 000 in transaction 16, which are not shown as cash outflows, as the inventory was purchased on credit. It is only when the supplier is paid for the inventory in transaction 19 that C600 000 is shown as a cash outflow. The C7 000 paid for advertising in transaction 12 and the C8 000 paid for the technician's salary in transactions 15 and 21 as well as the C750 paid for internet access in transactions 9 and 17 all give rise to cash outflows on the cash basis of accounting. In transaction 22, the C18 000 interest paid is also shown as a cash outflow from operating activities.

Transactions 4 and 5 comprise an outflow of cash from *investing* activities. In transaction 4, C120 000 is transferred out of the business bank account to a fixed deposit investment. You will learn in later chapters in this book that long-term investments are not regarded as cash. In transaction 5, C240 000 is paid to purchase furniture and fittings that will be used for five years.

The transactions that do not affect the statement of cash inflows and outflows, other than those mentioned above (transactions 8, 10, 16 and 20 where goods were bought and sold on credit) are numbered 7 and 11. These two transactions do not have any economic impact on the entity.

Pause and reflect...

The statement of cash inflows and outflows of Smart Concepts for the period ended 31 March 20X5 reports a net cash *inflow* of C970 500, implying that the business performed well during that period. Do you think that this represents a true measure of the *performance* of Smart Concepts for the period?

Response

This does not represent a true measure of *performance* for the period. The cash inflows include contributions from the owner of C900 000 and the loan from the bank of C600 000 (both financing activities). The full C48 000 received for the technical support contracts is included as a cash inflow, yet the work is to be performed over a two-year period. The cash outflows include C240 000 paid for furniture and fittings which will be used for five years (and is an investing activity). Also included is C48 000 paid for rent up to the end of April 20X5 and a distribution to the owner of C60 000. The statement of cash inflows and outflows does provide useful information about the entity's cash flows (especially when presented in terms of IAS 7 *Statement of Cash Flows*, and which you will learn about in Chapter 18). However, as the statement of cash inflows and outflows includes cash flows that do not relate to the current period and to operating activities, it is not a good measure of performance.

We could address some of the issues mentioned above by preparing a statement of ***operating*** cash inflows and outflows. This will allow us to focus on the main revenue-producing activities of the entity and exclude the effect of investing and financing activities.

Example: Operating cash inflows and outflows

Consider the same transactions as in the previous example.

You are required to:

Prepare a statement of operating cash inflows and outflows for Smart Concepts for the three-month period ended 31 March 20X5.

 **Solution: Operating cash inflows and outflows**

SMART CONCEPTS
STATEMENT OF OPERATING CASH INFLOWS AND OUTFLOWS
FOR THE PERIOD ENDED 31 MARCH 20X5

		C
Cash inflows		548 000
Sales	*(375 000 + 125 000)*	500 000
Service fees		48 000
Cash outflows		(707 500)
Rent	*(12 000 × 4)*	48 000
Computer parts & stationery supplies	*(5 000 + 12 000)*	17 000
Internet	*(750 + 750)*	1 500
Advertising		7 000
Salaries	*(8 000 + 8 000)*	16 000
Inventory	*(10 000 × 60)*	600 000
Interest	*(600 000 × 0.12 × 3/12)*	18 000
Net cash outflow		(159 500)

If you look carefully at the statement of operating cash inflows and outflows, you will notice that the cash inflows do not include the financing activities (the contribution from the owner and the loan from the bank). Further, the cash outflows do not include the investing activities (the fixed deposit investment and the purchase of the furniture and fittings). However, the cash inflows *include* C48 000 received for technical support contracts where the work will be performed over a two-year period, but *do not include* the C375 000 of credit sales from transaction 20. The cash outflows include C48 000 paid for rent up to the end of April, and C600 000 paid to Computer World for 60 computers, whereas 75 computers were sold during the period.

We cannot measure an entity's financial performance on the basis of cash flows alone. A different and more useful measure of an entity's financial performance is the ***accrual basis*** of accounting. The accrual basis depicts the effects of transactions in the periods in which those effects occur, even if the related cash inflows and outflows occur in a different period. We will address the accrual basis in more detail in Section 2.6 of this chapter.

2.3 The entity concept

Recall from Chapter 1 that a sole proprietor and a partnership can be referred to as *unincorporated* entities, while a company can be referred to as an *incorporated* entity.

The importance and relevance of the entity concept is best understood by considering the situation of a sole proprietor or the partners in a partnership. From a legal point of view, the owner of a sole proprietorship and the partners of a partnership are the *same* legal entity as the respective business entity, but for accounting purposes, they are *separate* accounting entities apart from the business entity.

The shareholders of a company are *separate* legal entities apart from the business entity, but are also separate accounting entities. A company is incorporated as a separate legal entity in terms of statute.

Table 2.2 The entity concept

Transaction	*Recording of transaction*
Transactions of the business entity with external parties	Recorded as transactions of the business entity
Transactions carried out by the owner on behalf of the business entity	Recorded as transactions of the business entity
Transactions carried out by the owner on own behalf	Not recorded as transactions of the business entity

Financial statements are prepared from the perspective of the business entity, utilising the entity concept.

The entity concept entails:

- identification of the business entity
- separation of the recording of transactions relating to the business entity as an accounting entity, and the owner as the proprietor of the entity.

In other words, irrespective of the form of entity, the transactions of the business entity must be accounted for separately and distinctly from its owner or owners. The financial statements of the business entity should not mix the owner's personal transactions with the business transactions. If the entity concept is not followed, the information reported in the financial statements of the business entity will not be useful to the users in making their decisions. The practical application of the entity concept is summarised in Table 2.2.

2.4 Financial reporting

2.4.1 The objective of general purpose financial reporting

The objective of general purpose financial reporting forms the basis of the *Conceptual Framework*, with other aspects of the *Framework* flowing from it. It is defined as follows:

The objective of general purpose financial reporting is to provide financial information about the reporting entity that is useful to existing and potential investors, lenders and other creditors in making decisions about providing resources to the entity.

It is directed at users who provide resources to a reporting entity but lack the ability to require the entity to provide them with the information they need to make decisions about their investments. You will recall from Chapter 1 that existing and potential investors, lenders and other creditors are referred to as the ***primary users*** of general purpose financial reports. Remember also that primary users are also a subset of external users.

In addition to ***general purpose*** financial reports, many types of reports are produced relating to the financial position, financial performance and cash flows of an entity, such as investors' analysis reports, due diligence reports and management reports. Such reports are normally prepared for a ***special purpose***. The focus of this book is on general purpose financial reports.

 **Pause and reflect...**

Does management need to rely on general purpose financial reports?

Response

Management does not need to rely on general purpose financial reports, as all the financial information needed may be obtained internally.

2.4.2 Information presented in general purpose financial reports

It is not possible for general purpose financial reports to provide all the information that the primary users need. Those users need to consider relevant information from other sources, for example general economic conditions and political events, as well as industry and company outlooks.

General purpose financial reports do provide information about an entity's ***financial position*** and ***financial performance***. This is achieved by presenting a set of ***financial statements*** including the following components:

- A statement of financial position (which provides information about the financial position of an entity).
- A statement of profit or loss (which provides information about the financial performance as reflected by accrual accounting).
- A statement of changes in equity (which provides information about changes in the financial position of an entity).
- A statement of cash flows (which provides information about the financial performance as reflected by past cash flows).

Financial statements also show the results of ***management's stewardship*** of the resources entrusted to it. In large listed companies, management and shareholders are different groups of people. The shareholders are the owners of the company and management manages the company on their behalf. The stewardship function refers to the relationship that exists between management and the shareholders, and the responsibility of management to the shareholders.

Diagram 2.1 illustrates the relationship between the components of a set of financial statements. The statement of financial position reflects the financial position of an entity at the *end of a period*. The statement of profit or loss reflects the financial performance *during a period* using accrual accounting, and the statement of cash flows reflects financial performance based on cash flows. The statement of changes in equity reflects the impact on equity resulting from financial performance *and* from other transactions, such as contributions by and distributions to owners.

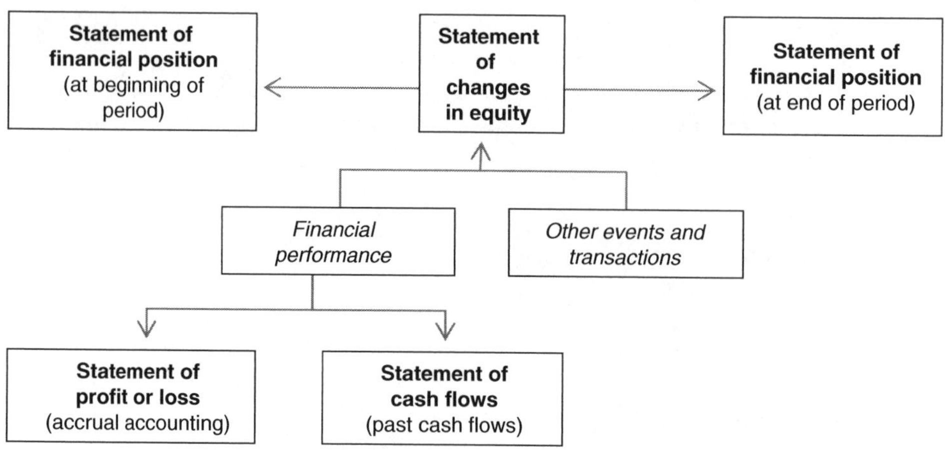

Diagram 2.1 Relationship between the components of financial statements

In the sections that follow, we will examine in more detail the financial statements and the measurement of financial performance as reflected by accrual accounting and cash flows.

2.5 The financial statements

In this section, we will learn about the statement of financial position, the statement of profit or loss and the statement of changes in equity. Financial statements portray the financial effects of transactions and other events by grouping them into broad categories according to their economic characteristics. These categories are termed the elements of the financial statements. The elements directly related to the measurement of the financial position in the statement of financial position are ***assets***, ***liabilities*** and ***equity***. The elements directly related to the measurement of financial performance in the statement of profit or loss are ***income*** and ***expenses***.

2.5.1 The statement of financial position and the elements: assets, liabilities and equity

The elements directly related to the measurement of the financial position in the statement of financial position are assets, liabilities and equity. These elements are all defined in the IASB's *Conceptual Framework*.

Assets

An **asset** is:

- a resource controlled by the entity
- as a result of past events
- from which future economic benefits are expected to flow to the entity.

For **a resource to be controlled** by the entity, physical form and right of ownership are not essential. Many assets, for example property or equipment, have a physical form and are associated with the right of ownership. However, intangibles such as patents and copyrights may have no physical form other than a certificate of registration. They are, however, assets if they are controlled by the entity and future economic benefits are expected to flow from them. Equipment held on a lease is not legally owned by the lessee, but the substance of the agreement may give the lessee control over the benefits which are expected to flow from the equipment.

Financial assets, such as accounts receivable, are also a resource controlled by the entity. In the case of accounts receivable, when the entity has sold goods or provided a service to customers on credit, the resource controlled is the right to collect cash from the customers.

In addition to tangible assets, intangible assets and financial assets, there are other assets, for example rent paid in advance, which also represents a resource controlled by the entity, namely the right to occupy the property.

Pause and reflect...

a) A business entity sells goods *on credit* or on account to its customers. Selling on credit means that the customer agrees to pay the business entity for the goods at a later date. These customers are known as *accounts receivable* or *debtors* of the business. Are the accounts receivable a resource controlled by the entity?

b) A business entity takes out an insurance policy and pays the premium in advance for a one-year period. Is the insurance paid in advance a resource controlled by the entity?

Response

a) The accounts receivable are a resource controlled by the entity as the entity has the right to collect the amounts owing from the customers.

b) By paying cash in advance for a service, in this case the insurance cover, the entity has the right to receive that service in the future. It is a resource controlled by the entity, referred to as *insurance paid in advance*.

The assets of an entity result from **past transactions or events**. Entities normally obtain assets by purchasing or producing them. Events expected to occur in the future do not in themselves give rise to assets; for example, an intention to purchase a vehicle does not, in itself, meet the definition of an asset.

The **inflow of future economic benefits** from an asset is the ability to contribute, directly or indirectly, to the flow of cash to the entity. An entity uses its assets to produce or purchase goods or services wanted or needed by customers. As these goods or services meet the customers' wants or needs, they are prepared to pay for them and thus contribute to the cash flow of the entity. Cash itself embodies future benefits because of its command over other resources.

The future economic benefits embodied in an asset may flow to the entity in a number of ways:

- The asset may be used in the production of goods or services sold by the entity.
- It may be exchanged for other assets.
- It may be used to settle a liability.
- It may be distributed to the owners of the entity.

 **Pause and reflect...**

Do accounts receivable meet the definition of an asset?

Response

Accounts receivable are a resource controlled by the entity (the right to collect the amounts owing from the customers), as a result of past events (the sale of goods on credit), from which future economic benefits are expected to flow to the entity (cash to be received from the customers). Accounts receivable therefore do meet the definition of an asset.

Liabilities

A liability is:

- a present obligation of the entity
- arising from past events
- the settlement of which is expected to result in an outflow from the entity of resources embodying economic benefits.

A fundamental characteristic of a liability is that the entity has a **present obligation**. Obligations may be legally enforceable or may arise from normal business practice or custom. A legally enforceable obligation arises, for example, when the entity has purchased goods or services from suppliers on credit. The amounts owing are referred to as accounts payable. In addition, a legally enforceable obligation may arise when customers have paid for goods or services in advance, for example subscribers paying for magazine subscriptions. The present obligation of the entity is to provide those goods or services in the future. On the other hand, if an entity decides to rectify defects in its products after the warranty period has expired, there is no legally enforceable obligation, but the amounts that are expected to be expended in respect of goods already sold are liabilities.

 **Pause and reflect...**

a) A business entity buys goods on *credit* or on *account* from its suppliers. Buying on credit means that the business entity agrees to pay the supplier for the goods at a later date. These suppliers are known as *accounts payable* or *creditors* of the business entity. Are the accounts payable an obligation of the entity?

b) A daily newspaper offers subscribers one-year subscription agreements to have a newspaper delivered to their home every weekday. The newspaper receives C1 200 cash from a subscriber for a one-year subscription agreement. Is the cash received from the subscriber an obligation of the entity?

Response

a) The accounts payable are an obligation of the entity as the entity has an obligation to pay cash to the suppliers.

b) By receiving cash in advance for a service, the entity has an obligation to provide that service in the future. It is an obligation of the entity, referred to as *subscriptions received in advance.*

Liabilities result from **past transactions or events.** As mentioned above, the purchase of goods gives rise to accounts payable, and the receipt of a loan gives rise to an obligation to repay it.

The settlement of an obligation involves an **outflow of future economic benefits** in order to satisfy the claim of the other party. Settlement of a present obligation may occur in a number of ways. These include:

- payment of cash;
- transfer of other assets;
- provision of services;
- replacement of that obligation with another one.

A distinction needs to be drawn between a present obligation and a future commitment. A decision to acquire assets in the future does not, of itself, give rise to a present obligation.

 **Pause and reflect...**

Do accounts payable meet the definition of a liability?

Response

Accounts payable are an obligation of the entity (the obligation to pay the amount owing to the suppliers), as a result of a past event (the purchase of the goods on credit), the settlement of which is expected to result in an outflow from the entity of resources embodying economic benefits (cash will be paid to the suppliers). Accounts payable therefore do meet the definition of a liability.

Equity

Equity is the residual interest in the assets of the entity after deducting all its liabilities.

Equity is often referred to as the net assets or net wealth of the entity. Assume that a business entity has assets of C10 000 000 and liabilities of C4 000 000 at 31 December 20X5. The assets of C10 000 000 are resources controlled by the entity and the liabilities of C4 000 000 represent the obligation of the entity to outside parties. The residual of C6 000 000 is the equity or the owner's interest in the entity.

If the assets of C10 000 000 comprise accounts receivable of C7 500 000 and cash in the bank of C2 500 000, and the liabilities of C4 000 000 are all accounts payable, a simple statement of financial position can be prepared as follows:

STATEMENT OF FINANCIAL POSITION
AT 31 DECEMBER 20X5

	C
ASSETS	
Accounts receivable	7 500 000
Bank	2 500 000
	10 000 000
EQUITY AND LIABILITIES	
Equity	6 000 000
Liabilities	
Accounts payable	4 000 000
	10 000 000

Commercial, industrial and other business activities can be undertaken by sole proprietorship, partnerships or companies. Although equity in each of these entity forms will have different sub-classifications, the definition is appropriate for all such entities. A detailed discussion of the sub-classifications of equity appears in Chapter 15, *Owner's equity and non-current liabilities*.

2.5.2 The statement of profit or loss and the elements: income and expenses

The elements directly related to the measurement of financial performance in the statement of profit or loss are income and expenses. The IASB's *Conceptual Framework* also defines income and expenses.

Income

Income is defined as increases in economic benefits during the accounting period in the form of:

- inflows or enhancements of assets, or
- decreases in liabilities

that result in increases in equity, other than those relating to contributions from equity participants.

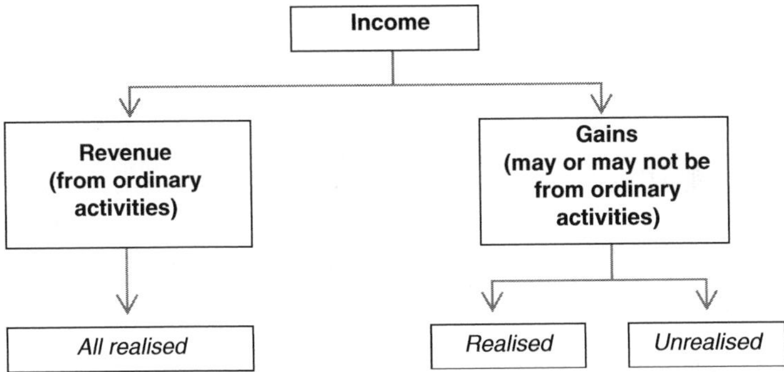

Diagram 2.2 Definition of income

Various kinds of *assets* may be received by earning income, such as cash or receivables received in exchange for goods and services supplied. Income may also be earned by the *settlement of a liability*; for example, a publisher may earn income by distributing magazines to subscribers who have paid for them in advance.

The definition of income encompasses both ***revenue*** and ***gains***. Revenue arises in the course of the *ordinary* activities of an entity and includes sales, fees, interest and royalties. Gains represent increases in economic benefits and may or may not arise in the course of the ordinary activities of an entity.

Income also includes realised and unrealised gains, for example a *realised* gain such as the profit on the sale of property, plant or equipment, and an *unrealised* gain resulting from the revaluation of property, plant and equipment. This can be illustrated as shown in Diagram 2.2.

 **Pause and reflect...**

What is the difference between a realised and an unrealised gain?

Response

A realised gain arises from a transaction where the underlying asset has been sold for cash or on credit (i.e. realised). For an unrealised gain, the underlying asset has not been sold (i.e. not realised).

 **Example: Income definition**

On 1 April 20X5, a daily newspaper receives C1 200 from a subscriber for a 12-month period, from 1 April 20X5 to 31 March 20X6. The year end of the newspaper entity is 31 December 20X5.

You are required to:

Discuss whether any income is recognised for the year ended 31 December 20X5 and, if so, what the amount of the income is.

Solution: Income definition

The cash received of C1 200 refers to the contract period from 1 April 20X5 to 31 March 20X6. Income of C900 (C1 200 × 9/12) is recognised as earned for the year ended 31 December 20X5. There is a *decrease in a liability* (the subscriptions that were received in advance and recognised when the cash was received now decrease) that results in an *increase in equity* (income earned increases equity), and it is not a contribution from an equity participant.

(Start of contract period) 01/04/X5	*9 months*	*(End of reporting period)* 31/12/X5	*3 months*	*(End of contract period)* 31/03/X6
Step 1 Liability of C1 200 recognised on receipt of cash (Subscriptions received in advance)	*Step 2.1* Income of C900 recognised as *earned* in statement of profit or loss for the period ended 31/12/X5	*Step 2.2* Liability of C300 remaining in statement of financial position at 31/12/X5 (C1 200 − C900)		

Step 1 – Remember from the discussion of a liability that when cash is received in advance for a service, the entity has an obligation to provide that service in the future. A liability is recognised representing an obligation of the entity, referred to here as *subscriptions received in advance.*

Step 2.1 – At 31 December 20X5, nine months of the 12-month contract period have passed and therefore income of C900 (C1 200 × 9/12) is recognised as earned. Income is earned by an increase in an asset or a decrease in a liability; in this case a decrease in the liability, being subscriptions received in advance.

Step 2.2 – As a result of Step 2.1, the remaining liability for subscriptions received in advance in the statement of financial position at 31 December 20X5 is C300 (C1 200 − C900).

Pause and reflect...

What amount of income is recognised in respect of this contract for the year ended 31 December 20X6?

Response

Income of C300 (C1 200 × 3/12) is recognised as earned for the year ended 31 December 20X6. This represents the income for the remaining three months of the contract from 1 January 20X6 to 31 March 20X6.

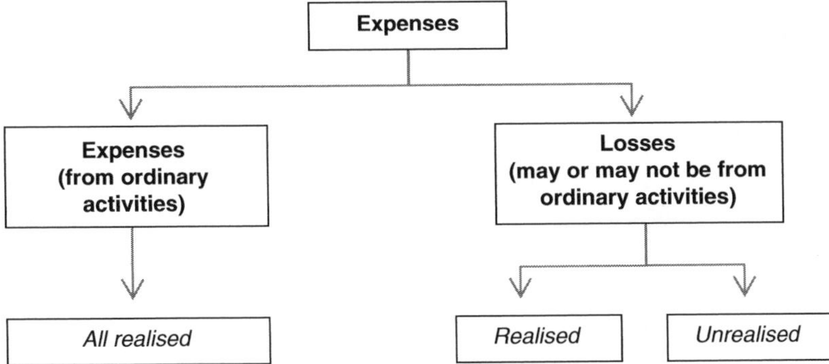

Diagram 2.3 Definition of expenses

Expenses

Expenses are defined as decreases in economic benefits during the accounting period in the form of:

- outflows or depletions of assets, or
- incurrences of liabilities

that result in decreases in equity other than those relating to distributions to equity participants.

An *asset may be given up* by the incurrence of expenses, such as the payment of cash for goods and services received. Expenses may also result in the *incurrence of a liability*, for example wages owing for services performed in the current period.

The definition of expenses encompasses both ***expenses that arise in the ordinary course of activities*** of the entity, as well as ***losses***. Expenses that arise in the course of the ordinary activities of the entity include, for example, the cost of goods sold, the cost of supplies used, rent and wages, and the consumption of benefits embodied in property, plant and equipment. Losses represent decreases in economic benefits, and may or may not arise in the ordinary activities of the entity.

Expenses also include realised and unrealised losses, for example a realised loss such as the loss from flood damage and an unrealised loss resulting from a decrease in the value of property, plant and equipment. This can be illustrated as shown in Diagram 2.3.

Example: Expenses definition

On 1 October 20X5, an entity pays C1 200 for an insurance policy for a 12-month period from 1 October 20X5 to 30 September 20X6. The year end of the entity is 31 December 20X5.

You are required to:

Discuss whether an expense is recognised for the year ended 31 December 20X5 and, if so, what the amount of the expense is.

Solution: Expense definition

The cash paid of C1 200 relates to the contract period from 1 October 20X5 to 30 September 20X6. An expense of C300 (C1 200 × 3/12) is recognised for the year ended 31 December 20X5. There is an *outflow of assets* (the insurance prepaid that was recognised when the cash was paid now decreases) that results in a *decrease in equity* (expenses incurred decrease equity) and it is not a distribution to an equity participant.

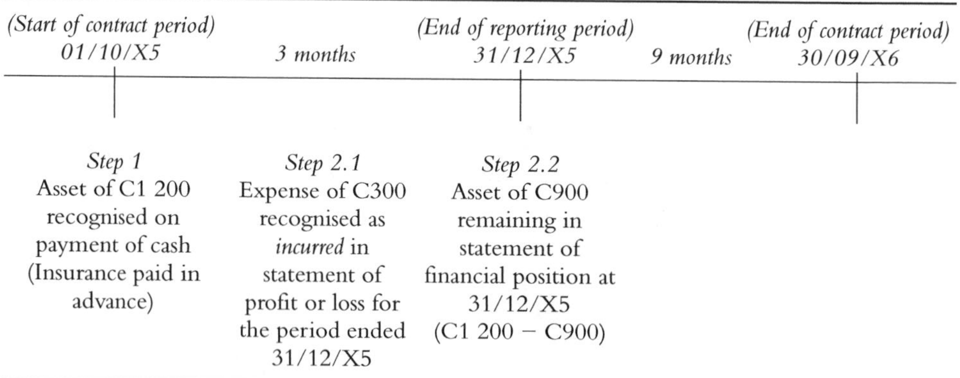

Step 1 – Remember from the discussion of an asset that when cash is paid in advance for a service, the entity has a resource that it controls. An asset is recognised representing a resource of the entity, referred to here as *insurance paid in advance.*

Step 2.1 – At 31 December 20X5, three months of the 12-month contract period have passed and therefore an expense of C300 (C1 200 × 3/12) is recognised as incurred. Expenses are incurred by a decrease in an asset or an increase in a liability – in this case, a decrease in the asset, insurance in advance.

Step 2.2 – As a result of Step 2.1, the remaining asset for insurance paid in advance in the statement of financial position at 31 December 20X5 is C900 (C1 200 – C300).

Pause and reflect...

What amount of expense is recognised in respect of this contract for the year ended 31 December 20X6?

Response

An expense of C900 (C1 200 × 9/12) is recognised as incurred for the year ended 31 December 20X6. This represents the expense for the remaining nine months of the contract from 1 January 20X6 to 30 September 20X6.

Assume during the year ended 31 December 20X5 that a business entity earns income of C1 500 000 and incurs expenses of C1 000 000. If the income of C1 500 000 all comprises fees for services provided and the expenses of C1 000 000 comprise administrative expenses of C600 000 and distribution expenses of C400 000, a simple statement of profit or loss can be drawn up as follows:

STATEMENT OF PROFIT OR LOSS
FOR THE YEAR ENDED 31 DECEMBER 20X5

		C
Income		
Fees		1 500 000
Expenses		(1 000 000)
Administative	600 000	
Distribution	400 000	
Profit of the period		500 000

Concepts in context

Comair Limited
Extract from notes to the financial statements

Trade and other payables	**R 000**
Trade payables	802 754
Unflown ticket liability	217 729
Other	38 027
	1 058 510

Unflown ticket liability is all monies received from passengers prior to the reporting period and relating to flights not yet flown.

What concepts in context can you see here?

Remember from the discussion of a liability that when cash is received in advance for a service, the entity has an obligation to provide that service in the future. A liability is recognised representing an obligation of the entity, which we have referred to in this book as income received in advance.

Comair state in their financial statements that 'unflown ticket liability is all monies received from passengers prior to the reporting period and relating to flights not yet flown'. Comair are reporting a liability in their statement of financial position representing their obligation to fly passengers in the future. Comair have used the term 'unflown ticket liability' rather than 'income received in advance'. There are many acceptable terms used in practice.

Comair Limited is an airline based in South Africa that operates scheduled services on domestic routes as a British Airways franchisee and also as a low-cost carrier under its own kulula.com brand.

Source: www.comair.co.za/Media/Comair/files/2013/Comair-Limited-Intergrated-Annual-Report-2013.pdf (Accessed 19 August 2014).

2.5.3 The statement of changes in equity

There are no elements unique to the statement of changes in equity (as assets, liabilities and equity are related to the statement of financial position and income and expenses are related to the statement of profit or loss). Rather, the statement of changes in equity reports the effect of transactions during the period that have increased or decreased equity.

Changes in an entity's equity between two reporting dates result from the entity's financial performance *and* from other transactions or events, such as the contribution of capital by the owners or distributions of cash to the owners.

The statement of changes in equity thus presents line items showing:

- the profit or loss for the period;
- contributions by owners;
- distributions to owners.

Assume the business entity referred to in the previous example had a balance of equity at the beginning of the period of C4 400 000. Contributions to capital by owners amounted to C1 000 000 and distributions to owners amounted to C100 000. The income and expenses are the same as in the previous example. A simple statement of changes in equity could then be drawn up as follows:

STATEMENT OF CHANGES IN EQUITY
FOR THE YEAR ENDED 31 DECEMBER 20X5

	Capital
	C
Balance at 1 January 20X5	4 400 000
Contributions by owners	1 000 000
Distributions to owners	(100 000)
Profit for the period	500 000
Balance at 31 December 20X5	5 800 000

2.5.4 The purpose, components and elements of financial statements summarised

Objective	*Components*	*Elements*
To provide useful information about:		
Financial position	Statement of financial position	Assets, liabilities, equity
Financial performance	Statement of profit or loss	Income, expenses
Changes in financial position	Statement of changes in equity	No defined elements
Cash flows	Statement of cash flows	No defined elements, but classified as operating, investing and financing activities

In addition to the above, financial statements present accounting policies and explanatory notes that are necessary to assist in understanding the financial statements. You will remember that *understandability* is one of the enhancing qualitative characteristics or attributes that make financial statements useful to users.

2.6 The accrual basis of accounting

The accrual basis of accounting is one of the ***general features*** listed in IAS 1 *Presentation of Financial Statements*. We have previously mentioned the accrual basis of accounting as a more useful measure of the financial performance of a business entity compared to the cash basis.

There are eight general features listed in IAS 1 (including the accrual basis). These will be discussed in detail in Chapter 6, *Preparation and presentation of financial statements*. However, an understanding of the accrual basis of accounting is essential for the preparation of even the most elementary financial statements and is addressed here in detail.

When the accrual basis of accounting is used, items are recognised as assets, liabilities or equity and as income or expenses when they satisfy the ***definitions*** and ***recognition criteria*** for those elements in the accounting framework. The definitions of the elements have already been described in this chapter. The recognition criteria will be addressed in Chapter 6.

The implication of the accrual basis is that the effects of transactions are recognised when they *occur*, even if cash is received or paid in a different period, and they are recorded in the accounting records and reported in the financial statements of the periods to which they *relate*.

Only amounts that are ***earned*** in or relate to a period are recognised as income and included in the statement of profit or loss. Goods or services may be provided for cash; in other words, the provision of the goods or services and the receipt of cash occur in the same period, and the amount received is recognised as income. If the goods or services have been provided and cash has not been received, the amount is still regarded as earned and is recognised as income. Conversely, cash received in the current period for goods or services provided in a previous period is not recognised as income when received. The relevant amount would have been recognised as income in the period when the goods or services were provided.

Turning our attention to expenses, only amounts that are ***incurred*** in or relate to a period are recognised as an expense and included in the statement of profit or loss. When dealing with expenses, it is only goods or services that are **used** in the period under review that are recognised as expenses. The use of the goods or services and the payment of cash may occur in the same period, and the amount paid is recognised as an expense. If the goods or services have been used and cash has not been paid, the amount is still regarded as incurred and is recognised as an expense. Conversely, cash paid in the current period for goods or services used in a previous period is not recognised as an expense when paid. The relevant amount would have been recognised as an expense when the goods or services were used.

Example: Accrual basis of accounting

A legal practice consults with 100 clients in a financial period of one month. The practice charges each client C500. The practice operates from rented premises, and the landlord charges the practice rent of C10 000 per month.

Scenario 1: The practice receives the full C50 000 from clients in the current month and the practice pays the landlord the full C10 000 for rent in the current month.
Scenario 2: The practice receives C30 000 from clients in the current month as some clients have not yet paid their accounts, and the practice neglects to pay the landlord in the current month.
Scenario 3: The practice receives C70 000 from clients in the current month as certain clients decide to pay in advance for future consultations and the practice pays the landlord C20 000 in the current month by paying the following month's rent in advance.

You are required to:

For each of the above scenarios, prepare a cash basis statement of cash flows and an accrual basis statement of profit or loss. For the accrual basis, indicate the effect on the statement of financial position.

Solution: Accrual basis of accounting

Scenario 1

	C
Cash received from clients	50 000
Cash paid for rent	10 000

CASH BASIS		**ACCRUAL BASIS**		
Statement of cash flows		*Statement of profit or loss*		*Statement of financial position effect*
	C		C	
Cash inflows		**Income**		
Fees	50 000	Fees	50 000	No statement of financial position effect
Cash outflows		**Expenses**		
Rent	(10 000)	Rent	(10 000)	No statement of financial position effect
Net cash flow	40 000	**Profit for the period**	40 000	

Scenario 2

	C
Cash received from clients	30 000
Cash paid for rent	—

CASH BASIS		**ACCRUAL BASIS**		
Statement of cash flows		*Statement of profit or loss*		*Statement of financial position effect*
	C		C	
Cash inflows		**Income**		
Fees	30 000	Fees	50 000	Asset, *fees receivable*, of C20 000 representing a *resource controlled* by the entity, in respect of the amount owing by clients

Cash outflows		**Expenses**		
Rent	—	Rent	(10 000)	Liability, *rent payable*, of C10 000 representing an *obligation* of the entity, in respect of the amount owing to the landlord
Net cash flow	30 000	**Profit for the period**	40 000	

Scenario 3

	C
Cash received from clients	70 000
Cash paid for rent	20 000

CASH BASIS		ACCRUAL BASIS		
Statement of cash flows (Cash basis)		*Statement of profit or loss (Accrual basis)*		*Statement of financial position effect*
	C		*C*	
Cash inflows		**Income**		
Fees	70 000	Fees	50 000	Liability, *fees received* in *advance*, of C20 000 representing an *obligation* of the entity, in respect of the fees received in advance from clients
Cash outflows		**Expenses**		
Rent	(20 000)	Rent	(10 000)	Asset, *rent paid in advance*, of C10 000 representing a *resource controlled* by the entity, in respect of the rent paid in advance to the landlord
Net cash flow	50 000	**Profit for the period**	40 000	

Considering the cash received and income first, if the practice charges each client C500, the income earned for the period should be C50 000. In *scenario 1*, all the clients pay the practice in the current month, in which case the income earned of C50 000 will equal the C50 000 cash received. In *scenario 2*, the practice receives less than C50 000 in the current month, in this case C30 000, because some clients have not yet paid their accounts. In *scenario 3*, the practice receives more than C50 000, in this case C70 000, as certain clients decide to pay in advance for future consultations. In both of these cases, the statement of profit or loss will still reflect C50 000 as income from fees as that is the amount which has been earned in the period from services provided. The recognition of income on the statement of profit or loss is a measure of *accomplishment* for the period and is not dependent on the cash received.

Turning to the rent the practice has to pay for its office space, the landlord charges the practice rent of C10 000 per month, the practice's rent expense should be C10 000.

In *scenario 1*, the practice pays the landlord the full C10 000 in the current month, in which case the expense incurred of C10 000 will equal the cash paid of C10 000. *In scenario 2*, the practice neglects to pay the C10 000 in the current month and in *scenario 3* it pays C20 000 by paying the following month's rent in advance. In both of these cases, the statement of profit or loss will reflect C10 000 as rent expense as that is the amount which has been incurred in the period and which needs to be matched with the income earned. The recognition of expenses on the statement of profit or loss is a measure of *sacrifice* for the period and is not dependent on the cash paid.

Concepts in context

Comair Limited
Extract from revenue recognition policy note

Revenue comprises all airline-related and non-airline revenue earned. Revenue arising from the provision of transportation services to passengers is recognised on an accrual basis in the period in which the services are rendered and the passenger has flown. Unflown ticket revenue is recognised as a liability until such time as the passenger has flown.

What concepts in context can you see here?

You have learnt in this chapter that transactions are recognised on the accrual basis when they *occur*, even if cash is received or paid in a different period.

Can you understand what Comair are doing? Many people book and pay for their airline tickets many weeks or months ahead of travel. Comair are recognising revenue from airline ticket sales in the period when the passenger has flown; in other words, when the service is provided, even though the cash may have been received in an earlier period. In addition, when the cash is received, it is recognised as a liability, representing the obligation of Comair to fly the passengers in the future.

Comair Limited is an airline based in South Africa that operates scheduled services on domestic routes as a British Airways franchisee and also as a low-cost carrier under its own kulula.com brand.

Source: www.comair.co.za/Media/Comair/files/2013/Comair-Limited-Intergrated-Annual-Report-2013.pdf (Accessed 19 August 2014).

2.7 Analysing transactions and the preparation of financial statements from concepts

The following is a record of the transactions of Simon Smart, a computer retailer, for the three-month period from 1 January 20X5 to 31 March 20X5. Transactions 1 to 23 are the same as in the previous example, and transactions 24 to 29 are now included as internal transactions.

Example: Analysing transactions and the preparation of financial statements from concepts

External transactions

Starting the business

1 On 2 January, Simon Smart started a business as a computer retailer. He drew C950 000 from a savings account and opened a bank account in the name of Smart Concepts into which he paid C950 000.
2 On 2 January, Smart Concepts negotiated a loan from Techno Bank for an amount of C600 000. The loan is repayable in four equal annual instalments, beginning on 31 December 20X5. The interest rate is 12 per cent per annum, payable quarterly in arrears.
3 On 2 January, Simon located premises from which to operate in Hyde Park. The monthly rent for the premises is C12 000. Smart Concepts paid four months' rent in advance.
4 On 2 January, Simon transferred C120 000 from the bank account into a fixed deposit account earning interest at 5 per cent per annum.
5 On 2 January, Smart Concepts purchased furniture and fittings for C240 000. This was paid for from funds in the bank account. The expected useful life of the furniture and fittings is five years.
6 On 5 January, Smart Concepts purchased supplies of stationery for C5 000 as well as supplies of computer parts for C12 000. All of these were paid for in cash.
7 On 7 January, Smart Concepts opened an account with Computer World, the supplier of its inventory.

Trading and operating transactions for January

8 On 10 January, Smart Concepts purchased inventory of 60 computers from Computer World at a cost of C10 000 each. The total amount owing is to be paid by 25 March.
9 On 12 January, Simon paid a service provider C750 for internet access.
10 On 25 January, Smart Concepts sold 15 computers on credit to a customer for C12 500 each. An amount of C125 000 is due by 15 March and the balance by 15 April.

Trading and operating transactions for February

11 On 1 February, Smart Concepts employed a computer technician at a salary of C8 000 per month.
12 On 8 February, Smart Concepts paid C7 000 for an advertisement in a newspaper, advertising the computers available for sale.
13 On 12 February, Smart Concepts sold 30 computers to customers for C12 500 each. The customers paid cash for them.
14 On 25 February, Smart Concepts received cash of C48 000 in respect of technical support contracts taken out by customers. The contracts are for a two-year period.
15 On 28 February, Smart Concepts paid the computer technician his salary for February.

Trading and operating transactions for March

16 On 4 March, Smart Concepts purchased inventory of a further 75 computers from Computer World at a cost of C10 000 each. The total amount owing is to be paid by 25 May.

17 On 5 March, Smart Concepts paid a service provider C750 for internet access.
18 On 15 March, Smart Concepts received C125 000 from the customer in transaction 10.
19 On 25 March, Smart Concepts paid Computer World an amount of C600 000.
20 On 29 March, Smart Concepts sold 30 computers on credit to customers for C12 500 each. The full amount owing is due by 30 April.
21 On 30 March, Smart Concepts paid the computer technician his salary for March.

Rewarding the providers of finance

22 On 30 March, Smart Concepts paid the interest on the loan from Techno Bank for the three-month period.
23 On 30 March, Simon authorised a distribution to himself of C60 000 for personal use.

Internal transactions

24 On 31 March, Simon examined the records of the business and established that technical support in respect of contracts to the value of C6 000 had been provided to customers.
25 On 31 March, Smart Concepts accounted for the interest on the fixed deposit earned for the period.
26 On 31 March, Smart Concepts recognised the rent expense incurred for the period.
27 On 31 March, the water account for C1 500 and the electricity account for C2 500 had been received but not paid.
28 On 31 March, Simon counted stationery supplies on hand costing C2 000 and also counted computer parts on hand costing C3 500.
29 On 31 March, Smart Concepts accounted for the usage of the furniture and fittings for the period.

You are required to:

Prepare, for Smart Concepts, the statement of profit or loss and the statement of changes in equity for the three months ended 31 March 20X5, and the statement of financial position at 31 March 20X5. You should develop the answer considering the entity concept, the definitions of the elements of the financial statements and applying the accrual basis of accounting.

Solution: Analysing transactions and preparation of financial statements from concepts

Each transaction needs to be analysed bearing in mind the entity concept, the definitions of the elements of the financial statements and the accrual basis of accounting. We suggest that you set up an outline of the statement of profit or loss, statement of changes in equity and statement of financial position, and enter each item, or components of that item, on the financial statements as the transaction is analysed.

You should use the following approach to analyse each transaction:

- Identify which elements of the financial statements are affected; in other words, does the transaction affect assets, liabilities, income, expenses or owner's equity? For example, a transaction may affect an asset and income, an asset and a liability, or maybe two assets.
- Identify the specific asset, liability, income, expense or owner's equity item affected; in other words, the asset, i.e. accounts receivable; income, i.e. sales; the asset, inventory; and the liability, accounts payable.
- Decide if the identified item is increasing or decreasing, and record the effect on the financial statements using the workings column.

SMART CONCEPTS
STATEMENT OF PROFIT OR LOSS
FOR THE THREE MONTHS ENDED 31 MARCH 20X5

	Workings	C
Income		945 000
Sales	*(187 500 + 375 000 + 375 000)*	937 500
Service fees	*(Internal transaction 24)*	6 000
Interest	*(120 000 × 0.05 × 3/12)*	1 500
Expenses		(856 000)
Cost of sales	*(150 000 + 300 000 + 300 000)*	750 000
Internet	*(750 + 750)*	1 500
Advertising	*(External transaction 12)*	7 000
Salaries	*(8 000 + 8 000)*	16 000
Rent	*(48 000 × ¾)*	36 000
Water and electricity	*(1 500 + 2 500)*	4 000
Stationery supplies	*(5 000 – 2 000)*	3 000
Computer parts	*(12 000 – 3 500)*	8 500
Depreciation	*(240 000/5 yrs × 3/12)*	12 000
Interest	*(600 000 × 0.12 × 3/12)*	18 000
Profit for the period		89 000

SMART CONCEPTS
STATEMENT OF CHANGES IN EQUITY
FOR THE PERIOD ENDED 31 MARCH 20X5

	C
Balance at 1 January 20X5	—
Profit for the period	89 000
Distributions	(60 000)
Contribution to capital	950 000
Balance at 31 March 20X5	979 000

SMART CONCEPTS
STATEMENT OF FINANCIAL POSITION
AT 31 MARCH 20X5

	Workings	*C*
ASSETS		2 375 000
Furniture and fittings	*(240 000 – 12 000)*	228 000
Fixed deposit investment	*(External transaction 4)*	120 000
Inventory	*(600 000 – 150 000 – 300 000 + 750 000 – 300 000)*	600 000
Accounts receivable	*(187 500 – 125 000 + 375 000)*	437 500
Stationery supplies	*(5 000 – 3 000)*	2 000
Computer parts	*(12 000 – 8 500)*	3 500
Rent paid in advance	*(48 000 – 36 000)*	12 000
Interest receivable	*(120 000 x 0.5 x 3/12)*	1 500
Bank	*(950 000 + 600 000 – 48 000 – 120 000 – 240 000 – 17 000 – 750 – 7 000 + 375 000 + 48 000 – 8 000 – 750 + 125 000 – 600 000 – 8 000 – 18 000 – 60 000)*	970 500
		2 375 000
EQUITY AND LIABILITIES		
Equity		
Capital	*[(From SOCIE*) or (0 + 89 000 – 60 000 + 950 000)]*	979 000
Liabilities		1 396 000
Borrowings	*(External transaction 2)*	600 000
Accounts payable	*(600 000 + 750 000 – 600 000)*	750 000
Service fees received in advance	*(48 000 – 6 000)*	42 000
Water and electricity payable	*(1 500 + 2 500)*	4 000
		2 375 000

* SOCIE = Statement of changes in equity.

The analysis of each transaction follows, together with a detailed explanation.

Starting the business

1 On 2 January, Simon Smart started a business as a computer retailer. He drew C950 000 from a savings account and opened a bank account in the name of Smart Concepts into which he paid C950 000.	
Analysis of transaction	The asset, *bank*, is increased by C950 000, and owner's equity, *capital*, is increased by C950 000.

Remember that the financial statements are prepared from the perspective of the business entity, utilising the entity concept. When Simon Smart withdraws C950 000 from his personal savings account, the business entity is not affected. When C950 000 is paid into the bank account of the business entity, Smart Concepts, the first transaction takes place. The cash in the bank embodies future economic benefits because of its command over other resources. Each transaction must affect at least two elements of the financial statements, or classifications of the same element twice.

Trading and operating transactions for January

2 On 2 January, Smart Concepts negotiated a loan from Techno Bank for an amount of C600 000. The loan is repayable in four equal annual instalments, beginning on 31 December 20X5. The interest rate is 12 per cent per annum, payable quarterly in arrears.

Analysis of transaction	The asset, *bank*, is increased by C600 000, and the liability, *borrowings*, is increased by C600 000.

The borrowing is a liability as it is a present obligation of the entity (an amount owing to an outside party) arising from a past event (the loan transaction) and is expected to result in an outflow of resources on settlement (cash will be paid to the bank in settlement of the loan).

3 On 2 January, Simon located premises from which to operate in Hyde Park. The monthly rent for the premises is C12 000. Smart Concepts paid four months' rent in advance.

Analysis of transaction	The asset, *rent paid in advance*, is increased by C48 000, and the asset, *bank*, is decreased by C48 000.

By paying four months' rent in advance, the business has a right to occupy the premises for the months of January, February, March and April. This right is an asset, as it is a resource controlled by the entity (the right of occupation) as a result of a past event (the rental agreement with the landlord) and from which future economic benefits are expected to flow (income will be earned by selling computers from the premises). The asset, *rent paid in advance*, is therefore increased on the statement of financial position. The amount of C48 000 has been paid and therefore the asset, *bank*, is decreased by the same amount. You will notice that items on the financial statements that are affected by more than one transaction have brackets behind the narration in a working column to expedite the calculation of the final balance.

4 On 2 January, Simon transferred C120 000 from the bank account into a fixed deposit account earning interest at 5 per cent per annum.

Analysis of transaction	The asset, *fixed deposit*, is increased by C120 000, and the asset, *bank*, is decreased by C120 000.

The transfer of funds from the bank account to a fixed deposit account results in the increase in one asset, *fixed deposit*, and the decrease of another asset, *bank*. Interest is earned on a time proportion basis and will be recognised as income at the end of the period.

5 On 2 January, Smart Concepts purchased furniture and fittings for C240 000. This was paid for from funds in the bank account. The expected useful life of the furniture and fittings is five years.

Analysis of transaction	The asset, *furniture and fittings*, is increased by C240 000, and the asset, *bank*, is decreased by C240 000.

The furniture and fittings comply with the definition of an asset. The furniture and fittings are a resource controlled by the entity (ownership of the furniture and fittings) arising from a past event (the purchase transaction) and from which future economic benefits are expected to flow to the entity (the furniture and fittings will be used in operating the business).

6 On 5 January, Smart Concepts purchased supplies of stationery for C5 000 as well as supplies of computer parts for C12 000. All of these were paid for in cash.

Analysis of transaction	The assets, *stationery supplies* and *computer parts* are increased by C5 000 and C12 000 respectively, and the asset, *bank*, is decreased by C17 000.

Supplies comply with the definition of an asset and are recorded as such on purchase. The supplies are a resource controlled by the entity (ownership of the supplies) as a result of a past event (the purchase transaction) and from which future economic benefits are expected to flow (the supplies will be used in the operations of the entity). An expense will be recognised only when the supplies are used.

7 On 7 January, Smart Concepts opened an account with Computer World, the supplier of its inventory.

Analysis of transaction	Not applicable.

The opening of the account with the supplier is a transaction that has no economic impact on the entity and therefore the financial statements are not affected.

Trading and operating transactions for January

8 On 10 January, Smart Concepts purchased inventory of 60 computers from Computer World at a cost of C10 000 each. The total amount owing is to be paid by 25 March.

Analysis of transaction	The asset, *inventory*, is increased by C600 000, and the liability, *accounts payable*, is increased by C600 000.

The asset, *inventory*, is increased when inventory is purchased. The inventory is a resource controlled by the entity (ownership of the inventory) arising from a past event (the purchase transaction) and from which future economic benefits are expected to flow (the inventory will be sold to customers). The amount owing to Computer World is represented by an increase in the liability, *accounts payable*. It is a present obligation of the entity (the amount owing to the supplier) arising from a past event (the purchase transaction), and is expected to result in an outflow of resources upon settlement (cash will be paid to Computer World).

9 On 12 January, Smart Concepts paid a service provider C750 for internet access.

Analysis of transaction	The expense, *internet*, is increased by C750, and the asset, *bank*, is decreased by C750.

Purchase of internet access gives rise to an expense. Applying the accrual basis of accounting, the purchase of the service (in this case, internet access) and the payment of the cash occur in the same period, and the amount paid is recognised immediately as an expense. There is a decrease in economic benefits in the form of, in this case, the decrease of an asset, *bank* (the amount paid to the service provider). An asset is not created, bearing in mind the threshold quality of materiality and the cost/benefit constraint.

10 On 25 January, Smart Concepts sold 15 computers on credit to a customer for C12 500 each. An amount of C125 000 is due by 15 March and the balance by 15 April.

Analysis of transaction	The asset, *accounts receivable*, is increased by C187 500, and income, *sales*, is increased by C187 500. In addition, the expense, *cost of sales*, is increased by C150 000, and the asset, *inventory*, is decreased by C150 000.

Smart Concepts earns income by selling computers to customers. The sales in this transaction are *on credit* and the customer is going to pay part of the purchase consideration before the end of the current three-month period and the remainder during the next period. Income, in the form of revenue from sales, is recognised immediately in terms of the accrual basis. Remember that the accrual basis requires income to be recognised as it is *earned*, irrespective of when the cash is received. An asset, *accounts receivable*, is increased and the sales revenue included as income in the statement of profit or loss. There has been an increase in economic benefits in the form of, in this case, the increase of an asset (the amount owing by the customer as accounts receivable).

The expense side of the transaction must also be recognised. The accrual basis of accounting requires expenses to be recognised when *incurred*, irrespective of when the cash is paid. A cost of sales expense is recognised in the period when the goods are sold. There has been a decrease in economic benefits in the form of, in this case, an outflow of an asset (the inventory sold). Remember from transaction 8 that no expense was recognised when the inventory was purchased.

Trading and operating transactions for February

11 On 1 February, Smart Concepts employed a computer technician at a salary of C8 000 per month.

Analysis of transaction	Not applicable.

The employment of a technician is also a transaction that has no economic impact on the entity and therefore the financial statements are not affected.

12 On 8 February, Smart Concepts paid C7 000 for an advertisement in a newspaper, advertising the computers available for sale.

Analysis of transaction	The expense, *advertising*, is increased by C7 000, and the asset, *bank*, is decreased by C7 000.

Inserting an advertisement into the newspaper gives rise to an expense. Applying the accrual basis of accounting, the purchase of the service (in this case, advertising) and the payment of the cash occur in the same period, and the amount paid is recognised immediately as an expense. It results in a decrease in economic benefits in the form of, in this instance, the outflow of an asset (the cash paid to the newspaper).

13 On 12 February, Smart Concepts sold 30 computers to customers for C12 500 each. The customers paid cash for them.

Analysis of transaction	The asset, *bank*, is increased by C375 000, and income, *sales*, is increased by C375 000. In addition, the expense, *cost of sales*, is increased by C300 000 and the asset, *inventory*, is decreased by C300 000.

The sales in this transaction are *for cash*. The sale of the goods and the receipt of the cash occur in the same period, and income, in the form of revenue from sales, is recognised immediately. There has been an increase in economic benefits in the form of, in this case, the enhancement of an asset (the cash in the bank). As in transaction 10, the cost of sales must be recognised at the time the sale is made.

14 On 25 February, Smart Concepts received cash of C48 000 in respect of technical support contracts taken out by customers. The contracts are for a two-year period.

Analysis of transaction	The asset, *bank*, is increased by C48 000, and the liability, *service fees received in advance*, is increased by C48 000.

This transaction requires a careful examination of the accrual basis. Cash has been received and the asset, *bank*, is increased. The provision of technical support, however, is going to take place partly in the current period and partly in future periods. The accrual basis requires income to be recognised only when it is *earned* and as the technical support will be provided over a two-year period, the income for the current period can only be recognised at the end of the period when the value of the work that has been performed is known.

On receipt of the cash, a liability, *service fees received in advance*, is created, representing the obligation of Smart Concepts to provide customers with technical support. The service fees received in advance are a liability as there is a present obligation of the entity (obligation to provide technical support) as a result of a past event (the contract) that will result in an outflow of economic benefits. (Smart Concepts will use its resources to service the customers' computers.)

15 On 28 February, Smart Concepts paid the computer technician his salary for February.

Analysis of transaction	The expense, *salaries*, is increased by C8 000, and the asset, *bank*, is decreased by C8 000.

Payment to the technician gives rise to an expense for the same reason as the payment for internet access and the advertisement. Applying the accrual basis of accounting, the services of the employee and the payment of the cash occur in the same period, and the amount paid is recognised immediately as an expense. This results in a decrease in economic benefits in the form of, in this instance, the outflow of an asset (the cash paid to the employee).

Trading and operating transactions for March

16 On 4 March, Smart Concepts purchased inventory of a further 75 computers from Computer World at a cost of C10 000 each. The total amount owing is to be paid by 25 May.

Analysis of transaction	The asset, *inventory*, is increased by C750 000, and the liability, *accounts payable*, is increased by C750 000.

This transaction is identical to transaction 8.

17 On 5 March, Smart Concepts paid a service provider C750 for internet access.

Analysis of transaction	The expense, *internet*, is increased by C750, and the asset, *bank*, is decreased by C750.

 This transaction is identical to transaction 9.

18 On 15 March, Smart Concepts received C125 000 from the customer in transaction 10.

Analysis of transaction	The asset, *bank*, is increased by C125 000, and the asset, *accounts receivable*, is decreased by C125 000.

The customer to whom the computers were sold in transaction 10 now pays part of the amount owing by him. If you look back at transaction 10, you will notice that in terms of the accrual basis, the income was recognised at the time the sale was made. Income cannot be recognised again now that the cash has been received.

19 On 25 March, Smart Concepts paid Computer World an amount of C600 000.	
Analysis of transaction	The liability, *accounts payable*, is decreased by C600 000, and the asset, *bank*, is decreased by C600 000.

 This transaction involves the settlement of a liability. Note that no expense is recognised here as the expense (in this case, cost of sales) is recognised when the inventory is sold and not when the liability is settled.

20 On 29 March, Smart Concepts sold 30 computers on credit, to customers, for C12 500 each. The full amount owing is due by 30 April.	
Analysis of transaction	The asset, *accounts receivable*, is increased by C375 000, and income, *sales*, is increased by C375 000. In addition, the expense, *cost of sales*, is increased by C300 000, and the asset, *inventory*, is decreased by C300 000

 This transaction is identical to transaction 10.

21 On 30 March, Smart Concepts paid the computer technician his salary for March.	
Analysis of transaction	The expense, *salaries*, is increased by C8 000, and the asset, *bank*, is decreased by C8 000.

This transaction is identical to transaction 15.

Rewarding the providers of finance

22 On 30 March, Smart Concepts paid the interest on the loan from Techno Bank for the three-month period.	
Analysis of transaction	The expense, *interest*, is increased by C18 000, and the asset, *bank*, is decreased by C18 000.

The interest is payable quarterly *in arrears*, which means that the interest payments are made at the *end* of each three-month period. Applying the accrual basis of accounting, the interest charged by the bank and the payment of the cash occur in the same period, and the amount paid is recognised immediately as an expense. The payment of the interest gives rise to an expense as there is a decrease in economic benefits in the form of, in this case, the outflow of an asset, *bank*. The amount of the interest expense is C18 000 (C600 000 × 0.12 × 3/12). The amount of the loan is C600 000, the interest rate is 12 per cent per annum, and we recognise the interest expense for a three-month period.

23 On 30 March, Simon authorised a distribution to himself of C60 000 for personal use.

Analysis of transaction	Owner's equity, *distributions*, is increased by C60 000, and the asset, *bank*, is decreased by C60 000.

The C60 000 distributed to Simon decreases the asset, *bank*, but no expense is shown on the statement of profit or loss, as the amount is a distribution to the owner. The definition of an expense refers to decreases in economic benefits that result in decreases in equity *other* than those relating to distributions to equity participants. The entity concept also applies here, as an amount distributed to the owner cannot create a business expense. Note that an *increase* in distributions results in a *decrease* in owner's equity and is therefore shown as a decrease in the statement of changes in equity.

Internal transactions

24 On 31 March, Simon examined the records of the business and established that technical support in respect of contracts to the value of C6 000 had been provided to customers.

Analysis of transaction	The liability, *service fees received in advance*, is decreased by C6 000, and income, *service fees*, is increased by C6 000.

When Smart Concepts received cash of C48 000 in respect of technical support contracts taken out by customers (see transaction 14), a liability was established representing an obligation of the entity to provide a service in the future. At the end of the period, the service records show that C6 000 of the work has been performed.

The accrual basis of accounting requires income to be recognised in the period when earned and therefore ***income*** of C6 000 for service fees is recognised in the statement of profit or loss and the ***liability***, service fees received in advance, is decreased in the statement of financial position.

25 On 31 March, Smart Concepts accounted for the interest on the fixed deposit earned for the period.

Analysis of transaction	The asset, *interest receivable*, is increased by C1 500, and income, *interest*, is increased by C1 500.

The transfer to the fixed deposit investment was made at the beginning of January. No interest has been received from the bank, but interest for three months has been earned. As mentioned previously, interest is earned on the time-apportioned basis.

The accrual basis of accounting requires income to be recognised when *earned* even if the cash is received in a different period. Interest of C1 500 (C120 000 × 0.05 × 3/12) is therefore recognised as ***income*** in the statement of profit or loss, and an interest receivable is recognised as an ***asset*** in the statement of financial position representing the amount of interest owing to Smart Concepts. You will notice that the same item, *interest*, appears in the statement of profit or loss as ***income*** and in the statement of financial position as an ***asset***.

26 On 31 March, Smart Concepts recognised the rent expense incurred for the period.

Analysis of transaction	The expense, *rent*, is increased by C36 000, and the asset, *rent paid in advance*, is decreased by C36 000.

When Smart Concepts paid C48 000 for four months' rent in advance (see transaction 3), an asset, *rent paid in advance*, was created, representing the right to occupy the premises from the beginning of January to the end of April.

The accrual basis of accounting requires expenses to be recognised in the period when *incurred* and therefore an ***expense*** of C36 000 for rent in respect of the three-month period to the end of March is recognised in the statement of profit or loss, and the ***asset***, *rent paid in advance*, is reduced by C36 000 in the statement of financial position.

27 On 31 March, the water account for C1 500 and the electricity account for C2 500 had been received but not paid.

Analysis of transaction	The expense, *water and electricity*, is increased by C4 000, and the liability, *water and electricity payable*, is increased by C4 000.

The water and electricity accounts have been received, but will only be paid in the following month. However, both are expenses incurred in the current period.

The accrual basis of accounting requires expenses to be recognised when *incurred*, even if the cash is paid in a different period. An ***expense*** for water and electricity is therefore recognised in the statement of profit or loss, and *water and electricity payable* is recognised as a ***liability*** in the statement of financial position representing the amount owing to service providers. You will notice that the same item, *water and electricity*, appears in the statement of profit or loss as an expense, and in the statement of financial position as a liability.

28 On 31 March, Simon counted stationery supplies on hand costing C2 000 and also counted computer parts on hand costing C3 500.

Analysis of transaction	The expense, *stationery supplies*, is increased by C3 000, and the asset, *stationery supplies*, is decreased by C3 000. In addition, the expense, *computer parts*, is increased by C8 500, and the asset, *computer parts*, is decreased by C8 500.

When the supplies were purchased in transaction 6, an amount of C5 000 was recorded as an asset, *stationery supplies*, and an amount of C12 000 as an asset, *computer parts*.

At the end of the period, C2 000 of the stationery supplies is still unused, implying that C3 000 has been used during the period. The amount used must be shown as an expense, and the balance unused must be reflected as an asset. This is effected by recognising an ***expense*** of C3 000 for stationery supplies in the statement of profit or loss, and reducing the ***asset***, *stationery supplies*, on the statement of financial position to C2 000. Similarly, at the end of the period, C3 500 of the computer parts is still unused, implying that C8 500 has been used during the period. Again, the amount used must be shown as an expense, and the balance unused must be reflected as an asset. This is effected by recognising an ***expense*** of C8 500 for computer parts in the statement of profit or loss, and reducing the ***asset***, *computer parts*, on the statement of financial position to C3 500. Note that the same items, *stationery supplies and computer parts*, appear in the statement of profit or loss as expenses and in the statement of financial position as assets.

29 On 31 March, Smart Concepts accounted for the usage of the furniture and fittings for the period.

Analysis of transaction	The expense, *depreciation*, is increased by C12 000, and the asset, *furniture and fittings*, is decreased by C12 000.

> The furniture and fittings are expected to have a useful life of five years. Even though the full purchase price of C240 000 was paid in cash during the current period, the cost of the asset is expensed over the periods when the asset is used. An ***expense*** of C12 000 (C240 000/5 x 3/12) is thus recognised for the usage of the asset, known as *depreciation*, in the statement of profit or loss, and the carrying amount of the ***asset***, furniture and fittings is reduced by C12 000.

2.8 Cash basis compared to accrual basis of accounting

It is appropriate at this stage to compare the statement of cash inflows and outflows prepared using the cash basis of accounting, and the statement of profit or loss prepared using the accrual basis of accounting in order to assess which provides a better measure of performance.

In Section 2.2 of this chapter, we prepared two statements of cash inflows and outflows, one showing total cash inflows and outflows, and the other showing operating cash inflows and outflows. Then in Section 2.7 of the chapter, we prepared a statement of profit or loss using the accrual basis of accounting. The information presented in these statements can be summarised in Table 2.3.

The advantage of the cash basis of accounting is that it is factual, and cash flows, particularly the prediction of future cash flows, are of interest to investors. The cash basis assists investors to understand how an entity receives and uses its cash, and also explains the cash flows in relation to an entity's operating, investing and financing activities.

On the other hand, there are some major disadvantages to consider. When measured over short periods of time, the cash basis may seriously misrepresent the long-run cash-generating ability of the entity. For example, many business entities encounter large cash outflows in one period to acquire resources such as property and equipment that will be used to produce goods and services in future periods. In addition, the entity may acquire or use resources in the current period that were paid for in a previous period or which may be paid for only in a future period. Similarly, the entity may provide goods and services in the current period in respect of which the cash was received in a previous period or for which the cash will be received only in a future period.

The accrual basis statement of profit or loss provides information on the results of an entity's operations for the relevant period. Income earned by the entity for goods or services provided is included as a measure of *accomplishment* in the period when the goods are sold or the service provided and not when the cash is received (unless the goods or services are provided for cash). The expenses incurred by the entity are included as a measure of *effort* in the period when used or consumed and not when the cash is paid (unless the expenses are paid in cash).

Table 2.3 Cash basis compared to accrual basis

CASH BASIS OF ACCOUNTING			**ACCRUAL BASIS OF ACCOUNTING**	
	Statement of cash inflows and outflows	*Statement of operating cash inflows and outflows*	*Statement of profit or loss*	
Cash inflows	2 098 000	548 000	Income	945 000
Cash outflows	(1 127 500)	(707 500)	Expenses	(856 000)
Net cash flow	970 500	(159 500)	Profit for the period	89 000

The accrual basis is used in all components of a set of financial statements except in the statement of cash flows. In other words, the statement of profit or loss, the statement of financial position and the statement of changes in equity all rely on the accrual basis. According to the *Conceptual Framework*, accrual accounting 'provides a better basis for assessing the entity's past and future performance than information solely about cash receipts and payments during that period'.

Revision example

Perfect Paws is dog parlour owned and managed by Brian Beagle. The entity began trading on 1 April 20X6. The following transactions relate to Perfect Paws for the month of April 20X6:

1 On 1 April, Brian Beagle opened a business bank account and contributed capital of C51 000 in cash to start the business.
2 On 1 April, Beagle arranged to rent premises, and Perfect Paws paid rent of C1 800 in advance for the months of April, May and June of 20X6.
3 On 1 April, Perfect Paws purchased grooming equipment as a cost of C30 000. The grooming equipment has an expected useful life of five years and no value at the end of its life.
4 On 1 April, Beagle took out an insurance policy and paid C3 000 for cover from 1 April 20X6 to 31 July 20X6.
5 On 3 April, Perfect Paws purchased supplies on credit costing C580.
6 During the week ended 9 April, Perfect Paws received C3 400 in cash for grooming services provided.
7 On 11 April, Perfect Paws paid for the supplies purchased on 3 April.
8 During the week ended 16 April, Perfect Paws completed grooming services for a poodle breeder on credit for C1 700.
9 On 17 April, Perfect Paws purchased additional supplies on credit costing C340.
10 On 20 April, Perfect Paws received cash of C600 in advance from a client to groom her show dogs once a month from April to June 20X6.
11 During the week ended 26 April, Perfect Paws completed grooming services including nail clipping and brushing for the German Shepherd Club on credit for C1 200.
12 On 27 April, Perfect Paws received C1 700 from the poodle breeder.
13 On 28 April, Perfect Paws paid the April telephone account of C80.
14 On 29 April, Perfect Paws paid the assistant's salary of C650 for April.
15 On 29 April, Perfect Paws distributed cash of C1 000 to Brian Beagle.
16 On 30 April, Perfect Paws recognised the rent and insurance expense for March 20X6.
17 On 30 April, Perfect Paws recognised C200 income in respect of grooming the show dogs for the client in transaction 10.
18 On 30 April, Perfect Paws recognised the usage of the equipment for March 20X6.
19 On 30 April, Brian Beagle counted supplies on hand at the end of the month costing C520.

You are required to:

a) Prepare a statement of profit or loss for Perfect Paws for the month of April 20X6.
b) Prepare a statement of changes in equity for Perfect Paws for the month of April 20X6.
c) Prepare a statement of financial position for Perfect Paws at 30 April 20X6.

Solution: Revision example

a) Statement of profit or loss

PERFECT PAWS
STATEMENT OF PROFIT OR LOSS
FOR THE MONTH ENDED 30 APRIL 20X5

	Workings	*C*
Income		
Fees	*(3 400 + 1 700 + 1 200 + 200)*	6 500
Expenses		(2 980)
Telephone	*(80)*	80
Salary	*(650)*	650
Supplies	*(580 + 340 − 520)*	400
Rent	*(1 800/3)*	600
Insurance	*(3 000/4)*	750
Depreciation	*(30 000/5 × 1/12)*	500
Profit for the period		3 520

b) Statement of changes in equity

PERFECT PAWS
STATEMENT OF CHANGES IN EQUITY
FOR THE MONTH ENDED 30 APRIL 20X5

	Workings	*C*
Balance at 1 April 20X5		—
Capital contribution		51 000
Distributions		(1 000)
Profit for the period	*(from statement of profit or loss)*	3 520
Balance at 30 April 20X5		53 520

c) Statement of financial position

PERFECT PAWS
STATEMENT OF FINANCIAL POSITION
AT 30 APRIL 20X5

	Workings	*C*
ASSETS		
Grooming equipment	*(30 000 − 500)*	29 500
Supplies	*(580 + 340 − 400)*	520
Accounts receivable	*(1 700 + 1 200 − 1 700)*	1 200
Expenses paid in advance	*(1 800 + 3 000 − 600 − 750)*	3 450
Bank	*(51 000 − 30 000 − 1 800 − 3 000 + 3 400 − 580 + 600 + 1 700 − 1 000 − 80 − 650)*	19 590
		54 260

EQUITY AND LIABILITIES		
Equity		
Capital	*(51 000 + 3 520 − 1 000) or from SOCIE*	53 520
Liabilities		
Accounts payable		340
Fees received in advance	*(600 − 200)*	400
		54 260

Bibliography

Ernst & Young. 2010. *Conceptual Framework: Objectives and Qualitative Characteristics*. Supplement to IFRS Outlook, Issue 86. www.ey.com/Publication/vwLUAssets/Supplement_86_GL_IFRS/$FILE/Supplement_86_GL_IFRS.pdf (Accessed 18 August 2014).

Mueller, GG & Kelley, L. 1991. *Introductory Financial Accounting*. Englewood Cliffs, NJ: Prentice Hall Inc.

The International Accounting Standards Board. 2010. *The Conceptual Framework*.

The International Accounting Standards Board. 2012. IAS 1 *Presentation of Financial Statements*.

3 The accounting equation and the analysis of transactions

Business focus

The accounting equation, which tells us that assets are equal to the sum of liabilities and owners' equity, and the resulting double-entry system are taken for granted by most accountants. This is probably because these principles have been applied for well over 500 years since their use by the Franciscan Friar Luca Pacioli during the fifteenth century.

Why, however, was a complex system keeping track of transactions through entries on two sides of an equation used rather than a simple list of each of the elements of what are now modern financial statements? One reason is that it incorporates an accuracy check. The fact that the elements of the accounting equation must always be in balance provides some assurance that the relevant 'elements' affected by the transaction have been accounted for. Another explanation is the accounting equation reflects the use of scales – a measurement instrument in use at the time. More critically, the proliferation of the accounting technique may be the result of the political and social power of the Franciscan Order that allowed its accounting techniques to become the most widely applied, to the extent that alternatives were no longer even considered. Whatever the reason, no matter how complex the transactions and irrespective of the sophistication of the accounting software, the basic principle of 'assets are equal to the sum of liabilities and owner's equity' always applies.

In this chapter

Have you noticed when analysing a transaction that there are always *at least* two accounts affected? This chapter furthers your knowledge of analysing transactions by exploring the duality of accounting transactions while at the same time reinforcing the three fundamental accounting concepts from Chapter 2 – the entity concept, the definitions of the elements of the financial statements and the accrual basis of accounting.

Dashboard

- Look at the *Learning outcomes* so that you know what you should be able to do after studying this chapter.
- Read the *Business focus* to place this chapter's contents in a real-world context.
- Preview *In this chapter* to focus your mind on the contents of the chapter.

- Read the *text* in detail.
  - Pay attention to the *definitions*, and apply your mind to the *Pause and reflect* scenarios.
  - Ensure that you understand the effects of transactions on the accounting equation in Section 3.3 before moving on to the Smart Concepts case study in Section 3.5.
  - It is important that you relate the analysis of each transaction of the Smart Concepts case study in Chapter 2 (Section 2.7) to the effect of each transaction on the accounting equation in this chapter (Section 3.5).
- Prepare solutions to the examples as you read through the chapter.
- Prepare a solution to the *Revision example* at the end of the chapter without reference to the suggested one. Compare your solution to the suggested solution provided.

Learning outcomes

After studying this chapter, you should be able to do the following:

1. Distinguish between internal and external transactions.
2. Explain the logic of the accounting equation.
3. Analyse the effects of transactions on the accounting equation.
4. Analyse transactions using the accounting equation and prepare a set of financial statements.
5. Reconcile the profit for the period.

The accounting equation and the analysis of transactions

3.1 Transactions

In Chapter 2, *Fundamental accounting concepts*, we analysed the transactions or events of Smart Concepts for the period from 1 January 20X5 to 31 March 20X5. For each transaction, we determined whether an asset, liability or the owner's equity was affected and whether income was earned or an expense incurred. Remember that assets, liabilities, owner's equity, income and expense are the elements of the financial statements.

Transactions are therefore economic events which have an impact on the financial position of an entity. Transactions can be categorised as either external or internal.

- ***External transactions*** are economic events that occur between the entity and another business entity or person.
- ***Internal transactions*** are internal adjustments made to the financial position of an entity in order to apply the accrual basis of accounting.

When we revisit Smart Concepts later in this chapter, we will identify the external and internal transactions.

Pause and reflect . . .

Think about some of the transactions that we processed in the Smart Concepts example in Chapter 2:

a) The owner, Simon Smart, invested C950 000 in the business entity (transaction 1).
b) Smart Concepts paid C48 000 in respect of four months' rent in advance (transaction 3).
c) Smart Concepts recognised the rent expense incurred for the period (transaction 26).

Can you identify and explain which of the above transactions are external and which are internal?

Response

a) This is an external transaction because the owner and the business entity are separate accounting entities.
b) This is an external transaction because the landlord is another business entity or person.
c) This is an internal transaction because it takes into account the accrual basis of accounting by recognising an expense of C36 000 (C12 000 × 3 months) for the period from 1 January 20X5 to 31 March 20X5.

3.2 The accounting equation

A business entity is financed from two primary sources – ***owner's funds*** and ***borrowed funds***. Owner's funds are sourced from the *owners*, also known as investors, and borrowed funds are sourced from *lenders*. All funding can be categorised into one of these two sources.

Table 3.1 Funding of a business entity

Source of financing	*Known as*
Owner's funds – owners/investors	Owner's equity
Borrowed funds – lenders	Liabilities

Table 3.2 The accounting equation

Sum of assets	=	Claims against the entity
Sum of assets	=	Total source of finance
Assets	=	Funds provided by lenders and investors
Assets	=	Borrowed funds and owner's funds
Assets	=	Liabilities + owner's equity
A	=	L + OE

Owner's funds are known as ***owner's equity***, and the investment of funds into a business entity by an owner is referred to as the *capital contribution* or the *investment of capital.* Borrowed funds are known as ***liabilities***. See Table 3.1. Both the owner's funds and borrowed funds are used to purchase assets to enable the entity to operate.

You learnt in Chapter 2 that assets are the economic resources of the entity, liabilities are the obligations of the entity, and the owner's equity represents the owner's interest in the entity. Both the lenders and the owners are entities that are separate from the business entity. As such, both the liabilities and the owner's equity represent claims against the entity.

We can therefore develop an equation to measure the financial position of a business entity as in Table 3.2.

The elements of the financial statements that appear on the *statement of financial position* are assets, liabilities and owner's equity. The equation 'Assets = Liabilities + Owner's equity' (A = L + OE) is known as the accounting equation. This is a simple representation of the financial position of an entity, with the assets reflected on the left and the liabilities and owner's equity on the right. We are going to use this equation to help us analyse transactions that take place in a business.

Pause and reflect . . .

Look at this simple statement of financial position:

STATEMENT OF FINANCIAL POSITION
AT 31 DECEMBER 20X5

	C
ASSETS	
Accounts receivable	7 500 000
Bank	2 500 000
	10 000 000

EQUITY AND LIABILITIES	
Equity	6 000 000
Liabilities	
Accounts payable	4 000 000
	10 000 000

What do you notice about the structure of the statement of financial position and what you have just learnt about the accounting equation?

Response

The statement of financial position shows *assets* of C10 000 000 and *equity* and *liabilities* of C10 000 000. The equity and liabilities comprises equity of C6 000 000 and liabilities of C4 000 000. In other words, the statement of financial position portrays the accounting equation (Assets = Liabilities + Owner's equity or, as it is presented, Assets = Owner's equity + Liabilities).

3.3 Effects of transactions on the accounting equation

The accounting equation has two sides, which we can label the *left* side and the *right* side. Incorporating these labels, we can begin to develop an accounting equation worksheet, which we can use to analyse transactions. Each transaction needs to be analysed to determine its effect on the accounting equation. The accounting equation must always be in balance. It is often thought of as a scale, as depicted in Diagram 3.1. The accounting equation and the scale must always balance. This concept is discussed further in the paragraphs that follow.

It is possible to identify four sets of transactions, all of which maintain the equality of the accounting equation. These are the following transactions:

- Increase the left side (assets) and increase the right side (liabilities + owner's equity) of the equation.
- Decrease the left side (assets) and decrease the right side (liabilities + owner's equity) of the equation.
- Increase the left side (assets) and decrease the left side (assets) of the equation.
- Increase the right side (liabilities + owner's equity) and decrease the right side (liabilities + owner's equity) of the equation.

We will now examine some typical external and internal transactions that occur in a business entity to determine the effect they have on the elements of the accounting equation. The transactions are listed in Table 3.3.

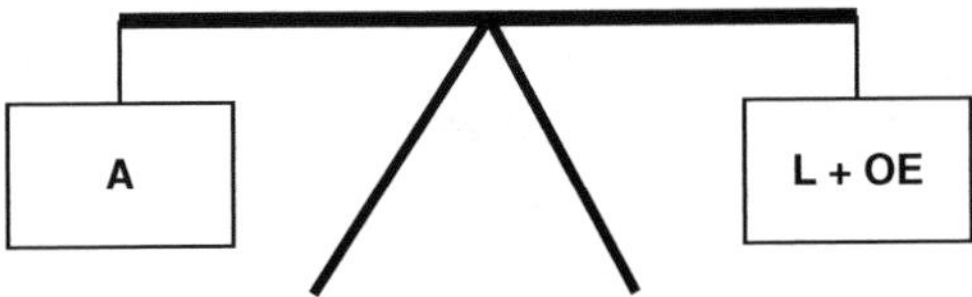

Diagram 3.1 The equality of the accounting equation

Table 3.3 Effects of transactions on the accounting equation

	Transaction	*Effect on the accounting equation*				
		A	**=**	**L**	**+**	**OE**
	External transactions					
a	Owner invests funds in the entity	+	=			+ C
b	Entity borrows funds from lender	+	=	+		
c	Entity buys assets for cash	+ –	=			
d	Entity buys assets on credit	+	=	+		
e	Entity sells goods/provides a service for cash	+	=			+ I
f	Entity sells goods/provides a service on credit	+	=			+ I
g	Recognition of cost of goods sold	–	=			– E
h	Entity receives cash from customer for amount owing	+ –	=			
i	Entity pays expenses in cash	–	=			– E
j	Entity pays lender/supplier in cash	–	=	–		
k	Cash received in advance of earning income	+	=	+		
l	Cash paid in advance of incurrence of expense	+ –	=			
m	Distribution of funds to owner	–	=			– D
	Internal transactions					
n	Recognition as income of cash received in advance (k)		=	–		+ I
o	Income earned and cash receipt outstanding	+	=			+ I
p	Recognition as an expense of cash paid in advance (l)	–	=			– E
q	Expense incurred and cash payment outstanding		=	+		– E
r	Recognition of usage of an asset	–	=			– E

Capital invested by owner	C
Income earned	I
Expense incurred	E
Distribution to owner	D

a Owner invests funds in the business (A ↑ = L + OE ↑)
The *asset column is increased* on the left side of the equation to reflect the inflow of cash. The other side of the transaction is to *increase the owner's equity column* on the right side of the equation, representing the investment or capital contribution by the owner. The owner's equity column represents the claim the owner has against the entity, or the owner's interest in the entity.

b Entity borrows funds from lender (A ↑ = L ↑ + OE)
Again, the *asset column is increased* on the left side of the equation to reflect the inflow of cash. The other side of the transaction is to *increase the liability column* on the right side of the equation. The liability column represents the claim the lender has against the entity, or the amount the entity owes the lender.

c Entity buys assets for cash (A ↑ ↓ = L + OE)
The asset purchased is a resource controlled by the entity. The *asset column is increased* on the left side of the equation to reflect the asset purchased. The asset purchased is financed from cash funds within the entity, therefore the other side of the transaction is then to *decrease the asset column*, also on the left side of the equation. The overall effect of this transaction is an increase and a decrease in the asset column by the same amount.

d Entity buys assets on credit (A ↑ = L ↑ + OE)
Again, the asset purchased is a resource controlled by the entity and the *asset column is increased* on the left side of the equation to reflect the asset purchased. The asset purchased is financed by a lender or supplier, therefore the other side of the transaction is to *increase the liability column* on the right side of the equation, representing the obligation to the lender or supplier.

e Entity sells goods/provides a service for cash (A ↑ = L + OE ↑)
This transaction results in income being earned. You also learnt in Chapter 2 that income gives rise to increases in economic benefits during the accounting period in the form of *increases in assets* or *decreases in liabilities* that result in increases in equity, other than those relating to contributions from equity participants.

On the left side of the equation, we *increase the asset column* due to the inflow of cash. The other side of the transaction is to *increase the owner's equity column* on the right side of the equation, reflecting the income earned. Income is a measure of accomplishment, and income earned increases the owner's interest in the business. Note that in this transaction, the earning of income on the accrual basis and the receipt of cash occur simultaneously.

f Entity sells goods/provides a service on credit (A ↑ = L + OE ↑)
The only difference between this transaction and the previous one is that the transaction in (e) was concluded for cash, whereas this transaction is on credit. Remember that the accrual basis requires that income be recognised when the goods are sold or the service provided even if the cash is received in a different period. Remember also that the definition of income refers to the *increase in assets* – the asset that increases in transaction (e) is cash, whereas the asset that increases in this transaction is accounts receivable.

On the left side of the equation, we *increase the asset column* due to an increase in accounts receivable. The other side of the transaction is to *increase the owner's equity column* on the right side of the equation, reflecting the income earned.

g Recognition of cost of goods sold (A ↓ = L + OE ↓)
When an entity sells goods, as opposed to providing a service, the cost of the goods sold must be recognised as an expense. You also learnt in Chapter 2 that expenses give rise to decreases in economic benefits during the accounting period in the form of *decreases of assets* or *increases of liabilities* that result in decreases in equity, other than those relating to distributions to equity participants.

On the left side of the equation, we *decrease the asset column* to record the decrease in inventory. The other side of the transaction is to *decrease the owner's equity column* on the right side of the equation to record the expense, cost of sales. Just as owner's equity is increased to record income earned, it must be decreased to record expenses incurred.

h Entity receives cash from customer for amount owing (A ↑ ↓ = L + OE)
The receipt of cash from a customer or client does not give rise to income being earned as the income was recognised as earned when the goods were sold or the service was provided.

On the left side of the equation, we *increase the asset column* to record an increase in cash. In this instance, we also *decrease the asset column* representing a decrease in another asset, accounts receivable.

i Entity pays expenses in cash (A ↓ = L + OE ↓)

This transaction results in an expense being incurred. Expenses are defined as decreases in economic benefits during the accounting period in the form of *decreases in assets* or *increases in liabilities* that result in decreases in equity, other than those relating to distributions to equity participants.

On the left side of the equation, we *decrease the asset column* due to the outflow of cash. The other side of the transaction is to *decrease the owner's equity column* on the right side of the equation to record the expense incurred.

j Entity pays lender/supplier in cash (A ↓ = L ↓ + OE)

The paying of cash to a lender/supplier does not give rise to an expense being incurred, since an obligation is being settled.

On the left side of the equation, we *decrease the asset column* due to the outflow of cash. The other side of the transaction is to *decrease the liability column* on the right side of the equation, representing the decrease in the obligation.

k Cash received in advance of earning income (A ↑ = L ↑ + OE)

When cash is received in advance of earning income, a liability is created at the time of receipt of the cash, representing the obligation of the entity to provide goods or services in the future. At the end of the period, an internal transaction is needed to recognise that part of the liability earned during the period. (See transaction (n).)

On the left of the accounting equation, we *increase the asset column* due to the inflow of cash. The other side of the transaction is to *increase the liability column* on the right side of the equation, representing the liability, income received in advance.

I Cash paid in advance of incurrence of expense (A ↑↓ = L + OE)

When cash is paid in advance of the incurrence of expenses, an asset is created at the time of payment of the cash, representing the right of the entity to receive services in the future. At the end of the period, an internal transaction is needed to recognise that part of the asset that is used or expired during the period. (See transaction (p).)

On the left side of the accounting equation, we *increase the asset column* representing the asset, expenses paid in advance, and also *decrease the asset column* due to the outflow of cash.

m Distribution of funds to owner (A ↓ = L + OE ↓)

The distribution of funds to the owner results in an outflow of resources from the entity. This decreases owner's equity as it reduces the owner's interest in the entity. It is, however, important to remember that the distribution of funds to the owner does not result in the incurrence of an expense. This is because of the entity concept, which separates the activities of the entity and the owner.

On the left side of the equation, we *decrease the asset column* due to the outflow of cash. The other side of the transaction is to *decrease the owner's equity column* on the right side of the equation, representing the distribution to the owner.

n Recognition as income of cash received in advance (A = L ↓ + OE ↑)

When cash is received prior to the goods or services being provided (see transaction (k)), a liability is established representing the obligation of the entity to provide the goods or services in the future. At the end of a period, part of the liability will be recognised as income earned (based on the goods sold or service provided), and part will remain a liability to be recognised as income in future periods. The accrual basis of accounting requires the amount earned to be recognised as income in the period when the goods or services are provided.

On the right side of the accounting equation, we *decrease the liability column* by the amount of income earned. The other side of the transaction is to *increase the owner's equity column* to record the income earned.

o **Income earned and cash receipt outstanding (A ↑ = L + OE ↑)**
The accrual basis of accounting requires that income is recognised in the period when the transaction occurs, even if the cash is received in a different period. If, at the end of the period, income has been earned but is unrecorded because payment has not been received, an internal transaction is needed to record the income earned during the period.

On the left side of the equation, we *increase the asset column* to record the income receivable – that is, the right to receive the amount owing in the future. The other side of the transaction is to *increase the owner's equity column* on the right side of the equation, reflecting the income earned. Owner's equity is increased because income earned increases the owner's interest in the entity.

p **Recognition as an expense of cash paid in advance (A ↓ = L + OE ↓)**
When cash is paid prior to services being provided (see transaction (I)), an asset is established at the time of payment of the cash, representing the right of the entity to benefit from the services in the future. At the end of a period, part of the asset will be incurred as an expense (based on the goods or services received), and part will remain as an asset to be recognised as an expense in future periods. The accrual basis of accounting requires the amount incurred to be recognised as an expense in the period when the services are used.

On the left side of the accounting equation, we *decrease the asset column* by the amount of the expense incurred. The other side of the transaction is to *decrease the owner's equity column* on the right side of the equation to record the expense incurred and the decrease in the owner's interest in the entity.

q **Expense incurred and cash payment outstanding (A = L ↑ + OE ↓)**
The accrual basis of accounting requires that expenses be recognised in the period when the transaction occurs, even if the cash is paid in a different period. If, at the end of the period, incurred expenses are unrecorded because payment has not been made, an internal transaction is needed to record the expense incurred during the period.

On the right side of the equation, we *increase the liability column* to record the expense payable – that is, the obligation to pay the amount owing in the future. The other side of the transaction is to *decrease the owner's equity column*, also on the right side of the equation, reflecting the expense incurred. Owner's equity is decreased because expenses incurred decrease the owner's interest in the entity.

It is important to note that the expense is recognised and owner's equity decreased irrespective of whether cash has been paid (see transaction (i)) or the amount is owed and a liability created (this transaction).

r **Recognition of usage of an asset (A ↓ = L + OE ↓)**
When cash is paid to acquire an item that will result in future economic benefits, this item is treated as an asset on purchase. The cost of these assets must be recognised as an expense as they are used to produce income. Once an asset has been used, it becomes an expense.

On the left side of the accounting equation, the *asset column is decreased* by the portion of the asset used. The other side of the transaction is to *decrease the owner's equity column* on the right side of the equation to record the expense incurred and the decrease in the owner's interest in the entity.

 **Pause and reflect . . .**

Compare transaction (i) (expense paid in cash) with transaction (q) (expense incurred and cash payment outstanding). In both cases, an expense is recognised according to the accrual basis of accounting. Can you relate the effect on the accounting equation to the definition of an expense that you learnt in Chapter 2?

Response

In transaction (i), the expense is recognised in the form of a *decrease in the asset*, bank, and in transaction (q), the expense is recognised in the form of an *increase in the liability*, expenses payable. This relates back to the definition of an expense in the *Conceptual Framework*, where an expense is defined as a decrease in economic benefits during the accounting period in the form of *decreases in assets* or *increases in liabilities* that decrease equity, other than distributions to owners. ***An expense can only be recognised if an asset decreases or a liability increases.***

 **Pause and reflect . . .**

Compare transaction (f) (goods sold or services provided on credit) with transaction (n) (recognition as income of cash received in advance). In both cases, income is recognised according to the accrual basis of accounting. Can you relate the effect on the accounting equation to the definition of income that you learnt in Chapter 2?

Response

In transaction (f), the income is recognised in the form of an *increase in the asset*, accounts receivable, and in transaction (n), the income is recognised in the form of a *decrease in the liability*, income received in advance. This relates back to the definition of income in the *Conceptual Framework*, where income is defined as an increase in economic benefits during the accounting period in the form of *increases in assets* or *decreases in liabilities* that increase equity, other than contributions from owners. ***Income can only be recognised if an asset increases or a liability decreases.***

3.4 Use of the accounting equation

In Chapter 1, *The accounting environment*, we mentioned that accounting is an information system which selects and processes data and then produces information about an economic entity. We mentioned further that data is processed through the accounting process. In Chapter 2, you learnt how to process data and prepare financial statements through a conceptual analysis of the transactions. We will now build on this by seeing how the accounting equation can help us process the data and produce information in the form of a statement of profit or loss, a statement of changes in equity and statement of financial position.

Table 3.4 Columns in the accounting equation worksheet

Assets					=	*Liabilities*			+	*Owner's equity*
Bank	+	Accounts receivable	+	Motor vehicles	=	Accounts payable	+	Borrowings	+	Owner's equity

Table 3.5 Components of owner's equity

		Owner's equity				
Capital	+	(Income	–	Expenses)	–	Distributions
			= Profit			

3.4.1 The accounting equation worksheet

The elements of the accounting equation need to be broken down into different classifications known as ***accounts***. We need a separate column on the accounting equation worksheet for each account (see Table 3.4). Assets are typically classified into accounts such as bank, accounts receivable, inventory, motor vehicles, computer, and office equipment and supplies. Liabilities are typically classified into accounts such as accounts payable and borrowings. The individual accounts are used to classify the transactions in a useful manner and assist in the preparation of the financial statements.

The financial statements can be prepared with the use of the accounting equation. This is set up as a worksheet showing the elements broken down into the different columns or accounts. Each transaction is entered into the worksheet after determining the effect it has on the entity's financial position. At the end of the accounting period, a new financial position is determined taking into account all the transactions that have taken place. The ***statement of financial position*** of the entity can then be prepared from the summarised information in the accounting equation worksheet. The totals of each column represent the amounts of each asset, liability and the owner's equity for the statement of financial position.

To assist in the preparation of the ***statement of profit or loss***, the accounting equation worksheet can be modified with specific columns further analysing owner's equity. When a transaction is analysed and entered into the worksheet, it is very important to understand which transactions affect owner's equity, and whether it is a capital investment by the owner, the earning of income, the incurrence of an expense or a distribution to the owner (see Table 3.5). The statement of profit or loss can then be prepared taking the information from the *income* and *expense* columns in the accounting equation worksheet.

3.4.2 Principles learnt from the accounting equation

You may have noticed while working through the transactions on the previous pages that owner's equity is affected by four types of transactions only:

C Investment of **c**apital by the owner increases owner's equity
I Earning of **i**ncome increases owner's equity
E Incurrence of **e**xpenses decreases owner's equity
D **D**istribution of funds to the owner decreases owner's equity

Table 3.6 Movement in owner's equity

Owner's equity	
Balance at beginning of period	Bal BOP
Add capital investment by owner	+ C
Add income	+ I
Less expenses	− E
Less distributions to owner	− D
Balance at end of period	Bal EOP

Only the earning of *income* and the incurrence of *expenses* affect profit. Funds invested by the owner do not represent income, and distributions to the owner do not represent expenses. To determine profit in the ***statement of profit or loss*** from the information in the accounting equation, therefore, the owner's equity column needs to be analysed to identify those transactions that result in income being earned and expenses being incurred.

The movement in owner's equity for a period can therefore be summarised as shown in Table 3.6. It is very important that you fully understand the impact that each component has on the ending balance in owner's equity.

The statement of changes in equity, which was introduced in Chapter 2, is prepared to provide information to users about the changes in an entity's wealth during the period. You will recall from Chapter 2 that the statement of changes in equity presented line items showing the following:

- the *income* earned and the *expenses* incurred, as reflected by the profit or loss for the period;
- *contributions* by owners;
- *distributions* to owners.

You should therefore realise that the statement of changes in equity provides information about the four types of transactions that affect equity.

3.5 Analysis of transactions using the accounting equation worksheet and the preparation of financial statements from the worksheet

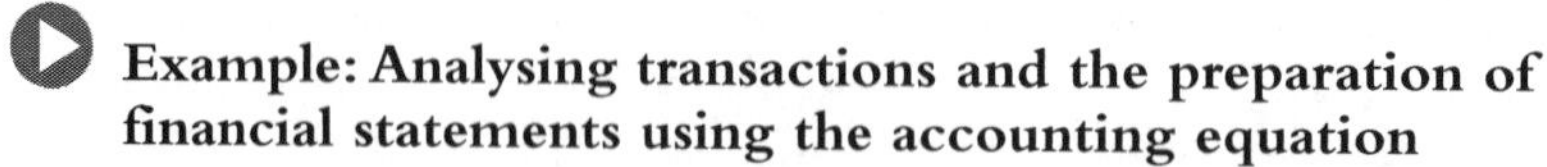

Example: Analysing transactions and the preparation of financial statements using the accounting equation

The following is a record of the transactions of Smart Concepts, a computer retailer, for the period from 1 January 20X5 to 31 March 20X5. These are the same transactions that we analysed on a conceptual level in Chapter 2. You must not forget the concepts taught in the previous chapters when analysing transactions using the accounting equation. The explanation which follows this example incorporates the analysis of the transaction on a conceptual level with an explanation of the effect of each transaction on the accounting equation.

External transactions

Starting the business

1. On 2 January, Simon Smart started a business as a computer retailer. He drew C950 000 from a savings account and opened a bank account in the name of Smart Concepts into which he paid C950 000.
2. On 2 January, Smart Concepts negotiated a loan from Techno Bank for an amount of C600 000. The loan is repayable in four equal annual instalments, beginning on 31 December 20X5. The interest rate is 12 per cent per annum, payable quarterly in arrears.
3. On 2 January, Simon located premises from which to operate in Hyde Park. The monthly rent for the premises is C12 000. Smart Concepts paid four months' rent in advance on 2 January.
4. On 2 January, Simon transferred C120 000 from the bank account into a fixed deposit account earning interest at 5 per cent per annum.
5. On 2 January, Smart Concepts purchased furniture and fittings for C240 000. This was paid for from funds in the bank account. The expected useful life of the furniture and fittings is five years.
6. On 5 January, Smart Concepts purchased supplies of stationery for C5 000 as well as supplies of computer parts for C12 000. All of them were paid for in cash.
7. On 7 January, Smart Concepts opened an account with Computer World, the supplier of its inventory.

Trading and operating transactions for January

8. On 10 January, Smart Concepts purchased inventory of 60 computers from Computer World at a cost of C10 000 each. The total amount owing is to be paid by 25 March.
9. On 12 January, Smart Concepts paid a service provider C750 for internet access.
10. On 25 January, Smart Concepts sold 15 computers on credit to a customer for C12 500 each. An amount of C125 000 is due by 15 March and the balance by 15 April.

Trading and operating transactions for February

11. On 1 February, Smart Concepts employed a computer technician at a salary of C8 000 per month.
12. On 8 February, Smart Concepts paid C7 000 for an advertisement in a newspaper, advertising the computers available for sale.
13. On 12 February, Smart Concepts sold 30 computers to customers for C12 500 each. The customers paid cash for them.
14. On 25 February, Smart Concepts received cash of C48 000 in respect of technical support contracts taken out by customers. The contracts are for a two-year period.
15. On 28 February, Smart Concepts paid the computer technician his salary for February.

Trading and operating transactions for March

16 On 4 March, Smart Concepts purchased inventory of a further 75 computers from Computer World at a cost of C10 000 each. The total amount owing is to be paid by 25 May.
17 On 5 March, Smart Concepts paid a service provider C750 for internet access.
18 On 15 March, Smart Concepts received C125 000 from the customer in transaction 10.
19 On 25 March, Smart Concepts paid Computer World an amount of C600 000.
20 On 29 March, Smart Concepts sold 30 computers on credit to customers for C12 500 each. The full amount owing is due by 30 April.
21 On 30 March, Smart Concepts paid the computer technician his salary for March.

Rewarding the providers of finance

22 On 30 March, Smart Concepts paid the interest on the loan from Techno Bank for the three-month period.
23 On 30 March, Simon authorised a distribution to himself of C60 000 for personal use.

Internal transactions

24 On 31 March, Simon examined the records of the business and established that technical support in respect of contracts to the value of C6 000 had been provided to customers.
25 On 31 March, Smart Concepts accounted for the interest on the fixed deposit earned for the period.
26 On 31 March, Smart Concepts recognised the rent expense incurred for the period.
27 On 31 March, the water account for C1 500 and the electricity account for C2 500 had been received but not paid.
28 On 31 March, Simon counted stationery supplies on hand costing C2 000 and also counted computer parts on hand costing C3 500.
29 On 31 March, Smart Concepts accounted for the usage of the furniture and fittings for the period.

You are required to:

a) Enter the above transactions in the accounting equation worksheet.
b) Prepare a statement of profit or loss and statement of charges in equity for Smart Concepts for the three-month period ended 31 March 20X5 and a statement of financial position at 31 March 20X5.

Solution: Analysing transactions and preparation of financial statements using the accounting equation

In part (a), all of the transactions are analysed on a detailed accounting equation worksheet, first, to illustrate the mechanics of preparing such a worksheet, and second, so

a) Accounting equation worksheet

	ASSETS									= LIABILITIES				+ OWNER'S EQUITY			
No.	Bank +	Rent paid in advance +	Fixed deposit investment +	Accounts receivable +	Stationery supplies +	Computer parts +	Furniture and fittings +	Inventory +	Interest receivable	Water and electricity payable +	Service fees received in advance +	Accounts payable +	Borrowings	Capital +	Income −	Expenses −	Distributions
1	950													950			
2	600												600				
3	(48)	48															
4	(120)		120														
5	(240)						240										
6	(17)				5	12											
7																	
8								600				600					
9	(0.75)															(0.75)	
10				187.5				(150)							187.5	(150)	
11																	
12	(7)															(7)	
13	375							(300)							375.0	(300)	
14	48										48						
15	(8)															(8)	
16								750				750					
17	(0.75)															(0.75)	
18	125			(125)													
19	(600)											(600)					
20				375				(300)							375.0	(300)	
21	(8)															(8)	
22	(18)															(18)	
23	(60)																(60)
	970.5	48	120	437.5	5	12	240	600			48	750	600	950	937.5	(792.5)	(60)
24											(6)				6.0		
25									1.5						1.5		
26		(36)														(36)	
27										4						(4)	
28					(3)	(8.5)										(11.5)	
29							(12)									(12)	
	970.5 +	12 +	120 +	437.5 +	2 +	3.5 +	228 +	600 +	1.5	4 +	42 +	750 +	600	950 +	945.0 +	(856) +	(60)

ASSETS = 2 375 | LIABILITIES = 1 396 | OWNER'S EQUITY = 979

that you are able to see the process from beginning to end. After the financial statements are prepared in part (b), each transaction is analysed individually with a detailed explanation.

b) Financial statements

SMART CONCEPTS
STATEMENT OF PROFIT OR LOSS
FOR THE THREE MONTHS ENDED 31 MARCH 20X5

		C
Income	*(From the income column on the worksheet)*	945 000
Sales	*(187 500 + 375 000 + 375 000)*	937 500
Service fees		6 000
Interest	*(120 000 × 0.05 × 3/12)*	1 500
Expenses	*(From the expences column on the worksheet)*	(856 000)
Cost of sales	*(150 000 + 300 000 + 300 000)*	750 000
Internet	*(750 + 750)*	1 500
Advertising		7 000
Salaries	*(8 000 + 8 000)*	16 000
Rent	*(48 000 × 3/4)*	36 000
Water and electricity	*(1 500 + 2 500)*	4 000
Stationery supplies	*(5 000 – 2 000)*	3 000
Computer parts	*(12 000 – 3 500)*	8 500
Depreciation	*(240 000/5 × 3/12)*	12 000
Interest	*(600 000 × 0.12 × 3/12)*	18 000
Profit for the period		89 000

SMART CONCEPTS
STATEMENT OF CHANGES IN EQUITY
FOR THE PERIOD ENDED 31 MARCH 20X5

		C
Balance at 1 January 20X5		—
Profit for the period	*(From the statement of profit or loss)*	89 000
Distributions	*(From the distributions column on the worksheet)*	(60 000)
Contribution to capital	*(From the capital column on the worksheet)*	950 000
Balance at 31 March 20X5		979 000

SMART CONCEPTS
STATEMENT OF FINANCIAL POSITION
AT 31 MARCH 20X5

		C
ASSETS	*(From totals of each asset column on the worksheet)*	2 375 000
Furniture and fittings		228 000
Fixed deposit investment		120 000
Inventory		600 000
Accounts receivable		437 500
Stationery supplies		2 000
Computer parts		3 500
Rent paid in advance		12 000
Interest receivable		1 500
Bank		16 000
		970 500
		2 375 000
EQUITY AND LIABILITIES		
Equity		
Capital	*(From the statement of changes in equity) or (0 + 89 000 − 60 000 + 950 000)*	979 000
Liabilities	*(From the totals of each liability column on the worksheet)*	1 396 000
Borrowings		600 000
Accounts payable		750 000
Service fees received in advance		42 000
Water and electricity payable		4 000
		2 375 000

In the following explanations, the analysis of each transaction is repeated from Chapter 2. However, the detailed explanation of the analysis of the transaction has been omitted. Please refer to Chapter 2 to see this again. Each transaction is then processed through the accounting equation with an accompanying explanation.

External transactions

Starting the business

1 On 2 January, Simon Smart started a business as a computer retailer. He drew C950 000 from a savings account and opened a bank account in the name of Smart Concepts into which he paid C950 000.					
Analysis of transaction	The asset, *bank*, is increased by C950 000, and owner's equity, *capital*, is increased by C950 000.				
The accounting equation	***Assets***	=	***Liabilities***	+	***Owner's equity***
	Bank				**Capital**
	950 000				950 000

There is a C950 000 *increase in assets on the left side* of the equation and a C950 000 *increase in owner's equity on the right side* of the equation. The equality of the accounting equation is maintained.

2 On 2 January, Smart Concepts negotiated a loan from Techno Bank for an amount of C600 000. The loan is repayable in four equal annual instalments, beginning on 31 December 20X5. The interest rate is 12 per cent per annum, payable quarterly in arrears.

Analysis of transaction

The asset, *bank*, is increased by C600 000, and the liability, *borrowings*, is increased by C600 000.

The accounting equation

Assets	=	***Liabilities***	+	***Owner's equity***
Bank		**Borrowings**		
600 000		600 000		

There is a C600 000 *increase in assets on the left side* of the equation and a C600 000 *increase in liabilities on the right side* of the equation. The equality of the accounting equation is maintained.

3 On 2 January, Simon located premises from which to operate in Hyde Park. The monthly rent for the premises is C12 000. Smart Concepts paid four months' rent in advance.

Analysis of transaction

The asset, *rent paid in advance*, is increased by C48 000, and the asset, *bank*, is decreased by C48 000.

The accounting equation

Assets		=	***Liabilities***	+	***Owner's equity***
Bank	**Rent paid in advance**				
(48 000)	48 000				

There is a C48 000 *increase in assets on the left side* of the equation and a C48 000 *decrease in assets also on the left side* of the equation. The equality of the accounting equation is maintained. Note that an expense is not recognised as incurred on the accrual basis of accounting, as the property has not yet been used for the three-month period.

4 On 2 January, Simon transferred C120 000 from the bank account into a fixed deposit account earning interest at 5 per cent per annum.

Analysis of transaction

The asset, *fixed deposit*, is increased by C120 000, and the asset, *bank*, is decreased by C120 000.

The accounting equation	*Assets*		=	*Liabilities*	+	*Owner's equity*
	Bank	**Fixed deposit investment**				
	(120 000)	120 000				

There is a C120 000 *increase in assets on the left side* of the equation and a C120 000 *decrease in assets also on the left side* of the equation. The equality of the accounting equation is maintained.

5 On 2 January, Smart Concepts purchased furniture and fittings for C240 000. This was paid for from funds in the bank account. The expected useful life of the furniture and fittings is five years.

Analysis of transaction The asset, *furniture and fittings*, is increased by C240 000, and the asset, *bank*, is decreased by C240 000.

The accounting equation	*Assets*		=	*Liabilities*	+	*Owner's equity*
	Bank	**Furniture and fittings**				
	(240 000)	240 000				

There is a C240 000 *increase in assets on the left side* of the equation and a C240 000 *decrease in assets also on the left side* of the equation. The equality of the accounting equation is maintained.

6 On 5 January, Smart Concepts purchased supplies of stationery for C5 000 as well as supplies of computer parts for C12 000. All the supplies were paid for in cash.

Analysis of transaction The assets, *stationery supplies* and *computer parts*, are increased by C5 000 and C12 000 respectively, and the asset, *bank*, is decreased by C17 000.

The accounting equation	*Assets*			=	*Liabilities*	+	*Owner's equity*
	Bank	**Stationery supplies**	**Computer parts**				
	(17 000)	5 000	12 000				

There is a C5 000 and a C12 000 *increase in assets on the left side* of the equation and a C17 000 *decrease in assets also on the left side* of the equation. The equality of the accounting equation is maintained.

7 On 7 January, Smart Concepts opened an account with Computer World, the supplier of its inventory.

Analysis of transaction	Not applicable.

The opening of the account with the supplier is a transaction that has no economic impact on the entity and therefore the financial statements are not affected.

Trading and operating transactions for January

8 On 10 January, Smart Concepts purchased inventory of sixty computers from Computer World at a cost of C10 000 each. The total amount owing is to be paid by 25 March.

Analysis of transaction	The asset, *inventory*, is increased by C600 000, and the liability, *accounts payable*, is increased by C600 000.				
The accounting equation	***Assets***	=	***Liabilities***	+	***Owner's equity***
	Inventory		**Accounts payable**		
	600 000		600 000		

There is a C600 000 *increase in assets on the left side* of the equation and a C600 000 *increase in liabilities on the right side* of the equation. The equality of the accounting equation is maintained.

9 On 12 January, Simon paid a service provider C750 for internet access.

Analysis of transaction	The expense, *internet*, is increased by C750, and the asset, *bank*, is decreased by C750.				
The accounting equation	***Assets***	=	***Liabilities***	+	***Owner's equity***
	Bank				**Internet expense**
	(750)				(750)

There is a C750 *decrease in assets on the left side* of the equation and a C750 *decrease in owner's equity on the right side* of the equation. The equality of the accounting equation is maintained. Note, importantly, that although expenses are increasing (an internet expense of C750 has been incurred), an *increase in expenses* leads to a *decrease in owner's equity*.

10 On 25 January, Smart Concepts sold 15 computers on credit to a customer for C12 500 each. An amount of C125 000 is due by 15 March and the balance by 15 April.

Analysis of transaction The asset, *accounts receivable*, is increased by C187 500, and income, *sales*, is increased by C187 500. In addition, the expense, *cost of sales*, is increased by C150 000, and the asset, *inventory*, is decreased by C150 000.

The accounting equation

Assets		=	*Liabilities*	+	*Owner's equity*	
Accounts receivable	**Inventory**				**Sales**	**Cost of sales**
187 500					187 500	
	(150 000)					(150 000)

There is a C187 500 *increase in assets on the left side* of the equation and a C187 500 *increase in owner's equity on the right side* of the equation. The equality of the accounting equation is maintained. Note that income is increasing (sales income of C187 500 has been earned) and an *increase in income* leads to an *increase in equity*.

There is also a C150 000 *decrease in assets on the left side* of the equation and a C150 000 *decrease in owner's equity on the right side* of the equation. The equality of the accounting equation is maintained. Note again, that although expenses are increasing (a cost of sales expense of C150 000 has been incurred), an *increase in expenses* leads to a *decrease in owner's equity*.

Trading and operating transactions for February

11 On 1 February, Smart Concepts employed a computer technician at a salary of C8 000 per month.

Analysis of transaction Not applicable.

The employment of a technician is also a transaction that has no economic impact on the entity and therefore the financial statements are not affected.

12 On 8 February, Smart Concepts paid C7 000 for an advertisement in a newspaper, advertising the computers available for sale.

Analysis of transaction The expense, *advertising*, is increased by C7 000, and the asset, *bank*, is decreased by C7 000.

The accounting equation

Assets	=	***Liabilities***	+	***Owner's equity***
Bank				**Advertising expense**
(7 000)				(7 000)

There is also a C7 000 *decrease in assets on the left side* of the equation and a C7 000 *decrease in owner's equity on the right side* of the equation. The equality of the accounting equation is maintained. Note again that although expenses are increasing (an advertising expense of C7 000 has been incurred), an *increase in expenses* leads to a *decrease in owner's equity*.

13 On 12 February, Smart Concepts sold 30 computers to customers for C12 500 each. The customers paid cash for them.

Analysis of transaction The asset, *bank*, is increased by C375 000, and income, *sales*, is increased by C375 000. In addition, the expense, *cost of sales*, is increased by C300 000, and the asset, *inventory*, is decreased by C300 000.

The accounting equation

Assets		=	***Liabilities***	+	***Owner's equity***	
Bank	**Inventory**				**Sales**	**Cost of sales**
375 000					375 000	
	(300 000)					(300 000)

There is a C375 000 *increase in assets on the left side* of the equation and a C375 000 *increase in owner's equity on the right side* of the equation. The equality of the accounting equation is maintained. Note that income is increasing (sales income of 375 000 has been earned) and an *increase in income* leads to an *increase in equity*.

There is also a C300 000 *decrease in assets on the left side* of the equation and a C300 000 *decrease in owner's equity on the right side* of the equation. The equality of the accounting equation is maintained. Note again that although expenses are increasing (a cost of sales expense of C300 000 has been incurred), an *increase in expenses* leads to a *decrease in owner's equity*.

14 On 25 February, Smart Concepts received cash of C48 000 in respect of technical support contracts taken out by customers. The contracts are for a two-year period.

Analysis of transaction	The asset, *bank*, is increased by C48 000, and the liability, *service fees received in advance*, is increased by C48 000.

The accounting equation

Assets	=	*Liabilities*	+	*Owner's equity*
Bank		**Service fees in advance**		
48 000		48 000		

There is a C48 000 *increase in assets on the left side* of the equation and a C48 000 *increase in liabilities on the right side* of the equation. The equality of the accounting equation is maintained. Note that no income is recognised as earned on the accrual basis of accounting as the services have not yet been provided.

15 On 28 February, Smart Concepts paid the computer technician his salary for February.

Analysis of transaction	The expense, *salaries*, is increased by C8 000, and the asset, *bank* is decreased by C8 000.

The accounting equation

Assets	=	*Liabilities*	+	*Owner's equity*
Bank				**Salaries expense**
(8 000)				(8 000)

There is a C8 000 *decrease in assets on the left side* of the equation and a C8 000 *decrease in owner's equity on the right side* of the equation. The equality of the accounting equation is maintained. Note again that although expenses are increasing (a salaries expense of C8 000 has been incurred), an *increase in expenses* leads to a *decrease in owner's equity*.

Trading and operating transactions for March

16 On 4 March, Smart Concepts purchased inventory of a further 75 computers from Computer World at a cost of C10 000 each. The total amount owing is to be paid by 25 May.

Analysis of transaction	The asset, *inventory*, is increased by C750 000, and the liability, *accounts payable*, is increased by C750 000.

The accounting equation

Assets	=	***Liabilities***	+	***Owner's equity***
Inventory		**Accounts payable**		
750 000		750 000		

There is a C750 000 *increase in assets on the left side* of the equation and a C750 000 *increase in liabilities on the right side* of the equation. The equality of the accounting equation is maintained.

17 On 5 March, Smart Concepts paid a service provider C750 for internet access.

Analysis of transaction	The expense, *internet*, is increased by C750, and the asset, *bank*, is decreased by C750.

This transaction is identical to transaction 9.

18 On 15 March, Smart Concepts received C125 000 from the customer in transaction 10.

Analysis of transaction	The asset, *bank*, is increased by C125 000, and the asset, *accounts receivable*, is decreased by C125 000.

The accounting equation	*Assets*		=	*Liabilities*	+	*Owner's equity*
	Bank	**Accounts receivable**				
	125 000	(125 000)				

There is a C125 000 *increase in assets on the left side* of the equation and a C125 000 *decrease in assets also on the left side* of the equation. The equality of the accounting equation is maintained.

19 On 25 March, Smart Concepts paid Computer World an amount of C600 000.

Analysis of transaction	The liability, *accounts payable*, is decreased by C600 000, and the asset, *bank*, is decreased by C600 000.

The accounting equation	*Assets*	=	*Liabilities*	+	*Owner's equity*
	Bank		**Accounts Payable**		
	(600 000)		(600 000)		

There is a C600 000 *decrease in assets on the left side* of the equation and a C600 000 *decrease in liabilities on the right side* of the equation. The equality of the accounting equation is maintained.

20 On 29 March, Smart Concepts sold 30 computers on credit to customers for C12 500 each. The full amount owing is due by 30 April.

Analysis of transaction	The asset, *accounts receivable*, is increased by C375 000, and income, *sales*, is increased by C375 000. In addition, the expense, *cost of sales*, is increased by C300 000, and the asset, *inventory*, is decreased by C300 000.

This transaction is identical in nature to transaction 10.

21 On 30 March, Smart Concepts paid the computer technician his salary for March.

Analysis of transaction	The expense, *salaries*, is increased by C8 000, and the asset, *bank*, is decreased by C8 000.

 This transaction is identical to transaction 15.

Rewarding the providers of finance

22 On 30 March, Smart Concepts paid the interest on the loan from Techno Bank for the three-month period.

Analysis of transaction	The expense, *interest*, is increased by C18 000, and the asset, *bank*, is decreased by C18 000.

The accounting equation	***Assets***	=	***Liabilities***	+	***Owner's equity***
	Bank				**Interest expense**
	(18 000)				(18 000)

There is a C18 000 *decrease in assets on the left side* of the equation and a C18 000 *decrease in owner's equity on the right side* of the equation. The equality of the accounting equation is maintained. Note again that although expenses are increasing (an interest expense of C18 000 has been incurred), an *increase in expenses* leads to a *decrease in owner's equity*.

23 On 30 March, Simon authorised a distribution to himself of C60 000 for personal use.

Analysis of transaction	Owner's equity, *distributions*, is increased by C60 000, and the asset, *bank*, is decreased by C60 000.

The accounting equation	***Assets***	=	***Liabilities***	+	***Owner's equity***
	Bank				**Distribution**
	(60 000)				(60 000)

There is a C60 000 *decrease in assets on the left side* of the equation and a C60 000 *decrease in owner's equity on the right side* of the equation. The equality of the accounting equation is maintained. Note, importantly, and similar to expenses, that although distributions are increasing (a distribution of C60 000 has been made), an *increase in distributions* leads to a *decrease in owner's equity*.

Internal transactions

24 On 31 March, Simon examined the records of the business and established that technical support in respect of contracts to the value of C6 000 had been provided to customers.

Analysis of transaction	The liability, *service fees received in advance*, is decreased by C6 000, and income, *service fees*, is increased by C6 000.

The accounting equation	*Assets*	=	*Liabilities*	+	*Owner's equity*
			Service fees in advance		**Service fees income**
			(6 000)		6 000

There is a C6 000 *decrease in liabilities on the right side* of the equation and a C6 000 *increase in owner's equity also on the right side* of the equation. The equality of the accounting equation is maintained. Note that income is increasing (service fee income of C6 000 has been earned) and an *increase in income* leads to an *increase in equity*.

25 On 31 March, Smart Concepts accounted for the interest on the fixed deposit earned for the period.

Analysis of transaction	The asset, *interest receivable*, is increased by C1 500, and income, *interest* is increased by C1 500.

The accounting equation	*Assets*	=	*Liabilities*	+	*Owner's equity*
	Interest receivable				**Interest income**
	1 500				1 500

There is a C1 500 *increase in assets on the left side* of the equation and a C1 500 *increase in owner's equity on the right side* of the equation. The equality of the accounting equation is maintained. Note that income is increasing (interest income of C1 500 has been earned) and an *increase in income* leads to an *increase in equity*.

26 On 31 March, Smart Concepts recognised the rent expense incurred for the period.

Analysis of transaction	The expense, *rent*, is increased by C36 000, and the asset, *rent paid in advance*, is decreased by C36 000.

The accounting equation	*Assets*	=	*Liabilities*	+	*Owner's equity*
	Rent paid in advance				**Rent expense**
	(36 000)				(36 000)

There is a C36 000 *decrease in assets on the left side* of the equation and a C36 000 *decrease in owner's equity on the right side* of the equation. The equality of the accounting equation is maintained. Note again that although expenses are increasing (a rent expense of C36 000 has been incurred), an *increase in expenses* leads to a *decrease in owner's equity*.

27 On 31 March, the water account for C1 500 and the electricity account for C2 500 had been received but not paid.

Analysis of transaction

The expense, *water and electricity*, is increased by C4 000, and the liability, *water and electricity payable*, is increased by C4 000.

The accounting equation	*Assets*	=	*Liabilities*	+	*Owner's equity*
			Water and electricity payable		**Water and electricity expense**
			4 000		(4 000)

There is a C4 000 *increase in liabilities on the right side* of the equation and a C4 000 *decrease in owner's equity also on the right side* of the equation. The equality of the accounting equation is maintained. Note again that although expenses are increasing (a water and electricity expense of C4 000 has been incurred), an *increase in expenses* leads to a *decrease in owner's equity*.

28 On 31 March, Simon counted stationery supplies on hand costing C2 000 and also counted computer parts on hand costing C3 500.

Analysis of transaction

The expense, *stationery supplies*, is increased by C3 000, and the asset, *stationery supplies*, is decreased by C3 000. In addition, the expense, *computer parts*, is increased by C8 500, and the asset, *computer parts*, is decreased by C8 500.

The accounting equation	*Assets*		= *Liabilities* +	*Owner's equity*	
	Stationary supplies	**Computer parts**		**Stationary supplies expense**	**Computer parts expense**
	(3 000)	(8 500)		(3 000)	(8 500)

There is a combined C11 500 *decrease in assets on the left side* of the equation and a combined C11 500 *decrease in owner's equity on the right side* of the equation. The equality of the accounting equation is maintained. Note again that although expenses are increasing (a stationery supplies expense of C3 000 and a computer parts expense of C8 500 have been incurred), an *increase in expenses* leads to a *decrease in owner's equity*.

29 On 31 March, Smart Concepts accounted for the usage of the furniture and fittings for the period.

Analysis of transaction	The expense, *depreciation*, is increased by C12 000, and the asset, *furniture and fittings* is decreased by C12 000.		
The accounting equation	*Assets*	= *Liabilities* +	*Owner's equity*
	Furniture and fittings (12 000)		**Depreciation expense** (12 000)

There is a C12 000 *decrease in assets on the left side* of the equation and a C12 000 *decrease in owner's equity on the right side* of the equation. The equality of the accounting equation is maintained. Note again, that although expenses are increasing (a depreciation expense of C8 000 has been incurred), an *increase in expenses* leads to a *decrease in owner's equity*.

3.6 Conceptual proof of profit

Changes in an entity's equity between two reporting dates reflect the increase or decrease in its net assets or wealth during the period under review. Except for changes resulting from transactions with owners (capital contributions and distributions), the overall change in equity represents the profit or loss generated by the entity's activities during the period.

The *profit for the period* can be calculated without details of the income and expenses, provided the following information is available:

- the opening balance in owner's equity;
- the closing balance in owner's equity;
- the investment of capital by the owner;
- distributions to the owner.

Table 3.7 Conceptual proof of profit

Balance at end of year	Bal EOY
Balance at beginning of year	Bal BOY
	Movement
Add distributions	+ D
Less capital invested by owner	– C
Profit for the period	P

The movement in the owner's equity account is first calculated by subtracting the opening balance from the closing balance. The movement in the account is due to investments by the owner (which increase owner's equity), income earned (which increases owner's equity), expenses incurred (which decrease owner's equity) and distributions to the owner (which decrease owner's equity). Profit for the period (the effect of income less expenses) therefore can be calculated by reversing the effects of the investments and distributions; in other words, by subtracting the amount of the investments and adding back the amount of the distributions. This is illustrated in Table 3.7.

Example: Calculation of profit using the principles learnt from the accounting equation

A business entity had the following assets and liabilities at the beginning and at the end of the year:

	Assets	*Liabilities*
	C	*C*
Beginning of the year (BOY)	650 000	200 000
End of the year (EOY)	700 000	100 000

There are no items of other comprehensive income.

You are required to:

Determine the profit or loss of the business entity during the year under each of the following unrelated assumptions:

a) There were no capital contributions by the owner and no distributions to the owner during the year.
b) There were no capital contributions by the owner, but a distribution to the owner of C15 000 per month was made to cover personal living expenses.
c) There were no distributions to the owner, but a capital contribution by the owner of C200 000 was made during the year.
d) A capital contribution by the owner of C200 000 was made during the year and a distribution to the owner of C15 000 per month was made to cover personal living expenses.

Solution: Calculation of profit using the principles learnt from the accounting equation

To calculate the profit for the period in the above example, the following information is required:

- opening balance in owner's equity;
- closing balance in owner's equity;
- any contributions by the owner;
- any distributions to the owner.

Since we know the opening and closing balances for the assets and liabilities, we can use the accounting equation to calculate the owner's equity balances at the respective dates. After calculating the opening and closing balances in owner's equity, we need to determine the movement in owner's equity for the year by subtracting the opening balance from the closing balance.

This movement represents contributions by the owner, plus profit, less distributions. Therefore, if we adjust for the investments and distributions, the balancing figure will be the profit for the period.

Owner's equity calculation

	Owner's equity	=	*Assets*	–	*Liabilities*
	C		*C*		*C*
BOY	?	=	650 000	–	200 000
	450 000	=	650 000	–	200 000
EOY	?	=	700 000	–	100 000
	600 000	=	700 000	–	100 000

Profit calculation

a) No contribution and no distribution

		C
	Ending owner's equity	600 000
	Opening owner's equity	(450 000)
=	Profit	150 000

In the first situation, there were no contributions from or distributions to the owner during the year, therefore the movement in the owner's equity account represents the profit for the period.

b) Distribution but no contribution

			C
	Ending owner's equity		600 000
	Opening owner's equity		(450 000)
=	Movement		150 000
+	Distribution	*(C15 000 × 12)*	180 000
=	Profit		330 000

In the second situation, there was a distribution to the owner of C180 000 during the year. Therefore, we reverse the effect of the distribution to calculate the profit for the period.

c) Contribution but no distribution

		C
	Ending owner's equity	600 000
	Opening owner's equity	(450 000)
=	Movement	150 000
–	Capital contributed by owner	(200 000)
=	Loss	(50 000)

In the third situation, there was a contribution of C200 000 by the owner during the year, therefore we reverse the effect of the contribution to calculate the profit for the period.

d) Contribution and distribution

			C
	Ending owner's equity		600 000
	Opening owner's equity		(450 000)
=	Movement		150 000
+	Distribution	*(C15 000 × 12)*	180 000
–	Capital invested by owner		(200 000)
=	Profit		130 000

In the fourth situation, C180 000 was distributed to the owner during the year, who contributed an additional C200 000, therefore we reverse the effect of the distribution and of the contribution to calculate the profit for the period.

Revision example

Rooms for Rent was formed by Ronnie Roome in 20X3 with the intention of buying old properties and converting them into student accommodation. The accounting records of Rooms for Rent show the following assets and liabilities at 31 December 20X3 and 20X4.

	20X3	*20X4*
	C	C
Accounts payable	16 500	20 100
Accounts receivable	26 400	11 200
Bank	50 600	49 200
Rent receivable	—	2 000
Rent received in advance	—	3 000
Land and buildings	—	3 630 000
Loan	—	2 475 000
Office equipment	61 600	137 500
Supplies (asset)	15 400	12 100
Vehicles	136 400	98 200

Rooms for Rent purchased their first property during March 20X4 at a cost of C3 630 000. The purchase price was funded by paying cash of C1 155 000 and by a loan from the bank for C2 475 000.

During the year, additional office equipment was purchased and a vehicle was sold.

Ronnie Roome contributed an additional C990 000 to the entity during the year. The entity earned sufficient profits during 20X4 to enable a distribution to Ronnie of C66 000 per month.

You are required to:

Calculate the profit earned by Rooms for Rent for the year ended 31 December 20X4.

Solution: Revision example

	20X3	*20X4*
	C	C
Assets	290 400	3 940 200
Bank	50 600	49 200
Rent receivable	—	2 000
Accounts receivable	26 400	11 200
Supplies	15 400	12 100
Vehicles	136 400	98 200
Office equipment	61 600	137 500
Land and buildings	—	3 630 000
Liabilities	16 500	2 498 100
Rent received in advance	—	3 000
Accounts payable	16 500	20 100
Loan	—	2 475 000
Owner's equity at end of year	273 900	1 442 100

		C
Owner's equity at 31/12/X4		1 442 100
Owner's equity at 31/12/X3		(273 900)
Movement		1 168 200
Add distribution	*(C66 000 × 12)*	792 000
Less contribution to capital		(990 000)
Profit for 20X4		970 200

There is not enough information given in the question to enable you to determine the income and expenses, and to calculate profit by preparing a statement of profit or loss. The first step is thus to calculate the owner's equity at the end of the year and at the beginning of the year. The second step then calculates the total movement in equity to be C1 168 200. This amount includes all movements in equity for the year (income earned, expenses incurred, contributions from the owner and distributions to the owner). If we reverse the effect of the contributions (subtract) and the distributions (add back), we can calculate the effect of income and expenses on equity – that is, the profit for the period.

Bibliography

The International Accounting Standards Board. 2012. IAS 1 *Presentation of Financial Statements*.

PART II

The accounting process

4 Recording external transactions

Business focus

In more primitive trading times, bookkeeping was not such a big issue because the person who manufactured or produced the goods was usually the one selling or trading them in the marketplace. However, the Renaissance period saw a huge increase in both trade and banking systems brought about by the Roman-built transport systems and the growth of more sophisticated societies like those in Italy, and particularly in Venice, where, in the 1400s, the merchants developed an accounting system to record these more complex financial dealings.

A Franciscan friar and mathematician from that era, Luca Pacioli, widely regarded as the 'father of accounting', was the first to codify this accounting system in his book, published in 1494 and titled *Summa de arithmetica, geometria, proportioni et proportionalita*, which means 'The collected knowledge of arithmetic, geometry, proportion and proportionality'. This documented system has become known as the 'double-entry accounting' system. The chapters on the accounting system became the only accounting textbook for the next 100 years, and its principles are still followed by accountants today.

Writing in Latin, Pacioli named the act of entrusting *credere* (which means 'to entrust') and the corresponding obligation on the firm *debere* (which means 'to owe'). So, from the point of view of the firm, he could see that this principle of duality held true for every financial transaction it entered into. For him, it was not just a formula but also an aspect of existence where one side could not exist without the other. In a closed system, every *debere* must have a corresponding *credere*, and vice versa.

His work included most of the accounting cycle as we know it today. He described the use of journals and ledgers, and warned that a person should not go to sleep at night until the debits equalled the credits! His ledger had accounts for assets, liabilities, capital, income and expenses – the account categories that are still reported on an entity's statement of financial position and statement of profit or loss today, over 500 years later. He demonstrated year-end closing entries, and proposed that a trial balance be used to prove a balanced ledger.

In this chapter

In Chapter 2, *Fundamental accounting concepts*, you learnt how to analyse and process transactions by applying the definitions of an asset, a liability, equity, income and expenses and also by applying the accrual basis of accounting. In Chapter 3, *The accounting equation and the analysis of transactions*, you learnt the principles of the accounting equation and how to process transactions using an accounting equation worksheet. In this chapter, we build on what you have learnt in the previous chapters and introduce the principles of the double-entry system with debits and credits. We then go on to the bookkeeping process of recording transactions in a journal, posting to a ledger and preparing a trial balance.

Dashboard

- Look at the *Learning outcomes* so that you know what you should be able to do after studying this chapter.
- Read the *Business focus* to place this chapter's contents in a real-world context.
- Preview *In this chapter* to focus your mind on the contents of the chapter.
- Read the *text* in detail.
    - Pay attention to the *definitions*, and apply your mind to the *Pause and reflect* scenarios.
    - Make sure that you read Section 4.2 carefully, which explains the principles of the double-entry system, before working through the Smart Concepts case study in Section 4.4. You will find it helpful to refer to the summary in Diagram 4.3 when working through the case study.
    - The Smart Concepts case study in Section 4.4 integrates the analysis of transactions from Chapter 2 (Section 2.7) and the effect on the accounting equation in Chapter 3 (Section 3.5) with the double-entry accounting system, the journal and the ledger. It is important for you to relate these concepts together as you work through each transaction.
- Prepare solutions to the examples as you read through the chapter.
- Prepare a solution to the *Revision example* at the end of the chapter without reference to the suggested one. Compare your solution to the suggested solution provided.

Learning outcomes

After studying this chapter, you should be able to do the following:

1 Explain the accounting process.
2 Describe the double-entry accounting system.
3 Analyse transactions using the double-entry accounting system.
4 Explain the purpose and structure of the general journal and prepare one.
5 Explain the purpose and structure of the general ledger and prepare one.
6 Demonstrate the process of balancing the accounts and preparing a trial balance.

Recording external transactions

4.1 The accounting process

We mentioned in Chapter 1, *The accounting environment*, that accounting is an information system that selects data, processes that data and produces information about an economic entity. In this chapter, we turn our attention to the *processing of data* using a traditional bookkeeping system with a journal and a ledger, often referred to as the double-entry accounting system.

The principles that you have learnt in previous chapters do not change – in fact you will see that double-entry accounting is a direct outcome of the accounting equation and applies the definitions of the elements of the financial statements and the accrual basis of accounting. It is necessary before explaining the principles of the double-entry system to refer again to our definition of accounting and place it in the context of the accounting process. Refer to Diagram 4.1, remembering that accounting is an information system that selects data, processes that data and produces information about an economic entity. Only **data** which has an economic impact on the entity is analysed as a transaction in order to determine the effect on the accounting equation. Data is **processed** through the accounting system by means of an activity known as *bookkeeping*. This involves recording the effects of the transactions in a *journal*, from there transferring the recorded effects into accounts in a *ledger*, and then summarising the information in each account by preparing a *trial balance*. The final stage of the accounting process, the **producing of information** for users, involves adjusting the information in the ledger accounts to conform to the accrual basis of accounting, then preparing the financial statements and finally closing the accounts for the period. These last steps of the accounting process are covered in Chapters 5 to 7. Chapter 5, *Recording internal transactions,* deals with adjusting entries; Chapter 6, *Preparation and presentation of the financial statements*, covers the preparation of financial statements; and Chapter 7, *Closing entries*, completes the accounting process.

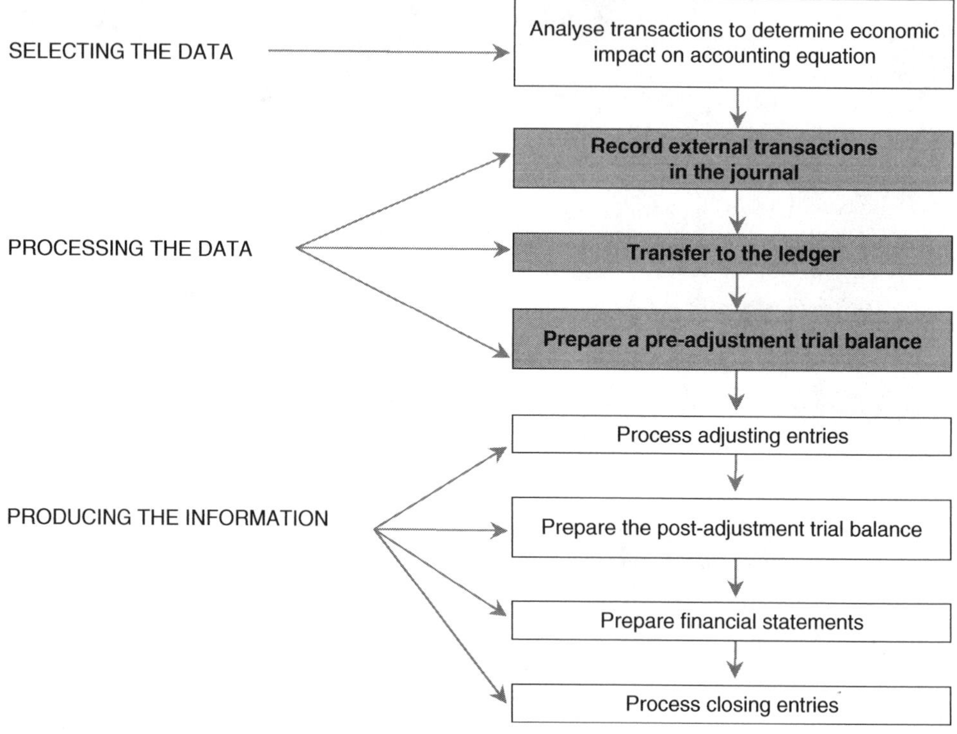

Diagram 4.1 The accounting process

4.2 Double-entry accounting

You learnt in Chapter 3 that every transaction affects and is recorded in two or more accounts. Also, in recording each transaction, the equality of the accounting equation must be maintained at all times. The left-hand side of the accounting equation represents the entity's assets, and the right-hand side the claims against the entity, or the entity's liabilities and owner's equity. Each asset, liability or owner's equity account can be split down the middle, with a left-hand side and a right-hand side.

In double-entry accounting, increases in assets are recorded on the *left-hand side* of asset accounts, for no reason other than that assets are typically shown on the left-hand side of the accounting equation. It follows, therefore, that increases in liabilities and owner's equity are recorded on the *right-hand side* of those accounts in order to maintain the equality of the accounting equation. In other words, if assets are increased with left-hand entries, the accounting equation will balance only if increases in liabilities and owner's equity are recorded on the opposite or right-hand side. Conversely, decreases in assets are recorded on the right-hand side of asset accounts, and decreases in liabilities and equity are recorded on the left-hand side.

Furthermore, the Venetian merchants that developed this system over 500 years ago decided to call the left-hand side of each account the ***debit*** side, abbreviated to ***Dr***, and the right-hand side of each account the ***credit*** side, abbreviated to ***Cr***. The words 'debit' and 'credit' originate from the Latin words *debere* and *credere* respectively. Remember that an account is simply a representation of a column in the accounting equation worksheet. We can summarise these principles as shown in Diagram 4.2.

Assets		=	**Liabilities**		+	**Owner's equity**	
Left/Dr	*Right/Cr*		*Left/Dr*	*Right/Cr*		*Left/Dr*	*Right/Cr*
Increase	Decrease		Decrease	Increase		Decrease	Increase

Diagram 4.2 Principles of the double-entry system

Left-hand side of accounting equation		=	**Right-hand side of accounting equation**				
Assets		=	***Claims against the entity***				
Assets		=	Liabilities		+	Owner's equity	
Left	*Right*		*Left*	*Right*		*Left*	*Right*
+	–		–	+		–	+
Dr	*Cr*		*Dr*	*Cr*		*Dr*	*Cr*

Capital	
Left	*Right*
–	+
Dr	*Cr*
Income	
Left	*Right*
–	+
Dr	*Cr*
Expense	
Left	*Right*
+	–
Dr	*Cr*
Distribution	
Left	*Right*
+	–
Dr	*Cr*

Diagram 4.3 Principles of the double-entry system

The Venetian accounting system was translated from Latin into English in the sixteenth century. At that time, the Latin words *debere* and *credere* were translated into 'debits' and 'credits' in English, therefore, while from an accounting perspective, 'debit' and 'credit' are labels used to describe the left- and right-hand side of accounts, these words often have different meanings in the English language.

It is very important to understand debits and credits in an accounting context without trying to relate them to good and bad, or positive and negative. For example, the word 'credit' in a non-accounting context can mean the achievement of success, a grade in an exam, funds made available in the context of buying or selling goods on credit, or the use of a credit card. The word 'debit' is used by banks to refer to a charge on a business entity's or individual's account (a debit order). Further, it is important not to confuse the word 'debt', meaning an amount owing, with the accounting word 'debit'. Diagram 4.3 summarises the principles of the double-entry system, which are then discussed in detail.

Looking at each element of the accounting equation in Diagram 4.3, we can expand on the double-entry principles as follows:

- **Assets** are on the left-hand side of the equation, thus:
    - Increases in assets are recorded on the left side of the asset account as a debit.
    - Decreases in assets are recorded on the right side of the asset account as a credit.
- **Liabilities** are on the right-hand side of the equation, thus:
    - Increases in liabilities are recorded on the right side of the liability account as a credit.
    - Decreases in liabilities are recorded on the left side of the liability account as a debit.
- **Owner's equity**, although also on the right-hand side of the equation, requires more thought. As you should recall, there are only four types of transactions that affect owner's equity – investments by the owner, distributions to the owner, the earning of income and the incurrence of expenses. Investments by and distributions to the owner do not affect the statement of profit or loss, and therefore:
    - Increases in owner's equity as a result of investments by the owner are recorded on the right side of the capital account as a credit.
    - Decreases in owner's equity as a result of distributions to the owner are recorded on the left side of the distributions account as a debit.

The earning of income and the incurrence of expenses do affect the statement of profit or loss and also the owner's equity.

- **Income** increases owner's equity, which is on the right side of the equation, thus:
    - Increases in income (which increase owner's equity) are recorded on the right side of the income account as a credit.
    - Decreases in income (which decrease owner's equity) are recorded on the left side of the income account as a debit.
- **Expenses** decrease owner's equity, which again, it is emphasised, is on the right side of the equation, thus:
    - Increases in expenses (which decrease owner's equity) are recorded on the left side of the expense account as a debit.
    - Decreases in expenses (which increase owner's equity) are recorded on the right side of the expense account as a credit.

You will notice that the principle which governs the recording of movements in income and expense items is based on the effect that the transaction has on owner's equity. As the earning of income increases owner's equity, increases in income are recorded on the right side of the income account as a credit, because increases in owner's equity are recorded on the right side as a credit. Conversely, as the incurrence of expenses decreases owner's equity, increases in expenses are recorded on the left side of expense accounts as a debit, because decreases in owner's equity are recorded on the left side as a debit.

These are the principles of the double-entry system – the language of accounting. You may find that you need to memorise them now, but soon you will be using this language fluently.

 **Pause and reflect...**

You know that assets represent future economic benefits and that expenses are outflows of economic benefits, yet assets increase with a debit entry and so do expenses. Why is this so?

Response

Assets are on the left side of the accounting equation and therefore increases in assets are recorded on the left side of the asset account as a debit. Expenses decrease owner's equity, which, you will recall, is on the right side of the equation. Increases in expenses (which decrease owner's equity) are thus recorded on the left side of the expense account as a debit.

4.3 The general journal and general ledger

Before applying the principles of double-entry accounting to the Smart Concepts case study, it is necessary to introduce the recording process in the general journal and general ledger. A detailed explanation of the use of the journal and ledger will follow in Section 4.5.

4.3.1 Use of the general journal

If you refer to Diagram 4.1 earlier in this chapter, you will notice that after a transaction has been analysed to determine its effect on the accounting equation, the processing begins by recording the effects of the transaction in a journal. In a double-entry bookkeeping system, before transactions are recorded in the ledger, they are first entered in a journal.

The journal that we are going to use here is referred to as a general journal. We will learn about other journals in Chapter 9, *Analysis journals*. The journals are known collectively as books of ***original entry***.

The general journal links the debit and credit of each transaction by providing, in one place, a complete record of each transaction, in chronological order. Each transaction is analysed and recorded in the general journal in a manner which identifies which *accounts* are affected and the *amount* by which each account is to be changed.

Double-entry principles are to be followed for each transaction:

- Two or more accounts are affected.
- Total debits equal total credits.
- Equality of the accounting equation is maintained.

No transaction may be entered in the ledger unless it has first been entered in a journal. In a double-entry bookkeeping system, the journal does not replace the ledger.

4.3.2 Format of the general journal

A typical format of the general journal is shown below. For each transaction, it provides places for recording the following:

- the date;
- the name of the accounts to be debited or credited;
- a reference to the account in the ledger to which the transaction is to be transferred (the folio column);
- the amount;
- an explanation of the transaction, known as the narration.

GENERAL JOURNAL OF (NAME OF ENTITY)

Date	*Description*	*Fol*	*Dr*	*Cr*
1 May 20X5	Name of account to be debited	GL1	21 400	
	Name of account to be credited	GL2		21 400
	Narration			

The details are entered in the journal as each transaction is analysed. You should be able to analyse the transaction in your mind by thinking about the underlying concepts and the accounting equation. Each journal entry represents one line in the accounting equation worksheet – the journal entry is simply a bookkeeping representation of the effects of a transaction on the elements of the equation.

You should note that when transactions are recorded in the general journal, no entry is made in the folio column. When the transactions are transferred to the ledger, the relevant ledger account number is then entered.

4.3.3 Use of the general ledger

If you refer to Diagram 4.1 again, you will see that, after the transaction has been recorded in a journal, the recorded effects are transferred to a ledger. This part of the accounting process is referred to as ***posting***. Posting of journal entry information from the journal to the ledger may be done daily, weekly, monthly or at other intervals. Smart Concepts posts from the journal to the ledger quarterly.

The ledger that we are going to use here is known as the general ledger. Other ledgers will be introduced in Chapter 9. The ledger is known as a book of ***final entry***.

The general ledger comprises a number of different accounts, which accumulate the effects of transactions recorded in the journal. Each account in the ledger is simply a formal representation of a column in the accounting equation worksheet. In the posting procedure, the amount in the debit column in the journal is posted to the debit of the named account in the general ledger. Similarly, the amount in the credit column in the journal is posted to the credit of the named account in the general ledger.

4.3.4 Format of the general ledger

The format of a typical general ledger account is shown below. The account has a debit side and a credit side; in other words, a left side and a right side, just as you found in the accounting equation worksheet. Given its shape, it is normally referred to as a ***T account***.

Dr		ACCOUNT NAME (GL 1)					*Cr*
Date	*Details*	*Fol*	*C*	*Date*	*Details*	*Fol*	*C*
10/02/X5	Name of account credited	GJ1	21 500	15/02/X5	Name of account debited	GJ1	10 000

On each side, it provides places for recording the following:

- the date;
- the name of the other account affected in the transaction;
- a reference to the page number in the journal where the transaction was recorded;
- the amount.

Posting to the general ledger takes place by referring to the journal and transferring the recorded effects to each ledger account. The folio column is completed as each entry is posted from the journal. If the posting process is interrupted, the bookkeeper can look at the folio column in the journal to see which was the last entry posted.

4.4 Analysis of transactions using double-entry accounting

The following is a record of the *external transactions* of Smart Concepts for the period from 1 January 20X5 to 31 March 20X5. Note that only the external transactions are analysed here – the *internal transactions* are analysed at a later stage in the accounting process.

By now, you should be familiar with the activities of Simon Smart and his business entity, Smart Concepts. In Chapter 2, we processed the transactions and prepared financial statements using the concepts found in the *Conceptual Framework*. In Chapter 3, we again processed the transactions and prepared financial statements using the accounting equation. We are now going to begin processing the data by analysing the transactions using the principles of double-entry accounting.

 **Example: External transactions**

Starting the business

1 On 2 January, Simon Smart started a business as a computer retailer. He drew C950 000 from a savings account and opened a bank account in the name of Smart Concepts into which he paid C950 000.

2 On 2 January, Smart Concepts negotiated a loan from Techno Bank for an amount of C600 000. The loan is repayable in four equal annual instalments, beginning on 31 December 20X5. The interest rate is 12 per cent per annum, payable quarterly in arrears.

3 On 2 January, Simon located premises from which to operate in Hyde Park. The monthly rent for the premises is C12 000. Smart Concepts paid four months' rent in advance on 2 January.

4 On 2 January, Simon transferred C120 000 from the bank account into a fixed deposit account earning interest at 5 per cent per annum.

5 On 2 January, Smart Concepts purchased furniture and fittings for C240 000. This was paid for from funds in the bank account. The expected useful life of the furniture and fittings is five years.

6 On 5 January, Smart Concepts purchased supplies of stationery for C5 000 as well as supplies of computer parts for C12 000. All of them were paid for in cash.
7 On 7 January, Smart Concepts opened an account with Computer World, the supplier of its inventory.

Trading and operating transactions for January

8 On 10 January, Smart Concepts purchased inventory of 60 computers from Computer World at a cost of C10 000 each. The total amount owing is to be paid by 25 March.
9 On 12 January, Smart Concepts paid a service provider C750 for internet access.
10 On 25 January, Smart Concepts sold 15 computers on credit to a customer for C12 500 each. An amount of C125 000 is due by 15 March and the balance by 15 April.

Trading and operating transactions for February

11 On 1 February, Smart Concepts employed a computer technician at a salary of C8 000 per month.
12 On 8 February, Smart Concepts paid C7 000 for an advertisement in a newspaper, advertising the computers available for sale.
13 On 12 February, Smart Concepts sold 30 computers to customers for C12 500 each. The customers paid cash for them.
14 On 25 February, Smart Concepts received cash of C48 000 in respect of technical support contracts taken out by customers. The contracts are for a two-year period.
15 On 28 February, Smart Concepts paid the computer technician his salary for February.

Trading and operating transactions for March

16 On 4 March, Smart Concepts purchased inventory of a further 75 computers from Computer World at a cost of C10 000 each. The total amount owing is to be paid by 25 May.
17 On 5 March, Smart Concepts paid a service provider C750 for internet access.
18 On 15 March, Smart Concepts received C125 000 from the customer in transaction 10.
19 On 25 March, Smart Concepts paid Computer World an amount of C600 000.
20 On 29 March, Smart Concepts sold 30 computers on credit to customers for C12 500 each. The full amount owing is due by 30 April.
21 On 30 March, Smart Concepts paid the computer technician his salary for March.

Rewarding the providers of finance

22 On 30 March, Smart Concepts paid the interest on the loan from Techno Bank for the three-month period.
23 On 30 March, Simon authorised a distribution to himself of C60 000 for personal use.

You are required to:

Set up an accounting equation worksheet with each asset, liability and equity column having a left/debit side and a right/credit side. Record the transactions of Smart Concepts for the period from 1 January 20X5 to 31 March 20X5 on the worksheet, applying the principles of double-entry accounting.

No	ASSETS																=	LIABILITIES						OWNER'S EQUITY							
	Bank		*Rent paid in advance*		*Fixed deposit investment*		*Accounts receivable*		*Stationery supplies*		*Computer parts*		*Furniture & fittings*		*Inventory*			*Fees in advance*		*Accounts payable*		*Borrowings*		*Capital*		*Income*		*Expenses*		*Distribution*	
	+ *L Dr*	– *R Cr*	+ *L Dr*	– *R Cr*	+ *L Dr*	– *R Cr*	+ *L Dr*	– *R Cr*	+ *L Dr*	– *R Cr*	+ *L Dr*	– *R Cr*	+ *L Dr*	– *R Cr*	+ *L Dr*	– *R Cr*		– *L Dr*	+ *R Cr*	– *L Dr*	+ *R Cr*	– *L Dr*	+ *R Cr*	– *L Dr*	+ *R Cr*	– *L Dr*	+ *R Cr*	+ *L Dr*	– *R Cr*	+ *L Dr*	– *R Cr*
1	950																=								950						
2	600																=						600								
3		48	48														=														
4		120			120												=														
5		240											240				=														
6		17							5		12						=														
7																															
8															600		=				600										
9		0.75															=											0.75			
10							187.5									150	=										187.5	150			
11																															
12		7															=											7			
13	375															300	=										375	300			
14	48																=		48												
15		8															=											8			
16															750		=				750										
17		0.75															=											0.75			
18	125							125									=														
19		600															=			600											
20							375									300	=										375	300			
21		8															=											8			
22		18															=											18			
23		60															=													60	
*Bal	970.5		48		1 120		437.5		5		12		240		600				48		750		600		950		937.5	792.5		60	
	ASSETS = 2 433																**=**	**LIABILITIES = 1 398**						**OWNER'S EQUITY = 1 035**							

*Bal = Net balance on each account/column.

Solution: Analysis of transactions using double-entry accounting

All of the transactions are analysed on a detailed accounting equation worksheet, first, to illustrate the mechanics of preparing such a worksheet, and second, so that you are able to see the process from beginning to end. Each transaction is then analysed individually with a detailed explanation. The explanation incorporates the analysis of the transaction on a conceptual level, the effect of each transaction on the accounting equation as well as the application of double-entry principles, the journal and the ledger.

Starting the business

1 On 2 January, Simon Smart started a business as a computer retailer. He drew C950 000 from a savings account and opened a bank account in the name of Smart Concepts into which he paid C950 000.

Analysis of transaction	The asset, *bank*, is increased by C950 000, and owner's equity, *capital*, is increased by C950 000.
The accounting equation	***Assets*** = ***Liabilities*** + ***Owner's equity*** **Bank** 950 000 — **Capital** 950 000
Double entry	***Debit*** To increase an asset requires a left or debit entry, thus ***debit*** bank C950 000 ***Credit*** To increase owner's equity requires a right or credit entry, thus ***credit*** capital C950 000
Journal	Bank (A) — *Dr* 950 000 Capital (OE) — *Cr* 950 000
Ledger	*Dr* **Bank** *Cr*: 950 000 (Dr side) *Dr* **Capital** *Cr*: 950 000 (Cr side)

2 On 2 January, Smart Concepts negotiated a loan from Techno Bank for an amount of C600 000. The loan is repayable in four equal annual instalments, beginning on 31 December 20X5. The interest rate is 12 per cent per annum, payable quarterly in arrears.

Analysis of transaction	The asset, *bank*, is increased by C600 000, and the liability, *borrowings*, is increased by C600 000.

The accounting equation	*Assets* = *Liabilities* + *Owner's equity* **Bank** 600 000 — **Borrowings** 600 000
Double entry	***Debit*** To increase an asset requires a left or debit entry, thus ***debit*** bank C600 000 ***Credit*** To increase equity liability requires a right or credit entry, thus ***credit*** borrowings C600 000
Journal	Bank (A) — *Dr* 600 000 Borrowings (L) — *Cr* 600 000
Ledger	*Dr* **Bank** *Cr*: 600 000 (Dr) *Dr* **Borrowings** *Cr*: 600 000 (Cr)

3 On 2 January, Simon located premises from which to operate in Hyde Park. The monthly rent for the premises is C12 000. Smart Concepts paid four months' rent in advance.

Analysis of transaction	The asset, *rent paid in advance*, is increased by C48 000, and the asset, *bank*, is decreased by C48 000.
The accounting equation	*Assets* = *Liabilities* + *Owner's equity* **Bank** (48 000) — **Rent paid in advance** 48 000
Double entry	***Debit*** To increase an asset requires a left or debit entry, thus ***debit*** rent paid in advance C48 000 ***Credit*** To decrease an asset requires a right or credit entry, thus ***credit*** bank C48 000
Journal	Rent paid in advance (A) — *Dr* 48 000 Bank (A) — *Cr* 48 000
Ledger	*Dr* **Rent paid in advance** *Cr*: 48 000 (Dr) *Dr* **Bank** *Cr*: 48 000 (Cr)

4 On 2 January, Simon transferred C120 000 from the bank account into a fixed deposit account earning interest at 5 per cent per annum.

Analysis of transaction

The asset, *fixed deposit*, is increased by C120 000, and the asset, *bank*, is decreased by C120 000.

The accounting equation

Assets		=	***Liabilities***	+	***Owner's equity***
Bank	**Fixed deposit investment**				
(120 000)	120 000				

Double entry

Debit To increase an asset requires a left or debit entry, thus ***debit*** fixed deposit investment C120 000

Credit To decrease an asset requires a right or credit entry, thus ***credit*** bank C120 000

Journal

	Dr	*Cr*
Fixed deposit investment (A)	120 000	
Bank (A)		120 000

Ledger

Dr **Fixed deposit investment**	*Cr*
120 000	

Dr **Bank**	*Cr*
	120 000

5 On 2 January, Smart Concepts purchased furniture and fittings for C240 000. This was paid for from funds in the bank account. The expected useful life of the furniture and fittings is five years.

Analysis of transaction

The asset, *furniture and fittings*, is increased by C240 000, and the asset, *bank*, is decreased by C240 000.

The accounting equation

Assets		=	***Liabilities***	+	***Owner's equity***
Bank	**Furniture and fittings**				
(240 000)	240 000				

Double entry	***Debit*** To increase an asset requires a left or debit entry, thus ***debit*** furniture and fittings C240 000 ***Credit*** To decrease an asset requires a right or credit entry, thus ***credit*** bank C240 000

Journal

	Dr	*Cr*
Furniture and fittings (A)	240 000	
Bank (A)		240 000

Ledger

Dr **Furniture and fittings** *Cr*		*Dr* **Bank** *Cr*	
240 000			240 000

6 On 5 January, Smart Concepts purchased supplies of stationery for C5 000 as well as supplies of computer parts for C12 000. All of them were paid for in cash.

Analysis of transaction

The assets, *stationery supplies* and *computer parts*, are increased by C5 000 and C12 000 respectively, and the asset, *bank*, is decreased by C17 000.

The accounting equation

Assets			=	*Liabilities*	+	*Owner's equity*
Bank	**Stationery supplies**	**Computer parts**				
(17 000)	5 000	12 000				

Double entry

Debit To increase an asset requires a left or debit entry, thus ***debit*** stationery supplies C5 000 and debit computer parts C12 000

Credit To decrease an asset requires a right or credit entry, thus ***credit*** bank C17 000

Journal

	Dr	*Cr*
Stationery supplies (A)	5 000	
Computer parts (A)	12 000	
Bank (A)		17 000

Ledger

Dr **Stationery supplies** *Cr*		*Dr* **Bank** *Cr*	
5 000			17 000

Dr **Computer parts** *Cr*	
12 000	

7 On 7 January, Smart Concepts opened an account with Computer World, the supplier of its inventory.	
Analysis of transaction	Not applicable.

The opening of the account with the supplier is a transaction that has no economic impact on the entity and therefore the financial statements are not affected.

Trading and operating transactions for January

8 On 10 January, Smart Concepts purchased inventory of 60 computers from Computer World at a cost of C10 000 each. The total amount owing is to be paid by 25 March.	
Analysis of transaction	The asset, *inventory*, is increased by C600 000, and the liability, *accounts payable*, is increased by C600 000.

The accounting equation

Assets	=	***Liabilities***	+	***Owner's equity***
Inventory		**Accounts payable**		
600 000		600 000		

Double entry

Debit To increase an asset requires a left or debit entry, thus ***debit*** inventory C600 000

Credit To increase a liability requires a right or credit entry, thus ***credit*** accounts payable C600 000

Journal

	Dr	*Cr*
Inventory (A)	600 000	
Accounts payable (L)		600 000

Ledger

Dr **Inventory**	*Cr*
600 000	

Dr **Accounts payable**	*Cr*
	600 000

9 On 12 January, Simon paid a service provider C750 for internet access.	
Analysis of transaction	The expense, *internet*, is increased by C750, and the asset, *bank*, is decreased by C750.
The accounting equation	***Assets*** = ***Liabilities*** + ***Owner's equity*** **Bank** (750) — **Internet expense** (750)
Double entry	***Debit*** To increase an expense requires a left or debit entry, thus ***debit*** internet C750 ***Credit*** To decrease an asset requires a right or credit entry, thus ***credit*** bank C750
Journal	Internet (E) — *Dr* 750 Bank (A) — *Cr* 750
Ledger	*Dr* **Internet** *Cr*: 750 (Dr) *Dr* **Bank** *Cr*: 750 (Cr)

Journal:

	Dr	*Cr*
Internet (E)	750	
Bank (A)		750

10 On 25 January, Smart Concepts sold 15 computers on credit to a customer for C12 500 each. An amount of C125 000 is due by 15 March and the balance by 15 April.	
Analysis of transaction	The asset, *accounts receivable*, is increased by C187 500, and income, *sales*, is increased by C187 500. In addition, the expense, *cost of sales*, is increased by C150 000, and the asset, *inventory*, is decreased by C150 000.

The accounting equation

Assets		= ***Liabilities*** +	***Owner's equity***	
Accounts receivable	**Inventory**		**Sales**	**Cost of sales**
187 500			187 500	
	(150 000)			(150 000)

Double entry

Debit To increase an asset requires a left or debit entry, thus ***debit*** accounts receivable C187 500

Credit To increase owner's equity requires a right or credit entry, thus ***credit*** sales C187 500

Debit To increase an expense requires a left or debit entry, thus ***debit*** cost of sales C150 000

Credit To decrease an asset requires a right or credit entry, thus ***credit*** inventory C150 000

Journal

	Dr	*Cr*
Accounts receivable (A)	187 500	
Sales (I)		187 500
Cost of sales (E)	150 000	
Inventory (A)		150 000

Ledger

Dr	**Accounts receivable**	*Cr*	*Dr*	**Sales**	*Cr*
187 500					187 500

Dr	**Cost of sales**	*Cr*	*Dr*	**Inventory**	*Cr*
150 000					150 000

Trading and operating transactions for February

11 On 1 February, Smart Concepts employed a computer technician at a salary of C8 000 per month.

Analysis of transaction Not applicable.

The employment of a technician is also a transaction that has no economic impact on the entity and therefore the financial statements are not affected.

12 On 8 February, Smart Concepts paid C7 000 for an advertisement in a newspaper, advertising the computers available for sale.

Analysis of transaction The expense, *advertising*, is increased by C7 000, and the asset, *bank*, is decreased by C7 000.

The accounting equation	***Assets***	=	***Liabilities***	+	***Owner's equity***
	Bank				**Advertising expense**
	(7 000)				(7 000)

Double entry

Debit To increase an expense requires a left or debit entry, thus ***debit*** advertising C7 000

Credit To decrease an asset requires a right or credit entry, thus ***credit*** bank C7 000

Journal

	Dr	*Cr*
Advertising (E)	7 000	
Bank (A)		7 000

Ledger

Dr	**Advertising**	*Cr*	*Dr*	**Bank**	*Cr*
7 000					7 000

13 On 12 February, Smart Concepts sold 30 computers to customers for C12 500 each. The customers paid cash for the computers.

Analysis of transaction

The asset, *bank*, is increased by C375 000, and income, *sales*, is increased by C375 000. In addition, the expense, *cost of sales*, is increased by C300 000, and the asset, *inventory*, is decreased by C300 000.

The accounting equation	***Assets***		=	***Liabilities***	+	***Owner's equity***	
	Bank	**Inventory**				**Sales**	**Cost of sales**
	375 000					375 000	
		(300 000)					(300 000)

Double entry

Debit To increase an asset requires a left or debit entry, thus ***debit*** bank C375 000

Credit To increase owner's equity requires a right or credit entry, thus ***credit*** sales C375 000

Debit To increase an expense requires a left or debit entry, thus ***debit*** cost of sales C300 000

Credit To decrease an asset requires a right or credit entry, thus ***credit*** inventory C300 000

Journal

	Dr	Cr
Bank (A)	375 000	
Sales (I)		375 000
Cost of sales (E)	300 000	
Inventory (A)		300 000

Ledger

Dr **Bank**	*Cr*	*Dr* **Sales**	*Cr*
375 000			375 000

Dr **Cost of sales**	*Cr*	*Dr* **Inventory**	*Cr*
300 000			300 000

14 On 25 February, Smart Concepts received cash of C48 000 in respect of technical support contracts taken out by customers. The contracts are for a two-year period.

Analysis of transaction

The asset, *bank*, is increased by C48 000, and the liability, *service fees received in advance*, is increased by C48 000.

The accounting equation

Assets	=	***Liabilities***	+	***Owner's equity***
Bank		**Service fees in advance**		
48 000		48 000		

Double entry

Debit To increase an asset requires a left or debit entry, thus ***debit*** bank C48 000

Credit To increase a liability requires a right or credit entry, thus ***credit*** service fees in advance C48 000

Journal

	Dr	Cr
Bank (A)	48 000	
Service fees received in advance (L)		48 000

Ledger

Dr **Bank**	*Cr*	*Dr* **Service fees in advance**	*Cr*
48 000			48 000

15 On 28 February, Smart Concepts paid the computer technician his salary for February.			
Analysis of transaction	The expense, *salaries*, is increased by C8 000, and the asset, *bank*, is decreased by C8 000.		
The accounting equation	***Assets*** =	***Liabilities*** +	***Owner's equity***
	Bank		**Salaries expense**
	(8 000)		(8 000)
Double entry	***Debit*** To increase an expense requires a left or debit entry, thus ***debit*** salaries C8 000 ***Credit*** To decrease an asset requires a right or credit entry, thus ***credit*** bank C8 000		
Journal		*Dr*	*Cr*
	Salaries (E)	8 000	
	Bank (A)		8 000
Ledger	*Dr* **Salaries** *Cr* 8 000 |		*Dr* **Bank** *Cr* | 8 000

Trading and operating transactions for March

16 On 4 March, Smart Concepts purchased inventory of a further 75 computers from Computer World at a cost of C10 000 each. The total amount owing is to be paid by 25 May.			
Analysis of transaction	The asset, *inventory*, is increased by C750 000, and the liability, *accounts payable*, is increased by C750 000.		
The accounting equation	***Assets*** =	***Liabilities*** +	***Owner's equity***
	Inventory	**Accounts payable**	
	750 000	750 000	

Double entry	***Debit*** To increase an asset requires a left or debit entry, thus ***debit*** inventory C750 000 ***Credit*** To increase a liability requires a right or credit entry, thus ***credit*** accounts payable C750 000

Journal

	Dr	*Cr*
Inventory	750 000	
Accounts payable (L)		750 000

Ledger

Dr **Inventory** *Cr*		*Dr* **Accounts payable** *Cr*	
750 000			750 000

17 On 5 March, Smart Concepts paid a service provider C750 for internet access.

Analysis of transaction	The expense, *internet*, is increased by C750, and the asset, *bank*, is decreased by C750.

This transaction is identical to transaction 9.

18 On 15 March, Smart Concepts received C125 000 from the customer in transaction 10.

Analysis of transaction	The asset, *bank*, is increased by C125 000, and the asset, *accounts receivable*, is decreased by C125 000.

The accounting equation

Assets		= ***Liabilities***	+ ***Owner's equity***
Bank	**Accounts receivable**		
125 000	(125 000)		

Double entry	***Debit*** To increase an asset requires a left or debit entry, thus ***debit*** bank C125 000 ***Credit*** To decrease an asset requires a right or credit entry, thus ***credit*** accounts receivable C125 000

Journal

	Dr	*Cr*
Bank (A)	125 000	
Accounts receivable (A)		125 000

Ledger

Dr **Bank**	*Cr*	*Dr* **Accounts receivable**	*Cr*
125 000			125 000

19 On 25 March, Smart Concepts paid Computer World an amount of C600 000.

Analysis of transaction

The liability, *accounts payable*, is decreased by C600 000, and the asset, *bank*, is decreased by C600 000.

The accounting equation

Assets	=	*Liabilities*	+	*Owner's equity*
Bank		**Accounts payable**		
(600 000)		(600 000)		

Double entry

Debit To decrease a liability requires a left or debit entry, thus ***debit*** accounts payable C600 000

Credit To decrease an asset requires a right or credit entry, thus ***credit*** bank C600 000

Journal

	Dr	*Cr*
Accounts payable (L)	600 000	
Bank (A)		600 000

Ledger

Dr **Accounts payable**	*Cr*	*Dr* **Bank**	*Cr*
600 000			600 000

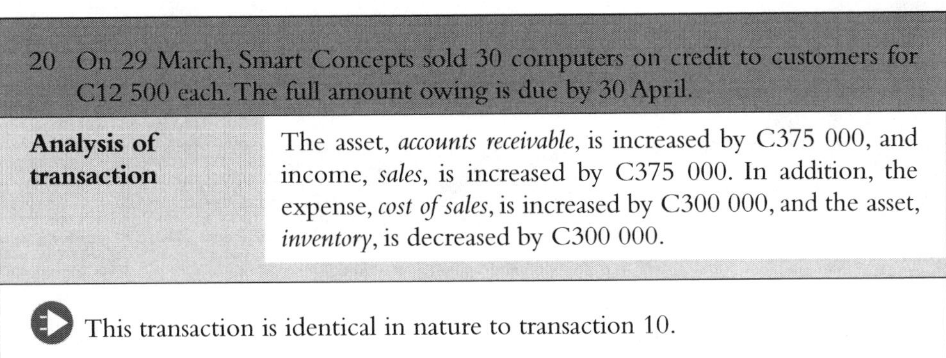

20 On 29 March, Smart Concepts sold 30 computers on credit to customers for C12 500 each. The full amount owing is due by 30 April.

Analysis of transaction

The asset, *accounts receivable*, is increased by C375 000, and income, *sales*, is increased by C375 000. In addition, the expense, *cost of sales*, is increased by C300 000, and the asset, *inventory*, is decreased by C300 000.

This transaction is identical in nature to transaction 10.

21 On 30 March, Smart Concepts paid the computer technician his salary for March.

Analysis of transaction	The expense, *salaries*, is increased by C8 000, and the asset, *bank*, is decreased by C8 000.

This transaction is identical to transaction 15.

Rewarding the providers of finance

22 On 30 March, Smart Concepts paid the interest on the loan from Techno Bank for the three-month period.

Analysis of transaction

The expense, *interest*, is increased by C18 000, and the asset, *bank*, is decreased by C18 000.

The accounting equation

Assets	=	*Liabilities*	+	*Owner's equity*
Bank				**Interest expense**
(18 000)				(18 000)

Double entry

Debit To increase an expense requires a left or debit entry, thus ***debit*** interest C18 000

Credit To decrease an asset requires a right or credit entry, thus ***credit*** bank C18 000

Journal

	Dr	*Cr*
Interest (E)	18 000	
Bank (A)		18 000

Ledger

Dr **Interest**	*Cr*
18 000	

Dr **Bank**	*Cr*
	18 000

23 On 30 March, Simon authorised a distribution to himself of C60 000 for personal use.

Analysis of transaction	Owner's equity, *distributions*, is increased by C60 000, and the asset, *bank*, is decreased by C60 000.

The accounting equation	***Assets***	=	***Liabilities***	+	***Owner's equity***
	Bank				**Distribution**
	(60 000)				(60 000)

Double entry	***Debit***	To decrease owner's equity requires a left or debit entry, thus ***debit*** distributions C60 000
	Credit	To decrease an asset requires a right or credit entry, thus ***credit*** bank C60 000

Journal		*Dr*	*Cr*
	Distributions (OE)	60 000	
	Bank (A)		60 000

Ledger	*Dr*	**Distributions** *Cr*	*Dr*	**Bank** *Cr*
	60 000			60 000

4.5 Recording of transactions in a general journal and general ledger

You have learnt in the previous sections about the principles of the double-entry system as well as the format of a general journal and general ledger. We have *analysed each transaction* showing its effect on the *accounting equation*, the resultant *double entry* as well as the applicable *journal* entry and *ledger* posting.

It is important that you are able to process a set of transactions using a manual book-keeping system; in other words, record the transactions in a journal, post the transactions to a ledger and prepare a trial balance. We examine this process in the sections and examples that follow.

It is very important to be able to identify accounts as an asset, liability, owner's equity, income or expense as this determines the debit or credit in the double-entry system. In this book, we include either an 'A', 'L', 'OE', 'I' or 'E' behind the account name to identify it as an asset, liability, owner's equity, income or expense respectively. This helps you identify the account as a statement of financial position account or a statement of profit or loss account when preparing the financial statements. It is also essential to distinguish accounts of the same or similar name that appear as statement of financial position accounts and as statement of profit or loss accounts.

For example, if an entity pays insurance in advance, we debit an *asset* account that we have called 'Insurance paid in advance (A)'. When the entity recognises the insurance used for the period, we debit an *expense* account 'Insurance (E)' and credit the 'Insurance paid in advance (A)'. Similarly, if an entity receives fees in advance, we credit a *liability* account that we have called 'Fees received in advance (L)'. When the entity recognises the fees earned for the period, we debit the liability account 'Fees received in advance (L)' and credit an *income* account 'Fees (I)'.

Pause and reflect...

Think of 'rent'. Is 'rent' an asset, a liability, income or an expense? Could it be all of these?

Response

Rent is recognised as an *asset* if the entity is a tenant and pays rent in advance to a landlord. At the end of the period, the entity recognises the rent incurred for the period as an *expense*.

Rent is recognised as a *liability* if the entity is a landlord and receives rent in advance from a tenant. At the end of the period, the entity recognises the rent earned for the period as *income*.

This emphasises the importance of identifying an account as an asset, liability, income or expense.

4.5.1 Recording transactions in a general journal

The format of a general journal was explained in Section 4.3.2. Remember that the general journal is the book of prime or first entry. In other words, all transactions need to be recorded in the journal before being posted to the ledger.

Example: Recording transactions in a general journal

Refer to the external transactions listed in the Smart Concepts case study in Section 4.4 for the period from 1 January 20X5 to 31 March 20X5.

You are required to:

Record the external transactions for the period from 1 January 20X5 to 31 March 20X5 in the general journal of Smart Concepts.

Solution: Recording transactions in a general journal

GENERAL JOURNAL OF SMART CONCEPTS (GJ 1)

Date	*Description*	*Fol*	*Dr*	*Cr*
20X5				
January				
02	Bank (A)	A1	950 000	
	Simon Smart capital (OE)	OE1		950 000
	Investment by owner			
02	Bank (A)	A1	600 000	
	Borrowings (L)	L1		600 000
	Raising of loan from Techno Bank			
02	Rent paid in advance (A)	A2	48 000	
	Bank (A)	A1		48 000
	Payment of four months' rent in advance			
02	Fixed deposit investment (A)	A3	120 000	
	Bank (A)	A1		120 000
	Transferred cash to fixed deposit			

02	Furniture and fittings (A) Bank (A) *Purchase of furniture and fittings for cash*	A4 A1	240 000	 240 000
05	Stationery supplies (A) Computer parts (A) Bank (A) *Purchase of stationery and computer parts for cash*	A5 A6 A1	5 000 12 000	 17 000
10	Inventory (A) Accounts payable (L) *Purchase of inventory on credit*	A7 L2	600 000	 600 000
12	Internet expense (E) Bank (A) *Purchase of data bundle for cash*	E1 A1	750	 750
25	Accounts receivable (A) Sales income (I) *Sale of 15 computers to customer on credit*	A8 I1	187 500	 187 500
	Cost of sales expense (E) Inventory (A) *Recording the cost of inventory sold*	E2 A7	150 000	 150 000

GENERAL JOURNAL OF SMART CONCEPTS (GJ 2)

Date	*Description*	*Fol*	*Dr*	*Cr*
February 08	 Advertising expense (E) Bank (A) *Advertising paid for in cash*	 E3 A1	 7 000	 7 000
12	Bank (A) Sales income (I) *Sale of 30 computers to customers for cash*	A1 I1	375 000	 375 000
	Cost of sales expense (E) Inventory (A) *Recording the cost of inventory sold*	E2 A7	300 000	 300 000
25	Bank (A) Service fees received in advance (L) *Receipts from clients for technical support contracts to be provided over the next two years*	A1 L3	48 000	 48 000
28	Salaries expense (E) Bank (A) *Payment of salary expense*	E4 A1	8 000	 8 000
March 04	 Inventory (A) Accounts payable (L) *Purchase of inventory on credit*	 A7 L2	 750 000	 750 000
05	Internet expense (E) Bank (A) *Purchase of data bundle for cash*	E1 A1	750	 750
15	Bank (A) Accounts receivable (A) *Receipt from customer*	A1 A8	125 000	 125 000

GENERAL JOURNAL OF SMART CONCEPTS (GJ 2)

Date	Description	Fol	Dr	Cr
25	Accounts payable (L)	L2	600 000	
	Bank (A)	A1		600 000
	Payment to supplier			
29	Bank (A)	A1	375 000	
	Sales income (I)	I1		375 000
	Sale of 30 computers to customers for cash			
	Cost of sales (E)	E2	300 000	
	Inventory	A7		300 000
	Recording the cost of inventory sold			
30	Salaries expense (E)	E4	8 000	
	Bank (A)	A1		8 000
	Payment of salaries			
30	Interest expense (E)	E5	18 000	
	Bank (A)	A1		18 000
	Payment of interest on borrowings			
30	Distributions (OE)	OE2	60 000	
	Bank (A)	A1		60 000
	Distribution to owner			

Ensure that for each journal entry, you are able to *analyse the transaction*, determine its effect on the *accounting equation* and the resultant *double entry* leading to the entry recorded in the *journal*. These explanations were provided in the detailed explanation for each transaction within the solution to the example in Section 4.4.

Looking at the format of the general journal, please note that the debit side of the entry is always recorded above the credit side (and not the other way around). The narration after each journal entry is a simple description of the transaction, and many alternative narrations are acceptable. The folio references refer to the ledger accounts in the general ledger. Each ledger account will have a unique folio reference. We have chosen the style here of allocating an 'A' reference to all asset accounts and an 'L' reference to all liability accounts, and so on. Again, there are many acceptable styles for the folio references.

Note that 'bank' refers to the cash resources of the entity and is thus labelled as an asset (A). A bank account could be in overdraft, in which case it would be a liability.

4.5.2 Recording transactions in a general ledger

The format of the general ledger and the process of posting from a journal were explained in Section 4.3.4. Remember that the general ledger is the book of final or second entry. Transactions are recorded in the general journal during the period and are posted to the general ledger at the end of the period.

 **Example: Recording transactions in a general ledger**

Refer to the journal entries in Section 4.5.1.

You are required to:

Post all of the journal entries from the general journal to the general ledger of Smart Concepts for the period from 1 January 20X5 to 31 March.

Solution: Recording transactions in a general ledger

Dr **BANK (GL A1)** *Cr*

Date	*Details*	*Fol*	*C*	*Date*	*Details*	*Fol*	*C*
02/01	Capital	GJ1	950 000	02/01	Rent paid in advance	GJ1	48 000
02/01	Borrowings	GJ1	600 000	02/01	Fixed deposit investment	GJ1	120 000
12/02	Sales income	GJ2	375 000	02/01	Furniture and fittings	GJ1	240 000
25/02	Service fees in advance	GJ2	48 000	05/01	Stationery supplies	GJ1	5 000
15/03	Accounts receivable	GJ2	125 000	05/01	Computer parts	GJ1	12 000
				12/01	Internet expense	GJ1	750
				08/02	Advertising expense	GJ2	7 000
				28/02	Salaries expense	GJ2	8 000
				05/03	Internet expense	GJ2	750
				25/03	Accounts payable	GJ2	600 000
				30/03	Salaries expense	GJ2	8 000
				30/03	Interest expense	GJ2	18 000
				30/03	Distributions	GJ2	60 000
				31/03	Balance	c/d	970 500
			2 098 000				2 098 000
01/04	Balance	b/d	970 500				

Dr **RENT PAID IN ADVANCE (GL A2)** *Cr*

Date	*Details*	*Fol*	*C*	*Date*	*Details*	*Fol*	*C*
02/01	Bank	GJ1	48 000	31/03	Balance	c/d	48 000
			48 000				48 000
01/04	Balance	b/d	48 000				

Dr **FIXED DEPOSIT INVESTMENT (GL A3)** *Cr*

Date	*Details*	*Fol*	*C*	*Date*	*Details*	*Fol*	*C*
02/01	Bank	GJ1	120 000	31/03	Balance	c/d	120 000
			120 000				120 000
01/04	Balance	b/d	120 000				

Dr **FURNITURE AND FITTINGS (GL A4)** *Cr*

Date	*Details*	*Fol*	*C*	*Date*	*Details*	*Fol*	*C*
02/01	Bank	GJ1	240 000	31/03	Balance	c/d	240 000
			240 000				240 000
01/04	Balance	b/d	240 000				

Dr			STATIONERY SUPPLIES (GL A5)				*Cr*
Date	*Details*	*Fol*	*C*	*Date*	*Details*	*Fol*	*C*
05/01	Bank	GJ1	5 000				
				31/03	Balance	c/d	5 000
			5 000				5 000
01/04	Balance	b/d	5 000				

Dr			COMPUTER PARTS (GL A6)				*Cr*
Date	*Details*	*Fol*	*C*	*Date*	*Details*	*Fol*	*C*
05/01	Bank	GJ1	12 000				
				31/03	Balance	c/d	12 000
			12 000				12 000
01/04	Balance	b/d	12 000				

Dr			INVENTORY (GL A7)				*Cr*
Date	*Details*	*Fol*	*C*	*Date*	*Details*	*Fol*	*C*
10/01	Accounts payable	GJ1	600 000	25/01	Cost of sales expense	GJ1	150 000
04/03	Accounts payable	GJ2	750 000	12/02	Cost of sales expense	GJ2	300 000
				29/03	Cost of sales expense	GJ2	300 000
				31/03	Balance	c/d	600 000
			1 350 000				1 350 000
01/04	Balance	b/d	600 000				

Dr			ACCOUNTS RECEIVABLE (GL A8)				*Cr*
Date	*Details*	*Fol*	*C*	*Date*	*Details*	*Fol*	*C*
25/01	Sales income	GJ1	187 500	15/03	Bank	GJ2	125 000
29/03	Sales income	GJ2	375 000	31/03	Balance	c/d	437 500
			562 500				562 500
01/04	Balance	b/d	437 500				

Dr			BORROWINGS (GL L1)				*Cr*
Date	*Details*	*Fol*	*C*	*Date*	*Details*	*Fol*	*C*
				02/01	Bank	GJ1	600 000
31/03	Balance	c/d	600 000				
			600 000				600 000
				01/04	Balance	b/d	600 000

Dr			ACCOUNTS PAYABLE (GL L2)				*Cr*
Date	*Details*	*Fol*	*C*	*Date*	*Details*	*Fol*	*C*
25/03	Bank	GJ2	600 000	10/01	Inventory	GJ1	600 000
31/03	Balance	c/d	750 000	04/03	Inventory	GJ2	750 000
			1 350 000				1 350 000
				01/04	Balance	b/d	750 000

Dr			SERVICE FEES RECEIVED IN ADVANCE (GL L3)				*Cr*
Date	*Details*	*Fol*	*C*	*Date*	*Details*	*Fol*	*C*
				25/02	Bank	GJ2	48 000
31/03	Balance	c/d	48 000				
			48 000				48 000
				01/04	Balance	b/d	48 000

Dr			CAPITAL (GL OE1)				*Cr*
Date	*Details*	*Fol*	*C*	*Date*	*Details*	*Fol*	*C*
				02/01	Bank	GJ1	950 000
31/03	Balance	c/d	950 000				
			950 000				950 000
				01/04	Balance	b/d	950 000

Dr			DISTRIBUTIONS (GL OE2)				*Cr*
Date	*Details*	*Fol*	*C*	*Date*	*Details*	*Fol*	*C*
30/03	Bank	GJ2	60 000				
				31/03	Balance	c/d	60 000
			60 000				60 000
31/03	Balance	b/d	60 000				

Dr			SALES INCOME (GL I1)				*Cr*
Date	*Details*	*Fol*	*C*	*Date*	*Details*	*Fol*	*C*
				25/01	Accounts receivable	GJ1	187 500
				12/02	Bank	GJ2	375 000
31/03	Balance	c/d	937 500	29/03	Accounts receivable	GJ2	375 000
			937 500				937 500
				31/03	Balance	b/d	937 500

Dr			INTERNET EXPENSE (GL E1)				Cr
Date	Details	Fol	C	Date	Details	Fol	C
12/01	Bank	GJ1	750				
05/03	Bank	GJ2	750	31/03	Balance	c/d	1 500
			1 500				1 500
31/03	Balance	b/d	1 500				

Dr			COST OF SALES EXPENSE (GL E2)				Cr
Date	Details	Fol	C	Date	Details	Fol	C
25/01	Inventory	GJ1	150 000				
12/02	Inventory	GJ2	300 000				
29/03	Inventory	GJ2	300 000	31/03	Balance	c/d	750 000
			750 000				750 000
31/03	Balance	b/d	750 000				

Dr			ADVERTISING EXPENSE (GL E3)				Cr
Date	Details	Fol	C	Date	Details	Fol	C
08/02	Bank	GJ2	7 000				
				31/03	Balance	c/d	7 000
			7 000				7 000
31/03	Balance	b/d	7 000				

Dr			SALARIES EXPENSE (GL E4)				Cr
Date	Details	Fol	C	Date	Details	Fol	C
28/02	Bank	GJ2	8 000				
30/03	Bank	GJ2	8 000	31/03	Balance	c/d	16 000
			16 000				16 000
31/03	Balance	b/d	16 000				

Dr			INTEREST EXPENSE (GL E5)				Cr
Date	Details	Fol	C	Date	Details	Fol	C
30/03	Bank	GJ2	18 000				
				31/03	Balance	c/d	18 000
			18 000				18 000
31/03	Balance	b/d	18 000				

As explained in Section 4.3.4, there are some conventions that you need to be aware of when posting transactions from the journal to the ledger. The information entered into the 'details' column is always the name of the other account in the journal entry. Using transaction 22 on 30 March 20X5 as an example, the analysis of the transaction gives rise to a journal entry to debit *interest expense* and credit *bank* for C18 000.

Thus, on the debit side of the interest expense ledger account (E5), the word 'bank' is entered in the details column, indicating that the credit side of the entry is in the bank ledger account (A1). Looking at the bank ledger account (A1) on the credit side, the words 'interest expense' are entered in the details column, indicating that the debit side of the entry is in the interest expense account (E5).

The folio column in the ledger is a reference to the journal where the transaction was recorded. This transaction was recorded in GJ 2.

The amount of C18 000 is entered in the amount column on the debit side of the interest expense ledger account and the credit side of the bank ledger account.

4.6 The trial balance

4.6.1 Balancing the accounts

The rules of double-entry bookkeeping have been used to journalise and post the transactions. Increases to each account have been entered on one side (debit for assets, distributions and expenses; credit for liabilities, capital and income) and decreases on the opposite side (credit for assets, distributions and expenses; debit for liabilities, capital and income). This makes it easy to determine the balance on each account. Regardless of whether the account is an asset, liability or owner's equity, the account balance is the difference between its increases and decreases, or its debit side and credit side. The balance on the account at the end of a period is the same as the equivalent accounting equation column.

When balancing each account in the general ledger, you should be aware of whether the balance in the account is *normally* a debit or credit. The normal balance results from the principles of double-entry bookkeeping (Table 4.1).

The procedure to balance an account is as follows:

Step 1

Total the side of the ledger account as indicated by the 'normal balance' and enter this amount between two horizontal lines beneath the last entry in the account, on both the debit and credit sides.

Step 2

Calculate the account balance.

Table 4.1 Normal balance of ledger accounts

Elements of the financial statements	*Increases recorded as*	*Decreases recorded as*	*Normal balance*
Asset	Dr	Cr	Dr
Liability	Cr	Dr	Cr
Owner's equity			
Capital	Cr	Dr	Cr
Distributions	Dr	Cr	Dr
Income	Cr	Dr	Cr
Expenses	Dr	Cr	Dr

- If the *normal balance is a debit*, you will find that the total debits are higher than the total credits. The excess of the debits over the credits is first written *above the total on the credit* side as 'balance c/d' (*c/d* means carried down) and then written *below the total on the debit* side as 'balance b/d' (*b/d* means brought down).
- If the *normal balance is a credit*, you will find that the total credits are higher than the total debits. The excess of the credits over the debits is first written *above the total on the debit* side as 'balance c/d' (*c/d* means carried down) and then written *below the total on the credit* side as 'balance b/d') (*b/d* means brought down).

We will use the accounts receivable account in the general ledger to illustrate this procedure.

Step 1

Total the debit side and enter '562 500' between the horizontal lines on the debit and credit sides.

Dr **ACCOUNTS RECEIVABLE (GL A8)** *Cr*

Date	*Details*	*Fol*	*C*	*Date*	*Details*	*Fol*	*C*
25/01	Sales (I)	GJ1	187 500	15/03	Bank	GJ2	125 000
29/03	Sales (I)	GJ2	375 000				
			562 500				***562 500***

Step 2

As the normal balance of an asset account is a debit, the account balance is the excess of the debits of C562 500 over the credits C125 000, giving a balance of C437 500. This amount is entered as a balance c/d on the credit side and as a balance b/d on the debit side.

Dr **ACCOUNTS RECEIVABLE (GL A8)** *Cr*

Date	*Details*	*Fol*	*C*	*Date*	*Details*	*Fol*	*C*
25/01	Sales (I)	GJ1	187 500	15/03	Bank	GJ2	125 000
29/03	Sales (I)	GJ2	375 000	***31/03***	***Balance***	***c/d***	***437 500***
			562 500				562 500
01/04	***Balance***	***b/d***	***437 500***				

4.6.2 Preparing the trial balance

The last stage in processing the data is to summarise the information in the general ledger by preparing a trial balance (see Diagram 4.1). In double-entry bookkeeping, every transaction is recorded with equal debits and credits. This equality is tested by preparing a trial balance, which lists the balance on each account. This procedure is equivalent to checking that the two sides of the bottom line of the accounting equation have equal totals. To prepare a trial balance, you need to do the following:

- Balance each account in the general ledger.
- List all the accounts with their balances from the general ledger.
- Total the debit and credit column of the trial balance.

If the trial balance does not balance, an error has been made. However, the fact that the sum of the debit balances equals the sum of the credit balances is not proof that the bookkeeping procedures have been free from error. The composition of items in the general ledger can be incorrect if, for example, an item has been posted to, say, the debit of an asset account instead of to the debit of an expense account.

Example: Trial balance

Refer to the ledger accounts in Section 4.5.2.

You are required to:

Prepare the trial balance of Smart Concepts at 31 March 20X5.

Solution: Trial balance

SMART CONCEPTS
PRE-ADJUSTMENT TRIAL BALANCE AT 31 MARCH 20X5

Description	*Folio*	*Dr*	*Cr*
Bank	A1	970 500	
Rent paid in advance	A2	48 000	
Fixed deposit investment	A3	120 000	
Furniture and fittings	A4	240 000	
Stationery supplies	A5	5 000	
Computer parts	A6	12 000	
Inventory	A7	600 000	
Accounts receivable	A8	437 500	
Borrowings	L1		600 000
Accounts payable	L2		750 000
Service fees received in advance	L3		48 000
Simon Smart capital	OE1		950 000
Distributions	OE2	60 000	
Sales income	I1		937 500
Internet expense	E1	1 500	
Cost of sales expense	E2	750 000	
Advertising expense	E3	7 000	
Salaries expense	E4	16 000	
Interest expense	E5	18 000	
		3 285 500	3 285 500

Note that the trial balance is referred to as a ***pre-adjustment*** trial balance as the internal transactions or adjusting entries are still to be processed.

It has been prepared by listing all the accounts with their balances from the general ledger and then totalling the debit and credit columns of the trial balance. Please make sure that you are able to balance a ledger account as described in Section 4.6.1.

The total of C3 285 500 on the debit side is the total of all the asset accounts, expense accounts and the distributions account. Similarly, the total of C3 285 500 on the credit side is the total of all the liability accounts, income accounts and the capital account. There is no other significance to these totals than that they are equal.

 **Pause and reflect...**

Errors can occur in the recording of transactions in the journal and posting to the ledger. Consider the following errors and the effect of each error on the balancing of the trial balance.

a) When the owner, Simon Smart, invested C950 000 in the business entity (transaction 1), the capital account was debited with C950 000 and the bank account was credited with C950 000.
b) When Smart Concepts purchased furniture and fittings for C240 000 (transaction 5), the furniture and fittings account was debited with C24 000 and the bank account was credited with C24 000.
c) When Smart Concepts paid an internet service provider an amount of C750 (transaction 9), both the internet expense account and the bank account were debited with C750.
d) When Smart Concepts paid Computer World an amount of C600 000 (transaction 19), the accounts payable account was debited with C600 000 and the bank account was credited with C60 000.

Response

a) The incorrect account was debited (the capital account instead of the bank account) and the incorrect account was credited (the bank account instead of the capital account). However, the trial balance will balance as the debit of C950 000 equals the credit of C950 000 and the equality of the accounting equation is maintained.
b) The correct accounts were debited and credited, but an incorrect amount was processed. However, the trial balance will balance as the debit of C24 000 equals the credit of C24 000, and the equality of the accounting equation is maintained.
c) The internet expense account was correctly debited with C750 but the bank account was also incorrectly debited with the same amount. The debit side of the trial balance will exceed the credit side by C1 500, and the trial balance will not balance.
d) The correct amount of C600 000 was debited to the accounts payable account, but the incorrect amount of C60 000 was credited to the bank account. The debit side of the trial balance will exceed the credit side of the trial balance by C540 000, and the trial balance will not balance.

Revision example

Perfect Paws is a dog parlour owned and managed by Brian Beagle. The business entity began trading on 1 April 20X6. The following transactions relate to Perfect Paws for the month of April 20X6:

1. On 1 April, Brian Beagle opened a business bank account and contributed capital of C51 000 in cash to start the business.
2. On 1 April, Beagle arranged to rent premises, and Perfect Paws paid rent of C1 800 in advance for the months of April, May and June of 20X6.
3. On 1 April, Perfect Paws purchased grooming equipment at a cost of C30 000. This equipment has an expected useful life of five years and no value at the end of its life.
4. On 1 April, Beagle took out an insurance policy and paid C3 000 for cover from 1 April 20X6 to 31 July 20X6.
5. On 3 April, purchased supplies on credit costing C580.
6. During the week ended 9 April, received C3 400 in cash for grooming services provided.
7. On 11 April, paid for the supplies purchased on 3 April.
8. During the week ended 16 April, completed grooming services for a poodle breeder on credit for C1 700.
9. On 17 April, purchased additional supplies on credit costing C340.
10. On 20 April, received cash of C600 in advance from a client to groom her show dogs once a month from April to June 20X6.
11. During the week ended 26 April, completed grooming services including nail clipping and brushing for the German Shepherd Club on credit for C1 200.
12. On 27 April, received C1 700 from the poodle breeder.
13. On 28 April, paid the April telephone account of C80.
14. On 29 April, paid the assistant's salary of C650 for April.
15. On 29 April, distributed cash of C1 000 to Brian Beagle.

You are required to:

a) Enter all of the above transactions in the general journal of Perfect Paws for the month of April 20X6.
b) Post all of the journal entries to the general ledger of Perfect Paws.
c) Prepare a trial balance of Perfect Paws at 30 April 20X6.

Solution: Revision example

a) General journal

GENERAL JOURNAL OF PERFECT PAWS (GJ 1)

Date	*Description*	*Fol*	*Dr*	*Cr*
20X6				
April				
1	Bank (A)	A5	51 000	
	Capital (OE)	OE1		51 000
	Contribution made to start the business			

GENERAL JOURNAL OF PERFECT PAWS (GJ 1)

Date	*Description*	*Fol*	*Dr*	*Cr*
1	Expenses paid in advance (A) Bank (A) *Payment of rent for the months of April, May and June*	A4 A5	1 800	 1 800
1	Grooming equipment (A) Bank (A) *Purchase of grooming equipment*	A1 A5	30 000	 30 000
1	Expenses paid in advance (A) Bank (A) *Payment of insurance for period 1 April to 31 July 20X6*	A4 A5	3 000	 3 000
3	Supplies (A) Accounts payable (L) *Purchase of supplies*	A2 L1	580	 580
9	Bank (A) Fees income (I) *Fees received for grooming services*	A5 I1	3 400	 3 400
11	Accounts payable (L) Bank (A) *Payment for supplies purchased on 3 April*	L1 A5	580	 580
16	Accounts receivable (A) Fees income (I) *Fees for grooming services provided on credit*	A3 I1	1 700	 1 700
17	Supplies (A) Accounts payable (L) *Purchase of supplies*	A2 L1	340	 340
20	Bank (A) Fees received in advance (L) *Payment received for grooming services for the period April to June 20X6*	A5 L2	600	 600
26	Accounts receivable (A) Fees income (I) *Fees for grooming services*	A3 I1	1 200	 1 200
27	Bank (A) Accounts receivable (A) *Receipt of amount owing for grooming services*	A5 A3	1 700	 1 700
28	Telephone expense (E) Bank (A) *Payment of April telephone account*	E1 A5	80	 80
29	Salaries expense (E) Bank (A) *Payment of assistant's salary for April*	E2 A5	650	 650
29	Distributions (OE) Bank *Distribution to owner*	OE2 A5	1 000	 1 000

b) General ledger

Dr **CAPITAL (GL 0E1)** *Cr*

Date	*Details*	*Fol*	*C*	*Date*	*Details*	*Fol*	*C*
30/04/X6	Balance	c/d	51 000	01/04/X6	Bank	GJ1	51 000
			51 000				51 000
				30/04/X6	Balance	b/d	51 000

Dr **DISTRIBUTIONS (GL 0E2)** *Cr*

Date	*Details*	*Fol*	*C*	*Date*	*Details*	*Fol*	*C*
29/04/X6	Bank	GJ1	1 000	30/04/X6	Balance	c/d	1 000
			1 000				1 000
30/04/X6	Balance	b/d	1 000				

Dr **GROOMING EQUIPMENT (GL A1)** *Cr*

Date	*Details*	*Fol*	*C*	*Date*	*Details*	*Fol*	*C*
01/04/X6	Bank	GJ1	30 000	30/04/X6	Balance	c/d	30 000
			30 000				30 000
30/04/X6	Balance	b/d	30 000				

Dr **SUPPLIES (GL A2)** *Cr*

Date	*Details*	*Fol*	*C*	*Date*	*Details*	*Fol*	*C*
03/04/X6	Accounts payable	GJ1	580	30/04/X6	Balance	c/d	920
17/04/X6	Accounts payable	GJ1	340				
			920				920
30/04/X6	Balance	b/d	920				

Dr **ACCOUNTS RECEIVABLE (GL A3)** *Cr*

Date	*Details*	*Fol*	*C*	*Date*	*Details*	*Fol*	*C*
16/04/X6	Fees income	GJ1	1 700	27/04/X6	Bank	GJ1	1 700
26/04/X6	Fees income	GJ1	1 200	30/04/X6	Balance	c/d	1 200
			2 900				2 900
30/04/X6	Balance	b/d	1 200				

Dr **EXPENSES PAID IN ADVANCE (GL A4)** *Cr*

Date	*Details*	*Fol*	*C*	*Date*	*Details*	*Fol*	*C*
01/04/X6	Bank	CJ1	1 800	30/04/X6	Balance	c/d	4 800
01/04/X6	Bank	CJ1	3 000				
			4 800				4 800
30/04/X6	Balance	b/d	4 800				

BANK (GL A5)

Dr Date	Details	Fol	C	Date	Details	Fol	C *Cr*
01/04/X6	Capital	GJ1	51 000	01/04/X6	Expenses paid in advance	GJ1	1 800
09/04/X6	Fees income	GJ1	3 400	01/04/X6	Grooming equipment	GJ1	30 000
20/04/X6	Fees received in advance	GJ1	600	01/04/X6	Expenses paid in advance	GJ1	3 000
27/04/X6	Accounts receivable	GJ1	1 700	11/04/X6	Accounts payable	GJ1	580
				28/04/X6	Telephone expense	GJ1	80
				29/04/X6	Salaries expense	GJ1	650
				29/04/X6	Distributions	GJ1	1 000
				30/04/X6	Balance	c/d	19 590
			56 700				56 700
30/04/X6	Balance	b/d	19 590				

ACCOUNTS PAYABLE (GL L1)

Dr Date	Details	Fol	C	Date	Details	Fol	C *Cr*
11/04/X6	Bank	GJ1	580	03/04/X6	Supplies	GJ1	580
30/04/X6	Balance	c/d	340	17/04/X6	Supplies	GJ1	340
			920				920
				30/04/X6	Balance	b/d	340

FEES RECEIVED IN ADVANCE (GL L2)

Dr Date	Details	Fol	C	Date	Details	Fol	C *Cr*
30/04/X6	Balance	c/d	600	20/04/X6	Bank	GJ1	600
			600				600
				30/04/X6	Balance	b/d	600

FEES INCOME (GL I1)

Dr Date	Details	Fol	C	Date	Details	Fol	C *Cr*
30/04/X6	Balance	c/d	6 300	09/04/X6	Bank	GJ1	3 400
				16/04/X6	Accounts receivable	GJ1	1 700
				26/04/X6	Accounts receivable	GJ1	1 200
			6 300				6 300
				30/04/X6	Balance	b/d	6 300

Dr		TELEPHONE EXPENSE (GL E1)					*Cr*
Date	*Details*	*Fol*	*C*	*Date*	*Details*	*Fol*	*C*
28/04/X6	Bank	GJ1	80	30/04/X6	Balance	c/d	80
			80				80
30/04/X6	Balance	b/d	80				

Dr		SALARIES EXPENSE (GL E2)					*Cr*
Date	*Details*	*Fol*	*C*	*Date*	*Details*	*Fol*	*C*
29/04/X6	Bank	GJ1	650	30/04/X6	Balance	c/d	650
			650				650
30/04/X6	Balance	b/d	650				

c) Trial balance

PERFECT PAWS
PRE-ADJUSTMENT TRIAL BALANCE AT 31 MARCH 20X5

Description	*Folio*	*Dr*	*Cr*
Capital	OE1		51 000
Distributions	OE2	1 000	
Grooming equipment	A1	30 000	
Supplies	A2	920	
Accounts receivable	A3	1 200	
Expenses paid in advance	A4	4 800	
Bank	A5	19 590	
Accounts payable	L1		340
Fees received in advance	L2		600
Fees income	I1		6 300
Telephone expense	E1	80	
Salaries expense	E2	650	
		58 240	58 240

In this example, the expenses paid in advance relate to rent paid in advance and insurance paid in advance. These have been combined into one account, 'expenses paid in advance'. It is also acceptable to have separate accounts for 'rent paid in advance' and 'insurance paid in advance'.

Note that as this is a pre-adjustment trial balance, the expenses paid in advance have not yet been expensed.

Bibliography

Baskerville, P. 2013. *Basic Accounting Concepts: Q&A*. Queensland, Australia: Nowmaster.
The International Accounting Standards Board. 2010. *The Conceptual Framework*.
The International Accounting Standards Board. 2012. IAS 1 *Presentation of Financial Statements*.

5 Recording internal transactions

Business focus

Accounting scandals, creative accounting and fraud are recurrent. They range from the South Sea Bubble in 1720 to Parmalat, Enron and Worldcom today. They occur in all eras and in all countries. As accounting forms a central element of any business success or failure, the role of accounting is crucial in understanding such business scandals.

Accounting enables businesses to keep a set of records to give investors and other users a picture of how well or badly the entity is doing. However, sometimes when businesses are doing badly, management are tempted to use accounting to enhance the apparent performance of the firm in an unjustified way. In addition, management may use 'creative accounting' to exploit the flexibility within accounting to serve a range of managerial interests legally, such as to boost profits or increase assets.

Alternatively, management may engage in false accounting or fraud. Here management will step outside the principles that govern accounting. Often this will be because management has got into serious financial difficulties and is looking for any way to postpone corporate collapse. Management may use prohibited accounting techniques, falsify records or even document fictitious transactions. In some cases, companies start with creative accounting, but end up committing fraud.

The inappropriate use of internal transactions or adjusting entries is one of the ways to perpetuate creative accounting or commit fraud. Management intent on creative accounting could recognise cash received in advance as income before it has been earned, thus increasing profit. Similarly, the recognition as an expense of cash paid in advance could be deferred, also increasing profit. This chapter will give you a good understanding of the authentic use of adjusting entries.

In this chapter

Life for an accountant could be easy if the work for an accounting period was done after processing the data for that period. However, at the end of a period, most entities have received some cash in advance of earning the income and have also earned some income where the cash receipt is outstanding. Similarly, most entities have paid some cash in advance of the incurrence of expenses and have also incurred some expenses where the cash payment is outstanding. This chapter explores these issues in detail.

Dashboard

- Look at the *Learning outcomes* so that you know what you should be able to do after studying this chapter.
- Read the *Business focus* to place this chapter's contents in a real-world context.
- Preview *In this chapter* to focus your mind on the contents of the chapter.
- Read the *text* in detail.
    - Pay attention to the *definitions*, and apply your mind to the *Pause and reflect* scenarios.
    - Focus on Diagram 5.2, which identifies and classifies the four *main* adjusting entries. Use this classification as you read the explanation of each adjustment.
    - Look back at the relevant internal transaction of the Smart Concepts case study in Chapters 2, 3 and 4 as you come across each one in Sections 5.2 and 5.3 of this chapter.
- Prepare solutions to the examples as you read through the chapter.
- Prepare a solution to the *Revision example* at the end of the chapter without reference to the suggested one. Compare your solution to the suggested solution provided.

Learning outcomes

After studying this chapter, you should be able to do the following:

1 Explain the objective of internal transactions.
2 Identify the four main types of adjustments and explain the impact of each on the accounting equation.
3 Record internal transactions in the journal, post to the ledger and prepare a post-adjustment trial balance.
4 Explain the accounting procedure when receipts and payments of cash are recorded into income and expense accounts.

Recording internal transactions

5.1 Adjusting entries in the context of the accounting process

Diagram 5.1 illustrates the accounting process that you were introduced to in Chapter 4, *Recording external transactions*. You will recall that, after processing the data, the final stage of the accounting process is the producing of information for users. This involves processing adjusting entries to conform to the accrual basis of accounting, then preparing the financial statements and, finally, processing the closing entries for the period.

This chapter continues the accounting process from Chapter 4, where we completed the processing of the data for a period by preparing a trial balance. We now need to refer to that trial balance as a ***pre-adjustment*** trial balance to distinguish it from the trial balance that we will prepare after the next stage in the accounting process – the ***post-adjustment*** trial balance.

The current chapter examines the adjustment process, where we record and post the internal transactions. Chapter 6 covers the preparation of financial statements and Chapter 7 completes the accounting process with closing entries.

5.1.1 The accrual basis of accounting and internal transactions

At the end of an accounting period, all the ***external*** transactions will have been processed through the accounting system – that is, recorded in a journal, posted to the ledger and a trial balance prepared. At this point, the ***internal*** transactions will not have been processed.

Remember that internal transactions are adjustments made to the financial position of an entity in order to comply with the accrual basis of accounting. The adjusting entries are therefore no more than internal adjustments to ensure that the statement of profit or loss reports income which has been *earned* and expenses which have been *incurred* during the period.

5.1.2 The accrual basis of accounting and the time-period concept

The activities of a business entity are identified as occurring during specific time periods, such as a week, a month, six months or a year. This is done so that timely information can

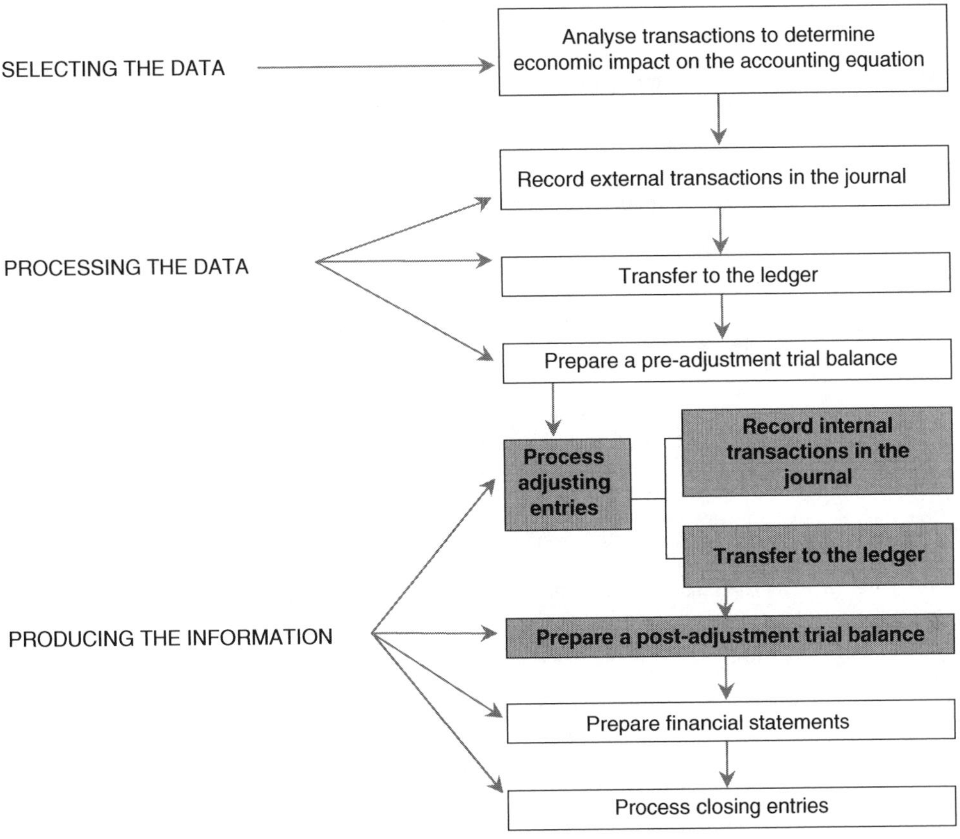

Diagram 5.1 The accounting process, highlighting the processing of adjusting entries

be made available to management and other users for decision-making purposes. A consequence of the time-period concept is that the natural trading cycles of a business are divided into reporting periods, and financial reports are prepared for each one. As mentioned above, the statement of profit or loss measures profit for a reporting period as the difference between the income recognised as earned and the expenses recognised as incurred in that period. Adjusting entries, or internal transactions, need to be processed in each reporting period in order to comply with the accrual basis of accounting.

5.2 Classification of the adjustments

The purpose of adjusting entries is to ensure that the statement of profit or loss reports income which has been *earned* and expenses which have been *incurred* during the period, even if the related receipts and payments of cash occurred in a different period. Remember that if the cash received during the period equals the income earned, there will be no adjusting entries in respect of income and, likewise, if the cash paid equals the expenses incurred, there will be no adjustments in respect of those expenses. If the cash received *does not* equal the income, only two other scenarios exist – either the cash is received before the income is earned or the cash receipt is outstanding when the income has been earned. Similarly, if the cash paid *does not* equal the expenses, either the cash is paid before

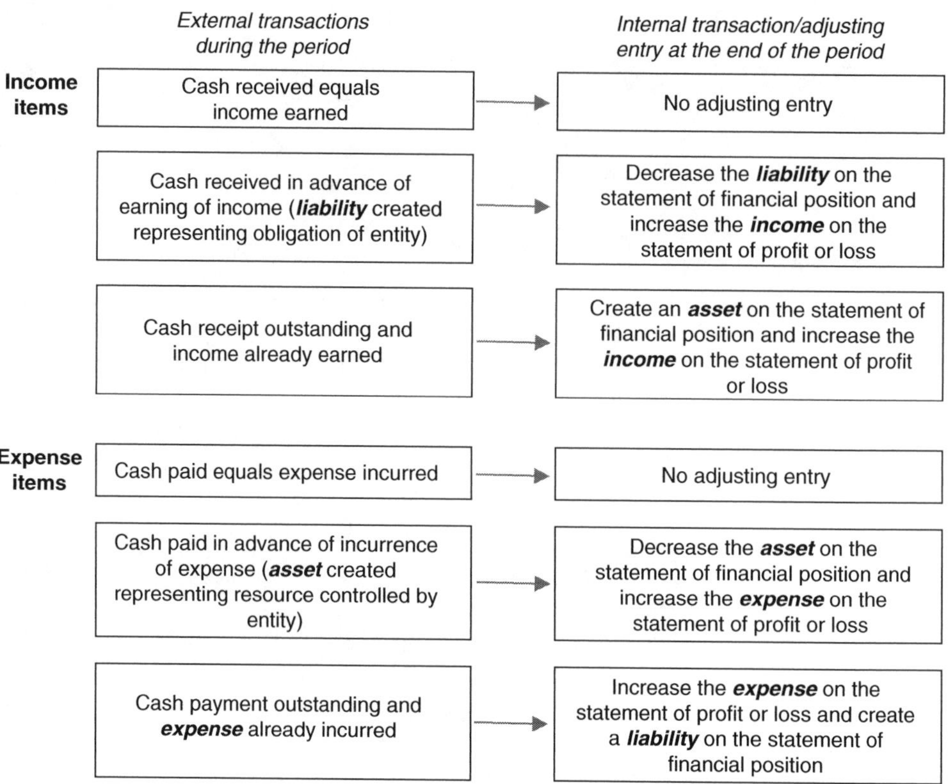

Diagram 5.2 Classification of the adjustments

the expense is incurred or the cash payment is outstanding when the expense has been incurred.

We can therefore summarise the above paragraph and classify the adjustments as shown in Diagram 5.2 above.

5.2.1 Cash received in advance of earning income (income received in advance)

When cash is received in advance of earning income, a liability is created at the time of receipt of the cash, representing the obligation of the entity to provide goods or services in the future. This is referred to as ***income received in advance*** or ***unearned income***. At the end of the period, an adjusting entry, or internal transaction, is needed to recognise that part of the liability earned during the period. Transaction 14 of the Smart Concepts example is the relevant external transaction.

Transaction 14 (25/02/X5)

On 25 February, Smart Concepts received cash of C48 000 in respect of technical support contracts taken out by customers. The support contracts are for a two-year period.

At the end of the period, part of the cash received will be *earned*, based on the service provided, and part will remain *unearned*. Transaction 24 is the relevant internal transaction.

Transaction 24 (31/03/X5)

On 31 March, Simon examined the records of the business and established that technical support in respect of contracts to the value of C6 000 had been provided to customers.

These transactions can be analysed as follows:

Assets		=	*Liabilities*		+	*Owner's equity*	
Bank			Service fees in advance (L)			Service fees (I)	
+/L/Dr	−/R/Cr		−/L/Dr	+/R/Cr		−/L/Dr	+/R/Cr
14 48 000				48 000			
24			6 000				6 000
				42 000			6 000

When the cash was received in advance, the asset, *bank*, was increased by C48 000, and the liability, *service fees received in advance*, was increased by C48 000. However, by the end of March, C6 000 of the liability had been discharged and the income earned. The liability, *service fees received in advance*, is decreased by C6 000 with a debit entry, and *income, service fees* is increased by the same amount with a credit entry. The service fees account in the above worksheet shows a credit balance of C6 000, which will appear as income on the statement of profit or loss for the period. The income received in advance account shows the balance of the obligation of C42 000, which will be shown as a liability on the statement of financial position.

5.2.2 Cash receipt outstanding and income already earned (income receivable)

Income needs to be recognised when earned, which may occur before the cash is received. If at the end of the period the cash receipt is outstanding but the income has already been earned, an adjusting entry, or internal transaction, is needed to record the income earned during the period. This is known as the recognition of ***income receivable*** or ***accrued income***.

Transaction 4 of the Smart Concepts example records the transfer of C120 000 from the bank account to a fixed deposit account, earning interest at 5 per cent per annum. At the end of the period, no cash has been received from the bank on the fixed deposit investment, but interest for three months has been earned. Transaction 25 is the relevant internal transaction.

Transaction 25 (31/03/X5)

On 31 March, Smart Concepts accounted for the interest on the fixed deposit earned for the period.

This transaction can be analysed as follows:

Assets		=	*Liabilities*	+	*Owner's equity*	
Interest receivable (A)					Interest (I)	
+/L/Dr	−/R/Cr				−/L/Dr	+/R/Cr
25 1 500						1 500
1 500						1 500

At the end of the period, interest income of C1 500 has been earned (C120 000 × 0.05 × 3/12). The asset, *interest receivable*, is increased by C1 500 with a debit entry representing the amount owed to Smart Concepts at the end of March, and income, *interest*, is increased by C1 500 with a credit entry. The interest receivable account in the above worksheet shows a debit balance of C1 500, which will appear as an asset on the statement of financial position at the end of March. The interest income account on the above worksheet shows a credit balance of C1 500, which will appear as income on the statement of profit or loss for the period.

5.2.3 Cash paid in advance of incurrence of expenses (expenses paid in advance)

When cash is paid in advance of incurrence of expenses, an asset is created at the time of payment of the cash representing the right of the entity to receive goods or services in the future. This is referred to as ***expenses paid in advance*** or ***prepaid expenses***. At the end of the period, an adjusting entry, or internal transaction, is needed to recognise that part of the asset that was used or expired during the period. Transaction 3 of the Smart Concepts example is the relevant external transaction.

Transaction 3 (2/01/X5)

On 2 January, Simon located premises in Hyde Park. The monthly rent for the premises is C12 000. Smart Concepts paid four months' rent in advance on 2 January.

The benefit of the rent paid in advance expires on a time basis and at the end of the period, part will be incurred as an expense, and part will remain as an asset. Transaction 26 is the relevant internal transaction.

Transaction 26 (31/03/X5)

On 31 March, Smart Concepts recognised the rent expense incurred for the period.

Assets				=	*L*	*+ Owner's equity*	
Bank		Rent paid in advance (A)				Rent (E)	
+/L/Dr	−/R/Cr	+/L/Dr	−/R/Cr			+/L/Dr	−/R/Cr
3	48 000	48 000					
26			36 000			36 000	
		12 000				36 000	

When the cash was paid in advance, the asset, *rent paid in advance*, was increased by C48 000, and the asset, *bank*, was decreased by C48 000. However, by the end of March, C36 000 of the asset had expired and the expense incurred. The expense, *rent*, is increased by C36 000 with a debit entry, and the asset, *rent paid in advance*, is decreased by C48 000 with a credit entry. The rent expense account in the above worksheet shows a debit balance of C36 000, which will appear as an expense on the statement of profit or loss for the period. The rent paid in advance account also shows a debit balance of C12 000 representing the right of occupation for one month, which will be shown as an asset on the statement of financial position.

5.2.4 Cash payment outstanding and expense already incurred (expenses payable)

Expenses need to be recognised when incurred, which may be before the cash has been paid. If at the end of a period the cash payment is outstanding but the expense has already been incurred, an adjusting entry, or internal transaction, is needed to record the expense incurred during the period. This is known as the recognition of ***expenses payable*** or ***accrued expenses***.

Each month, Smart Concepts uses water and electricity to operate the business and earn income. At the end of the period, no cash has been paid for these expenses, which have already been incurred. Transaction 27 is the relevant internal transaction.

Transaction 27 (31/03/X5)

On 31 March, the water account for C1 500 and the electricity account for C2 500 had been received but not paid.

This can be analysed as follows:

Assets	=	*Liabilities*		+	*Owner's equity*	
		Water and electricity payable (L)			Water and electricity(E)	
		−/L/Dr	+/R/Cr		+/L/Dr	−/R/Cr
27			4 000		4 000	
			4 000		4 000	

At the end of the period, water and electricity expenses totalling C4 000 have been incurred. The expense, *water and electricity*, is increased by C4 000 with a debit entry, and the liability, *water and electricity payable*, is increased by C4 000 with a credit entry. The water and electricity expense account in the above worksheet shows a debit balance of C4 000, which will appear as an expense on the statement of profit or loss for the period. The water and electricity payable account shows a credit balance of C4 000, which will appear as a liability on the statement of financial position at the end of March.

5.2.5 Other period-end adjustments

The accrual basis of accounting requires assets purchased for use by a business entity to be recognised as an expense when used. This typically applies to non-current assets, such as equipment and vehicles, and also to current assets used in the business, such as consumable stores.

Recognition of current assets used

When cash is paid to acquire consumable stores such as office or parts supplies, the items are treated as assets on purchase. The consumable stores are a resource controlled by the entity (they have been bought and are available for use), from a past event (the purchase transaction) and will contribute to an inflow of resources in the future (the consumable stores will be used in the operations of the business entity). At the end of the period, an adjusting or internal entry is needed to recognise that part of the asset used during the period. Transaction 6 of the Smart Concepts example is the relevant external transaction.

Transaction 6 (05/01/X5)

On 5 January, Smart Concepts purchased supplies of stationery for C5 000, as well as supplies of computer parts for C12 000. All the supplies were paid for in cash.

If no records are kept showing the amount used, it is necessary to count the remaining supplies on hand and then deduct the cost of the remaining supplies from the cost of the supplies purchased. Transaction 28 is the relevant internal transaction.

Transaction 28 (31/03/X5)

On 31 March, Simon counted stationery supplies on hand costing C2 000 and also counted computer parts on hand costing C3 500.

These transactions can be analysed as follows:

Assets				=	*L*	+	*Owner's equity*	
Stationery supplies (A)		Bank					Stationery supplies (E)	
+/L/Dr	−/R/Cr	+/L/Dr	−/R/Cr				+/L/Dr	−/R/Cr
6 5 000			5 000					
28	3 000						3 000	
2 000							3 000	
Computer parts (A)		Bank					Computer parts (E)	
+/L/Dr	−/R/Cr	+/L/Dr	−/R/Cr				+/L/Dr	−/R/Cr
6 12 000			12 000					
28	8 500						8 500	
3 500							8 500	

When the stationery supplies and computer parts were purchased, the assets, stationery supplies and computer parts were increased by C5 000 and C12 000 respectively, and the asset, *bank*, was decreased by a total of C17 000. At the end of March, stationery supplies costing C2 000 and computer parts costing C3 500 remain on hand, therefore stationery supplies costing C3 000 and computer parts costing C8 500 were used during the period. The expenses, *stationery supplies* and *computer parts*, are increased by C3 000 and C8 500 respectively with debit entries, and the assets, *stationery supplies* and *computer parts*, are decreased by C3 000 and C8 500 respectively with credit entries.

The stationery supplies asset account in the above worksheet shows a debit balance of C2 000, which will appear as an asset on the statement of financial position at the end of March. The stationery supplies expense account shows a debit balance of C3 000, which will be shown as an expense on the statement of profit or loss for the period.

The computer parts asset account in the above worksheet shows a debit balance of C3 500, which will appear as an asset on the statement of financial position at the end of March. The computer parts expense account shows a debit balance of C8 500, which will be shown as an expense on the statement of profit or loss for the period.

Recognition of non-current assets used

The use of non-current assets such as machines, vehicles, furniture or even professional libraries represents a consumption of benefits inherent in the assets. The cost of these assets must be charged as an expense during the periods over which the assets are expected to be available for use by an entity. This asset usage expense is known as ***depreciation***. This is consistent with the accrual basis of accounting, which recognises expenses when incurred (in this case, as the asset is used) even if the cash is paid in a different period (for example on purchase of the asset or on repayment of a loan to acquire the asset).

Non-current assets in the form of furniture and fittings were purchased by Smart Concepts. Transaction 5 of the Smart Concepts example is the relevant external transaction.

Transaction 5 (02/01/X5)

On 2 January, Smart Concepts purchased furniture and fittings for C240 000. This was paid for from funds in the bank account. The expected useful life of the furniture and fittings is five years.

The portion of the cost of the asset used which is recognised as an expense is based on various factors, such as the estimated useful life of the asset. The concept of deprecation is addressed in detail in Chapter 10, *Property, plant and equipment*. Transaction 29 is the relevant internal transaction.

Transaction 29 (31/03/X5)

On 31 March, Smart Concepts accounted for the usage of the furniture and fittings for the period.

These transactions can be analysed as follows:

Assets				=	*L*	+	*Owner's equity*	
Furniture and fittings (A)		Bank					Depreciation (E)	
+/*L*/*Dr*	−/*R*/*Cr*	+/*L*/*Dr*	−/*R*/*Cr*				+/*L*/*Dr*	−/*R*/*Cr*
5 240 000			240 000					
29	12 000						12 000	
228 000							12 000	

The furniture and fittings are expected to have a useful life of five years. They have been used for three months, and a usage expense needs to be charged to the statement of profit or loss for that period. C12 000 of the furniture and fittings has been used (C240 000/5 years × 3/12). The expense, *depreciation*, is increased by a total of C12 000 with a debit entry. The asset, *furniture and fittings*, is reduced by C12 000 with a credit entry.

Pause and reflect...

Look back at the debit and credit of each of the internal transactions described in the previous section. What do you notice about the accounts debited and credited in each one, and why is this significant?

Response

For each internal transaction, one side of the entry affected a *statement of profit or loss* account, and the other side affected a *statement of financial position* account. This is because the internal transactions are processed to comply with the accrual basis of accounting so that income is recognised as earned, and expenses recognised as incurred even if the related cash is received or paid in a different period. When income is earned, an asset increases or a liability decreases. Similarly, when an expense is incurred, an asset decreases or a liability increases. This is summarised as follows:

Situation	*Summarised adjusting entry*	*Affects*
Where cash was received in advance of earning the income	Dr Liability Cr Income	Statement of financial position Statement of profit or loss
Where the cash receipt is outstanding and the income is already earned	Dr Asset Cr Income	Statement of financial position Statement of profit or loss
Where the cash was paid in advance of the incurrence of the expense	Dr Expense Cr Asset	Statement of profit or loss Statement of financial position
Where the cash payment is outstanding and the expense is already incurred	Dr Expense Cr Liability	Statement of profit or loss Statement of financial position

5.3 Processing of internal transactions at the end of the accounting period

The previous section classified the internal transactions and explained the concept underlying each adjustment. Diagram 5.1 at the beginning of this chapter showed that adjusting the accounts is the first step in producing information. Much of the work of the accountant involves producing information, which begins by deciding what internal transactions are required.

The accountant is given the trial balance, often prepared by a bookkeeper.

In Chapter 4, the external transactions (1–23) of Smart Concepts for the period from 1 January 20X5 to 31 March 20X5 were journalised and posted to the ledger. A trial balance was then prepared at 31 March 20X5. As mentioned previously, this trial balance is known as the ***pre-adjustment trial balance*** as it is prepared *before* the adjusting entries have been processed. The internal transactions, or adjusting entries, are then entered in the journal and posted to the ledger, and a second trial balance, known as the ***post-adjustment trial balance***, is prepared.

Example: Processing of internal transactions at the end of an accounting period

The pre-adjustment trial balance of Smart Concepts at 31 March 20X5 (as shown in Chapter 4) is repeated below:

SMART CONCEPTS
PRE-ADJUSTMENT TRIAL BALANCE AT 31 MARCH 20X5

Description	*Folio*	*Dr*	*Cr*
Bank	A1	970 500	
Rent paid in advance	A2	48 000	
Fixed deposit investment	A3	120 000	
Furniture and fittings	A4	240 000	
Stationery supplies	A5	5 000	
Computer parts	A6	12 000	
Inventory	A7	600 000	
Accounts receivable	A8	437 500	
Borrowings	L1		600 000
Accounts payable	L2		750 000
Service fees in advance	L3		48 000
Simon Smart capital	OE1		950 000
Distributions	OE2	60 000	
Sales income	I1		937 500
Internet expense	E1	1 500	
Cost of sales expense	E2	750 000	
Advertising expense	E3	7 000	
Salaries expense	E4	16 000	
Interest expense	E5	18 000	
		3 285 500	3 285 500

Transactions 24–29 are the internal transactions relating to Smart Concepts:

24 On 31 March, Simon examined the records of the business and established that technical support in respect of contracts to the value of C6 000 had been provided to customers.
25 On 31 March, Smart Concepts accounted for the interest on the fixed deposit earned for the period.
26 On 31 March, Smart Concepts recognised the rent expense incurred for the period.
27 On 31 March, the water account for C1 500 and the electricity account for C2 500 had been received but not paid.
28 On 31 March, Simon counted stationery supplies on hand costing C2 000 and also counted computer parts on hand costing C3 500.
29 On 31 March, Smart Concepts accounted for the usage of the furniture and fittings for the period.

You are required to:

Journalise the above adjustments, post to the relevant ledger accounts and prepare a post-adjustment trial balance.

Solution: Processing of internal transactions at the end of the accounting period

The conceptual explanation of each of the internal transactions was given in the previous section. It is important for you to be able to identify the adjustments required at the end of a period and classify them as described in that section.

GENERAL JOURNAL OF SMART CONCEPTS (GJ 3)

Date	*Description*	*Fol*	*Dr*	*Cr*
20X5				
March				
31	Service fees received in advance (L)	L3	6 000	
	Service fees income (I)	I2		6 000
	Recognition of service fees earned (24)			
31	Interest receivable (A)	A9	1 500	
	Interest income (I)	I3		1 500
	Recognition of income receivable (25)			
31	Rent expense (E)	E6	36 000	
	Rent paid in advance (A)	A2		36 000
	Recognition of expenses incurred (26)			
31	Water & electricity expense (E)	E7	4 000	
	Water & electricity payable (L)	L4		4 000
	Recognition of expenses payable (27)			
31	Stationery supplies expense (E)	E8	3 000	
	Computer parts expense (E)	E9	8 500	
	Stationery supplies (A)	A5		3 000
	Computer parts (A)	A6		8 500
	Current assets used (28)			
31	Depreciation expense (E)	E10	12 000	
	Furniture and fittings (A)	A4		12 000
	Non-current assets used (29)			

These transactions are then posted to the ledger. The ledger accounts affected by each entry are shown, with the **adjustment highlighted**.

Recognition of income received in advance

Dr **SERVICE FEES RECEIVED IN ADVANCE (GL L3)** *Cr*

Date	*Details*	*Fol*	*C*	*Date*	*Details*	*Fol*	*C*
31/03	**Service fees income**	**GJ3**	**6 000**	25/02	Bank	GJ2	48 000
31/03	Balance	c/d	42 000				
			48 000				48 000
				01/04	Balance	b/d	42 000

Dr **SERVICE FEES INCOME (GL I2)** *Cr*

Date	*Details*	*Fol*	*C*	*Date*	*Details*	*Fol*	*C*
31/03	Balance	c/d	6 000	**31/03**	**Service fees received in advance**	**GJ3**	**6 000**
			6 000				6 000
				31/03	Balance	b/d	6 000

Recognition of income receivable

Dr	INTEREST RECEIVABLE (GL A9)						*Cr*
Date	*Details*	*Fol*	*C*	*Date*	*Details*	*Fol*	*C*
31/03	**Interest income**	**GJ3**	**1 500**	31/03	Balance	c/d	1 500
			1 500				1 500
01/04	Balance	b/d	1 500				

Dr	INTEREST INCOME (GL I3)						*Cr*
Date	*Details*	*Fol*	*C*	*Date*	*Details*	*Fol*	*C*
31/03	Balance	c/d	1 500	**31/03**	**Interest receivable**	**GJ3**	**1 500**
			1 500				1 500
				31/03	Balance	b/d	1 500

Recognition of expenses paid in advance

Dr	RENT PAID IN ADVANCE (GL A2)						*Cr*
Date	*Details*	*Fol*	*C*	*Date*	*Details*	*Fol*	*C*
02/01	Bank	GJ1	48 000	**31/03**	**Rent expense**	**GJ3**	**36 000**
				31/03	Balance	c/d	12 000
			48 000				48 000
01/04	Balance	b/d	12 000				

Dr	RENT EXPENSE (GL E6)						*Cr*
Date	*Details*	*Fol*	*C*	*Date*	*Details*	*Fol*	*C*
31/03	**Rent paid in advance**	**GJ3**	**36 000**	31/03	Balance	c/d	36 000
			36 000				36 000
31/03	Balance	b/d	36 000				

Recognition of expenses payable

Dr	WATER AND ELECTRICITY PAYABLE (GL L4)						*Cr*
Date	*Details*	*Fol*	*C*	*Date*	*Details*	*Fol*	*C*
31/03	Balance	c/d	4 000	**31/03**	**Water and electricity expense**	**GJ3**	**4 000**
			4 000				4 000
				01/04	Balance	b/d	4 000

Dr			WATER AND ELECTRICITY EXPENSE (GL E7)				Cr
Date	Details	Fol	C	Date	Details	Fol	C
31/03	**Water and electricity payable**	**GJ3**	**4 000**	31/03	Balance	c/d	4 000
			4 000				4 000
31/03		b/d	4 000				

Recognition of current assets used

Dr			STATIONERY SUPPLIES (GL A5)				Cr
Date	Details	Fol	C	Date	Details	Fol	C
05/01	Bank	GJ1	5 000	**31/03**	**Stationery supplies expense**	**GJ3**	**3 000**
				31/03		c/d	2 000
			5 000				5 000
01/04	Balance	b/d	2 000				

Dr			STATIONERY SUPPLIES EXPENSE (GL E8)				Cr
Date	Details	Fol	C	Date	Details	Fol	C
31/03	**Stationery supplies**	**GJ3**	**3 000**	31/03	Balance	c/d	3 000
			3 000				3 000
31/03	Balance	b/d	3 000				

Dr			COMPUTER PARTS (GL A6)				Cr
Date	Details	Fol	C	Date	Details	Fol	C
05/01	Bank	GJ1	12 000	**31/03**	**Computer parts expense**	**GJ3**	**8 500**
				31/03	Balance	c/d	3 500
			12 000				12 000
01/04	Balance	b/d	3 500				

Dr			COMPUTER PARTS EXPENSE (GL E9)				Cr
Date	Details	Fol	C	Date	Details	Fol	C
31/03	**Computer parts**	**GJ3**	**8 500**	31/03	Balance	c/d	8 500
			8 500				8 500
31/03	Balance	b/d	8 500				

Recognition of non-current assets used

Dr		FURNITURE AND FITTINGS (GL A4)					*Cr*
Date	*Details*	*Fol*	*C*	*Date*	*Details*	*Fol*	*C*
02/01	Bank	GJ1	240 000	**31/03**	**Depreciation expense**	**GJ3**	**12 000**
				31/03	Balance	c/d	228 000
			240 000				240 000
01/04	Balance	b/d	228 000				

Dr		DEPRECIATION EXPENSE (GL E10)					*Cr*
Date	*Details*	*Fol*	*C*	*Date*	*Details*	*Fol*	*C*
31/03	**Furniture and fittings**	**GJ3**	**12 000**	31/03	Balance	c/d	12 000
			12 000				12 000
31/03	Balance	b/d	12 000				

After the internal transactions have been recorded and posted, a ***post-adjustment trial balance*** is prepared in order to assist in preparing the financial statements. Smart Concepts' post-adjustment trial balance is presented below.

SMART CONCEPTS
POST-ADJUSTMENT TRIAL BALANCE AT 31 MARCH 20X5

Description	*Folio*	*Dr*	*Cr*
Bank	A1	970 500	
Rent paid in advance	A2	12 000	
Fixed deposit investment	A3	120 000	
Furniture and fittings	A4	228 000	
Stationery supplies	A5	2 000	
Computer parts	A6	3 500	
Inventory	A7	600 000	
Accounts receivable	A8	437 500	
Interest receivable	A9	1 500	
Borrowings	L1		600 000
Accounts payable	L2		750 000
Service fees received in advance	L3		42 000
Water and electricity payable	L4		4 000
Simon Smart capital	OE1		950 000
Distributions	OE2	60 000	
Sales income	I1		937 500
Service fees income	I2		6 000
Interest income	I3		1 500
Internet expense	E1	1 500	
Cost of sales expense	E2	750 000	

Description	Folio	Dr	Cr
Advertising expense	E3	7 000	
Salaries expense	E4	16 000	
Interest expense	E5	18 000	
Rent expense	E6	36 000	
Water and electricity expense	E7	4 000	
Stationery supplies expense	E8	3 000	
Computer parts expense	E9	8 500	
Depreciation expense	E10	12 000	
		3 291 000	3 291 000

Concepts in context

Nestlé Group

Extract from accounting policies note

The consolidated financial statements have been prepared on an accrual basis and under the historical cost convention, unless otherwise stated.

Extract from consolidated balance sheet

	CHF million
Current assets	
Prepayments and accrued income	762
Current liabilities	
Accruals and deferred income	3 185

What concepts in context can you see here?

You have learnt in this chapter that internal transactions are adjustments processed to comply with the accrual basis of accounting. We classified the adjustments as those relating to income – received in advance (liability) or receivable (asset) and to expenses – paid in advance (asset) or payable (liability). Nestlé complies with the accrual basis of accounting, and its balance sheet (statement of financial position) reflects all four classifications.

Nestlé's current assets include prepayments and accrued income (referring to expenses paid in advance and income receivable respectively). Its current liabilities include accruals and deferred income (referring to expenses payable and income received in advance respectively).

Nestlé S.A. is a Swiss multinational food and beverage company headquartered in Vevey, Switzerland. It has many well-known brands including Kit-Kat, Milo and Nespresso.

Source: www.nestle.co.uk/asset-library/documents/library/documents/annual_reports/2013-annual-report-en.pdf/ (Accessed 30 August 2014).

Pause and reflect...

In this chapter, we have been consistent in our use of the terminology *income received in advance, income receivable, expenses paid in advance* and *expenses payable.*

Can you come up with alternative terms for these concepts? Look at some published financial statements on the internet and see what you can find.

Response

You should have found the following common alternatives:

- the liability, income received in advance – unearned income or deferred income;
- the asset, income receivable – accrued income;
- the asset, expenses paid in advance – prepaid expenses or deferred expenses;
- the liability, expenses payable – accrued expenses.

5.4 Recording receipts and payments into income and expense accounts

We have emphasised throughout this book that when cash is received in advance of earning income, a liability is created, representing the obligation to provide the service in the future. Similarly, when cash is paid in advance of the incurrence of expenses, an asset is created, representing the right to receive a service in the future. At the end of the period, adjustments are made to recognise the income earned and the expense incurred during the period. This procedure was described in the previous sections.

Some business entities may decide to record all cash receipts for services provided with credits to income accounts, and all cash paid for services acquired with debits to expense accounts. We will now address this procedure and the corresponding adjusting entries.

5.4.1 Recording of receipts into income accounts

When cash is received in advance of earning income and it is known that the service will be provided in full by the end of the period, the credit may be recorded in an income account as opposed to a liability account. If the service is provided by the end of the period, no adjusting entry is required as the amount earned is correctly reflected in an income account.

On the other hand, the income account may also be credited on receipt of the cash even if the service is not to be provided in full by the end of the period. Then, if any amount of the income represented by the cash received remains unearned at the end of the period, an adjustment is made to transfer the amount unearned to a liability account.

To illustrate this, recall transaction 14 of Smart Concepts where C48 000 was received in respect of technical support contracts taken out by customers. At the end of the period (transaction 24), services to the value of C6 000 had been provided. Both methods (of recording the receipt in a liability account or an income account) are illustrated below, together with the relevant adjusting entry.

Assets			=	*Liabilities*		+	*Owner's equity*	
Receipt recorded as a liability								
	Bank			**Service fees in advance (L)**			**Service fees (I)**	
	+/L/Dr	−/R/Cr		−/L/Dr	+/R/Cr		−/L/Dr	+/R/Cr
14	48 000				48 000			
24				6 000				6 000
Bal					42 000			6 000
Receipt recorded as income								
	Bank			**Service fees in advance (L)**			**Service fees (I)**	
	+/L/Dr	−/R/Cr		−/L/Dr	+/R/Cr		−/L/Dr	+/R/Cr
14	48 000							48 000
24					42 000		42 000	
Bal					42 000			6 000

The required internal transaction, or adjusting entry, depends on how the external transaction or original entry was recorded. When the C48 000 cash received was **recorded as a liability**, the adjusting entry reduced the liability by the amount *earned* of C6 000 and transferred this amount to the income account, *service fees*. The statement of financial position liability account, *service fees received in advance*, reported a balance of C42 000 representing the income *unearned* at the end of the period, and the statement of profit or loss income account, *service fees*, showed C6 000 being the amount *earned* during the period.

On the other hand, when the cash received was **recorded as income**, the adjusting entry reduced the income by the amount *unearned* of C42 000 and transferred this amount to the liability account, *service fees received in advance*. Again, the statement of financial position liability account, *service fees*, reported a balance of C42 000 *unearned* at the end of the period, and the statement of profit or loss income account, *service fees*, showed a balance of C6 000 *earned* during the period.

5.4.2 Recording of payments into expense accounts

When cash is paid in advance of the incurrence of expenses and it is known that the service will be received in full by the end of the period, the debit may be recorded in an expense account as opposed to an asset account. If the service is received by the end of the period, no adjusting entry is required as the amount incurred is correctly reflected in an expense account.

On the other hand, the expense account may also be debited on payment of the cash even if the service is not to be received in full by the end of the period. Then if any amount of the expense represented by the cash paid remains unexpired at the end of the period, an adjustment is made to transfer the amount unused to an asset account.

To illustrate this, recall transaction 3 of Smart Concepts where C48 000 was paid at the beginning of January in respect of rental from January to April. At the end of the period (transaction 26), rent of C36 000 had expired. Both methods (of recording the payment in an asset account or an expense account) are illustrated below, together with the relevant adjusting entry.

Assets						=	*L*	+	*Owner's equity*	

Payment recorded as an asset

	Rent paid in advance (A)		Bank		Rent (E)	
	+/L/Dr	−/R/Cr	+/L/Dr	−/R/Cr	+/L/Dr	−/R/Cr
3	48 000			48 000		
26		36 000			36 000	
Bal	12 000				36 000	

Payment recorded as an expense

	Rent paid in advance (A)		Bank		Rent (E)	
	+/L/Dr	−/R/Cr	+/L/Dr	−/R/Cr	+/L/Dr	−/R/Cr
3				48 000	48 000	
26	12 000					12 000
Bal	12 000				36 000	

The required internal transaction, or adjusting entry, depends on how the external transaction or original entry was recorded. When the C48 000 cash paid was **recorded as an asset**, the adjusting entry reduced the asset by the amount *expired* of C36 000, and transferred this amount to the expense account, *rent expense*. The statement of financial position account, *rent paid in advance*, reported a balance of C12 000, representing the expense *prepaid* at the end of the period and the statement of profit or loss expense account, *rent*, showed C36 000, being the amount *incurred* during the period.

On the other hand, when the cash paid was **recorded as an expense**, the adjusting entry reduced the expense by the *unexpired* amount of C12 000 and transferred this amount to the asset account, *rent paid in advance*. Again, the statement of financial position asset account, *rent paid in advance*, reported a balance of C12 000 *prepaid* at the end of the period, and the statement of profit or loss expense account, *rent*, showed a balance of C36 000 *incurred* during the period.

 **Revision example**

Bake for Me is a business entity offering baking classes. It is owned and managed by Mary Flour. The pre-adjustment trial balance of Bake for Me at 31 December 20X4 is presented below.

BAKE FOR ME
PRE-ADJUSTMENT TRIAL BALANCE
AT 31 DECEMBER 2014

	Dr	*Cr*
Baking equipment	14 000	
Baking supplies on hand	900	
Accounts receivable	6 250	
Insurance paid in advance	1 200	
Bank	10 800	
Capital – M Flour		24 350
Distributions – M Flour	2 000	

	Dr	Cr
Accounts payable		3 500
Fees received in advance		2 300
Fees income		14 500
Wages expense	7 500	
Rent expense	2 000	
	44 650	44 650

The following internal transactions need to be taken into account:

1 Insurance that expired during the year ended 31 December 20X4 amounted to C200.
2 Fees earned for baking classes that were received in advance amount to C800.
3 Fees earned for baking classes held and not yet billed totalled C1 500.
4 Wages unpaid at the end of December totalled C600.
5 Equipment usage expense for the year ended 31 December 20X4 totalled C500.
6 Baking supplies on hand at 31 December 20X4 amounted to C375.

You are required to:

a) Record the above internal transactions in the journal of Bake for Me.
b) Prepare the post-adjustment trial balance of Bake for Me at 31 December 20X4.

Solution: Revision example

a) Journal entries

GENERAL JOURNAL OF BAKE FOR ME (GJ 1)

Date	*Description*	*Fol*	*Dr*	*Cr*
20X4 December				
31	Insurance expense (E)		200	
	Insurance paid in advance (A)			200
	Insurance expense for the year			
31	Fees received in advance (L)		800	
	Fees income (I)			800
	Recognition of fees earned			
31	Accounts receivable (A)		1 500	
	Fees income (I)			1 500
	Recognition of income receivable			
31	Wages expense (E)		600	
	Wages payable (L)			600
	Recognition of expenses payable			
31	Depreciation expense (E)		500	
	Baking equipment (A)			500
	Usage of baking equipment for the year			
31	Baking supplies expense (E)		525	
	Baking supplies (A)			525
	Baking supplies used during the year			

b) Post-adjustment trial balance

BAKE FOR ME
POST-ADJUSTMENT TRIAL BALANCE AT 31 DECEMBER 20X4

		Dr	*Cr*
Baking equipment		13 500	
Baking supplies	*(900 – 525)*	375	
Accounts receivable	*(6 250 + 1 500)*	7 750	
Insurance paid in advance	*(1 200 – 200)*	1 000	
Bank		10 800	
Capital – M Flour			24 350
Drawings – M Flour		2 000	
Accounts payable			3 500
Fees received in advance	*(2 300 – 800)*		1 500
Wages payable			600
Fees income	*(14 500 + 800 + 1 500)*		16 800
Wages expense		8 100	
Rent expense		2 000	
Insurance expense		200	
Depreciation expense		500	
Baking supplies expense		525	
		46 750	46 750

Bibliography

Jones, M. 2011. *Creative Accounting, Fraud and International Accounting Scandals*. Chichester, UK: John Wiley & Sons, Ltd.

6 Preparation and presentation of financial statements

Business focus

The goal of the IFRS Foundation and the IASB is to 'develop, in the public interest, a single set of high-quality, understandable, enforceable and globally accepted financial reporting standards based upon clearly articulated principles'. Prior to the introduction of IFRS, each jurisdiction developed its own set of 'generally accepted accounting principles' with the result that transactions concluded in different countries could be accounted for and disclosed differently despite being virtually identical in terms of their economic substance. Needless to say, for capital providers to make informed investment decisions, comparability of financial statements is of great importance. This is especially true for deregulated capital markets where investors are able to operate across borders and buy and sell shares in almost any listed company.

All member countries of the Group of Twenty (G20), the forum for the governments and central bank governors from 20 major economies, have made a public commitment to supporting a single set of high-quality global accounting standards. Of the G20 jurisdictions, 14 have adopted IFRS for all or most listed companies, with a notable exception being the United States.

The G20's members include 19 individual countries – Argentina, Australia, Brazil, Canada, China, France, Germany, India, Indonesia, Italy, Japan, Republic of Korea, Mexico, Russian Federation, Saudi Arabia, South Africa, Turkey, United Kingdom, United States and the European Union.

In this chapter

Have you seen the financial report of a listed company? If you go online and open the web page of any listed company, you will find their published financial report, usually within a tab or link called 'investor relations'. The preparation of the financial statements, which are part of the financial report, requires extensive knowledge of financial accounting and IFRS. This chapter provides an introduction to that process.

Dashboard

- Look at the *Learning outcomes* so that you know what you should be able to do after studying this chapter.
- Read the *Business focus* to place this chapter's contents in a real-world context.

- Preview *In this chapter* to focus your mind on the contents of the chapter.
- Read the *text* in detail.
    - Pay attention to the *definitions*, and apply your mind to the *Pause and reflect* scenarios.
    - Take note of the expanded and alternative formats for presenting financial performance in Section 6.6. This section introduces the statement of profit or loss and other comprehensive income.
    - Section 6.7 demonstrates a technique to enable you to prepare a set of financial statements from a pre-adjustment trial balance and a list of adjustments. Work through the example carefully to ensure that you are able to do this.
- Prepare solutions to the examples as you read through the chapter.

Learning outcomes

After studying this chapter, you should be able to do the following:

1 Explain the role and purpose of financial statements in the accounting process.
2 Recall the objectives of financial reporting and of financial statements.
3 Recall and apply the general features of financial statements.
4 Explain and apply the recognition criteria of the elements of financial statements.
5 Explain and apply the classification of assets and liabilities.
6 Prepare a statement of profit or loss *or* a statement of profit or loss and other comprehensive income, statement of financial position and statement of changes in equity.
7 Develop an effective approach to answering exam questions related to the preparation of financial statements.

Preparation and presentation of financial statements

6.1 Financial statements in the context of the accounting process

You have already been exposed to the accounting process as shown in Diagram 6.1. Chapter 2, *Fundamental accounting concepts*, and Chapter 3, *The accounting equation and the analysis of transactions*, focused on the analysis of transactions, while Chapter 4, *Recording external transactions*, described the journal, ledger and pre-adjustment trial balance.

This chapter continues the accounting process from Chapter 5, *Recording internal transactions*, where we processed the adjusting entries and prepared a post-adjustment trial balance. The current chapter examines the preparation of financial statements from the post-adjustment trial balance before completing the accounting process with closing entries in Chapter 7, *Closing entries*.

6.2 Purpose of financial statements

IAS 1 *Presentation of Financial Statements* prescribes the basis for presentation of *general purpose* financial statements prepared in accordance with International Financial Reporting Standards (IFRS). IAS 1 describes the objective of financial statements.

The objective of financial statements is to provide information about an entity's financial position, performance and cash flows that is useful to a wide range of users in making economic decisions.

It is useful at this point to compare the objective of general purpose financial reporting as set out in the *Conceptual Framework* with the objective of general purpose financial statements as set out in IAS 1 (Table 6.1). Refer back to Chapter 2 for a discussion of the objective of general purpose financial reporting.

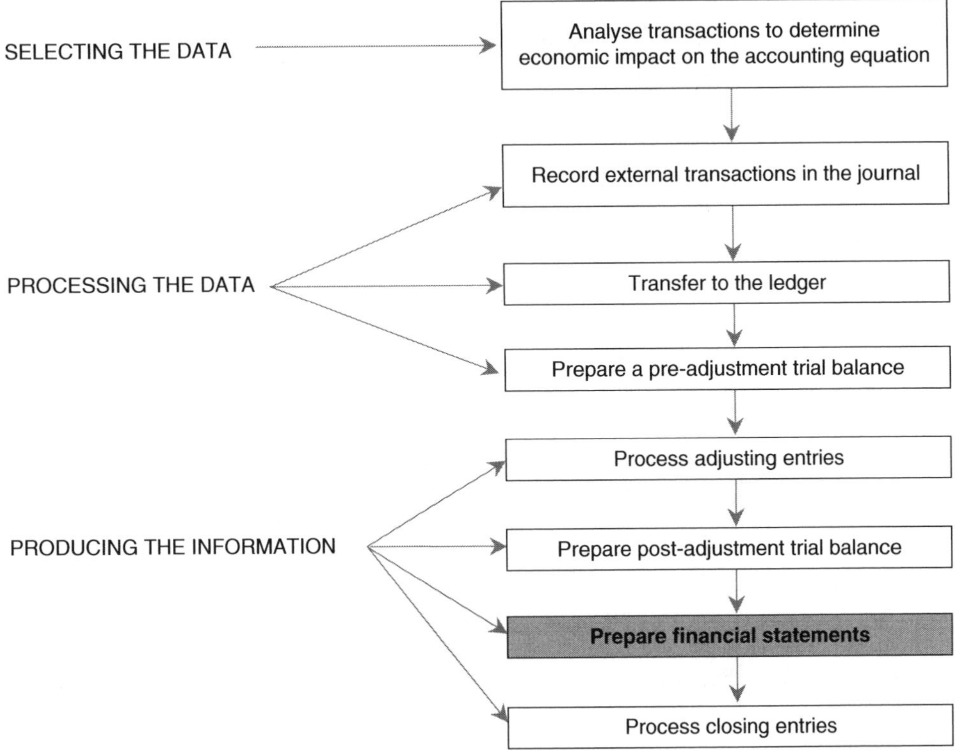

Diagram 6.1 The accounting process, highlighting the preparation of financial statements

Table 6.1 The objective of general purpose financial reporting and financial statements compared

Objective of general purpose financial reporting (Conceptual Framework)	*Objective of general purpose financial statements (IAS 1)*
Provide financial information about the reporting entity that is useful to existing and potential investors, lenders and other creditors in making decisions about providing resources to the entity	Provide information about the financial position, performance and cash flows of an entity that is useful to a wide range of users in making economic decisions

 **Pause and reflect...**

What do you notice when comparing the two definitions?

Response

The *Conceptual Framework* refers to general purpose *financial reporting* whereas IAS 1 refers to the general purpose *financial statements*. The financial statements are a component of the larger financial report, often referred to as an annual report.

> The *Conceptual Framework* also refers to *investors, lenders and other creditors* while IAS 1 refers to a *wide range of users*. You will recall from Chapter 1, *The accounting environment*, that investors, lenders and creditors are known as the ***primary users*** of financial statements. ***Other users*** such as regulators and members of the public may find general purpose financial reports useful, although they are not primarily directed at them.

6.3 General features

IAS 1 describes eight ***general features*** that need to be applied in the presentation of financial statements. These requirements are intended to ensure that an entity's financial statements are a ***faithful representation*** of its financial position, performance and cash flows in accordance with the *Conceptual Framework*.

The features dealt with in IAS 1 relate to fair presentation, the accrual basis of accounting, going concern, consistency of presentation, comparative information, materiality and aggregation, offsetting and, finally, frequency of reporting.

We have already explained the accrual basis of accounting in detail in Chapter 2. An understanding of the accrual basis of accounting is essential for the preparation of even the most elementary financial statements. The going concern assumption is listed as an underlying assumption in the preparation of financial statements according to the *Conceptual Framework*.

6.3.1 Fair presentation

A requirement of IAS 1 is that the financial statements should fairly present the financial position, performance and cash flows of an entity.

According to IAS 1, fair presentation requires the faithful representation of the effects of transactions, other events or conditions in accordance with the definitions and recognition criteria for assets, liabilities, income and expenses as set out in the *Conceptual Framework*.

The above requirement is presumed to be achieved by the application of appropriate IFRSs.

6.3.2 Accrual basis

Financial statements, other than the statement of cash flows, are prepared using the accrual basis of accounting. This principle is applied throughout this book.

6.3.3 Going concern

Financial statements are normally prepared on a going-concern basis, which assumes that the entity will continue in operation for the foreseeable future. This is also an underlying assumption of the *Conceptual Framework*. Financial statements should be prepared on this basis unless management either intends to liquidate the entity or to cease trading or has no alternative but to do so.

The statement of financial position therefore does not report liquidation values of assets. Rather, assets are reported on the statement of financial position at cost or carrying amount.

The going concern principle is ignored if the business is expected to be liquidated and assets and liabilities on the statement of financial position are measured at the amounts expected to be received or settled on liquidation.

6.3.4 Consistency of presentation and comparative information

Remember from Chapter 1 that one of the enhancing qualitative characteristics is that of *comparability*. Users need to be able to compare different entities when making investment decisions and also compare the financial statements of a particular entity over time. As such, IAS 1 requires a consistent presentation and classification of items in the financial statements from one period to the next.

IAS 1 further requires comparative information to be reported in respect of the previous period for all amounts reported in the financial statements. As the focus of this book is on a conceptual introduction to financial accounting and not on disclosure, comparative information has not been incorporated.

6.3.5 Materiality and aggregation

An item is regarded as being material if it can affect users' decisions. IAS 1 requires each material class of similar items as well as items of a dissimilar nature to be presented separately. Immaterial items should be aggregated with similar items, and need not be presented separately.

6.3.6 Offsetting

The process of offsetting means subtracting an expense from an income or subtracting a liability from an asset, and showing the net amount. IAS 1 states that assets and liabilities as well as income and expenses should be reported separately and not be offset.

 **Pause and reflect...**

Can you think of an example that applies the principle that income and expenses should not be offset?

Response

If an entity buys goods for C300 and then sells them for C500, the statement of profit or loss reports income (sales) of C500 and an expense (cost of sales) of C300. It is incorrect to report a net sales amount of C200.

6.3.7 Frequency of reporting

IAS 1 requires an entity to present a complete set of financial statements at least annually.

6.4 Recognition of the elements of financial statements

According to the *Conceptual Framework*, recognition is the process of incorporating in the statement of financial position or statement of profit or loss an item that meets the ***definition*** of an element *and* satisfies the ***recognition criteria***. As you know from the accounting process, before the financial statements are prepared, transactions are recorded in a journal and posted to a ledger. Thus, recognition effectively means the recording of an external or internal transaction, leading to its incorporation in the financial statements.

You were introduced to the ***elements*** of financial statements in Chapter 2 – assets, liabilities, income, expenses and equity. Before these elements may be recognised in the accounting records, the *definition* of the elements *and* the *recognition criteria* must be met. An item that meets the *definition* of an element is *recognised* if:

- the flow of future economic benefits caused by this element are probable; and
- the element has cost or value that can be measured reliably.

It is important to note that the use of estimates in measurement is an essential part of the preparation of financial statements and does not undermine their reliability. When, however, a reliable estimate cannot be made, the item is not recognised in the statement of financial position or the statement of profit or loss.

The recognition criteria for assets, liabilities, income and expenses are described in the *Conceptual Framework* and are discussed below. There are no specific recognition criteria for equity, as equity is the residual interest in the assets of an entity after deducting all of its liabilities.

6.4.1 Recognition of assets

An asset is recognised in the statement of financial position:

- when the inflow of future economic benefits is probable; *and*
- the asset has a cost or value that can be measured reliably.

The inflow of economic benefits needs to be *probable* – in other words, more rather than less likely. Note, however, that even if the probability of future benefits is high, recognition of an asset cannot occur unless there is a cost of value that can be *reliably measured.*

An asset is not recognised in the statement of financial position when expenditure has been incurred for which it is considered improbable that economic benefits will flow to the entity beyond the current period. In this situation, the transaction results in the recognition of an expense on the statement of profit or loss.

Applying these principles to the Smart Concepts case study, each asset on the statement of financial position must satisfy the definition of an asset and the recognition criteria for an asset in accordance with the *Conceptual Framework*. This process is illustrated by the purchase of the furniture and fittings (transaction 5).

First, the item must meet the **definition** of an asset. Furniture and fittings are a resource controlled by the entity (Smart Concepts controls the furniture and fittings for their economic life), as a result of past events (Smart Concepts purchased the furniture and fittings) and from which future economic benefits are expected to flow to the entity (the furniture and fittings will facilitate the selling of computers). The furniture and fittings therefore satisfy the definition of an asset.

Second, the item must meet the **recognition criteria** for an asset. It is probable that future economic benefits will flow to the entity (Smart Concepts utilises the furniture and fittings to display the computers), and the asset has a cost or value that can be reliably measured (the furniture and fittings were purchased for C240 000), thus the furniture and fittings satisfy the recognition criteria for assets, and their recognition on the statement of financial position is appropriate.

6.4.2 Recognition of liabilities

A liability is recognised in the statement of financial position:

- when the outflow of resources embodying economic benefits from the settlement of a present obligation is probable; *and*
- the amount of the settlement can be measured reliably.

As with an asset, the outflow of economic benefits needs to be probable and the amount must be measured reliably.

Applying these principles to the Smart Concepts example, each liability on the statement of financial position must satisfy the definition of a liability and the recognition criteria for a liability in accordance with the accounting framework. This process is illustrated by the purchase of inventory on credit from Computer World (transaction 8).

First, the item must meet the **definition** of a liability. The commitment to pay Computer World is a present obligation of the entity (Smart Concepts has undertaken to pay the supplier for the inventory received), arising from past events (Smart Concepts purchased the inventory on credit from the supplier) and the settlement of which is expected to result in an outflow from the entity of resources embodying economic benefits (Smart Concepts will pay the supplier in cash for the inventory received). The commitment to pay Computer World therefore satisfies the definition of a liability.

Second, the item must meet the **recognition criteria** for a liability. It is probable that an outflow of resources embodying economic benefits will result from the settlement of a present obligation (Smart Concepts is obligated to pay the supplier in cash by 25 March), and the amount at which the settlement will take place can be measured reliably (Smart Concepts is obligated to pay the supplier C600 000). Thus, the commitment to pay Computer World satisfies the recognition criteria for a liability, and its recognition on the statement of financial position is appropriate.

6.4.3 Recognition of income

It is important to note that the recognition of income is linked to a *change* in the carrying amount of an asset or liability. The focus is thus on the *reliable measurement* of the income as opposed to the probable increase in future benefits. This relates back to the definition of income in the *Conceptual Framework*.

Income is recognised in the statement of profit or loss:

- when an increase in future economic benefits related to an increase in an asset or a decrease in liability has arisen
- that can be measured reliably.

Pause and reflect...

Look back at the following transactions involving the recognition of income in the Smart Concepts case study in previous chapters, and make sure that you can identify the increase in assets or decrease in liabilities:

10 On 25 January, Smart Concepts sold 15 computers on credit to a customer for C12 500 each.
13 On 12 February, Smart Concepts sold 30 computers to customers for C12 500 each. The customers paid cash for them.
24 On 31 March, Simon examined the records of the business and established that technical support in respect of contracts to the value of C6 000 had been provided to customers.
25 On 31 March, Smart Concepts accounted for the interest on the fixed deposit earned for the period.

Response

In each of these transactions, income has been recognised with a corresponding increase in assets or a decrease in liabilities:

10 The asset, *accounts receivable*, was increased.
13 The asset, *cash*, was increased.
24 The liability, *fees received in advance*, was decreased.
25 The asset, *interest receivable*, was increased.

6.4.4 Recognition of expenses

Expenses are recognised in the statement of profit or loss:

- when a decrease in future economic benefits related to a decrease in an asset or an increase in a liability has arisen
- that can be measured reliably.

As you saw with the recognition of income, the recognition of expenses is linked to a *change* in the carrying amount of an asset or liability. The focus is thus on the reliable measurement of the expense as opposed to the probable decrease in future benefits. This relates back to the definition of an expense in the *Conceptual Framework*.

 **Pause and reflect...**

Look back at the following transactions involving the recognition of expenses in the Smart Concepts case study in previous chapters, and make sure that you can identify the decrease in assets or increase in liabilities:

9 On 12 January, Smart Concepts paid a service provider C750 for internet access.
26 On 31 March, Smart Concepts recognised the rent expense incurred for the period.
27 On 31 March, the water account for C1 500 and the electricity account for C2 500 had been received but not paid.

Response

In each of these transactions, an expense has been recognised with a corresponding decrease in assets or an increase in liabilities:

9 The asset, *cash*, was decreased.
26 The asset, *rent paid in advance,* was decreased.
27 The liability, *water and electricity payable*, was increased.

6.5 Classification of assets and liabilities

In earlier chapters, you were introduced to the basic format of a statement of financial position and a statement of profit or loss. The statement of financial position has two sections – **assets** (the resources of the entity) and **equity and liabilities** (the sources of finance). The statement of financial position is derived directly from the accounting equation: Assets = Liabilities + Owner's equity.

In order to understand the classification of assets and liabilities, it is necessary to review the operating cycle of an entity.

The operating cycle of an entity is the time between the acquisition of inventory and its ultimate realisation in cash. The operating cycle can be illustrated as shown in Diagram 6.2.

Inventory, accounts receivable and cash are typical assets which circulate in the operating cycle. Inventory is purchased from suppliers and then realised by sale to customers. When inventory is sold on credit to customers, accounts receivable are created which will ultimately result in a cash inflow when the customers settle their accounts. This completes the operating cycle. Cash is used to pay the suppliers for inventory purchased, and the cycle begins again with the purchase of inventory.

When examining the financial statements of an entity, you will notice that the assets are classified into two different types: ***non-current assets*** and ***current assets***.

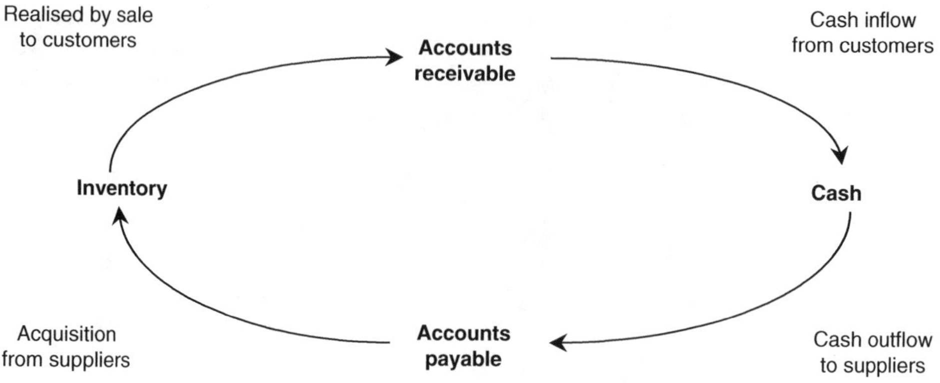

Diagram 6.2 The operating cycle

According to IAS 1, an asset is classified as a current asset when:

- it is expected to be realised within 12 months after the end of the reporting period; ***or***
- it holds the asset mainly for the purpose of trading; ***or***
- it expects to realise the asset, or intends to sell or consume it, in its normal operating cycle; ***or***
- it is cash or a cash equivalent.

All other assets are classified as non-current assets.

The operating cycle of many entities is shorter than 12 months, and the inventory and accounts receivable will normally be realised within that time. However, such items remain current assets even when they are not expected to be realised within 12 months after the reporting period. In other words, inventory is classified as a current asset even if it is only expected to be realised beyond 12 months after the reporting date.

Examples of current assets include inventory, accounts receivable, supplies, bank and cash, expenses paid in advance and income receivable. Examples of non-current assets include land, buildings, motor vehicles, plant and machinery, furniture and computer equipment.

Turning our attention to liabilities, the financial statements of an entity classify liabilities into two different types: ***non-current liabilities*** and ***current liabilities***.

According to IAS 1, a liability is classified as a current liability when:

- it is due to be settled within 12 months after the end of the reporting period; ***or***
- it holds the liability mainly for the purpose of trading; ***or***
- it expects to settle the liability in its normal operating cycle; ***or***
- the entity does not have an unconditional right to defer settlement of the liability for at least 12 months after the end of the reporting period.

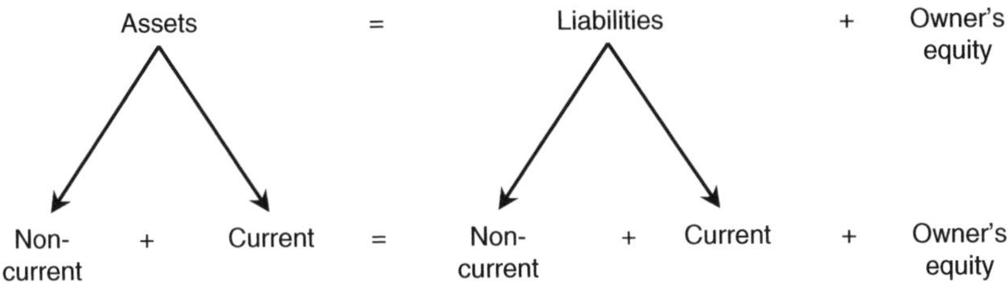

Diagram 6.3 The expanded accounting equation

All other liabilities are non-current liabilities.

Current liabilities are therefore categorised in a similar way to current assets. Current liabilities such as accounts payable and expenses payable are normally settled within 12 months of the reporting date. However, such items remain as current liabilities even if they are due to be settled after more than 12 months from the reporting date.

Examples of current liabilities include accounts payable, income received in advance and expenses payable. Examples of non-current liabilities include loans and mortgage bonds.

The accounting equation can therefore be expanded as shown in Diagram 6.3.

Pause and reflect...

a) An entity that trades as an antique dealer buys inventory with a cost of C75 000 on 1 October 20X0. The inventory is not expected to be sold until early 20X2. The entity has a year end of 31 December. Explain how the inventory will be classified on the statement of financial position at 31 December 20X0.

b) An entity raises a loan for C120 000 on 1 October 20X0. The loan is to be repaid in three equal annual instalments of C40 000 each on 30 September 20X1, 20X2 and 20X3. The entity has a year end of 31 December. How will the loan be classified on the statement of financial position at 31 December 20X0?

Response

a) At 31 December 20X0, the inventory is expected to be realised beyond 12 months after the end of the reporting period. However, as inventory is being held primarily for the purposes of being traded, inventory of C75 000 is classified as a current asset.

b) At 31 December 20X0, C40 000 of the loan is due to be settled within 12 months after the end of the reporting period, and C80 000 of the loan is due to be settled beyond 12 months after the end of the reporting period. C40 000 will therefore be classified as a current liability and C80 000 will be classified as a non-current liability.

6.6 The financial statements

6.6.1 Structure and content of financial statements

You are already familiar with the components of the financial statements (the statement of financial position, statement of profit or loss, statement of cash flows, statement of changes in equity, as well as accounting policies and explanatory notes).

IAS 1 requires each component to be clearly identified and also requires the following information to be displayed for a proper understanding of the financial statements:

- the name of the entity and any change from the preceding statement of financial position date;
- the statement of financial position date (referred to as the reporting date) and the period covered by the financial statements;
- the presentation currency;
- the level of rounding used in presenting amounts in the financial statements.

Judgement is required in determining the best way of presenting such information.

We mentioned in Section 6.2 that the financial statements are a structured representation of the financial position and the financial performance of an entity. We will examine in more detail how these are presented in the financial statements.

6.6.2 The statement of profit or loss and other comprehensive income

Measurement of financial performance

Profit or loss is the most common measure of the financial performance of an entity and we have focused our attention thus far on the statement of profit or loss to represent financial performance. However, a full representation of financial performance requires consideration of not only income earned and expenses incurred in the determination of profit or loss, but also of gains and losses recognised directly in equity.

Throughout the Smart Concepts case study, we have used a separate statement of profit or loss, both for the sake of clarity and because there are no transactions in the example giving rise to items of other comprehensive income. It is important now to revisit the concepts of *profit or loss* and *other comprehensive income* as well as the different presentation options of IAS 1.

IAS1 requires an entity to present items of income and expense either in two separate statements – the ***statement of profit or loss*** (displaying items of profit or loss) *and* the ***statement of comprehensive income*** (displaying components of comprehensive income); *or* in a single combined statement – the ***statement of profit or loss and other comprehensive income***. Many entities find this name too long and cumbersome and simply refer to the single combined statement as the ***statement of comprehensive income***. The combined statement (irrespective of its name) has a *profit and loss* section and an *other comprehensive income* section.

This can be represented as shown in Diagram 6.4.

The statement of profit or loss and other comprehensive income (as a combined statement) or the separate statement of profit or loss and statement of comprehensive income provide information about the *performance* of an entity.

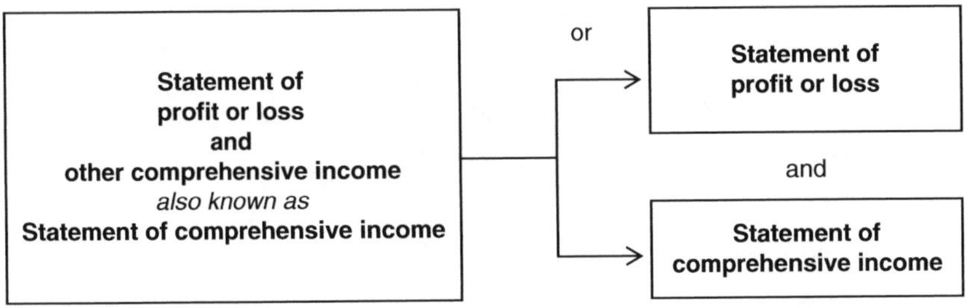

Diagram 6.4 Presentation formats of statement of profit or loss and other comprehensive income

Most of the transactions that give rise to items of income and expense that comprise the components of other comprehensive income are beyond the scope of this book. In fact, you will be exposed only to one such component, known as a revaluation of property, plant and equipment. You will be introduced to the concept of a revaluation later in this chapter, and will revisit revaluations in more detail in Chapter 10, *Property, plant and equipment* and Chapter 17, *Companies*.

In this book, we refer to and use a separate *statement of profit or loss* in all financial statements except where there is a transaction involving a revaluation of property, plant and equipment, when we will use a combined statement and refer to it as the *statement of comprehensive income*.

It is now important to understand which items of income and expense are recognised in profit or loss and which items are recognised in other comprehensive income, and how these are reported. These terms are defined in IAS 1.

Profit or loss is defined as the total of income less expenses, excluding the components of other comprehensive income.

Other comprehensive income is defined as items of income and expense that are not recognised in profit or loss.

Profit or loss, as a measure of performance, is generally measured by the income earned from ordinary activities less the expenses incurred from ordinary activities. However, the distinction between items recognised in profit or loss and those recognised in other comprehensive income is often driven by accounting standards rather than conceptual reasons.

The profit or loss and other comprehensive income are then combined to give the total comprehensive income.

Total comprehensive income comprises all components of profit or loss and all components of other comprehensive income.

Table 6.2 Presentation of statement of profit or loss and other comprehensive income

Combined statement		*Two separate statements*	
	Statement of profit or loss and other comprehensive income or **Statement of comprehensive income**		**Statement of profit or loss**
	Income		Income
–	Expenses	–	Expenses
=	**Profit or loss**	=	**Profit or loss**
			Statement of comprehensive income
			Profit or loss
+/–	Other comprehensive income	+/–	Other comprehensive income
=	Total comprehensive income	=	Total comprehensive income

Table 6.2 incorporates these definitions.

In order to illustrate the concept of other comprehensive income, we are going to consider a revaluation of an item of property, plant and equipment. Assume that a business entity buys a property for C1 000 000. After a period of, say, two years, an independent valuer assesses the property to be worth C1 200 000. We can then say that the *fair value* of the property is C1 200 000 and that there has been an increase in the value of the property of C200 000. If the business entity chooses to measure the property at its fair value, this is referred to as a *revaluation*. (The choice between measurement at cost or at revaluation will be discussed in detail in Chapter 10.)

An important question to consider now is whether the revaluation of C200 000 represents income. There is an increase in economic benefits during the period in the form of an enhancement of an asset (the value of the property has increased), which results in an increase in equity (the revaluation, you will see, does increase equity), other than a contribution from equity participants (there is no contribution of capital). The revaluation therefore does represent income.

 **Pause and reflect...**

Is the revaluation of C200 000 an income item that is included in profit or loss for the period or is it an item of other comprehensive income?

Response

Profit or loss generally measures performance from ordinary activities. The C200 000 does not represent income earned from ordinary activities during the period. It is therefore income in the form of a gain and is reported as an item of other comprehensive income.

Assume further, during the period, that the profit or loss of the business entity comprises income earned of C1 500 000, and expenses incurred of C1 000 000. In addition, the property was revalued by C200 000.

If two separate statements are presented, a simple statement of profit or loss and statement of comprehensive income could be drawn up as follows:

STATEMENT OF PROFIT OR LOSS
FOR THE PERIOD ENDED 31 DECEMBER 20X5

	C
Income	1 500 000
Expenses	(1 000 000)
Profit for the period	500 000

STATEMENT OF COMPREHENSIVE INCOME
FOR THE PERIOD ENDED 31 DECEMBER 20X5

	C
Profit for the period	500 000
Other comprehensive income	
Revaluation	200 000
Total comprehensive income	700 000

If a single statement is presented, a simple statement of profit or loss and other comprehensive income could be drawn up as follows:

STATEMENT OF PROFIT OR LOSS AND OTHER COMPREHENSIVE INCOME
FOR THE PERIOD ENDED 31 DECEMBER 20X5

	C
Income	1 500 000
Expenses	(1 000 000)
Profit for the period	500 000
Other comprehensive income	
Revaluation	200 000
Total comprehensive income	700 000

The previous paragraphs have explained and illustrated the alternative presentations of income and expenses – that is, as two separate statements (statement of profit or loss and statement of comprehensive income) or as a single statement (statement of profit or loss and other comprehensive income). IAS 1 allows a choice between the two alternatives. In this textbook, as most of the scenarios do not involve items of other comprehensive income, and for the purposes of illustrating concepts, a separate ***statement of profit or loss*** will be used. When the scenario does involve an item of comprehensive income, a single statement with the shortened name of ***statement of comprehensive income*** will be used.

Formats

IAS 1 does not prescribe a standard format for the presentation of the statement of profit or loss. We will examine some common formats here, depending on the nature of the entity's operations.

Table 6.3 Statement of comprehensive income formats

Elements		*Retail entity*	*Service entity*	*Combined retail and service entity*
		Statement of comprehensive income		
		C	*C*	*C*
Income	→	Sales	Fees	Sales
		less		*less*
Expense	→	Cost of sales		Cost of sales
		Gross profit		**Gross profit**
				Other income
Income	→			Fees
		less	*less*	*less*
Expense	→	Operating expenses	Operating expenses	Operating expenses
	→	Finance costs	Finance costs	Finance costs
		Profit for the period	**Profit for the period**	**Profit for the period**
Income or expense	→	**Other comprehensive income**	**Other comprehensive income**	**Other comprehensive income**
		Total comprehensive income	**Total comprehensive income**	**Total comprehensive income**

You will recall from Chapter 1 that there are different types of business entity, such as a service entity and a retail entity. A service entity provides services to clients, whereas a retail entity buys goods from suppliers and then sells them to customers. Some entities, such as Smart Concepts, are involved in both retail and service activities. The format of the statement of comprehensive income needs to be adapted to take into account the nature of the entity's activities. The order of presentation and the descriptions used for line items are changed when necessary in order to achieve a fair presentation of each entity's particular circumstances.

You also learnt in Chapter 2 that the elements of the financial statements in the accounting framework that relate to the statement of profit or loss are income and expenses. It is important to relate the elements to the line items on the statement of comprehensive income in order to understand the format of the statement of comprehensive income. Table 6.3 links the elements of income and expense to alternative formats for a retail entity, a service entity and a combined retail and service entity.

Note how the format of the statement of profit or loss differs depending on the nature of the entity's activities. For a **retail entity**, the sales and cost of sales are grouped together, resulting in a subtotal known as the ***gross profit***. This is the trading profit of the entity. The operating expenses and finance costs are then subtracted to give the profit for the period. Note that the finance costs are not an operating expense and are listed separately from the operating expenses. The statement of comprehensive income of a **service entity** shows the income, normally comprising fees, less the operating expenses and finance costs, resulting in the profit for the period. Looking at a **combined retail and service entity**, the 'trading' section is presented as for the retail entity. Other income, such as fees, is included after the gross profit before the subtraction of the operating expenses and finance costs.

The presentation option shown in Table 6.4 is that of a single statement of comprehensive income. Looking at the combined retail and service entity, we could present a separate statement of profit or loss and statement of comprehensive income as follows.

Table 6.4 Format with separate statement of profit or loss and statement of comprehensive income

Elements		*Combined retail and service entity*
		Statement of profit or loss
		C
Income	→	Sales
		less
Expense	→	Cost of sales
		Gross profit
		Other income
Income	→	Fees
		less
Expense	→	Operating expenses
	→	Finance costs
		Profit for the period
	→	**Statement of comprehensive income**
		C
		Profit for the period
Income or expense		**Other comprehensive income**
		Total comprehensive income

As there are no items of other comprehensive income in the Smart Concepts case study, and to be consistent with the presentation in previous chapters, the separate statement of profit or loss of Smart Concepts is shown below.

SMART CONCEPTS
STATEMENT OF PROFIT OR LOSS
FOR THE THREE MONTHS ENDED 31 MARCH 20X5

		C
Sales		937 500
Cost of sales		(750 000)
Gross profit		187 500
Other income		7 500
Service fees	6 000	
Interest	1 500	
Operating expenses		(88 000)
Internet	1 500	
Advertising	7 000	
Salaries	16 000	
Rent	36 000	
Water and electricity	4 000	
Stationery supplies and computer parts	11 500	
Depreciation	12 000	
Finance cost		
Interest		(18 000)
Profit for the period		89 000

 The statement of profit or loss for Smart Concepts follows the suggested format for a combined retail and service entity. Smart Concepts' trading activities comprise the selling of computers, and the gross profit of C187 500 is separately identified as a line item. There are two items of other income in this case – the service fees and the interest. Note also that the finance costs, comprising interest of C18 000, are disclosed separately from the operating expenses.

Concepts in context

Massmart
Extract from condensed consolidated income statement for the 53 weeks ended December 2013

	Rm
Sales	72 263.4
Cost of sales	(58 926.4)
Gross profit	13 337.0
Other income	249.5
Depreciation and amortisation	(731.1)
Impairment of assets	(41.6)
Employment costs	(5 423.5)
Occupancy costs	(2 555.3)
Foreign exchange profit	67.8
Other operating costs	(2 750.3)
Operating profit	2 152.5
Finance costs	(283.8)
Finance income	28.7
Net finance costs	(255.1)
Profit before tax	1 897.4
Taxation	(555.3)
Profit for the year	1 342.1

What concepts in context do you see here?

Having read this chapter, the overall format of Massmart's income statement should look familiar to you. Note that Massmart has chosen to call it an *income statement* rather than a *statement of profit or loss*. IAS 1 allows entities this choice.

The reporting of sales, cost of sales and gross profit are exactly the same as you have seen in this book. Massmart also has a subtotal – 'operating profit' – and has disclosed a net finance cost beneath that. It is important for you to realise that there are many acceptable presentation formats.

Massmart is a South African retail and wholesale distributor, with stores in South Africa and sub-Saharan Africa. It is the third-largest distributor of consumer goods in Africa, and owns brands such as Makro, Builders Warehouse and Game. Its ultimate holding company is Walmart Stores Inc.

Source: www.massmart.co.za/iar2013/ (Accessed 3 October 2014).

6.6.3 The statement of financial position

As stated in Section 6.2, a major purpose of financial statements is to provide information about an entity's financial position (the other to provide information about its financial performance). The statement of financial position provides information about an entity's assets, liabilities and owner's equity.

The statement of financial position is prepared from the post-adjustment trial balance using the asset, liability and equity elements of the financial statements – remember that assets are *resources* of the entity, liabilities are the *obligations* of the entity and equity represents the owner's interest in the entity.

The items on the statement of financial position are classified as explained in Section 6.5 above. The format of the statement of financial position is not prescribed and may be changed to achieve fair presentation.

SMART CONCEPTS
STATEMENT OF FINANCIAL POSITION
AT 31 MARCH 20X5

	C
ASSETS	
Non-current assets	348 000
Furniture and fittings	228 000
Fixed deposit investment	120 000
Current assets	2 027 000
Inventory	600 000
Accounts receivable	437 500
Stationery supplies	2 000
Computer parts	3 500
Interest receivable	1 500
Rent paid in advance	12 000
Bank	970 500
	2 375 000
EQUITY AND LIABILITIES	
Equity	
Capital	979 000
Non-current liabilities	
Long-term borrowings	450 000
Current liabilities	946 000
Short-term borrowings	150 000
Accounts payable	750 000
Service fees received in advance	42 000
Water and electricity payable	4 000
	2 375 000

Note the format of the statement of financial position. Both the assets and liabilities are categorised as either non-current or current. The distinction between non-current assets and current assets, as well as between non-current liabilities and current liabilities, was discussed earlier in this chapter. You will note the separation of the borrowings into long-term and short-term components. This is because C150 000 of the total borrowing of C600 000 is repayable in less than 12 months, thus the C150 000 represents a current liability. The service fees received in advance are also classified as current as they are considered to be part of the entity's normal operating cycle.

Concepts in context

Massmart

Extract from condensed consolidated statement of financial position for the 53 weeks ended December 2013

	Rm
ASSETS	
Non-current assets	10 111.8
Property, plant and equipment	5 988.1
Goodwill and other intangible assets	2 928.8
Investments and loans	522.8
Deferred taxation	672.1
Current assets	16 036.1
Inventories	10 115.5
Trade, other receivables and prepayments	3 712.5
Taxation	12.0
Cash and bank balances	2 196.1
Total	26 147.9
EQUITY AND LIABILITIES	
Total equity	5 369.6
Non-current liabilities	2 206.4
Long-term interest-bearing borrowings	1 178.7
Other non-current liabilities and provisions	941.1
Deferred taxation	86.6
Current liabilities	18 571.9
Trade, other payables and provisions	17 101.2
Taxation	331.3
Bank overdrafts	607.8
Short-term interest-bearing borrowings	531.6
Total	26 147.9

What concepts in context do you see here?

Having read this chapter, you should be familiar with the structure, format and most of the contents of Massmart's statement of financial position. Certain line items are beyond the scope of this book (such as deferred taxation) and you will learn about other items in more detail in later chapters.

You have learnt about the classification of assets and liabilities into two types – non-current and current. Look back at the definition of current assets in Section 6.5 and relate this to what you see on Massmart's statement of financial position. 'Inventories', for example, are held mainly for the purpose of trading and 'trade, other receivables and prepayments' are expected to be realised within 12 months after the end of the reporting period.

Do the same for current liabilities. Note that Massmart reports a non-current liability – 'long-term interest-bearing borrowings' – and a current liability – 'short-term interest-bearing borrowings'. You should appreciate that the current liability is the portion of the borrowings that is due to be settled within 12 months after the end of the reporting period.

Massmart is a South African retail and wholesale distributor, with stores in South Africa and sub-Saharan Africa. It is the third-largest distributor of consumer goods in Africa, and owns brands such as Makro, Builders Warehouse and Game. Its ultimate holding company is Walmart Stores Inc.

Source: www.massmart.co.za/iar2013/ (Accessed 3 October 2014).

6.6.4 The statement of changes in equity

The statement of changes in equity reflects the increases or decreases in the net assets or wealth of an entity for a period of time. IAS 1 *Presentation of Financial Statements* requires the statement of changes in equity to present changes in equity separated into the following:

- owner changes in equity;
- non-owner changes in equity.

Owner changes in equity arise from transactions with owners in their capacity as owners. They incorporate contributions to capital by owners (which increases equity) and distributions to owners (which decreases equity).

Non-owner changes in equity arise from income and expense transactions. You learnt in the previous section that income increases equity and expenses decrease it. The profit for the period, or the total comprehensive income (if there are items of other comprehensive income), is thus included on the statement of changes in equity as a line item.

SMART CONCEPTS
STATEMENT OF CHANGES IN EQUITY
FOR THE PERIOD ENDED 31 MARCH 20X5

	C
Balance at 1 January 20X5	—
Profit for the period	89 000
Distributions	(60 000)
Contribution to capital	950 000
Balance at 31 March 20X5	979 000

6.7 Exam technique

A common exam question is one where you are given a pre-adjustment trial balance with additional information. You would usually be expected to draft the statement of profit or loss and/or the statement of financial position and/or the statement of changes in equity for the entity. The pre-adjustment trial balance of Smart Concepts is reproduced below, together with the internal transactions presented as 'additional information'. The solution explains how to approach such a question in an exam and how to present your answer with appropriate workings.

Example: Exam technique

The pre-adjustment trial balance of Smart Concepts at 31 March 20X5 is shown below:

SMART CONCEPTS
PRE-ADJUSTMENT TRIAL BALANCE AT 31 MARCH 20X5

Description	*Folio*	*Dr*	*Cr*
Bank	A1	970 500	
Rent paid in advance	A2	48 000	
Fixed deposit investment	A3	120 000	
Furniture and fittings	A4	240 000	
Stationery supplies	A5	5 000	
Computer parts	A6	12 000	
Inventory	A7	600 000	
Accounts receivable	A8	437 500	
Borrowings	L1		600 000
Accounts payable	L2		750 000
Service fees received in advance	L3		48 000
Simon Smart capital	OE1		950 000
Distributions	OE2	60 000	
Sales	I1		937 500
Internet expense	E1	1 500	
Cost of sales expense	E2	750 000	
Advertising expense	E3	7 000	
Salaries expense	E4	16 000	
Interest expense	E5	18 000	
		3 285 500	3 285 500

Additional information

24 On 31 March, Simon examined the records of the business and established that technical support in respect of contracts to the value of C6 000 had been provided to customers.

25 On 31 March, Smart Concepts accounted for the interest on the fixed deposit earned for the period.

26 On 31 March, Smart Concepts recognised the rent expense incurred for the period.

27 On 31 March, the water account for C1 500 and the electricity account for C2 500 had been received but not paid.

28 On 31 March, Simon counted stationery supplies on hand costing C2 000, and also counted computer parts on hand costing C3 500.

29 On 31 March, Smart Concepts accounted for the usage of the furniture and fittings for the period.

You are required to:

a) Prepare the statement of profit or loss of Smart Concepts for the three-month period ended 31 March 20X5.

b) Prepare the statement of changes in equity of Smart Concepts for the three-month period ended 31 March 20X5.
c) Prepare the statement of financial position of Smart Concepts at 31 March 20X5.

Solution: Exam technique

In an exam, you would not usually have enough time to journalise the adjustments, post to the ledger and extract the post-adjustment trial balance before drafting the financial statements. In any event, none of these steps would be required of you. You will need to manually adjust the trial balance for the adjustments in the additional information. This procedure is explained below, including guidance on how to effect the adjustments on the trial balance.

Additional information – point 24

On 31 March, Simon examined the records of the business and established that technical support to the value of C6 000 had been performed on customers' computers.

Income of C6 000 is now earned. Smart Concepts received cash of C48 000 in respect of technical support contracts taken out by customers. This was originally recorded as a debit to bank and a credit to service fees received in advance. The liability therefore needs to be reduced and income increased as C6 000 of the services have been provided:

- Decrease service fees received in advance (Dr) C6 000
- Increase service fees income (Cr) C6 000

Additional information – point 25

On 31 March, Smart Concepts accounted for the interest on the fixed deposit earned for the period.

C120 000 × 0.05 for three months = C1 500 interest earned but not yet received:

- Increase interest receivable (Dr) C1 500
- Increase interest income (Cr) C1 500

Since these accounts were not on the pre-adjustment trial balance, you need to include them to be able to make the adjustment.

Additional information – point 26

On 31 March, Smart Concepts recognised the rent expense incurred for the period.

This requires an adjustment to the rent paid in advance. Before the adjustment is made, examine the trial balance to see how the payment was originally recorded. In this example, it was recorded in the *rent paid in advance* account, therefore an adjustment is required for the portion used:

- Increase rent expense (Dr) C36 000
- Decrease rent paid in advance (Cr) C36 000

Additional information – point 27

On 31 March, the water account for C1 500 and the electricity account for C2 500 had been received but not paid.

These are expenses incurred but not yet paid:

- Increase water and electricity expense (Dr) C4 000
- Increase water and electricity payable (Cr) C4 000

Since these accounts were not on the pre-adjustment trial balance, you need to include them to be able to make the adjustment.

Additional information – point 28

On 31 March, Simon counted stationery supplies on hand costing C2 000, and also counted computer parts on hand costing C3 500.

C3 000 of the stationery supplies asset and C8 500 of the computer parts asset have been used and need to be expensed:

- Increase stationery supplies expense (Dr) C3 000
- Decrease stationery supplies (Cr) C3 000
- Increase computer parts expense (Dr) C8 500
- Decrease computer parts (Cr) C8 500

Additional information – point 29

On 31 March, Smart Concepts accounted for the usage of the furniture and fittings for the period.

Non-current assets are accounted for as being used (depreciated):

- Increase depreciation expense (Dr) C12 000
- Decrease furniture and fittings (Cr) C12 000

For illustrative purposes, the adjustments are summarised on the trial balance as follows:

Description	*Dr*		*Cr*	
Bank	970 500			
Rent paid in advance	48 000	*– 36 000*[26]		
Fixed deposit investment	120 000			
Furniture and fittings	240 000	*– 12 000*[29]		
Stationery supplies	5 000	*– 3 000*[28]		
Computer parts	12 000	*– 8 500*[28]		
Inventory	600 000			
Accounts receivable	437 500			
Borrowings			600 000	
Accounts payable			750 000	
Service fees received in advance			48 000	*– 6 000*[24]
Simon Smart capital			950 000	
Distributions	60 000			
Sales			937 500	
Internet expense	1 500			
Cost of sales expense	750 000			
Advertising expense	7 000			
Salaries expense	16 000			

Description	*Dr*	*Cr*
Interest expense	18 000	
Service fee income		*6 000*[24]
Interest receivable	*1 500*[25]	
Interest income		*1 500*[25]
Rent expense	*36 000*[26]	
Water and electricity expense	*4 000*[27]	
Water and electricity payable		*4 000*[27]
Stationery supplies expense	*3 000*[28]	
Computer parts expense	*8 500*[28]	
Depreciation expense	*12 000*[29]	

a) Statement of profit or loss

SMART CONCEPTS
STATEMENT OF PROFIT OR LOSS
FOR THE THREE MONTHS ENDED 31 MARCH 20X5

		C
Sales	*(From TB)*	937 500
Cost of sales	*(From TB)*	(750 000)
		187 500
Gross profit		
Other income		7 500
Service fees	*(6 000 (24))*	6 000
Interest	*(120 000 × 0.05 × 3/12 (25))*	1 500
Operating expenses		(88 000)
Internet	*(From TB)*	1 500
Advertising	*(From TB)*	7 000
Salaries	*(From TB)*	16 000
Rent	*(36 000 (26))*	36 000
Water and electricity	*(1 500 + 2 500 (27))*	4 000
Stationery supplies and computer parts	*(3 000 + 8 500 (28))*	11 500
Depreciation	*(240 000/5 × 3/12 (29))*	12 000
Finance cost		
Interest	*(From TB)*	(18 000)
Profit for the period		89 000

b) Statement of changes in equity

SMART CONCEPTS
STATEMENT OF CHANGES IN EQUITY
FOR THE PERIOD ENDED 31 MARCH 20X5

	C
Balance at 1 January 20X5	—
Profit for the period	89 000
Distributions	(60 000)
Contribution to capital	950 000
Balance at 31 March 20X5	979 000

c) Statement of financial position

SMART CONCEPTS
STATEMENT OF FINANCIAL POSITION
AT 31 MARCH 20X5

		C
ASSETS		
Non-current assets		348 000
Furniture and fittings	*(240 000 – 12 000 (29))*	228 000
Fixed deposit investment	*(From TB)*	120 000
Current assets		2 027 000
Inventory	*(From TB)*	600 000
Accounts receivable	*(From TB)*	437 500
Stationery supplies	*(2 000 (28))*	2 000
Computer parts	*(3 500 (28))*	3 500
Interest receivable	*(1 500 (25))*	1 500
Rent paid in advance	*(48 000 – 36 000 (26))*	12 000
Bank	*(From TB)*	970 500
		2 375 000
EQUITY AND LIABILITIES		
Equity		
Capital		979 000
Non-current liabilities		
Long-term borrowings	*(600 000 – 150 000)*	450 000
Current liabilities		946 000
Short-term borrowings	*(600 000 – 450 000)*	150 000
Accounts payable	*(From TB)*	750 000
Service fees received in advance	*(48 000 – 6 000 (24))*	42 000
Water and electricity payable	*(4 000 (27))*	4 000
		2 375 000

Bibliography

IASB. 2011. *IFRS Application around the World*. www.ifrs.org/Use-around-the-world/Pages/Analysis-of-the-G20-IFRS-profiles.aspx (Accessed 9 September 2014).

Picker, R; Leo, K; Loftus, J *et al.* 2013. *Applying International Financial Reporting Standards*. Milton, Queensland, Australia: Wiley.

The International Accounting Standards Board. 2010. *The Conceptual Framework*.

The International Accounting Standards Board. 2012. IAS 1 *Presentation of Financial Statements*.

7 Closing entries

Business focus

WorldCom is one of the most well-documented cases of fraud, with accounting irregularities estimated at USD11 billion. While the exact nature and extent of the fraud perpetrated at this multinational company are beyond the scope of this text, one major area of fraud involved the allocation of accounts when preparing financial statements.

Management engaged in the unauthorised re-allocation of various line costs as prepaid capacity. Line costs paid to local telephone companies to facilitate long-distance, including international, telephone calls, constitute one of the largest expenses for a telecommunications operation. By capitalising these costs as prepaid capacity (a type of prepaid expense) during the year or as part of the processes of closing off accounts for the purpose of preparing financial statements, management was able to defer material operating costs. Rather than expense these as incurred, these costs were effectively amortised over time, allowing WorldCom to report significantly better profits and impressive operating ratios. What this example of fraud at WorldCom tells us is that although closing entries are a largely mechanical and relatively simple accounting process, this by no means detracts from their importance.

In this chapter

Assets and liabilities are statement of financial position accounts, and the closing balances at the end of one period become the opening balances at the beginning of the next period. Income and expenses, however, are statement of profit or loss accounts that relate to *income earned for a period* and *expenses incurred for a period*. These accounts do not have balances that carry forward from one period to the next, and the account balances need to be cleared before transactions of the following period can be posted. This is referred to as the closing entry process, which is the topic of this chapter.

Dashboard

- Look at the *Learning outcomes* so that you know what you should be able to do after studying this chapter.
- Read the *Business focus* to place this chapter's contents in a real-world context.

- Preview *In this chapter* to focus your mind on the contents of the chapter.
- Read the *text* in detail.
  - Apply your mind to the *Pause and reflect* scenarios.
  - Try to visualise the flow of income and expenses from the ledger accounts through the trading account, the profit or loss account and finally to the owner's capital account.
- Prepare solutions to the examples as you read through the chapter.
- Prepare a solution to the *Revision example* at the end of the chapter without reference to the suggested one. Compare your solution to the suggested solution provided.

Learning outcomes

After studying this chapter, you should be able to do the following:

1 Explain the role performed by closing entries in the accounting process.
2 Describe the procedure to close the income and expense accounts, as well as the distributions account.
3 Prepare closing entries.
4 Prepare accounting entries in respect of accrued items in the following period.

Closing entries

7.1 Closing entries in the context of the accounting process

By now you should be familiar with the stages of the accounting process. Part II of this book, dealing with the accounting process, has covered the recording of transactions in Chapter 4, and adjusting entries in Chapter 5, and has demonstrated how to prepare financial statements from the post-adjustment trial balance in Chapter 6. Chapter 7 completes the accounting process with the processing of closing entries (Diagram 7.1).

7.2 The need for closing entries

7.2.1 Updating the owner's equity

You will recall from Chapter 3 that owner's equity is affected by four types of transactions – contributions by the owner, distributions to the owner, the earning of income and the incurrence of expenses.

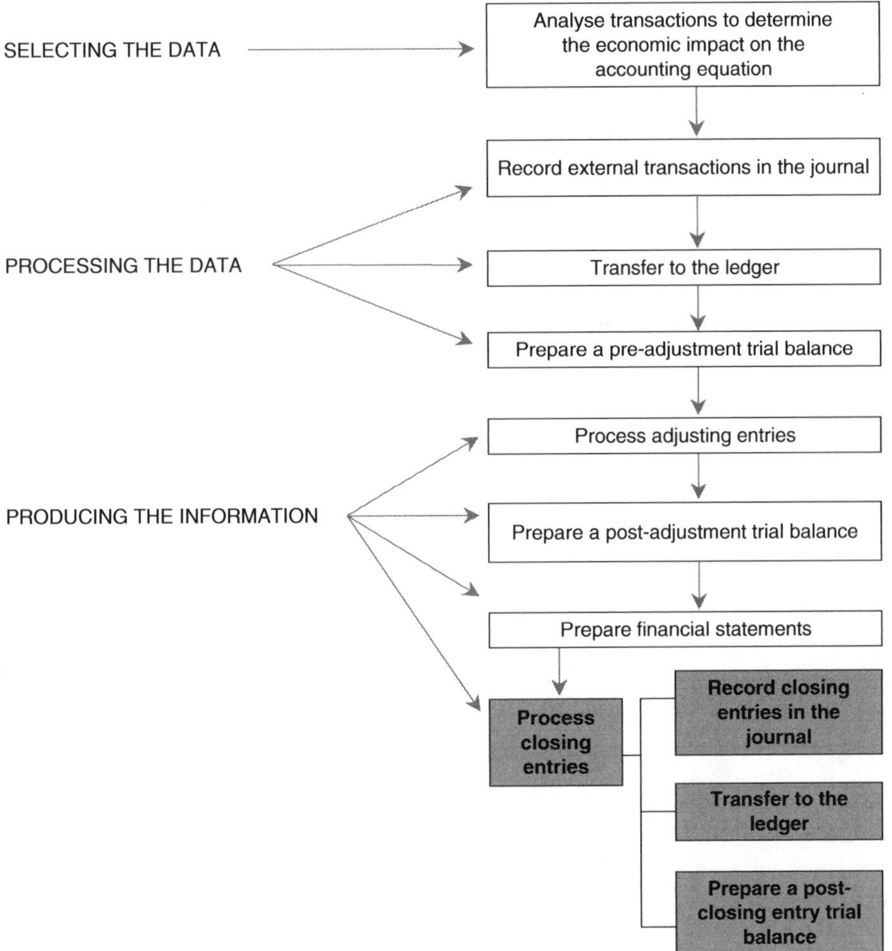

Diagram 7.1 The accounting process, highlighting closing entries

During an accounting period, movements in income and expense items are recorded in separate accounts for each type of income and expense, and not entered directly to the owner's capital account. The same applies to distributions, which are also recorded in a separate distributions account. Only contributions by the owner are entered directly into the capital account.

The closing entries serve the purpose of transferring the end-of-period balances in the income and expense accounts, as well as the distributions account, to the capital account so that the balance on the capital account in the statement of financial position represents the correct amount of the owner's interest in the business.

7.2.2 Clearing the income, expense and distributions accounts

Processing of closing entries also clears the income, expense and distributions accounts so that the following accounting period can begin with zero balances in those accounts.

As you are aware, the statement of profit or loss reports the profit of a period as being the difference between *income earned* and *expenses incurred*. The information for the income and expense items on the statement of profit or loss is taken from the balances on each income and expense account in the post-adjustment trial balance. These accounts therefore need to be closed at the end of each period so that the following period can begin with zero balances.

The statement of changes in equity reports the opening capital balance, the profit for the period and the amount of the distributions to the owner. The distributions account therefore also needs to be cleared in preparation for the next period.

7.3 Procedure to close the accounts

The balances on the income and expense accounts are transferred to owner's equity through temporary accounts known as the ***trading*** account and the ***profit or loss*** account. These accounts accumulate the income and expenses of the period before transferring the profit (or loss) to the owner's capital account. As mentioned above, the balance on the distributions account is transferred directly to the owner's capital account.

The post-adjustment trial balance, which was used to prepare the financial statements in Chapter 6, is shown below. The accounts which need to be closed off or cleared are highlighted. All other accounts are either the asset or liability accounts, which are not closed off, or the owner's capital account to which the balances on the income, expense and distributions accounts are being transferred.

SMART CONCEPTS
POST-ADJUSTMENT TRIAL BALANCE AT 31 MARCH 20X5

Description	*Folio*	*Dr*	*Cr*
Bank	A1	970 500	
Rent paid in advance	A2	12 000	
Fixed deposit investment	A3	120 000	
Furniture and fittings	A4	228 000	
Stationery supplies	A5	2 000	
Computer parts	A6	3 500	
Inventory	A7	600 000	

Description	*Folio*	*Dr*	*Cr*
Accounts receivable	A8	437 500	
Interest receivable	A9	1 500	
Borrowings	L1		600 000
Accounts payable	L2		750 000
Service fees received in advance	L3		42 000
Water and electricity payable	L4		4 000
Simon Smart capital	OE1		950 000
Distributions	**OE2**	**60 000**	
Sales income	**I1**		**937 500**
Service fees income	**I2**		**6 000**
Interest income	**I3**		**1 500**
Internet expense	**E1**	**1 500**	
Cost of sales expense	**E2**	**750 000**	
Advertising expense	**E3**	**7 000**	
Salaries expense	**E4**	**16 000**	
Interest expense	**E5**	**18 000**	
Rent expense	**E6**	**36 000**	
Water and electricity expense	**E7**	**4 000**	
Stationery supplies expense	**E8**	**3 000**	
Computer parts expense	**E9**	**8 500**	
Depreciation expense	**E10**	**12 000**	
		3 291 000	**3 291 000**

7.3.1 Closing the sales and cost of sales accounts

The accounts relating to the *trading* activities of the entity, namely the sales and cost of sales accounts, need to be closed off to the ***trading account***.

Sales

The income account relevant to the trading activities of an entity is the sales account, which has a right-hand or credit balance. To clear the sales account therefore requires a left-hand or debit entry to the account (by an amount equal to the credit balance), with the credit side of the entry appearing in the trading account.

The only income account on Smart Concepts' trial balance that is relevant to the trading activities of the entity is the sales account.

A	*= L +*	*Owner's equity*			
		Sales (I)		Trading	
		−/L/Dr	+/R/Cr	−/L/Dr	+/R/Cr
Bal			937 500		
c/e		937 500			937 500
					937 500

The balance in the sales account of C937 500 is closed off to the trading account. This requires a debit entry to the sales account of C937 500 and a credit entry to the trading account of the same amount. The balance in the sales account has been reduced to zero and the trading account temporarily shows a balance of C937 500, before the cost of sales account is closed off.

Cost of sales

The expense account relevant to the trading activities of an entity is the cost of sales account, which has a left-hand or debit balance. To clear the cost of sales account therefore requires a right-hand or credit entry to the account (by an amount equal to the debit balance), with the debit side of the entry appearing in the trading account.

The only expense account on Smart Concepts' trial balance that is relevant to the trading activities of the entity is the cost of sales account.

	A	*= L +*	*Owner's equity*			
			Cost of sales (E)		Trading	
			+/L/Dr	*−/R/Cr*	*−/L/Dr*	*+/R/Cr*
Bal						937 500
c/e			750 000	750 000	750 000	
						187 500

The balance in the cost of sales account of C750 000 is closed off to the trading account. This requires a credit entry to the cost of sales account of C750 000 and a debit entry to the trading account of the same amount. The balance in the cost of sales account has been reduced to zero and the trading account temporarily shows a balance of C187 500.

7.3.2 Closing the trading account

After the balances on the sales and cost of sales accounts have been closed off or reduced to zero, the balance on the trading account represents the gross profit. This gross profit is then transferred to the profit or loss account.

	A	*= L +*	*Owner's equity*			
			Trading		Profit or loss	
			−/L/Dr	*+/R/Cr*	*−/L/Dr*	*+/R/Cr*
c/e				937 500		
c/e			750 000			
Bal				187 500		
c/e			187 500			187 500
Bal						187 500

The balance in the trading account of C187 500 is closed off to the profit or loss account. This requires a debit entry to the trading account of C187 500 and a credit entry to the profit or loss account of the same amount. The balance in the trading account has been reduced to zero and the balance in the profit or loss account temporarily shows a balance of C187 500 before the other income and expense accounts are closed off.

7.3.3 Closing the other income and expense accounts

We have already closed off the income and expense accounts relating to the *trading* activities of the entity. You will recall that these accounts are the sales account and the cost of sales account. The next step in the process is to close off the other income and expense accounts.

Income accounts

All income accounts have right-hand or credit balances, therefore to clear an income account requires a left-hand or debit entry to the relevant income account (by an amount equal to the credit balance), with the credit side of the entry appearing in the profit or loss account. The only remaining income accounts on Smart Concepts' trial balance are the service fees account and the interest account.

A = *L* +	*Owner's equity*					
	Service fees (I)		Interest (I)		Profit or loss	
	−/*L*/*Dr*	+/*R*/*Cr*	−/*L*/*Dr*	+/*R*/*Cr*	−/*L*/*Dr*	+/*R*/*Cr*
Bal		6 000		1 500		187 500
c/e	6 000		1 500			7 500
						195 000

The service fees and interest accounts are reduced by C6 000 and C1 500 respectively with debit entries. The total amount of C7 500 is transferred to the credit side of the profit or loss account. The balances in both income accounts have been reduced to zero and the profit or loss account temporarily shows a balance of C195 000, before the expense items are closed off.

Expense accounts

All expense accounts have left-hand or debit balances, therefore to clear an expense account requires a right-hand or credit entry to the relevant expense account (by an amount equal to the debit balance), with the debit side of the entry appearing in the profit or loss account.

There are a number of remaining expense accounts on Smart Concepts' trial balance, namely petrol, advertising, salaries, interest, rent, water and electricity, office supplies, parts supplies and depreciation.

A = *L* +									*Owner's equity*											
	Internet (E)		*Advertising (E)*		*Salaries (E)*		*Interest (E)*		*Rent (E)*		*Water and electricity (E)*		*Stationery supplies (E)*		*Computer parts (E)*		*Depreciation (E)*		*Profit or loss*	
	Dr	*Cr*	*Dr*	*Cr*	*Dr*	*Cr*	*Dr*	*Cr*	*Dr*	*Cr*	*Dr*	*Cr*	*Dr*	*Cr*	*Dr*	*Cr*	*Dr*	*Cr*	*Dr*	*Cr*
Bal	1.5		7		16		18		36		4		3		8.5		12			195
c/e		1.5		7		16		18		36		4		3		8.5		12	106	
																				89

The amounts above have been rounded to C000s. All the expense accounts are reduced by the amount of the balance in the respective accounts with credit entries. The total expenses of C106 000 are transferred to the debit side of the profit or loss account. The balances in all the expense accounts have been reduced to zero and the profit or loss account temporarily shows a balance of C89 000, after the expense items are closed off.

7.3.4 Closing the profit or loss account

After the balances on the income and expense accounts have been closed off or reduced to zero, the balance on the profit or loss account represents the profit or loss for the period. Where income exceeds expenses, the profit or loss account will reflect a credit balance representing the profit for the period. Conversely, where expenses exceed income, the profit or loss account will show a debit balance representing the net loss for the period.

A = *L* +	*Owner's equity*			
	Profit or loss		Capital (OE)	
	–/*L*/*Dr*	+/*R*/*Cr*	–/*L*/*Dr*	+/*R*/*Cr*
Bal				950 000
c/e (Gross profit)		187 500		
c/e (Other income)		7 500		
c/e (Other expenses)	106 000			
Bal		89 000		
c/e	89 000			89 000
Bal				1 039 000

The balance in the profit or loss account is closed off to the owner's capital account. This requires a debit entry to the profit or loss account of C89 000 and a credit entry to the owner's capital account of the same amount. The balance in the profit or loss account has been reduced to zero and the balance in the owner's capital account increased by the profit for the period.

Recall that in Chapter 2, we described equity as the owner's interest in the business. When we processed the transactions for Simon Smart's business on a conceptual level, we added the profit for the period to the owner's equity, as it increases the owner's interest in the business. We have now reached the same point in the accounting process, with the profit being transferred from the profit or loss account to the owner's capital account.

7.3.5 Closing the distributions account

The distributions account has a left-hand or debit balance, therefore to reduce this account to zero and to transfer the distributions for the period to the owner's capital account requires a right-hand or credit entry to the distributions account (by an amount equal to the debit balance), with the debit side of the entry posted to the owner's capital account.

	A	= *L* +	*Owner's equity*			
			Distributions (OE)		Capital (OE)	
			+/*L*/*Dr*	−/*R*/*Cr*	−/*L*/*Dr*	+/*R*/*Cr*
Bal			60 000			1 039 000
c/e				60 000	60 000	
Bal						979 000

 The distributions account is reduced by C60 000 with a credit entry. This amount is transferred to the debit side of the owner's capital account. The balance on the capital account is now C979 000, the amount that will appear on the statement of financial position.

Having closed off the distributions account, the balance on the capital account is now fully representative of the equity of the business. All the transactions affecting equity – contributions by the owner, earning of income, incurrence of expenses and distributions to the owner – have now been incorporated in the capital account. It is important that you do not lose sight of these concepts when processing data through the journals and ledger.

7.4 Processing of closing entries at the end of the period

The previous section provided a conceptual explanation of the closing entries and their impact on equity. As with the adjusting entries, the closing entries need to be entered in the general journal and posted to the general ledger. This is the last step in the accounting process, and the last phase of the year-end procedures.

Example: Processing of closing entries at the end of the period

This example takes the trial balance of Smart Concepts, prepared *after* the adjusting entries have been processed, and shows the mechanics of entering the closing entries in the journal and posting to the ledger. The same trial balance that was used for the conceptual explanation above is reproduced here.

SMART CONCEPTS
POST-ADJUSTMENT TRIAL BALANCE AT 31 MARCH 20X5

Description	*Folio*	*Dr*	*Cr*
Bank	A1	970 500	
Rent paid in advance	A2	12 000	
Fixed deposit investment	A3	120 000	
Furniture and fittings	A4	228 000	
Stationery supplies	A5	2 000	
Computer parts	A6	3 500	
Inventory	A7	600 000	
Accounts receivable	A8	437 500	
Interest receivable	A9	1 500	
Borrowings	L1		600 000

Description	*Folio*	*Dr*	*Cr*
Accounts payable	L2		750 000
Service fees received in advance	L3		42 000
Water and electricity payable	L4		4 000
Simon Smart capital	OE1		950 000
Distributions	**OE2**	**60 000**	
Sales income	**I1**		**937 500**
Service fees income	**I2**		**6 000**
Interest income	**I3**		**1 500**
Internet expense	**E1**	**1 500**	
Cost of sales expense	**E2**	**750 000**	
Advertising expense	**E3**	**7 000**	
Salaries expense	**E4**	**16 000**	
Interest expense	**E5**	**18 000**	
Rent expense	**E6**	**36 000**	
Water and electricity expense	**E7**	**4 000**	
Stationery supplies expense	**E8**	**3 000**	
Computer parts expense	**E9**	**8 500**	
Depreciation expense	**E10**	**12 000**	
		3 291 000	3 291 000

You are required to:

Enter the closing entries in the general journal of Smart Concepts and post to the general ledger.

 Solution: Processing of closing entries at the end of the period

When journalising the closing entries, you should bear in mind the objective, which is to transfer to the owner's capital account the effects of the income, expenses and distributions for the period.

As there are likely to be a number of income and expense items, the closing entries are usually made in the form of cumulative journal entries, as demonstrated below.

GENERAL JOURNAL OF SMART CONCEPTS (GJ4)

Date	*Description*	*Fol*	*Dr*	*Cr*
20X5				
March				
31	Sales income (I)	I1	937 500	
	Trading (T*)	T		937 500
	Closing entry for trading income item			
31	Trading (T)	T	750 000	
	Cost of sales (E)	E2		750 000
	Closing entry for trading expense item			
31	Trading (T)	T	187 500	
	Profit or loss (T*)	PL		187 500
	Transfer of gross profit to profit or loss			

GENERAL JOURNAL OF SMART CONCEPTS (GJ4)

Date	*Description*	*Fol*	*Dr*	*Cr*
31	Service fees income (I)	I2	6 000	
	Interest income(I)	I3	1 500	
	Profit or loss (T)	PL		7 500
	Closing entry for other income items			
31	Profit or loss (T)	PL	106 000	
	Internet expense (E)	E1		1 500
	Advertising expense (E)	E3		7 000
	Salaries expense (E)	E4		16 000
	Interest expense (E)	E5		18 000
	Rent expense (E)	E6		36 000
	Water and electricity expense (E)	E7		4 000
	Stationery supplies expense (E)	E8		3 000
	Computer parts expense (E)	E9		8 500
	Depreciation expense (E)	E10		12 000
	Closing entry for other expense items			
31	Profit or loss (T)	PL	89 000	
	Capital (OE)	OE1		89 000
	Transfer of profit to capital			
31	Simon Smart capital (OE)	OE1	60 000	
	Distributions (OE)	OE2		60 000
	Transfer of distributions to capital			

* Temporary account.

Dr **SALES INCOME (GL I1)** *Cr*

Date	*Details*	*Fol*	*C*	*Date*	*Details*	*Fol*	*C*
31/03	Balance	c/d	937 500	25/01	Accounts receivable	GJ1	187 500
				12/02	Bank	GJ2	375 000
				29/03	Accounts receivable	GJ2	375 000
			937 500				937 500
31/03	**Trading**	**GJ4**	**937 500**	31/03	Balance	b/d	937 500

Dr **SERVICE FEES INCOME (GL I2)** *Cr*

Date	*Details*	*Fol*	*C*	*Date*	*Details*	*Fol*	*C*
31/03	Balance	c/d	6 000	31/03	Service fees received in advance	GJ3	6 000
			6 000				6 000
31/03	**Profit or loss**	**GJ4**	**6 000**	31/03	Balance	b/d	6 000

Dr			INTEREST INCOME (GL I3)				*Cr*
Date	*Details*	*Fol*	*C*	*Date*	*Details*	*Fol*	*C*
31/03	Balance	c/d	1 500	31/03	Interest receivable	GJ3	1 500
			1 500				1 500
31/03	**Profit or loss**	**GJ4**	**1 500**	31/03	Balance	b/d	1 500

Dr			INTERNET EXPENSE (GL E1)				*Cr*
Date	*Details*	*Fol*	*C*	*Date*	*Details*	*Fol*	*C*
12/01	Bank	GJ1	750	31/03	Balance	c/d	1 500
05/03	Bank	GJ2	750				
			1 500				1 500
31/03	Balance	b/d	1 500	**31/03**	**Profit or loss**	**GJ4**	**1 500**

Dr			COST OF SALES EXPENSE (GL E2)				*Cr*
Date	*Details*	*Fol*	*C*	*Date*	*Details*	*Fol*	*C*
25/02	Inventory	GJ1	150 000	31/03	Balance	c/d	750 000
12/02	Inventory	GJ2	300 000				
29/03	Inventory	GJ2	300 000				
			750 000				750 000
31/03	Balance	b/d	750 000	**31/03**	**Trading**	**GJ4**	**750 000**

Dr			ADVERTISING EXPENSE (GL E3)				*Cr*
Date	*Details*	*Fol*	*C*	*Date*	*Details*	*Fol*	*C*
08/02	Bank	GJ2	7 000				
				31/03	Balance	c/d	7 000
			7 000				7 000
31/03	Balance	b/d	7 000	**31/03**	**Profit or loss**	**GJ4**	**7 000**

Dr			SALARIES EXPENSE (GL E4)				*Cr*
Date	*Details*	*Fol*	*C*	*Date*	*Details*	*Fol*	*C*
28/02	Bank	GJ2	8 000	31/03	Balance	c/d	16 000
30/03	Bank	GJ2	8 000				
			16 000				16 000
31/03	Balance	b/d	16 000	**31/03**	**Profit or loss**	**GJ4**	**16 000**

Dr				INTEREST EXPENSE (GL E5)			*Cr*
Date	*Details*	*Fol*	*C*	*Date*	*Details*	*Fol*	*C*
30/03	Bank	GJ2	18 000	31/03	Balance	c/d	18 000
			18 000				18 000
31/03	Balance	b/d	18 000	**31/03**	**Profit or loss**	**GJ4**	**18 000**

Dr				RENT EXPENSE (GL E6)			*Cr*
Date	*Details*	*Fol*	*C*	*Date*	*Details*	*Fol*	*C*
31/03	Rent paid in advance	GJ3	36 000	31/03	Balance	c/d	36 000
			36 000				36 000
31/03	Balance	b/d	36 000	**31/03**	**Profit or loss**	**GJ4**	**36 000**

Dr				WATER AND ELECTRICITY EXPENSE (GL E7)			*Cr*
Date	*Details*	*Fol*	*C*	*Date*	*Details*	*Fol*	*C*
31/03	Water and electricity liability	GJ3	4 000	31/03	Balance	c/d	4 000
			4 000				4 000
31/03	Balance	b/d	4 000	**31/03**	**Profit or loss**	**GJ4**	**4 000**

Dr				STATIONERY SUPPLIES EXPENSE (GL E8)			*Cr*
Date	*Details*	*Fol*	*C*	*Date*	*Details*	*Fol*	*C*
31/03	Stationery supplies	GJ3	3 000	31/03	Balance	c/d	3 000
			3 000				3 000
31/03	Balance	b/d	3 000	**31/03**	**Profit or loss**	**GJ4**	**3 000**

Dr				COMPUTER PARTS EXPENSE (GL E9)			*Cr*
Date	*Details*	*Fol*	*C*	*Date*	*Details*	*Fol*	*C*
31/03	Computer parts	GJ3	8 500	31/03	Balance	c/d	8 500
			8 500				8 500
31/03	Balance	b/d	8 500	**31/03**	**Profit or loss**	**GJ4**	**8 500**

Dr **DEPRECIATION EXPENSE (GL E10)** *Cr*

Date	*Details*	*Fol*	*C*	*Date*	*Details*	*Fol*	*C*
31/03	Furniture and fittings	GJ3	12 000	31/03	Balance	c/d	12 000
			12 000				12 000
31/03	Balance	b/d	12 000	**31/03**	**Profit or loss**	**GJ4**	**12 000**

Dr **TRADING (GL T)** *Cr*

Date	*Details*	*Fol*	*C*	*Date*	*Details*	*Fol*	*C*
31/03	**Cost of sales**	**GJ4**	**750 000**	**31/3**	**Sales revenue**	**GJ4**	**937 500**
31/03	**Profit or loss**	**GJ4**	**187 500**				
			937 500				937 500

Dr **PROFIT OR LOSS (GL PL)** *Cr*

Date	*Details*	*Fol*	*C*	*Date*	*Details*	*Fol*	*C*
31/03	**Internet expense**	**GJ4**	**1 500**	**31/03**	**Trading**	**GJ4**	**187 500**
31/03	**Advertising expense**	**GJ4**	**7 000**	**31/03**	**Service fees income**	**GJ4**	**6 000**
31/03	**Salaries expense**	**GJ4**	**16 000**	**31/03**	**Interest income**	**GJ4**	**1 500**
31/03	**Interest expense**	**GJ4**	**18 000**				
31/03	**Rent expense**	**GJ4**	**36 000**				
31/03	**Water and electricity expense**	**GJ4**	**4 000**				
31/03	**Stationery supplies expense**	**GJ4**	**3 000**				
31/03	**Computer parts expense**	**GJ4**	**8 500**				
31/03	**Depreciation expense**	**GJ4**	**12 000**				
31/03	**Capital**	**GJ4**	**89 000**				
			195 000				195 000

Dr **DISTRIBUTIONS (GL OE2)** *Cr*

Date	*Details*	*Fol*	*C*	*Date*	*Details*	*Fol*	*C*
30/03	Bank	GJ2	60 000	31/03	Balance	c/d	60 000
			60 000				60 000
31/03	Balance	b/d	60 000	**31/03**	**Simon Smart capital**	**GJ4**	**60 000**

Dr		**SIMON SMART CAPITAL (GL OE1)**					*Cr*
Date	*Details*	*Fol*	*C*	*Date*	*Details*	*Fol*	*C*
				02/01	Bank	GJ1	950 000
31/03	Balance	c/d	950 000				
			950 000				950 000
31/03	**Distributions**	**GJ4**	**60 000**	31/03	Balance	b/d	950 000
31/03	Balance	c/d	979 000	**31/03**	**Profit or loss**	**GJ4**	**89 000**
			1 039 000				1 039 000
				01/04	Balance	b/d	979 000

You will notice that all the income and expense accounts have zero balances, as does the distributions account. The only accounts with balances at this stage are the statement of financial position asset and liability accounts, and the owner's capital account. The accounting process for the current period is complete and a final post-closing entry trial balance can be drawn up to ensure that there were no bookkeeping errors in the processing of the closing entries.

SMART CONCEPTS
POST-CLOSING TRIAL BALANCE AT 31 MARCH 20X5

Description	*Folio*	*Dr*	*Cr*
Bank	A1	970 500	
Rent paid in advance	A2	12 000	
Fixed deposit investment	A3	120 000	
Furniture and fittings	A4	228 000	
Stationery supplies	A5	2 000	
Computer parts	A6	3 500	
Inventory	A7	600 000	
Accounts receivable	A8	437 500	
Interest receivable	A9	1 500	
Borrowings	L1		600 000
Accounts payable	L2		750 000
Service fees received in advance	L3		42 000
Water and electricity payable	L4		4 000
Capital	OE1		979 000
Distributions	**OE2**	—	
Sales income	**I1**		—
Service fees income	**I2**		—
Interest income	**I3**		—
Internet expense	**E1**	—	
Cost of sales expense	**E2**	—	
Advertising expense	**E3**	—	
Salaries expense	**E4**	—	
Interest expense	**E5**	—	
Rent expense	**E6**	—	
Water and electricity expense	**E7**	—	
Stationery supplies expense	**E8**	—	
Computer parts expense	**E9**	—	
Depreciation expense	**E10**	—	
		2 375 000	2 375 000

7.5 Treatment of accrued items in the following period

Having completed the accounting process for one period, it is appropriate to consider the impact, if any, that the internal transactions or adjusting entries at the end of one period will have on the recording of transactions in the following period.

You will recall from Chapter 5 that the adjusting entries are classified according to the relationship between cash received and income, and cash paid and expenses. When cash is received in advance of the earning of income and a liability is recorded on receipt of the cash, the adjusting entry transfers the amount *earned* to an income account, leaving the amount *unearned* in the liability account. This process will continue each period until the income has been earned and the liability reduced to zero. No special treatment is required in this situation at the beginning of the following period.

When cash is paid in advance of the incurrence of expenses and an asset recorded on payment of the cash, the adjusting entry transfers the amount incurred to an expense account, leaving the amount prepaid in the asset account. This process will continue each period until the expense has been incurred and the asset reduced to zero. Again, no special treatment is required in this situation at the beginning of the following period.

7.5.1 Income receivable (accrued income)

However, where the cash receipt is outstanding at the period end and the income has already been earned, the adjusting entry creates an asset in respect of the income receivable and recognises the income that has been earned during the period. This income will be received in cash at some time during the following period and the relevant income account will then be credited, as with all other receipts of this nature. You should now realise that this will result in double counting the income adjusted at the end of the previous period. It is for this reason that income receivable is reversed at the beginning of the new period. Consider the accrual of the interest revenue at the end of March in the Smart Concepts example.

		Dr	*Cr*
31/03/X5	Interest receivable (A)	1 500	
	Interest income (I)		1 500
	Recognition of income receivable		

The income of C1 500 is correctly recognised as earned for the period ended 31 March 20X5. Assume that no reversing entry is processed and that on 30 June 20X5 the interest for the quarter ended 31 March of C1 500 as well as the interest for the quarter ended 30 June of C1 500 is received from the bank. The receipt of the interest will be recorded as follows:

		Dr	*Cr*
30/06/X5	Bank (A)	3 000	
	Interest income (I)		3 000

The result of these two entries is that the interest income for the period from 1 April to 30 June is C3 000. To avoid this situation arising, a reversing entry is recorded at the beginning of each new period, so that when the cash is received it does not result in the double counting of the income. The reversing entry is recorded as follows:

		Dr	*Cr*
01/04/X5	Interest income (I)	1 500	
	Interest receivable (A)		1 500
	Reversal of asset at end of previous period		

Taking into account the two entries shown above, the interest income for the three-month period ended 30 June 20X5 is C1 500 (C3 000 – C1 500).

 **Pause and reflect...**

Is there a different way that we could ensure the interest income is allocated to the correct period?

Response

The reversing entry could be avoided if the receipt of the accrued income is specifically identified, and the asset credited upon receipt of the cash in the subsequent period (and not the income). The net effect of these entries can be illustrated as follows:

		Dr	*Cr*
30/06/X5	Bank	3 000	
	Interest receivable (A)		1 500
	Interest income (I)		1 500
	Receipt of cash for interest receivable at 31/03/X5 and for interest income for the period ended 30/06/X5		

7.5.2 Expenses payable (accrued expenses)

Following the same logic, where the cash payment is outstanding at the period end and the expense has already been incurred, the adjusting entry creates a liability in respect of the expense payable and recognises the expense that has been incurred during the period. This expense will be paid in cash at some time during the following period and, when paid, the relevant expense account will be debited, as with all other expenses of this nature. Again, you should realise that this will result in double counting the expense adjusted at the end of the previous period. It is for this reason that accrued expenses are reversed at the beginning of the new period. Consider here the accrual of the water and electricity expense at the end of March in the Smart Concepts example:

		Dr	*Cr*
31/03/X5	Water and electricity expense (E)	4 000	
	Water and electricity payable (L)		4 000
	Recognition of expenses payable		

The expense of C4 000 is correctly recognised as incurred for the quarter ended 31 March 20X5. Assume that no reversing entry is processed and that during the quarter ended 30 June 20X5 the amount of C4 000 is paid, as well as the amount for that period of, say, C3 000. The payment of the two amounts (on 10 April and 30 June 20X5 respectively) will be recorded as follows:

		Dr	*Cr*
10/04/X5	Water and electricity expense (E)	4 000	
	Bank (A)		4 000
	Payment of liability at 31/03/X5		
30/06/X5	Water and electricity expense (E)	3 000	
	Bank (A)		3 000
	Payment of expense for three months ended 30/06/X5		

The result of these two entries is that the water and electricity expense for the period from 1 April 20X5 to 30 June 20X5 is C7 000. To avoid this situation arising, a reversing entry is recorded at the beginning of each new period, so that when the cash is paid it does not result in the double counting of the expense. The reversing entry is recorded as follows:

		Dr	*Cr*
01/04/X5	Water and electricity payable (L)	4 000	
	Water and electricity expense (E)		4 000
	Reversal of liability at end of previous period		

Taking into account the three entries shown above, the water and electricity expense for the three-month period ended 30 June 20X5 is C3 000 (C7 000 − C4 000).

Pause and reflect...

Is there a different way that we could ensure the water and electricity expense is allocated to the correct period?

Response

The reversing entry could be avoided if the payment of the accrued expense is specifically identified and the *liability* debited upon payment of the accrual (and not the expense). The net effect of these entries can be illustrated as follows:

		Dr	*Cr*
10/04/X5	Water and electricity payable (L)	4 000	
	Bank (A)		4 000
	Payment of cash for water and electricity payable at 31/03/X5		
30/06/X5	Water and electricity expense (E)	3 000	
	Bank (A)		3 000
	Payment of cash for water and electricity expense for the period ended 30/06/X5		

Revision example

Daisy Davis is retired. She decided at the beginning of last spring to enter the business of landscaping small courtyard gardens. The business trades under the name of The Yellow Daisy and the financial year end of the business is 31 March.

On 1 October 20X8, Daisy paid C24 000 into the business bank account. She then purchased gardening tools and equipment for the business at a total cost of C28 000. She paid cash for the tools and equipment, utilising part of the cash invested and borrowed C8 000 at an interest rate of 15 per cent per annum from a bank. It is estimated that the tools and equipment can be sold for C2 400 at the end of their useful life of two years.

Daisy Davis uses public transport to visit client's homes and hires a small van when she needs to transport larger quantities of plants and soil.

In order to exercise control over the financial affairs of her business, Daisy prepares a trial balance at the end of every quarter. Closing entries are processed at the end of the financial year when financial statements are prepared.

Details of transactions for the first six months of trading are as shown below. All amounts relate to the relevant period.

	01/10/X8–31/12/X8	*01/01/X9–31/03/X9*
	C	*C*
Fees invoiced on credit	49 600	45 200
Receipts from clients	46 400	48 400
Wages paid	4 400	4 800
Office costs paid	400	800
Transport and van hire costs paid	2 000	2 000
Supplies purchased on credit	4 800	2 000
Repayment of loan	4 000	4 000
Payment of accounts payable	4 000	2 800
Distribution to owner	31 300	24 500

The following additional information is relevant:

- Upon enquiry, Daisy visits the client's home and provides a free quote. She sends out invoices upon completion of the landscaping work.
- At the end of March 20X9, thieves stole Daisy's gardening tools and equipment. The insurance company agreed to pay out C17 200, which was received early in May 20X9.
- Supplies on hand at 31 December 20X8 amounted to C2 000. There were no supplies on hand at 31 March 20X9.
- The loan is repayable in equal instalments on 31 December 20X8 and 31 March 20X9. Interest on the loan is payable quarterly in arrears on 1 January and 1 April.

You are required to:

a) Prepare a post-adjustment trial balance of The Yellow Daisy at 31 December 20X8.
b) Record all the closing entries in the journal of The Yellow Daisy at 31 March 20X9.
c) Prepare the statement of changes in equity of The Yellow Daisy for the six months ended 31 March 20X9.
d) Prepare the statement of financial position of The Yellow Daisy at 31 March 20X9.

 **Solution: Revision example**

a) Post-adjustment trial balance

THE YELLOW DAISY
POST-ADJUSTMENT TRIAL BALANCE AT 31 DECEMBER 20X8

		Dr	*Cr*
Bank	*(24 000 + 8 000 − 28 000 + 46 400 − 4 400 − 400 − 2 000 − 4 000 − 4 000 − 31 300)*	4 300	
Tools and equipment	*(28 000 − 3 200)*	24 800	
Accounts receivable	*(49 600 − 46 400)*	3 200	
Supplies		2 000	

		Dr	*Cr*
Loan	*(8 000 – 4 000)*		4000
Accounts payable	*(4 800 – 4 000)*		800
Interest payable	*(8 000 × 0.15 × 3/12)*		300
Fees income			49 600
Wages expense		4 400	
Office expense		400	
Interest expense	*(8 000 × 0.15 × 3/12)*	300	
Supplies expense	*(4 800 – 2 000)*	2 800	
Depreciation expense	*(28 000 – 2 400) × 3/24*	3 200	
Transport and van hire expense		2 000	
Capital			24 000
Distributions		31 300	
		78 700	78 700

b) Closing entries at 31 March 20X9

THE YELLOW DAISY
JOURNAL

Description	*Workings*	*Dr*	*Cr*
Fees income (I)	*(49 600 + 45 200)*	94 800	
Profit or loss (T)			94 800
Closing entry for income			
Profit or loss (T)		32 450	
Wages expense (E)	*(4 400 + 4 800)*		9 200
Office expense (E)	*(400 + 800)*		1 200
Supplies expense (E)	*[2 800 + (2 000 + 2000 – 0)]*		6 800
Depreciation expense (E)	*(3 200 + 3 200)*		6 400
Loss on tools and equipment (E)	*(21 600* – 17 200)*		4 400
	**(28 000 – 3 200 – 3 200)*		
Interest expense (E)	*(300 + 150*)*		450
	**[(8 000 – 4 000) × 0.15 × 3/12]*		
Transport and van expense (E)	*(2 000 + 2 000)*		4 000
Closing entry for expenses			
Profit or loss	*(94 800 – 32 450)*	62 350	
Capital			62 350
Transfer of profit to capital			
Capital		55 800	
Distributions	*(31 300 + 24 500)*		55 800
Transfer of distributions to capital			

c) Statement of changes in equity

THE YELLOW DAISY
STATEMENT OF CHANGES IN EQUITY
FOR THE SIX MONTHS ENDED 31 MARCH 20X9

	C
Balance at 1 October 20X8	—
Profit for the period	62 350
Distributions	(55 800)
Contribution to capital	24 000
Balance at 31 March 20X9	30 550

d) Statement of financial position

THE YELLOW DAISY
STATEMENT OF FINANCIAL POSITION
AT 31 MARCH 20X9

		C
ASSETS		
Current assets		
Insurance claim receivable		17 200
Bank	*(4 300 − 300 + 48 400 − 4 800 − 800 − 2 000 − 4 000 − 2 800 − 24 500)*	13 500
		30 700
EQUITY AND LIABILITIES		
Equity		
Capital		30 550
Current liabilities		
Interest payable		150
		30 700

Bibliography

Scharff, M. 2005. Understanding WorldCom's accounting fraud: Did Groupthink play a role? *Journal of Leadership and Organizational Studies* 11(3): 109–118.

PART III

The accounting process expanded

8 Purchase and sale transactions

Business focus

Is it possible that images of bookkeepers processing sales transactions on desktops, printing out invoices and attaching them to delivery notes and quotations are becoming clichéd? Accounting software has been quick to take advantage of advances in cloud computing and the proliferation of smartphones and tablets. Sage Evolution Mobile is one example of technology that allows for a completely mobile sales force. Employees have live access to secure client, inventory and business information allowing for 'in the moment' quoting, negotiation of discounts and generation of invoices. Rather than print the invoice, the customer simply signs the tablet or smartphone, triggering the automatic emailing of the invoice to the customer and updating of the sales system. Managers – irrespective of their location – can monitor the activities of their sales consultants, making use of real-time 'dashboards' to keep track of sales volumes, inventory levels, most popular products and accounts receivable balances.

In this chapter

You have already been exposed to purchase and sale transactions in Chapters 2 to 7. However, this was in the context of learning about the analysis of transactions, the accounting equation and the accounting process for the recording of those transactions in a journal and ledger. In this chapter, we go much further and examine some of the issues relating to purchase and sale transactions, such as the perpetual and periodic inventory systems, discounts and returns.

Dashboard

- Look at the *Learning outcomes* so that you know what you should be able to do after studying this chapter.
- Read the *Business focus* to place this chapter's contents in a real-world context.
- Preview *In this chapter* to focus your mind on the contents of this chapter.
- Read the *text* in detail.
  - Pay attention to the *definitions* and apply your mind to the *Pause and reflect* scenarios.
  - As this is a long chapter, the contents have been carefully arranged to enable you to read and study it in manageable portions.

Dashboard (cont.)

- Ensure that you have read and understood Section 8.4 relating to the perpetual system *before* moving on to Section 8.5, which relates to the periodic system.
- When studying the perpetual system in Section 8.4, first focus your attention on Section 8.4.1 (the recording of goods purchased) and once you have understood this, then move onto 8.4.2 (the recording of sales and cost of sales).
- When studying the periodic system in Section 8.5, focus on the similarities between the perpetual and periodic systems, and also the differences, such as the use of a purchases account, the calculation of cost of sales and the closing entries.
- As you read the chapter, take careful note of the treatment of cash discounts, settlement discounts and trade discounts.
- Prepare solutions to the examples as you read through the chapter.
- Prepare solutions to the *Revision examples* at the end of the chapter without reference to the suggested ones. After you have prepared your own solutions, compare them to the suggested solutions provided.

Learning outcomes

After studying this chapter, you should be able to do the following:

1. Compare service and retailing entities.
2. Describe the differences between a perpetual and a periodic inventory system.
3. Record purchase and sale transactions using a perpetual inventory system, including transactions involving settlement discount, cash discount and trade discount.
4. Record purchase and sale transactions using a periodic inventory system, including transactions involving settlement discount, cash discount and trade discount.

Purchase and sale transactions

8.1 The nature of business activities

You will recall from the Smart Concepts example in Parts I and II of this book that computers were purchased and sold, and technical support contracts were offered to customers. The purchase and sale of computers represent the retail aspect of Smart Concepts' business, whereas the technical support contracts represent the service activities of its business. It is appropriate at this stage to briefly review the nature of a service entity as distinct from a retailer. A brief summary of the nature of a retail and service entity, followed by a discussion of a combined entity, is provided below.

8.1.1 Service entity

In this type of business entity, a service is performed for a commission or fee. Profit for the period is the difference between fees or commissions earned and the operating and financing expenses incurred. Remember that operating expenses include all the expenses incurred, such as administration and distribution expenses.

Although a service entity does not hold goods for *resale*, it may indeed hold goods that will be *consumed* in the process of providing services. If such goods are kept on hand, these are referred to as ***supplies*** or sometimes ***inventory of supplies***.

Concepts in context

British Sky Broadcasting Group
(Extract from) Consolidated income statement
For the year ended 30 June 2013

	£m
Revenue	7 235
Operating expenses	(5 944)
Operating profit	1 291

(Extract from) Notes to the consolidated financial statements
For the year ended 30 June 2013

Revenue	**£m**
Retail subscription	5 951
Wholesale subscription	396
Advertising	440
Installation, hardware and service	87
Other (including Sky Bet and public access Wi-Fi)	361
	7 235

What concepts in context can you see here?

Sky is a service entity and, as you have learnt, you do not see a line item for cost of sales in the income statement (or statement of profit or loss). Sky provides a note to revenue detailing the composition of their revenue. As you can see, all the components of revenue involve providing a service.

British Sky Broadcasting Group plc (commonly known as BSkyB and trading as Sky) is a satellite broadcasting, broadband and telephone services company headquartered in London.

Source: corporate.sky.com/documents/publications-and-reports/2013/annual-report-2013.pdf (Accessed 29 June 2016).

8.1.2 Retail entity

As mentioned above, a retail entity is involved in the purchase and sale of goods. Profit from this type of entity is the difference between revenue earned from sales and the *cost of the goods sold* as well as the operating and financing expenses.

As opposed to a service entity, a retail entity does hold a stock of goods for resale. The stock of goods on hand is referred to as ***inventory*** or ***stock*** of the business.

Inventory refers to goods held for resale to customers, or for use in the production of goods held for resale or for use in the provision of services.

Inventory includes, for example, merchandise purchased by a retailer and held for resale. For a manufacturer, inventory would also include raw materials awaiting use in the production process, work in progress being produced and finished goods. As with a service entity, a retailer may also hold goods that are consumed in the process of sale or production as opposed to being held for resale, and are also referred to as *inventory* or *supplies*.

8.1.3 Combining a retail and a service entity

Smart Concepts is an example of a business entity that combines retail (buying and selling computers) and service activities (offering technical support contracts to customers). The retail activity generates an income item, sales revenue, and an expense item – cost of sales. You have learnt in previous chapters that the trading results of such an entity are represented by the gross profit, calculated as the difference between sales and cost of sales. The service activity generates an income item – service revenue. The service revenue is added to the gross profit followed by the deduction of the operating and financing expenses to calculate the profit or loss for the period.

Irrespective of whether the entity's activities involve sales, services or a combination thereof, the entity may also earn other income (e.g. rental income), which needs to be included in the statement of profit or loss before the deduction of operating and financing expenses.

Pause and reflect ...

A business entity has earned revenue from sales of C100 and revenue from services of C50. It also earned rental income of C10 when it rented out an unused portion of its premises. The cost of goods sold amounts to C60, operating expenses amount to C20 and the interest expense amounts to C5. How will this be reported in the statement of profit or loss for the period?

Response

STATEMENT OF PROFIT OR LOSS

	C
Sales revenue	100
Cost of sales	(60)
Gross profit	40
Service revenue	50
Other income	
Rent income	10
Operating expenses	(20)
Finance costs	
Interest expense	(5)
Profit for the period	75

Concepts in context

The Bidvest Group Limited
(Extract from) Notes to the consolidated financial statements
For the year ended 30 June 2013

Revenue	**R000**
Sale of goods	119 925 966
Rendering of services	12 485 927
Commissions and fees earned	1 005 102
Gross billings relating to clearing and forwarding transactions	22 887 951
Insurance	248 253
	156 553 199

What concepts in context can you see here?

Bidvest is an example of a company that provides both goods and services. You can see in the above note that its revenue is derived from the sale of goods, the rendering of services as well as other types of service revenue.

The Bidvest Group Limited is an international investment holding company, headquartered in Johannesburg, South Africa, with investments across the food service, broad services, trading and distribution industries. The group owns or has significant holdings in over 300 companies and operates across five continents.

Source: www.bidvest.com/ar/bidvest_ar2013/pdf/full.pdf (Accessed 20 June 2014).

8.2 Recording sales and purchases of inventory

One of the main issues relating to the purchase and sale of goods is the measurement of the revenue from sales and the measurement of the cost of the inventory purchased.

IFRS 15 *Revenue from Contracts with Customers* requires an entity to determine the transaction price. This reflects an entity's expectations about the consideration to which it will be entitled from the customer.

The transaction price is the amount to which an entity expects to be entitled in exchange for transferring goods or services to a customer, excluding amounts collected on behalf of third parties.

Determining the transaction price in day-to-day retail transactions does not usually present a problem. However, where goods are bought or sold and discounts are involved, this introduces a ***variable consideration*** that needs to be taken into account in determining the transaction price. The definition of a variable consideration in IFRS 15 is wide and far reaching and is beyond the scope of this book. For our purposes, the discussion here is focused on discounts as a form of variable consideration. The discounts could take one of the following forms:

- a settlement discount, where goods are bought or sold on credit and a discount is offered for early settlement;
- a cash discount, offered at the point of purchase or sale;
- a trade discount, also offered at the point of purchase or sale, and normally associated with purchases and sales between a retailer and supplier in a particular industry.

It is very important for you to be able to understand the difference between each of these types of discount and the scenario where each one may arise.

These issues will be examined in detail in the example that follows, after we have discussed perpetual and periodic inventory systems.

8.3 Perpetual and periodic inventory systems

Recording inventory transactions can be done through two different systems – the perpetual inventory system and the periodic inventory system.

8.3.1 Perpetual inventory system

A perpetual inventory system is used by the vast majority of large entities with significant numbers of purchase and sale transactions. The system allows management to have better control over inventory by providing immediate and up-to-date information about inventory on hand.

When a perpetual inventory system is used, the inventory account is updated for all inventory transactions. The inventory account is increased with the cost of goods purchased and is decreased with the cost of goods sold. In theory, the balance on the inventory account reflects the cost of inventory on hand. Owing to theft, however, this balance does not always reflect the actual cost of inventory on hand. This issue is discussed in more detail in Chapter 11, *Inventory and cost of sales*.

The actual physical inventory on hand at the end of the period is counted to verify the accuracy of the balance on the inventory account. This count is often referred to as a 'stock count' or 'stock taking'. This is also explored further in Chapter 11.

After reading the above paragraphs, you should realise that a perpetual inventory system has been used in the Smart Concepts example described in the previous chapters. The use of the perpetual system to record purchase and sale transactions will be explained in detail in Section 8.4 of this chapter.

8.3.2 Periodic inventory system

A periodic inventory system is more suitable to smaller entities that do not have large numbers of purchase and sale transactions. The owner is usually more involved in day-to-day operations and often knows what inventory is on hand at any time.

When a periodic inventory system is used, inventory purchased is recorded in a temporary account, referred to simply as a purchases account. The purchases account only reflects the purchases of goods for resale and is not reduced when goods are sold. In addition to the purchases account, an inventory account is also used, but this is only updated at the end of the period when inventory is physically counted. It is at this time that the cost of goods sold can be determined. The fact that the inventory account is not continuously updated means that it will not reflect the theoretical balance of inventory on hand. The procedure for using a periodic inventory system is explained in detail in Section 8.5 of this chapter.

Pause and reflect . . .

Have you thought about how a perpetual inventory system works when you buy goods from a retail store such as a supermarket?

Response

When you arrive at the checkout counter, you pass the goods you have selected to the checkout assistant, who scans the barcode of each item with an optical scanner. The barcode contains a lot of information relating to the relevant item. Upon scanning the barcode, the accounting system performs the following operations:

- records the sale by debiting bank and crediting sales revenue;
- records the cost of sales, by debiting cost of sales and, at the same time, updates the perpetual inventory records by crediting inventory.

You will recall that a retailer operates by purchasing goods from suppliers and selling them to customers at a marked-up price. The goods that are bought and sold are referred to as inventory. The inventory can be purchased for cash or on credit. We shall now examine the recording of purchase and sale transactions with particular emphasis on the measurement of revenue from sales and purchases of inventory as well as on the differences between a perpetual and a periodic inventory system.

8.4 Recording of purchase and sale transactions using a perpetual inventory system

Simon Smart has a second business entity, Sharp Moves, which focuses on the fast-growing market for mobile computing, and sells a range of tablets, mobile phones and accessories. The activities of Sharp Moves will be used to illustrate the recording of purchase and sale transactions using the perpetual system, as well as to compare the perpetual and periodic inventory systems.

The summarised post-closing trial balance of Sharp Moves at 31 May 20X5 is as follows:

SHARP MOVES
TRIAL BALANCE AT 31 MAY 20X5

Description	*Dr*	*Cr*
Inventory	240	
Bank	2 600	
Owner's equity		2 840
	2 840	2 840

Listed below are the transactions of Sharp Moves for the month of June 20X5. Please note when reading through these transactions that transactions 3 and 8 include two possible *alternatives*.

#	*Date*	*Transaction*	*C*
		Opening inventory and purchases	
–	01/06/X5	Opening inventory consists of 4 items at a cost of C60 each	240
1	04/06/X5	Purchased 15 items at C60 each on account from Mobile Magic. Mobile Magic does not offer settlement discounts	900
2	08/06/X5	Purchased 20 items at C62.50 each on account from Plug & Go Limited, which allows a 4 per cent settlement discount if payment is received within 15 days	1 250 (50) 1 200
3a	23/06/X5	Paid Plug & Go Limited the amount owing to them *within the settlement discount period*, taking advantage of the settlement discount	1 200
3b	24/06/X5	Paid Plug & Go Limited the amount owing to them *after the settlement discount period*	1 250
4	25/06/X5	Purchased 20 items at C75 each for cash. Received a 20 per cent discount for paying cash	1 500 (300) 1 200
5	30/06/X5	Purchased 100 items on account from Digital World. The normal selling price from Digital World is C75 an item. Sharp Moves is a good customer, so Digital World grants a trade discount of 20 per cent	7 500 (1 500) 6 000
		Sales	
6	06/06/X5	Sold 2 items at C100 each on credit. No discount was offered to the customers. The cost of the 2 items was C60 each	200
7	09/06/X5	Sold 15 items at C100 each on account to a customer. Sharp Moves allows a 5 per cent settlement discount if payment is received within 15 days. The cost of the 15 items was C60 each	1 500 (75) 1 425
8a	24/06/X5	Received from the customer in transaction 7 the amount owing by him *within the settlement discount period*, taking advantage of the settlement discount	1 425
8b	25/06/X5	Received from the customer in transaction 7 the amount owing by him *after the settlement discount period*	1 500
9	27/06/X5	Sold 20 items at C100 each for cash. The customers were offered a cash discount of 5 per cent. The cost of the 20 items was C60 each	2 000 (100) 1 900

#	Date	Transaction	C
10	30/06/X5	Sold 75 items on account to Fleet Street Computers. The normal selling price is C100 each. Fleet Street Computers is a good customer and is allowed a 20 per cent trade discount on all purchases. The cost of the 75 items was C60 each	7 500 (1 500) 6 000
		Operating expenses	
11	30/06/X5	Administration expenses amounted to C1 200	
12	30/06/X5	Marketing and selling expenses amounted to C1 400	

You will notice that the cost per item in this example is a constant C60. This has been done in order to be able to illustrate some important concepts relating to the purchase and sale of inventory. In Chapter 11, you will come across examples where the cost per item of inventory is not constant.

8.4.1 The recording of goods purchased

In the following paragraphs, we are going to describe how Sharp Moves records transactions relating to the purchase of inventory, assuming a **perpetual inventory system** is used. We will also focus on the purchase of inventory where discounts are concerned.

The perpetual inventory system takes its name from the fact that the inventory account is perpetually up to date – that is, the cost of inventory on hand is known at any point in time. As you already know, the inventory account is updated after each purchase and sale of inventory, the cost of the goods sold being recorded at the time of sale. The balance on the inventory account must be verified against physical inventory figures.

Credit purchases and settlement discount

A retail entity does not usually purchase its inventory for cash. It is normal practice for the entity to open an account with its suppliers. The buying department is responsible for selecting suppliers to supply the entity with inventory and will negotiate the best prices and payment terms with them.

Suppliers may offer a settlement discount to encourage early payment of the account, and this is indicated on the invoice as part of the terms of payment. Potential settlement discounts receivable have to be estimated at the date of purchase and the cost of the inventory purchased should be reduced accordingly.

The settlement discount offered by a supplier serves as an incentive for the purchasing entity to pay early. If the purchasing entity does not pay within the given settlement period, the settlement discount that it forfeits is regarded as a cost of financing.

The total amount payable therefore includes a potential interest expense. In other words, the amount payable to the supplier (100 per cent) includes a financing component (say 4 per cent), which is only recognised if the payment to the supplier is not made within the specified period. The purchase of inventory is therefore recognised at the fair value at the transaction date, being 96 per cent of the amount payable.

Pause and reflect ...

Can you think of the journal entry in the accounting records of the purchasing entity if goods are purchased from a supplier for C100 with a 4 per cent settlement discount offered for early payment?

Response

Dr Inventory (A) 96
Dr Settlement discount allowance (–L) 4
Cr Accounts payable (L) 100

Let us now start analysing the transactions of Sharp Moves relating to the purchase of inventory.

Transaction 1 *04/06/X5* *Purchased 15 items at C60 each on account from Mobile Magic. Mobile Magic does not offer settlement discounts.*

1	*Assets*		=	*Liabilities*		+ *Owner's equity*
	Inventory			Accounts payable		
	+/L/Dr	−/R/Cr		−/L/Dr	+/R/Cr	
	900				900	

This transaction for the purchase of inventory is similar to the ones that you analysed in the Smart Concepts example. There is a debit entry to the inventory account on the left side of the equation, and a credit entry to the accounts payable account on the right side of the equation.

Transaction 2 *08/06/X5* *Purchased 20 items at C62.50 each on account from Plug & Go Limited which allows a 4 per cent settlement discount if payment is received within 15 days.*

Look closely at transaction 2. Do you see how it differs from transaction 1? In transaction 2, the supplier allows a settlement discount and this is going to affect how the purchase of inventory is recorded.

2	*Assets*		=	*Liabilities*				+ *Owner's equity*
	Inventory			Settlement discount allowance		Accounts payable		
	+/L/Dr	−/R/Cr		+/L/Dr	−/R/Cr	−/L/Dr	+/R/Cr	
	1 200			50			1 250	

The inventory purchased is recorded as an asset at its cost of C1 200 and therefore the inventory account is increased with a debit entry on the left side of the equation. The inventory was purchased on credit from Plug & Go Limited. The accounts payable account is increased with a credit entry on the right side of the equation by the full amount of the obligation owing to Plug & Go Limited. The potential settlement discount is recorded with a debit entry as a contra-liability, as a settlement discount allowance.

As you have seen above, the potential settlement discount offered by the supplier was recorded with a debit entry to a settlement discount allowance account at the date of purchase. Although it has a debit balance, the settlement discount allowance account is neither an asset nor an expense. It is a measurement account relating to the liability, accounts payable, and the two accounts together (the accounts payable with a credit balance of C1 250 and the settlement discount allowance with a debit balance of C50) represent the fair value of the transaction.

Pause and reflect . . .

Assuming that Sharp Moves prepares a statement of financial position immediately after the above transaction, how would the amount owing to Plug & Go Limited be reported?

Response

It will be reported as a current liability, accounts payable, at an amount of C1 200 (1 250 − 50).

Two scenarios now exist:

a) If the supplier **is paid within the settlement discount period**, the purchasing entity is *granted the settlement discount* and would not have obtained finance from the supplier. The settlement discount allowance is thus reversed on settlement of the amount owing (transaction 3a below).
b) On the other hand, if the supplier **is not paid within the settlement period**, the purchasing entity *forfeits the settlement discount* and the substance of the transaction is that the purchasing entity obtained finance from the supplier (transaction 3b below).

Transaction 3a *23/06/X5* *Paid Plug & Go Limited amount owing to them within the settlement discount period, taking advantage of the 4 per cent settlement discount.*

3a	*Assets*		=	*Liabilities*			+ *Owner's equity*
	Bank			Settlement discount allowance		Accounts payable	
	+/L/Dr	−/R/Cr	+/L/Dr	−/R/Cr	−/L/Dr	+/R/Cr	
Balance			50			1 250	
3a		1 200		50	1 250		

The invoiced amount owing to Plug & Go Limited was C1 250, therefore the accounts payable account is reduced by a debit entry of C1 250 to reflect that the obligation has been settled. The amount of cash paid to settle the account was C1 200 as Sharp Moves took advantage of the 4 per cent settlement discount offered by Plug & Go Limited. The bank account is reduced by this amount with a credit entry on the left side of the equation. As the amount was paid within the settlement period, there is no finance expense and the settlement discount allowance is reversed with a credit of C50.

Transaction 3b *24/06/X5* *Paid Plug & Go Limited amount owing to them after the settlement discount period.*

3b	*Assets*		=	*Liabilities*				+	*Owner's equity*
	Bank			Settlement discount allowance		Accounts payable		Interest expense	
	+/L/Dr	*−/R/Cr*		*+/L/Dr*	*−/R/Cr*	*−/L/Dr*	*+/R/Cr*	*+/L/Dr*	*−/R/Cr*
Balance				50			1 250		
3b		1 250				1 250			
3b					50			50	

The amount owing to Plug & Go Limited was C1 250, therefore the accounts payable account is reduced with a debit entry of C1 250 to reflect that the obligation has been settled. The amount of cash paid to settle the account was C1 250 as Sharp Moves did not take advantage of the 4 per cent settlement discount offered by Plug & Go Limited. The bank account is reduced by this amount with a credit entry on the left side of the equation. As the amount was paid after the settlement discount period, the substance of the transaction is that Sharp Moves obtained finance from Plug & Go Limited.The difference of C50 represents the financing component, therefore the settlement discount allowance is again reversed, but this time an interest expense is recognised with a debit entry (a reduction in equity) on the right side of the equation.

The scenarios described above relating to the **settlement discount on goods purchased** can be summarised as shown in Diagram 8.1.

Cash purchases and cash discounts

Purchase transactions are measured after taking into account the amount of point of sale discounts. Cash discounts are point of sale discounts and the purchase is recognised at the *net* amount payable at the transaction date.

Transaction 4 *25/06/X5* *Purchased 20 items at C75 each for cash. Received a 20 per cent discount for paying cash.*

4	*Assets*			= *Liabilities* + *Owner's equity*
Bank		Inventory		
+/L/Dr	*−/R/Cr*	*+/L/Dr*	*−/R/Cr*	
	1 200	1 200		

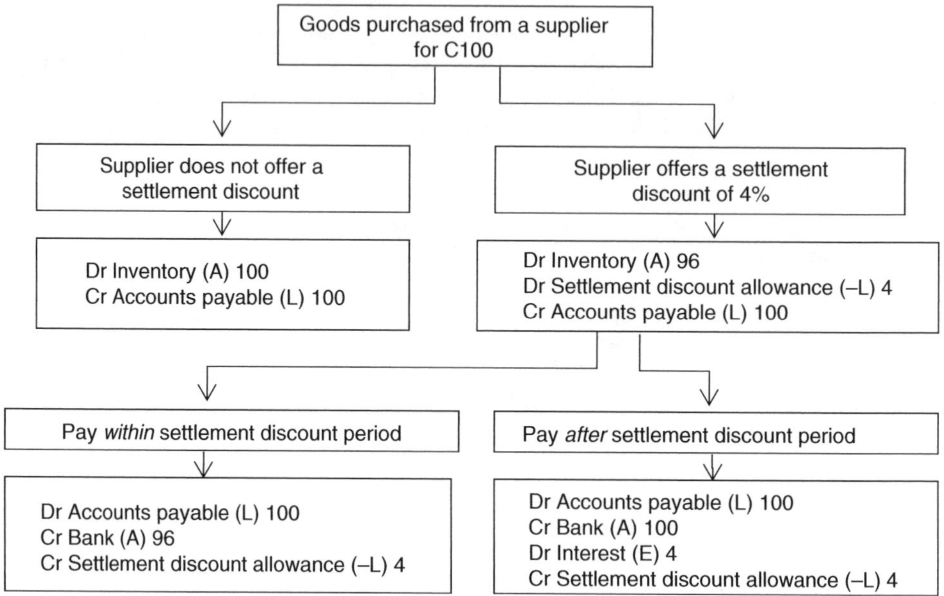

Diagram 8.1 Settlement discount on purchase transactions

The inventory purchased had a list price of C1 500. As the supplier has allowed a 20 per cent cash discount, the consideration paid amounts to C1 200. The inventory account is increased with a debit entry on the left side of the equation at the fair value of C1 200, to reflect the increase in the asset. The bank account must be reduced with a credit entry, also on the left side of the equation, by C1 200 to record the payment. Note that the amount of the cash discount – in this case C300 – is not separately recorded.

Trade discount

As mentioned above, purchase transactions are measured after taking into account the amount of point of sale discounts. Trade discounts, just like cash discounts, are point of sale discounts and thus the purchase is recognised at the *net* amount payable at the transaction date. In addition, IAS 2, *Inventory* requires that trade discounts be deducted when determining the cost of goods purchased.

Transaction 5	*30/06/X5*	*Purchased 100 items on account from Digital World. The normal selling price from Digital World is C75 an item. Sharp Moves is a good customer so Digital World grants a trade discount of 20 per cent.*

5	*Assets*		=	*Liabilities*		+	*Owner's equity*
	Inventory			Accounts payable			
	+/L/Dr	−/R/Cr		−/L/Dr	+/R/Cr		
	6 000				6 000		

The invoice price of the goods purchased is C6 000 after deducting the trade discount (100 items × C75 × 0.80). Inventory is increased by this amount with a debit entry on the left side of the equation to reflect the increase in the asset. Since the goods purchased have not been paid for, accounts payable on the right side of the equation is increased with a credit entry to reflect the increase in the liability.

Journal entries for goods purchased

Before moving on to the recording of goods sold and cost of sales, it is appropriate at this point to review the general journal entries that have been processed in relation to the goods purchased. The following is the journal of Sharp Moves for the month of June 20X5, showing all of the above transactions:

GENERAL JOURNAL OF SHARP MOVES

#	*Date*	*Description*	*Dr*	*Cr*
1	04/06/X5	Inventory (A)	900	
		Accounts payable (L)		900
		Purchase of 15 items at C60 each on credit		
2	04/06/X5	Inventory (A)	1 200	
		Settlement discount allowance (–L)	50	
		Accounts payable (L)		1 250
		Purchase of 20 items at C62.50 each on credit subject to a 4 per cent settlement discount		
3a	04/06/X5	Accounts payable (L)	1 250	
		Bank (A)		1 200
		Settlement discount allowance (–L)		50
		Cash paid to Plug & Go Limited within the settlement discount period		
or				
3b	04/06/X5	Accounts payable (L)	1 250	
		Bank(A)		1 250
		Interest (E)	50	
		Settlement discount allowance (–L)		50
		Settled account with Plug & Go Limited after the settlement discount period		
4	04/06/X5	Inventory (A)	1 200	
		Bank (A)		1 200
		Purchase of 20 items at C75 each for cash less 20 per cent cash discount		
5	04/06/X5	Inventory (A)	6 000	
		Accounts payable (L)		6 000
		Purchase of 100 items at C75 each on credit less 20 per cent trade discount		

8.4.2 The recording of sales and cost of sales

You know that a retail entity earns revenue by selling goods and that these sales can be either cash or credit sales. In the following paragraphs, we are going to describe how Sharp

Moves records transactions relating to revenue from sales, assuming a **perpetual inventory system** is used. We will also focus on revenue from sales where discounts are concerned. The recording of revenue from sales is identical for both the perpetual and periodic systems.

As you learnt in the Smart Concepts example in Parts I and II of this book, *both* the revenue and the expense aspects of the transaction must be recorded at the time of sale when using the perpetual system.

The cost of goods sold in a retail entity is reported on the statement of profit or loss as a trading expense as opposed to an operating expense. It is typically referred to as cost of sales and is recorded differently depending on whether a perpetual or periodic system is being used.

Credit sales and settlement discount

Before a sale is made on credit, the customer needs to open an account. The entity will investigate the creditworthiness of the customer before allowing goods to be sold on credit.

Once the account has been approved, the customer is given specific credit terms. This means that the customer can purchase goods from the entity up to a predetermined level and that payment must be made before a certain date.

The selling entity may offer a settlement discount to encourage early settlement of the account and this is indicated on the invoice as part of the terms of payment. Potential settlement discounts allowable have to be estimated at the date of sale, and the amount of sales revenue should be reduced accordingly.

The settlement discount offered by a seller serves as an incentive for the customer to pay early. If the customer does not pay within the given settlement period, the settlement discount that it forfeits is regarded by the selling entity as financing income.

The total amount receivable therefore includes a potential interest income. In other words, the amount receivable from the customer (100 per cent) includes a financing component (say 5 per cent), which is only recognised if the receipt from the customer is not forthcoming within the specified period. The income from sales is therefore recognised at the fair value at the transaction date, being 95 per cent of the amount receivable.

 **Pause and reflect ...**

Can you think of the journal entry in the accounting records of the selling entity if goods are sold to a customer for C100 with a 5 per cent settlement discount offered for early payment?

Response

Dr Accounts receivable (A) 100
Cr Sales (I) 95
Cr Settlement discount allowance (–A) 5

We can now turn our attention to analysing the transactions of Sharp Moves relating to revenue from sales. The sales transactions are repeated here for ease of use:

#	*Date*	*Transaction*	*C*
		Sales	
6	06/06/X5	Sold 2 items at C100 each on credit. No discount was offered to the customers. The cost of the 2 items was C60 each	200
7	09/06/X5	Sold 15 items at C100 each on account to a customer. Sharp Moves allows a 5 per cent settlement discount if payment is received within 15 days. The cost of the 15 items was C60 each	1 500 (75) 1 425
8a	24/06/X5	Received from the customer in transaction 7 the amount owing by him *within the settlement period*, taking advantage of the settlement discount	1 425
8b	25/06/X5	Received from the customer in transaction 7 the amount owing by him *after the settlement period*	1 500
9	27/06/X5	Sold 20 items at C100 each for cash. The customers were offered a cash discount of 5 per cent for paying cash. The cost of the 20 items was C60 each	2 000 (100) 1 900
10	30/06/X5	Sold 75 items on account to Fleet Street Computers. The normal selling price is C100 each. Fleet Street Computers is a good customer and is allowed a 20 per cent trade discount on all purchases. The cost of the 75 items was C60 each	7 500 (1 500) 6 000

Transaction 6 *06/06/X5* *Sold 2 items at C100 each on credit. No discount was offered to the customers. The cost of the 2 items was C60 each.*

6	*Assets*		=	*Liabilities*	+	*Owner's equity*	
	Accounts receivable					Sales income	
	+/L/Dr	*−/R/Cr*				*−/L/Dr*	*+/R/Cr*
	200						200

This sales revenue transaction is similar to the ones that you analysed in the Smart Concepts example. There is a debit entry to the accounts receivable account on the left side of the equation, and a credit entry to the sales revenue account on the right side of the equation.

The expense part of the transaction is to record the cost of sales.

6	*Assets*		=	*Liabilities*	+	*Owner's equity*	
	Inventory					Cost of sales expense	
	+/L/Dr	*−/R/Cr*				*+/L/Dr*	*−/R/Cr*
		120				120	

Again, this cost of sales transaction is similar to the ones that you analysed in the Smart Concepts example. There is a debit entry to the cost of sales expense account on the right side of the equation, and a credit entry to the inventory account on the left side of the equation. The cost of the 2 items sold is C120 (2 × C60).

As with the purchase of inventory transactions, look closely at transaction 7 and see how it differs from transaction 6. In transaction 7, Sharp Moves allows a settlement discount, which is going to affect how the sales revenue transaction is recorded.

Transaction 7 *09/06/X5* *Sold 15 items at C100 each on account to a customer. Sharp Moves allows a 5 per cent settlement discount if payment is received within 15 days. The cost of the 15 items was C60 each.*

7	*Assets*			=	*Liabilities*	+	*Owner's equity*	
Accounts receivable		Settlement discount allowance					Sales income	
+/L/Dr	−/R/Cr	−/L/Dr	+/R/Cr				−/L/Dr	+/R/Cr
1 500			75					1 425

Once the sale has taken place, the customer owes C1 500 to Sharp Moves. The amount owed is an asset, and the accounts receivable account on the left side of the equation is increased with a debit entry by the full amount receivable from the customer. The revenue from sales is recorded at its fair value of C1 425 and therefore the sales revenue account is increased with a credit entry on the right side of the equation. The potential settlement discount offered to the customer is recorded with a credit entry to a settlement discount allowance account at the date of sale.

As you have seen above, the potential settlement discount offered to the customer was recorded with a credit entry to a settlement discount allowance account at the date of sale. Although it has a credit balance, the settlement discount allowance account is neither a liability nor income. It is a measurement account relating to the asset, accounts receivable and the two accounts together (the accounts receivable with a debit balance of C1 500 and the settlement discount allowance with a credit balance of C75) represent the fair value of the transaction.

The expense part of the transaction is to record the cost of sales. Note that the measurement of the cost of sales is not affected by the measurement of the sales revenue transaction.

7	*Assets*	=	*Liabilities*	+	*Owner's equity*	
Inventory					Cost of sales expense	
+/L/Dr	−/R/Cr				+/L/Dr	−/R/Cr
	900				900	

As you now know, when inventory is sold it must be treated as a cost of sales expense (a debit entry on the left side of the equation) and removed as an asset (a credit entry on the left side of the equation). The cost of the 15 items sold is C900 (15 × C60).

Pause and reflect ...

Assuming that Sharp Moves prepares a statement of financial position immediately after the above transaction, how would the amount owing from the customer be reported?

Response

It will be reported as a current asset, accounts receivable, at an amount of C1 425 (1 500 − 75).

Again, two scenarios now exist:

a) If the customer **pays within the settlement period**, the customer is *granted the settlement discount* and the selling entity would not have granted finance to the customer. The settlement discount allowance is thus reversed on receipt of the amount owing (transaction 8a).
b) On the other hand, if the customer **does not pay within the settlement period**, the customer *forfeits the settlement discount*, and the substance of the transaction is that the selling entity granted finance to the customer (transaction 8b).

Transaction 8a *24/06/X5* *Received from the customer in transaction 7 the amount owing by him within the settlement discount period, taking advantage of the 5 per cent settlement discount.*

8a	*Assets*						*= L + OE*
	Bank		Accounts receivable		Settlement discount allowance		
	+/L/Dr	*−/R/Cr*	*+/L/Dr*	*−/R/Cr*	*−/L/Dr*	*+/R/Cr*	
Balance			1 500			75	
8a	1 425			1 500	75		

The invoiced amount receivable from the customer was C1 500, therefore the accounts receivable account is reduced by C1 500 with a credit entry to reflect that the amount has been received. The amount of cash received to settle the account was C1 425 as the customer took advantage of the 5 per cent settlement discount offered by Sharp Moves. The bank account is increased by this amount with a debit on the left side of the equation. As the amount was received within the settlement period, there is no finance income and the settlement discount allowance is reversed with a debit of C75.

Transaction 8b *25/06/X5* *Received from the customer in transaction 7 the amount owing by them after the settlement discount period.*

8b	*Assets*						*= L*	*+ OE*	
	Bank		Accounts receivable		Settlement discount allowance			Interest income	
	+/L/Dr	−/R/Cr	+/L/Dr	−/R/Cr	−/L/Dr	+/R/Cr		−/L/Dr	+/R/Cr
Balance			1 500			75			
8b	1 500			1 500					
8b					75				75

The amount receivable from the customer was C1 500, therefore the accounts receivable account is reduced by C1 500 to reflect that the amount has been received. The amount of cash received to settle the account was C1 500 as the customer did not take advantage of the 5 per cent settlement discount offered by Sharp Moves. The bank account is increased by this amount with a debit entry on the left side of the equation. As the amount was received after the settlement discount period, the substance of the transaction is that Sharp Moves granted finance to the customer. The difference of C75 represents the financing component, therefore the settlement discount allowance is reversed but this time interest income is recognised with a credit entry (an increase in equity) on the right side of the equation.

The scenarios described above relating to the **settlement discount on goods sold** can be summarised as shown in Diagram 8.2.

Cash sales and cash discounts

Sale transactions are measured after taking into account the amount of point of sale discounts. Cash discounts are point of sale discounts, and the sale is recognised at the *net* amount receivable at the transaction date.

Transaction 9 *27/06/X5* *Sold 20 items at C100 each for cash. The customers were offered a cash discount of 5 per cent for paying cash.*

9	*Assets*		*=*	*Liabilities*	*+*	*Owner's equity*	
	Bank					Sales income	
	+/L/Dr	−/R/Cr				−/L/Dr	+/R/Cr
	1 900						1 900

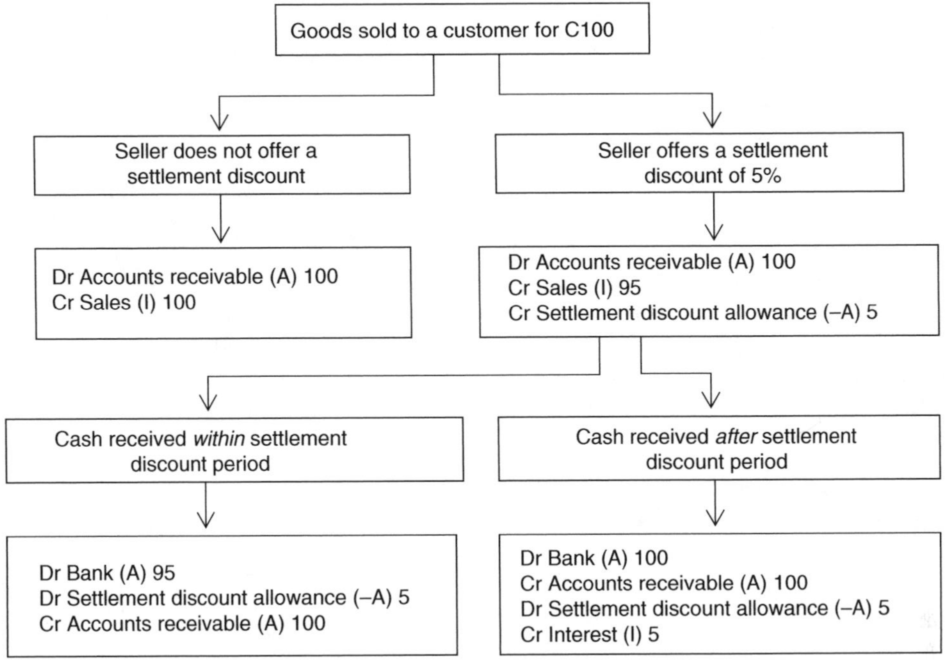

Diagram 8.2 Settlement discount on sales transactions

The inventory sold had a list price of C2 000. As Sharp Moves has allowed a 5 per cent cash discount, the consideration received amounts to C1 900. The bank account is increased with a debit entry on the left side of the equation to reflect the receipt. The sales revenue account is increased with a credit entry on the right side of the equation at the fair value of C1 900 to record the amount earned.

The expense part of the transaction is to record the cost of sales.

9	*Assets*	=	*Liabilities*	+	*Owner's equity*	
	Inventory				Cost of sales expense	
	+/L/Dr	*–/R/Cr*			*+/L/Dr*	*–/R/Cr*
		1 200			1 200	

As you now know, when inventory is sold it must be recognised as a cost of sales expense and removed as an asset. The cost of the 20 items sold is C1 200 (20 × C60).

Trade discount

As with purchase transactions, sale transactions are measured after taking into account the amount of point of sale discounts. Trade discounts, just like cash discounts, are point of sale discounts and thus the sale is recognised at the *net* amount receivable at the transaction date.

Transaction 10 *30/06/X5* *Sold 75 items on account to Fleet Street Computers. The normal selling price is C100 each. Fleet Street Computers is a good customer and is allowed a 20 per cent trade discount on all purchases.*

10	*Assets*	=	*Liabilities*	+	*Owner's equity*
	Accounts receivable				Sales income

Accounts receivable +/L/Dr	Accounts receivable −/R/Cr	Sales income −/L/Dr	Sales income +/R/Cr
6 000			6 000

The invoice price of the goods sold is C6 000 after deducting the trade discount. Since the goods sold have not been paid for, accounts receivable on the left side of the equation is increased with a debit entry to reflect the increase in the asset. Sales revenue is increased with a credit entry of the same amount on the right side of the equation to reflect the increase in equity.

The expense part of the transaction is to record the cost of sales.

10	*Assets*	=	*Liabilities*	+	*Owner's equity*
	Inventory				Cost of sales expense

Inventory +/L/Dr	Inventory −/R/Cr	Cost of sales expense +/L/Dr	Cost of sales expense −/R/Cr
	4 500	4 500	

Again, when inventory is sold it must be recognised as a cost of sales expense and removed as an asset. The cost of the 75 items sold is C4 500 (75 × C60).

Concepts in context

Clover Industries Limited
(Extract from) Notes to the consolidated financial statements

Revenue recognition

Revenue is recognised to the extent that it is probable that the economic benefits will flow to the Group and the revenue can be reliably measured. Revenue is measured at the fair value of the consideration received or receivable, taking into account discounts and rebates.

What concepts in context can you see here?

Clover Industries' revenue recognition policy states that revenue is recognised at fair value after the deduction of discounts and rebates. Relate this to what you have learnt in this chapter – that revenue is recognised net of all discounts (cash, settlement and trade discounts), in other words, at fair value.

Clover Industries Limited is a branded foods and beverage group, listed on the main board of the Johannesburg Stock Exchange. The group produces and distributes a diverse range of dairy and consumer products.

Source: www.clover.co.za/annual-report (Accessed on 12 November 2015).

Journal entries for sales and cost of sales

It is now appropriate to review the journal entries that have been processed in relation to the goods sold and cost of sales. The following is an extract from the journal of Sharp Moves for the month of June 20X5, showing all of the revenue and cost of sales transactions:

GENERAL JOURNAL OF SHARP MOVES

#	*Date*	*Description*	*Dr*	*Cr*
6	06/06/X5	Accounts receivable (A)	200	
		Sales (I)		200
		Sold 2 items at C100 each on credit		
	06/06/X5	Cost of sales (E)	120	
		Inventory (A)		120
		Cost of goods sold		
7	09/06/X5	Accounts receivable (A)	1 500	
		Sales (I)		1 425
		Settlement discount allowance (–A)		75
		Sold 15 items at C100 each on account subject to a 5 per cent settlement discount		
	09/06/X5	Cost of sales (E)	900	
		Inventory (A)		900
		Cost of goods sold		
8a	24/06/X5	Bank (A)	1 425	
		Settlement discount allowance (–A)	75	
		Accounts receivable (A)		1 500
		Cash received from the customer within the settlement discount period		
or				
8b	25/06/X5	Bank (A)	1 500	
		Accounts receivable (A)		1 500
		Settlement discount allowance (–A)	75	
		Interest (I)		75
		Cash received from the customer after the settlement discount period		
9	27/06/X5	Bank (A)	1 900	
		Sales (I)		1 900
		Sold 20 items at C100 each less a 5 per cent cash discount		
	27/06/X5	Cost of sales (E)	1 200	
		Inventory (A)		1 200
		Cost of goods sold		
10	30/06/X5	Accounts receivable (A)	6 000	
		Sales (I)		6 000
		Sold 20 items at C100 each on account less a 20 per cent trade discount		
	30/06/X5	Cost of sales (E)	4 500	
		Inventory (A)		4 500
		Cost of goods sold		

8.4.3 Ledger accounts for goods purchased and sold

The general journal for the purchase transactions was shown in Section 8.4.1, and the general journal for the sales and cost of sales transactions was shown in Section 8.4.2. Once all the journal entries have been posted to the ledger, the relevant ledger accounts reflecting all of the transactions will appear as shown below. The ledger accounts shown here are abridged ledger accounts, without date and folio columns. Remember that the transactions have been recorded in this section using a ***perpetual system***.

INVENTORY

Details	*C*	*Details*	*C*
Balance b/d	240	Cost of sales	120
Accounts payable	900	Cost of sales	900
Accounts payable	1 200	Cost of sales	1 200
Bank	1 200	Cost of sales	4 500
Accounts payable	6 000	Balance c/d	2 820
	9 540		9 540
Balance b/d	2 820		

COST OF SALES

Details	*C*	*Details*	*C*
Inventory	120	Balance c/d	6 720
Inventory	900		
Inventory	1 200		
Inventory	4 500		
	6 720		6 720
Balance b/d	6 720		

ACCOUNTS RECEIVABLE

Details	*C*	*Details*	*C*
Sales	200	Bank	1 425
Sales	1 425	Balance c/d	6 200
Sales	6 000		
	7 625		7 625
Balance b/d	6 200		

SALES

Details	*C*	*Details*	*C*
Balance	9 525	Accounts receivable	200
		Accounts receivable	1 425
		Bank	1 900
		Accounts receivable	6 000
	9 525		9 525
		Balance	9 525

8.4.4 Summary of goods purchased and sold

It is useful at this stage to reflect on all the transactions that have been processed (Diagram 8.3). This will assist you in understanding the presentation of the statement of profit or loss in Section 8.4.5.

8.4.5 Statement of profit or loss presentation

In addition to the above transactions, Sharp Moves had incurred administration expenses during the period of C1 200, and marketing and selling expenses of C1 400.

#	Details	Qty	Inventory		Sales	
			Cost	Total	SP	Total
			C	C	C	C
0	Opening inventory	4	60	240		
		155		9 300		
1	Purchases	15	60	900		
2	Purchases	20	60	1 200		
4	Purchases	20	60	1 200		
5	Purchases	100	60	6 000		
	Goods available for sale / cost of goods available for sale	159		9 540		
	Goods sold / cost of sales	(112)		(6 720)		
	Sales	(2)	60	(120)	100	200
	Sales	(15)	60	(900)	95	1 425
	Sales	(20)	60	(1 200)	95	1 900
	Sales	(75)	60	(4 500)	80	6 000
	Closing inventory/sales	47	60	2 820		9 525

Diagram 8.3 Summary of goods purchased and sold

Pause and reflect . . .

a) Do you understand the difference between the 'cost of goods available for sale' and the 'cost of sales'?
b) Can you see a relationship between the opening inventory, the goods purchased, the goods sold and the closing inventory?

Response

a) The 'cost of goods available for sale' is the cost of the opening inventory + the cost of the goods purchased during the period. In other words, it is the cost of the goods that the entity had available for sale to customers during the period. The 'cost of sales', on the other hand, is the cost of the goods actually sold during the period.
b) Opening inventory + goods purchased − goods sold = closing inventory. Looking at quantity,
   4 + 154 − 112 = 47.
   In currency, C240 + C9 300 − C6 720 = C2 820.
   This relationship is very important in understanding the periodic inventory system.

Two statements of profit or loss are presented below. The first includes the effects of transactions 3a and 8a (where the payment to the supplier and the receipt from the customer occurred **within the settlement discount period**). The second includes the effects of transactions 3b and 8b (where the payment to the supplier and the receipt from the customer occurred **after the settlement discount period** and thus an interest expense and an interest income respectively were recorded).

Statement of profit or loss with no financing transactions (3a and 8a)

SHARP MOVES
STATEMENT OF PROFIT OR LOSS
FOR THE MONTH ENDED 30 JUNE 20X5

	Workings	*C*
Sales		9 525
Cost of sales		(6 720)
Opening inventory		240
Purchases	*(900 + 1 200 + 1 200 + 6 000)*	9 300
Cost of goods available for sale		9 540
Closing inventory	*(47 × C60)*	(2 820)
Gross profit		2 805
Operating expenses		(2 600)
Administration expenses		1 200
Marketing and selling expenses		1 400
Profit for the period		205

Statement of profit or loss with financing transactions (3b and 8b)

SHARP MOVES
STATEMENT OF PROFIT OR LOSS
FOR THE MONTH ENDED 30 JUNE 20X5

	Workings	*C*
Sales		9 525
Cost of sales		(6 720)
Opening inventory		240
Purchases	*(900 + 1 200 + 1 200 + 6 000)*	9 300
Cost of goods available for sale		9 540
Closing inventory	*(47 × C60)*	(2 820)
Gross profit		2 805

Other income	
Interest income	75
Operating expenses	(2 600)
Administration expenses	1 200
Marketing and selling expenses	1 400
Finance costs	
Interest expense	(50)
Profit for the period	230

The interest income of C75 arises from transaction 8b where cash for goods sold was received from the customer after the settlement discount period. On the other hand, the interest expense of C50 arises from transaction 3b where cash for goods purchased was paid to the supplier after the settlement discount period. Notice how, apart from the inclusion of interest income and interest expense, nothing else changes.

8.4.6 Closing entries for a perpetual inventory system

The closing entry process was explained in Chapter 7, *Closing entries*. For completeness, and to compare with the closing entries for the periodic inventory system, this section again describes the closing entry process for a perpetual inventory system.

The relevant accounts here are the inventory account, the cost of sales account and the sales account. We learnt earlier in this chapter that the cost of sales is recorded each time that a sale is made. The sales and the cost of sales will both be transferred to the trading account, and the gross profit will be determined from it.

The trial balance of Sharp Moves using the **perpetual system** and *with no financing transactions* (3a and 8a) at the end of June 20X5 is shown below.

SHARP MOVES
TRIAL BALANCE AT 30 JUNE 20X5

Description	*Dr*	*Cr*
Bank	925	
Inventory	2 820	
Accounts receivable	6 200	
Accounts payable		6 900
Owner's equity		2 840
Cost of sales	6 720	
Administration expenses	1 200	
Marketing and selling expenses	1 400	
Sales		9 525
	19 265	19 265

Sales

The sales account as income will have a credit balance representing the sales during the period. To reduce this account to zero, the balance must be transferred by a debit entry to the sales account with the credit entered in the trading account.

Cost of sales

The cost of sales account as an expense will have a debit balance representing the cost of goods sold during the period. To reduce this account to zero, the balance must be transferred by a credit to the cost of sales account with the debit entered in the trading account.

Inventory

As the inventory account in the perpetual system is updated each time goods are bought or sold, the balance of C2 820 in the inventory account on the trial balance is the amount that will appear as an asset on the statement of financial position. As you have seen in Chapter 7, *Closing entries*, there is thus no need to include the inventory account in the closing entry process when using the perpetual system.

The effect of the closing entries in the perpetual system can be demonstrated as follows. Again, only those accounts affecting trading activities have been included.

	Assets		= L +		*Owner's equity*			
	Inventory		Sales		COS		Trading	
	+/L/Dr	−/R/Cr	−/L/Dr	+/R/Cr	+/L/Dr	−/R/Cr	−/L/Dr	+/R/Cr
Bal	2 820			9 525	6 720			
c/e 1			9 525					9 525
c/e 2						6 720	6 720	
Bal	2 820							2 805

Closing entry 1 transfers the sales to the trading account, while closing entry 2 transfers the cost of sales to the trading account. The balance on the trading account then reflects the gross profit for the period of C2 805.

You should know from Chapter 7, *Closing entries*, that the trading account is then closed off by transferring the gross profit to the profit and loss account, followed by the closing off of the income and expense accounts, also to the profit and loss account. The profit and loss account is then closed off by transferring the profit or loss for the period to the capital account.

The completed ledger accounts, incorporating the closing entries that have been ***highlighted*** are shown below.

INVENTORY

Details	*C*	*Details*	*C*
Balance b/d	240	Cost of sales	120
Accounts payable	900	Cost of sales	900
Accounts payable	1 200	Cost of sales	1 200
Bank	1 200	Cost of sales	4 500
Accounts payable	6 000	Balance c/d	2 820
	9 540		9 540
Balance b/d	2 820		

COST OF SALES

Details	*C*	*Details*	*C*
Inventory	120	Balance c/d	6 720
Inventory	900		
Inventory	1 200		
Inventory	4 500		
	6 720		6 720
Balance b/d	6 720	***Trading***	***6 720***

TRADING

Details	*C*	*Details*	*C*
Cost of sales	***6 720***	***Sales***	***9 525***
Profit or loss	***2 805***		
	9 525		9 525

SALES

Details	*C*	*Details*	*C*
Balance c/d	9 525	Accounts receivable	200
		Accounts receivable	1 425
		Bank	1 900
		Accounts receivable	6 000
	9 525		9 525
Trading	***9 525***	Balance b/d	9 525

 **Pause and reflect . . .**

What do you notice about the inventory account compared to the sales, cost of sales and trading accounts?

Response

There are no closing entries reflected in the inventory account. Remember this, and compare it to the inventory account that you will see when doing closing entries for a periodic system in Section 8.5.6 of this chapter.

8.5 Recording of purchase and sale transactions using a periodic inventory system

The previous sections have described the recording of inventory transactions using a perpetual inventory system. In this section, we will examine the principles relating to a **periodic** inventory system. The recognition and measurement principles that you learnt for the perpetual system do not change. It is only the procedures to record the purchases of inventory and cost of sales that differ.

More specifically, when using a periodic system:

- A ***purchases account*** is used to accumulate the cost of goods purchased for resale (as opposed to an inventory account in the perpetual system).
- The cost of goods sold is ***not*** recorded at the time of sale (whereas the cost of goods sold is recorded at the time of sale in a perpetual system).

8.5.1 The purchases account

The purchases account is neither an asset account nor an expense account, but a temporary account which records and accumulates the cost of goods purchased during the period.

When inventory is purchased, the purchases account is debited and the bank account or the accounts payable account is credited (depending on whether the purchase was for cash or on credit). Any additional costs incurred, such as freight, duty or transport, are also recorded in the purchases account.

At the end of the period, those goods which are sold become part of the cost of sales expense, and those which are still on hand will form part of the closing inventory, an asset on the statement of financial position. We will now explain how this is achieved.

8.5.2 Cost of sales

At the time the sale is made, only the revenue aspect of the transaction is recorded and not the cost of goods sold. Similarly, if goods sold are returned, only the revenue is reversed. At the end of the accounting period, the cost of all goods sold during that period is calculated. The following information is needed to compute the cost of goods sold:

- the cost of inventory on hand at the beginning of the period;
- the cost of inventory purchased during the period;
- the cost of inventory on hand at the end of the period (determined by performing a physical count).

 **Pause and reflect . . .**

How would Sharp Moves determine the cost of its closing inventory?

Response

Employees at Sharp Moves would physically count the number of items of inventory on hand at the end of the period. Based on the quantity of opening inventory as well as the quantities of goods bought and sold during the current period, a total of 47 units is counted at the end of the period (4 + 154 − 112). Each item cost C60 and therefore the cost of the closing inventory is C2 820.

Note that the cost of sales as calculated here is the same as the balance on the cost of sales account when using the perpetual inventory system.

SHARP MOVES
COST OF SALES CALCULATION

		C
Opening inventory		240
Add Purchases	(transactions 1, 2, 4 and 5)	9 300
Cost of goods available for sale		9 540
Less Closing inventory	(47 × C60)	(2 820)
Cost of sales		6 720

It is important at this stage to compare what we have learnt about cost of goods sold and closing inventory using the perpetual inventory system with that of using the periodic inventory system.

In a **perpetual inventory system**, we balance to *closing inventory*:

Opening inventory 240	+	Purchases 9 300	–	Cost of sales 6 720	=	Closing inventory 2 820

The cost of sales of C6 720 is the balance in the cost of sales account after processing the cost of sales transactions during the period. The balance of C2 820 in the inventory account needs to be verified by a physical inventory count.

In a **periodic inventory system**, we balance to *cost of sales*:

Opening inventory 240	+	Purchases 9 300	–	Closing inventory 2 820	=	Cost of sales 6 720

The closing inventory of C2 820 is computed by a physical count and then used to *determine* the cost of sales of C6 720. The closing inventory is recorded in the accounting records through the closing entry process. Since we need to perform a physical count in order to *calculate* the closing inventory balance, we cannot use a physical count to *check* the closing inventory balance.

8.5.3 Journal entries for goods purchased and sold

As mentioned above, the recognition and measurement principles are the same whether we use the perpetual or the periodic system; it is only the recording of the purchase of inventory and the cost of sales that differs. It follows that all the accounting entries are also the same, except for these two differences.

The general journal of Sharp Moves for the month of June 20X5 is repeated here, showing the **entries for goods purchased** using the periodic inventory system. Note that for the settlement discount transaction, only transaction 3a is considered (the supplier paid within the settlement discount period).

GENERAL JOURNAL OF SHARP MOVES

#	*Date*	*Description*	*Dr*	*Cr*
1	04/06/X5	**Purchases (T)**	900	
		Accounts payable (L)		900
		Purchase of 15 items at C60 each on credit		
2	04/06/X5	**Purchases (T)**	1 200	
		Settlement discount allowance (–L)	50	
		Accounts payable (L)		1 250
		Purchase of 20 items at C62.50 each on credit subject to a 4 per cent settlement discount		
3a	04/06/X5	Accounts payable (L)	1 250	
		Bank (A)		1 200
		Settlement discount allowance (–L)		50
		Cash paid to Plug & Go Limited within the settlement discount period		

#	Date	Description	Dr	Cr
4	04/06/X5	**Purchases (T)**	1 200	
		Bank (A)		1 200
		Purchase of 20 items at C75 each for cash less 20 per cent cash discount		
5	04/06/X5	**Purchases (T)**	6 000	
		Accounts payable (L)		6 000
		Purchase of 100 items at C75 each on credit less a 20 per cent trade discount		

Looking at transactions 1, 2, 4 and 5, you will notice that on purchase of inventory, a temporary account – ***purchases*** – is debited (and not the inventory account as in the perpetual system). Note that a 'T' is used to describe the purchases account, which indicates that this account is a temporary one. It is increased with a debit entry but it is neither an asset nor an expense.

Turning to the **entries for goods sold**, the general journal of Sharp Moves for the month of June 20X5 is again repeated here using the periodic inventory system. Note that for the settlement discount transaction, only transaction 8a is considered (cash received from the customer within the settlement discount period).

GENERAL JOURNAL OF SHARP MOVES

#	Date	Description	Fol	Dr	Cr
6	06/06/X5	Accounts receivable (A)		200	
		Sales (I)			200
		Sold 2 items at C100 each on credit			
7	09/06/X5	Accounts receivable (A)		1 500	
		Sales (I)			1 425
		Settlement discount allowance (–A)			75
		Sold 15 items at C100 each on account subject to a 5 per cent settlement discount			
8a	24/06/X5	Bank (A)		1 425	
		Settlement discount allowance (–A)		75	
		Accounts receivable (A)			1 500
		Cash received from the customer within the settlement discount period			
9	27/06/X5	Bank (A)		1 900	
		Sales (I)			1 900
		Sold 20 items at C100 each less a 5 per cent cash discount			
10	30/06/X5	Accounts receivable (A)		6 000	
		Sales (I)			6 000
		Sold 75 items at C100 each on credit less a 20 per cent trade discount			

Remember that for a periodic system, only the revenue aspect of the transaction is recorded. The entries here are therefore identical to those processed using the perpetual system, except for the omission of the cost of sales entries.

8.5.4 Ledger accounts for goods purchased and sold

Following on from the journal entries, the relevant ledger accounts for the periodic inventory system are shown below:

INVENTORY

Details	*C*	*Details*	*C*
Balance b/d	240	Balance c/d	240
	240		240
Balance b/d	240		

PURCHASES

Details	*C*	*Details*	*C*
Accounts payable	900	Balance c/d	9 300
Accounts payable	1 200		
Bank	1 200		
Accounts payable	6 000		
	9 300		9 300
Balance b/d	9 300		

SALES

Details	*C*	*Details*	*C*
Balance c/d	9 525	Bank	200
		Accounts receivable	1 425
		Bank	1 900
		Accounts receivable	6 000
	9 525		9 525
		Balance b/d	9 525

COST OF SALES

Details	*C*	*Details*	*C*

Using the periodic system, the inventory account shows the opening balance in inventory at the beginning of the period. The goods purchased during the period are instead recorded in the purchases account. The sales account is identical to what you saw using the perpetual system. Note that no transactions are entered into the cost of sales account during the period.

8.5.5 Statement of profit or loss presentation

The presentation of the statement of profit or loss is the same using a perpetual system or a periodic system. The statement of profit or loss (with no financing transactions) that was shown in Section 8.4.5 is repeated here.

Statement of profit or loss with no financing transactions (3a and 8a)

SHARP MOVES
STATEMENT OF PROFIT OR LOSS
FOR THE MONTH ENDED 30 JUNE 20X5

	Workings		C
Sales			9 525
Cost of sales			(6 720)
Opening inventory		240	
Purchases	*(900 + 1 200 + 1 200 + 6 000)*	9 300	
Cost of goods available for sale		9 540	
Closing inventory	*(47 × C60)*	(2 820)	
Gross profit			2 805
Operating expenses			(2 600)
Administration expenses		1 200	
Marketing and selling expenses		1 400	
Profit for the period			205

8.5.6 Closing entries for a periodic inventory system

The closing entry process explained in Chapter 7, *Closing entries*, and described again in Section 8.4.6, applied to the ***perpetual inventory system***. This section describes the process for a ***periodic inventory system***.

Recall that when using the **perpetual inventory system**, the inventory account was continuously kept up to date with corresponding entries in the cost of sales account. Thus to calculate the gross profit, we simply closed off the sales account and cost of sales account to the trading account.

However, when using the **periodic inventory system**, the inventory account at the end of the period still reflects the cost of the opening inventory *and* the cost of sales account has a zero balance as the cost of sales is not recorded as goods are sold. We therefore need to record the cost of the closing inventory in the inventory account *and* record the cost of sales in the cost of sales account. We are then in the same position as with the perpetual system and can close off the sales account and cost of sales account to the trading account.

 **Pause and reflect ...**

Do we have all the information to record the cost of sales in a cost of sales account?

Response

Although no entries have been processed in a cost of sales account during the period, we do have all the information we need to calculate the cost of sales.

The inventory account reflects the inventory on hand at the beginning of the period (i.e. the opening inventory balance).

The purchases account, which is a temporary account, shows the total purchases during the period.

The physical stock count will determine the quantity of goods on hand, which is then multiplied by the cost of each item to determine the cost of the closing inventory (i.e. the closing inventory balance).

The trial balance of Sharp Moves at the end of June 20X5 using the **periodic system** and assuming *no financing transactions* (3a and 8a) is shown below. It is important to note that the inventory of C240 on the trial balance is the *opening* inventory – in other words, the balance at the beginning of the period. In the periodic system, the inventory account is used to record the inventory on hand at the end of a period and then remains unchanged until the end of the following period when the new ending inventory is recorded. Therefore, by examining the trial balance at 30 June 20X5, we can immediately establish that the closing entries have not been processed as the inventory account shows the balance at the beginning of the period.

SHARP MOVES
TRIAL BALANCE AT 30 JUNE 20X5

Description	*Dr*	*Cr*
Bank	925	
Inventory (01/06/X5)	240	
Accounts receivable	6 200	
Accounts payable		6 900
Owner's equity		2 840
Purchases	9 300	
Administration expenses	1 200	
Marketing and selling expenses	1 400	
Sales		9 525
	19 265	19 265

Opening inventory

The inventory account will have a debit balance representing the *opening inventory* at the beginning of the period. This balance must be transferred out of the inventory account so that the *closing inventory* can be entered into the account. This is achieved by a credit entry to the inventory account (by an amount equal to the balance of the opening inventory) with the debit side of the entry appearing in the cost of sales account.

Purchases and other costs

The purchases account, as well as the accounts used to record other costs of purchase in the periodic system, will have a debit balance at the end of the period. To reduce these accounts to zero requires credit entries to the purchases and related accounts (by amounts equal to the debit balances) with the debit side of the entries appearing in the cost of sales account.

Closing inventory

The inventory account, which has a zero balance after the transfer of the opening inventory, must be re-established with the amount of the closing inventory, which will appear as an asset on the statement of financial position. To increase an asset account requires a debit entry to the inventory account (by an amount of the closing inventory) with the credit side of the entry appearing in the cost of sales account.

Sales

The sales account has a credit balance at the end of the period, representing the revenue earned from goods sold during the period. To reduce an income account requires a debit entry to the sales account (by an amount equal to the credit balance) with the credit side of the entry also appearing in the trading account.

The effect of the above closing entries can be shown as follows. Only those accounts affecting the trading activities of the entity have been included.

	Assets =		*L* +			*Owner's equity*				
	Inventory		Purchases		Cost of sales		Sales		Trading	
	+/L/Dr	−/R/Cr	+/L/Dr	−/R/Cr	+/L/Dr	−/R/Cr	−/L/Dr	+/R/Cr	−/L/Dr	+/R/Cr
Bal	240		9 300					9 525		
c/e 1		240			240					
c/e 2				9 300	9 300					
c/e 3	2 820					2 820				
Bal	2 820				6 720			9 525		
c/e 4						6 720			6 720	
c/e 5							9 525			9 525
Bal	2 820									2 805

The effect of closing entries 1 and 2 is to transfer the cost of the opening inventory as well as the cost of purchases to the cost of sales account. This amounts to C9 540 and represents the *cost of goods available for sale* during the period. Closing entry 3 records the closing inventory as a debit in the inventory account and as a credit in the cost of sales account. The debit in the inventory account establishes the asset for the statement of financial position, and the credit to the cost of sales account reduces the cost of goods available for sale by C2 820 to arrive at *the cost of sales* for the period of C6 720. Closing entry 4 closes off the cost of sales for the period by placing a credit to the cost of sales account of C6 720 and a debit of the same amount to the trading account. Closing entry 5 closes off the sales for the period by placing a debit to the sales account of C9 525 and a credit of the same amount to the trading account. This leaves the trading account with a credit balance of C2 805, representing the gross profit for the period. The remainder of the closing entry process is the same as you learnt in Chapter 7, and as you saw with the perpetual inventory system in Section 8.4.6.

The closing entries have been ***highlighted*** in the ledger accounts below:

INVENTORY

Details	C	*Details*	C
Balance b/d	240	***Cost of sales***	***240***
Cost of sales	***2 820***	Balance c/d	2 820
	3 060		3 060
Balance b/d	2 820		

PURCHASES

Details	C	*Details*	C
Accounts payable	900	***Cost of sales***	***9 300***
Accounts payable	1 200		
Bank	1 200		
Accounts payable	6 000		
	9 300		9 300

SALES

Details	C	*Details*	C
Trading	***9 525***	Bank	200
		Accounts receivable	1 425
		Bank	1 900
		Accounts receivable	6 000
	9 525		9 525

TRADING

Details	C	*Details*	C
Cost of sales	***6 720***	***Sales***	***9 525***
Profit or loss	***2 805***		
	9 525		9 525

COST OF SALES

Details	C	*Details*	C
Inventory (Opening)	***240***	***Inventory (Closing)***	***2 820***
Purchases	***9 300***	Balance	6 720
	9 540		9 540
Balance	6 720	***Trading***	***6 720***

 **Pause and reflect . . .**

What do you notice about the entries in the cost of sales ledger account?

Response

The entries in the cost of sales ledger account represent the components of the cost of sales computation – the opening inventory and the purchases on the debit side, and the closing inventory on the credit side.

8.6 Cost of inventory

Although the concepts relating to the cost of inventory are examined in detail in Chapter 11, *Inventory and cost of sales*, it is important to mention them briefly now in the context of purchase and sale transactions.

According to IAS 2, the cost of inventory includes all costs of purchase and other costs incurred in bringing the inventories to their present location and condition.

The cost of purchase of inventory thus comprises the following:

- the invoice price;
- import duties and other taxes that are not recoverable from the tax authority;
- transport;
- handling and other costs.

 **Pause and reflect . . .**

Sharp Moves purchases 100 items at an invoice price of C50 each. Import duties of C700 are incurred and paid to the tax authority, and C300 is paid to transport the goods from the harbour to Sharp Moves' premises. What is the cost per item to be used to record the inventory and subsequent cost of sales in the accounting records of Sharp Moves?

Response

	C
Invoice price: 100 items × C50	5 000
Import duties	700
Transport	300
	6 000

The cost incurred to bring the inventory to its present location and condition amounts to C6 000, therefore the cost per item is C60 (C6 000/100 items).

When using a **perpetual inventory system**, the other costs such as import duties and transport costs are debited to the inventory account as part of the cost of the inventory.

When using a **periodic inventory system**, the approach taken in this book is for these other costs to be debited to the purchases account. In this way, all the costs relating to the purchase of inventory are accumulated in one account – the purchases account. An alternative accounting treatment is for the other costs to be debited to separate accounts, for example the import duties debited to an import duties account and the transport costs debited to a transport costs account.

8.7 Purchase and sale returns

It is common for a buyer to return goods to a seller because of faults or simply because the item is not required.

From the perspective of the buyer, these are referred to as **purchases returns**. If the goods were bought on credit, the accounts payable account is debited and either the inventory account (for a perpetual system) or the purchases account (for a periodic system) is credited. An alternative accounting treatment for the periodic system is to credit a purchases returns account.

From the perspective of the seller, these are referred to as **sales returns**. If the goods were sold on credit, the accounts receivable account is credited and the sales account is debited. An alternative accounting treatment is to debit a sales returns account. When using the perpetual system, an entry is also required to reverse the cost of sales by debiting inventory and crediting cost of sales.

Diagram 8.4 incorporates the accounting entries relating to other costs as well as returns with the entries learnt throughout the chapter.

Transaction	*Perpetual*	*Periodic*
Purchase of goods on credit	Dr Inventory (A) Cr Accounts payable (L)	Dr Purchases (T) Cr Accounts payable (L)
Other costs paid in cash (e.g. transport)	Dr Inventory (A) Cr Bank (A)	Dr Purchases (T) Cr Bank (A)
Return of goods purchased on credit	Dr Accounts payable (L) Cr Inventory (A)	Dr Accounts payable (L) Cr Purchases (T) or Purchases returns (T)
Sale of goods on credit	Dr Accounts receivable (A) Cr Sales (I) *and*	Dr Accounts receivable (A) Cr Sales (I)
Recording cost of goods sold	Dr Cost of sales (E) Cr Inventory (A)	Computed at end of period
Return of goods sold on credit	Dr Sales (I) Cr Accounts receivable (A) *and*	Dr Sales (I) or Sales returns (–I) Cr Accounts receivable (A)
Recording of cost of goods returned	Dr Inventory (A) Cr Cost of sales (E)	Incorporate in computation at end of period

Diagram 8.4 Accounting entries using perpetual and periodic inventory systems

Revision example

The Gallery, an exclusive outlet selling original works of art, started trading on 1 February 20X8.

On 5 February 20X8, The Gallery purchased inventory of two artworks on credit from Art Dealers Limited at a cost of C1 000. Artwork A cost C600 and artwork B cost C400.

Art Dealers Limited allows a settlement discount of 4 per cent if payment is made within ten days. The Gallery paid the amount owing on 10 February 20X8.

On 15 February 20X8, The Gallery sold artwork A on credit to Mr Aye for a selling price of C780. On 20 February, The Gallery sold artwork B on credit to Mr Bee for a selling price of C520. A settlement discount of 5 per cent is allowed if payment is received within ten days.

The full amount owing by Mr Aye was received on 20 February 20X8 and the full amount owing by Mr Bee was received on 5 March 20X8.

Operating expenses for the two-month period from 1 February to 31 March 20X8 amounted to C101.

The Gallery uses a perpetual inventory system. As there are a relatively small number of customers, the entity does not use an accounts receivable subsidiary ledger.

You are required to:

a) Prepare all the journal entries in the accounting records of The Gallery for the months of February and March 20X8.

b) Show how accounts receivable will be reported in the statement of financial position at 28 February 20X8.

c) Prepare a statement of profit or loss for the two-month period ended 31 March 20X8.

Solution: Revision example

a) Journal entries

GENERAL JOURNAL OF THE GALLERY

Date	*Description*	*Dr*	*Cr*
20X8			
Feb 5	Inventory (A)	960	
	Settlement discount allowance (–L)	40	
	Accounts payable (L)		1 000
	Purchase of goods for resale subject to a 4 per cent settlement discount (C600 × 0.96 + C400 × 0.96)		
Feb 10	Accounts payable (L)	1 000	
	Bank (A)		960
	Settlement discount allowance (–L)		40
	Cash paid to Art Dealers Limited within the settlement discount period		
Feb 15	Accounts receivable (Mr Aye) (A)	780	
	Sales (I)		741
	Settlement discount allowance (–A)		39
	Sold goods on credit subject to a 5 per cent settlement discount		

	Cost of sales (E)	576	
	Inventory (A)		576
	Cost of goods sold (C600 × 0.96)		
Feb 20	Accounts receivable (Mr Bee) (A)	520	
	Sales (I)		494
	Settlement discount allowance (–A)		26
	Sold goods on credit subject to a 5 per cent settlement discount		
	Cost of sales (E)	384	
	Inventory (A)		384
	Cost of goods sold (C400 × 0.96)		
	Bank (A)	741	
	Settlement discount allowance (–A)	39	
	Accounts receivable (Mr Aye) (A)		780
	Cash received from customer within the settlement discount period		
Mar 5	Bank (A)	520	
	Accounts receivable (Mr Bee) (A)		520
	Settlement discount allowance (–A)	26	
	Interest (I)		26
	Cash received from customer after the settlement period		

b) Extract from statement of financial position

THE GALLERY
(EXTRACT FROM) STATEMENT OF FINANCIAL POSITION
AT 28 FEBRUARY 20X8

	Workings	*C*
Current assets		
Accounts receivable	*(520 − 26)*	494

c) Statement of profit or loss

THE GALLERY
STATEMENT OF PROFIT OR LOSS
FOR THE TWO MONTHS ENDED 31 MARCH 20X8

	Workings	*C*
Sales	*(741 + 494)*	1 235
Cost of sales	*(576 + 384)*	(960)
Gross profit		275
Other income		
Interest		26
Operating expenses		(101)
Profit for the period		200

Bibliography

Ernst & Young. 2014. *A Closer Look at the New Revenue Recognition Standard*. www.ey.com/Publication/vwLUAssets/EY-applying-rev-june2014/$FILE/EY-applying-rev-june2014.pdf (Accessed 6 July 2014).

The International Accounting Standards Board. 2004. IAS 2 *Inventories*.

The International Accounting Standards Board. 2014. IFRS 15 *Revenue from Contracts with Customers*.

9 Analysis journals

Business focus

Analysis journals are the primary means of capturing transactions in most accounting systems. Users of accounting software interact with inter alia cash journals, sales journals, purchases journals and payroll journals in order to process transactions. Each entry is tagged with a description or narration and allocated to specific accounts in the same manner as outlined in this chapter. Multiple analysis journals and cash journals, each of which are assigned to different users, improve the efficiency of transaction processing while allowing transactions to be organised according to their nature. This is what happens today, in the twenty-first century. Consider the following extracts (originally written in Latin) from *Summa*, by Luca Pacioli, written in the fifteenth century:

> The memorandum book ... is a book in which the merchant shall put down all his transactions, small or big, as they take place, day by day, hour by hour. In this book he will put down in detail everything that he sells or buys, and every other transaction without leaving out a jot; who, what, when, where, mentioning everything to make it fully as clear as I have already said in talking about the inventory, so that there is no necessity of saying it over again in detail.
>
> ...
>
> The bookkeeper will put everything in order before he transcribes a transaction in the journal. In this way, when the owner comes back he will see all the transactions, and he may put them in a better order if he thinks necessary. Therefore, this book is very necessary to those who have a big business.
>
> ...
>
> After you have proceeded in this way through all the accounts of the Ledger and Journal and found that the two books correspond in debit and credit. It will mean that all the accounts are correct and the entries entered correctly.

You will see how the fundamentals of bookkeeping and the analysis journal that you will encounter in this chapter have not changed in over 500 years!

In this chapter

This chapter focuses on the procedural aspects of recording multiple transactions in analysis journals.

This chapter is useful for those who want exposure to the bookkeeping procedures involved in maintaining multiple journals for cash receipts and payments, purchases and sales. The chapter can also be skipped and the flow of the book resumed in Chapter 10, *Property, plant and equipment*.

Dashboard

- Look at the *Learning outcomes* so that you know what you should be able to do after studying this chapter.
- Read the *Business focus* to place this chapter's contents in a real-world context.
- Preview *In this chapter* to focus your mind on the contents of the chapter.
- Read the *text* in detail.
  - Apply your mind to the *Pause and reflect* scenarios.
  - Make continual reference to Diagram 9.1 as you read the chapter. This diagram places all the analysis journals and subsidiary ledgers in context.
  - Ensure that you understand the relationship between the accounts receivable and payable control accounts in the *general* ledger and the respective *subsidiary* ledgers. This is explained in Section 9.2.
  - The numerous columns in the analysis journals may look daunting. As long as you keep in mind the underlying double entry, you will be able to understand and remember which columns to use for a particular transaction.
- Prepare solutions to the examples as you read through the chapter.
- Prepare solutions to the *Revision examples* at the end of the chapter without reference to the suggested ones. Compare your solutions to the suggested solutions provided.

Learning outcomes

After studying this chapter, you should be able to do the following

1 Describe the function of the analysis journals.
2 Explain the relationship between subsidiary ledgers and the control accounts.
3 Prepare the sales, purchases, cash receipts and cash payments journals.
4 Explain the process for using the sales returns, purchases returns and petty cash journals.
5 Describe the interaction of computerised accounting systems with the analysis journals.

Analysis journals

9.1 The use of analysis journals

When the accounting process was introduced in Chapter 4, *Recording external transactions*, the general journal was used as the book of prime entry to record the transactions of a business. This resulted in the posting of many debits and credits to the general ledger. There is, however, a more efficient way to process the financial data of a business entity. This chapter will introduce accounting systems that reduce the time and effort involved in recording the transactions and the subsequent postings to the general ledger.

For both practical and pedagogical reasons, this chapter describes the workings of a manual accounting system. The principles of a computerised system are similar, so you will quickly and easily follow the workings of a particular computerised system that you may encounter in practice.

The accounting systems referred to are the analysis journals. These assist the book-keeper in reducing the number of postings to the general ledger.

The accounting process does not change as a result of introducing the analysis journals (see Diagram 9.1). Rather, the recording of the transactions in the journals and the posting to the general ledger are refined to speed up the processing of data phase in the accounting process.

Analysis journals are created for each major group of transactions typically entered into by a business entity. The primary analysis journals are used to record the effects of the following transaction groups:

- the sale of goods and the rendering of services on credit;
- the purchase of goods and the acquisition of services on credit;
- the receipt of cash;
- the payment of cash.

The secondary analysis journals are used to record the effects of the following transaction groups:

- the return of goods sold and adjustments in relation to services rendered;
- the return of goods purchased and adjustments in relation to services acquired;
- petty cash funds.

The above transactions occur frequently, and 'common elements' are debited or credited to the general ledger in each case. It is therefore more efficient to use an analysis journal, with cumulative postings taking place at the end of the period. The general journal is retained for recording all other transactions that do not fall into a typical group.

9.2 Subsidiary ledgers and control accounts

In addition to the analysis journals, this chapter will introduce the use of subsidiary ledgers. Efficient business operations require up-to-date information on amounts due from individual customers and to each supplier.

The general ledger accounts for accounts receivable and accounts payable provide details on the total amount owing by customers and to suppliers. The general ledger could be expanded to include accounts for each customer and supplier. However, this would make it voluminous and unwieldy.

Separate and distinct ledgers, referred to as subsidiary ledgers, are created to provide data relating to each customer and supplier. A subsidiary ledger is not part of the general ledger (see Diagram 9.1). It represents only the details of one general ledger account.

The *general ledger* account is a summary or aggregation of the accounts in the relevant *subsidiary ledger*. The aggregated accounts in the general ledger are known as the accounts receivable control and the accounts payable control.

The posting to the control accounts in the general ledger constitutes part of the double-entry accounting system, and the control accounts will therefore appear on the general ledger trial balance.

The postings to the individual customer and supplier accounts in the subsidiary ledgers can be regarded as an analysis of the entries posted to the accounts receivable and accounts payable control accounts. These postings do not form part of the double-entry system and therefore do not form part of the general ledger trial balance. This is because the purpose of a subsidiary ledger is to give a detailed breakdown of the control account in the general ledger. The general ledger is where the complete double entry is posted.

You will notice that the subsidiary ledger has the same format as a general ledger account – that is, columns for the date, details, folio and amount. However, the detail column will not record the other side of the entry; instead, it will record the document number on which the transaction was recorded. The folio reference will still be used to indicate the page in the journal where the transaction was first recorded, but, since there are many journals, the initials of the specific journal will be used together with the page number. For example, page 2 of a sales journal will have the reference 'SJ2'.

9.3 Procedures for using the primary analysis journals

Simon Smart decided in late 20X5 to diversify his business interests further and expand into the growing home entertainment market. On 2 January 20X6, Simon opened a new

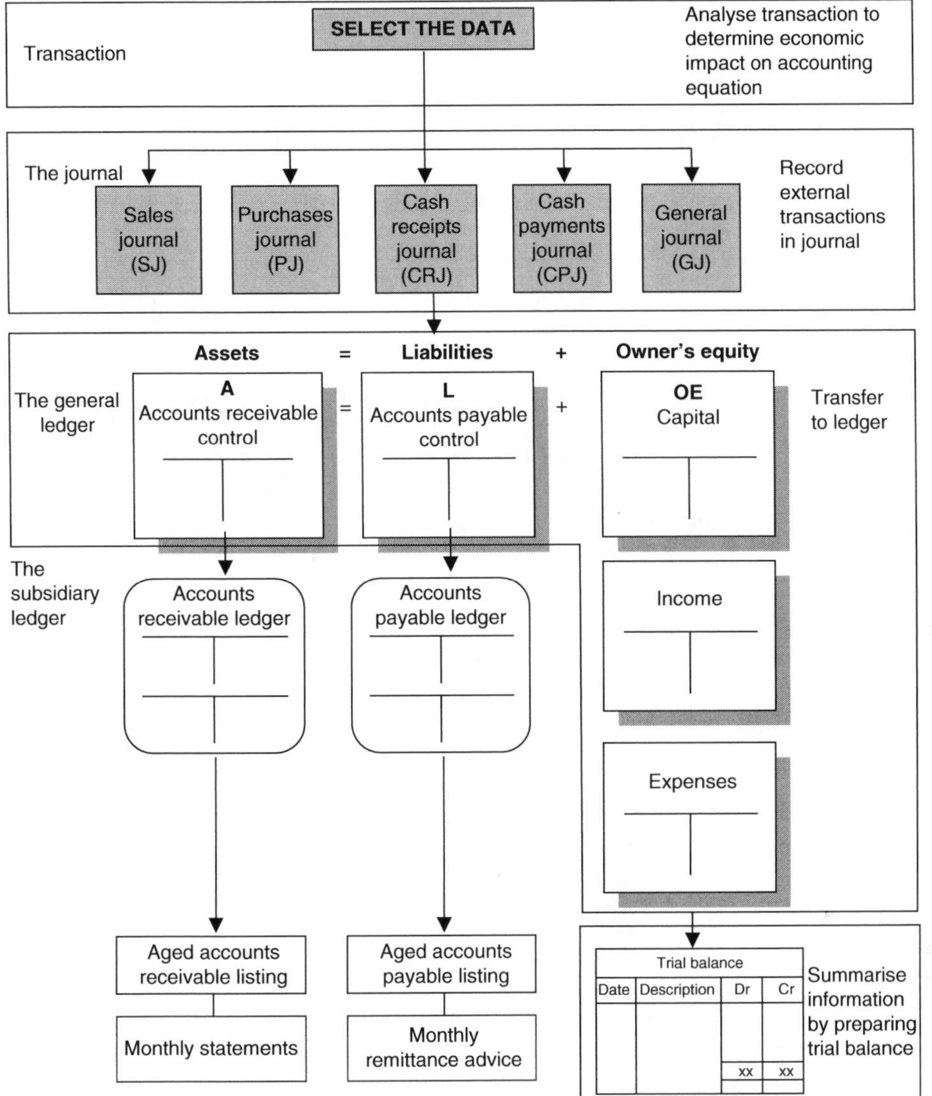

Diagram 9.1 The expanded accounting process to trial balance

business, Bright Life, selling gaming products including video games, consoles, joysticks and related accessories. In the following sections, we will analyse how Bright Life records its transactions using analysis journals.

9.3.1 Sales journal

Use

The transactions that are recorded in the sales journal are sales made to customers *on credit*. *Cash* sales are recorded in the cash receipts journal, which is discussed in Section 9.3.3 below.

Consider a credit customer such as a supermarket that places orders with the sales department of a food manufacturer. The order is an instruction to supply the customer with specific goods. This instruction is passed on to the stores department to select the items to be delivered to the customer. Staff in the distributions department produce a delivery note to accompany the goods. This is a document detailing the goods to be delivered, the date of delivery and the customer to whom they are delivered. When the customer (the supermarket in this case) receives the goods, the delivery note is signed as acknowledgement of receipt. It is at this point that control usually passes and the revenue can be recognised as earned. The signed delivery note is then passed on to the accounts department, which produces a sales invoice and records the sale in the accounting records. The invoice has all the information from the delivery note as well as the prices charged for the goods supplied.

The sales journal can also be referred to as a columnar journal. There are columns in the journal to record the date, invoice number, name of the customer, folio-posting reference and amount of the sales transaction. In a perpetual inventory system, there is an additional column to record the cost of sales.

At the end of the month, the balance in the accounts receivable control account should equal the total of the balances in the accounts receivable subsidiary ledger.

Procedure for using the sales journal

- Enter each invoice (representing a credit sale of merchandise) as a line item in the sales journal.
- Post the amount of each invoice to the debit side of each individual customer's account in the accounts receivable subsidiary ledger.
- At the end of the month, post the total of these transactions to the general ledger.

Posting

	Perpetual inventory system	*Periodic inventory system*
General ledger	Dr Accounts receivable control (A) Cr Sales (I) ***and*** Dr Cost of sales (E) Cr Inventory (A)	Dr Accounts receivable control (A) Cr Sales (I)
Accounts receivable subsidiary ledger	Dr Individual customers' accounts	Dr Individual customers' accounts

The recording process will be illustrated through the use of the sales transactions of Bright Life. The perpetual system is illustrated first, followed by the periodic system.

Example: Sales journal

For the month of January 20X6, Bright Life made the following credit sales to customers:

1 01/01/X6 Sold goods on credit to F Jones for C1 000 (invoice 23). Cost C500.
2 08/01/X6 Sold goods on credit to S Pillay for C500 (invoice 24). Cost C250.

3 19/01/X6 Sold goods on credit to M Nakita for C2 000 (invoice 25). Cost C1 000.
4 30/01/X6 Sold goods on credit to F Jones for C1 500 (invoice 26). Cost C750.

Bright Life does not allow settlement discount to its customers.

You are required to:

Prepare a sales journal using the following:

a) A perpetual inventory system.
b) A periodic inventory system.

Solution: Sales journal

a) Perpetual system

Sales journal – January 20X6 **SJ2**

Date	*Invoice*	*Customer*	*Fol*	*Sales*	*Cost of sales*
01/01/X6	23	F Jones	ARL15	1 000	500
08/01/X6	24	S Pillay	ARL25	500	250
19/01/X6	25	M Nakita	ARL35	2 000	1 000
30/01/X6	26	F Jones	ARL15	1 500	750
				5 000	2 500
				Dr GL: AR control **Cr** GL: Sales	**Dr** GL: COS **Cr** GL: Inventory

Accounts receivable subsidiary ledger
Individual customer accounts
(The individual sales are posted to the subsidiary ledger accounts on a continuous basis)

General ledger
Financial statement accounts
General ledger posting:
Dr Accounts receivable control (GL255)
Cr Sales (GL580)
and
Dr Cost of sales (GL660)
Cr Inventory (GL325)
(The total sales and cost of sales are posted at the end of the month to the general ledger)

F Jones (ARL15)

Date	*Details*	*Fol*	*C*	*Date*	*Details*	*Fol*	*C*
01/01	23	SJ2	1 000				
30/01	26	SJ2	1 500				

Accounts receivable control (GL255)

Date	*Details*	*Fol*	*C*	*Date*	*Details*	*Fol*	*C*
31/01	Sales	SJ2	5 000				

S Pillay (ARL25)

Date	*Details*	*Fol*	*C*	*Date*	*Details*	*Fol*	*C*
08/01	24	SJ2	500				

Sales (GL580)

Date	*Details*	*Fol*	*C*	*Date*	*Details*	*Fol*	*C*
				31/01	Accounts receivable	SJ2	5 000

M Nakita (ARL35)

Date	Details	Fol	C	Date	Details	Fol	C
19/01	25	SJ2	2 000				

Inventory (GL325)

Date	Details	Fol	C	Date	Details	Fol	C
				31/01	Cost of sales	SJ2	2 500

Cost of sales (GL660)

Date	Details	Fol	C	Date	Details	Fol	C
31/01	Inventory	SJ2	2 500				

Note that the individual credit sales have been posted to the individual customers' accounts in the accounts receivable subsidiary ledger, and the month-end postings have been made to the general ledger accounts.

b) Periodic system

Sales journal – January 20X6 **SJ2**

Date	*Invoice*	*Customer*	*Fol*	*Sales*
01/01/X6	23	F Jones	ARL15	1 000
08/01/X6	24	S Pillay	ARL25	500
19/01/X6	25	M Nakita	ARL35	2 000
30/01/X6	26	F Jones	ARL15	1 500
				5 000
				Dr GL: AR control **Cr** GL: Sales

Accounts receivable subsidiary ledger

Individual customer accounts

(The individual sales are posted to the subsidiary ledger accounts on a continuous basis)

General ledger

Financial statement accounts

General ledger posting:

Dr Accounts receivable control (255)

Cr Sales (580)

(The total sales are posted at the end of the month to the general ledger)

F Jones (ARL15)

Date	Details	Fol	C	Date	Details	Fol	C
01/01	23	SJ2	1 000				
30/01	26	SJ2	1 500				

S Pillay (ARL25)

Date	Details	Fol	C	Date	Details	Fol	C
08/01	24	SJ2	500				

M Nakita (ARL35)

Date	Details	Fol	C	Date	Details	Fol	C
19/01	25	SJ2	2 000				

Accounts receivable control (GL255)

Date	Details	Fol	C	Date	Details	Fol	C
31/01	Sales	SJ2	5 000				

Sales (GL580)

Date	Details	Fol	C	Date	Details	Fol	C
				31/01	Accounts receivable	SJ2	5 000

 Again, note that the individual credit sales have been posted to the individual customers' accounts in the accounts receivable subsidiary ledger, and the month-end postings have been made to the general ledger accounts.

Pause and reflect . . .

Have you thought how you decide what columns are needed in the sales journal?

Response

You just need to think of the underlying accounting entry. For the perpetual system, there are two entries. First, there is a debit to accounts receivable control and credit to sales. Second, there is a debit to cost of sales and a credit to inventory. We therefore need a column for the sales (the debit to accounts receivable is for the same amount) and a column for the cost of sales (the credit to inventory is for the same amount).

9.3.2 Purchases journal

Use

The transactions that are recorded in the purchases journal are purchases made *on credit* from suppliers. *Cash* purchases are recorded in the cash payments journal, which is discussed in Section 9.3.4 below.

An entity not only buys goods for resale on credit. In addition, non-current assets and other supplies and services are purchased on credit. The buying department is responsible for placing orders with a supplier. The order details the goods required, the price negotiated for the goods and the delivery address. The supplier then sends the goods ordered to the entity. The staff in the receiving department are responsible for matching the goods received against the authorised order before signing the supplier's delivery note as acceptance of the goods. Once this is done, a goods received note (GRN) is prepared for the items received. This is an internal document evidencing the receipt of goods from a supplier. The GRN is matched to the order and sent to the accounts department, where these documents are filed in an outstanding GRN file until the supplier's invoice arrives. Once this occurs, all three documents are matched and recorded in the accounting records. The supplier's invoice gives the details and the price of the goods purchased.

Procedure for using the purchases journal

- Enter each invoice received from the supplier as a separate line item.
- The total amount owing will be entered into the accounts payable column. The items charged on the invoice must be analysed and allocated to the appropriate column, for example purchases.
- Post the total of each invoice to the credit side of each individual supplier's account in the accounts payable subsidiary ledger.
- At the end of the month, post totals (except for the sundry items) to the general ledger. Sundry items must be posted to the debit side of the appropriate general ledger accounts.

Posting

	Perpetual inventory system	*Periodic inventory system*
General ledger	Dr Inventory (A) Dr Stationery (A) Dr Other individual accounts in the general ledger with the items recorded in the sundries column Cr Accounts payable control (L)	Dr Purchases (T) Dr Stationery (A) Dr Other individual accounts in the general ledger with the items recorded in the sundries column Cr Accounts payable control (L)
Accounts payable subsidiary ledger	Cr Individual suppliers' accounts	Cr Individual suppliers' accounts

The recording process will be illustrated through the use of the purchases transactions of Bright Life.

Example: Purchases journal

For the month of January 20X6, Bright Life made the following credit purchases from suppliers:

5 01/01/X Purchased goods for resale from Games for Africa for C1 000 (invoice 242)
6 02/01/X6 Purchased stationery from Paper Limited for C220 (invoice 128)
7 07/01/X6 Purchased goods for resale from Master's Music for C1 200 (invoice 891)
8 14/01/X6 Purchased a computer for the accountant from Computer World for C8 000 (invoice 315)
9 21/01/X6 Purchased refreshments from Mr Thirsty for C50 (invoice 99)
10 24/01/X6 Purchased goods for resale from Games for Africa for C1 500 (invoice 281)

Bright Life's suppliers do not grant settlement discounts.

You are required to:

Prepare a purchases journal using the following:

a) A perpetual inventory system
b) A periodic inventory system

Solution: Purchases journal

a) Perpetual system

Purchases journal – January 20X6									**PJ4**
Date	*Inv*	*Details*	*Fol*	*Accounts payable*	*Inventory*	*Stationery*	*Sundry accounts*		
							Detail	*Fol*	*Amount*
01/01	242	Games for Africa	APL1	1 000	1 000				
02/01	128	Paper Limited	APL2	220		220			
07/01	891	Master's Music	APL3	1 200	1 200				
14/01	315	Computer World	APL4	8 000			Computer	GL75	8 000
21/01	99	Mr Thirsty	APL5	50			Refreshments	GL45	50
24/01	281	Games for Africa	APL1	1 500	1 500				
				11 970	3 700	220			8 050
				Cr GL: AP control	**Dr** GL: Inventory	**Dr** GL: Stationery	**Dr** Individual accounts detailed		

Accounts payable subsidiary ledger
Individual customer accounts
(The individual purchases are posted to the subsidiary ledger accounts on a daily basis)

General ledger
Financial statement accounts
(The totals are posted at the end of the month to the general ledger as indicated below each column in the purchases journal)

Games for Africa (APL1)

Date	*Details*	*Fol*	*C*	*Date*	*Details*	*Fol*	*C*
				01/01	242	PJ4	1 000
				24/01	281	PJ4	1 500

Accounts payable control (GL90)

Date	*Details*	*Fol*	*C*	*Date*	*Details*	*Fol*	*C*
				31/01	Purchases	PJ4	11 970

Paper Limited (APL2)

Date	*Details*	*Fol*	*C*	*Date*	*Details*	*Fol*	*C*
				02/01	128	PJ4	220

Inventory (GL325)

Date	*Details*	*Fol*	*C*	*Date*	*Details*	*Fol*	*C*
31/01	Accounts payable	PJ4	3 700				

Master's Music (APL3)

Date	*Details*	*Fol*	*C*	*Date*	*Details*	*Fol*	*C*
				07/01	891	PJ4	1 200

Stationery (GL50)

Date	*Details*	*Fol*	*C*	*Date*	*Details*	*Fol*	*C*
31/01	Accounts payable	PJ4	220				

Computer World (APL4)

Date	*Details*	*Fol*	*C*	*Date*	*Details*	*Fol*	*C*
				14/01	315	PJ4	8 000

Computer equipment (GL75)

Date	*Details*	*Fol*	*C*	*Date*	*Details*	*Fol*	*C*
31/01	Accounts payable	PJ4	8 000				

Mr Thirsty (APL5)

Date	*Details*	*Fol*	*C*	*Date*	*Details*	*Fol*	*C*
				21/01	99	PJ4	50

Refreshments (GL45)

Date	*Details*	*Fol*	*C*	*Date*	*Details*	*Fol*	*C*
31/01	Accounts payable	PJ4	50				

The individual credit purchases have been posted to the individual suppliers' accounts in the accounts payable subsidiary ledger and the month-end postings have been made to the general ledger accounts.

b) Periodic system

Purchases journal – January 20X6 — **PJ4**

Inv	*Date*	*Details*	*Fol*	*Accounts payable*	*Inventory*	*Stationery*	*Sundry*		
							Detail	*Fol*	*Amount*
242	01/01	Games for Africa	APL1	1 000	1 000				
128	02/01	Paper Limited	APL2	220		220			
891	07/01	Master's Music	APL3	1 200	1 200				
315	14/01	Computer World	APL4	8 000			Computer	GL75	8 000
99	21/01	Mr Thirsty	APL5	50			Refreshments	GL45	50
281	24/01	Games for Africa	APL1	1 500	1 500				
				11 970	3 700	220			8 050
				Cr GL: AP control	**Dr** GL: Inventory	**Dr** GL: Stationery	**Dr** Individual accounts detailed		

Accounts payable *subsidiary ledger*
Individual customer accounts
(The individual purchases are posted to the subsidiary ledger accounts on a daily basis)

Games for Africa (APL1)

Date	*Details*	*Fol*	*C*	*Date*	*Details*	*Fol*	*C*
				01/01	242	PJ4	1 000
				24/01	281	PJ4	1 500

Paper Limited (APL2)

Date	*Details*	*Fol*	*C*	*Date*	*Details*	*Fol*	*C*
				02/01	128	PJ4	220

Master's Music (APL3)

Date	*Details*	*Fol*	*C*	*Date*	*Details*	*Fol*	*C*
				07/01	891	PJ4	1 200

Computer World (APL4)

Date	*Details*	*Fol*	*C*	*Date*	*Details*	*Fol*	*C*
				14/01	315	PJ4	8 000

Mr Thirsty (APL5)

Date	*Details*	*Fol*	*C*	*Date*	*Details*	*Fol*	*C*
				21/01	99	PJ4	50

General ledger
Financial statement accounts
(The totals are posted at the end of the month to the general ledger as indicated below each column in the purchases journal)

Accounts payable control (GL90)

Date	*Details*	*Fol*	*C*	*Date*	*Details*	*Fol*	*C*
				31/01	Purchases	PJ4	11 970

Inventory (GL60)

Date	*Details*	*Fol*	*C*	*Date*	*Details*	*Fol*	*C*
31/01	Accounts payable	PJ4	3 700				

Stationery (GL50)

Date	*Details*	*Fol*	*C*	*Date*	*Details*	*Fol*	*C*
31/01	Accounts payable	PJ4	220				

Computer equipment (GL75)

Date	*Details*	*Fol*	*C*	*Date*	*Details*	*Fol*	*C*
31/01	Accounts payable	PJ4	8 000				

Refreshments (GL45)

Date	*Details*	*Fol*	*C*	*Date*	*Details*	*Fol*	*C*
31/01	Accounts payable	PJ4	50				

Again, the individual credit purchases have been posted to the individual suppliers' accounts in the accounts payable subsidiary ledger and the month-end postings have been made to the general ledger accounts.

Pause and reflect . . .

Have you thought how you decide what columns are needed in the purchases journal?

Response

Again, you just need to think of the underlying accounting entry. It is different from the sales journal situation in that a number of separate accounts are debited with a single credit to the accounts payable control account. For the perpetual system, there are debits to each major category purchased, such as inventory, supplies and furniture, and then a credit to the accounts payable control with the total. We therefore need columns for each of the categories of items purchased and a column for accounts payable control.

9.3.3 Cash receipts journal

Use

The transactions that are recorded in the cash receipts journal are cash sales, receipts from customers in settlement of amounts owing, and sundry receipts (such as cash from the sale of a non-current asset, interest received from the bank or cash introduced by the owner at the start of a business). When cash is received from a cash sale, it is usually entered using a cash register. At the end of the day, the sales as recorded by the cash register are totalled up and matched to the cash in the register. If cash is received from a customer in settlement of amounts owing or from another source, such as cash from the sale of a non-current asset, a cash receipt is issued. The cash receipt will detail the amount of cash received, from whom it was received and the reason, for example payment of an account. Cheques received from customers are entered into a cheque register on a daily basis. The cheque register will list the cheques received, detailing the amounts received and from whom they were received. At the end of each day, the total cash sales, individual cash receipts and cheques received are recorded in the accounting records.

Procedure for using the cash receipts journal

- Enter each cash amount received as a line item.
- Where cash is received from a credit customer, the cash received is entered into the analysis column (and subsequently into the bank column when deposited and in the accounts receivable control column).
- The analysis column is used to record all cash received until it is banked. If a perpetual system is being used, the cost price of the goods sold for cash will be entered in the cost of sales column. The cost of sales column is not part of the double entry to record cash received.
- Post the amounts received from individual customers to the credit side of each individual customer's account in the accounts receivable subsidiary ledger.
- At the end of the month, post totals, except for the sundry items, to the general ledger. Sundry items must be posted to the credit side of the appropriate general ledger accounts.

Posting

	Perpetual inventory system	*Periodic inventory system*
General ledger	Dr Bank (A) Cr Accounts receivable control (A) Cr Sales (I) Cr Other individual accounts in the general ledger with the items recorded in the sundry column *and* Dr Cost of sales (E) Cr Inventory (A)	Dr Bank (A) Cr Accounts receivable control (A) Cr Sales (I) Cr Other individual accounts in the general ledger with the items recorded in the sundry column
Accounts receivable subsidiary ledger	Cr Individual customers' accounts	Cr Individual customers' accounts

The recording process will be illustrated through the use of the cash receipts transactions of Bright Life. The perpetual system is illustrated first, followed by the periodic system.

Example: Cash receipts journal

For the month of January 20X6, Bright Life received the following amounts in cash:

11 01/01/X6 The owner, Mr S Smart, invested C20 000 into the business (deposit slip 1)

12 15/01/X6 Sold goods for cash C200 (cost price C100, cash sale slip 18)

13 15/01/X6 Received C1 000 from F Jones (receipt 90)

14 25/01/X6 Sold goods for cash for C800 and allowed a 10 per cent cash discount (cost price C400, cash sale slip 19)

15 25/01/X6 Received interest of C20 from the bank (receipt 91)

16 28/01/X6 Received payment from S Pillay for amount due (receipt 92)

You are required to:

Prepare a cash receipts journal using the following:

a) A perpetual inventory system
b) A periodic inventory system

Solution: Cash receipts journal

a) Perpetual system

Cash receipts journal – January 20X6 **CRJ7**

Doc	*Date*	*Account name*	*Fol*	*Sales*	*Accounts receivable control*	*Sundries*	*Cost of sales*	*Analysis*	*Bank*
DS01	01/01	Capital - S Smart	GL10			20 000			20 000
CSS18	15/01	Sales		200			100	200	
Rec90	15/01	F Jones	ARL15		1 000			1 000	1 200
CSS19	25/01	Sales		720			400	720	
Rec91	25/01	Interest received	GL70			20		20	740
Rec92	28/01	S Pillay	ARL25		500				500
				920	1 500	20 020	500		22 440
				Cr GL: Sales	**Cr** GL: AR control	**Cr** Individual accounts	**Dr** GL: COS **Cr** GL: Inventory		**Dr** GL: Bank

Remember from Chapter 8, *Purchase and sale transactions*, that sales are recorded net of cash sale discounts.

Accounts receivable subsidiary ledger
Individual customer accounts
(The individual receipts from customers are posted to the subsidiary ledger accounts on a daily basis)

F Jones (ARL15)

Date	*Details*	*Fol*	*C*	*Date*	*Details*	*Fol*	*C*
01/01	23	SJ2	1 000	15/02	Rec90	CRJ7	1 000
30/01	26	SJ2	1 500	31/01	Bal	c/d	1 500
			2 500				2 500
01/02	Bal	b/d	1 500				

S Pillay (ARL25)

Date	*Details*	*Fol*	*C*	*Date*	*Details*	*Fol*	*C*
08/01	24	SJ2	500	28/01	Rec92	CRJ7	500
				31/01	Bal	c/d	—
			500				500
01/02	Bal	b/d	—				

M Nakita (ARL35)

Date	*Details*	*Fol*	*C*	*Date*	*Details*	*Fol*	*C*
19/01	25	SJ2	2 000				
				31/01	Bal	c/d	2 000
			2 000				2 000
01/02	Bal	b/d	2 000				

General ledger
Financial statement accounts
(The totals are posted at the end of the month to the general ledger as indicated below each column in the receipts journal)

Accounts receivable control (GL255)

Date	*Details*	*Fol*	*C*	*Date*	*Details*	*Fol*	*C*
31/01	Sales	SJ2	5 000	31/01	Bank	CRJ7	1 500
				31/01	Bal	c/d	3 500
			5 000				5 000
01/02	Bal	b/d	3 500				

Sales (GL580)

Date	*Details*	*Fol*	*C*	*Date*	*Details*	*Fol*	*C*
				31/01	Accounts receivable	SJ2	5 000
31/01	Bal	c/d	5 970	31/01	Bank	CRJ7	970
			5 970				5 970
				31/01	Bal	b/d	5 970

Inventory (GL325)

Date	*Details*	*Fol*	*C*	*Date*	*Details*	*Fol*	*C*
31/01	Accounts Payable	PJ4	3 700	31/01	Cost of sales	SJ2	2 500
				31/01	Cost of sales	CRJ7	500
				31/01	Bal	c/d	700
			3 700				3 700
01/02	Bal	b/d	700				

Cost of sales (GL660)

Date	*Details*	*Fol*	*C*	*Date*	*Details*	*Fol*	*C*
31/01	Inventory	SJ2	2 500				
31/01	Inventory	CRJ7	500	31/01	Bal	c/d	3 000
			3 000				3 000
31/01	Bal	b/d	3 000				

Capital – S Smart (GL10)

Date	*Details*	*Fol*	*C*	*Date*	*Details*	*Fol*	*C*
				01/01	Bank	CRJ7	20 000

Bank (GL150)

Date	*Details*	*Fol*	*C*	*Date*	*Details*	*Fol*	*C*
31/01	Deposits	CRJ7	22 440				

Interest received (GL70)

Date	*Details*	*Fol*	*C*	*Date*	*Details*	*Fol*	*C*
				25/01	Bank	CRJ7	20

The individual receipts from customers have been posted to the individual customers' accounts in the accounts receivable subsidiary ledger. In addition, the month-end postings have been made to the general ledger accounts.

b) Periodic system

Cash receipts journal – January 20X6 **CRJ7**

Doc	Date	Account name	Fol	Sales	Accounts Receivable control	Sundries	Analysis	Bank
DS01	01/01	Capital – S Smart	GL10			20 000		20 000
CSS18	15/01	Sales		200			200	
Rec90	5/01	F. Jones	ARL15		1 000		1 000	1 200
CSS19	25/01	Sales		720			720	
Rec91	25/01	Interest received	GL70			20	20	740
Rec92	8/01	S. Pillay	ARL25		500			500
				920	1 500	20 020		22 440
				Cr GL: Sales	**Cr** GL: AR control	**Cr** Individual accounts		**Dr** GL: Bank

Accounts receivable subsidiary ledger
Individual customer accounts
(The individual receipts from customers are posted to the subsidiary ledger accounts on a daily basis)

F Jones (ARL15)

Date	Details	Fol	C	Date	Details	Fol	C
01/01	23	SJ2	1 000	15/02	Rec90	CRJ7	1 000
30/01	26	SJ2	1 500	31/01	Bal	c/d	1 500
			2 500				2 500
01/02	Bal	b/d	1 500				

S Pillay (ARL25)

Date	Details	Fol	C	Date	Details	Fol	C
08/01	24	SJ2	500	28/01	Rec92	CRJ7	500
				31/01	Bal	c/d	—
			500				500
01/02	Bal	b/d	—				

M Nakita (ARL35)

Date	Details	Fol	C	Date	Details	Fol	C
19/01	25	SJ2	2 000				
				31/01	Bal	c/d	2 000
			2 000				2 000
01/02	Bal	b/d	2 000				

General ledger
Financial statement accounts
(The totals are posted at the end of the month to the general ledger as indicated below each column in the receipts journal)

Accounts receivable control (GL255)

Date	Details	Fol	C	Date	Details	Fol	C
31/01	Sales	SJ2	5 000	31/01	Bank	CRJ7	1 500
				31/01	Bal	c/d	3 500
			5 000				5 000
01/02	Bal	b/d	3 500				

Sales (GL580)

Date	Details	Fol	C	Date	Details	Fol	C
				31/01	Accounts receivable	SJ2	5 000
31/01	Bal	c/d	5 920	31/01	Bank	CRJ7	920
			5 920				5 920
				31/01	Bal	b/d	5 920

Capital – S Smart (GL10)

Date	Details	Fol	C	Date	Details	Fol	C
				01/01	Bank	CRJ7	20 000
31/01	Bal	c/d	20 000				
			20 000				20 000
				01/02	Bal	b/d	20 000

Interest received (GL70)

Date	Details	Fol	C	Date	Details	Fol	C
				25/01	Bank	CRJ7	20

Bank (GL150)

Date	Details	Fol	C	Date	Details	Fol	C
31/01	Deposits	CRJ7	22 440				

 The individual receipts from customers have been posted to the individual customers' accounts in the accounts receivable subsidiary ledger. In addition, the month-end postings have been made to the general ledger accounts.

Pause and reflect . . .

There is a sales column in both the sales journal and the cash receipts journal. Can you identify the types of sales transactions that are recorded in each journal?

Response

The sales journal records sales on credit whereas the cash receipts journal records cash sales.

9.3.4 Cash payments journal

Use

The transactions that are recorded in the cash payments journal are payments made out of the bank account for purchases, settlement of balances on suppliers' accounts, salaries, wages and sundry payments. Payments are only made once all documentation is received. The accounts payable clerk in the accounts department then makes out a cheque requisition. This, together with the supporting documents, is passed on to the accountant who is an authorised cheque signatory to review and prepare the cheque. The payment is then recorded in the accounting records.

For an entity to maintain proper control over its disbursements, all payments should be made by way of cheque. This is because a cheque has to be signed by an authorised person before payment can be made.

Procedure for using the cash payments journal

- Enter each cheque drawn, or reduction in the bank balance, as a line item.
- Post amounts paid to each individual supplier to the debit side of each individual supplier's account in the subsidiary accounts payable ledger.
- At the end of the month, post totals, except for the sundry items, to the general ledger. Sundry items must be posted to the debit side of the appropriate general ledger accounts.

Posting

	Perpetual inventory system	*Periodic inventory system*
General ledger	Dr Inventory (A) Dr Accounts payable control (L) Dr Salaries (E) Dr Other individual accounts in the general ledger with the items recorded in the sundry column Cr Bank (A)	Dr Purchases (T) Dr Accounts payable control (L) Dr Salaries (E) Dr Other individual accounts in the general ledger with the items recorded in the sundry column Cr Bank (A)
Accounts payable subsidiary ledger	Dr Individual suppliers' accounts	Dr Individual suppliers' accounts

The recording process will be illustrated through the use of the cash payments transactions of Bright Life. The perpetual inventory system is illustrated first, followed by the periodic system.

Example: Cash payments journal

For the month of January 20X6, Bright Life made the following payments:

17 01/01/X6 Purchased C200 of goods for resale and paid by cheque (cheque 141)
18 15/01/X6 Paid Games for Africa C1 000 (cheque 142)
19 18/01/X6 Purchased C500 worth of goods for resale and paid by cheque. Received a 10 per cent cash discount (cheque 143)
20 27/01/X6 Paid Computer World the amount outstanding (cheque 144)
21 30/01/X6 Paid salaries for the month, C2 000 (cheque 145)
22 30/01/X6 Paid the January rent C1 500 (cheque 146)

You are required to:

Prepare a cash payments journal using the following:

a) A perpetual inventory system
b) A periodic inventory system

Solution: Cash payments journal

a) Perpetual system

Cash payments journal – January 20X6 **CPJ7**

Doc	*Date*	*Details*	*Fol*	*Inventory*	*Salaries*	*Accounts payable*	*Sundries*	*Bank*
CHQ141	01/01	Inventory		200				200
CHQ142	15/01	Games for Africa	APL1			1 000		1 000
CHQ143	18/01	Inventory		450				450
CHQ144	27/01	Computer World	APL4			8 000		8 000
CHQ145	30/01	Salaries			2 000			2 000
CHQ146	30/01	Rent	GL95				1 500	1 500
				650	2 000	9 000	1 500	13 150
				Dr GL: Inventory	**Dr** GL: Salaries	**Dr** GL: AP control	**Dr** Individual accounts	**Cr** GL: Bank

Remember from Chapter 8 that purchases of inventory are recorded net of cash discounts.

Accounts payable subsidiary ledger

Individual customer accounts

(The individual payments made to suppliers are posted to the subsidiary ledger accounts on a daily basis)

Games for Africa (APL1)

Date	*Details*	*Fol*	*C*	*Date*	*Details*	*Fol*	*C*
15/01	142	CPJ7	1 000	01/01	242	PJ4	1 000
31/01	Bal	c/d	1 500	24/01	281	PJ4	1 500
			2 500				2 500
				01/02	Bal	b/d	1 500

Paper Limited (APL2)

Date	*Details*	*Fol*	*C*	*Date*	*Details*	*Fol*	*C*
				02/01	182	PJ4	220
31/01	Bal	c/d	220				
			220				220
				01/02	Bal	b/d	220

Master's Music (APL3)

Date	*Details*	*Fol*	*C*	*Date*	*Details*	*Fol*	*C*
				07/01	891	PJ4	1 200
31/01	Bal	c/d	1 200				
			1 200				1 200
				01/02	Bal	b/d	1 200

Computer World (APL4)

Date	*Details*	*Fol*	*C*	*Date*	*Details*	*Fol*	*C*
27/01	144	CPJ7	8 000	14/01	315	PJ4	8 000
31/01	Bal	c/d	—				
			8 000				8 000
				01/02	Bal	b/d	—

Mr Thirsty (APL5)

Date	*Details*	*Fol*	*C*	*Date*	*Details*	*Fol*	*C*
				21/01	99	PJ4	50
31/01	Bal	c/d	50				
			50				50
				01/02	Bal	b/d	50

General ledger

Financial statement accounts

(The totals are posted at the end of the month to the general ledger as indicated below each column in the cash payments journal)

Accounts payable control (GL90)

Date	*Details*	*Fol*	*C*	*Date*	*Details*	*Fol*	*C*
31/01	Bank	CPJ7	9 000	31/01	Purchases	PJ4	11 970
31/01	Bal	c/d	2 970				
			11 970				11 970
				01/02	Bal	b/d	2 970

Inventory (GL325)

Date	*Details*	*Fol*	*C*	*Date*	*Details*	*Fol*	*C*
31/01	Accounts payable	PJ4	3 700	31/01	Cost of sales	SJ2	2 500
31/01	Bank	CPJ7	650	31/01	Cost of sales	CRJ7	500
				31/01	Bal	c/d	1 350
			4 350				4 350
01/02	Bal	b/d	1 350				

Salaries (GL55)

Date	*Details*	*Fol*	*C*	*Date*	*Details*	*Fol*	*C*
31/01	Bank	CPJ7	2 000				
				31/01	Bal	c/d	2 000
			2 000				2 000
31/01	Bal	b/d	2 000				

Rent (GL95)

Date	*Details*	*Fol*	*C*	*Date*	*Details*	*Fol*	*C*
30/01	Bank	CPJ7	1 500				
				31/01	Bal	c/d	1 500
			1 500				1 500
31/01	Bank	b/d	1 500				

Bank (GL150)

Date	*Details*	*Fol*	*C*	*Date*	*Details*	*Fol*	*C*
31/01	Deposits	CRJ7	22 440	31/01	Payments	CPJ7	13 150
				31/01	Bal	c/d	9 290
			22 440				22 440
01/02	Bal	b/d	9 290				

The individual payments to suppliers have been posted to the individual suppliers' accounts in the accounts payable subsidiary ledger. In addition, the month-end postings have been made to the general ledger accounts.

b) Periodic system

Cash payments journal – January 20X6 **CPJ7**

Doc	*Date*	*Details*	*Fol*	*Purchases*	*Salaries*	*Accounts payable*	*Sundries*	*Bank*
CHQ141	01/01	Purchases		200				200
CHQ142	15/01	Games for Africa	APL1			1 000		1 000
CHQ143	18/01	Purchases		450				450
CHQ144	27/01	Computer World	APL4			8 000		8 000
CHQ145	30/01	Salaries			2 000			2 000
CHQ146	30/01	Rent	GL95				1 500	1 500
				650	2 000	9 000	1 500	13 150
				Dr GL: Purchases	**Dr** GL: Salaries	**Dr** GL: AP control	**Dr** Individual accounts	**Cr** GL: Bank

Accounts payable subsidiary ledger
Individual supplier accounts
(The individual payments made to suppliers are posted to the subsidiary ledger accounts on a daily basis)

Games for Africa (APL1)

Date	*Details*	*Fol*	*C*	*Date*	*Details*	*Fol*	*C*
15/01	142	CPJ7	1 000	01/01	242	PJ4	1 000
31/01	Bal	c/d	1 500	24/01	281	PJ4	1 500
			2 500				2 500
				01/02	Bal	b/d	1 500

Paper Limited (APL2)

Date	*Details*	*Fol*	*C*	*Date*	*Details*	*Fol*	*C*
				02/01	182	PJ4	220
31/01	Bal	c/d	220				
			220				220
				01/02	Bal	b/d	220

Master's Music (APL3)

Date	*Details*	*Fol*	*C*	*Date*	*Details*	*Fol*	*C*
				07/01	891	PJ4	1 200
31/01	Bal	c/d	1 200				
			1 200				1 200
				01/02	Bal	b/d	1 200

General ledger
Financial statement accounts
(The totals are posted at the end of the month to the general ledger as indicated below each column in the cash payments journal)

Accounts payable control (GL90)

Date	*Details*	*Fol*	*C*	*Date*	*Details*	*Fol*	*C*
31/01	Bank	CPJ7	9 000	31/01	Purchases	PJ4	11 970
31/01	Bal	c/d	2 970				
			11 970				11 970
				01/02	Bal	b/d	2 970

Purchases (GL60)

Date	*Details*	*Fol*	*C*	*Date*	*Details*	*Fol*	*C*
31/01	Accounts payable	PJ4	3 700				
31/01	Bank	CPJ7	650	31/01	Bal	c/d	4 350
			4 350				4 350
31/01	Bal	b/d	4 350				

Salaries (GL55)

Date	*Details*	*Fol*	*C*	*Date*	*Details*	*Fol*	*C*
31/01	Bank	CPJ7	2 000				
				31/01	Bal	c/d	2 000
			2 000				2 000
31/01	Bal	b/d	2 000				

Computer World (APL4)

Date	*Details*	*Fol*	*C*	*Date*	*Details*	*Fol*	*C*
27/01	144	CPJ7	8 000	14/01	315	PJ4	8 000
31/01	Bal	c/d	—				
			8 000				8 000
				01/02	Bal	b/d	—

Rent (GL95)

Date	*Details*	*Fol*	*C*	*Date*	*Details*	*Fol*	*C*
30/01	Bank	CPJ7	1 500				
				31/01	Bal	c/d	1 500
			1 500				1 500
31/01	Bank	b/d	1 500				

Mr Thirsty (APL5)

Date	*Details*	*Fol*	*C*	*Date*	*Details*	*Fol*	*C*
				21/01	99	PJ4	50
31/01	Bal	c/d	50				
			50				50
				01/02	Bal	b/d	50

Bank (GL150)

Date	*Details*	*Fol*	*C*	*Date*	*Details*	*Fol*	*C*
31/01	Deposits	CRJ7	22 440	31/01	Payments	CPJ7	13 150
				31/01	Bal	c/d	9 290
			22 440				22 440
01/02	Bal	b/d	9 290				

 The individual payments to suppliers have been posted to the individual suppliers' accounts in the accounts payable subsidiary ledger. In addition, the month-end postings have been made to the general ledger accounts.

Pause and reflect . . .

Look carefully at the cash payments journal (either the perpetual inventory system or the periodic inventory system). Explain the following:

a) On 1 January when inventory was purchased, why is there is no entry in the folio column?
b) On 15 January when Bright Life paid Games for Africa, why does the folio column record an entry to the accounts payable ledger?
c) On 30 January when the rent is paid, why does the folio column record an entry to the general ledger?

Response

a) When the inventory was purchased, the underlying accounting entry is a debit to inventory/purchases and a credit to bank. No subsidiary ledger is involved and the posting to the general ledger accounts takes place in total at the end of the period.
b) When Bright Life paid Games for Africa, both the accounts payable control account in the general ledger as well as the Games for Africa account in the accounts payable ledger need to be reduced or debited. The folio reference to APL1 results in a posting to the debit of the Games for Africa account in the accounts payable ledger while the posting to the accounts payable account in the general ledger takes place in total at the period end, with the posting reference beneath the column total (Dr AP control).
c) When the rent is paid, a folio reference to the rent account in the general ledger is needed, as there is no separate column for rent in this cash payment journal. Rent is entered into the sundries column, and thus the posting to the debit of the rent account in the general ledger is done on a transaction-by-transaction basis and not in total.

9.4 Procedures for using the secondary analysis journals

9.4.1 Sales returns journal

This is used to record goods returned from customers, or allowances granted in respect of items such as overcharges and trade discounts not deducted. A credit note is issued as evidence that the amount is authorised and is to be recorded. The format of the sales return journal is very similar to that of the sales journal. However, when we post to the accounts receivable subsidiary ledger and the general ledger, the reverse entry is posted.

Procedure for using the sales returns journal

- Enter each credit note (representing a reduction in the amount owing by a customer) as a line item.
- Post the amount of each credit note to the credit side of each individual customer's account in the accounts receivable subsidiary ledger.
- At the end of the month, post the total of these transactions to the general ledger.

Posting

	Perpetual inventory system	*Periodic inventory system*
General ledger	Dr Sales returns (– I) Cr Accounts receivable control (A) ***and*** Dr Inventory (A) Cr Cost of sales (E)	Dr Sales returns (– I) Cr Accounts receivable control (A)
Accounts receivable subsidiary ledger	Cr Individual customers' accounts	Cr Individual customers' accounts

9.4.2 Purchases returns journal

This is used to record goods returned to suppliers, or allowances granted in respect of items such as overcharges or trade discounts not granted. The supplier will issue a credit note as evidence of the reduction. The format of the purchases returns journal is the same as that of the purchases journal. However, when we post to the accounts payable subsidiary ledger and the general ledger, the reverse entry is posted.

Procedure for using the purchases returns journal

- Enter each credit note received from a supplier as a separate line item.
- The total amount of the credit note will be entered in the control column. The reduction granted on the credit note must be analysed and allocated to the appropriate column.
- Post the total amount of each credit note to the debit side of each individual supplier's account in the accounts payable subsidiary ledger.
- At the end of the month, post totals, except for the sundry items, to the general ledger.

Posting

	Perpetual inventory system	*Periodic inventory system*
General ledger	Dr Accounts payable control (L) Cr Inventory (A) Cr Stationery (A) Cr Other individual accounts in the general ledger with the items recorded in the sundry column	Dr Accounts payable control (L) Cr Purchases returns (T) Cr Stationery (A) Cr Other individual accounts in the general ledger with the items recorded in the sundry column
Accounts payable subsidiary ledger	Dr Individual suppliers' accounts	Dr Individual suppliers' accounts

9.4.3 Petty cash journal

This is used to record all payments made in cash, usually of small amounts. A petty cash voucher is made out and attached to the receipt from the supplier as evidence of the amount paid. The format is the same as the cash payments journal, except that the bank column is changed to petty cash.

Procedure for using the petty cash journal

This is the same as for the cash payments journal, except it is recorded from the petty cash voucher.

	Perpetual inventory system	*Periodic inventory system*
General ledger	Dr Inventory (A) Dr Stationery (E) Dr Wages (E) Dr Other individual accounts in the general ledger with the items recorded in the sundry column Cr Petty cash (A)	Dr Purchases (A) Dr Stationery (E) Dr Wages (E) Dr Other individual accounts in the general ledger with the items recorded in the sundry column Cr Petty cash (A)

9.5 Computerised accounting systems

This chapter has focused on the workings of a manual accounting system. The principles of a computerised accounting system are similar, although each such system will have a different interface based on the operating system, much like the difference between an Apple and an Android smartphone. Once you have understood the principles of a manual accounting system, you will be able to apply that knowledge to any computerised system.

All large business entities today use a computerised accounting system with the software typically customised for their own needs. Small business entities often use one of the commercially available accounting software packages, but many still choose to use a manual system.

The accounting software performs all the tedious tasks of posting from the journal to the general ledger and subsidiary ledgers. The posting process is mechanical and is a task which a computer is capable of doing much faster than any human being. However, the principles of basic bookkeeping have not changed as a result of the accounting software. Manual and computerised accounting systems perform basically the same processes; the accounting principles and concepts are the same, with differences lying in the mechanics of the process.

Computer accounting packages group similar transactions together for input into the system. A typical computerised accounting system will have a section for entering credit sales, credit purchases, cash receipts, cash payments, petty cash payments and other transactions. It is therefore structured in a similar way to the traditional manual system, which uses analysis journals.

The main difference between manual and computerised systems is speed. Accounting software processes data and creates reports much faster than manual systems. Calculations are done automatically in software programs, minimising errors and increasing efficiency.

Revision examples

Example 1

Craig Crayon decided that his school accounting knowledge was sufficient to see him through the first term of accounting at university. He decided to take on a bookkeeping job instead of attending accounting lectures and tutorials. The trial balance he prepared did not balance and you (who attended all your lectures) found the following errors:

- The total of the sales column in the sales journal, amounting to C10 250, was posted as C10 520 to the correct accounts in the general ledger. In addition, one transaction for C700 was not posted to the customer's account in the accounts receivable ledger.
- The total of the entertainment expense column in the cash payments journal, amounting to C370, was posted to the incorrect side of the entertainment expense account in the general ledger. All other postings from the cash payments journal were correct.
- The bank column in the cash payments journal was undercast by C120 and posted to the general ledger at the incorrect amount.

Which of the following statements is correct?

In the trial balance prepared by Craig Crayon:

a) Total credits exceeded total debits by C250.
b) Total credits exceeded total debits by C740.
c) Total credits exceeded total debits by C620.
d) Total debits exceeded total credits by C860.
e) Total debits exceeded total credits by C80.

Example 2

Mr B Burn operates a business entity trading as Colourful Candles. He uses analysis journals to record the transactions of the business. No discounts are offered on credit sales.

The following transactions occurred during March 20X5:

March 3 Sold goods on credit to W Wick for C600
March 12 Sold goods for cash to C Wax for C250
March 25 Received in cash the full amount owed by W Wick
March 30 Sold goods on credit to F Flame for C375

Which of the following statements is correct?

In posting the transactions from the special journals to the ledger accounts:

a) Nothing would be posted to the accounts receivable subsidiary ledger account of W Wick because payment in full was received in the same month as the sale.
b) An amount of C250 would be posted to the accounts receivable subsidiary ledger account of C Wax.
c) An amount of C600 would be posted from the cash receipts journal to the credit side of the sales account in the general ledger.
d) An amount of C975 would be posted from the sales journal to the credit side of the sales account in the general ledger.
e) An amount of C1 225 would be posted from the sales journal to the debit side of the accounts receivable control account in the general ledger.

 **Solution: Revision examples**

Example 1

c)

Working

	Dr	*Cr*
Entertainment posted to incorrect side (370 × 2)		740
Bank column undercast		(120)
		620

Example 2

d)

Working

Credit sales of C600 + C375

Bibliography

Project VRM. *Why Double-Entry Bookkeeping is Actually Cool.* blogs.law.harvard.edu/vrm/2014/09/30/why-bookkeeping-is-actually-cool/ (Accessed 24 November 2014).

PART IV

Recognition and measurement of the elements of financial statements

10 Property, plant and equipment

Business focus

The road to the Reserve Bank is paved with gold

One of the world's largest gold producers, Anglo Gold Ashanti, produced almost four million ounces of gold during 2012. The jewellery sector accounted for 43 per cent of global gold demand during 2012, while the investment sector (including bar and coin stockpiles, and exchange-traded funds) constituted 35 per cent of the total demand. Industrial applications consumed 10 per cent of global production and central banks took up 12 per cent of the world's total output. Gold used to make necklaces and earrings is one thing. Have you ever considered how central banks, like the South African Reserve Bank or the European Central Bank, account for their stockpiles of gold bullion?

One argument is that the bullion meets the definition of property, plant and equipment. The bullion may be seen as a type of commodity which is not exactly akin to cash or cash equivalents. It is not held for sale in the ordinary course of business or as a material to be consumed in the production process or the rendering of services, implying that bullion is not inventory. Bullion is, however, a tangible item that is used during more than one financial period. It is held for use in the supply of services such as the exchange rates for leasing to other financial institutions. As such, it may well be the case that bullion ought to be accounted for as property, plant and equipment: recognised initially at cost and adjusted for the effects of depreciation, impairment and revaluations.

In this chapter

Property, plant and equipment often represent a major portion of the total assets of an entity and are therefore significant in the presentation of an entity's financial position. This gives rise to significant challenges in financial reporting – that is, how to measure financial performance when a substantial component of costs in the current period also affects subsequent reporting periods. One of the main goals in accounting for property, plant and equipment is thus how to allocate the cost of items of property, plant and equipment over those periods in which future benefits from these items are expected to be recognised in the financial statements.

In addition, the determination of whether an expenditure represents an asset or an expense can have a significant effect on an entity's financial position and results of its operations.

When reading this chapter, you will notice a number of practical issues when applying the basic accounting principles for property, plant and equipment, such as the date on which an entity should recognise items of property, plant and equipment; the types of costs to be included upon initial measurement of property, plant and equipment; how depreciation is calculated and allocated to different periods and how the revaluation model is applied.

Dashboard

- Look at the *Learning outcomes* so that you know what you should be able to do after studying the chapter.
- Read the *Business focus* to place the chapter content in a real-world context.
- Preview *In this chapter* to focus your mind on the contents of the chapter.
- Read the *text* in detail.
- Pay attention to the definitions, and apply your mind to the *Pause and reflect* scenarios.
- Make sure that you fully understand the issues relating to the recognition of property, plant and equipment in Section 10.2.2, specifically the difference between costs recognised as an asset and those recognised as an expense.
- Take note of the use of the different methods to calculate depreciation in Section 10.4 and the use of the residual value in these calculations.
- Section 10.8 examines the revaluation model. If you are not studying the revaluation model as part of your course or module, you can omit this section.
- Prepare solutions to all the examples as you read through the chapter.
- Prepare solutions to the *Revision examples* at the end of the chapter, without reference to the suggested solutions. Compare your solutions to the suggested solutions provided.
- Do revision example 1 only if you are not studying the revaluation model. If you are studying the revaluation model, you need to do revision example 2 as well.

Learning outcomes

After studying this chapter, you should be able to do the following:

1 Explain the nature of property, plant and equipment.
2 Recall and explain the definition and recognition criteria for property, plant and equipment.
3 Recall the measurement principles relating to the cost of property, plant and equipment at initial recognition.
4 Differentiate between subsequent expenditure being recognised as either an asset or an expense.
5 Calculate and record depreciation.
6 Record the reassessment of the useful life and residual value of property, plant and equipment.

7 Record the disposal of property, plant and equipment.
8 Calculate and process the accounting entries relating to an impairment of property, plant and equipment.
9 Calculate and process the accounting entries relating to revaluation increases and decreases.

Property, plant and equipment

10.1 The nature of property, plant and equipment

The definition of an asset was discussed in detail in Chapter 2, *Fundamental accounting concepts*. You should refer back to that chapter to ensure that you understand this definition.

Further, in Chapter 6, *Preparation of the financial statements*, we mentioned that the assets of an entity are split into two different types: non-current assets and current assets. Examples listed in Chapter 6 of non-current assets included land, buildings, plant and machinery, furniture, computer equipment and motor vehicles. These examples are all ***tangible*** non-current assets and are collectively referred to as property, plant and equipment, the focus of this chapter.

An entity can also have other non-current assets, for example ***intangible assets*** (such as goodwill, patents and copyrights) and ***investment properties*** (a property that is held to earn rental income or for capital appreciation instead of being used by the entity in the production or supply of goods or services, or for administration use).

The accounting for investment properties is beyond the scope of this text. You will be exposed to goodwill in later chapters.

An asset is defined in the Conceptual Framework as a resource controlled by the entity as a result of past events and from which future economic benefits are expected to flow to the entity.

10.2 Definition and recognition of property, plant and equipment

You will recall that an asset needs to meet both the **definition** and **recognition criteria** in order to be recognised as an asset on the statement of financial position.

10.2.1 Definition

The applicable accounting standard is IAS 16 *Property, Plant and Equipment.*

IAS 16 defines property, plant and equipment as *tangible* assets that:

- are held by an entity for use in the production or supply of goods or services, for rental to others, or for administration purposes; and
- are expected to be used during more than one period.

In order to meet the definition of property, plant and equipment, an item must first meet the definition of an ***asset*** as defined above. The asset must be ***tangible*** – in other words, a physical asset such as land rather than a non-physical one such as a patent. Further, the asset must have a ***specific use*** within the entity, namely for use in production/supply, rental or administration. Lastly, as the asset is non-current, there is an expectation that it will be used for ***more than one period***.

Pause and reflect ...

Can you think of examples of non-current assets that are held by an entity:

- for the production of goods?
- for the supply of goods?
- for the supply of services?
- for rental to others?

Response

There are many examples that you could have come up with, such as:

- plant and machinery held for the production of goods;
- delivery vehicles held for the supply of goods;
- the cleaning equipment of a car-wash service held for the supply of services;
- motor vehicles belonging to a car-hire entity held for rental to others;
- office furniture held for the administration of the entity.

10.2.2 Recognition criteria

IAS 16 requires that an item of property, plant and equipment should be recognised as an asset if, and only if,

- it is probable that **future economic benefits** associated with the item will flow to the entity; and
- the cost of the item can be **measured** reliably.

The **future economic benefits** can be associated with the item of property, plant and equipment either directly or indirectly. For example, an item of manufacturing plant or a delivery vehicle will generate direct future economic benefits. On the other hand, there may be cases where items of property, plant and equipment are acquired for safety or environmental reasons, such as installing a filter to meet environmental protection requirements. Although the acquisition of the filter does not directly increase the future economic benefits of any particular existing item of property, plant and equipment, the installation of the filter is necessary in order for the entity to obtain the future economic benefits from other assets it owns.

Concepts in context

Flybe Group plc
Extract from accounting policy note for property, plant and equipment

Subsequent costs, such as long-term scheduled maintenance and major overhaul of aircraft, are capitalised and amortised over the length of period benefiting from these costs. All other costs relating to maintenance are charged to the income statement as incurred.

What concepts in context can you see here?

Take a careful look at Flybe's accounting policy and relate it to what you are reading in this section. This policy note is referring to the general recognition principle of

IAS 16. Note that the long-term scheduled maintenance and major overhaul costs are recognised as an asset whereas the day-to-day maintenance is recognised as an expense

Flybe is one of Europe's largest independent regional airlines, flying over 200 routes from more than 100 airports across 23 countries.

Source: www.flybe.com/corporate/pdf/Flybe-Group-plc-Annual-Report-2012-13.pdf (Accessed 15 May 2014).

The reliable **measurement** of the cost is usually satisfied because of the exchange transaction relating to the purchase of the asset. Refer back to Chapter 2 to ensure that you have a good understanding of the recognition criteria of an asset.

The recognition principle discussed above is a *general* recognition principle for property, plant and equipment. It applies to costs incurred ***initially*** to acquire an item of property, plant and equipment, and when costs are incurred ***subsequently*** to add to it, replace part of it, repair it or service it.

It is important to note that the standard does not differentiate between initial recognition of property, plant and equipment and subsequent costs. In other words, when costs are incurred in relation to an item of property, plant and equipment, management is required to apply the general recognition principle in order to decide whether the costs incurred should be recognised as an asset (capitalised as part of the cost of the asset on the statement of financial position) or recognised as an expense (included in the statement of profit or loss). If the recognition principle of IAS 16 is met (it is probable that future benefits associated with the item will flow to the entity and the cost of the item can be measured reliably), the costs incurred are recognised as an asset.

Parts of some items of property, plant and equipment may require replacement or repair at regular intervals, such as the replacement of the lining of a furnace or the replacement of the seats and galley of an aircraft. These replacement costs are recognised as an asset if the recognition principles are met.

However, and for practical reasons, costs of day-to-day servicing are recognised as an expense when incurred. These costs are primarily the costs of labour, consumables and small parts, and are often referred to as 'repairs and maintenance' in the statement of profit or loss.

Example: Recognition criteria

Smart Concepts purchased a delivery vehicle on 1 June 20X5. The vehicle cost C220 000. On 1 July 20X5, a satellite navigation system was installed at a cost of C12 000. On 15 December 20X5, the windscreen wipers and the indicator lamps were replaced at a cost of C1 200.

You are required to:

Discuss how Smart Concepts should recognise the above costs in accordance with IAS 16 *Property, Plant and Equipment.*

Solution: Recognition criteria

The cost of C220 000 *incurred initially* to acquire the motor vehicle is recognised as an asset as it meets the definition and recognition criteria for property, plant and equipment.

(It is a tangible asset that will be used to supply goods to customers for more than one financial period.) It is probable that future economic benefits will flow to the entity (the vehicle is used to deliver goods to customers) and the cost can be measured reliably (the amount of C220 000 is known).

The cost of C12 000 incurred to install the navigation system on 1 July 20X5 and the cost of the service on 15 December 20X5 are referred to as *subsequent expenditure* as discussed above. We have to apply the general recognition criteria to these costs incurred to ascertain whether the costs should be recognised as an asset or as an expense.

Although the satellite navigation system on its own is not directly used to deliver goods to customers, it will allow the related asset – the delivery vehicle – to earn more economic benefits in the future than it would without a navigation system. Future economic benefits will flow to the entity (the ability of the business entity to deliver the goods to its customers is enhanced) and the cost can be measured reliably (the amount of C12 000 is known). The satellite navigation system is therefore also recognised as an asset.

The cost of C1 200 incurred for replacing the windscreen wipers and the indicator lamps is recognised as an expense when incurred. Although this cost will result in future economic benefits, the standard had to be practical and hence the requirement that all 'day-to-day servicing' is expensed.

Example: Journal entries on initial and subsequent recognition

Consider the same example as above and record the journal entries in the general journal of Smart Concepts. All costs incurred were paid in cash.

Solution: Journal entries on initial and subsequent recognition

GENERAL JOURNAL OF SMART CONCEPTS

Date	*Description*	*Dr*	*Cr*
01/06/X5	Delivery vehicle: cost (A)	220 000	
	Bank (A)		220 000
	Recognition of initial cost of delivery vehicle		
01/07/X5	Delivery vehicle: cost (A)	12 000	
	Bank (A)		12 000
	Recognition of subsequent expenditure incurred as part of the cost of delivery vehicle		
15/12/X5	Repairs and maintenance (E)	1 200	
	Bank (A)		1 200
	Payment of costs incurred to replace the windscreen wipers and indicator lamps		

10.3 Measurement at initial recognition

IAS 16 states that an item of property, plant and equipment that qualifies for recognition as an asset should be measured at its ***cost***.

10.3.1 Elements of cost

The cost of an item of property, plant and equipment comprises its purchase price, including import duties and non-refundable purchase taxes, and any costs directly attributable to bringing the asset to the location and condition necessary for it to be capable of operating in the manner intended by management.

Any trade discounts are deducted in arriving at the purchase price. Examples of directly attributable costs include the cost of site preparation; delivery and handling costs; installation and assembly costs; net costs of testing whether the asset is functioning properly; and professional fees such as those of architects and engineers.

Only non-refundable purchase taxes are included in the cost of property, plant and equipment. If the entity is a registered VAT vendor, the VAT paid will be recovered and therefore does not form part of the cost. However, if the entity is not a registered VAT vendor, the VAT paid would not be recoverable and would need to be included as part of the cost of the asset.

The elements of the cost of an item of property, plant and equipment are shown in Diagram 10.1.

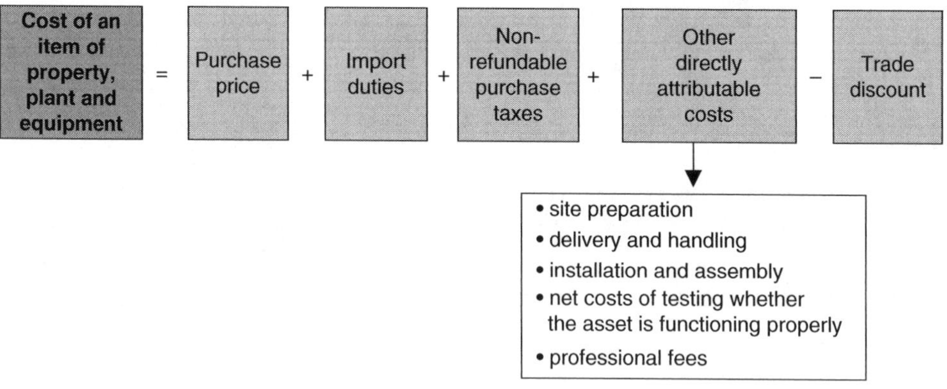

Diagram 10.1 Elements of cost of an item of property, plant and equipment

Recognition of costs in the carrying amount of an item of property, plant and equipment ceases when the item is in the location and condition necessary for it to be capable of operating in the manner intended by management. Costs incurred for an item of property, plant and equipment while it is capable of operating in the manner intended by management, but which has not yet been brought into use, are therefore not included in the carrying amount of the item. These costs are expensed in the statement of profit or loss. Similarly, initial operating losses are also expensed in the statement of profit or loss.

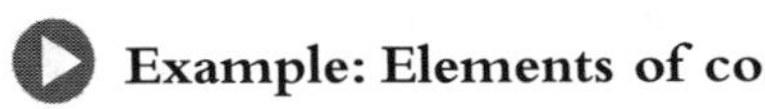

Example: Elements of cost

Smart Concepts purchased equipment for the repair of computers at an invoice price of C45 600 (inclusive of VAT at 20 per cent). Transport costs of C1 254 (inclusive of VAT at 20 per cent) were paid. Installation fees amounted to C1 000 (exclusive of VAT as the consultants are not registered for VAT purposes).

You are required to:

Compute the cost of the equipment
a) If Smart Concepts is a registered vendor for VAT purposes.
b) If Smart Concepts is not a registered vendor for VAT purposes.

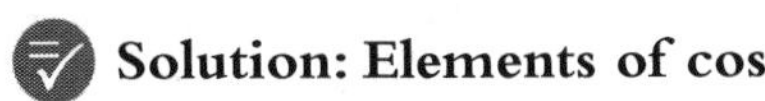

Solution: Elements of cost

a) If Smart Concepts is a registered vendor for VAT purposes

		C
Invoice price	*(45 600 × 100/120)*	38 000
Transport costs	*(1 254 × 100/120)*	1 045
Installation fees		1 000
		40 045

b) If Smart Concepts is not a registered vendor for VAT purposes

	C
Invoice price	45 600
Transport costs	1 254
Installation fees	1 000
	47 854

Example: Elements of cost

Computer World purchased a new item of equipment for the assembly of computer screens on 1 July 20X5. The equipment cost an amount of C640 000. The cost of testing the equipment amounted to C72 500. Five screens that were produced during the testing phase were sold to schools for C5 000 each. Commission of C2 500 was paid to the sales agent. The testing phase was complete by 31 July 20X5 and the equipment was in a condition capable of operating in the manner intended by management on that date. The equipment operated at less than full capacity during August 20X5 and further modifications were made at a cost of C4 000. Initial operating losses during August and September 20X5 amounted to C14 000.

You are required to:

Identify the elements of the cost of the equipment.

 **Solution: Elements of cost**

		C
Cost/invoice price		640 000
Costs of testing		72 500
Net proceeds from sale of test products	*(25 000 – 2 500)*	(22 500)
Further modifications		—
Initial operating losses		—
		690 000

The cost of testing whether an asset is functioning properly is a directly attributable cost required to be included in the cost of the item of equipment. The net proceeds from selling any items produced while bringing the asset to the location and condition necessary for it to be capable of operating in the manner intended by management are deducted from the costs of testing the asset. The cost of testing the equipment of C72 500 is thus included in the cost, reduced by the net proceeds from the sale of the test products of C22 500 (C25 000 – C2 500). The cost of the further modifications and the initial operating losses were incurred after the equipment was in a condition capable of operating in the manner intended by management. The cost of the further modifications of C4 000 and the initial operating losses of C14 000 are therefore recognised as expenses when incurred, and are not included in the carrying amount of the equipment.

You have seen that the point at which an item of property, plant and equipment is in the location and condition necessary for it to be capable of operating in the manner intended by management is important for determining when costs are to be included in the carrying amount of the asset or expensed in the statement of profit or loss. Costs incurred after this point are referred to as subsequent expenditure, and are evaluated in terms of the subsequent recognition criteria of IAS 16.

10.3.2 Measurement of cost

The cost of an item of property, plant and equipment is the amount of cash or cash equivalents paid or the fair value of the consideration given to acquire an asset at the time of its acquisition or construction.

The cost of an item of property, plant and equipment is the ***cash price equivalent*** at the recognition date. If payment is deferred beyond normal credit terms, the difference between the cash price equivalent and the total payments is recognised as interest expense over the period of credit (see Diagram 10.2).

Normal credit terms refer to the period of time that a supplier will normally give its clients to repay a similar amount before the supplier starts charging interest on the amount owed for the purchase.

The amount that would have been paid in cash on the acquisition date is recorded as the cost of the asset. The interest is then recognised as an expense over the period for which the finance was obtained.

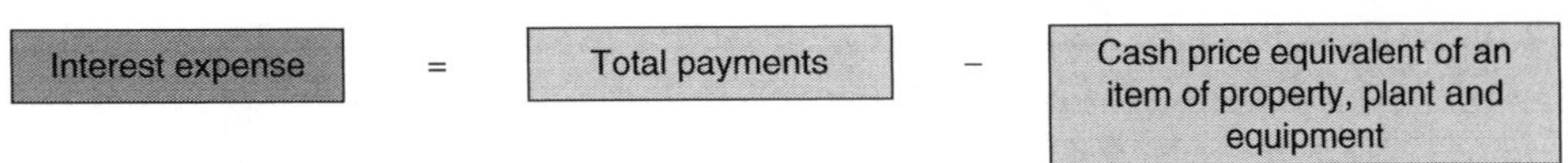

Diagram 10.2 Finance costs for an item of property, plant and equipment

Example: Measurement of cost

Smart Concepts purchased a photocopier for the office at an invoice price of C112 000 on 1 April 20X5. Delivery and installation costs of C8 000 were paid to the supplier. Smart Concepts is to finance the photocopy machine by raising a loan of C120 000 from Investors Bank at 15 per cent interest per annum. The loan is to be repaid in 12 monthly instalments of C10 831, starting at the end of April 20X5. The entity has a 31 December year end.

You are required to:

a) Show the relevant journal entries for the month of April 20X5.
b) Show the relevant journal entries for the month of December 20X5.
c) Show extracts from the statement of profit or loss for the period ended 31 December 20X5 and from the statement of financial position at that date, relating to the borrowing.

Solution: Measurement of cost

The *total payments* over the credit term amount to C129 972 (C10 831 × 12). The cost of the asset to be recorded at recognition date is its *cash price equivalent* of C120 000, which includes the invoice price of C112 000, as well as the delivery and installation costs of C8 000. The total finance cost to be recorded as *interest expense* is C9 972, calculated as total payments of C129 972 less the cash price equivalent of C120 000.

It is necessary to complete an amortisation schedule in order to calculate the amount of interest expense to recognise each period, as well as the amount by which the liability is to be reduced.

	Balance at beginning of period	*Payment*	*Interest expense*	*Reduction in liability*	*Balance at end of period*
20X5					
April	120 000	10 831	1 500	9 331	110 669
May	110 669	10 831	1 383	9 448	101 221
June	101 221	10 831	1 265	9 566	91 656
July	91 656	10 831	1 146	9 685	81 970
August	81 970	10 831	1 025	9 806	72 164
September	72 164	10 831	902	9 929	62 235
October	62 235	10 831	778	10 053	52 182
November	52 182	10 831	652	10 179	42 003
December	42 003	10 831	525	10 306	31 697
			9 176		
20X6					
January	31 697	10 831	396	10 435	21 262
February	21 262	10 831	266	10 565	10 697
March	10 697	10 831	134	10 697	—
		129 972	9 972	120 000	

It is important to understand that the balance of the liability at each date represents the present value of future cash flows relating to the loan. In other words, the balance of C110 669 at the end of April 20X5 is the present value of the 11 payments of C10 831 from the end of May 20X5 to the end of March 20X6, discounted at the rate of 1.25 per cent per month (15 per cent/12).

You will notice that each instalment of C10 831 represents partly the interest expense for the period and partly a reduction in the liability. Looking at the month of April, the balance at the beginning of the month (the date that the loan was raised) was C120 000. At the end of April, the first payment of C10 831 is made. The payment of C10 831 comprises the interest expense for the month of C1 500 (C120 000 × 15 per cent × 1/12) and the reduction in the liability of C9 331 (C10 831 − C1 500). The balance at the end of April/beginning of May is then C110 669 (C120 000 − C9 331). The same procedure is then followed for May where the payment at the end of the month of C10 831 results in an interest expense of C1 383 (C110 669 × 15 per cent × 1/12) and a reduction in the liability of C9 448 (C10 831 − C1 383), resulting in a balance at the end of the month of C101 221 (C110 669 − C9 448).

You will also notice that, as the balance in the liability decreases, the amount of the interest expense also decreases.

a) Journal entries for April 20X5

GENERAL JOURNAL OF SMART CONCEPTS

Date	*Description*	*Dr*	*Cr*
01/04/X5	Bank (A)	120 000	
	Borrowings (L)		120 000
	Loan raised to purchase photocopier		
01/04/X5	Photocopier: Cost (A)	120 000	
	Bank (A)		120 000
	Recognition of cost of asset		
30/04/X5	Interest (E)	1 500	
	Borrowings (L)	9 331	
	Bank (A)		10 831
	Payment of instalment for April 20X5 and allocation of payment between interest and liability		

b) Journal entries for December 20X5

GENERAL JOURNAL OF SMART CONCEPTS

Date	*Description*	*Dr*	*Cr*
31/12/X5	Interest (E)	525	
	Borrowings (L)	10 306	
	Bank (A)		10 831
	Payment of instalment for December 20X5 and allocation of payment between interest and liability		

c) Statement of profit or loss and statement of financial position extracts

SMART CONCEPTS
STATEMENT OF PROFIT OR LOSS
FOR THE PERIOD ENDED 31 DECEMBER 20X5

	C
Finance costs	
Interest expense	9 176

SMART CONCEPTS
STATEMENT OF FINANCIAL POSITION
AT 31 DECEMBER 20X5

	C
Current liabilities	
Short-term borrowings	31 697

The interest expense of C9 176 comprises the total of the finance costs for the months of April to December of 20X5.

You will recall from Chapter 6 that a liability is classified as current when the amount is due to be settled within 12 months of the statement of financial position date. In this example, the balance at 31 December 20X5 of C31 697 will be settled by the end of March 20X6 and is thus shown as a current liability. The following calculation proves that the balance of C31 697 is the present value of the future cash flows:

Date of cash flow	*Amount of cash flow*	*PV at (15%/12)*
	C	C
31/01/X6	10 831	10 697
28/02/X6	10 831	10 565
31/03/X6	10 831	10 435
		31 697

10.4 Depreciation expense

The use of an item of property, plant and equipment represents a consumption of the benefits inherent in the asset. This expense is known as depreciation. The accounting terminology relating to the acquisition and use of items of property, plant and equipment has specific meanings, which need to be understood before we can continue with our discussion of depreciation.

These terms are defined in IAS 16 as follows:

- ***Depreciation*** is the systematic allocation of the depreciable amount of an asset over its useful life.
- ***Depreciable amount*** is the cost of an asset, less its residual value.

- ***Useful life*** is either:
  - the period of time an asset is expected to be available for use by the entity; or
  - the number of production or similar units expected to be obtained from the asset by the entity.
- ***Residual value*** is the estimated amount that the entity would currently obtain from the disposal of the asset (net of costs of disposal) if the asset were already of the age and in the condition expected at the end of its useful life.
- ***Carrying amount*** is the amount at which the asset is recognised after deducting any accumulated depreciation.

10.4.1 Depreciable amount, depreciation period, useful life and carrying amount

Let us consider the photocopier purchased by Smart Concepts on 1 April 20X5. Delivery and installation took place during April 20X5, and the machine was available for use from 1 May 20X5. Use of the new machine only began on 1 June 20X5, as Smart Concepts had rented another photocopier until the end of May 20X5. The amount initially recognised as the ***cost*** of the machine is C120 000. For the moment, let us assume that the ***estimated useful life*** is four years, which is the period of time that the machine is expected to be available for use. It has a ***residual value*** of C15 000, which is the estimated amount that the entity would currently obtain if the machine were already four years old.

Depreciable amount

IAS 16 requires the depreciable amount of an asset to be allocated on a systematic basis over its useful life.

 **Pause and reflect ...**

What is the depreciable amount of Smart Concept's photocopier?

Response

The depreciable amount is C105 000 (the difference between the original cost of C120 000 and the residual value of C15 000); *therefore* the amount of C105 000 is allocated over the useful life of four years as a depreciation charge.

We will learn about different methods of depreciation in the section that follows, but for the purposes of our discussion at present, let us assume that the *straight-line* method of depreciation is used. This means that the depreciable amount of C105 000 (see Diagram 10.3) will be charged as depreciation of C26 250 (C105 000/4 years) each year, apportioned as discussed in the following section.

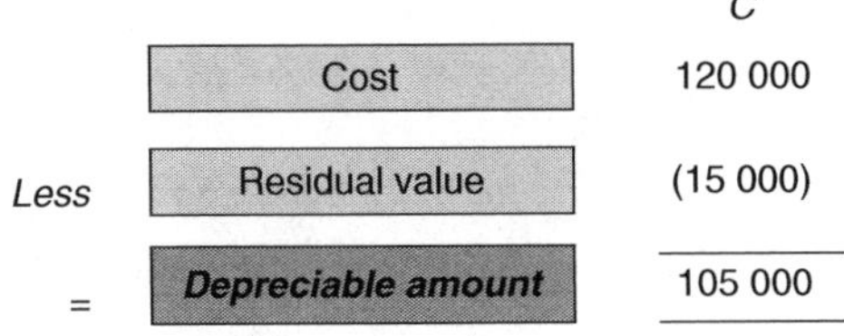

Diagram 10.3 Depreciable amount

Depreciation period

Depreciation of an asset begins when it is *available for use*, which is when it is in the location and condition necessary for it to be *capable of operating in the manner intended by management*. Depreciation of an asset ceases when the asset is derecognised, for example when it is sold. Accounting for the disposal of property, plant and equipment is covered in Section 10.5 below. It is important to note that depreciation does not cease when an asset is idle. This is done so that the financial statements reflect the consumption of the asset's service potential that occurs while the asset is held and is available for use.

 **Pause and reflect ...**

a) On what date will depreciation of Smart Concept's photocopier begin?
b) What is the depreciation expense for the year ended 31 December 20X5?

Response

a) Depreciation will begin on 1 May 20X5, the date from which it is available for use. Note that depreciation is charged during the month of May 20X5 even though the asset is idle.
b) The depreciation expense for the year ending 31 December 20X5 amounts to C17 500 (C105 000/4 years × 8/12).

Useful life

The future economic benefits embodied in an item of property, plant and equipment are consumed by an entity principally through the use of the asset. However, other factors, such as technical or commercial obsolescence and wear and tear while an asset remains idle, often result in the reduction of the economic benefits that might have been obtained from the asset. All of the following factors therefore need to be considered in determining the useful life of an asset:

- the expected usage of the asset by the entity;
- the expected physical wear and tear, which depends on operational factors such as the number of shifts for which the asset is to be used and the repair and maintenance programme;

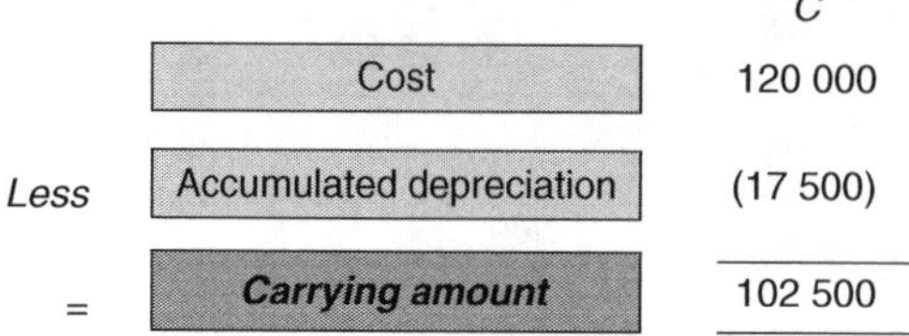

Diagram 10.4 Carrying amount

- technical or commercial obsolescence arising from changes or improvements in technology, or from a change in the market demand for the product or service output of the asset.

As mentioned above, we are assuming an estimated useful life of four years for the purposes of the discussion at present.

Carrying amount

We have seen that the depreciation expense for the year ending 31 December 20X5 amounts to C17 500. The C17 500 represents the *accumulated depreciation*; in other words, that part of the depreciable amount of C105 000 that has been charged as depreciation. Remember that the carrying amount is the amount at which the asset is recognised after deducting any accumulated depreciation (see Diagram 10.4).

 **Pause and reflect ...**

What is the carrying amount of Smart Concept's photocopier at 31 December 20X5?

Response

The carrying amount at 31 December is C102 500, comprising the cost of C120 000 less the accumulated depreciation of C17 500. As the economic benefits embodied in an asset are consumed by the entity, the carrying amount of the asset is reduced to reflect this consumption by charging an expense for depreciation.

To sum up, we have seen that the purpose of the depreciation expense is one of cost allocation. Depreciation is that part of the cost of the asset which has been or is being charged to the statement of profit or loss, and the carrying amount on the statement of financial position is that part of the original cost that has not yet been charged against income. In other words, the carrying amount represents future benefits yet to be consumed as depreciation.

10.4.2 Methods of depreciation

A variety of depreciation methods can be used to allocate, on a systematic basis, the depreciable amount of an asset over its useful life. The depreciation method should reflect the pattern in which the future economic benefits are to be consumed by the entity. These methods include the ***straight-line*** method, the ***diminishing balance*** method and the ***units of production*** method. Each method will be examined in detail. Straight-line depreciation results in a constant charge over the useful life of the asset. The diminishing balance method results in a decreasing charge over the useful life of the asset. The units of production method results in a charge based on the expected use or output.

Straight-line method

The straight-line method results in a constant charge over the useful life of the asset. This method is appropriate if the asset's usefulness is considered to be equal in each accounting period. The depreciation charge is calculated as:

$$\text{Depreciation expense} = \frac{\text{Cost} - \text{residual value}}{\text{Useful life}}$$

Note that the residual value is subtracted from the cost so that the depreciable amount is allocated over the useful life. For the photocopier with a cost of C120 000 and a residual value of C15 000, the depreciation expense each period will be C26 250, assuming a useful life of four years ((C120 000 − 15 000)/4). As discussed above, the charge is apportioned for a part period, resulting in a depreciation charge of C17 500 for the first year.

Diminishing balance method

The diminishing balance method results in a decreasing charge over the useful life of the asset. This method applies a fixed percentage to the carrying amount of the asset at the beginning of each period. The carrying amount at the beginning of the first period is the cost, as no depreciation has yet been charged. The depreciation charge is simply:

$$\text{Depreciation expense} = \text{Carrying amount} \times \%\ \text{rate}$$

Note that the depreciation rate is applied to the cost (and thereafter the carrying amount) and not to the depreciable amount, as with the straight-line method. The effect of the residual value is taken into account in the determination of the fixed percentage, according to the following formula:

$$\%\,\text{rate} = \left(1 - \sqrt[n]{\frac{r}{c}}\right)$$

In this formula, n = the useful life of the asset in years, r = the residual value of the asset and c = the cost of the asset. Applying the formula to the machine that we are working with results in a depreciation rate of 40.539 per cent.

$$\left(1 - \sqrt[4]{\frac{15000}{120000}}\right)$$

This has been rounded down to 40.5 per cent for ease of calculation.

Consider the photocopier with a cost of C120 000 and a residual value of C15 000. The asset was available for use on 1 May 20X5 and thus is used for eight months in the financial year ending 31 December 20X5 (1 May 20X5 to 31 December 20X5). It will be used for 12 months for each of the financial years ending 31 December 20X6, 20X7 and 20X8 and then for four months for the financial year ending 31 December 20X9 (1 January 20X9 to 30 April 20X9). Because of the part periods, it is necessary to calculate the depreciation expense by applying the 40.5 per cent diminishing balance rate to the cost on 1 May 20X5 and thereafter to the carrying amount at the end of each year of the asset's life. As one year of the asset's life extends over two financial years, the depreciation expense needs to be apportioned as shown in Diagram 10.5.

The depreciation expense for the year ended 31 December 20X5 is C32 400 (the first 8 months of the 12 months to 30 April 20X6). The depreciation expense for the year ended 31 December 20X6 is C35 478 (C16 200 for the last 4 months of the 12 months to 30 April 20X6 and C19 278 for the first 8 months of the 12 months to 30 April 20X7). The same pattern is repeated to calculate the depreciation expense for the year ended 31 December 20X7 and 20X8. The depreciation expense for the year ended 31 December 20X9 is C3 412 (representing the depreciation expense for the last four months of the asset's useful life from 1 January 20X9 to 30 April 20X9). These amounts are incorporated into the diminishing balance calculation in Diagram 10.6.

Units of production method

Where the potentially available benefits from the asset can be expressed in terms of a maximum potential output, the depreciable amount can be allocated to each period based on the output produced. Output can be measured in a variety of ways, such as units, kilogrammes or kilometres. The depreciation charge is calculated as:

$$\text{Depreciation expense} = \text{Depreciable amount} \times \frac{\text{Output in period}}{\text{Total estimated output}}$$

01/05/X5	Cost		120 000
	Depreciation from 01/05/X5 – 30/04/X6	(120 000 × 40.5%)	(48 600)
	01/05/X5 – 31/12/X5	(48 600 × 8/12)	32 400
	01/01/X6 – 30/04/X6	(48 600 × 4/12)	16 200
30/04/X6	Carrying amount		71 400
	Depreciation from 01/05/X6 – 30/04/X7	(71 400 × 40.5%)	(28 917)
	01/05/X6 – 31/12/X6	(28 917 × 8/12)	19 278
	01/01/X7 – 30/04/X7	(28 917 × 4/12)	9 639
30/04/X7	Carrying amount		42 483
	Depreciation from 01/05/X7 – 30/04/X8	(42 483 × 40.5%)	(17 206)
	01/05/X7 – 31/12/X7	(17 206 × 8/12)	11 471
	01/01/X8 – 30/04/X8	(17 206 × 4/12)	(5 735)
30/04/X8	Carrying amount		25 277
	Depreciation from 01/05/X8 – 30/04/X9	(25 277 × 40.5%)	(10 237)
	01/05/X8 – 31/12/X8	(10 237 × 8/12)	6 825
	01/01/X9 – 30/04/X9	(10 237 × 4/12)	3 412
30/04/X9	Carrying amount		15 040

Diagram 10.5 Calculation for diminishing balance depreciation

			Straight line	*Diminishing balance*	*Units of production*
01/05/X5	Cost		120 000	120 000	120 000
20X5	Depreciation	*(× 8/12)	*(17 500)	*(32 400)	(16 800)
31/12/X5	Carrying amount		102 500	87 600	103 200
20X6	Depreciation		*(26 250)	(35 478)	(29 400)
31/12/X6	Carrying amount		76 250	52 122	73 800
20X7	Depreciation		(26 250)	(21 110)	(26 250)
31/12/X7	Carrying amount		50 000	31 012	47 550
20X8	Depreciation		(26 250)	(12 560)	(27 300)
31/12/X8	Carrying amount		23 750	18 452	20 250
20X9	Depreciation	*(× 4/12)	*(8 750)	*(3 412)	(5 250)
30/04/X9	Carrying amount		15 000	15 040	15 000

Diagram 10.6 Comparison of depreciation methods

Assume that the photocopier in our example has an estimated total output of 5 000 000 copies over its useful life. If 800 000 copies were made in the first year, the depreciation charge for that year is C16 800 (C105 000 × (800 000/5 000 000)). Assume that the units of output are 1 400 000 in 20X6, 1 250 000 in 20X7, 1 300 000 in 20X8 and 250 000 in 20X9.

 **Pause and reflect ...**

What predominant factor influences the choice of depreciation method?

Response

The entity selects the method that most closely reflects the expected pattern of consumption of the future economic benefits embodied in the asset.

10.4.3 Comparison of the depreciation methods

Diagram 10.6 below completes and compares the depreciation calculation relating to the photocopier purchased by Smart Concepts, using the depreciation methods referred to in Section 10.4.2. Note that the carrying amount of the asset at the end of its useful life is equal to the originally estimated residual value of C15 000. The difference on the diminishing balance method is due to rounding.

 **Pause and reflect ...**

You will notice that depreciation on the photocopier is recognised from 1 May 20X5 to 31 December 20X5 even though the asset is idle for the month of May. What is the implication of the idle month for the depreciation calculation using the units of production method?

Response

Depreciation calculated using the units of production method is a function of output and not a function of time. In the idle month, no units are produced, and thus the asset's service potential is not decreased, therefore no depreciation is recorded for the idle month when using the units of production method.

10.4.4 Accounting entries

When the concept of depreciation was first introduced in Part II of this book, the accounting entry was described as a debit to depreciation expense and a credit to the asset. The depreciation expense decreases equity on the right side of the accounting equation, which gives rise to the debit to depreciation expense. The charging of depreciation, as you are now aware, is an allocation of the cost of the asset over its useful life and therefore the asset account on the left side of the accounting equation is reduced by a right or credit entry.

However, for presentation purposes, the original cost of the asset and the related accumulated depreciation are normally shown separately on the statement of financial position. For this reason, a separate column in the accounting equation worksheet, and hence a separate account in the ledger, is used for the accumulated depreciation. The accounting entry for recording depreciation expense then becomes:

Dr Depreciation expense
Cr Accumulated depreciation

The accumulated depreciation column appears on the left side of the accounting equation as a contra-asset. A contra-asset account can be thought of as a negative asset. To increase the accumulated depreciation therefore requires a right or credit entry. The accounting equation is therefore expanded to accommodate the accumulated depreciation and appears as follows:

		Assets			=	*Liabilities*	+	*Owner's equity*
Non-current assets	+	Current assets	−	***Accumulated depreciation***				

To illustrate the accounting entries for depreciation, refer again to our example of the photocopier, which was recorded at a total cost of C120 000 at the beginning of April 20X5. For the purposes of this illustration, we will work with the straight-line method. The entries for all the methods are naturally the same; only the amounts differ.

	Assets				= L +	*Owner's equity*
	Machinery		Accumulated depreciation		Depreciation expense	
	+/L/Dr	−/R/Cr	−/L/Dr	+/R/Cr	+/L/Dr	−/R/Cr
Bal	120 000					
20X5				17 500	17 500	
31/12/X5	120 000			17 500	17 500	
c/e						17 500
20X6				26 250	26 250	
31/12/X6	120 000			43 750	26 250	
c/e						26 250

The cost of the machine is shown as an asset of C120 000. For the year ending 31 December 20X5, depreciation of C17 500 is charged. The equity account, depreciation expense, is increased with a left or debit entry of C17 500 and the contra-asset, accumulated depreciation, is increased by the same amount with a right or credit entry. At the end of December 20X5, the depreciation expense of C17 500 is closed off to the profit and loss account as part of the normal year-end procedures. The machinery account shows a debit balance of C120 000, which is reported as an asset on the statement of financial position. The accumulated depreciation account reflects a credit balance of C17 500, which is set off against the cost of C120 000 to report a carrying amount of C102 500 on the statement of financial position. The same procedure is repeated for the year ended 31 December 20X6.

10.4.5 Depreciation of significant parts

Each part of an item of property, plant and equipment with a cost that is significant in relation to the total cost of the item is required to be depreciated separately. Examples of this include an aircraft, where the airframe, engines and interior are identified as significant parts, or an item of industrial plant, where the mechanised components and the casing are significant parts.

Separate but significant parts of an item of property, plant and equipment may have the same useful life and depreciation method. Such parts are grouped together for depreciation purposes. For example, the significant parts of an aircraft may be identified as the fuselage, the wings, the engines, the tyres and the interior fittings. If the fuselage and the wings are considered to have the same useful life and depreciation method, they may be grouped together as a significant part.

Once the significant parts have been identified, the remainder of the non-significant parts are grouped together for the calculation of depreciation. Using the example of the aircraft, the remainder of the cost (after identifying the engines, the tyres, the interior fittings and the combination of the fuselage and wings) is grouped together as a significant part.

For this purpose, it is also important to understand that land and buildings are separable assets even when acquired together. The cost of the land and the cost of the buildings are recorded as separate assets as they can be classified as different significant parts with different useful lives.

Land is generally not depreciated, whereas buildings are depreciable assets. This is because land usually does not have a limited useful life, and the land's ability to generate future economic benefits is not reduced every year. Although buildings can be used for a long time, they have a limited useful life and should be depreciated over the period that they are expected to generate future economic benefits.

Example: Depreciation of significant parts

On 1 January 20X7, Computer World purchased new business premises for C10 000 000. The following significant parts were identified:

Significant part	*C*	*Useful life and depreciation method*
Land	500 000	Unlimited useful life, not depreciated
Building structure	6 000 000	Useful life of 40 years, depreciated using the straight-line method
Other fittings (such as partitions and air conditioning system)	1 600 000	Useful life of 8 years, depreciated using the straight-line method
Windows	1 000 000	Useful life of 10 years, depreciated using the straight-line method
Lifts	900 000	Depreciated at 10 per cent per annum using the diminishing balance method

The estimated residual value of all the significant parts is zero.

You are required to:

Calculate the depreciation and carrying amount of the business premises for the year ended 31 December 20X7.

Solution: Depreciation of significant parts

Component	*Cost*		*Depreciation*	*Carrying amout*
Land	500 000	(Land not depreciated)	—	500 000
Building structure	6 000 000	(6 000 000 × 1/40)	150 000	5 850 000
Other fittings	1 600 000	(1 600 000 × 1/8)	200 000	1 400 000
Windows	1 000 000	(1 000 000 × 1/10)	100 000	900 000
Lifts	900 000	(900 000 × 10%)	90 000	810 000
Total	10 000 000		540 000	9 460 000

The total cost of the business premises is C10 000 000. The building structure, other fittings, windows and lifts are identified as separate significant parts as each has a cost that is significant in relation to the total cost of the item *and* each has a different useful life. Each significant part is depreciated separately over its useful life using the specified depreciation method. Although the windows and lifts both have a useful life of ten years, they are not grouped together as an individual part as the depreciation methods are different.

Pause and reflect ...

Think back to the recognition principle described for property, plant and equipment earlier in this chapter (Section 10.2.2). If the building in the above example is painted once every eight years and the windows are cleaned once a month, how should these subsequent costs be recognised, bearing in mind the general recognition principle of IAS 16 *Property, Plant and Equipment*?

Response

It is important to distinguish between repairs and day-to-day servicing. Repair costs are capitalised if the recognition principles are met. Judgement is required in applying the recognition criteria to the specific circumstances of the entity. The cost of painting the building once every eight years should be capitalised as a separate significant part of the building as it is probable that future economic benefits will flow to the entity, but the cost of cleaning the windows once a month should be expensed in the statement of profit or loss.

 **Concepts in context**

Flybe Group Plc
Extract from accounting policy note for property, plant and equipment

Property, plant and equipment are stated at their cost, less accumulated depreciation and impairment losses. Aircraft and engines and other associated equipment are classified as aircraft. All other equipment is classified as plant and equipment. An element of the cost of a new aircraft is attributed on acquisition to prepaid maintenance of its engines and airframe and is amortised over a period from one to five years from the date of purchase to the date of the next scheduled maintenance event for the component.

What concepts in context can you see here?

You learn in this section that in many cases it is not appropriate to simply apply a depreciation rate, useful life and residual value to an asset as a whole, where the asset has different significant parts with different depreciation rates, useful lives and residual values. The policy note of Flybe is identifying this issue – see that even the prepaid maintenance of its engines and airframes is dealt with as a separate significant part.

Flybe is one of Europe's largest independent regional airlines, flying over 200 routes from more than 100 airports across 23 countries.

Source: www.flybe.com/corporate/pdf/Flybe-Group-plc-Annual-Report-2012-13.pdf (Accessed 15 May 2014).

10.5 Reassessment of useful life and residual value

The amount of depreciation charged to the statement of profit or loss every year is based on estimates of the useful life of the asset, the residual value of the asset and the pattern of consumption of the economic benefits relating to that asset. The useful life, residual value and depreciation method need to be reviewed annually and, if expectations are *significantly* different from original estimates, the depreciation charge for the *current* and *future* periods should be adjusted, using the new estimates.

The useful life may be extended by subsequent expenditure on the asset which improves the condition of the asset beyond its originally assessed standard of performance. On the

31/12/X7	Carrying amount		50 000
20X8	Depreciation	((50 000 − 12 000)/40 months × 12 months)	(11 400)
31/12/X8	Carrying amount		38 600
20X9	Depreciation	((50 000 − 12 000)/40 months × 12 months)	(11 400)
31/12/X9	Carrying amount		27 200
20Y0	Depreciation	((50 000 − 12 000)/40 months × 12 months)	(11 400)
31/12/Y0	Carrying amount		15 800
20Y1	Depreciation	((50 000 − 12 000)/40 months × 4 months)	(3 800)
30/04/Y1	Carrying amount		12 000

Diagram 10.7 Revised depreciation charge

other hand, technological changes may reduce the useful life of the asset. This is particularly the case with high-technology assets like computers.

We will refer again to Smart Concepts and the photocopier purchased for C120 000 on 1 April 20X5 and that was available for use from 1 May 20X5. The straight-line depreciation method will be used for the purposes of this illustration. Referring to the calculation in Diagram 10.5, the carrying amount of the asset at the end of December 20X7 is C50 000 (C120 000 − C17 500 − C26 250 − C26 250), and the remaining useful life is one year and four months (01/01/X8 to 30/04/X9). Assume, when preparing the financial statements at the end of 20X8, that the useful life and residual value were reviewed. It was considered that the *total useful life* of the photocopier is six years (compared to the original estimate of four years), thus extending the *remaining useful life* to three years and four months, and that the residual value is C12 000. The revised depreciation charge for the current year and future years is calculated as follows:

$$\text{Revised depreciation charge} = \frac{\text{Carrying amount} - \text{residual value}}{\text{Remaining useful life}}$$

The depreciation expense for the years from 20X8 to 20Y1 is shown in Diagram 10.7.

Pause and reflect . . .

In the above example, the useful life and residual value were reviewed at the year end – that is, on 31 December 20X8. Would the measurement of the depreciation expense for the year ended 31 December 20X8 and future years change if the estimate of the useful life and residual value were reviewed on 30 June 20X8?

Response

If the estimate of useful life and/or residual value changes, the depreciation charge for the current and future periods is adjusted. It does not matter whether the review takes place on 30 June 20X8 or 31 December 20X8 – the depreciation expense for the year ending 31 December 20X8 is adjusted.

10.6 Disposals

A disposal can happen when an asset is sold or whenever the asset is scrapped, given away or stolen. The cost of an item of property, plant and equipment and the related accumulated depreciation must be eliminated from the statement of financial position on disposal of the asset. This is referred to as the ***derecognition*** of the asset. ***Profits*** or ***losses*** on disposal are determined as the difference between the proceeds on disposal and the carrying amount of the asset, and are recognised as an income or expense in the statement of profit or loss (see Diagram 10.8).

There are four steps to follow when derecognising an item of property, plant and equipment. These are shown in Diagram 10.9, together with the accompanying accounting entries.

A temporary account, referred to as the disposal account, is used to record the disposal of an item of property, plant and equipment. Each of the four steps described above results in either a debit or credit to the disposal account. Once all the entries are processed, the disposal account will have a zero balance.

This procedure will be demonstrated in the examples that follow.

Example 1: Disposal for cash

At 1 January 20X6, the equipment account of Computer World reflected a balance of C100 000, and on that date the accumulated depreciation account reflected a balance of C40 000. Equipment is depreciated at 20 per cent per annum on the diminishing balance basis. On 30 June 20X6, the equipment was sold for C50 000 cash. The financial year ends on 31 December 20X6.

	Proceeds on disposal
Less	Carrying amount
=	Profit or loss

Diagram 10.8 Determination of profit or loss on disposal

	Step	*Accounting entry*
1	The cost is eliminated as an asset from the accounting records	Dr Disposal Cr Asset
2	The accumulated depreciation is eliminated as a contra-asset from the accounting records	Dr Accumulated depreciation Cr Disposal
3	The proceeds on disposal are recorded	Dr Cash Cr Disposal
4	The profit or loss on disposal is recorded	Dr Disposal Cr Profit on disposal (for a profit) *or* Dr Loss on disposal Cr Disposal (for a loss)

Diagram 10.9 Disposal of an item of property, plant and equipment

You are required to:

a) Show the effect of the disposal of the equipment using an 'A = L + OE' worksheet.
b) Prepare journal entries to record the disposal of the equipment.

Solution 1: Disposal for cash

a) A = L + OE worksheet

	Assets						= *L* +	*Owner's equity*			
	Cash		Equipment		Accumulated depreciation			Disposal		Loss on disposal	
	+/L/Dr	−/R/Cr	+/L/Dr	−/R/Cr	−/L/Dr	+/R/Cr		L/Dr	R/Cr	+/L/Dr	−/R/Cr
01/01			100			40					
Depreciation						6					
30/06						46					
1				100				100			
2					46				46		
3	50								50		
4									4	4	
Balance										4	

The balance on the accumulated depreciation of C40 000 must be updated by C6 000 to reflect the accumulated depreciation at the date of disposal. Entry 1 reverses the cost of the equipment sold from the asset account; entry 2 reverses the accumulated depreciation from the contra-asset account; and entry 3 records the proceeds in the cash account. Entry 4 records the loss on disposal of C4 000 as the balancing figure in the disposal account, which is transferred to the loss on disposal account. (Figures in the worksheet are stated in C000.)

b) Journal entries to record the disposal on 30 June 20X6

Date	*Description*	*Dr*	*Cr*
30/06/X6	Depreciation (E)	6 000	
	Equipment: Accumulated depreciation (–A)		6 000
	Recognition of depreciation on equipment for six months		
	Disposal (T*)	100 000	
	Equipment: Cost (A)		100 000
	Transfer of cost of asset to disposal account on the disposal of the asset		
	Equipment: Accumulated depreciation (–A)	46 000	
	Disposal (T*)		46 000
	Transfer of the balance on the accumulated depreciation account to the disposal account on disposal of the asset		
	Bank	50 000	
	Disposal (T*)		50 000
	Recording of the proceeds received on sale of the asset		
	Loss on disposal (E)	4 000	
	Disposal (T*)		4 000
	Recording of the loss on disposal and closing off the disposal account		

*T = Temporary account.

Example 2: Disposal with a trade-in

At 1 January 20X6, the machinery account of Computer World reflected a balance of C200 000. At that date, the accumulated depreciation account had a credit balance of C38 000. Machinery is depreciated at 10 per cent per annum on the reducing balance method. On 30 June 20X6, new machinery costing C500 000 was purchased for cash from SA Manufacturers. On that date, the existing machinery was traded in for C150 000.

You are required to:

Show the effect of the disposal of the machinery using an 'A = L + OE' worksheet.

Solution 2: Disposal with a trade-in

	Assets						*= L +*	*Owner's equity*		
	Cash		Machinery		Accumulated depreciation		Disposal		Loss on disposal	
	+/L/Dr	*−/R/Cr*	*+/L/Dr*	*−/R/Cr*	*−/L/Dr*	*+/R/Cr*	*L/Dr*	*R/Cr*	*+/L/Dr*	*−/R/Cr*
01/01			200.0			38.0				
Depreciation						8.1				
30/06			200.0			46.1				
1				200.0			200.0			
2					46.1			46.1		
3a			150.0					150.0		
3b		350.0	350.0							
4								3.9	3.9	
Balance			500.0						3.9	

As in the previous example, the balance on accumulated depreciation needs to be updated to the date of disposal. C8 100 is the depreciation for six months based on the carrying amount of C162 000 at 1 January 20X6. Entries 1 and 2 follow the same principle as in the previous example, reversing the cost and accumulated depreciation to the disposal account. New machinery costing C500 000 is purchased, and old plant is traded in for an amount of C150 000, therefore entry 3a debits the machinery account with C150 000 (the trade-in value) and credits the disposal account with the same amount. Entry 3b records the payment of the additional C350 000 to the supplier of the machinery. The loss on disposal of C3 900 is the balancing figure in the disposal account, which is transferred to the loss on disposal account. (Figures in the worksheet are stated in C000s.)

Concepts in context

Exxaro Resources Ltd
Extract from 'Property, plant and equipment' note

Company	*Notes*	*Buildings and infrastructure Rm*	*Machinery, plant and equipment Rm*	*Extensions under construction Rm*	*Total Rm*
2013					
Gross carrying amount					
At beginning of year		20	327	438	785
Additions			17	118	135
Disposals of items of property, plant and equipment		(12)	(39)		(51)
Transfer between classes			335	(335)	
At end of year		8	640	221	869
Accumulated depreciation					
At beginning of year		4	154		158
Depreciation charges		–	138		138
Disposals of items of property, plant and equipment		(1)	(28)		(29)
At end of year		3	264		267
Net carrying amount at end of year		5	376	221	602

What concepts in context have you learnt here?

You know that the carrying amount of property, plant and equipment is equal to its cost less accumulated depreciation. When assets are disposed of, both the cost and accumulated depreciation must be eliminated. If you look at the note, you can see that Exxaro disposed of machinery, plant and equipment that had a cost of R39 000 000 and accumulated depreciation of R28 000 000 at the date of sale.

Exxaro Resources is a large coal and heavy minerals mining company in South Africa. The company operates facilities and offices in Africa, Asia, Europe and Australia.

Source: www.exxaro.com/wp-content/uploads/2012/11/EXXARO_AFS-final_web.pdf (Accessed 15 May 2014).

10.7 Impairment of assets

IAS 16 needs to be read together with IAS 36 *Impairment of Assets*, which provides guidance on the recognition and measurement of impairments. The objective of IAS 36

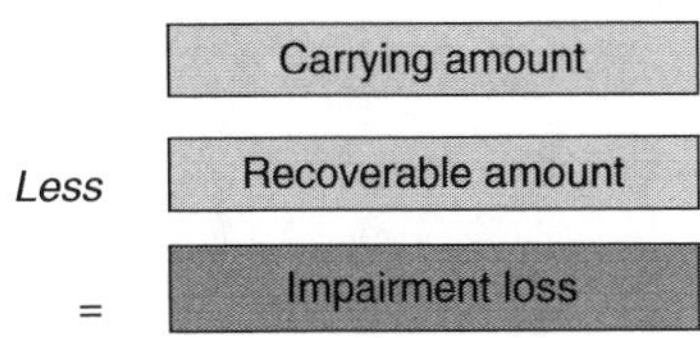

Diagram 10.10 Determination of an impairment loss

is to ensure that an entity's assets are not overstated. If the ***carrying amount*** of an asset exceeds its ***recoverable amount***, the carrying amount will probably not be recovered in the future, either through *use* or *sale*. The asset is described as impaired (see Diagram 10.10), and IAS 36 requires the entity to recognise an impairment loss in the statement of profit or loss.

We will now examine more closely the definition of the recoverable amount and its component parts, an asset's 'fair value less costs of disposal' and 'value in use'.

The recoverable amount is defined in IAS 36 as the higher of an asset's ***fair value less costs of disposal*** and its ***value in use***.

This effectively means that the recoverable amount is calculated at the higher of the future economic benefits expected through the *sale* of the asset or through the *use* of the asset. The 'fair value less costs of disposal' and 'value in use' are also defined in IAS 36.

Fair value less costs of disposal is defined in IAS 36 as the amount obtainable from the sale of an asset in an arm's-length transaction between knowledgeable willing parties, less the costs of disposal.

The best evidence of an asset's net selling price is a price in a sale agreement. If there is no sale agreement but the asset is traded in an active market, the net selling price would be equal to its market price. On the other hand, if there is no sale agreement or active market for an asset, the net selling price is based on the best information available to reflect the amount the entity could obtain for the disposal of the asset in an arm's-length transaction.

It is important to remember that costs of disposal are deducted in arriving at ***net*** selling price. Examples of such costs are legal costs and costs of removing the asset.

Value in use is defined in IAS 36 as the present value of estimated cash flows expected from the continuing use of the asset and from its disposal at the end of its useful life.

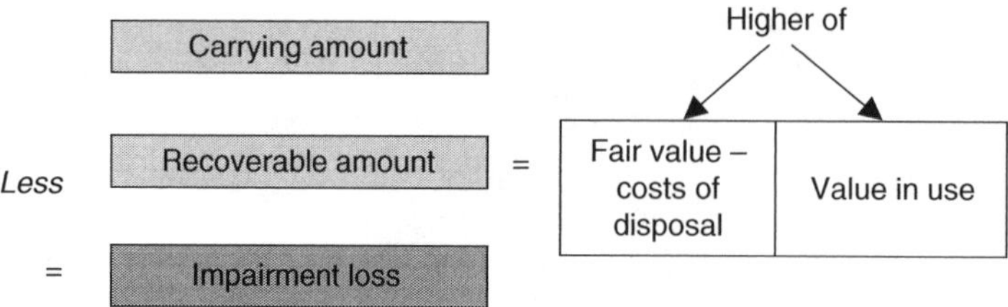

Diagram 10.11 Recoverable amount

The calculation of value in use involves predictions about future cash flows as well as an estimation of an appropriate discount rate.

We can now extend Diagram 10.10 to incorporate the definition of the recoverable amount shown in Diagram 10.11.

Pause and reflect ...

Why do you think that the recoverable amount is calculated using the *higher* of the future economic benefits from the *sale* and from the *use* of an asset?

Response

The recoverable amount is defined as the higher of an asset's ***fair value less costs of disposal*** (future economic benefits from *sale*) and its ***value in use*** (future economic benefits from *use*). The reason for this is simply that for any asset, an entity can choose to continue using it or sell it. Business sense dictates that if the future economic benefits from use are higher than the future economic benefits from sale, the entity will choose to use the asset. Conversely, if the future economic benefits from sale are higher than the future economic benefits from use, the entity will choose to sell the asset.

The higher of these two amounts is the recoverable amount that should be compared to the carrying amount of the asset. The recoverable amount is therefore the maximum benefit that can be obtained from the specific asset by either selling it or using it.

An entity should assess at each statement of financial position date whether or not there are indications that items of property, plant and equipment may be impaired. Such indicators include external factors such as:

- a large decline in the asset's market value;
- changes in the technological, market economic or legal environment in which the entity operates.

Such indicators also include internal factors such as:

- obsolescence or physical damage;
- evidence that the economic performance of the asset is, or will be, worse than expected.

If such indications exist, calculations should be made of the recoverable amount, as described in the previous paragraphs. If the carrying amount exceeds the recoverable amount, the asset is impaired and the carrying amount needs to be written down to the recoverable amount. If the recoverable amount exceeds the carrying amount, the requirements of IAS 36 do not apply and no impairment is recognised.

Example: Impairment of property, plant and equipment measured using the cost model

Computer World has an item of plant with a cost of C100 000 and accumulated depreciation of C60 000. The plant is measured using the cost model and is depreciated at 10 per cent per annum on the straight-line basis. There are indications at the end of the financial year on 31 December 20X6 that the asset may be impaired. The selling price in an active market is C27 500 and costs of disposal are estimated at C500. The estimated cash flows, as well as the present value of C1 at 10 per cent, are shown below.

Year ending	*Cash flow*	*Years*	*PV of C1 at 10%*
31/12/X7	15 000	1	0.909
31/12/X8	12 000	2	0.826
31/12/X9	8 000	3	0.751

You are required to:

a) Calculate the recoverable amount of the plant.
b) Account for the impairment of the plant using the 'A = L + OE' worksheet.

Solution: Impairment of property, plant and equipment measured using the cost model

a) Calculation of recoverable amount

		C
Carrying amount		40 000
Recoverable amount – higher of		(29 555)
• Fair value less costs of disposal	27 000	
• Value in use	29 555	
Impairment loss		10 445

b) Accounting for the impairment of the plant

	Assets				= L +	*Owner's equity*	
	Plant		Accumulated depreciation/ impairment			Impairment loss expense	
	+/L/Dr	−/R/Cr	−/L/Dr	+/R/Cr		+/L/Dr	−/R/Cr
Balance	100 000			60 000			
Impairment				10 445		10 445	
Balance	100 000			70 445		10 445	

The impairment is accounted for by recognising an expense of C10 445 and increasing the accumulated depreciation/impairment by the same amount. The impairment loss expense is closed off to the profit and loss account and reported in the statement of profit or loss as an expense.

Workings

Date of cash flow	*Amount of cash flow*	*PV of C1 at 10%*
	C	C
31/12/X7	15 000	13 635
31/12/X8	12 000	9 912
31/12/X9	8 000	6 008
		29 555

10.8 Measurement after recognition

You will recall from Section 10.3 of this chapter that property, plant and equipment that qualifies for recognition as an asset is measured at its ***cost***. We now turn our attention to the measurement models available to measure property, plant and equipment after initial recognition at cost. IAS 16 provides two possible treatments, the *cost model* or the *revaluation model*.

An entity can choose either model, but must then apply that model to an entire class of assets. For example, a motor manufacturer may not use the cost model for a machine that assembles cars, and the revaluation model for a machine that applies paint to them. This is because machines are considered a separate *class* of property, plant and equipment, and therefore both machines must be measured using the same model, say the cost model. However, using the cost model for machines would not prevent the entity measuring its property using the revaluation model. This is because machines are a different class of asset to property.

10.8.1 Cost model

In applying the cost model, an item of property, plant and equipment is carried at its cost less any accumulated depreciation and accumulated impairment losses.

The discussion in this chapter thus far relating to the recognition and measurement of property, plant and equipment has been on the cost model.

10.8.2 Revaluation model

In applying the revaluation model, an item of property, plant and equipment is carried at a revalued amount, which is its fair value at the date of revaluation less any subsequent accumulated depreciation and accumulated impairment losses.

The fair value is the price that would be received to sell an asset in an orderly transaction between market participants at the measurement date.

The fair value of land and buildings is usually their market value, normally determined by an appraisal undertaken by professionally qualified valuers. The fair value of items of plant and equipment is also their market value, determined by appraisal.

According to IAS 16, a revaluation increase is ***credited directly to equity*** in a ***revaluation surplus*** account.

When preparing the financial statements of a sole proprietor, the balance on the revaluation surplus account is transferred to the owner's capital account. In Part V of this book, dealing with the different forms of entity, you will learn how to record a revaluation surplus in the accounting records of a partnership and a company.

You will recall that in Parts I and II of this book, you were introduced to the concept of a revaluation. This was done in order to illustrate the presentation of the statement of profit or loss and other comprehensive income. To review briefly, IAS 1 requires total comprehensive income to comprise the profit for the period and other comprehensive income. The revaluation surplus is identified in IAS 1 as a component of other comprehensive income. As such, the revaluation surplus is reported on the statement of comprehensive income under the heading of other comprehensive income.

The following example deals with the revaluation of a non-depreciable asset.

Example 1: Revaluation of non-depreciable property, plant and equipment

At 31 December 20X6, Computer World has land with a cost of C500 000. The land was purchased two years previously. Land is measured using the revaluation model and is not depreciated. The land is revalued to C550 000. The profit for the period is C120 000.

You are required to:

a) Account for the revaluation of the plant using the 'A = L + OE' worksheet.
b) Prepare an extract from the statement of comprehensive income for the year ended 31 December 20X6.

Solution 1: Revaluation of non-depreciable property, plant and equipment

a) Revaluation of the plant

	Assets		= L +	*Owner's equity*	
	Land			Revaluation surplus	
	+/L/Dr	−/R/Cr		−/L/Dr	+/R/Cr
Bal	500 000				
1	50 000				50 000
Bal	550 000				50 000

Entry 1 increases the carrying amount of the land to its revalued amount of C550 000, with the surplus on revaluation being placed to the credit of a revaluation surplus account.

b) Extract from the statement of comprehensive income

COMPUTER WORLD **EXTRACT FROM STATEMENT OF COMPREHENSIVE INCOME** **FOR THE YEAR ENDED 31 DECEMBER 20X6**	
	C
Profit for the period	120 000
Other comprehensive income:	
Revaluation of land	50 000
Total comprehensive income	170 000

Turning our attention to the revaluation of depreciable assets, IAS 16 provides two options for dealing with the balance on accumulated depreciation when an item of property, plant and equipment is revalued. We will consider one of those methods here, where the accumulated depreciation is eliminated against the cost of the asset.

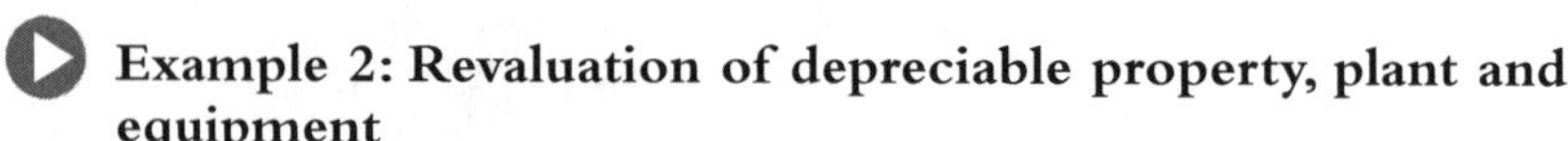

Example 2: Revaluation of depreciable property, plant and equipment

At 31 December 20X6, Computer World has an item of plant with a cost of C100 000 and accumulated depreciation of C20 000. Plant is measured using the revaluation model and is depreciated at 10 per cent per annum on the straight-line basis. The plant is revalued to C90 000, and the remaining useful life of the plant is unchanged.

The profit for the period is C120 000.

You are required to:

a) Account for the revaluation of the plant using the 'A = L + OE' worksheet.
b) Prepare an extract from the statement of comprehensive income for the year ended 31 December 20X6.
c) Prepare an extract from the statement of changes in equity for the year ended 31 December 20X6.
d) Calculate the depreciation in the first year after revaluation.

Solution 2: Revaluation of depreciable property, plant and equipment

a) Account for revaluation of the plant

	Assets				=	*Owner's equity*
	Plant		Accumulated depreciation		Revaluation surplus	
	+/L/Dr	−/R/Cr	−/L/Dr	+/R/Cr	−/L/Dr	+/R/Cr
Bal	100 000			20 000		
1		20 000	20 000			
	80 000					
2	10 000					10 000
Bal	90 000					10 000

Entry 1 eliminates, or reverses, the balance of accumulated depreciation against the cost of the plant. The plant account then reflects the carrying amount of C80 000. Entry 2 increases the carrying amount of the plant to its revalued amount of C90 000, with the surplus on revaluation being placed to the credit of a revaluation surplus account.

b) Extract from the statement of comprehensive income

COMPUTER WORLD
EXTRACT FROM STATEMENT OF COMPREHENSIVE INCOME
FOR THE YEAR ENDED 31 DECEMBER 20X6

	C
Profit for the period	120 000
Other comprehensive income:	
Revaluation of plant	10 000
Total comprehensive income	130 000

c) Extract from statement of changes in equity

COMPUTER WORLD
EXTRACT FROM STATEMENT OF CHANGES IN EQUITY
FOR THE YEAR ENDED 31 DECEMBER 20X6

	Capital	*Revaluation surplus*	*Total*
	C	*C*	*C*
Balance	×	×	×
Total comprehensive income	120 000	10 000	130 000
	×	×	×

d) Depreciation in the first year after revaluation

As the useful life of the plant is unchanged, the revalued carrying amount of C90 000 will be written off over the *remaining* useful life of eight years at C11 250 per year (C90 000/8 yrs). The additional depreciation to be provided each year over the plant's remaining life of eight years amounts to C1 250 (C11 250 – C10 000). This represents the depreciation on the revaluation of C10 000 over the remaining eight years (C1 250 × 8 yrs = C10 000).

10.8.3 Revaluation increases and decreases

Property, plant and equipment measured using the revaluation model need to be revalued on a regular basis. It is important to realise that a revaluation can result in an increase in the carrying amount (known as a revaluation increase) or a decrease in the carrying amount (known as a revaluation decrease) (see Diagram 10.12).

Revaluation decrease compared to impairment

A revaluation decrease is not the same as an impairment. In principle, an entity must first revalue an asset in terms of IAS 16 before testing for impairment under IAS 36. Therefore, if a revaluation decrease is determined under IAS 16 in relation to the selling price and

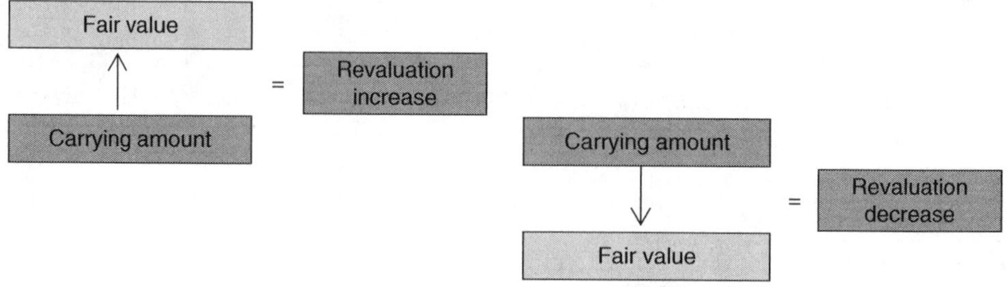

Diagram 10.12 Revaluation increases and decreases

disposal costs are immaterial, no impairment can be recognised under IAS 36. This is a subtle yet important principle and is illustrated in the following example.

Example: Revaluation decrease

At 31 December 20X6, Computer World has land with a carrying amount of C500 000. Land is measured using the revaluation model and is not depreciated. The fair value of the land is C480 000 and disposal costs are immaterial. The value in use is:

a) C490 000
b) C470 000

You are required to:

Determine the revaluation decrease and the impairment loss, if any, in each of the above two scenarios.

Solution: Revaluation decrease

a) FV = C480 000 and value in use = C490 000

We first determine the revaluation decrease under IAS 16:

Carrying amount	500 000
Fair value	480 000
Revaluation decrease	20 000

We then assess whether there is an impairment loss by comparing the *revised carrying amount* with the recoverable amount (higher of fair value and value in use). The recoverable amount is C490 000 and as it exceeds the carrying amount, no impairment loss is recognised.

Revised carrying amount	480 000
Recoverable amount – higher of	490 000
Fair value	480 000
Value in use	490 000
Impairment loss	—

b) FV = C480 000 and value in use = C470 000

Again, we first determine the revaluation decrease under IAS 16:

Carrying amount	500 000
Fair value	480 000
Revaluation decrease	20 000

We then assess whether there is an impairment loss by comparing the *revised carrying amount* with the recoverable amount (higher of fair value and value in use). The recoverable amount is C480 000 and, as this is the same as the carrying amount, again no impairment loss is recognised.

Revised carrying amount	480 000
Recoverable amount – higher of	480 000
Fair value	480 000
Value in use	470 000
Impairment loss	—

Accounting for revaluation increases and decreases

There are many, often complex, implications of revaluation increases and decreases relating to items of property, plant and equipment, especially depreciable property, plant and equipment. These issues will not be addressed in detail. However, for a basic understanding, the principles of IAS 16 are set out below, followed by some examples of revaluation increases and decreases relating to non-depreciable property, plant and equipment.

If an asset's carrying amount **increases** as a result of a revaluation, the increase is:

- recognised in ***other comprehensive income*** as a revaluation surplus; or
- recognised in ***profit or loss*** as a revaluation income if it reverses a previous revaluation decrease recognised in profit or loss.

If an asset's carrying amount **decreases** as a result of a revaluation, the decrease is:

- first recognised in other comprehensive income as a decrease to any revaluation surplus that may exist; then
- after any revaluation surplus is reduced to nil, the decrease is recognised in profit or loss as a revaluation expense.

Example 1: Revaluation increase of non-depreciable property, plant and equipment followed by a revaluation decrease

Land is purchased at a cost of C100 000 on 1 January 20X5. Land is not depreciated and is measured using the revaluation model. At 31 December 20X6, the land is revalued to C130 000.

Two years later, at 31 December 20X8, the fair value of the land is measured at:

a) C120 000
b) C90 000

Costs of disposal are immaterial.

You are required to:

Provide the journal entries to record the revaluation increase at 31 December 20X6 and the revaluation decrease at 31 December 20X8, for each scenario in (a) and (b) above.

Solution 1: Revaluation increase of non-depreciable property, plant and equipment followed by a revaluation decrease

				Dr	*Cr*
	31/12/X6	Land (A)	*(130 000 – 100 000)*	30 000	
		Revaluation surplus (OE)			30 000
a)	31/12/X8	Revaluation surplus (OE)	*(130 000 – 120 000)*	10 000	
		Land (A)			10 000
b)	31/12/X8	Revaluation surplus (OE)	*(Amount in revaluation surplus)*	30 000	
		Revaluation loss (E)	*(40 000 – 30 000)*	10 000	
		Land (A)	*(130 000 – 90 000)*		40 000

In situation (a), the whole of the revaluation decrease is allocated against the revaluation surplus as it does not exceed the balance of C30 000 in the revaluation surplus account. However, in situation (b), the amount allocated against the revaluation surplus is limited to the balance of C30 000 in that account, and the excess of C10 000 is recognised as an expense.

Workings

		(a)	*(b)*
1/1/X5	Cost	100 000	100 000
	Revaluation increase	30 000	30 000
31/12/X6	Fair value	130 000	130 000
31/12/X8	Fair value	120 000	90 000
	Revaluation decrease	10 000	40 000
	Reversal of revaluation surplus	10 000	30 000
	Revaluation loss (expense)	—	10 000

Example 2: Revaluation decrease of non-depreciable property, plant and equipment followed by a revaluation increase

Land is purchased at a cost of C100 000 on 1 January 20X5. Land is not depreciated and is measured using the revaluation model. At 31 December 20X6, the land is revalued to C80 000.

Two years later, at 31 December 20X8 the fair value of the land is measured at:

a) C90 000
b) C110 000

You are required to:

Provide the journal entries to record the revaluation decrease at 31 December 20X6 and the revaluation increase at 31 December 20X8.

Solution 2: Revaluation decrease of non-depreciable property, plant and equipment followed by a revaluation increase

			Dr	*Cr*
31/12/X6	Revaluation loss (E)	*(100 000 – 80 000)*	20 000	
	Land (A)			20 000
a) 31/12/X8	Land (A)	*(90 000 – 80 000)*	10 000	
	Revaluation gain (I)			10 000
b) 31/12/X8	Land (A)	*(110 000 – 80 000)*	30 000	
	Revaluation gain (I)	*(Amount of revaluation loss)*		20 000
	Revaluation surplus (OE)	*(30 000 – 20 000)*		10 000

In situation (a), the whole of the revaluation increase of C10 000 is recognised as income as it reverses part of the revaluation decrease of C20 000 previously recognised as an expense. However, in situation (b), the amount recognised as income is limited to the C20 000 previously recognised as an expense, and the excess of C10 000 is credited to equity in a revaluation surplus account.

Workings

		(a)	*(b)*
1/1/X5	Cost	100 000	100 000
	Revaluation decrease	(20 000)	(20 000)
31/12/X6	Fair value	80 000	80 000
31/12/X8	Fair value	90 000	110 000
	Revaluation increase	10 000	30 000
	Reversal of revaluation decrease/revaluation gain (income)	10 000	20 000
	Revaluation surplus	—	10 000

Revision example 1

The following account balances appeared in the accounting records of Sparks Spare Parts on 1 October 20X4:

	C
Land and building, cost	350 000
Motor vehicles, cost	106 000
Computer equipment, cost	36 000
Accumulated depreciation – buildings	7 600
Accumulated depreciation – motor vehicles	52 310
Accumulated depreciation – computer equipment	16 000

The accounting policies for depreciation are as follows:

1 Land with a cost price of C160 000 is not depreciated.
2 Buildings are depreciated at 2 per cent per annum using the straight-line method.
3 Motor vehicles and related significant parts are depreciated at 30 per cent per annum using the diminishing balance method.
4 Computer equipment is depreciated on a straight-line basis and is expected to have a useful life of three years with a zero residual value.

On 30 June 20X5, Sparks Spare Parts traded in a delivery van for C23 000 on a used newer model. The second van cost C65 000 and the difference on the purchase price was paid by cheque. The original van was purchased on 30 November 20X2 for C50 000.

An account for C3 515 was received from Fix-it Garage on 2 August 20X5 in respect of work done on the second delivery van. The account comprised the following amounts:

	C
40 000 km service	415
New tyres	3 100
	3 515

The old tyres had a zero carrying amount and were scrapped.

Owing to an increase in sales demand, another sales assistant was hired, and a new computer was purchased for C6 800 cash on 1 September 20X5. Installation and transport costs of C400 were due to Computer World.

No other purchases or sales took place.

All transactions (including cash transactions) are journalised and all calculations are made to the nearest whole currency unit.

You are required to:

a) Journalise the above transactions for the year ended 30 September 20X5. The journal entries for depreciation at the year end need not be shown.
b) Prepare an extract from the statement of financial position of Sparks Spare Parts in respect of non-current assets at 30 September 20X5.

 **Solution: Revision example 1**

a) Journal of Sparks Spare Parts for the year ended 30 September 20X5

Date	*Description*	*Dr*	*Cr*
20X5			
June 30	Depreciation: motor vehicles (E)	5 906	
	Motor vehicles: accumulated depreciation: (–A)		5 906
	Depreciation on vehicle traded in		
	Asset disposal (T)	50 000	
	Motor vehicles: cost (A)		50 000
	Cost of van traded in		

	Motor vehicles: accumulated depreciation: (–A)	29 656	
	Asset disposal (T)		29 656
	Accumulated depreciation on van traded in		
	Motor vehicles: cost (A)	65 000	
	Bank (A)		42 000
	Asset disposal (T)		23 000
	New van purchased and old van traded in		
	Asset disposal (T)	2 656	
	Profit on sale of non-current assets (I)		2 656
	Profit on van traded in		
Aug 2	Motor vehicles: cost (A)	3 100	
	Motor vehicle repairs (E)	415	
	Accounts payable (L)		3 515
	Motor vehicle repairs		
Sept 1	Computer equipment: cost (A)	7 200	
	Bank (A)		6 800
	Accounts payable (L)		400
	Purchase of new computer		

b) Extract from the statement of financial position in respect of non-current assets at 30 September 20X5

SPARKS SPARE PARTS
STATEMENT OF FINANCIAL POSITION AS AT 30 SEPTEMBER 20X5

Non-current assets	*Cost*	*Accumulated depreciation*	*Carrying amount*
	C	C	C
Land and buildings	350 000	11 400	338 600
Motor vehicles	124 100	41 822	82 278
Computer equipment	43 200	28 200	15 000
	517 300	81 422	435 878

Workings

Van traded in

Accumulated depreciation – van traded in

1/12/X2 – 30/09/X3	(50 000 × 30% × 10/12)	12 500
1/10/X3 – 30/09/X4	(*37 500 × 30%)	11 250
1/10/X4 – 30/06/X5	(**26 250 × 30% × 9/12)	5 906
		29 656

*(50 000 – 12 500); **(50 000 – 12 500 – 11 250)

Cost	50 000
Accumulated depreciation	(29 656)
Carrying amount	20 344
Proceeds	23 000
Profit on trade-in	2 656

Motor vehicles		*Cost*	*Accum. depn*
Balance 1/10/X4		106 000	52 310
Van traded in:			
Depreciation to date of trade-in			5 906
		106 000	58 216
Removal of cost and accumulated depreciation		(50 000)	(29 656)
		56 000	28 560
Depreciation on remaining MV (56 000 – 28 560) × 30%			8 232
		56 000	36 792
Van purchased		65 000	
Depreciation to year end	(65 000 × 30% × 3/12)		4 875
Expenditure on van		3 100	
Depreciation to year end	(3 100 × 30% × 2/12)		155
		124 100	41 822
Computer equipment			
Balance 1/10/X4		36 000	16 000
Depreciation on existing CE	(36 000/3)		12 000
Computer purchased		7 200	
Depreciation to year end	(7 200/3 × 1/12)		200
		43 200	28 200
Land and buildings			
Total land and buildings			350 000
Less Cost of land			(160 000)
Cost of building			190 000
Depreciation	(190 000 × 2%)		3 800

Revision example 2

The Golden Pumpkin is a store selling a range of organic farm produce. The following is a post-closing trial balance of The Golden Pumpkin at 31 May 20X4.

THE GOLDEN PUMPKIN
POST-CLOSING TRIAL BALANCE AT 31 MAY 20X4

	Dr	*Cr*
Furniture and equipment	160 000	
Accumulated depreciation: furniture and equipment		24 000
Motor vehicles	40 000	
Accumulated depreciation: motor vehicles		16 000
Accounts receivable	75 200	
Accounts payable		58 400
Inventory	56 300	
Bank	10 500	
Capital		243 600
	342 000	342 000

The following additional information is relevant:

Furniture and equipment

- A computerised cash till, purchased on 1 September 20X3 and included in the furniture and equipment on the above trial balance, was sold for cash on 30 November 20X4. The selling price was C34 000. The cash till was originally purchased at an invoice price of C37 500, and installation costs amounted to C2 500.
- The remaining furniture and equipment was revalued by C13 400 on 31 May 20X5.
- Furniture and equipment is depreciated at 20 per cent per annum on the diminishing balance method.

Motor vehicles

- The motor vehicles comprise two vans used to deliver goods to customers. Both vans were purchased on 1 June 20X0 at a total cost of C40 000. The residual value was estimated to be zero.
- On 1 June 20X4, the engines of the vans were overhauled at a total cost of C12 000. The estimated useful life was considered to be extended by two years, and the residual value was re-estimated to be C6 000.
- On 31 May 20X5, there were indications that the vans were impaired. Management's calculations reveal that the vans could be disposed of to a willing buyer for C25 000. The present value of future expected cash flows from the use of the vans over the remainder of their useful life amounts to C24 200, and the present value of the estimated residual value amounts to C2 800.
- Motor vehicles are depreciated at 10 per cent per annum on the straight-line basis.

You are required to:

a) Prepare all the journal entries relating to the furniture and equipment for the year ended 31 May 20X5. You should include the entries relating to depreciation expense, the sale of the cash till and the revaluation of the remaining equipment.
b) Prepare a schedule showing all movements in the carrying amount of the motor vehicles. You should begin from the date of purchase on 1 June 20X0 to the end of the current year on 31 May 20X5.
c) Prepare the non-current assets section only from the statement of financial position of The Golden Pumpkin at 31 May 20X5.
d) Discuss whether it is necessary to reduce the carrying amount of the equipment in the current year by accounting for depreciation expense when the carrying amount is increased by the revaluation.
e) Explain why it is necessary to account for the impairment of the motor vehicles when the carrying amount exceeds the recoverable amount.

Solution: Revision example 2

a) Journal entries relating to furniture and equipment

Date	*Description*	*Dr*	*Cr*
30/11/X4	Depreciation (E) Furniture and equipment: Accumulated depreciation (–A) *Depreciation on item sold* ((40 000 – 6 000) × 20% × 6/12)	3 400	 3 400

		Dr	Cr
	Furniture and equipment: Accumulated depreciation (–A) (6 000 + 3 400)	9 400	
	Furniture and equipment: Cost (A)		40 000
	Bank	34 000	
	Disposal (T)		3 400
	Disposal of cash till		
30/05/X5	Depreciation (E)	20 400	
	Furniture and equipment: Accumulated depreciation (–A)		
	Furniture and equipment: Cost (A)		20 400
	Depreciation on remaining items		
	((120 000 – 18 000) × 20%)		
	Furniture and equipment: Accumulated depreciation (–A)	38 400	
	Furniture and equipment: Cost (A)		38 400
	Reversal of accumulated depreciation on revaluation		
	Furniture and equipment: Cost (A)	13 400	
	Revaluation surplus (OE)		13 400
	Revaluation of furniture and equipment		

Workings

Furniture and equipment sold			
01/09/X3	Cost		40 000
01/09/X3 – 31/05/X4	Depreciation	*(40 000 × 20% × 9/12)*	(6 000)
			34 000
01/06/X4 – 30/11/X4	Depreciation	*(34 000 × 20% × 6/12)*	(3 400)
			30 600
	Selling price		34 000
	Profit		3 400

Furniture and equipment		*Cost/ Valuation*	*Accumulated depreciation*	*Revaluation*
01/06/X4	Balance	160 000	(24 000)	
01/06/X4 – 30/11/X4	Depreciation on item sold		(3 400)	
30/11/X4	Removal of cost and accumulated depreciation	(40 000)	9 400	
		120 000	(18 000)	
01/06/X4 – 31/05/X5	Depreciation on remaining F&E ((120 000 – 18 000) × 20%)		(20 400)	
		120 000	(38 400)	
31/05/X5	Revaluation			
	– Reversal of accumulated depreciation	(38 400)	38 400	
	– Revaluation surplus	13 400		13 400
		95 000		13 400

b) Motor vehicles schedule

				Life
01/06/X0	Cost		40 000	10
01/06/X0 – 31/05/X4	Depreciation	*(40 000 × 10% × 4 yrs)*	(16 000)	(4)
			24 000	6
01/06/X4	Improvement		12 000	2
			36 000	8
01/06/X4 – 31/05/X5	Depreciation	*(36 000 – 6 000)/8 yrs*	(3 750)	
			32 250	
31/05/X5	Impairment		(5 250)	
		(Recoverable amount = Greater of (24 200 + 2 800) or 25 000)	27 000	

c) Statement of financial position

THE GOLDEN PUMPKIN
STATEMENT OF FINANCIAL POSITION
AT 31 MAY 20X5

		C
ASSETS		
Non-current assets		
Furniture and equipment		95 000
– At revaluation		95 000
– Accumulated depreciation		—
Motor vehicles		27 000
– At cost	*(40 000 + 12 000)*	52 000
– Accumulated depreciation and impairment	*(16 000 + 3 750 + 5 250)*	(25 000)

d) Depreciation expense and revaluation

An asset is an embodiment of future economic benefits. As the economic benefits embodied in an asset are consumed by an entity, the carrying amount of the asset is reduced to reflect this consumption by charging an expense for depreciation. The depreciation charge is made even if the asset is revalued.

e) Impairment loss

The objective of IAS 36 is to ensure that an entity's assets are not overstated. If the carrying amount of the motor vehicle exceeds the recoverable amount, the carrying amount will probably not be recovered in the future either through use or sale. An impairment loss is required to be recognised.

Bibliography

Anglo Gold Ashanti Integrated Report. 2012. www.aga-reports.com/12/ir (Accessed 7 May 2013).

Deegan, C and Ward, AM. 2013. *Financial Accounting and Reporting: An International Approach.* London, McGraw-Hill.

Integritax Newsletter. *South African Institute of Chartered Accountants.* October 2010. www.saica.co.za/integritax/Archive%5CIntegritax_October_2010_Issue_134.pdf (Accessed 8 April 2014).

RSM Shiff, Hazenfratz & Co. Chapter 14: *Property, plant and equipment.* portal.idc.ac.il/FacultyPublication.Publication?PublicationID=2876&FacultyUserName=c2h1dnM= (Accessed 22 April 2014).

The International Accounting Standards Board. 2010. IAS 16 *Property, Plant and Equipment.*

The International Accounting Standards Board. 2010. IAS 36 *Impairment of Assets.*

The International Accounting Standards Board. 2010. *The Conceptual Framework.*

11 Inventory and cost of sales

Business focus

The Drakensberg Pumped Storage Scheme (in the South African province of KwaZulu-Natal) is a hydroelectric facility relying on water in four dams (the Driekloof, Kilburb, Woodstock and Driel dams) to generate electricity during periods of peak power demand. Water from each of the dams is released, turning a series of turbines which produce electricity available for supply into the national grid. Should the water in the dams be accounted for as inventory? Although the water is not held for sale in the ordinary course of business by the power utility, it could be construed as a 'material' to be consumed in the production process. The water in each of the dams is used to generate hydroelectric power, after which its potential energy is lost. In this way, any water still in the dam could be accounted for as 'energy in production'. Think carefully about this proposed accounting while working through this chapter. Do not forget to go back to the definition of assets and income in the *Conceptual Framework*.

In this chapter

Inventory often comprises a substantial part of the assets of a business entity, particularly a merchandising entity. It is usually sold within one year or operating cycle and is therefore classified as a current asset. The measurement of inventory can have a significant impact on determining and presenting the financial position and results of operations of entities. What is included in the cost of inventory, and how is this allocated to the cost of goods sold and the closing inventory? And then there is the issue of measuring inventory at the end of a period. Theft of inventory, or shrinkage as it is often called, is a significant problem facing many retailers. We learn how accounting helps us to manage this.

Dashboard

- Look at the *Learning outcomes* so that you know what you should be able to do after studying the chapter.
- Read the *Business focus* to place the chapter contents in a real-world context.
- Preview *In this chapter* to focus your mind on the contents of the chapter.
- Read the *text* in detail.
    - Pay attention to the definitions and apply your mind to the *Pause and reflect* scenarios.

  - Ensure that you fully understand Section 11.2 on the relationship between cost, gross profit and selling price before moving on, as this is essential to your understanding of the rest of the chapter.
  - Compare and contrast the accounting entries for inventory shortages in Section 11.4.3 to those for the write-down of inventory in Section 11.6.2, and note the similarities between the two.
  - Prepare solutions to all the examples as you read through the chapter. For the examples on inventory shortages in Section 11.4.3 and on the write-down of inventory in Section 11.6.2, pay particular attention to the various scenarios (periodic and perpetual system, with and without a shortage; write-down and no write-down).
- Prepare solutions to the *Revision examples* at the end of the chapter without reference to the suggested solutions. Compare your solutions to the suggested solutions provided.

Learning outcomes

After studying this chapter, you should be able to do the following:

1 Describe the nature of inventory.
2 Compute the relationship between cost, gross profit and selling price.
3 Determine the cost of inventory.
4 Account for goods in transit, goods on consignment and inventory shortages.
5 Compute the cost of sales and closing inventory using the inventory cost formulae.
6 Apply the 'lower of cost and net realisable value' measurement rule.
7 Calculate inventory errors.
8 Estimate the value of closing inventory.

Inventory and cost of sales

11.1 Recognition and classification of inventory

The recognition of inventory affects both the statement of profit or loss and the statement of financial position. The cost of inventory available for sale is allocated between the cost of sales expense (which is included on the statement of profit or loss of the current period) and the inventory asset (which is included on the statement of financial position of the current period and then carried forward to be included on the statement of profit or loss of a future period). Diagram 11.1 illustrates this point.

You are familiar with the definition of an asset in the *Conceptual Framework* – a resource controlled by the entity as a result of past events and from which future economic benefits are expected to flow to the entity.

The cost of inventory is recorded initially as an asset (using the perpetual system) or in a temporary purchases account (using the periodic system), and subsequently transferred to the statement of profit or loss as the inventory is sold. The inventory amount on the statement of financial position thus represents that portion of the inventory purchased in the past which has not yet been expensed – it is carried forward as an asset which will provide future economic benefits to the entity.

The applicable accounting standard is IAS 2 *Inventories*.

Diagram 11.1 Effect of inventory on statement of profit or loss and statement of financial position

IAS 2 defines inventories as assets that:

- are held for sale in the ordinary course of business;
- are held in the form of materials or supplies to be consumed within the business operation.

Pause and reflect . . .

What factors may indicate when *control* of inventory has passed from the seller to the buyer?

Response

This is an interesting issue and is often not as straightforward as it might first appear. IFRS 15 *Revenue* provides a list of factors that may indicate the point in time at which control passes. These include, but are not limited to:

- the selling entity has a present right to payment for the asset;
- the customer has legal title to the asset;
- the entity has transferred physical possession of the asset;
- the customer has the significant risks and rewards related to the ownership of the asset; and
- the customer has accepted the asset.

The focus in this chapter is on the purchase of inventory and the recognition of an asset (from the perspective of the purchasing entity) rather than on the sale of inventory and the recognition of income (from the perspective of the selling entity). When an entity sells inventory in a retail environment, for example Smart Concepts selling computers to customers, the application of the above factors does not normally cause a problem. However, when an entity buys inventory from a wholesaler or manufacturer and it is perhaps transported over a long distance, for example Smart Concepts buying inventory from a manufacturer in another city or country, the application of the factors can cause some difficulties. Some of these issues will be addressed in the sections that follow.

Returning to our discussion of the definition of an asset, inventory is a resource controlled by the entity (satisfied by one of the factors mentioned above) as a result of a past event (the purchase transaction), from which future economic benefits are expected to flow to the entity (sale of the inventory to customers).

Turning to the recognition criteria, it is probable that future economic benefits will flow to the entity (cash to be received when customers pay for the goods) and the cost can be measured reliably (the invoice price is known).

It is very important to distinguish between goods held for sale and consumable goods, commonly known as consumable stores. Although both are included in the definition of inventory, it is only the cost of the goods held for sale that is included in the determination

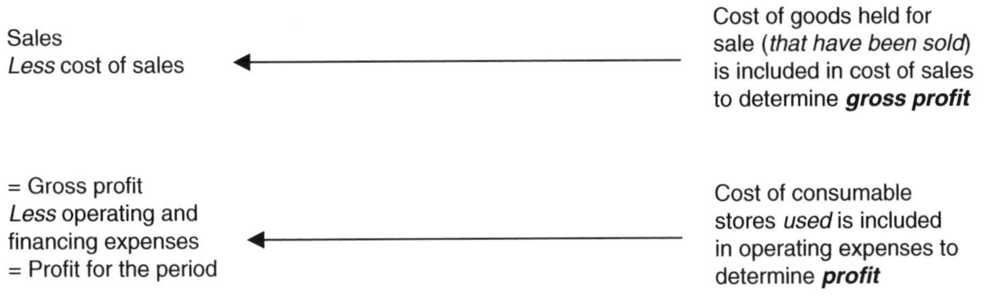

Diagram 11.2 Cost of goods held for sale and consumable stores

of the gross profit from trading activities. The cost of consumable stores is taken into account in calculating the profit for the period. This is illustrated in Diagram 11.2.

11.2 Relationship between cost, gross profit and selling price

The relationship between the cost of inventory, the mark-up applied to achieve the gross profit, and the selling price is crucial in a number of issues relating to accounting for inventory. In establishing the relationship, it is important to distinguish between the ***mark-up on cost*** and the gross profit percentage (GP %).

Assume that a business applies a ***mark-up on cost*** of 25 per cent to all of its goods. The following relationships can be established:

Cost	100	*mark-up on cost* = GP/C = 25% (25/100)
Gross profit	25	
Selling price	125	*expected GP %* = GP/SP = 20% (25/125)

On the other hand, assume that the ***expected GP %*** is 25%. The relationship between cost, gross profit and selling price is different and is established as follows:

Cost	75	*mark-up on cost* = GP/C = 33.33% (25/75)
Gross profit	25	
Selling price	100	*expected GP %* = GP/SP = 25% (25/100)

 **Pause and reflect . . .**

What is the difference between a mark-up on cost and an expected GP %?

Response

Management of a business entity may decide to focus on the mark-up it wants to add to the cost of goods in order to determine the selling price. A mark-up on cost of, say, 25 per cent is then applied to the cost of goods purchased, which leads to an expected GP % of 20 per cent. On the other hand, management may decide to focus on the GP % it wants to achieve, say 25 per cent. This is the expected GP %, which in turn determines the mark-up on cost, in this case 33.33 per cent.

In some situations (which you will encounter later in this chapter), you will need to calculate the expected GP % from a known mark-up on cost. In other situations, you may need to establish the mark-up applied to cost from a known GP %.

Pause and reflect . . .

a) An entity applies a constant mark-up on cost of 25 per cent to all of its goods. The sales amount to C500. What would you expect the cost of sales to be?

b) An entity marks up all of its goods to achieve an expected GP % of 25 per cent. The sales amount to C500. What would you expect the cost of sales to be?

Response

a) The relationship between cost, gross profit and selling price is as follows:

	%	C	
Cost	100	400	(500 × 100/125)
Gross profit	25	100	(500 × 25/125)
Selling price	125	500	

The cost of sales is therefore C400.

b) The relationship between cost, gross profit and selling price is as follows:

	%	C	
Cost	75	375	(500 × 75/100)
Gross profit	25	125	(500 × 25/100)
Selling price	100	500	

The cost of sales is therefore C375.

11.3 Measuring the cost of inventory

According to IAS 2, the cost of inventory of a merchandising entity comprises all ***costs of purchase*** and ***other costs*** incurred in bringing the inventory to its present location and condition (see Diagram 11.3).

11.3.1 Costs of purchase

The costs of purchase of inventory comprise the purchase price, import duties and other taxes (other than those which are recoverable, such as VAT) as well as transport and handling costs directly attributable to the acquisition of goods for resale. Trade discounts and rebates are deducted in determining the costs of purchase. We will now examine these costs in more detail.

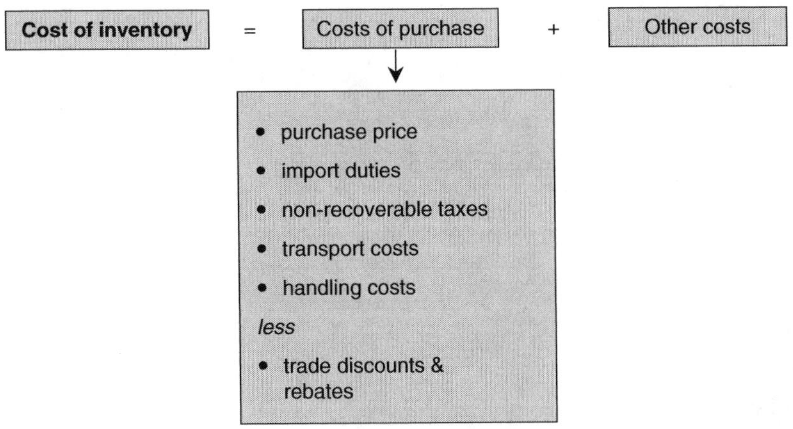

Diagram 11.3 Cost of inventory

Transaction	*Perpetual*	*Periodic*
Purchase of goods on credit	Dr Inventory (A)	Dr Purchases (T)
	Cr Accounts payable (L)	Cr Accounts payable (L)
Import duties paid in cash	Dr Inventory (A)	Dr Purchases (T)
	Cr Bank (A)	Cr Bank (A)

Diagram 11.4 Accounting entries for purchase of inventory and import duties using a perpetual and periodic inventory system

Purchase price and import duties

These costs are relatively straightforward to determine and are found on the invoice from the supplier and the import documentation. You should also remember the accounting entries for these items from Chapter 8, *Purchase and sale transactions*, which are summarised in Diagram 11.4.

You should recall from Chapter 8, *Purchase and sale transactions*, that inventory can be recorded using either a perpetual or a periodic system. Remember also that a perpetual system is used by larger business entities that have more sophisticated accounting systems, whereas a periodic system is used by smaller business entities that do not have sophisticated accounting systems.

Non-recoverable taxes

Many countries around the world have some form of transaction tax (commonly VAT) that is levied on the purchase of various goods and services. The only time that VAT will form part of the cost of inventory is if it may *not* be claimed back from the tax authorities. This happens, for example, where the entity fails to meet certain criteria laid down by the tax authorities (for example, if the entity is not registered as a vendor for VAT purposes).

Transaction	*Perpetual*	*Periodic*
Transport inwards paid in cash	Dr Inventory (A) Cr Bank (A)	Dr Transport in (T) Cr Bank (A)
Transport outwards paid in cash	Dr Transport (E) Cr Bank (A)	Dr Transport (E) Cr Bank (A)

Diagram 11.5 Accounting entries for transport costs using a perpetual and periodic inventory system

Thus, if the VAT *is not* recoverable, then the business entity has incurred a cost that is included in the cost of the inventory asset. On the other hand, if the VAT *is* able to be recovered at a later date from the tax authorities, then no cost has been incurred.

Transport costs

When referring to transport costs, business entities distinguish between two types of transport costs, commonly known as *transport inwards* and *transport outwards.*

Transport inwards refers to the cost of transporting the purchased inventory from the supplier's to the purchaser's premises. It is a cost that was incurred in 'bringing the inventory to its present location' and should therefore be included in the cost of inventory *asset* in the statement of financial position.

When a business sells inventory, it is a common business practice to offer to deliver the goods to the customer's premises. The cost of this delivery is known as **transport outwards**. It is a cost that is incurred in order to *sell* the inventory rather than to *purchase* it, and is thus *not* a cost that was incurred in 'bringing the inventory to its present location'. As such, it should be recorded as a selling *expense* in the statement of profit or loss.

The accounting entries are summarised in Diagram 11.5.

11.3.2 Other costs

Other costs are included in the cost of inventory only to the extent that they are incurred in bringing the inventories to their present location and condition – for example, the cost of customising an item for a customer. The cost of storing maturing inventory such as wine or cheese might also be included.

11.4 Other recognition and measurement issues

Most items present no problem in recognising and measuring the cost. There are, however, a few issues which require special attention. These include goods in transit at the end of the period, goods on consignment and inventory shortages.

11.4.1 Goods in transit

Goods in transit, as the name implies, are goods which have not physically arrived at the premises of the buying entity. The crucial issue from an accounting perspective is whether

control of the goods has passed from the supplier to the buyer (the reporting entity, in this case) as this determines whether the goods are to be included as inventory on the statement of financial position of the buying entity.

If control has not passed, then the goods in question remain the property of the seller and do not affect the financial statements of the buyer at all. If control *has* passed (and the goods have not been delivered), then the goods in question are regarded as 'in transit' and have to be recognised as an asset on the buyer's statement of financial position even though they are not at the buyer's premises and have thus not been included in the physical count of inventory.

Naturally, if the goods have been delivered, they will be included in the physical count of closing inventory to the extent that they remain unsold, and the problem of being 'in transit' falls away.

This can be expressed as shown in Diagram 11.6.

In deciding whether *control* has passed from the seller to the buyer, it is necessary, as discussed in Section 11.1 previously, to consider the factors mentioned in IFRS 15 including right of payment, legal title, physical possession, transfer of risks and rewards of ownership and acceptance of the goods.

The issue of goods in transit arises more often when goods are transported long distances and across international boundaries. The International Chamber of Commerce has produced a list of trading terms, called the International Chamber of Commerce Terms of Trade (commonly referred to as 'Incoterms') to assist in determining when the risks and rewards have transferred.

The Incoterms rules are complex and are beyond the scope of most financial accounting texts. However, for illustrative purposes, we will briefly discuss two of these terms here.

The term **'FOB' (Free on Board)** means that the risks and rewards transfer when the goods are loaded on board the vessel at the port of shipment. The buyer bears all costs

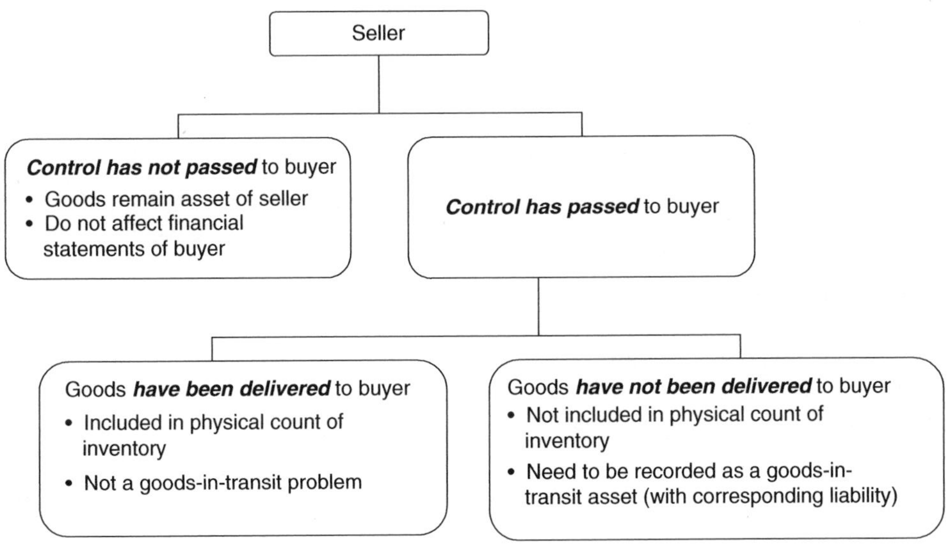

Diagram 11.6 Goods in transit

from that moment onwards (included in the cost of purchase of the inventory, as explained in Section 11.3). The term **'DAT' (Delivered at Terminal)** means that risks and rewards transfer when goods are unloaded at a named destination terminal. The seller bears all risks involved in bringing the goods to and unloading them at the terminal. Note that a 'terminal' includes places such as a quay, warehouse, container yard, rail or air cargo terminal.

Once it is confirmed that control has passed and the goods have not been delivered (and are therefore in transit), the purchase of the goods needs to be processed through the accounting records. As *control* has passed, the goods in transit are a resource, controlled by the entity, from which future economic benefits are expected to flow and therefore need to be recorded as an asset. For the same reason, the amount owing to the supplier is an obligation of the entity, which will result in an outflow of economic benefits in the future and must be recorded as a liability.

The entry is the same for both the ***periodic*** and ***perpetual*** systems, as the adjustment affects the *statement of financial position* only. The statement of profit or loss is not affected.

Assume that inventory costing C70 000 was in transit at the end of the financial year. The accounting entry can be shown as follows:

	Assets		=	*Liabilities*		+	*Owner's equity*
	Goods in transit			Accounts payable			
	+/L/Dr	−/R/Cr		−/L/Dr	+/R/Cr		
Recording of goods in transit	70 000				70 000		

Summary of entries to account for goods in transit

Periodic	*Perpetual*
Dr Goods in transit	Dr Goods in transit
Cr Accounts payable	Cr Accounts payable

11.4.2 Goods on consignment

Goods on consignment are goods delivered by the entity owning these goods (known as the consignor) to another entity (known as the consignee), who will sell these goods on behalf of the owner. The goods are not sold to the consignee and control of them remains with the consignor.

Goods on consignment held by the consignee at the end of the period must be included as inventory on the consignor's statement of financial position. Although future economic benefits will flow to the consignee when the goods are sold, the goods do not comprise a resource controlled by the consignee and are therefore correctly excluded from the consignee's statement of financial position.

 **Example: Goods on consignment**

Sharp Moves delivered ten printers on consignment to Peoples' Printers on 1 November 20X6. The printers cost C2 000 each, and Peoples' Printers sells them at a mark-up on cost of 25 per cent. Sharp Moves has agreed to pay Peoples' Printers a commission of 15 per cent of the selling price of the printers. At 31 December 20X6, Peoples' Printers had sold six of the printers for cash. A perpetual inventory system is used.

You are required to:

a) Prepare the relevant journal entries in the accounting records of Sharp Moves relating to the goods on consignment.
b) Prepare the relevant journal entries in the accounting records of Peoples' Printers relating to the goods on consignment.

Solution: Goods on consignment

a) Sharp Moves goods on consignment journal entries

GENERAL JOURNAL OF SHARP MOVES

Date	*Description*		*Dr*	*Cr*
31/12/X6	Bank (A)	*(15 000 − 2 250)*	12 750	
	Commission (E)	*(15 000 × 0.15)*	2 250	
	Sales (I)	*(2 000 × 125/100 × 6)*		15 000
	Cost of sales (E)	*(2 000 × 6)*	12 000	
	Inventory (A)	*(2 000 × 6)*		12 000

When the goods on consignment are delivered to Peoples' Printers on 1 November, there is no entry in the accounting records of either Sharp Moves or Peoples Printers. When the goods are sold by the consignee (in this case Peoples' Printers), the consignor (Sharp Moves) records the full selling price as sales revenue and the corresponding cost of sales as an expense, as well as the expense relating to the commission.

b) Peoples' Printers goods on consignment journal entries

GENERAL JOURNAL OF PEOPLES' PRINTERS

Date	*Description*	*Dr*	*Cr*
31/12/X6	Bank (A)	2 250	
	Commission (I)		2 250

There is no purchase or sale transaction to record in the accounting records of the consignee. The risks and rewards of ownership of the goods on consignment remained with the consignor until sold by the consignee, at which point the consignor recorded the sales revenue and the corresponding cost of sales. The consignee records the commission earned as income. The consignee must keep records to know what inventory is still on hand at the year end.

11.4.3 Inventory shortages

The detection and prevention of inventory shortages is a key area of management responsibility concerning the trading activities of a business. The inventory system used (periodic or perpetual) will influence management's ability to exercise the necessary levels of control. Whichever inventory system is used, physical inventory needs to be counted at regular intervals. A gross profit percentage is computed for the periodic system, whereas for the perpetual system the cost of the inventory counted is compared to the balance in the inventory account.

IAS 2 requires the amount of any shortage to be recognised as an expense in the period of the shortage.

The amount of the shortage is normally included in cost of sales.

The procedure to establish and account for inventory shortages using either the periodic or perpetual system is described below.

Periodic system

It is much more difficult to establish inventory shortages when using a periodic system than it is when using a perpetual system. As no entry is made to record the cost of inventory sold on a day-to-day basis, there is no inventory value in the accounting records to compare to the physical count. The only technique available to an owner or manager in this situation is to compare the ***actual gross profit percentage*** with the ***expected gross profit percentage***.

Assume that a business entity marks up its goods at 100 per cent above cost. The following relationships then exist between cost, gross profit and selling price:

Cost	100	*mark-up on cost* = GP/C = 100% (100/100)
Gross profit	100	
Selling price	200	*expected GP %* = GP/SP = 50% (100/200)

At the end of a period, the actual gross profit percentage is calculated and compared to the expected gross profit percentage. If the actual gross profit percentage is less than the expected gross profit percentage, management needs to investigate the difference and identify the reasons. Shortages may arise, for example, from theft, evaporation or inventory lost through fire or flood damage.

Assume further that sales are C400 000 and that cost of sales is computed at C205 000 (taking into account the cost of opening inventory of C50 000, purchases of C250 000 and closing inventory of C95 000). Cost of sales is therefore C205 000, gross profit is C195 000 and the actual GP % is 48.75 per cent (C195 000/C400 000). This is lower than the expected GP % of 50 per cent.

The difference between the actual GP % and expected GP % is 1.25 per cent, and this difference needs to be investigated. If it is known that goods costing C2 000 were lost through flood damage, this accounts for 0.5 per cent of the difference (C2 000/C400 000).

The remaining difference of 0.75 per cent is therefore an unknown shortage, presumably theft. The total difference can be summarised as follows:

Expected GP %	50.00%
Actual GP %	48.75%
Difference	1.25%
Known shortage – flood (C2 000/C400 000)	0.50%
Unknown shortage – theft (C3 000/C400 000)	0.75%
	1.25%

Note that, using the periodic system, the cost of the inventory shortage is included in the cost of sales by virtue of the fact that the cost of the inventory lost is included in either the opening inventory or purchases and not in the closing inventory.

The above transactions are represented in the form of the accounting equation as follows:

Assets = L +	*Owner's equity*					
	Cost of sales		Trading		Profit or loss	
	+/L/Dr	*−/R/Cr*	*−/L/Dr*	*+/R/Cr*	*−/L/Dr*	*+/R/Cr*
Sales				400 000		
Opening inventory	50 000					
Purchases	250 000					
Closing inventory		95 000				
	205 000					
Closing entry 1		205 000	205 000			
				195 000		
Closing entry 2			195 000			195 000
Closing entry 3 (to capital)					195 000	

The cost of sales account shows the cost of sales of C205 000, computed by taking into account the cost of opening inventory of C50 000, purchases of C250 000 and closing inventory of C95 000. The subtotal of C205 000 is closed off to the trading account as shown in closing entry 1. The trading account in turn shows the gross profit of C195 000, and this is closed off to the profit and loss account, as shown in closing entry 2. Finally, the profit of C195 000 (assuming no other expenses) is closed off to capital, as shown in closing entry 3.

Perpetual system

When a perpetual system is used, the cost of the closing inventory according to the physical count is compared to the balance in the inventory account in the general ledger. This is because the inventory account reflects the cost of all goods purchased and sold.

The inventory account is then adjusted to reflect the amount of the physical count by recording the difference as an inventory shortage. The entry to take into account the known inventory shortage debits an inventory shortage expense account and credits the inventory account.

Assume that the inventory account reflects a balance of C100 000 at the end of a period, whereas the physical count of inventory shows C95 000 to be on hand. In addition, assume sales of C400 000 and a mark-up on cost of 100 per cent, as in the example above. At a mark-up of 100 per cent above cost, sales of C400 000 results in a cost of sales of C200 000 (C400 000 × 100/200) and a gross profit of C200 000 (C400 000 × 100/200).

The adjusting entry debits the inventory shortage expense with the inventory shortage of C5 000 and credits the inventory account to reduce the balance on the inventory account from C100 000 to C95 000, the cost of the physical count of inventory. As previously mentioned, the inventory shortage expense is then normally closed off to cost of sales.

The difference between the original balance in the inventory account and the physical count of inventory amounts to C5 000, and this difference also needs to be investigated. If we again assume that goods costing C2 000 were lost through flood damage, the remaining C3 000 presumably results from theft. The same numerical reconciliation can be done as was illustrated with the periodic system.

The above transactions are represented in the form of the accounting equation as follows:

	Assets	= L +			*Owner's equity*			
	Inventory		Cost of sales		Trading		Profit and loss	
	+/L/Dr	−/R/Cr	+/L/Dr	−/R/Cr	−/L/Dr	+/R/Cr	−/L/Dr	+/R/Cr
Balance	50 000							
Purchases	250 000							
Cost of sales		200 000	200 000					
Sales						400 000		
	100 000							
Inventory shortage		5 000	5 000					
			205 000					
Closing entry 1				205 000	205 000			
						195 000		
Closing entry 2					195 000			195 000
Closing entry 3 (to capital)							195 000	
Balance	95 000							

Remember that when using a perpetual system, the inventory account reflects the cost of all goods purchased and sold. Inventory purchased (C250 000 in this example) is debited to the inventory account and, when inventory is sold, the cost of the inventory sold is debited to the cost of sales account and credited to the inventory account (C200 000 in this example). The subtotal of C100 000 in the inventory account is then compared to the physical count of inventory of C95 000, leading to the adjusting entry to record the inventory shortage of C5 000.

Note that, for clarity of explanation, the inventory shortage has been recorded directly to cost of sales in this worksheet.

The closing entries are the same as for the periodic system.

Summary of entries to account for inventory shortages

	Periodic	*Perpetual*
Recording the shortage	Included in cost of sales because of reduced closing inventory	Dr Inventory shortage (E) Cr Inventory (A)
Closing entry	—	Dr Cost of sales (E) Cr Inventory shortage (E)

Example: Inventory shortages

Assume that Sharp Moves has an opening inventory of ten data projectors at the beginning of July 20X7. During the three-month period to the end of September 20X7, 50 data projectors were purchased and 40 were sold. Data projectors cost C5 000 each and are sold for C10 000 each. Other expenses total C75 000. Sharp Moves marks up its goods at 100 per cent above cost.

You are required to:

a) Show the computation of the gross profit and the entries in the cost of sales account, trading account and profit and loss account if the **periodic** system is being used:

   i) assuming 20 data projectors were counted at the end of the period.
   ii) assuming 19 data projectors were counted at the end of the period.

b) Show the entries in the inventory account, cost of sales account, trading account and profit and loss account if the **perpetual** system is being used:

   i) assuming 20 data projectors were counted at the end of the period.
   ii) assuming 19 data projectors were counted at the end of the period.

Solution: Inventory shortages

a) Periodic inventory system

Periodic	*20 units on hand (no inventory shortage)*			*19 units on hand (inventory shortage)*		
Revenue from sales	40 × C10 000		400 000	40 × C10 000		400 000
Cost of sales			(200 000)			(205 000)
Opening inventory	10 × C5 000	50 000		10 × C5 000	50 000	
Purchases	50 × C5 000	250 000		50 × C5 000	250 000	
Cost of goods available for sale	60 × C5 000	300 000		60 × C5 000	300 000	
Closing inventory	20 × C5 000	(100 000)		19 × C5 000	(95 000)	
Gross profit			200 000			195 000
Other expenses			(75 000)			(75 000)
Profit for the period			125 000			120 000
Mark-up %	100%			100%		
Gross profit %	50%			48.75%		

i) No inventory shortage

Cost of sales

Details	*C*	*Details*	*C*
O/inventory	50 000	C/inventory	100 000
Purchases	250 000	Trading	200 000
	300 000		300 000

Trading

Details	*C*	*Details*	*C*
Cost of sales	200 000	Sales	400 000
Profit or loss	200 000		
	400 000		400 000

Profit or loss

Details	*C*	*Details*	*C*
Expenses	75 000	Trading	200 000
Capital	125 000		
	200 000		200 000

ii) Inventory shortage

Cost of sales

Details	*C*	*Details*	*C*
O/inventory	50 000	C/inventory	95 000
Purchases	250 000	Trading	205 000
	300 000		300 000

Trading

Details	*C*	*Details*	*C*
Cost of sales	205 000	Sales	400 000
Profit or loss	195 000		
	400 000		400 000

Profit or loss

Details	*C*	*Details*	*C*
Expenses	75 000	Trading	195 000
Capital	120 000		
	195 000		195 000

In situation (i) where there is no inventory shortage, the gross profit of C200 000 results in an actual GP % of 50 per cent (C200 000/C400 000), which is equal to the expected GP % based on a mark-up on cost of 100 per cent. In situation (ii) where there is a shortage of C5 000 (1 × C5 000), the gross profit of C195 000 results in an actual GP % of 48.75 per cent (C195 000/C400 000). The difference between the expected GP % of 50 per cent and the actual GP % of 48.75 per cent (C195 000/ C400 000) is attributable to an inventory shortage. The amount of the shortage is C5 000 (C400 000 × 1.25%).

Note also that the profit for the period of C120 000 in situation (ii) is C5 000 lower than the profit for the period of C125 000 in situation (i), reflecting the impact of the shortage.

b) Perpetual inventory system

i) No inventory shortage

Inventory

Details	*C*	*Details*	*C*
Balance b/d	50 000	Cost of sales	200 000
Accounts payable	250 000	Balance c/d	100 000
	300 000		300 000
Balance b/d	100 000		

ii) Inventory shortage

Inventory

Details	*C*	*Details*	*C*
Balance b/d	50 000	Cost of sales	200 000
Accounts payable	250 000	Cost of sales	5 000
		Balance c/d	95 000
	300 000		300 000
Balance b/d	95 000		

Cost of sales			
Details	*C*	*Details*	*C*
Inventory	200 000	Trading	200 000
	200 000		200 000

Cost of sales			
Details	*C*	*Details*	*C*
Inventory	200 000	Trading	205 000
Inventory	5 000		
	205 000		205 000

Trading			
Details	*C*	*Details*	*C*
Cost of sales	200 000	Sales	400 000
Profit and loss	200 000		
	400 000		400 000

Trading			
Details	*C*	*Details*	*C*
Cost of sales	205 000	Sales	400 000
Profit and loss	195 000		
	400 000		400 000

Profit or loss			
Details	*C*	*Details*	*C*
Expenses	75 000	Trading	200 000
Capital	125 000		
	200 000		200 000

Profit or loss			
Details	*C*	*Details*	*C*
Expenses	75 000	Trading	195 000
Capital	120 000		
	195 000		195 000

As you are aware, the cost of sales in a perpetual system is recorded each time a sale is made. In situation (i), the recorded cost of sales of C200 000 (representing 40 items sold at a cost of C5 000 each) results in a gross profit of C200 000 and an actual GP % of 50 per cent, which is equal to the expected GP %. In situation (ii), the recorded cost of sales is again C200 000 (40 × C5 000). However, the cost of sales needs to be increased, and the inventory decreased, to account for the inventory shortage. As with the periodic system, this results in an actual GP % of 48.75 per cent compared to the expected GP % of 50 per cent.

In this example, the inventory shortage expense has been recorded directly in the cost of sales account. We could have debited the inventory shortage expense account and then closed off this account to cost of sales.

The profit for the period in situation (ii) is C5 000 less than the profit in situation (i), as was the case with the periodic system. Note that the entry to credit inventory is not required in the periodic system, as the closing inventory is brought into the system at its reduced cost of C95 000 according to the inventory count.

In this example, the inventory shortage expense has been recorded directly in the cost of sales account. We could have debited the inventory shortage expense account and then closed off this account to cost of sales.

11.5 Cost formulae

Several different methods for determining the cost of sales and the cost of inventories on hand are used in practice. Each method may lead to widely differing results being reported. These methods are:

- specific identification;
- FIFO (first in, first out);
- weighted average cost.

It must be stressed that all these formulae are ***cost flow assumptions***, used to allocate the cost of goods available for sale between the statement of profit or loss and the statement of financial position. They do not necessarily represent the actual physical movement of goods.

11.5.1 Specific identification

IAS 2 indicates that, where items of inventory are dissimilar and not interchangeable, inventories should be measured by specific identification of costs. If practical, this is the best approach to adopt because no assumptions have to be made about the flow of costs in order to allocate either to cost of sales or closing inventory.

This method is only feasible when the inventory items are uniquely identifiable and of sufficient value to justify keeping such detailed records. For businesses such as a jewellery shop, a motorcar dealer or an antique shop, the individual inventory items are normally specifically identifiable and of high enough value to maintain the necessary records.

Assume that a jewellery shop holds, amongst other items, 110 diamond rings at the beginning of the current year. Of the 110 rings, 30 were purchased two years previously at C2 000 each, and a further 80 rings were acquired during the previous year at C5 500 each. During the current year, 40 rings were purchased at C10 000 each.

A total of 100 diamond rings were sold during the current year at C12 000 each. Applying the specific identification method, it is determined that of the 100 rings sold, 26 were from the batch purchased two years previously, 50 were from those acquired during the previous year, and 24 were of those purchased during the current year. We can then compute cost of sales and gross profit as follows:

Opening inventory	*((30 × C2 000 + (80 × C5 500))*	500 000
Purchases	*(40 × C10 000)*	400 000
Cost of goods available for sale		900 000
Closing inventory	*((4 × C2 000) + (30 × C5 500) + (16 × C10 000))*	(333 000)
Cost of sales	*((26 × C2 000) + (50 × C5 500) + (24 × C10 000))*	567 000
Revenue from sales	*(100 × C12 000)*	1 200 000
Gross profit		633 000

However, specific identification of costs is inappropriate when there are large numbers of inventory items which are *similar* or *interchangeable*. It is therefore necessary to apply a consistent policy to the allocation of costs, namely FIFO or weighted average cost.

11.5.2 FIFO

The FIFO method is based on the cost *flow assumption* that the first units acquired are the first ones sold. Often this assumption is justified by normal business practice, because many businesses attempt to maintain an orderly flow of goods so that they do not have old merchandise on hand. When using FIFO:

- cost of sales is represented by the cost of the ***earliest*** purchases;
- closing inventory is represented by the cost of the ***latest*** purchases.

In times of rising prices, this does not achieve a matching of current costs with current revenue on the statement of profit or loss. Outdated costs from the beginning of the period are matched against current revenue, resulting in an artificially high profit.

		Cost of inventory on hand at the beginning of the period + Cost of inventory purchased during the period
Weighted average cost per item	=	Total number of units available for sale

Diagram 11.7 Calculation of weighted average cost per item

11.5.3 Weighted average

The weighted average method is based on the cost *flow assumption* of the weighted average of the cost of similar items at the beginning of the period, and the cost of similar items purchased during the period. We can calculate a weighted average cost per item as shown in Diagram 11.7.

In times of rising prices:

- cost of sales is reported at an amount above the FIFO amount;
- closing inventory is reported at an amount below the FIFO amount.

Example 1: Cost formulae – periodic system

Bright Life's inventory records reveal the following information for the three-month period from July 20X5 to September 20X5:

	Date	*Quantity*	*C*
Opening inventory	01/07/X5	150	11
Purchases	15/07/X5	150	12
Sales	10/08/X5	200	20
Purchases	08/09/X5	150	13
Sales	20/09/X5	90	20

You are required to:

Compute the cost of sales and closing inventory, assuming that a periodic inventory system is used and:

a) Inventory is valued on the FIFO basis.
b) Inventory is valued on the weighted average basis.

Solution 1: Cost formulae – periodic system

Periodic	*a) FIFO*			*b) Weighted average*		
	Qty	*C*	*Total*	*Qty*	*C*	*Total*
Opening inventory	150	11.00	1 650	150	11.00	1 650
Purchases	150	12.00	1 800	150	12.00	1 800
Purchases	150	13.00	1 950	150	13.00	1 950
Cost of goods available for sale	450		5 400	450		5 400
Closing inventory (1)	160		2 070	160		1 920
Cost of sales (2)	290		3 330	290		3 480

Working (1)	150	13.00	1 950	Average price		
	10	12.00	120	5 400/450 = 12.00		
	160		2 070	160	12.00	1 920
Working (2)	150	11.00	1 650	Average price		
	140	12.00	1 680	5 400/450 = 12.00		
	290		3 330	290	12.00	3 480

 The quantity of closing inventory on hand at the end of the period is counted. Assuming no shortages, you should easily see that the quantity of items counted amounted to 160 (150 + 150 − 200 + 150 − 90). This is obviously the same for both the FIFO and the weighted average methods.

Using the FIFO basis, and looking at working (1), the cost of the closing inventory is measured at C2 070 (150 units of latest purchase at C13.00 per unit and then 10 units from the second purchase at C12.00 per unit). Remember that when using FIFO, the closing inventory is represented by the cost of the *latest* purchases. Looking at working (2), the cost of sales of C3 330 is represented by the cost of the *earliest* purchases (150 units of the opening inventory at C11.00 per unit and 140 units from the second purchase at C12.00 per unit).

Turning to the weighted average basis, and again looking at working (1), the cost of the closing inventory is measured at C1 920, (the weighted average cost of C12.00 × 160 units of closing inventory). The cost of sales of C3 480 is calculated in a similar way (C12.00 × 290).

Pause and reflect . . .

Once you had determined the cost of the closing inventory in the above example (by applying the FIFO or weighted average cost formula), was it possible to determine the cost of sales in another way?

Response

Using a periodic system, cost of sales can be calculated as follows:

	FIFO	*Weighted average*
Opening inventory	1 650	1 650
+ Purchases (1 800 + 1 950)	3 750	3 750
= Cost of goods available for sale	5 400	5 400
− Closing inventory	(2 070)	(1 920)
= Cost of sales	3 330	3 480

You should remember this from Chapter 8, *Purchase and sale transactions*, when we learnt that cost of sales = opening inventory + purchases − closing inventory. Once an entity has determined the cost of closing inventory by applying one of the cost formulae, it is not necessary to use the cost formulae again to determine the cost of sales. This can be a lengthy and costly exercise, which can be avoided by doing the above calculation.

Example 2: Cost formulae – perpetual system

The same details from Bright Life's inventory records as used in the periodic system example are shown below:

	Date	*Quantity*	*C*
Opening inventory	01/07/X5	150	11
Purchases	15/07/X5	150	12
Sales	10/08/X5	200	20
Purchases	08/09/X5	150	13
Sales	20/09/X5	90	20

You are required to:

Compute the cost of sales and closing inventory, assuming that a perpetual inventory system is used, and:

a) Inventory is valued on the FIFO basis.
b) Inventory is valued on the weighted average basis.

Solution 2: Cost formulae – perpetual system

Perpetual	*a) FIFO*			*b) Weighted average*		
	Qty	*C*	*Total*	*Qty*	*C*	*Total*
01/07 Opening inventory	150	11.00	1 650	150	11.00	1 650
15/07 Purchases	150	12.00	1 800	150	12.00	1 800
15/07 Balance	300		3 450	300	11.50	3 450
10/08 Sales (1)	(200)		(2 250)	(200)	11.50	(2 300)
10/08 Balance (2)	100		1 200	100	11.50	1 150
08/09 Purchases	150	13.00	1 950	150	13.00	1 950
20/09 Sales (3)	(90)		(1 080)	(90)	12.40	(1 116)
Closing inventory (4)	160		2 070	160	12.40	1 984

Workings

Working (1)	150	11.00	1 650	3 450/300	= 11.50	
	50	12.00	600			
	200		2 250	200	11.50	2 300
Working (2)	100	12.00	1 200	100	11.50	1 150
Working (3)	90	12.00	1 080	$\frac{(1\ 150 + 1\ 950)}{(100 + 150)}$	= 12.40	
	90		1 080	90	12.40	1 116
Working (4)	10	12.00	120			
	150	13.00	1 950			
	160		2 070	160	12.40	1 984

 Using the FIFO basis and looking at working (1), the cost of sales of the 200 units sold on 10 August is measured at C2 050 (150 units of the opening inventory at C11.00 and 50 units from the second purchase at C12 per unit). Looking at working (3), the same procedure is followed for the 90 units sold on 20 September where the cost of sales is measured at C1 080 (all 90 units from the second purchase at C12 per unit).

Turning to the weighted average basis, and again looking at working (1), the cost of sales of the 200 units sold on 10 August is measured at C2 300 (the weighted average cost of C11.50 × 200 units sold). Looking at working (3), the weighted average changes for the sale on 20 September where the cost of sales is measured at C1 116 (the new weighted average cost of C12.40 × 90 units sold).

Pause and reflect . . .

Compare the amount of the closing inventory and the amount of the cost of sales calculated using the FIFO method under the periodic system and the perpetual system. What do you see?

Response

Using the FIFO method, the closing inventory calculated using the periodic system and the perpetual system both result in a closing inventory of C2 070. The cost of sales using the periodic system amounts to C3 330, which is also the same as when using the perpetual system (C2 250 + C 1 080 = C 3 330).

Thus, FIFO periodic and FIFO perpetual give the same result.

The perpetual system involves significant additional record keeping as the cost of sales needs to be computed each time a sale is made. However, with the use of computer systems in the business world, the perpetual system is widely used as it results in more effective record keeping and better inventory control. Weighted average pricing is the most commonly used in conjunction with the perpetual system, as systems are able to recalculate average pricings instantly when new inventory is purchased and sold.

Concepts in context

Pick n Pay Limited

Extract from accounting policy note for inventory

Inventory comprises merchandise for resale and consumables. Inventory is measured at the lower of cost and net realisable value and is classified as a current asset as it is expected to be sold within the Group's normal operating cycle. Cost is calculated on the weighted-average basis and includes expenditure incurred in acquiring the inventories and bringing them to their existing location and condition, including distribution costs, and is stated net of relevant purchase incentives. The cost of merchandise sold includes shrinkage.

Obsolete, redundant and slow-moving items are identified on a regular basis and are written down to their estimated net realisable values. Net realisable value is the estimated selling price in the ordinary course of business, less the estimated costs of completion and selling expenses.

What concepts in context can you see here?

Pick n Pay are reporting that they measure inventory at the lower of cost and net realisable value, using the weighted average method. The policy note also refers to the costs included in the cost of purchase – exactly what you learnt earlier in this chapter.

Note also the reference to inventory being classified as a current asset as it is expected to be sold within the normal operating cycle. This relates to what you learnt in Chapter 6 about the operating cycle and the non-current / current classification of assets and liabilities.

Pick n Pay, established in 1967, is the second largest supermarket chain store in South Africa. It is also to be found in other regions of southern Africa.

Source: www.picknpayinvestor.co.za/financials/annual_reports/2015/index.php#null (Accessed 30 October 2015).

11.6 Measurement of inventory at period end

11.6.1 Lower of cost and net realisable value

Remember that inventory is an asset and that an asset is defined as a resource controlled by the entity, as a result of past events and from which future economic benefits are expected to flow to the entity. If the expected future economic benefits are less than the cost, IAS 2 requires the cost of the inventory to be written down to its net realisable value.

Inventory is measured at the ***lower*** of cost and net realisable value.

The writing down of inventories below cost to net realisable value is consistent with the view that assets should not be carried in excess of amounts expected to be realised from their sale or use.

Cost, as described earlier in this chapter, comprises all costs of purchase and other costs incurred in bringing the inventory to its present location and condition. It is then computed based on one of the cost formulae, namely specific identification, FIFO or weighted average.

Net realisable value is the estimated selling price in the ordinary course of business, less the estimated costs of completion and the estimated costs to make the sale.

When estimates of net realisable value are made, they are based on the most reliable evidence available at the time as to the amount the inventories are expected to realise. The costs of completion include any additional costs (over and above the original acquisition costs) in getting the goods into a saleable condition (see Diagram 11.8). Costs to make the sale include any additional selling expenses over and above normal selling expenses.

The cost of inventories may exceed the net realisable value if those inventories are damaged, if they have become wholly or partially obsolete, or if selling prices have declined. This situation may also arise if the estimated costs of completion or the estimated costs to be incurred to make the sale have increased.

If the net realisable value of the closing inventory is lower than cost, the cost of the inventory must be written down, representing the expected reduction in future economic benefits and an expense recognised in respect of the write-down.

Pause and reflect . . .

You have learnt that if the net realisable value of closing inventory is lower than cost, the inventory is written down and an expense is recognised. What would happen if the net realisable value of the closing inventory is higher than the cost?

Response

IAS 2 requires inventory to be valued at the lower of cost and net realisable value, therefore if the net realisable value of closing inventory is higher than cost, no adjustment is required. It would make no sense to write up inventory and recognise income as the inventory has not yet been realised.

	Estimated selling price in ordinary course of business
Less	Costs of completion
Less	Costs to make the sale
=	Net realisable value

Diagram 11.8 Computation of net realisable value

11.6.2 Accounting for the write-down of inventory

When preparing the financial statements, management needs to assess the net realisable value of individual items of inventory or, if more appropriate, of groups of items. If the net realisable value exceeds cost, the closing entries are processed as usual, based on either the periodic or perpetual system. These entries, which are described in detail in Chapter 8, *Purchase and sale transactions*, are summarised in Diagram 11.9 for ease of reference.

IAS 2 requires the amount of any write-down of inventory to net realisable value to be recognised as an expense in the period of the write-down.

As with the inventory shortage, the inventory write-down is normally included in cost of sales.

Periodic	*Perpetual*
Transfer of opening inventory and purchases	
Dr Cost of sales	
Cr Inventory	
Dr Cost of sales	
Cr Purchases	
Closing inventory entered into accounting system	
Dr Inventory	
Cr Cost of sales	
Transfer of cost of sales	***Transfer of cost of sales***
Dr Trading	Dr Trading
Cr Cost of sales	Cr Cost of sales
Transfer of sales	***Transfer of sales***
Dr Sales	Dr Sales
Cr Trading	Cr Trading

Diagram 11.9 Summary of closing entries for trading activities

Periodic system

If the net realisable value is lower than the cost, the closing inventory is entered into the accounting system at the reduced value. A lower closing inventory will lead to a higher cost of sales and a lower gross profit and profit for the period. The reduction in the gross profit, and therefore the GP %, will need to be taken into account in the reconciliation of the expected GP % to the actual GP %.

Perpetual system

As the inventory account in the perpetual system is updated each time goods are purchased or sold, the balance on the account represents the cost of inventory on hand at the end of the period. No specific entry is required to introduce the closing inventory into the accounting system, as with the periodic system. An adjusting entry will be required to reduce the balance in the inventory account from cost to net realisable value and to create an expense for the write-down, representing that part of the cost that will not be recovered in the future. The entry therefore debits inventory write-down expense and credits the inventory account. As previously mentioned, the inventory write-down expense is then normally closed off to cost of sales.

The higher cost of sales will result in a lower gross profit and GP % and, as with the periodic system, will need to be taken into account in the reconciliation of the expected GP % to the actual GP %.

Summary of entries on write-down of inventory

	Periodic	*Perpetual*
Recording the write-down	Included in cost of sales because of reduced closing inventory	Dr Inventory write-down (E) Cr Inventory (A)
Closing entry	—	Dr Cost of sales (E) Cr Inventory write-down (E)

Concepts in context

Pick n Pay Limited

(Extract from) Notes to the group financial statements

For the year ended 1 March 2015

Inventory	**Rm**
Merchandise for resale	4 767.5
Provision for shrinkage, obsolescence and mark-down of inventory	(158.1)
Consumables	45.1
	4 654.5

What concepts in context can you see here?

You have seen in the previous *Concepts in Context* in Section 11.5 of this chapter that Pick n Pay measure inventory at the lower of cost and net realisable value.

This note shows that inventory costing R158.1 million has been written down. Pick n Pay have chosen to credit a 'Provision for shrinkage, obsolescence and mark down of inventory' account, which is a contra-account to the inventory account. The amount is thus shown as a subtraction from the cost of inventory.

Note also that there are 'consumables' of R45.1 million. Remember that the definition of inventory includes items that are held in the form of materials or supplies to be consumed within the business operation

Pick n Pay, established in 1967, is the second largest supermarket chain store in South Africa. It is also to be found in other regions of southern Africa

Source: www.picknpayinvestor.co.za/financials/annual_reports/2015/index.php (Accessed 2 September 2015).

Example: Lower of cost and net realisable value (NRV)

The following details relate to Bright Life for the 20X6 year:

	Quantity	*C per item*	*Total*
Opening inventory	1 000	20	20 000
Purchases	2 500	20	50 000
Cost of sales	1 500	20	30 000
Sales	1 500	50	75 000
Closing inventory	2 000	20	40 000
Operating expenses	—	—	20 000

You are required to:

Show the relevant ledger accounts:

a) Using a periodic inventory system, and assuming that:
   i) the NRV of the closing inventory is C120 000.
   ii) the NRV of the closing inventory is C30 000.

b) Using a perpetual inventory system, and assuming that:
   i) the NRV of the closing inventory is C120 000.
   ii) the NRV of the closing inventory is C30 000.

Solution: Lower of cost and NRV

a) (i) Periodic inventory system (NRV C120 000)

Inventory

Details	C	*Details*	C
Balance b/d	20 000	Cost of sales	20 000
Cost of sales	40 000	Balance c/d	40 000
	60 000		60 000
Balance b/d	40 000		

Purchases

Details	C	*Details*	C
Bank/accounts payable	50 000	Cost of sales	50 000
	50 000		50 000

Cost of sales

Details	*C*	*Details*	*C*
Opening inventory	20 000	Closing inventory	40 000
Purchases	50 000	Trading	30 000
	70 000		70 000

Trading

Details	*C*	*Details*	*C*
Cost of sales	30 000	Sales	75 000
Profit or loss	45 000		
	75 000		75 000

Operating expenses

Details	*C*	*Details*	*C*
Balance b/d	20 000	Profit or loss	20 000
	20 000		20 000

Profit or loss

Details	*C*	*Details*	*C*
Operating expenses	20 000	Trading	45 000
Capital	25 000		
	45 000		45 000

a) (ii) Periodic inventory system (NRV C30 000)

Inventory

Details	*C*	*Details*	*C*
Balance c/d	20 000	Cost of sales	20 000
Cost of sales	30 000	Balance c/d	30 000
	50 000		50 000
Balance b/d	30 000		

Purchases

Details	*C*	*Details*	*C*
Bank/ accounts payable	50 000	Cost of sales	50 000
	50 000		50 000

Cost of sales

Details	*C*	*Details*	*C*
Opening inventory	20 000	Closing inventory	30 000
Purchases	50 000	Trading	40 000
	70 000		70 000

Trading

Details	*C*	*Details*	*C*
Cost of sales	40 000	Sales	75 000
Profit or loss	35 000		
	75 000		75 000

Operating expenses

Details	*C*	*Details*	*C*
Balance b/d	20 000	Profit or loss	20 000
	20 000		20 000

Profit or loss

Details	*C*	*Details*	*C*
Operating expenses	20 000	Trading	35 000
Capital	15 000		
	35 000		35 000

Part (a) of the question examines a periodic system. In situation (i), where the NRV of the closing inventory is higher than the cost (C120 000 compared to C40 000), the closing entries relating to the trading activities are processed as normal and the NRV of C120 000 is ignored. The gross profit is C45 000 and the profit for the period is C25 000. The actual GP % is 60 per cent (C45 000/C75 000), which is equal to the expected GP % of 60 per cent.

In situation (ii), the NRV of the closing inventory is lower than the cost (C30 000 compared to C40 000). The closing inventory is entered into the accounting records at the lower of cost and NRV, in this case at C30 000. This causes the cost of sales to increase to C40 000, the gross profit to decrease to C35 000, and the profit for the period to decrease to C15 000. The actual GP % is 46.67 per cent (C35 000/C75 000), which is less than the expected GP % of 60 per cent. As you are aware, any difference between the expected GP % and the actual GP % needs to be investigated and reconciled. In this situation, the difference can be entirely attributed to the inventory write-down of C10 000 (C75 000 × 13.33%), confirming that there are no unknown shortages.

In summary:

Expected GP %	60.00%
Actual GP %	46.67%
Difference	13.33%
Inventory write-down (C10 000/C75 000)	13.33%
Unknown shortage	—
	13.33%

b) (i) Perpetual inventory system (NRV C120 000)

Inventory			
Description	*C*	*Description*	*C*
Balance b/d	20 000	Cost of sales	30 000
Bank/Accounts payable	50 000	Balance c/d	40 000
	70 000		70 000
Balance b/d	40 000		

Trading			
Description	*C*	*Description*	*C*
Cost of sales	30 000	Sales	75 000
Profit or loss	45 000		
	75 000		75 000

Cost of sales			
Description	*C*	*Description*	*C*
Inventory	30 000	Trading	30 000
	30 000		30 000

Profit or loss			
Description	*C*	*Description*	*C*
Operating expenses	20 000	Trading	45 000
Capital	25 000		
	45 000		45 000

b) (ii) Perpetual inventory system (NRV C30 000)

Inventory

Description	*C*	*Description*	*C*
Balance b/d	20 000	Cost of sales	30 000
Bank/Accounts payable	50 000	Cost of sales	10 000
		Balance c/d	30 000
	70 000		70 000
Balance b/d	30 000		

Trading

Description	*C*	*Description*	*C*
Cost of sales	40 000	Sales	75 000
Profit or loss	35 000		
	75 000		75 000

Cost of sales

Description	*C*	*Description*	*C*
Inventory	30 000	Trading	40 000
Inventory	10 000		
	40 000		40 000

Profit or loss

Description	*C*	*Description*	*C*
Operating expenses	20 000	Trading	35 000
Capital	15 000		
	35 000		35 000

Part (b) of the question looks at a perpetual system. As with the periodic system, in situation (i) where the NRV of the closing inventory is higher than the cost, the NRV of C120 000 is ignored. As you should expect, the actual GP % is 60 per cent, which is equal to the expected GP % of 60 per cent.

In situation (ii), where the NRV of the closing inventory is lower than the cost, an adjusting entry is required to debit the inventory write-down expense and credit the inventory account. In this solution, the write-down has been allocated directly to cost of sales. As with the periodic system, this causes the actual GP % to be less than the expected GP %. The reconciliation in this case is identical to part (a) (ii).

11.7 Inventory errors

In determining the effect of inventory errors on the financial statements, it is important to understand the relationship between closing inventory and cost of sales, and the ultimate impact on gross profit.

In a **periodic** system, cost of sales is computed by adding opening inventory and purchases and subtracting closing inventory. Any overstatement in closing inventory will result in an understatement of cost of sales and overstatement of gross profit. Conversely, an understatement in closing inventory will result in an overstatement of cost of sales and an understatement of gross profit.

Turning to a **perpetual** system, the balance in the inventory account is made up of the opening balance and the purchases during the period, reduced by the cost of sales. Here, an understatement of cost of sales will lead to an overstatement of closing inventory. Similarly, an overstatement of cost of sales will result in an understatement of closing inventory.

 **Pause and reflect . . .**

Assuming an opening inventory of C10, purchases of C8, closing inventory of C6 as well as sales of C15, use your understanding of how cost of sales is computed in a periodic system to show the effect of the following errors on the cost of sales and gross profit:

a) An overstatement of opening inventory
b) An overstatement of closing inventory

Response

	Correct	*a) Overstatement of opening inventory by C1*	*b) Overstatement of closing inventory by C1*
Opening inventory	10	11	10
+ Purchases	8	8	8
− Closing inventory	(6)	(6)	(7)
= Cost of sales	12	13	11
Sales	15	15	15
Gross profit	3	2	4

You can see that in (a), the cost of sales is overstated by C1 and the gross profit is understated by C1. In (b), the cost of sales is understated by C1 and the gross profit is overstated by C1.

11.8 Estimating inventory

A business entity may in certain circumstances need to estimate the cost of closing inventory. It is important to understand the circumstances leading to the estimation of inventory. The cost of closing inventory may need to be estimated in relation to the following two different points in time:

- The closing inventory at some point in time in the current period where, for example, a fire destroys the inventory or a burglary results in the theft of inventory and this needs to be estimated so that an insurance claim can be submitted.
- The closing inventory at the end of a previous period, where inventory was not counted at the end of that period and financial statements need to be prepared.

The principle is the same in both cases. The cost of inventory is estimated by applying the historical, or estimated, relationship between cost, gross profit and selling price to the sales for the current period. This is done to estimate the cost of sales for the current period.

If it is the closing inventory at some point in the current period that needs to be estimated (because of an insurance claim, for example), then the estimated cost of sales is compared to the cost of goods available for sale to determine the inventory destroyed. If any inventory was salvaged, this must obviously be taken into account in calculating the insurance claim.

	Typical periodic inventory computation of cost of sales and gross profit		*Insurance claim*		*Inventory not counted at the end of previous period*
	Opening inventory		Opening inventory		***Opening inventory (?)***
+	Purchases	+	Purchases	+	Purchases
=	Cost of goods available for sale	=	Cost of goods available for sale	=	Cost of goods available for sale
−	Closing inventory	−	Inventory salvaged	−	Closing inventory
		−	***Inventory destroyed (?)***		
=	Cost of sales	=	Cost of sales	=	Cost of sales
	Revenue from sales		Revenue from sales		Revenue from sales
=	Gross profit	=	Gross profit	=	Gross profit

Diagram 11.10 Estimating inventory

If, on the other hand, the inventory was not counted at the end of the previous period, the closing inventory at a chosen date in the current period is counted. The cost of sales and cost of goods available for sale from the beginning of the period to the current date can then be computed. The closing inventory at the end of the previous period is then calculated as the opening inventory of the current period.

This logic is illustrated in Diagram 11.10.

Example: Estimating closing inventory

Hadit Traders' premises were destroyed by fire towards the end of the year. The following information was extracted from salvaged records:

	C
Opening inventory	30 000
Purchases (to date of fire)	60 000
Revenue from sales (to date of fire)	100 000

Inventory costing C5 000 was saved. Hadit Traders has constantly achieved a 25 per cent gross profit percentage in recent years.

You are required to:

Estimate the cost of inventory destroyed in the fire.

Solution: Estimating closing inventory

		C
Opening inventory	(Known)	30 000
Add Purchases	(Known)	60 000
Cost of goods available for sale		90 000
Less Inventory salvaged	(Known)	(5 000)
Less Inventory destroyed	?	***(10 000)***
Cost of sales	(C100 000 × 75/100)	75 000
Revenue from sales	(Known)	100 000
Gross profit		25 000

To calculate the amount of the insurance claim, the inventory on hand at the date of the fire needs to be estimated. It is known that a GP % of 25 per cent has been achieved in recent years. This translates into a relationship between cost, GP and selling price as follows:

Cost	75%	As the actual GP is 25 per cent, the selling price is set at 100 per cent, resulting in the cost being 75 per cent.
GP	25%	
SP	100%	

Given that sales to the date of the fire are C100 000, the cost of sales for the period is calculated at C75 000 (C100 000 × 75/100). The cost of goods available for sale is determined as C90 000, which means that the inventory on hand at the date of the fire was C15 000. Since inventory costing C5 000 was salvaged, the cost of the inventory destroyed is estimated at C10 000.

Revision example

Jersey Photo is an independent store selling photographic equipment. Jersey Photo applies a consistent mark-up of 50 per cent on the cost price of goods to calculate their selling price.

On 30 June 20X7 the store was destroyed by fire. The salvaged inventory was sold at cost price for C1 000.

The following balances were taken from the accounting records of Jersey Photo at 30 June 20X7:

	C
Accounts receivable control	21 800
Non-current assets at carrying amount	33 000
Purchases	45 700
Carriage inwards	3 900
Carriage outwards	2 300
Operating expenses	8 500
Sales	78 750
Inventory at 1 January 20X7	18 250

1 During April 20X7, a shop assistant misappropriated C750 from cash sale takings. He had failed to complete a cash sale docket at the time of sale. This fraud was discovered when the customer returned the goods to have a minor fault repaired. At the same time, the assistant had stolen goods costing C1 200. This amount includes the Carriage in respect of the goods stolen. To disguise the inventory shortage, the assistant had invoiced these goods to a fictitious customer for C1 800. No adjustments have been made to correct the above, and nothing can be recovered in respect of any of these items.

2 During two weeks in May 20X7, a 'cut-price sale' was held. The normal selling price of goods was reduced by 10 per cent. Sales during this period amounted to C8 100.

3 Goods costing C300 were donated to a local welfare organisation on 15 April 20X7. No entry has been made in respect of this transaction.

4 On 30 June 20X7, goods costing C4 500 had been ordered from a supplier. The goods were at the local railway station, and ownership had passed when they left the supplier's premises.

5 On 30 June 20X7, goods were sold and invoiced to a customer for C3 000. The customer arranged for these goods to be collected on 5 July 20X7.

You are required to:

a) Prepare the journal entries to record the transactions in (1), (3) and (4) above.
b) Prepare a statement showing the cost price of all the goods destroyed by the fire.

 **Solution: Revision example**

a) Journal entries

Date	*Description*	*Dr*	*Cr*
30/06/X7	Cash shortage (E)	750	
	Sales (I)		750
	Shortage iro cash stolen		
	Sales (I)	1 800	
	Accounts receivable (A)		1 800
	Reversal of fictitious invoice		
	Donations (E)	300	
	Purchases (T)		300
	Donation of inventory		
	Goods in transit (A)	4 500	
	Accounts payable (L)		4 500
	Recording of goods in transit		

b) Statement showing cost price of all goods destroyed in the fire

Opening inventory			18 250
+ Purchases		41 200	
+ Carriage inwards		3 900	
− Donation		(300)	44 800
= Cost of goods available for sale			63 050
Theoretical closing inventory	*(63 050 − 52 400)*		10 650
Inventory salvaged			(1 000)
Inventory shortage			(1 200)
Inventory destroyed			***(8 450)***
Cost of sales − normal SP	*((70 650^{w1} − 1 800 + 750) 100/150^{w2})*	46 400	
− reduced SP	*(8 100^{w1} × 100/135^{w2})*	6 000	52 400

		C
Cost of inventory destroyed		8 450
Customer's goods on premises	(3 000 × 100/150)	2 000
Total cost of all goods destroyed		10 450

Working (1): Allocation of sales		**Working (2): Calculation of relationship**	
Total sales	78 750	Cost	100
		Mark-up	50
Sales during 'normal' period	70 650	Normal selling price	150
		Mark-down	(15)
Sales during 'mark-down' period	8 100	Reduced selling price	135

Bibliography

The Incoterms rules. www.iccwbo.org/products-and-services/trade-facilitation/incoterms-2010/the-incoterms-rules/ (Accessed 7 June 2014).

The International Accounting Standards Board. 2010. *The Conceptual Framework.*

The International Accounting Standards Board. 2004. IAS 2 *Inventories.*

12 Accounts receivable

Business focus

Investors scramble to dump shares in African Bank

Accounts receivable and bad debts are not meaningless line items in the financial statements. When African Bank announced during May 2013 that its microlending business had exposed it to an increased level of credit risk (which means that the probability of default by its debtors was increasing), the share price plunged by almost 25 per cent in less than a week. The sell-off was not isolated. Capitec and Transaction Capital were forced to go on the defensive, issuing press releases shortly after the announcement by African Bank to explain why their book debt was of considerably better quality than that of their counterpart.

What this case shows us is that working capital (which includes trade receivables and payables, inventory and cash) and how it is managed is of great importance to investors. When it comes to banks in particular, the announcement of an increase in the allowance for doubtful debts can lead to significant financial losses by investors and have ripple effects for the rest of the sector.

In this chapter

Most entities show one amount for 'receivables' on the face of their statement of financial position, usually described as 'trade and other receivables'. This normally includes amounts owing from customers for goods sold on credit (accounts receivable), as well as other amounts owing to the entity such as loans to directors, rent receivable or interest receivable (often known collectively as other receivables). The focus of this chapter is on ***accounts receivable***, also known as ***trade receivables or debtors***.

A negative consequence of selling on credit is that customers do not always pay. Some customers fall on hard times and cannot pay, others dispute the amount owed while some are fraudulent and buy goods on credit and then disappear with no intention of paying. The amounts that will not be received are known as ***bad debts***.

Dashboard

- Look at the *Learning outcomes* so that you know what you should be able to do after studying the chapter. Take note that there is a difference between bad debts and doubtful debts.

- Read the *Business focus* to place the chapter contents in a real-world context.
- Preview *In this chapter* to focus your mind on the contents of the chapter.
- Read the *text* in detail.
- Pay attention to the *definitions*, and apply your mind to the *Pause and reflect* scenarios.
- Prepare solutions to the examples as you read through the chapter.
- Prepare a solution to the *Revision example* at the end of the chapter without reference to the suggested one. Compare your solution to the suggested solution provided.

Learning outcomes

After studying this chapter, you should be able to do the following:

1 Describe the nature of accounts receivable.
2 Explain the concept of a bad debts expense and an allowance for doubtful debts, and record the accounting entries for both.
3 Explain the concept of the recovery of debts previously written off, and record the accounting entry.

Accounts receivable

12.1 The nature of accounts receivable

The sale of goods and services on credit forms an integral part of economic activity, and many business entities have a large number of customers who buy on credit. When goods are sold on credit, the earning of revenue and the receipt of cash will not correspond. The accrual concept requires the revenue to be recognised in the period when the goods are sold and not when the cash is received. You learnt in earlier chapters how to account for the sale of goods on credit and the subsequent receipt of cash.

You also learnt in Chapter 9, *Analysis journals*, how to maintain an accounts receivable subsidiary ledger, along with the accounts receivable control account in the general ledger. Remember that the equality of the accounting equation is maintained in the general ledger. The balances on the accounts receivable subsidiary ledger are not included on the trial balance, as the subsidiary ledger serves only as a supplementary record of detailed information concerning each customer.

Accounts receivable are an asset. They represent a resource controlled by the entity (the right to collect an amount from a customer), from a past event (the credit sale), from which future economic benefits are expected to flow to the entity (the receipt of cash from the customers).

Pause and reflect ...

On 25 January 20X5, Smart Concepts sold computers for C187 500 to a customer. An amount of C125 000 was paid on 15 March and the balance is due by 15 April. We have discussed above how accounts receivable meet the definition of an asset. Think now about the recognition criteria in relation to accounts receivable.

Response

The future economic benefits are probable (it is a legally enforceable sale) and the amount still to be collected can be measured reliably at C62 500 (assume that proper accounting records are maintained). The accounts receivable are therefore included as an asset on the statement of financial position at C62 500. Later in this chapter we will consider what happens when it is not probable that the full amount of C62 500 will be received and how this affects the measurement of the accounts receivable.

Accounts receivable are also regarded as a financial instrument and, more specifically, a financial asset.

IAS 32 defines a financial instrument as any contract that gives rise to both a financial asset of one entity and a financial liability of another. The definition of a financial asset includes a contractual right to receive cash or another financial asset from another entity.

Accounts receivable are therefore classified as a financial asset because of the contractual right arising from a sale or service agreement to collect cash from customers.

It is important to note here that prepaid expenses are not a financial asset, as the future benefit is the right to receive goods or services and not the right to receive cash or another financial asset.

12.2 Bad debts and doubtful debts

When a business entity sells goods on credit, it takes the risk that some customers will not pay the amounts owing by them. If all efforts to collect the amount owing from a customer are unsuccessful, the amount owing is written off as uncollectable and is known as a ***bad debt***. At the end of the accounting period, an assessment is made of the future economic benefits that will flow to the entity from the accounts receivable – in other words, the amount of cash that will be received from customers. If some degree of non-payment is considered probable, an estimate must be made at the end of the period of the amount which is unlikely to be received. This is referred to as an ***allowance for doubtful debts***.

The accounting implications of recognising an amount as a *bad debt* and recognising an *allowance for doubtful debts* are different. This is discussed in the following sections.

12.2.1 Writing off bad debts

If a customer defaults on an amount owing, this will result in a decrease in the future economic benefits that will flow to the entity. The asset, accounts receivable, must be reduced to reflect this decrease and a corresponding ***bad debts*** expense is recognised. The basic accounting entry is therefore as follows:

Dr Bad debts (E)
Cr Accounts receivable (A)

If the entity uses an accounting system with a general ledger and subsidiary ledgers (as described in Chapter 9, *Analysis journals*), the accounting entry must credit the accounts receivable control account in the *general ledger* as well as the individual customer's account in the *accounts receivable subsidiary ledger* (ARSL). The accounting entry then becomes:

Dr Bad debts (E)
Cr Accounts receivable: GL (A)
Cr Individual customer: ARSL (A)

Remember from Chapter 9 that accounts for individual customers in the accounts receivable subsidiary ledger do not form part of the general ledger and are not part of the double entry. The total of these individual accounts needs to equal the balance on the accounts receivable control account in the general ledger and thus needs to reflect the entry in the general ledger account.

 **Example: Writing off bad debts**

Bright Life sold goods to a customer, Mr V, for an amount of C650 during October 20X5. By the end of December 20X5, Mr V had not paid, and all efforts to trace him were unsuccessful. A decision was taken at that stage to write off as uncollectable the full amount owing of C650.

You are required to:

Provide the journal entry to record the write-off of the bad debt.

Solution: Writing off bad debts

GENERAL JOURNAL OF BRIGHT LIFE

Date	*Description*	*Fol*	*Dr*	*Cr*
31/12/X5	Bad debts (E)	GL	650	
	Accounts receivable (A)	GL		650
	Mr V	*ARSL*		*650*
	Mr V's account written off as irrecoverable			

Accounts receivable is reduced by C650 to reflect the decrease in the future economic benefits as a result of Mr V's debt being written off as uncollectable. A corresponding bad debts expense of C650 is recognised. In addition, Mr V's account in the accounts receivable subsidiary ledger is reduced by C650.

Remember that the accounting equation balances with the debit to bad debts expense (reduces equity on the right side of the equation) and a credit to accounts receivable (reduces assets on the left side of the equation). The credit to Mr V's account in the accounts receivable subsidiary ledger is not part of the double entry.

12.2.2 Creating an allowance for doubtful debts

Accounts receivable are recognised as an asset if it is probable that future economic benefits will flow to the entity (that is, cash will be collected) and the value of the accounts receivable can be measured reliably.

If some degree of non-payment is considered probable, an estimate must be made at the end of the period of the amount which is unlikely to be received from customers. This estimate is known as the ***allowance for doubtful debts***. You will recall from Chapter 6, *Preparation and presentation of financial statements*, when discussing the recognition of assets that the use of estimates is an essential part of the preparation of financial statements and does not undermine their reliability.

An estimate of the future cash flows expected from the accounts receivable is necessary in order to determine the amount of the allowance for doubtful debts. Typically, information from the accounts receivable subsidiary ledger is used to prepare a report known as the *accounts receivable age analysis* (also referred to as a *debtors' age analysis*). This analysis is used to highlight the days for which the debts of each customer are outstanding and to direct management's attention to accounts that are slow to pay.

From this analysis, the entity determines the amount of the allowance for doubtful debts. In addition, this age analysis assists entities in making decisions on whether to continue supplying existing customers.

An accounts receivable age analysis for Bright Life at 31 March 20X6 is presented below.

BRIGHT LIFE
ACCOUNTS RECEIVABLE AGE ANALYSIS AT 31 MARCH 20X6

Customer name	*Total*	*Current*	*30–60 days*	*61–90 days*	*More than 90 days*
	C	C	C	C	C
Mr W	5 500	0	2 980	0	2 520
Ms X	2 000	1 400	600	0	0
Ms Y	1 500	580	420	500	0
Mr Z	5 020	5 020	0	0	0
	14 020	7 000	4 000	500	2 520

Pause and reflect . . .

Based on past experience, Bright Life makes the following estimates regarding the collectability of accounts receivable:

- accounts that are current – 99 per cent probability of being collected in full;
- accounts that are 30–60 days past due date – 97 per cent probability of being collected in full;
- accounts that are 61–90 days past due date – 90 per cent probability of being collected in full;
- accounts more than 90 days past due date – 60 per cent probability of being collected in full.

Can you determine the amount that should be recognised as an allowance for doubtful debts?

Response

The amount to be recognised as an allowance for doubtful debts is based on the *probability of collecting* each category of ageing. This is shown as follows:

Age of accounts receivable		*Probability of collecting*	*Expected cash flow*
	C		C
Current	7 000	99%	6 930
30–60 days	4 000	97%	3 880
61–90 days	500	90%	450
More than 90 days	2 520	60%	1 512
	14 020		12 772

The allowance for doubtful debts is then established by comparing the balance on accounts receivable with the expected cash flow:

Balance on accounts receivable	14 020
Expected future cash flow	12 772
Allowance required at end of period	1 248

On this basis, an allowance of C1 248 is recognised as an allowance for doubtful debts.

In determining an allowance for doubtful debts, information specific to a particular customer can also be taken into consideration, for example the customer's current financial status or a dispute with the customer.

The accounting entry to record the creation of an allowance for doubtful debts is:

Dr Doubtful debts (E)
Cr Allowance for doubtful debts (–A)

Pause and reflect . . .

What do you notice about the account debited and credited in this entry as compared to the entry to write off a bad debt?

Response

This entry debits a *doubtful debts expense* whereas when we wrote off a bad debt, we debited a *bad debts expense*. Both are expenses, but it is useful to distinguish the one from the other. The credit side of this entry is to the *allowance for doubtful debts*, but when we wrote off a bad debt, we credited *accounts receivable*. Accounts receivable is not credited because it is not yet certain which customers will not pay their accounts, neither are the amounts which will not be paid known with certainty. The amount of the estimate is therefore credited to an allowance.

Concepts in context

The Bidvest Group Limited

Extract from trade receivables note

Management identifies impairment of trade receivables on an ongoing basis. An impairment allowance in respect of doubtful debts is raised against trade receivables when their collectability is considered to be doubtful. In determining whether a particular receivable could be doubtful, the age, the customer's current financial status and disputes with the customer are taken into consideration.

What concepts in context can you see here?

When Bidvest refers to an impairment of trade receivables, this means that the expected cash flow from customers is less than the carrying amount of their trade receivables (trade receivables is another term for accounts receivable). Note the ageing of the receivables that you learnt about.

The Bidvest Group Limited is an international investment holding company with investments across the food service, broad services, trading and distribution industries.

Source: www.bidvest.com/ar/bidvest_ar2013/pdf/full.pdf/ (Accessed 20 June 2014).

The allowance for doubtful debts is regarded as an adjustment to the carrying amount of the asset, accounts receivable. Thus, the allowance for doubtful debts is sometimes referred to as a *measurement account* for accounts receivable, because it is used to adjust the measurement of the carrying amount of accounts receivable.

Remember that an asset is a resource controlled by the entity as a result of past events and from which future economic benefits are expected to flow to the entity. In the case of accounts receivable, the resource controlled by the entity is the right to collect the amount owing from the customer, the past event is the sale of the goods or the provision of services on credit, and the future economic benefit is the cash to be received from the customers. If the future economic benefits expected to be received by the entity are less than the balance on accounts receivable because some customers may not settle their accounts, the carrying amount of the asset must be reduced to reflect this.

Example: Creating an allowance for doubtful debts

Following on from the discussion above, the balance in the accounts receivable control account of Bright Life totalled C14 020 at 31/03/X6, the end of its first financial year. The future cash flows that are expected from accounts receivable amounts to C12 772.

You are required to:

Provide the journal entry to create an allowance for doubtful debts.

Solution: Creating an allowance for doubtful debts

GENERAL JOURNAL OF BRIGHT LIFE				
Date	*Description*	*Fol*	*Dr*	*Cr*
31/03/X6	Doubtful debts (E)		1 248	
	Allowance for doubtful debts (–A)			1 248
	Allowance for doubtful debts created			

The expected future cash flows amount to C12 772, requiring the carrying amount of the accounts receivable to be reduced by C1 248. The debit to doubtful debts expense results in an expense on the statement of profit or loss. The account credited, the allowance for doubtful debts, is known as a contra-account and is used because at the time the allowance is made it is not known which customers will not pay. It is therefore not possible to credit the accounts of specific customers in the accounts receivable subsidiary ledger, and because of this the accounts receivable control account also cannot be credited. Instead, the credit is placed to the allowance for doubtful debts.

An extract from the statement of financial position at the end of the period is given below. It shows that although C14 020 is legally owed to Bright Life at the end of the period, the future economic benefits likely to be received amount to C12 772. You will recall from Chapter 2, *Fundamental accounting concepts*, that the offsetting of items in the statement of profit or loss and the statement of financial position is not permitted. The measurement of the asset, accounts receivable, net of the allowance for doubtful debts, is not regarded as offsetting.

BRIGHT LIFE
(EXTRACT FROM) STATEMENT OF FINANCIAL POSITION
AT 31 MARCH 20X6

	C
Current assets	
Accounts receivable	14 020
Allowance for doubtful debts	(1 248)
	12 772

Concepts in context

The SPAR Group Limited
Extract from trade and other receivables note

	R
Trade receivables	5 392 300
Allowance for doubtful debts	(121 400)
Net trade receivables	5 270 900
Other receivables	570 400
Total trade and other receivables	5 841 300

What concepts in context do you see here?

You have learnt in this chapter that the allowance for doubtful debts is regarded as an adjustment to the carrying amount of the asset, accounts receivable. SPAR is doing exactly this, reporting that of the trade receivables amounting to R5 392 300, R121 400 is estimated to be doubtful and that the future cash flow expected from its trade receivables amounts to R5 270 900.

SPAR is an international retail chain and franchise with approximately 12 500 stores in 35 countries worldwide. It was founded in the Netherlands in 1932 by retailer Adriaan van Well.

Source: www.spar.co.za/getattachment/a6164404-0e5b-4110-bdd4-bf921af866be/00000000-0000-0000-0000-000000000000-(7).aspx/ (Accessed 20 June 2014).

12.2.3 Adjusting the allowance for doubtful debts

At the end of each period, a current estimate needs to be made regarding the allowance required for doubtful debts. The factors taken into account are the same as those considered when creating the allowance.

If an increase in the allowance is required, the allowance for doubtful debts account is credited, whereas to decrease the allowance, the allowance for doubtful debts account is debited. In both cases, the other account affected is the doubtful debts expense account. The accounting entries can be summarised as follows:

Dr Doubtful debts (E)
Cr Allowance for doubtful debts (–A)
(Increase in allowance)

Dr Allowance for doubtful debts (–A)
Cr Doubtful debts (E)
(Decrease in allowance)

This principle is also addressed in the following example.

Example: Writing off bad debts and adjusting the allowance for doubtful debts

An extract of the trial balance of Bright Life at 31/03/X7, its next financial year end, is presented below.

BRIGHT LIFE
(EXTRACT FROM) TRIAL BALANCE AT 31/03/X7

	Dr	*Cr*
Bad debts expense	350	
Accounts receivable	15 500	
Allowance for doubtful debts (01/04/X6)		1 248

Additional information

- The bad debts expense of C350 arose from the write-off of the account of a customer who purchased goods in August 20X6 and who, by December 20X6, had been declared insolvent.
- Ms Y has paid C1 000 of the C1 500 that was owing at 31 March 20X6. The balance of C500 is considered to be irrecoverable.
- The expected future cash flows from accounts receivable amounts to C13 550.

You are required to:

a) Prepare the necessary journal entries.
b) Post to the relevant ledger accounts.

c) Show how the bad debts expense will be presented in the statement of profit or loss and how the accounts receivable will be presented in the statement of financial position.

Solution: Writing off bad debts and adjusting the allowance for doubtful debts

a) Journal entries

GENERAL JOURNAL OF BRIGHT LIFE				
Date	*Description*	*Fol*	*Dr*	*Cr*
31/03/X7	Bad debts (E)	GL	500	
	Accounts receivable control (A)	GL		500
	Ms Y	*ARSL*		*500*
	Ms Y's account written off as irrecoverable			
31/03/X7	Doubtful debts (E)	GL	202	
	Allowance for doubtful debts (–A)	GL		202
	Allowance for doubtful debts increased			

The additional C500 written off as a bad debts expense at 31/03/X7 is recognised as an expense for the period from 01/04/X6 to 31/03/X7. Note that the expense is recognised in the year ending 31/03/X7 even though the income from the sale was recognised in the year ending 31/03/X6. This is an inevitable consequence of the accounting estimation process and, as mentioned previously, does not undermine reliability.

The computation to adjust the allowance for doubtful debts is made after taking into account any additional bad debts at the end of the period, such as Ms Y's account. The computation of the adjustment is as follows:

Balance on accounts receivable (15 500 – 500)	15 000
Expected future cash flow	13 550
Allowance for doubtful debts required at end of the current period (31/03/X7)	1 450
Balance in the allowance for doubtful debts account (31/03/X6)	(1 248)
Increase in the allowance	202

b) Ledger accounts

GENERAL LEDGER OF BRIGHT LIFE							
Accounts receivable control				**Allowance for doubtful debts**			
Details	*C*	*Details*	*C*	*Details*	*C*	*Details*	*C*
Balance b/d	15 500	Bad debts expense	500			Balance b/d	1 248
		Balance c/d	15 000	Balance c/d	1 450	Doubtful debts expense	202
	15 500		15 500		1 450		1 450
Balance b/d	15 000					Balance b/d	1 450

Bad debts expense				Doubtful debts expense			
Details	*C*	*Details*	*C*	*Details*	*C*	*Details*	*C*
Balance b/d	350	Profit or loss	850	Allowance for doubtful debts	202	Profit or loss	202
Accounts receivable	500						
	850		850		202		202

ACCOUNTS RECEIVABLE SUBSIDIARY LEDGER OF BRIGHT LIFE

Ms Y

Details	*C*	*Details*	*C*
Balance b/d	500	Bad debts expense	500
		Balance c/d	0
	500		500
Balance b/d	0		

c) Financial statement presentation

BRIGHT LIFE
(EXTRACT FROM) STATEMENT OF PROFIT OR LOSS
FOR THE YEAR ENDED 31 MARCH 20X7

		C
Operating expenses		
Bad debts	*(350 + 500)*	850
Doubtful debts		202

BRIGHT LIFE
(EXTRACT FROM) STATEMENT OF FINANCIAL POSITION
AT 31 MARCH 20X7

	C
Current assets	
Accounts receivable	15 000
Allowance for doubtful debts	(1 450)
	13 550

12.3 Bad debts recovered

When a customer's account is written off, that person's credit rating is jeopardised. Subsequently, and often long after the account has been written off, the defaulting customer may choose to pay all or part of the amount that was owing. It is good practice to first reinstate the receivable and then record the amount received. This is helpful when deciding whether to sell to this customer on credit in future.

Example: Bad debts recovered

During the next financial year, Ms Y's position changed and at the end of October 20X7 she paid C400 of the C500 originally owed by her.

You are required to:

Record the recovery of the bad debt in the general journal.

Solution: Bad debts recovered

GENERAL JOURNAL OF BRIGHT LIFE

Date	*Description*	*Fol*	*Dr*	*Cr*
31/10/X7	Accounts receivable (A)	GL	400	
	Ms Y	*ARSL*	*400*	
	Bad debts recovered (I)			400
	Reinstatement of part of amount owing by Ms Y			
31/10/X7	Cash	GL	400	
	Accounts receivable (A)	GL		400
	Ms Y	*ARSL*		*400*
	Amount recovered from Ms Y			

The accounts receivable is first reinstated with the corresponding entry increasing an income account, bad debts recovered. The cash received from the customer is then recorded, with an increase to cash and a decrease in the accounts receivable.

The bad debts recovered appears as income on the statement of profit or loss. It should not be set off against the bad debts expense, as this would distort the amount charged as a write-off during the current period.

Note that financial reporting requires many ***estimates***, and the accounting for bad debts is an estimation process.

If an amount recovered had originally included output VAT that was then claimed as input VAT at the time that the bad debt expense was recognised, then output VAT in respect of the recovered amount must again be recognised.

Revision example

Justin Thyme, trading as The Clock Shop, reports the following statement of financial position for the year ending 31 December 20X7 (with comparative figures for the year ended 31 December 20X6).

THE CLOCK SHOP
STATEMENT OF FINANCIAL POSITION AT 31 DECEMBER 20X7

	31/12/X7	*31/12/X6*
	C	*C*
ASSETS		
Non-current assets		
Furniture and fittings	52 000	50 000
Cost	66 000	60 000
Accumulated depreciation	(14 000)	(10 000)
Current assets	74 000	59 200
Inventory	32 000	30 000
Accounts receivable	30 000	19 200
Bank	12 000	10 000
	126 000	109 200
EQUITY AND LIABILITIES		
Equity		
Capital	104 000	94 200
Current liabilities		
Accounts payable	22 000	15 000
	126 000	109 200

The following information is available:

- Cash collected from customers during the year ended 31/12/X7, C145 000. All sales are on credit.
- Accounts receivable is reported net of the allowance for doubtful debts in the statement of financial position:
  - The allowance for doubtful debts amounts to C4 800 at 31/12/X6 and to C7 500 at 31/12/X7.
  - Bad debts of C1 500 were written off accounts receivable during the current year.
- A perpetual inventory system is used.
- Cash payments to suppliers of goods for resale, C95 000.
- Included in accounts payable are the following amounts owing to suppliers for purchase of goods for resale:
  - at 31/12/X6, C12 000.
  - at 31/12/X7, C20 000.
- Purchases of furniture and fittings (in cash), C6 000.
- Cash distributions to owner, C5 000.

You are required to:

Compute the following for the year ended 31 December 20X7:

a) Sales revenue.
b) Cost of sales.
c) Depreciation expense.
d) Profit for the period.

Solution: Revision example

a) Calculation of sales revenue

Accounts receivable

Date	*Details*	*C*	*Date*	*Details*	*C*
20X7			20X7	Bank[2] (collections)	145 000
Jan 1	Balance b/d[1]	24 000			
	Sales[4]	***160 000***		Bad debts expense[2] (write-off)	1 500
			Dec 31	Balance c/d[3]	37 500
		184 000			184 000
20X8					
Jan 1	Balance b/d[3]	37 500			

Allowance for doubtful debts (not required as part of answer)

Date	*Details*	*C*	*Date*	*Details*	*C*
20X7			20X7		
Dec 31	Balance c/d[2]	7 500	Jan 1	Balance b/d[2]	4 800
				Doubtful debts expense[4] (increase in allowance)	***2 700***
		7 500			7 500
			20X8		
			Jan 1	Balance b/d[2]	7 500

The sales revenue is calculated by reconstructing the accounts receivable account and determining the C160 000 for sales revenue as a balancing amount.

1 Net balance in the 20X6 SOFP: 19 200 + Doubtful debts allowance at 31/12/20X6: 4 800 = 24 000.
2 Given in the additional information.
3 Net balance in the 20X7 SOFP: 30 000 + Doubtful debts allowance at 31/12/20X7: 7 500 = 37 500.
4 Balancing amount.

b) Cost of sales

Accounts payable

Date	*Details*	*C*	*Date*	*Details*	*C*
20X7			20X7		
Dec 31	Bank (payments)[1]	95 000	Jan 1	Balance b/d[1]	12 000
			Dec 31	***Inventory (goods purchased)***[3]	***103 000***
	Balance c/d[1]	20 000			
		115 000			115 000
			20X8		
			Jan 1	Balance b/d[1]	20 000

Inventory

Date	*Details*	*C*	*Date*	*Details*	*C*
20X7			20X7		
Jan 1	Balance b/d[2]	30 000		***Cost of sales***[3]	***101 000***
Dec 31	Accounts payables (goods purchased)	103 000			
			Dec 31	Balance c/d[2]	32 000
		133 000			133 000
20X8					
Jan 1	Balance b/d[2]	32 000			

The cost of sales is calculated in two steps. First, we reconstruct the accounts payable account and determine the inventory purchased as the balancing amount. We then reconstruct the inventory account and, using the amount of inventory purchased, we determine the cost of sales as the balancing amount.

1 Given in the additional information.
2 Given in the SOFP.
3 Balancing amount.

c) Depreciation expense

	Ending accumulated depreciation	14 000
	Beginning accumulated depreciation	(10 000)
=	Depreciation expense	4 000

d) Profit for the period

	Closing owner's equity	104 000
	Opening owner's equity	(94 200)
		9 800
+	Distributions	5 000
=	Profit for the period	14 800

Bibliography

Business Report. 2013. Lenders scramble for distance from African Bank.

Financial statement. www.bidvest.com/ar/bidvest_ar2013/pdf/full.pdf (Accessed 20 June 2014).

Financial statement. www.spar.co.za/getattachment/a6164404-0e5b-4110-bdd4-bf921af866be/00000000-0000-0000-0000-000000000000-(7).aspx/ (Accessed 20 June 2014).

The International Accounting Standards Board. 2010. IAS 32 *Financial Instruments: Presentation*.

13 Cash and bank

Business focus

Have you ever stopped to consider the vast number of customer loyalty schemes that are currently on offer? There are many, including those offered by supermarket retailers and banks. Perhaps you are one of the numerous people who have a Barclaycard Freedom Rewards card and pay for everything with your credit card so that you can accumulate points. If so, how exactly would you account for this? For every £1 spent in supermarkets, petrol stations and Transport for London, you earn two points, and for every £1 spent elsewhere, you earn one point. The points can then be converted into vouchers to spend at a variety of partners, including well-known companies such as Amazon, Boots and iTunes. This raises the question: are the points a type of currency? They represent a resource, which, like cash on hand, provides a means of paying for goods or services. They may not be pounds or euros, but they can be converted into vouchers equivalent to a known number of pounds or euros. If you are still not convinced, ask yourself: what is the difference between the 100 points that I have accumulated and the £100 that I keep in my petty-cash box, other than the rate to convert them back into pounds? We answer this question with another question: what is a suitable definition of 'cash'?

In this chapter

The term 'cash' does not always mean notes and coins. We may refer to paying for goods or services *in cash*, yet this is often done by means of writing out a cheque or paying by electronic funds transfer (EFT) rather than handing over notes and coins. For accounting purposes, however, we credit the *bank* account when such payments are made. We explore these concepts in this chapter.

Cash is also a high-risk area of vulnerability when it comes to fraud. Temptations are great, and controls are often insufficient, leading to an abundance of opportunity for would-be fraudsters. Strict controls need to be in place to mitigate the risk of loss and, importantly, there must be practical oversight for them to be effective. One of the most important controls is the bank reconciliation, which is addressed in this chapter.

Dashboard

- Look at the *Learning outcomes* so that you know what you should be able to do after studying this chapter.

- Read the *Business focus* to place the chapter contents in a real-world context.
- Preview *In this chapter* to focus your mind on the contents of this chapter.
- Read the *text* in detail.
    - Pay attention to the *definitions,* and apply your mind to the *Pause and reflect* scenarios.
    - Ensure that you fully understand the relationship between the entries in the reporting entity's records and those in the bank's records (described in Section 13.3) before learning how to prepare a bank reconciliation (described in Section 13.4).
    - Take particular note of the objective of the bank reconciliation in Section 13.4.1. This is key to understanding the logic of a bank reconciliation.
    - Prepare solutions to the examples as you read through the chapter.
- Prepare a solution to the *Revision example* at the end of the chapter without reference to the suggested one. Compare your solution to the suggested solution provided.

Learning outcomes

After studying this chapter, you should be able to do the following:

1. Explain the use of the terms 'cash', 'bank' as well as 'cash and cash equivalents'.
2. List the internal controls over cash.
3. Distinguish between the accounting records of the reporting entity and the bank.
4. Explain why the bank balance in the general ledger can be different from the balance on the bank statement.
5. Explain the need for reconciling the bank account in the general ledger to the balance on the bank statement.
6. Prepare a bank reconciliation.

Cash and bank

13.1 What is cash?

A business entity receives payment for its goods and services in a number of ways. These include currency notes and coins, cheques, credit and debit card payments, and EFTs. The currency notes and coins need to be physically deposited into the bank account at the bank, whereas for card payments and EFTs the funds are transferred directly into the entity's bank account. Payments made for goods and services acquired are usually made by cheque or EFT. All of these receipts and payments are ultimately processed through the entity's bank account.

Goods and services can be bought *for cash* or *on credit*. Similarly, they can be sold *for cash* or *on credit*. When buying goods on credit, inventory is debited and the liability – accounts payable – is credited; when selling on credit, the asset – accounts receivable – is debited and the sale is credited. Buying or selling goods for cash does not necessarily mean that currency changes hands. For cash transactions, most business entities will use a bank account in the general ledger to record receipts and payments, whether these are in the form of currency notes and coins, cheques, EFTs or credit card transactions.

For presentation on the statement of financial position, IAS 1 *Presentation of Financial Statements*, uses the term '***cash and cash equivalents***'. Most large business entities follow this practice as well.

IAS 7 *Statement of Cash Flows* (which you will learn about in Chapter 18), defines these terms.

Cash includes cash on hand and demand deposits.

Cash equivalents are short-term, highly liquid investments that are readily convertible to known amounts of cash, and are subject to an insignificant risk of changes in value.

The IASB definition of cash thus includes both cash on hand (currency notes and coins) and demand deposits (current and savings accounts). A demand deposit refers to an account held at a bank, which may be withdrawn at any time by the account holder. The majority of demand deposit accounts are current (cheque) and savings accounts. Cash equivalents include short-term government bonds, money market investments and other short-term bank deposits.

13.2 The importance of control over cash

In all business entities, cash is a high-risk asset and vulnerable to fraud. You have no doubt read many stories in the newspapers of people found guilty of committing fraud, almost always involving the misappropriation of cash. If an employee is responsible for large amounts of cash, there is potential for fraud, especially if controls and oversight are lacking. Having controls in place and ensuring their compliance is therefore a top priority.

13.2.1 The fraud triangle

The fraud triangle is a model for explaining the factors that cause someone to commit fraud in the workplace. It consists of three components which, together, lead to fraudulent behaviour:

- a financial problem;
- opportunity;
- rationalisation.

An individual has a financial problem that he or she is unable to solve through legitimate means and thus contemplates committing an illegal act such as stealing cash as a way to do so. The person then sees an opportunity to use (effectively abuse) his or her position of trust to misappropriate cash with a perceived low chance of being caught. The majority of people who commit financial fraud are first-time offenders who do not view themselves as criminals, but as ordinary people who have fallen on hard times, and they use this to rationalise their illegal acts.

13.2.2 Internal control over cash

To prevent misappropriation of its cash resources, a business needs to ensure that an adequate internal control system is installed. The types of control referred to above include the following:

- Custody must be separated from recordkeeping for cash.
- All cash receipts should be deposited intact into the bank on a daily basis.
- All payments should be made by cheque or EFT (except for minor payments).
- Minor payments should be made from a petty-cash float, which is maintained on an imprest system.
- A bank reconciliation needs to be prepared on a regular basis to prove the accuracy of the records of both the reporting entity and the bank.

 **Pause and reflect . . .**

A small business entity may have only a few employees. Can you see any problem if the sales assistant banks the cash received and also prepares the bank reconciliation?

Response

The person who prepares the bank reconciliation should not be the same person who has access to, and control over, the cash. Segregation of duties is important to achieve proper internal control.

Concepts in context

Lindt & Sprüngli Group
Extract from cash and cash equivalents policy note

Cash and cash equivalents include cash on hand, cash in bank and other short-term, highly liquid investments with an original maturity period of up to ninety days.

Extract from balance sheet and financial statements notes

	CHF million
Current assets	
Cash and cash equivalents	619.4
Cash and cash equivalents	
Cash as bank and in hand	614.4
Short-term bank deposits	5.0
	619.4

What concepts in context do you see here?

You have read so far in this chapter that most business entities use the term 'cash and cash equivalents' to describe their cash resources. Here you see an extract from the balance sheet (statement of financial position) of the Lindt & Sprüngli Group that shows this principle. You should also remember that IAS 7 defines both 'cash' and 'cash equivalents'; cash includes cash on hand, and demand deposits and cash equivalents are short-term, highly liquid investments, as described in the notes to the financial statements of Lindt & Sprüngli.

Lindt & Sprüngli AG, more commonly known as Lindt, is a Swiss chocolate and confectionery company.

Source: www.lindt.co.uk/swf/eng/about-lindt/investors/ (Accessed 3 July 2014).

13.3 The records of the reporting entity and the bank

When working with cash and bank transactions, it is important to have an understanding of the relationship between the entries in the reporting entity's records and those in the bank's records. In the discussion that follows, increases and decreases in cash refer to the wider context and include EFTs and card transactions.

In the records of the reporting entity, *increases* in the bank balance brought about by deposits of cash into the bank are recorded with a *debit* to the bank account. As you are aware, this is because the balance in the bank is an asset, and assets increase with debit entries. Conversely, *decreases* in the bank balance caused by cheques being written out are recorded with a *credit* to the bank account, as assets decrease with credit entries.

From the bank's perspective, *deposits* of cash into the bank by the reporting entity are recorded with a *credit* to the account of the entity. This is because the amount deposited represents a liability of the bank, as the bank has an obligation to provide the cash when it is requested by the entity. Therefore, *cheques* written out by the entity are recorded with a *debit* to the entity's account, as liabilities decrease with debit entries.

You will remember from Chapter 9, *Analysis journals*, that the **reporting entity** records cash and bank transactions in a cash receipts and cash payments journal (manual or computerised) reflecting:

- receipts, in the form of:
  - cash and cheques deposited into the bank;
  - credit and debit card transactions;
  - EFT receipts.
- payments, in the form of:
  - cheques written out;
  - credit and debit card transactions;
  - EFT payments.
- other direct charges or deposits by the bank.

The **bank**, in turn, records the receipts and payments made by the reporting entity, and these are shown on the bank statement. The receipts and payments recorded by the bank should mirror those of the reporting entity.

- Card and EFT transactions are generated electronically, and, for large business entities, the respective records of the reporting entity and bank will be updated online with sophisticated computer systems. For smaller entities, the transactions are processed by the reporting entity as they appear on the bank statement.
- Currency, coins and cheques need to be deposited at the bank. Again, the procedure differs for large and small business entities. Large entities with significant amounts of cash will usually arrange for it to be collected from the business premises by an armed cash services company, whereas smaller entities will deposit the cash over the counter at the bank. Either way, a record of the deposit in the form of a deposit slip will be used by the bank to record the entry.
- Cheques made out by the reporting entity to pay suppliers for goods and other services are given or posted to the suppliers, who then present the cheques for payment by depositing them into their own bank accounts. It is only when the cheques are presented for payment that the bank is able to record the entry.

In addition, the bank itself may initiate:

- credits to the entity's account (i.e. an increase) such as interest earned;
- debits to the entity's account (i.e. a decrease) such as bank charges, interest incurred, direct debit and standing orders.

 **Pause and reflect . . .**

What situations give rise to interest *earned* and *incurred* in relation to a bank account?

Response

Interest is *earned* on a bank account when the entity maintains a positive balance in the account (debit balance from the entity's perspective and credit balance from the bank's perspective). The interest rate is often very low. Interest is *incurred* on a bank account when the account balance goes into overdraft (credit balance from the entity's perspective and debit balance from the bank's perspective).

 **Pause and reflect . . .**

What is the difference between a direct debit and a standing order?

Response

A direct debit is an agreement between you and a third party in which you authorise the company or third party to take money out of your bank account for services provided. This is commonly used for paying monthly accounts to service providers, for example internet access, mobile phones and utilities. Direct debits may be for fixed or variable amounts.

A standing order is an instruction given to your bank to pay funds across to a third party, at a fixed amount on a regular basis. The bank acts on your instructions and the third party is not given authority to debit your account as is the case with a direct debit. This could be used, for example, to make a monthly donation to a charity.

A direct debit is very similar to a standing order but a direct debit is more difficult to cancel than a standing order. To cancel a direct debit you need to approach the relevant company or third party and request that they instruct the bank to cancel the payments. For a standing order, you approach your bank yourself and instruct the bank to cancel the payments.

A summary comparing the records of the reporting entity and the bank is shown in Diagram 13.1.

A *favourable* balance in the reporting entity's bank account is an asset and thus has a debit balance. This corresponds to a credit balance on the entity's account in the bank's records, representing a liability from the bank's point of view. On the other hand, an *overdraft* in the reporting entity's bank account is a liability with a credit balance. This equates to a debit balance on the entity's account in the bank's records, an asset from the bank's perspective.

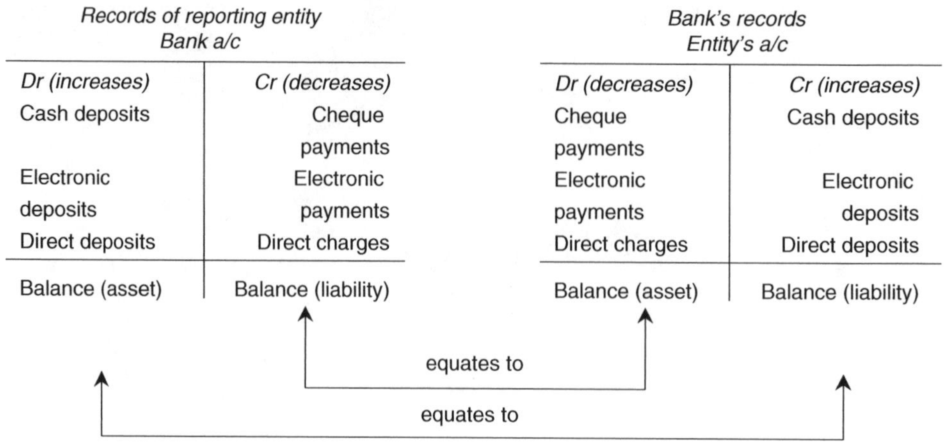

Diagram 13.1 Summary of entries in records of reporting entity and bank

Pause and reflect . . .

A bank manager explains to an account holder that the payment of the latest cheque resulted in a debit to the customer's account, yet the account remains in credit. What does this mean?

Response

The customer's account in the bank's records represents a liability from the bank's point of view. Thus, when a customer issues a cheque and the funds are paid from his or her bank account, this represents a decrease and therefore a debit to the liability from the bank's point of view. The fact that the account remains in credit means that there are sufficient funds in the bank account.

13.4 The bank reconciliation

Bank reconciliations are necessary because of timing differences between the date that receipt and payment transactions are recorded in the entity's records and the date that these transactions are responded to by the bank. Further differences arise because of bank-initiated entries and because of errors.

The differences between the bank balance in the entity's records and the balance per the bank statement can be identified as follows:

- deposits made and recorded by the entity which have not yet been acknowledged by the bank (i.e. not yet appearing as a credit on the entity's bank statement);
- cheques made out and recorded by the entity which have not yet been presented to the bank (i.e. not yet appearing as a debit on the entity's bank statement);

- bank-initiated entries:
  - direct charges (*debits*) by the bank;
  - direct deposits, including EFT receipts (*credits*) to the entity's account at the bank.
- errors:
  - in the entity's records;
  - in the bank's records.

13.4.1 The purpose of the bank reconciliation

If you understand the objective or purpose of reconciling the bank account balance in the reporting entity's records with the balance according to the bank statement, you should have no difficulty in following the bank reconciliation procedure. The purpose of the reconciliation is:

- *not* to make the bank account balance equal the bank statement balance;
- but rather to *explain and set out* the reasons for the bank account balance and bank statement balance not being equal.

13.4.2 Procedure to prepare a bank reconciliation

The first step towards preparing a bank reconciliation is to compare the entries in the cash journals with those on the bank statement. The second step is to update the bank account in the general ledger of the reporting entity by recording bank-initiated transactions (identified on the bank statement). The bank reconciliation is then prepared as the third step. This procedure is explained below, and then illustrated with examples.

Compare the cash journals to the bank statement

- Compare each deposit in the bank column of the cash receipts journal to the deposits listed on the bank statement.
- Compare each payment in the bank column of the cash payments journal to the payments listed on the bank statement.
- Identify any bank-initiated charges or deposits on the bank statement.
- Identify any errors in the entity's records or on the bank statement.

The procedure described here is essentially the same for a business entity using a manual bookkeeping system or an entity using computerised accounting software. Traditionally, the comparison of the cash journals with the bank statement was done manually by using a tick (✓) symbol to mark every transaction in the cash journals against the corresponding item on the bank statement. Currently, with electronic bank statements, this process can be performed by reconciliation software.

Amend the bank account in the general ledger of the reporting entity

Before preparing the bank reconciliation, the entity's records must be updated. This is done by recording the bank-initiated charges or deposits identified in the first step, and by correcting errors made in the entity's records.

Bank-initiated charges include commission on cheques and interest on overdrafts, as well as fees for unpaid cheques. Direct deposits arise when customers deposit their payments directly into the business bank account, often by way of EFT. Errors in the entity's records, for example deposits or cheques incorrectly entered, must also be corrected.

These items are journalised in the cash receipts or payments journal if the closing entries have not been processed. If the closing entries have been prepared and posted to the general ledger, the most convenient and practical way to journalise these amendments is to use the general journal.

It is very important to understand and appreciate which of the differences are accounted for by amending the records of the reporting entity and which are listed on the bank reconciliation. The principle is straightforward. The bank-initiated transactions, *already recorded by the bank* and identified on the bank statement, are *journalised in the entity's records*, along with the correction of errors made by the entity. The cheques and deposits, *already entered in the cash journals*, are *listed as reconciling items* on the bank reconciliation statement, along with the bank's errors. This is summarised in Diagram 13.2.

 **Pause and reflect . . .**

Another person's cheque is erroneously processed by the bank as a debit to the entity's account.

a) Explain whether or not a journal entry is required in the accounting records of the entity to correct this error.
b) Explain whether or not the error is listed on the bank reconciliation and, if so, whether it is added to or subtracted from the balance per the general ledger bank account.

Response

a) No journal entry is required in the accounting records of the entity. As the error is made by the bank, it is the bank's records that are in error, not those of the entity. A journal entry in the records of the entity is not required to correct this.
b) If the bank reconciliation begins with the balance per the general ledger bank account and the bank account balance is positive, the error must be subtracted to reconcile to the incorrect lower balance appearing on the bank statement.

Differences	*Treatment*
Receipts and payments appearing on the bank statement but not in the entity's records Errors made by entity	Adjusted in entity's records (before preparation of the bank reconciliation)
Outstanding cheques Outstanding deposits Errors made by bank	Listed on the bank reconciliation

Diagram 13.2 Summary of differences

 Example: Mechanics of a bank reconciliation

The following are the relevant extracts of the cash journals, bank account and bank statement of Bright Life for March 20X6. The information recorded in the books of Bright Life has been recorded correctly.

Cash receipts journal – March 20X6 **CRJ 2**

Date	*Doc*	*Account name*	*Fol*	*Sales*	*Accounts receivable control*	*Sundries*	*Allowance for settlement discount*	*Analysis*	*Bank*
01/03	DS 01	Capital	GL100			25 000		25 000	25 000
05/03	CSS 01	EFT cash sales		5 600				5 600	5 600
10/03	REC 01	Barons	DL09		4 000		200	3 800	
10/03	CSS 02	Cash sales		2 000				2 000	5 800
29/03	REC 02	Linus	DL74		6 000			6 000	
29/03	CSS 03	Cash sales		1 000				1 000	7 000
31/03	CSS 04	Cash sales		2 250				2 250	2 250
				10 850	10 000	25 000	200	—	45 650
				Cr GL: Sales	Cr GL: AR control	Cr Individual accounts	Dr GL: ASD		Dr GL: Bank

Cash payments journal – March 20X6 **CPJ 5**

Date	*Doc*	*Details*	*Fol*	*Purchases*	*Salaries*	*Accounts payable control*	*Sundries*	*Allowance for settlement discount*	*Bank*
01/03	0001	Rent	GL80				2 500		2 500
02/03	0002	Cash purchases		4 500					4 500
09/03	0003	EFT cash purchases		1 800					1 800
18/03	0004	Swift supplies	CL63			20 000		1 000	19 000
25/03	0005	EFT salaries			6 000				6 000
29/03	0006	Telephone	GL85				500		500
31/03	0007	Drawings	GL99				5 000		5 000
				6 300	6 000	20 000	8 000	1 000	39 300
Date				Dr GL: Purchases	Dr GL: Salaries	Dr GL: AP control	Dr Individual accounts	Cr GL: ASD	Cr GL: Bank

Bank (GL150)

Date	*Details*	*Fol*	*C*	*Date*	*Details*	*Fol*	*C*
20X6				20X6			
31/03	Deposits	CRJ 2	45 650	31/03	Payments	CPJ 5	39 300
				31/03	Balance c/d		6 350
			45 650				45 650
01/04	Balance b/d		6 350				

BB Limited	✉ Thames Business Park Valley Road SW6 3DP	**The Brall Bank** Reg. No. 56 00574/12 ☎ 402-6308
CURRENT ACCOUNT STATEMENT 31 March 20X6		Bright Life River Road Exeter EX1 2AM

Date	*Doc #*	*Details*	*Dr*	*Cr*	*Balance*
01/03	DEP	Deposit		25 000	25 000
06/03	EFT	EFT deposit		5 600	30 600
07/03	0001	Cheque	2 500		28 100
07/03	0002	Cheque	4 500		23 600
11/03	DEP	Deposit		5 800	29 400
13/03	0003	EFT payment	1 800		27 600
20/03	0004	Cheque	19 000		8 600
25/03	EFT	Electronic transfer – Ometer		1 500	10 100
25/03	DO	Direct debit – insurance	600		9 500
26/03	0005	EFT payment	6 000		3 500
30/03	DEP	Deposit		7 000	10 500
31/03	INT	Interest on credit balance		150	10 650
31/03	BC	Bank charges	200		10 450
31/03		***Month end balance***			***10 450***

You are required to:

a) Compare the cash journals of Bright Life for March 20X6 with the bank statement for March 20X6 and identify the differences between them.

b) Prepare the journal entries to record the bank-initiated transactions in the accounting records of Bright Life and then post the journal entries to the bank account in the general ledger.

c) Complete the bank reconciliation statement at 31 March 20X6.

Solution: Mechanics of a bank reconciliation

As mentioned above, the first step in preparing a bank reconciliation is to compare the entries in the cash journals with those on the bank statement. The relevant columns have been reproduced below for explanation purposes and ease of reference.

a) Comparison of cash journals and bank statements

CRJ Bank		*Bank statement Cr*		*CPJ Bank*		*Bank statement Dr*	
25 000	✓	25 000	✓	2 500	✗		
5 600	✓	5 600	✓	4 500	✗		
				1 800	✗	2 500	✗
5 800	✓			19 000	✗	4 500	✗
		5 800	✓	6 000	✗		
7 000	✓			500	***o/s chq***	1 800	✗
2 250	***o/s dep***			5 000	***o/s chq***	19 000	✗
45 650		1 500	***Direct credit***	39 300			
Debit GL 150				***Credit GL 150***		600	***Direct debit***
			7 000	✓		6 000	✗
			150	***Direct credit***			
						200	***Direct debit***

A ✓ symbol is used here to identify common entries in the cash receipts journal and the credit column on the bank statement. The amount of C2 250 appearing in the cash receipts journal and not on the bank statement is noted as an *outstanding deposit.* Amounts of C1 500 and C150 appearing on the bank statement and not in the cash receipts journal are noted as *direct credits.*

A ✗ symbol is used to compare the cash payments journal with the debit column on the bank statement. The amounts of C500 and C5 000 appearing in the cash payments journal and not on the bank statement are noted as *outstanding cheques.* Amounts of C600 and C200 appearing on the bank statement and not in the cash payments journal are noted as *direct debits.*

To ensure that all the differences have been identified, the following analysis can be done before the journal entries are processed in the entity's records, and before the bank reconciliation is prepared.

Date	*Description*	*Entity's records*	*Bank's records*
31/03/X6	Balance	6 350	10 450
25/03/X6	Electronic transfer – Ometer	1 500	
25/03/X6	Direct debit – insurance	(600)	
31/03/X6	Interest income	150	
31/03/X6	Bank charges	(200)	
31/03/X6	Outstanding deposit		
31/03/X6	Outstanding cheques		2 250
	– 0006		(500)
	– 0007		(5 000)
	Reconciled balance	7 200	7 200

The second step is to enter the direct debits and credits identified in the first step into the journal of Bright Life and to post the entries to the general ledger. Only the bank account in the general ledger is shown here.

b) Journal entries and bank account in general ledger

GENERAL JOURNAL OF BRIGHT LIFE

Date	*Description*	*Fol*	*Dr*	*Cr*
25/03/X6	Bank		1 500	
	Accounts receivable control			1 500
	Ometer			*1 500*
	Electronic payment received from Ometer			
25/03/X6	Bank		150	
	Interest income			150
	Interest earned on credit balance			
25/03/X6	Insurance expense		600	
	Bank			600
	Insurance direct debit			
25/03/X6	Bank charges		200	
	Bank			200
	March bank charges			

Dr **Bank (GL150)** *Cr*

Date	*Details*	*Fol*	*C*	*Date*	*Details*	*Fol*	*C*
20X6				20X6			
31/03	Balance	b/d	6 350	25/03	Insurance (debit order)	GJ	600
25/03	Accounts receivable (EFT)	GJ	1 500	31/03	Bank charges	GJ	200
31/03	Interest income	GJ	150	31/03	Balance	c/d	7 200
			8 000				8 000
01/04	Balance	b/d	7 200				

The third and final step is to prepare the bank reconciliation. It is normally prepared by starting with the ***adjusted*** balance as per the bank account in the entity's general ledger, and reconciling to the balance on the bank statement. It may also be prepared by reconciling from the balance on the bank statement to the ***adjusted*** balance in the general ledger. Both presentation formats are shown below.

In order to understand the bank reconciliation, remember the *purpose is not to make the bank account balance equal the bank statement balance*. Rather, it is to *explain and set out the reasons for the bank account balance and bank statement balance not being equal.*

c) Bank reconciliation

BRIGHT LIFE
BANK RECONCILIATION AT 31/03/X6

		C	*C*
Balance per bank account			7 200
Add	Outstanding cheques		5 500
	0006	500	
	0007	5 000	
Less	Outstanding deposits		(2 250)
	31/03	2 250	
Balance per bank statement			10 450

The balance per the bank account of C7 200 is the balance after the bank-initiated debits and credits have been journalised and posted to the general ledger. The outstanding cheques of C5 500 are added because the bank has not yet paid them. Conversely, the outstanding deposit is subtracted as the bank has not yet processed it.

Alternatively, the bank reconciliation may be prepared by reconciling from the balance on the bank statement to the adjusted balance in the general ledger.

BRIGHT LIFE
BANK RECONCILIATION AT 31/03/X6

		C	*C*
Balance per bank statement			10 450
Less	Outstanding cheques		(5 500)
	0006	500	
	0007	5 000	
Add	Outstanding deposits		2 250
	31/03	2 250	
Balance per bank account			7 200

When reconciling from the bank statement balance to the entity's records, the outstanding cheques are subtracted, as the entity has already recorded the cheques as payments. Conversely, the outstanding deposits are added because the entity has recorded the deposits as receipts.

Example: Mechanics of a bank reconciliation – subsequent month and an overdraft situation

The bank reconciliation performed in the previous example was for the first month of operations of Bright Life. There are certain additional considerations to take into account when preparing a bank reconciliation in subsequent months. The following are the relevant extracts of the cash journals, bank account and bank statement of Bright Life for April 20X6. The information recorded in the books of Bright Life has been recorded correctly.

Cash receipts journal – April 20X6 **CRJ 3**

Date	*Doc*	*Account name*	*Fol*	*Sales*	*Accounts receivable control*	*Sundries*	*Allowance for settlement discount*	*Analysis*	*Bank*
04/04	REC 03	Barons	DL 09		6 000		300	5 700	5 700
10/04	CSS 05	Cash sales		9 000				9 000	
10/04	CSS 06	Cash sales		3 000				3 000	12 000
15/04	REC 04	Promo Trade	DL 26		1 000			1 000	1 000
25/04	CSS 07	Cash sales		6 300				6 300	
25/04	REC 05	Linus	DL 74		8 000			8 000	14 300
30/04	CSS 08	Cash sales		500				500	500
				18 800	15 000		300		33 500
				Cr GL: Sales	Cr GL: AR control	Cr Individual accounts	Dr GL: ASD		Dr GL: Bank

Cash payments journal – April 20X6 **CPJ 6**

Doc	*Date*	*Details*	*Fol*	*Purchases*	*Salaries*	*Accounts payable control*	*Sundries*	*Allowance for settlement discount*	*Bank*
0008	01/04	Rent	GL 80				2 500		2 500
0009	04/04	EFT cash purchases		9 000					9 000
0010	11/04	Lights and water	GL 83				1 800		1 800
0011	14/04	Repairs	GL 87				900		900
0012	22/04	Swift Supplies	CL 63			28 000		700	27 300
0013	25/04	EFT salaries			6 000				6 000
0014	29/04	Telephone	GL 85				700		700
				9 000	6 000	28 000	5 900	700	48 200
				Dr GL: Purchases	Dr GL: Salaries	Dr GL: AP control	Dr Individual accounts	Cr GL: ASD	Cr GL: Bank

Bank (GL150)

Dr							*Cr*
Date	*Details*	*Fol*	*C*	*Date*	*Details*	*Fol*	*C*
20X6				20X6			
01/04	Balance	b/d	7 200	30/04	Payments	CPJ 6	48 200
30/04	Deposits	CRJ 3	33 500				
30/04	Balance	c/d	7 500				
			48 200				48 200
				01/05	Balance	b/d	7 500

BB

Limited

Thames Business Park
Valley Road
SW6 3DP

The Brall Bank
Reg. No. 56 00574/12
☎ 402-6308

CURRENT ACCOUNT STATEMENT
30 April 20X6

Bright Life
River Road
Exeter
EX1 2AM

Date	*Doc #*	*Details*	*Dr*	*Cr*	*Balance*
01/04		***Balance brought forward***			***10 450***
01/04	DEP	Deposit		2 250	12 700
03/04	0006	Cheque	500		12 200
04/04	0008	Cheque	2 500		9 700
04/04	DEP	Deposit		5 700	15 400
11/04	DEP	Deposit		12 000	27 400
12/04	0009	EFT payment	9 000		18 400

13/04	0010	Cheque	1 800		16 600
15/04	DEP	Deposit		1 000	17 600
15/04	0011	Cheque	900		16 700
16/04	RD	Cheque – refer to drawer	1 000		15 700
25/04	DO	Direct debit – insurance	600		15 100
25/04	0012	Cheque	27 300		−12 200
27/04	DEP	Deposit		13 400	1 200
27/04	0013	EFT payment	6 000		– 4 800
30/04	INT	Interest on credit balance		50	– 4 750
30/04	INT	Interest charged	10		– 4 760
30/04	BC	Bank charges	250		– 5 010
30/04		***Month end balance***			***– 5 010***

You are required to:

a) Compare the cash journals of Bright Life for April 20X6 with the bank statement for April 20X6 and identify the differences between them.

b) Prepare the journal entries to record the bank-initiated transactions in the accounting records of Bright Life and to post the journal entries to the bank account in the general ledger.

c) Complete the bank reconciliation at 30 April 20X6.

Solution: Mechanics of a bank reconciliation – subsequent month and an overdraft situation

To avoid repetition, only those aspects which were not addressed in the first example are explained here. Again, the relevant columns from the cash journals and bank statement have been reproduced below for explanation purposes and ease of reference.

a) Comparison of cash journals and bank statements

CRJ Bank		*Bank Statement Cr*		*CPJ Bank*		*Bank statement Dr*	
5 700	✓	2 250	*	2 500	✗	500	*
				9 000	✗	2 500	✗
12 000	✓			1 800	✗		
1 000	✓	5 700	✓	900	✗		
		12 000	✓	27 300	✗	9 000	✗
14 300	✓			6 000	✗	1 800	✗
500	*o/s dep*			700	*o/s chg*		
33 500		1 000	✓	48 200		900	✗
Debit GL 150				*Credit GL 150*		1 000	*Direct debit*
						600	*Direct debit*
						27 300	✗
		13 400	*(Bank error)*			6 000	✗
						10	*Direct debit*
		50	*Direct credit*			250	*Direct debit*

The two entries marked with an asterisk (*) appear on the April bank statement but not in the cash journals for April. The question that needs to be asked is how a deposit and a cheque payment can appear on the bank statement without being recorded in the cash journals. There are two possibilities. Either an error has been made by the reporting entity or by the bank, or the deposit and cheque payment were recorded in the cash journals in a previous month. In this case, the cheque of C500 and the deposit for C2 250 were recorded in the cash journals in March, and were both listed as 'outstanding' on the March bank reconciliation. As they were both processed by the bank during April, they are no longer outstanding. However, if a reconciling item in one month is not processed by the bank in the following month, that item will again appear on future bank reconciliations until it is processed by the bank.

As was done for the previous example, the following analysis is prepared as proof that all the differences have been taken into account.

Date	*Description*	*Entity's records*	*Bank's records*
30/04/X6	Balance	(7 500)	(5 010)
16/04/X6	RD cheque	(1 000)	
25/04/X6	Direct debit – Insurance	(600)	
27/04/X6	Bank error on deposit		900
30/04/X6	Interest income	50	
30/04/X6	Interest expense	(10)	
30/04/X6	Bank charges	(250)	
30/04/X6	Outstanding deposit		500
	Outstanding cheques		
	– 0007		(5 000)
	– 0014		(700)
	Reconciled balance	(9 310)	(9 310)

b) Journal entries and bank account in general ledger

GENERAL JOURNAL OF BRIGHT LIFE

Date	*Description*	*Fol*	*Dr*	*Cr*
16/04/X6	Accounts receivable control		1 000	
	Promo Trade		*1 000*	
	Bank			1 000
	Promo Trade cheque payment returned			
25/04/X6	Insurance		600	
	Bank			600
	Insurance direct debit			
30/04/X6	Interest expense		10	
	Bank			10
	Interest charged on debit balance			
30/04/X6	Bank charges		250	
	Bank			250
	April bank charges			
30/04/X6	Bank		50	
	Interest income			50
	Interest earned on credit balance			

Dr				**Bank (GL150)**			*Cr*
Date	*Details*	*Fol*	*C*	*Date*	*Details*	*Fol*	*C*
20X6				20X6			
30/04	Interest income	GJ	50	30/04	Balance	b/d	7 500
				16/04	Accounts receivable control	GJ	1 000
				25/04	Insurance	GJ	600
				30/04	Interest expense	GJ	10
30/04	Balance		9 310	30/04	Bank charges	GJ	250
			9 360				9 360
				01/05	Balance	b/d	9 310

c) Bank reconciliation

BRIGHT LIFE
BANK RECONCILIATION AT 30/04/X6

			C	C
Balance per bank account				(9 310)
Add	Outstanding cheques			5 700
	0007		5 000	
	0014		700	
Less	Outstanding deposits			(500)
	30/04		500	
Less	*Bank error*			(900)
	27/04 deposit	(14 300 − 13 400)	900	
Balance per bank statement				(5 010)

The bank error arose when Brall Bank credited the account of Bright Life with an amount of C13 400 when the amount actually deposited was C14 300. In other words, the bank has understated Bright Life's account by C900. If you think back to the purpose of the bank reconciliation, you will recall that it is not to make the balance in the entity's records equal the balance on the bank statement, but to set out the reasons why they are not equal. Therefore, as the bank statement balance is understated, the error of C900 must be subtracted when reconciling from the balance per the bank account in Bright Life's general ledger to the balance according to the statement from Brall Bank.

You will notice that the balance of C9 310 in Bright Life's bank account is a credit balance, representing an overdraft. On the bank reconciliation, this is shown in brackets as a negative number.

Pause and reflect ...

The bank statement in the above example reflected a debit entry on 16 April with the details 'refer to drawer'. What do you think this might be?

Response

A customer (in this case, Promo Trade) had paid the amount owing to Bright Life by issuing a cheque for C1 000 that Bright Life deposited on 15 April. This transaction was recorded in the cash receipts journal for April with the posting resulting in a debit to bank and a credit to the accounts receivable control account (as well as Promo Trade's account in the accounts receivable subsidiary ledger). When Brall Bank (Bright Life's bank) presented this cheque for payment through the clearing system, Promo Trade's bank would have responded that Promo Trade did not have sufficient funds in its account to make the payment. The cheque would then have been sent back to Bright Life with the April bank statement marked R/D (refer to drawer). In the process of preparing the bank reconciliation at the end of April, Bright Life reverses the entry made when the cheque was deposited by debiting the accounts receivable control (and Promo Trade's account in the accounts receivable subsidiary ledger) and credits bank.

Example: Bank reconciliation in successive month

The following information was obtained from the bank statements and cash journals of Bright Life for the two months ended 30 September and 31 October 20X6.

The cash journals are correct.

Cheques drawn in September		1 600
Cheques paid by the bank in September	1 460	
Cheques paid by the bank in October	80	
Cheques not yet presented for payment	60	
Cheques drawn in October		2 330
Cheques paid by the bank in October	2 160	
Cheques not yet presented for payment	170	
Deposits made in September		2 080
Deposits credited by the bank in September	1 960	
Deposits credited by the bank in October	120	
Deposits made in October		2 150
Deposits credited by the bank in October	2 000	
Deposits credited by the bank in November	150	
Bank charges		60
Bank charges debited by the bank in September	15	
Bank charges debited by the bank in October	45	

Another person's cheque for C65 was paid by the bank and debited to Bright Life's account in error in September, but reversed in the bank's records in October. The balance in the bank as per the bank statement at 30 September was C200.

You are required to:

a) Prepare the bank reconciliation at 30 September 20X6.
b) Draw up the bank account in the ledger of Bright Life for the month of October 20X6.
c) Prepare the bank reconciliation at 31 October 20X6.

Solution: Bank reconciliation in successive months

a) Bank reconciliation

BRIGHT LIFE
BANK RECONCILIATION AT 30/09/X6

		C	*C*
Balance per bank statement			200
Add	Bank error		65
	Cheque incorrectly debited	65	
Less	Cheques not yet presented		(140)
	(80 + 60)	140	
Add	Deposits not yet credited		120
	September deposit credited by bank in October	120	
Balance per bank account			245

b) Bank account in general ledger for October

Dr				*Bank*			*Cr*
Date	*Details*	*Fol*	*C*	*Date*	*Details*	*Fol*	*C*
20X6				20X6			
01/10	Balance	b/d	245	31/10	Payments	CPJ	2 330
31/10	Deposits	CRJ	2 150	31/10	Bank charges	GJ	45
				31/10	Balance	c/d	20
			2 395				2 395
01/11	Balance	b/d	20				

c) Bank reconciliation

BRIGHT LIFE
BANK RECONCILIATION AT 31/10/X6

		C	*C*
Balance per bank account			20
Add	Cheques not yet presented		230
	September	60	
	October	170	
Add	Deposits not yet credited		(150)
	October deposit credited by bank in November	150	
Balance per bank statement			100

 **Revision example**

The Cup Cake has a store that offers coffee and cupcakes to customers in the store as well as supplying cupcakes by order. The following is a correct list of the differences between the bank account in the ledger and the bank statement of The Cup Cake on 30 April 20X1.

	C
Deposit not credited by the bank	3 750
Outstanding cheques	210
106	128
128	328
133	

Cheque no 8322, drawn by the owner on his personal bank account for C2 861, was debited by the bank to the business bank account in error.

A month later, on 31 May 20X1, the bookkeeper identified the following factors which he considered relevant:

1 Of the outstanding cheques at 30 April 20X1, cheques no 128 and 133 appeared on the May bank statement.
2 The error made by the bank involving the owner's personal cheque had not yet been corrected.
3 The following cheques issued in May had not been presented for payment:
   – 210 for C400.
   – 234 for C1 536.
4 No entries appeared in the May cash journals to record the following which did appear on the May bank statement:
   a) A direct debit for an insurance premium of C500 paid by the bank on 15 May 20X1.
   b) A cheque for C651 from a customer in payment of her account which was returned by the bank marked 'R/D'.
   c) Interest on overdraft C50.
   d) Service fees C54.
5 A deposit of C8 261 on 28 May 20X1 (in respect of amounts received from debtors), correctly reflected on the bank statement, had been entered in the cash receipts journal as C8 621.
6 There were no outstanding deposits at 31 May 20X1.
7 The opening balance on the bank account in the ledger at 1 May 20X1 was C2 500 credit.
8 The bank statement for May 20X1 reflected a closing debit balance of C3 280.

You are required to:

a) Prepare a bank reconciliation at 31 May 20X1.
b) Complete the bank account in the ledger in as much detail as is possible, based on the information given.

 **Solution: Revision example**

Working – Bank balance before adjustment

31 May	Balance per bank statement – overdraft		(3 280)
	April cheque outstanding	(210)	
	Error by bank	2 861	
	May cheques outstanding (400 + 1 536)	(1 936)	
	Standing orders not entered	500	
	R/D cheque	651	
	Charges not entered (54 + 50)	104	
	Deposit error (8 621 – 8 261)	360	2 330
31 May	Balance per ledger		(950)

a) Bank reconciliation

THE CUP CAKE
BANK RECONCILIATION AT 31 MAY 20X1

		C	C
Balance per bank statement			(3 280)
Less	Cheques outstanding		(2 146)
	106	210	
	210	400	
	234	1 536	
Add	Error by bank		2 861
Balance per bank account			(2 565)

b) Bank account in general ledger

Dr **Bank (GL150)** *Cr*

Date	*Details*	*Fol*	*C*	*Date*	*Details*	*Fol*	*C*
				20X1 31 May	Balance	b/d	950
					Accounts receivable	GJ	360
					Interest	GJ	50
					Bank charges	GJ	54
					Accounts receivable	GJ	651
31 May	Balance	c/d	2 565		Insurance	GJ	500
			2 565				2 565
				01 June	Balance	b/d	2 565

Bibliography

Barclaycard Freedom Rewards. https://www.barclaycard.co.uk/personal/freedom-rewards?WT.mc_id=C021L011N91&WT.tsrc=DirectPartners&TC=MSE0720001&mpch=ads (Accessed 15 September 2016).

Chu, E. *The Fraud Examiner: Using Cash Control to Detect and Prevent Fraud*. Association of Certified Fraud Examiners. www.acfe.com/fraud-examiner.aspx?id=4294973010 (Accessed 1 July 2014).

Cressey, DR. 1973. *Other People's Money*. Montclair, NJ: Patterson Smith, 30.

Weil, S. 1989. *Accounting Skills: A Guide to the Mastery of Elementary Accounting*. Cape Town, South Africa: Juta, 73.

14 Accounts payable

Business focus

When you walk into a supermarket and see the thousands of items on the shelves, have you ever stopped to think about where those items came from and who the suppliers are? A company's relationship with its suppliers extends beyond buying the goods and paying the amount owing each month, and has much wider social responsibility implications.

Sainsbury's, the second largest supermarket chain in the United Kingdom, has over 23 million customer transactions each week, employs around 157 000 people and works with over 2 000 suppliers in over 70 countries. Sainsbury's invests a large amount of resources in managing its significant economic, social and environmental value chain.

The company has a close and longstanding relationship with its suppliers. It operates ten development groups for farmers and growers across dairy, beef, pork, lamb, veal, eggs, chicken, cheese and wheat and has invested over £40 million in these groups since 2006. The company also works with over 2 200 British farmers and has invested over £40 million in their British Farmer Development Groups since 2006 to promote and support good animal welfare and improve environmental and ethical standards.

In this chapter

Most entities show one amount for 'payables' on the face of their statement of financial position, usually described as 'trade and other payables'. This normally includes amounts owing to suppliers for goods purchased on credit as well as other amounts owing by the entity such as rent or interest payable (often known collectively as 'other payables'). The focus of this chapter is on ***accounts payable***, also known as ***trade payables*** or ***creditors.***

Dashboard

- Look at the *Learning outcomes* so that you know what you should be able to do after studying this chapter.
- Read the *Business focus* to place this chapter's contents in a real-world context.
- Preview *In this chapter* to focus your mind on the contents of the chapter.
- Read the *text* in detail.
    - Apply your mind to the *Pause and reflect* scenarios.
    - A key aspect of this chapter is the reconciliation of suppliers' statements and the preparation of a remittance advice, covered in Section 14.3.

- Prepare solutions to the examples as you read through the chapter.
- Prepare a solution to the *Revision example* at the end of the chapter without reference to the suggested one. Compare your solution to the suggested solution provided.

Learning outcomes

After studying this chapter, you should be able to do the following:

1 Describe the nature of accounts payable.
2 Classify liabilities.
3 Prepare a supplier's reconciliation statement.

Accounts payable

14.1 The nature of accounts payable

The purchase of goods and services on credit forms an integral part of economic activity, and many business entities have a large number of suppliers from whom they buy on credit. When goods are purchased on credit, the incurrence of a cost of sales expense and the payment of cash will not correspond. The accrual concept requires the expense to be recognised in the period when the goods are sold and not when the cash is paid. You learnt in Chapter 8, *Purchase and sale transactions,* about how to account for the purchase of goods on credit and the subsequent payment of cash.

You also learnt in Chapter 9, *Analysis journals*, about how to maintain an accounts payable subsidiary ledger along with the accounts payable control account in the general ledger. Remember that the equality of the accounting equation is maintained in the general ledger. The balances on the accounts payable subsidiary ledger are not included on the trial balance, as the subsidiary ledger serves only as a supplementary record of detailed information concerning each supplier.

The accounts payable are a liability. They represent an obligation of the entity (the obligation to pay an amount to a supplier) from a past event (the credit purchase), which is expected to result in an outflow of economic benefits (the payment of cash to the supplier).

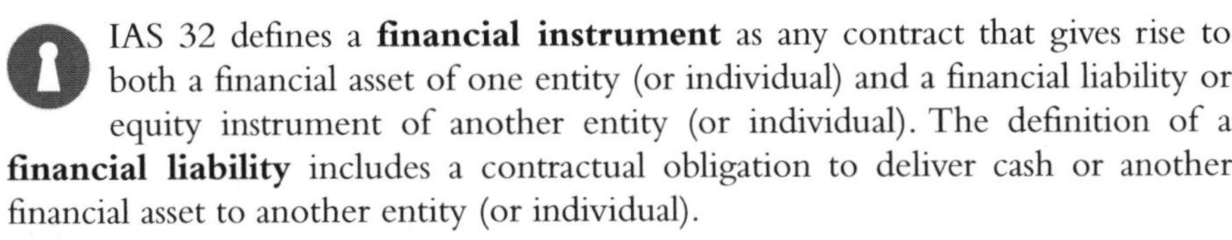

IAS 32 defines a **financial instrument** as any contract that gives rise to both a financial asset of one entity (or individual) and a financial liability or equity instrument of another entity (or individual). The definition of a **financial liability** includes a contractual obligation to deliver cash or another financial asset to another entity (or individual).

You were introduced to the definition of a financial asset in Chapter 12, *Accounts receivable*. A financial asset includes cash or a contractual right to receive cash or another financial asset from another entity (or individual).

Pause and reflect ...

On 5 January 20X5, Smart Concepts purchases stationery of C5 000 from a supplier. If the stationery is purchased on credit and the supplier agrees to accept a laptop computer valued at C5 000 in settlement of the amount owing:

a) does Smart Concepts recognise a liability?
b) if yes, is it a financial liability?

Response

a) Smart Concepts recognises a liability as it has an obligation to settle the amount owing to the supplier as a result of the purchase of the stationery on 5 January 20X5. The laptop is an asset of the business, therefore giving it to the supplier represents an outflow of economic benefits.
b) The liability is not a financial liability as Smart Concepts does not have an obligation to deliver cash or another financial asset.

There must be a contractual relationship between parties for a financial instrument to exist, thus liabilities which are not contractual in nature, such as amounts owing to the tax authority that are created as a result of statutory requirements, are not financial liabilities.

Note also that liabilities for payments received in advance are not financial liabilities as the obligation is to provide goods or services, and not cash or another financial asset.

The importance of identifying a financial liability relates to risk and the measurement of its fair value. These issues are beyond the scope of this text.

14.2 Classification of accounts payable

Current liabilities such as accounts payable and expenses payable are normally settled within 12 months of the financial reporting date. However, such items are classified as current liabilities even if they are due to be settled after more than 12 months from the financial reporting date, as they form part of the working capital used in the normal operating cycle of the business.

The distinction between non-current and current liabilities was addressed in Chapter 6, *Preparation and presentation of financial statements*.

IAS 1 requires an entity to classify a liability as current when:

- it expects to settle the liability in its normal operating cycle; or
- it holds the liability primarily for the purposes of trading; or
- the liability is due to be settled within 12 months after the reporting period; or
- the entity does not have an unconditional right to defer settlement of the liability for at least 12 months after the reporting period.

All other liabilities are classified as non-current.

Pause and reflect . . .

How would you classify accounts payable that are not expected to be settled within 12 months of the financial reporting date?

Response

Accounts payable not expected to be realised within 12 months of the financial reporting date should be classified as a current liability. This is because the raising of this liability and its subsequent payment is part of the entity's operating cycle.

Concepts in context

J Sainsbury plc
Extract from notes to consolidated financial statements for the 52 weeks ended 15 March 2014

	£m
Trade and other payables	
Trade payables	1 846
Other payables	590
Accruals and deferred income	256
	2 692

What concepts in context can you see here?

Sainsbury's discloses one amount, £2 692 million, as a current liability for trade and other payables on the face of the statement of financial position. This is supported by a note, which shows the breakdown of this amount. As discussed in this chapter, the trade payables are the accounts payable or creditors. Note also that there is a line item for accruals and deferred income. You should know from earlier chapters that this represents the expenses payable and the income received in advance.

Sainsbury's is the second largest supermarket chain in the United Kingdom and is headquartered in London.

Source: www.j-sainsbury.co.uk/media/2064053/sainsbury_s_annual_report_and_accounts_13-14.pdf (Accessed 1 October 2014).

14.3 Supplier's reconciliation statement

The accounts that an entity has with its suppliers are the most common and recurring of its current liabilities. Transactions are entered into on a daily basis with payments being made to the supplier at regular intervals. Since the volume of transactions is numerous, it is usual for the accounts to be checked against the suppliers' statements for correctness before payments are made. We will be looking at the purpose of and procedures for preparing a supplier's reconciliation in the following sections.

14.3.1 Purpose of a supplier's reconciliation statement

Each month, suppliers send statements to their customers indicating transactions for the month and the balance owing at the end of the month. Before the customer pays the account, the statement needs to be checked for correctness. There may be timing differences and errors. If such discrepancies arise, a reconciliation statement should be prepared. The details of the differences will be indicated on a ***remittance advice***, to be sent to the supplier at the time payment is made.

The purpose of a supplier's reconciliation statement is therefore to reconcile the amount owing to the supplier, as reflected in the supplier's account in the accounts payable subsidiary ledger, with the amount owing to the supplier, as reflected on the supplier's statement.

The supplier's reconciliation statement then becomes the remittance advice and informs the supplier how the firm arrived at the amount of the payment.

14.3.2 Reconciliation procedure

The preparation of a supplier's reconciliation statement involves two distinct steps:

1 Identification of errors and omissions in the accounting records of the reporting entity from the information in the supplier's statements that require adjustments by means of journal entries.
2 Identification of errors and omissions on the supplier's statement. These discrepancies result in a difference between the amount claimed by the supplier on the statement and the remittance to be made to the supplier. The business communicates the reasons for this difference to the supplier on a remittance advice, which accompanies the payment to the supplier. A remittance advice begins with the balance on the supplier's statement. If this figure is not given, the balance on the supplier's statement must first be calculated. Discount claimed from a supplier is also shown on the remittance advice.

Example: Supplier's reconciliation statement and remittance advice

Bright Life receives the following statement from Suppliers Limited, a wholesaler of home entertainment products, at the end of May 20X6:

Suppliers Limited

15 Eden Way
Edenglen
EX2 IFO

STATEMENT MAY 20X6

Date	*Doc #*	*Description*	*Dr*	*Cr*
			C	C
01/05	b/f	Balance	10 314	
01/05	C245	Credit note		114
08/05	S478	Invoice	2 708	
09/05	C314	Credit note		633
15/05	S528	Invoice	12 000	
18/05	P871	Payment		10 200
23/05	S574	Invoice	930	
24/05	C455	Credit note		50
28/05	S622	Invoice	11 833	
30/05	S789	Invoice	20 000	
31/05	c/f	Balance		36 788
			57 785	57 785

The Suppliers Limited ledger account in the accounts payable subsidiary ledger of Bright Life is as follows:

Dr		**SUPPLIERS LIMITED (GL 150)**					*Cr*
Date	*Details*	*Fol*	C	*Date*	*Details*	*Fol*	C
09/05	Inventory (credit note C314)		683	01/05	Balance	b/d	10 200
18/05	Bank		10 200	05/05	Inventory (invoice S478)		2 780
				15/05	Inventory (invoice S 528)		12 000
31/05	Balance	c/d	50 920	23/05	Inventory (invoice S574)		390
				24/05	Inventory (invoice C455)		50

				28/05	Inventory (invoice S622)		11 383
				30/05	Inventory (invoice S789)		25 000
			61 803				61 803
				01/06	Balance	b/d	50 920

On comparing the supplier's statement with the account in his records, Simon discovers the following:

1. Goods returned (credit note C455) to the value of C50 were entered in the accounting records as an invoice.
2. Goods purchased (invoice S574) for C930 were entered in the accounting records as C390.
3. Invoice S789 was subject to a trade discount of 20 per cent, which Bright Life did not take into account.
4. Credit note C245 relates to goods returned on 30 April 20X6.

In all other respects, the records of Bright Life are correct. Any further discrepancies are due to errors made by Suppliers Limited.

You are required to:

a) Prepare a remittance advice to send to Suppliers Limited on 18 June in full settlement of the amount outstanding at the end of May.
b) Prepare the journal entries to correct the errors in the accounting records of Bright Life (assume a perpetual inventory system is used).
c) Prepare Suppliers Limited's ledger account, starting with the balance of C50 920 as given, and post the journal entries as per (b) above.

Solution: Supplier's reconciliation statement and remittance advice

Workings

Doc #	*Description*		*The reporting entity (Bright Life)*	*The supplier (Suppliers Limited)*
Bal 31/05/X6	Closing balance		50 920	36 788
Invoice S478	Error on statement	(2 780 – 2 708)		72
Credit note C314	Error on statement	(683 – 633)		(50)
Invoice S574	Error on entry	(930 – 390)	540	
Credit note C455	Credit note entered as an invoice	(50 × 2)	(100)	
Invoice S622	Error on statement	(11 383 – 11 833)		(450)
Invoice S789	Trade discount		(5 000)	
Statement balance 31/05/X6	Error on statement due to casting	(C36 788 should be C46 788)		10 000
	Reconciled balance		46 360	46 360

To be able to answer the question, you may find it useful to reconcile the account. This is shown above by starting with the balance on Suppliers Limited's account in the accounting records of Bright Life in one column and the balance per Suppliers Limited's statement in another column. Any difference identified is then either a difference requiring adjustment in the records of Bright Life and therefore entered into the reporting entity's column, or it is an error in the records of Suppliers Limited and therefore entered into the supplier's column.

The errors in the reporting entity's column are then journalised in order to correct the balance in its accounting records. The journal entries need to be posted to the general ledger to correct the accounts payable control account, and to the accounts payable subsidiary ledger to correct the individual supplier's account.

The supplier needs to be notified of the errors in its account. These errors are the ones in the supplier's column of the supplier's reconciliation. To notify the supplier, the reporting entity prepares a remittance advice, which starts with the supplier's balance in the statement and adds and subtracts the errors from the balance to calculate the correct balance. If a discount is granted, this is deducted from the corrected balance before arriving at the amount to be paid to the supplier.

a) Remittance advice

BRIGHT LIFE
REMITTANCE ADVICE FOR ACCOUNT SUPPLIERS LIMITED
MAY 20X6

			C
Balance owing per your statement			36 788
Add	Error on invoice S478	(2 780 – 2 708)	72
	Casting error on statement		10 000
Less	Error on credit note C314	(683 – 633)	(50)
	Error on invoice S622	(11 833 – 11 383)	(450)
Our payment			46 360

b) Journal entries in accounting records of Bright Life

GENERAL JOURNAL OF BRIGHT LIFE

Date	*Description*	*Fol*	*Dr*	*Cr*
31/05	Accounts payable control (L)		100	
	Suppliers Limited		*100*	
	Inventory (A)			100
	Correction on credit note C455 entered as an invoice			
31/05	Inventory (A)		540	
	Accounts payable control (L)			540
	Suppliers Limited			*540*
	Correction on invoice S574 from Suppliers Limited			
31/05	Accounts payable control (L)		5 000	
	Suppliers Limited		*5 000*	
	Inventory (A)			5 000
	Correction on invoice S789 subject to trade discount			

c) Suppliers Limited ledger account in accounts payable subsidiary ledger

Dr			SUPPLIERS LIMITED				*Cr*
Date	*Details*	*Fol*	*C*	*Date*	*Details*	*Fol*	*C*
20X6				20X6			
31/05	Inventory		100	31/05	Balance	b/d	50 920
31/05	Inventory		5 000	31/05	Inventory		540
31/05	Balance	c/d	46 360				
			51 460				51 460
				01/06	Balance	b/d	46 360

Revision example

Healthy Hounds is a retail store specialising in good-quality healthy food for dogs. Healthy Hounds received a statement dated 31 May 20X0 from Epol Suppliers, which allows Healthy Hounds a 10 per cent trade discount on all transactions. Healthy Hounds uses a perpetual inventory system.

The statement received from Epol Suppliers reflected a debit balance of C19 031. The balance reflected in Healthy Hounds' ledger at 31 May 20X0 was C13 940.

When the account in the ledger was compared with Epol Suppliers' statement, the following discrepancies were noted. All invoices referred to below are stated net of trade discount, unless otherwise specified:

1 The credit side of the statement had been undercast by C1 570.
2 Invoice 2767 for a gross amount of C450 had been entered in the purchases journal as C504.
3 Credit note 223 for C125 was correctly recorded in the accounts payable subsidiary ledger, but was entered as an invoice on the statement.
4 Invoice 2863 for C432 was recorded in the purchases journal correctly, but entered in the accounts payable subsidiary ledger as if it were a credit note.
5 Invoice 2811 for a gross amount of C760 was entered on the statement as C648.
6 Invoice 2770 for C882 was incorrectly posted to Husky Traders, another of Healthy Hound's suppliers.
7 Invoice 2796 for C900 was debited twice on the statement.
8 During May, Epol Suppliers purchased goods from Healthy Hounds for C300. It was agreed that this amount should be deducted from the amount Healthy Hounds owes Epol Suppliers. Healthy Hounds entered this set-off in their accounting records, but Epol Suppliers' statement did not reflect this transaction.
9 The statement reflects invoice 2902 for C460. Healthy Hounds' goods-received note indicates that the goods were received on 31 May 20X0. The invoice was received only on 2 June 20X0.

You are required to:

a) Prepare the remittance advice to accompany the payment from Healthy Hounds to Epol Suppliers (to reach them before 30 June 20X0). All details of discount calculations must appear on the remittance advice.

b) Prepare the necessary journal entries to correct any mistakes in Healthy Hounds' accounting records. Control accounts are maintained.

Solution: Revision example

Workings

Doc #	*Description*		*The reporting entity (Healthy Hounds)*	*The supplier (Epol Suppliers)*
31/05/X0	Closing balance		13 940	19 031
1	Credit side of statement undercast			(1 570)
2	Error on entry of invoice 2767	(504 – 405)	(99)	
3	Credit note 223 entered as an invoice			(250)
4	Invoice 2863 recorded as a credit note		864	
5	Error on statement invoice 2811	(684 – 648)		36
6	Invoice 2770 posted to wrong account		882	
7	Invoice 2796 on statement twice			(900)
8	Goods purchased from Healthy Hounds set off			(300)
9	Invoice 2902 not recorded in accounting records		460	
31/05/X0	Reconciled balance		16 047	16 047

a) Remittance advice

HEALTHY HOUNDS
REMITTANCE ADVICE FOR ACCOUNT EPOL SUPPLIERS
MAY 20X0

Balance owing per your statement			19 031
Add	Error on invoice 2811 (684 – 648)	36	36
Less	Credit side of statement undercast	1 570	
	Credit note 223 entered as an invoice	250	
	Invoice 2796 on statement twice	900	
	Goods purchased from Healthy Hounds set off	300	(3 020)
Payment			16 047

b) Journal entries in Healthy Hounds records

Date	*Description*	*Fol*	*Dr*	*Cr*
31/05/X0	Accounts payable control (L)		99	
	Epol Suppliers		*99*	
	Purchases (T)/inventory (A)			99
	Invoice 2767 incorrectly entered			
	(450 gross × 0.90 = 405 net) (504 – 405 = 99)			

31/05/X0	*Epol Suppliers* *Invoice 2863 posted as a credit note in the subsidiary ledger*			*864*
31/05/X0	*Husky Traders* *Epol Suppliers* *Invoice 2770 posted to the incorrect account in the subsidiary ledger*		*882*	 *882*
31/05/X0	Purchases(T)/inventory (A) Accounts payable control (L) *Epol Suppliers* *Invoice 2902 omitted*		460	 460 *460*

Bibliography

J Sainsbury plc. 2104. *Annual Report and Financial Statements*. www.j-sainsbury.co.uk/media/1616189/sainsburys_ara.pdf (Accessed 1 October 2014).
The International Accounting Standards Board. 2010. *The Conceptual Framework*.
The International Accounting Standards Board. 2012. IAS 1 *Presentation of Financial Statements*.
The International Accounting Standards Board. 2014. IAS 32 *Financial Instruments: Presentation*.

15 Owner's equity and non-current liabilities

Business focus

Crowdfunding is a recent practice of funding a business entity by raising funds from a large number of people, normally via the internet. It is a way of raising finance by asking a large number of people for a small amount of funds. Until recently, finance for a new business idea involved asking a few people for large sums of money. Crowdfunding switches this idea around, using the internet to make contact with hundreds of thousands of potential funders. Typically, those seeking funds will set up a profile of their project on a recognised crowdfunding website. Much like traditional forms of finance, there is equity and debt crowdfunding.

With equity crowdfunding, people invest in a business entity in return for an equity share in the business. Cash is exchanged for shares or a small stake in the business entity. As with traditional equity funding, if the entity is successful, the value goes up; if not, it goes down.

With debt crowdfunding, lenders will receive their money back with interest. This allows for the lending of money while bypassing traditional banks. Lenders earn a financial return, but also benefit by having contributed to the success of an idea they believe in.

There is also a form of crowdfunding referred to as reward crowdfunding. People invest simply because they believe in the cause. Rewards are usually offered such as free gifts, tickets to events and acknowledgements. Reward crowd funders often have a personal motivation for contributing cash and expect no financial return other than having contributed to a venture they are passionate about.

In this chapter

The chapter includes a discussion of the costs of financing, repayment terms and security that may be offered in relation to funding from owners and lenders. For lenders, we focus on non-current liabilities, as current liabilities were addressed in Chapter 14, *Accounts payable*. The different components of equity for different entity forms are also discussed.

Owners of an entity need to know how their investment in the entity is faring. The owner's equity is the net worth of the entity. Increases in owner's equity are therefore also increases in the net worth of the entity. Knowing its net worth is particularly important if an owner wishes to dispose of his or her investment in the entity. Owners also need to know that the entity will be able to make regular returns to them, for example by way of dividends if the entity is a company or by way of distributions if the entity is a sole proprietorship.

Lenders who have advanced funding to an entity need to know that it will be able to pay the agreed interest and to make the agreed repayments of capital when they fall due.

Dashboard

- Look at the *Learning outcomes* so that you know what you should be able to do after studying this chapter.
- Read the *Business focus* to place this chapter's contents in a real-world context.
- Preview *In this chapter* to focus your mind on the contents of the chapter.
- Read the *text* in detail.
    - Pay attention to the definitions, and apply your mind to the *Pause and reflect* scenarios.
    - When reading about equity in the different entity forms in Section 15.3, relate what you already know about a sole proprietorship to the other entity forms.
    - Focus on comparing the nature of equity and liabilities as you read the chapter.
    - Prepare solutions to the examples as you read through the chapter.

Learning outcomes

After studying this chapter, you should be able to do the following:

1 Describe the sources of finance for a business entity.
2 Evaluate owner's equity as a form of finance.
3 Compare equity in the various entity forms.
4 Evaluate non-current liabilities as a form of finance.
5 Record accounting entries relating to non-current liabilities.

Owner's equity and non-current liabilities

15.1 Sources of finance

We learnt in Chapter 3, *The accounting equation and the analysis of transactions*, that a business entity is financed from two sources – funds provided by the owner and those provided by lenders. Funds provided by the owner are known as ***owner's equity*** and funds provided by lenders are known as ***liabilities***.

A business entity will raise finance in order to purchase assets. In general, non-current assets which are used for a long period of time should be financed by a long-term source of finance, such as owner's equity or non-current liabilities. On the other hand, current assets that will be used by the entity over a short period of time may be financed by a short-term source of finance, for example accounts payable or a bank overdraft. This chapter focuses on both of the following:

- owner's equity, specifically from the perspective of a sole proprietorship. It includes an introduction to the concept of equity of a partnership and a company;
- non-current liabilities.

15.2 Owner's equity as a form of finance

Equity is defined in the *Conceptual Framework*. You should remember the definition from Chapter 2, *Fundamental accounting concepts*:

Equity is the residual interest in the assets of the entity after deducting all its liabilities.

It includes both the funds invested in the business entity by the owner and the profit of the entity which has not been distributed to the owner. If you think back to the closing entry process in Chapter 7, *Closing entries*, you will remember that the profit is transferred to the owner's capital account after the income and expense items have been closed off to the profit or loss account. In addition, the distributions for the period are also closed off to the owner's capital account. Owner's equity is often referred to as the ***net worth*** of a business. When examining equity as a form of finance, it is appropriate to consider:

- the cost of the financing;
- the repayment terms;
- the security offered.

15.2.1 The cost of financing

The cost to a sole proprietorship of funds provided by the owner does not have a fixed cost, unlike for a non-current or long-term liability. The returns to the owner are represented by the entity's profit for the period, which is unlikely to equal the cash distributed to the owner. The amount distributed in cash depends on availability of cash resources and the extent to which cash is needed to finance future operations. As you are already aware, the distributions do not appear as an expense on the statement of profit or loss.

The sole proprietor who invests funds in a business takes the risk that the return on ownership interest will fluctuate from year to year. It is certainly more volatile than the return on a long-term loan where the interest rate is fixed. However, by bearing the higher risk, the sole proprietor also has the chance to achieve a higher return than the fixed return on a long-term loan.

 **Pause and reflect ...**

An owner of a business entity would like to recognise a distribution as an expense on the statement of profit or loss. By applying the definition of an expense in IAS 1, consider whether or not this is appropriate.

Response

Although the payment will result in an outflow of assets in the form of cash paid and will decrease equity, the definition of an expense in IAS 1 specifically excludes distributions to equity participants. Consequently, it is incorrect to recognise an expense in respect of the distribution.

15.2.2 The terms of repayment

The capital of the sole proprietor is not usually repaid until the activities of the business cease. There are few, if any, restrictions on the distribution to owners of amounts included in equity. It is important to bear in mind, however, that the owner and the business are the same legal entity and that the liabilities of the business cannot be avoided by simply withdrawing all the capital.

15.2.3 The security offered

As mentioned above, the individual who invests funds in a sole proprietorship is the ultimate risk bearer. On the cessation of business activities, the claims of liability holders take preference over the claim of the owner for the repayment of the amounts owing to him or her.

15.3 Equity in the different entity forms

The three forms of business entity identified in Chapter 1, *The accounting environment*, are the sole proprietorship, the partnership and the company. Parts I to IV of this book are concerned with the activities of a sole proprietorship. Processing data and producing year-end information are examined from the perspective of a sole proprietorship, as are the chapters dealing with the recognition and measurement of financial statement items. In Part V of this book, covering Chapters 16 and 17, we will explore the differences in accounting for the other entity forms. In these chapters, you will see that the major differences lie in the accounting for, and composition of, equity and in the allocation of profits to the owners. Most other items on the financial statements remain the same.

There is an accounting and legal relationship between the owner (or owners) and the business entity in each of the entity forms, which impacts upon the allocation of profit as

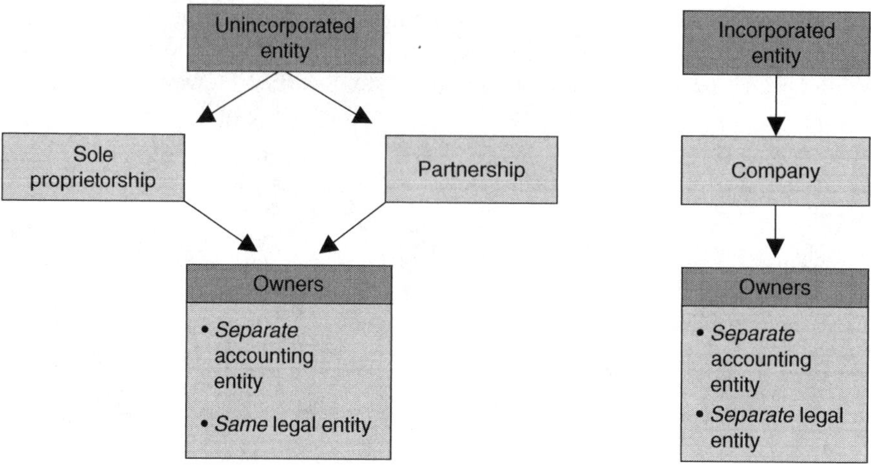

Diagram 15.1 Unincorporated and incorporated entities

well as the composition of equity. The accounting and legal relationship was described in Chapter 1 and is summarised in the following paragraph.

A sole proprietorship and a partnership can be referred to as ***unincorporated*** entities, whereas a company can be referred to as an ***incorporated*** entity. The owner of a sole proprietorship and the partners of a partnership are separate *accounting entities* from the business entity, but from a legal viewpoint, they are the same *legal entity*. The shareholders of a company are both *separate accounting* and *legal entities* from the business. The company is incorporated as a separate legal entity in terms of statute.

This can be represented as shown in Diagram 15.1.

Part V of this book, entitled *Entity forms*, deals with the accounting for partnerships and companies. Each chapter examines the specific accounting requirements of the different entity forms. Particular attention is given to the allocation of profit to the owners as well as the composition of equity. As an introduction, these aspects are addressed briefly in the remainder of this chapter.

15.3.1 Allocation of profit to the owners

Sole proprietorship

All the profits belong to the sole proprietor. The profit from the profit or loss account is allocated directly to equity – that is, to the capital account of the sole proprietor.

Partnership

The profit needs to be adjusted for unequal capital and labour contributions by the partners. The profit from the profit or loss account is transferred to an *appropriation* account where appropriations of profit are made to the partners' equity depending on the resources invested and services performed by each partner. The remaining profit is then also allocated to equity according to an agreed profit-sharing ratio.

Company

The profit earned also belongs to the business entity and only accrues to the owners (known as *shareholders*) when formally declared in the form of a dividend. The profit is transferred from the profit or loss account to a *retained earnings* account where dividends to shareholders are recorded.

15.3.2 Composition of owner's equity

The composition of owner's equity of a partnership and company is examined in detail in the following chapters. Table 15.1 provides a summary.

Table 15.1 Equity in different entity forms

Sole proprietorship	*Partnership*	*Company*
Capital account	Capital accounts Current accounts	Share capital Retained earnings Revaluation surplus

Pause and reflect ...

In Chapter 2, you were introduced to a statement of changes in equity for a sole proprietorship. What columns would you expect to see in a statement of changes in equity for a company?

Response

A statement of changes in equity for a company will have a column for each of the components of equity. The components of equity for a company are shown in Table 15.1. There will be columns for share capital and retained earnings and also a column for the revaluation surplus if any of the entity's assets have been revalued.

The statements of changes in equity for the partnership and company entity forms are discussed in more detail in the chapters dealing with these entity forms.

15.4 Non-current liabilities as a form of finance

According to IAS 1, a **non-current liability** is any liability that does not meet the definition of a current liability.

The definition of a **current liability** must therefore be used when deciding whether a liability is current or non-current. You have already seen this definition in previous chapters.

According to IAS 1, a liability is classified as a current liability when:

- it is due to be settled within 12 months after the end of the reporting period; *or*
- it holds the liability mainly for the purpose of trading; *or*
- it expects to settle the liability in its normal operating cycle; *or*
- the entity does not have an unconditional right to defer settlement of the liability for at least 12 months after the end of the reporting period.

Non-current liabilities include items such as long-term loans and loans secured by mortgage bonds. As with equity, there are three issues to examine when considering non-current liabilities:

- the cost of financing;
- the terms of repayment;
- the security offered to the lending institution.

We will examine each issue in turn.

15.4.1 The cost of financing

The cost of financing is the price paid to the lending institution for the use of the funds. The cost of financing is known as interest. The interest charged is payable to the lending institution at intervals determined by the terms agreed upon by the two parties. Interest charges are not dependent on an entity making a profit. Interest is an *expense* of the entity.

Nominal interest rate

The nominal interest rate is the rate at which interest will be paid on the ***nominal value*** or ***face value*** of the financial instrument. (The financial instrument is the contract that sets out the terms of the funding arrangement, as agreed by the lender and the borrower.)

Consider the situation where Smart Concepts is granted a loan facility of C300 000 by a financial institution on 1 January 20X7. Interest on the loan accrues at 6 per cent per annum, payable monthly in arrears. On 2 January 20X7, Smart Concepts utilised C100 000 of the loan facility. On 1 February 20X7, a further C150 000 was drawn against the loan facility. No further amounts were drawn or repaid during March 20X7. The interest expense for the three months ended 31 March 20X7 will be recorded as follows:

Assets		=	*Liabilities*	+	*Owner's equity*	
Bank					Interest expense	
+/L/Dr	−/R/Cr				+/L/Dr	−/R/Cr
	3 000				3 000	

GENERAL JOURNAL OF SMART CONCEPTS

Date	*Description*	*Fol*	*Dr*	*Cr*
31/03/X7	Interest (E) Bank (A) *Interest expense for the period*		3 000	3 000

The interest expense for the three months ended 31 March 20X7 is calculated by applying the nominal interest rate of 6 per cent to the amount of the loan utilised during the period. The interest expense is therefore calculated as 6 per cent of C100 000 for the period from 1 January 20X7 to 31 January 20X7, and 6 per cent of C250 000 in respect of the period from 1 February 20X7 to 31 March 20X7, which amounts to C3 000 ((C100 000 × 0.06 × 1/12) + (C250 000 × 0.06 × 2/12)). The interest expense will be increased by debiting the interest expense account. The other side of the entry is to decrease the asset, bank, by crediting the bank account.

Effective interest rate

The effective interest rate is the rate that, when used in a present value calculation, exactly discounts the expected future cash flows to equate to the initial carrying amount of the liability. The effective interest rate is the *internal rate of return* of the financial liability for the period of the contract.

Consider the example where Smart Concepts obtains a loan from its bank on 1 January 20X7. The nominal value of the loan is C1 000 000, the nominal interest rate is 5 per cent per annum and the loan matures in five years. The costs to establish the loan facility were C20 000 and the net proceeds received by Smart Concepts amounted to C980 000.

The first step in calculating the interest expense for each year is to set up a schedule of cash flows for the period of the loan contract.

01/01/X7	*31/12/X7*	*31/12/X8*	*31/12/X9*	*31/12/Y0*	*31/12/Y1*
980 000	(50 000)	(50 000)	(50 000)	(50 000)	(1 050 000)

Second, it is necessary to calculate the effective interest rate or the internal rate of return.

Pause and reflect . . .

Are you able to use your financial calculator to compute the effective interest rate? How is this done?

Response

Press the **CASH** button.

Enter the nominal rate of interest as the **i%** = 5% and press **EXE.**

Press **EXE** again on the **Cash=D.Editor x**.

Enter the cash flows from the schedule of cash flows, pressing **EXE** after each one. Note that the first cash flow of C980 000 is positive while the other cash flows are negative.

Press **ESC** after entering all the cash flows.

Scroll down to **IRR: Solve** and press **EXE**.

The IRR is 5.46795 per cent.

The rate that equates the initial cash inflow of C980 000 with cash outflows of C50 000 per year for four years and a final cash outflow of C1 050 000 is 5.46795 per cent.

The third step is to calculate the effective interest expense for each year. The effect of this is to allocate the cost of the loan over the period of the loan contract. This is done as shown in the following table:

Date	*Effective interest (a)*	*Nominal interest (b)*	*(a) − (b)*	*Balance*
01/01/X7				980 000
31/12/X7	53 586	50 000	3 586	983 586
31/12/X8	53 782	50 000	3 782	987 368
31/12/X9	53 989	50 000	3 989	991 357
31/12/Y0	54 207	50 000	4 207	995 564
31/12/Y1	54 437	50 000	4 437	1 000 000

The interest expense recorded each year is the effective interest expense as calculated above. The last entry on 31 December 20Y1 records the repayment of the nominal value of the loan.

GENERAL JOURNAL OF SMART CONCEPTS

Date	*Description*	*Fol*	*Dr*	*Cr*
01/01/X7	Bank (A)		980 000	
	Long-term loan (L)			980 000
31/12/X7	Interest expense (E)		53 586	
	Bank (A)			50 000
	Long-term loan (L)			3 586
31/12/X8	Interest expense (E)		53 782	
	Bank (A)			50 000
	Long-term loan (L)			3 782
31/12/X9	Interest expense (E)		53 989	
	Bank (A)			50 000
	Long-term loan (L)			3 989
31/12/Y0	Interest expense (E)		54 207	
	Bank (A)			50 000
	Long-term loan (L)			4 207

31/12/Y1	Interest expense (E)		54 437	
	Bank (A)			50 000
	Long-term loan (L)			4 437
	Long-term loan (L)		1 000 000	
	Bank (A)			1 000 000

The journal entries to record the raising of the loan, the interest expense each year and the repayment of the loan are shown above. Note that the loan is initially recorded on 1 January 20X7 at C980 000, the amount of the net proceeds received. The amount of C980 000 is in fact the present value at 1 January 20X7 of the future cash flows associated with the loan, discounted at the effective interest rate. This is proved in the following table:

Date	*Cash flow*	*PV factor (at 5.46795%)*	*PV*
31/12/X7	(50 000)	0.948155	47 408
31/12/X8	(50 000)	0.898999	44 950
31/12/X9	(50 000)	0.852390	42 620
31/12/Y0	(50 000)	0.808198	40 410
31/12/Y1	(1 050 000)	0.766298	804 612
			980 000

An extract from Smart Concepts' financial statements for the 20X7 financial year is presented below.

SMART CONCEPTS
(EXTRACT FROM) STATEMENT OF PROFIT OR LOSS
FOR THE YEAR ENDED 31 DECEMBER 20X7

Finance cost	C
Interest expense	53 586

SMART CONCEPTS
(EXTRACT FROM) STATEMENT OF FINANCIAL POSITION
AT 31 DECEMBER 20X7

Non-current liabilities	C
Long-term borrowings	983 586

15.4.2 The terms of repayment

At the time of a loan being advanced to an entity, it is usual for a future date to be decided on for its repayment. Remember, the repayment date must be more than a year after the statement of financial position date for the loan to be classified as non-current or long term. It is possible for a loan to be repaid over a period of time rather than at one point.

This results in a series of payments being made. Each time a repayment is made, the balance on which interest is calculated is reduced. When a portion of the loan is paid, we refer to it as a capital reduction.

15.4.3 The security offered

When a long-term loan is granted to an entity, the lending institution may require some guarantee that the interest and capital will be paid. The lending institution can ask for security on the loan as a guarantee of the payments being made. Security on a loan may take the form of a cession of rights or a pledge of an asset in favour of the lender.

In the event of the entity failing to make its interest payments or capital repayments, the lending institution has the right to take possession of the ceded or pledged assets and dispose of them. The proceeds that the lending institution receives will be used to settle the obligation and any additional monies will be given back to the entity. If the asset taken by the lending institution does not cover the loan, or if the loan was never secured, the lending institution could take action against the entity to recover its money.

Bibliography

UK Crowdfunding. www.ukcfa.org.uk/what-is-crowdfunding (Accessed 30 November 2014).

PART V

Entity forms

16 Partnerships

Business focus

It is very likely that you have already encountered and even done business with a partnership. The local doctor, dentist, lawyer, hairdresser and bookkeepers probably chose to run their businesses either as sole proprietorships or as partnerships. The relatively simple legal environment normally makes this form of business perfect for smaller concerns. This is not to say that partnerships are limited to only small and medium-sized operations. There are a number of business arrangements involving larger companies that in substance are very similar to partnerships.

Group 5, one of South Africa's largest construction companies, has entered into a type of partnership agreement with a Spanish company, Iberdrola Ingeniería, which has won a US$150 million contract for a 96MW solar power station to be constructed near Postmasburg. The agreement includes the development of the plant, a transformer substation and overhead power lines, as well as a 15-year maintenance arrangement. This transaction is more complex than the arrangement between, for example, a group of lawyers or dentists who decide to pool their resources to run a practice. Nevertheless, the underlying economics are similar. Two companies (which are juristic persons) or natural persons are combining their expertise and resources in order to carry out an economic activity where the work to be performed, the profits and the risks are shared in terms of a 'partnership arrangement'.

In this chapter

The accounting for partnerships highlights a number of important concepts which you have already been exposed to in previous chapters. We examine how the accounting records of a partnership are prepared as well as the accounting for the admission and retirement of partners.

We mentioned in Chapter 15, *Owner's equity and non-current liabilities*, that an important aspect of your understanding of partnerships and other entity forms is the distribution of profits to the owners and the composition of owner's equity in each entity form. These and other issues will be addressed in the sections that follow.

Dashboard

- Look at the *Learning outcomes* so that you know what you should be able to do after studying this chapter.
- Read the *Business focus* to place this chapter's contents in a real-world context.
- Preview *In this chapter* to focus your mind on the contents of the chapter.
- Read the *text* in detail.
    - Apply your mind to the *Pause and reflect* scenarios.
    - Read the characteristics of a partnership. Think about some of the partnerships which you may be aware of. This will assist you with contextualising the material in this chapter.
    - The chapter addresses the preparation of partnership financial statements in Section 16.4, the admission of a partner in Section 16.5 and the dissolution of a partnership in Section 16.6. Ensure that you understand each section before moving on to the next.
    - Take careful note of the appropriation of profits in Section 16.4, as this is unique to partnerships.
    - Study of the chapter could end after 16.4 or 16.5, depending on the requirements of the course.
- Prepare solutions to the examples as you read through the chapter.
- Prepare a solution to the *Revision example* at the end of the chapter without reference to the suggested one. Compare your solution to the suggested solution provided.

Learning outcomes

After studying this chapter, you should be able to do the following:

1. Describe the characteristics of a partnership.
2. Identify the sources of finance and explain the distinction between capital contributions and profits retained of a partnership.
3. Describe the formation process of a partnership.
4. Record the transactions relating to forming a partnership in the general journal and general ledger.
5. Account for the appropriation of the profit in the accounting records.
6. Prepare financial statements for a partnership.
7. Process the accounting entries for the admission of a new partner to an existing partnership.
8. Process the accounting entries to dissolve a partnership.

Partnerships

16.1 Characteristics of a partnership

The partnership form of a business entity is generally used for relatively small businesses that wish to take advantage of the combined financial capital, managerial talent and experience of two or more people. This form of entity is often found amongst professions such as doctors and dentists, and some firms of lawyers and accountants.

A partnership is a legal relationship which arises as a result of an agreement between two or more persons but not exceeding 20. (The membership of organised professions may, however, exceed 20). Each partner contributes cash and/or other assets to a legal undertaking with the objective of making a profit to the advantage of all concerned.

A partnership is *not a separate legal entity* and it has no legal standing apart from the members who constitute it. As a result, a partnership is also *not a separate taxable entity*. The profits are taxed in the hands of the individual partners.

The individual partners are the joint owners of the assets and are *jointly and severally* liable for the liabilities of the partnership. In other words, each partner could incur unlimited liability for all the debts and obligations of the partnership.

Joint and several liability means that each individual partner can be liable for all the debts of the partnership and not just for his or her own share of the respective liabilities.

No formalities are required in establishing a partnership. For example, a written agreement is not essential; it could also be oral or implied. It is, however, common practice and also desirable that it be in writing.

General provisions which are normally contained in partnership agreements are summarised below:

- the nature and amount of the capital contribution by each partner;
- the division of profits and losses between the partners;
- whether interest on capital or on drawings, or both, is to be allowed or charged before arriving at the profits divisible in the agreed proportions and, if so, at what rate;
- whether partners are to be allowed remuneration for their services before arriving at divisible profit and, if so, the amounts;
- whether or not current accounts are to bear interest and, if so, the interest rate;
- whether or not partners' drawings are limited;
- that financial statements be prepared at least once a year and signed by all the partners. (As the partnership may not necessarily comply with the International Financial Reporting Standards (IFRS), the agreement may specify exactly which statements are prepared as well as the required presentation and disclosure in the financial statements).

IFRS do not deal specifically with accounting for partnerships. IFRS focus on the nature of the transactions and balances, including rights to underlying assets and liabilities, rather than the structure in which the transactions are housed. As a result, although relevant IFRS have been taken into account in this chapter, the accounting may not be entirely consistent with IFRS. As there is no legislation mandating the adoption of IFRS by all partnerships, this chapter takes cognisance of generally accepted principles used by small and medium-sized entities that are, in substance, partnerships but which do not purport to comply in all material respects with IFRS.

Pause and reflect...

You know that a partnership is not a separate legal entity apart from its owners. Is it a separate accounting entity?

Response

A partnership, like a sole proprietorship, is a separate accounting entity apart from its owners. This is important as it means that profits earned by the business entity belong to the owners (unlike a company, where the profits earned belong to the business entity and need to be formally distributed to the owners).

16.2 Sources of finance for a partnership

A partnership, like any other business entity, can be financed from two sources – investors' funds and borrowed funds:

- Investors' funds come in the form of contributions by the partners to the ***equity*** of the partnership. The contributions may consist of cash or other assets.
- Borrowed funds may come from a variety of sources, such as a financial institution or a private individual. The amount borrowed is a ***liability*** of the partnership.

 **Pause and reflect...**

A partnership buys goods on credit from a supplier and then, due to financial difficulty, is unable to pay for them. Thinking of joint and several liability, who is the supplier able to sue and what are the implications for all of the partners of the partnership?

Response

The supplier can sue any one of the partners and may choose to sue the partner who is most likely to be able to pay the debt in his or her personal capacity. The partner who has been sued by the supplier has the right to claim a share or proportion of what is owed from the other partners, but may not be successful.

In addition to the capital contribution of a partner to a partnership, a partner may also make a loan to the business. As the partner and partnership are separate accounting entities, the amount borrowed from a partner is a liability of the partnership and is not part of the capital contribution.

16.2.1 Distinction between capital contribution and retained profit

The **capital contribution**, whether of a sole proprietor or a partner in a partnership, represents the long-term or relatively permanent contribution by the owner to the business. The capital contribution represents *part* of the partners' residual interest in the partnership (or a claim on the net assets of the business).

As the business trades, profits accrue to the owners and increase the owner's equity. Periodically, the owners withdraw cash from the business, which decreases the owners' equity. The cumulative excess of profit over distributions represents the **retained profit** in the business entity.

When accounting for a sole proprietor, all profits belong to the sole owner and there is no need to distinguish between capital contributed by the owner and retained profit. In a partnership, there are multiple owners and it is therefore necessary to record the equity of each partner separately. In order to distinguish between the capital contribution and the retained profit, a ***capital*** and ***current*** account is often opened for each partner.

The **capital** account reflects the fixed amount of capital contributed by each partner. This is normally provided for in the partnership agreement. In other words, the capital account represents the partners' long-term equity interests in the partnership.

The **current** account is used to record the allocation of profit to partners as well as the distributions to them. (You will learn later in this chapter that amounts allocated to partners can include salaries, interest on capital as well as a share of profits, but for the moment we will focus on the share of profits). The balance on the current account represents the difference between profits allocated to a partner and distributions to that partner. This balance is therefore the retained profit or loss attributable to the partner, or the partner's short-term equity interest in the partnership. A credit balance on the current account represents an amount 'owed' by the partnership to the partner (where share of profits to date is greater than distributions to date). On the other hand, a debit balance represents an amount 'owed' by the partner to the partnership (where distributions to date are greater than share of profits to date).

 **Pause and reflect...**

Is the current account part of equity or is it a liability?

Response

The partners and the partnership business are the same legal entity. As such, profits earned by the partnership and transferred to the current account belong to the partners. The current account is therefore part of equity.

16.2.2 Equity of a partnership

As we examine each entity form, it is important for you to appreciate and understand the composition of equity in the different entity forms. In a sole proprietorship, equity comprises the *capital* account of the owner, and all transactions between the business entity and the owner take place through this account.

In a partnership, equity comprises both the *capital* and *current* accounts of the partners. The combined balance on these accounts represents the interest of each partner in the net assets of the entity.

16.3 Formation of a partnership

As mentioned previously, partners contribute cash or other assets to the capital of the partnership. If non-cash assets are introduced into the partnership, a value must be placed on them. This will usually be the assets' *fair value* – the price that would be received from selling an asset, or paid to transfer a liability in an orderly transaction between independent buyers and sellers. For example, the current selling price of the same or a similar asset could be used to arrive at the fair value of the asset transferred to the partnership. As a safeguard, the partnership agreement may also specify that the partners must formally agree that the values placed on the non-cash assets are fair and reasonable. We will discuss here the formation of a partnership where two or more individuals decide to launch a business venture together.

Example: Formation of a partnership

Towards the end of 20X6, Simon Smart reviewed the business entities that he had formed during the previous two years. His principle business operation, Smart Concepts, was performing well, as were Bright Life and Sharp Moves. He realised that he did not have the capacity to devote to another business entity on his own. He therefore approached Gary Good with the idea of forming a partnership to begin a new business entity.

On 1 January 20X7, Simon Smart and Gary Good formed a partnership trading under the name of Intense Sports. The business is a retailer of endurance running and cycling equipment. Simon contributed C280 000 in cash, and Gary contributed land with a fair value of C250 000 and machinery with a fair value of C75 000. The land is being held for the future development of a retail outlet for Intense Sports.

You are required to:

a) Journalise the above transaction in the accounting records of Intense Sports Partnership.
b) Prepare the statement of financial position of Intense Sports partnership on 1 January 20X7.

Solution: Formation of a partnership

Assets		=	*Owners' equity*			
Bank			**Capital – Simon**		**Capital – Gary**	
+/L/Dr	*−/R/Cr*		*−/L/Dr*	*+/R/Cr*	*−/L/Dr*	*+/R/Cr*
280 000				280 000		
Land						
+/L/Dr	*−/R/Cr*					
250 000						250 000
Machinery						
+/L/Dr	*−/R/Cr*					
75 000						75 000
				280 000		325 000

On 1 January 20X7, the partners, Simon and Gary, invested cash and other assets into the business. The effect of this transaction is shown in the accounting equation above.

a) Journal entries

GENERAL JOURNAL OF INTENSE SPORTS PARTNERSHIP

Date	*Description*	*Fol*	*Dr*	*Cr*
01/01/X7	Bank (A)		280 000	
	Capital – Simon (OE)			280 000
	Capital contribution			
01/01/X7	Land (A)		250 000	
	Machinery (A)		75 000	
	Capital – Gary (OE)			325 000
	Capital contribution			

b) Statement of financial position

INTENSE SPORTS PARTNERSHIP
STATEMENT OF FINANCIAL POSITION
AT 1 JANUARY 20X7

	C
ASSETS	
Non-current assets	
Property, plant and equipment	325 000
Land	250 000
Machinery	75 000
Current assets	
Bank	280 000
	605 000
EQUITY AND LIABILITIES	
Equity	
Capital accounts	605 000
Simon	280 000
Gary	325 000
Liabilities	—
	605 000

16.4 Producing information for a partnership

You know from Chapter 1, *The accounting environment*, that the accounting information system selects data, processes that data and produces information about an economic entity. The *selection* and *processing* of data use the same concepts in all entity forms. In this section, we will review the accounting information system, concentrating on those aspects of *producing information* that are unique to a partnership.

16.4.1 Determination of profit

The profit of a partnership is determined in the same way as that of a sole proprietorship. The profit is computed according to the accrual basis of accounting, taking into account the principles in the *Conceptual Framework*.The procedural aspects of recording transactions in a journal, posting to a ledger and preparing a trial balance are performed as for a sole proprietorship. The internal transactions or adjusting entries are also identical in nature.

16.4.2 Appropriation of profit

After the adjusting entries have been processed and before the financial statements are prepared, the appropriating entries must be processed. An extract of the accounting process diagram referred to in Parts I and II of the book is shown below in Diagram 16.1, modified to take into account the appropriating entries.

You learnt in Chapter 1 and again in Chapter 15, *Owner's equity and non-current liabilities* that the sole proprietorship and the partnership are ***unincorporated*** entities, whereas the company is an ***incorporated*** entity. This stems from the legal nature of the relationship between the owner/s and the entity. As already mentioned in this chapter, for a sole proprietorship and partnership the owner/s and the business are the same legal entity, but the company is a separate legal entity which is distinct from its owner/s.

As a result of being an unincorporated entity, all the profit earned in a sole proprietorship belongs to the owner, and the profit is transferred from the profit or loss account to the owner's capital account with a closing entry. Distributions of the profit reduce the capital account, but, as you will recall, are recorded in a separate distributions account, which is then closed off to the capital account.

In a partnership, however, the procedure is complicated by the fact that there is more than one owner. As with a sole proprietorship, the partnership, being unincorporated, is not a separate legal entity, and profits cannot be retained by the business entity. The profit belongs to the partners and needs to be shared amongst them. As you will see later in this chapter, the relevant closing entry transfers the profit from the *profit or loss account* to the *appropriation account*, where the appropriations of profit are recorded before transferring the remaining profit to the *partners' current accounts*.

The objective of the appropriation of profit is to reward each partner for the services and resources provided to the firm as equity participants. The appropriation of profit is thus simply an accounting procedure which allocates the profit earned for the period to each partner by allocating ***salaries*** and ***interest on capital*** to the partners to compensate for unequal service and capital contributions.

In this context, partners' salaries and interest on capital are not recognised as an expense in the determination of profit but rather as an appropriation of profit that belongs to the partners. Remember that the definition of an expense excludes distributions to owners.

The appropriation of profits is illustrated in Diagram 16.2 and further explained in the example that follows.

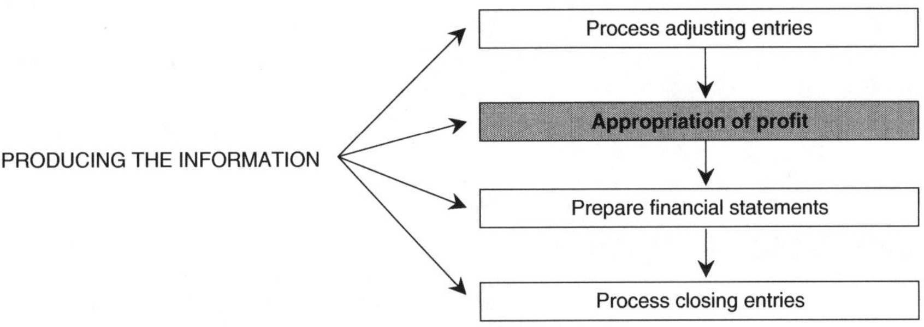

Diagram 16.1 Extract of accounting process highlighting the appropriating entries

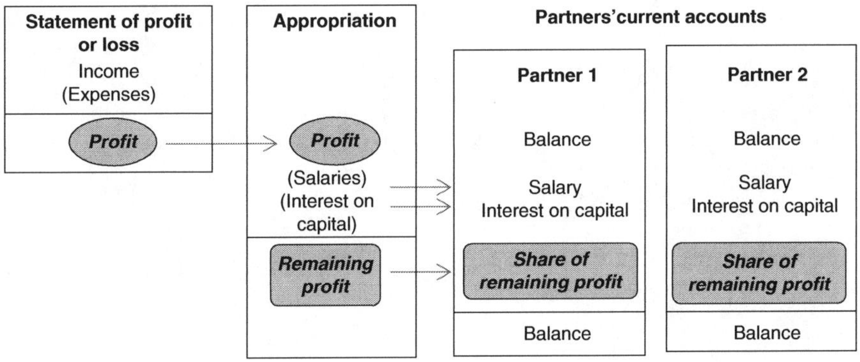

Diagram 16.2 Appropriation of profits

 **Pause and reflect...**

What do you think would happen if the partners in a partnership contributed the same amount of capital and provided the same service to the partnership?

Response

In this scenario, the profit transferred from the profit or loss account to the appropriation account would simply be allocated to the partners' current accounts in the agreed profit-sharing ratio without the need to account for salaries or interest on capital.

Salaries paid to partners may be recognised as an expense in the determination of profit if one or more of the partners work as an employee and are paid a market-related salary.

If a partner advances funds to a partnership as a lender in addition to the capital contribution, the interest on the loan is also recognised as an expense in the determination of profit.

Transactions with partners *as owners* are treated as appropriations of profit (and shown on the statement of changes in equity) whereas transactions with partners *as lenders* are treated as an expense (and shown on the statement of profit or loss).

Finally, it is important to note that interest paid on loans to outside parties and salaries paid to employees of the partnership must be treated as expenses in the determination of profit. Remember that in terms of the definition of an expense, neither of these items are distributions to owners.

 Example: Producing information for a partnership

The activities of Intense Sports for its first year of trading will be used to illustrate the appropriation of profits, financial statement preparation and closing entries of a partnership. The partnership agreement provides for the following:

- Interest on capital is calculated at 10 per cent per annum on the balances at the beginning of each year.
- Simon will be entitled to a salary of C132 000 per annum and Gary to C80 000 per annum, to be credited to their respective current accounts.
- Interest on drawings is calculated at 10 per cent per annum on the balances at the end of each year.
- Profit (or losses) will be shared in the ratio 3:2 between Simon and Gary.

The following additional information is available for the year ended 31 December 20X7.

INTENSE SPORTS PARTNERSHIP
TRIAL BALANCE
AT 31 DECEMBER 20X7

Description	*Folio*	*Dr*	*Cr*
Capital – Simon			280 000
Capital – Gary			325 000
Drawings – Simon		24 000	
Drawings – Gary		30 000	
Long-term borrowings			80 000
Land: cost		570 000	
Machinery: cost		100 000	
Machinery: accumulated depreciation			20 000
Inventory		70 000	
Accounts receivable		154 000	
Bank		354 000	
Accounts payable			141 000
Sales			1 980 000
Cost of sales		990 000	
Administration expense		60 000	
Marketing expense		59 000	
Telephone expense		18 000	
Rent		12 000	
Salaries expense – employees		340 000	
Light and water expense		25 000	
Depreciation expense		20 000	
		2 826 000	2 826 000

- Mega Bank advanced a long-term loan of C80 000 on 2 January 20X7 at an interest rate of 5 per cent per annum.
- Additional land costing C290 000 was purchased during the year.
- Additional machinery was acquired on 2 January 20X7 at a cost of C25 000. All the machinery has an estimated useful life of five years, with no residual value.

You are required to:

Prepare the financial statements of Intense Sports Partnership at 31 December 20X7.

The information from this example will now be used to illustrate the accounting entries for the appropriation of profits (Section 16.4.3) as well as the preparation of financial statements for a partnership (Section 16.4.5), before preparing the solution, as required.

16.4.3 Interest on capital, partners' salaries and drawings

Interest on capital

As discussed above, interest on capital is *not* recognised as an expense on the statement of profit or loss. It is an *appropriation of profit*, governed by the provisions of the partnership agreement. The objective is to reward partners for their capital investments. The interest rate may be fixed in the partnership agreement or based on current rates. The accounting entry to record interest on capital is as follows:

	Dr	*Cr*
Interest on capital (OE)	60 500	
Current: Simon (OE)		28 000
Current: Gary (OE)		32 500

Partners' salaries

Partners' salaries are also *not* recognised as an expense on the statement of profit or loss. Similar to interest on capital, partners' salaries are an *appropriation of profit* governed by the provisions of the partnership agreement. The partners are *owners* of the partnership and not *employees*. The objective is to reward partners for the time, effort and expertise that they devote to the entity. The entry to record partners' salaries is as follows:

	Dr	*Cr*
Partners' salaries (OE)	212 000	
Current a/c: Simon (OE)		132 000
Current a/c: Gary (OE)		80 000

It is important to note that both of the above entries are an *appropriation of profit* and not a *cash payment* to the partners. This appropriation or allocation of interest on capital and partners' salaries takes place at the end of the period, which could be a month, three months, six months or a year. Amounts drawn in cash by the partners during the period are charged to their respective drawings accounts. This will be discussed in detail below.

 **Pause and reflect...**

Can you remember why the interest on capital and partners' salaries is not recognised as an expense?

Response

Interest on capital and partners' salaries is an *appropriation* of profit already belonging to partners as owners of the business entity.

Interest on drawings

In the same way that interest on capital and partners' salaries are appropriations of profit credited to the partners' current accounts as a reward for resources and services provided, interest on drawings is debited to the current accounts to compensate other partners for unequal drawings or the timing of those drawings.

Interest on drawings is typically calculated from the date of the distribution to the end of the accounting period, but some other amount may be used if accurate records are not available, such as the average level of drawings during the period or the balance at the end of period.

According to the trial balance, Simon and Gary withdrew C24 000 and C30 000, respectively. The entry to record the cash paid to them is as follows:

	Dr	*Cr*
Drawings: Simon (OE)	24 000	
Drawings: Gary (OE)	30 000	
Bank (A)		54 000

As the partnership agreement states that interest on drawings is calculated at 10 per cent per annum on the balances at the end of the period, the entry to record interest on drawings is as follows:

	Dr	*Cr*
Current: Simon (OE)	2 400	
Current: Gary (OE)	3 000	
Interest on drawings (OE)		5 400

 **Pause and reflect...**

If the profit attributable to the partners accrues continuously over the accounting period, is it appropriate to charge the partners interest on drawings for the entire period?

Response

Conceptually, interest on drawings would only arise for the period of time when the partner had withdrawn the cash. However, it may not be practical to maintain that level of record keeping and the partners could agree, for example, to compute interest on drawings monthly or quarterly.

16.4.4 Interest on loans

As mentioned earlier in this chapter, interest on loans to outside parties is reported as an expense on the statement of profit or loss. The interest on the loan from the bank is therefore regarded as an expense in the determination of profit and *not as an appropriation* of profit. In our example, Mega Bank has advanced an amount of C80 000 to the partnership at an interest rate of 5 per cent per annum. The entry to record interest on the loan is as follows:

	Dr	*Cr*
Interest (E)	4 000	
Interest payable (L)		4 000

16.4.5 Preparation of the financial statements

Once the appropriating entries have been completed, the financial statements of the partnership can be prepared. The statement of profit or loss is presented in the same format as for a sole proprietor.

The only difference to the statement of financial position is the owner's equity section, which discloses the capital and current accounts for each partner.

The statement of changes in equity is expanded to include columns for the capital and current accounts of *each* partner and a column to accommodate the appropriation of profit.

Having illustrated the accounting entries for the appropriation of profits, we can now prepare a solution to the example: 'Producing information for a partnership'.

Solution: Producing information for a partnership

INTENSE SPORTS PARTNERSHIP
STATEMENT OF PROFIT OR LOSS
FOR THE YEAR ENDED 31 DECEMBER 20X7

		C
Sales		1 980 000
Cost of sales		(990 000)
Gross profit		990 000
Operating expenses		(534 000)
Administration	60 000	
Marketing	59 000	
Telephone	18 000	
Rent	12 000	
Salaries	340 000	
Lights and water	25 000	
Depreciation	20 000	
Operating profit		456 000
Finance cost		
Interest on loan		(4 000)
Profit for the period		452 000

INTENSE SPORTS PARTNERSHIP
STATEMENT OF CHANGES IN EQUITY
FOR THE YEAR ENDED 31 DECEMBER 20X7

	Capital		*Current*		*Appro-priation*	*Total*
	Simon	*Gary*	*Simon*	*Gary*		
	C	*C*	*C*	*C*	*C*	*C*
Balance at 1 January						
Profit for the period					452 000	452 000
Appropriation of profits						
Salaries			132 000	80 000	(212 000)	
Interest on capital			28 000	32 500	(60 500)	
Interest on drawings			(2 400)	(3 000)	5 400	
					184 900	
Share of remaining profit			110 940	73 960	(184 900)	
Contributions and distributions						
Contribution to capital	280 000	325 000				605 000
Distributions			(24 000)	(30 000)		(54 000)
Balance at 31 December	280 000	325 000	244 540	153 460	—	1 003 000

The appropriation column shows a balance of profit of C184 900 after the appropriations have been taken into account. This is shared between the partners in their agreed profit-sharing ratio and transferred to their current accounts by means of a closing entry, described in Section 16.4.6.

INTENSE SPORTS PARTNERSHIP
STATEMENT OF FINANCIAL POSITION
AT 31 DECEMBER 20X7

	Note	*C*	
ASSETS			
Non-current assets			
Property, plant and equipment	1		650 000
Current assets			578 000
Inventory		70 000	
Accounts receivable		154 000	
Bank		354 000	
			1 228 000
EQUITY AND LIABILITIES			
Equity			1 003 000
Capital accounts		605 000	
Simon		280 000	
Gary		325 000	
Current accounts		398 000	
Simon		244 540	
Gary		153 460	
Non-current liabilities			
Borrowing – Mega Bank			80 000
Current liabilities			145 000
Accounts payable		141 000	
Interest payable		4 000	
			1 228 000

INTENSE SPORTS PARTNERSHIP
NOTES TO THE FINANCIAL STATEMENTS
AT 31 DECEMBER 20X7

1) Property, plant and equipment

	Land	*Machinery*	*Total*
	C	C	C
Carrying amount at 31/12/X7	570 000	80 000	650 000
Cost	570 000	100 000	670 000
Accumulated depreciation	—	(20 000)	(20 000)

There is no carrying amount at the beginning of the year as this is the first period of trading.

16.4.6 Closing entries for a partnership

The closing entries to transfer the trading activities to the trading account and the operating activities to the profit or loss account are identical for a sole proprietor and a partnership. When accounting for a sole proprietor, the profit from the profit or loss account is transferred to the owner's capital account. In a partnership situation, however, the profit from the profit or loss account is transferred to the ***appropriation account***, where the appropriations of profit (as discussed above) are also transferred.

The appropriation account is used to accumulate the effects of the appropriations of profit in the same way that the profit or loss account accumulates the income and expenses for a period.

The closing entry to transfer the profit from the profit or loss account to the appropriation account is as follows:

	Dr	*Cr*
Profit or loss (T)	452 000	
Appropriation (T)		452 000

Further closing entries for a partnership are required to transfer the balances on the interest on capital, partners' salaries, and interest on drawings accounts to the appropriation account. These entries are as follows:

	Dr	*Cr*
Appropriation (T)	272 500	
Interest on capital (OE)		60 500
Partners' salaries (OE)		212 000
Interest on drawings (OE)	5 400	
Appropriation (T)		5 400

The objective of the appropriation has now been achieved. The partners have been fairly rewarded for resources invested and services rendered to the partnership. In addition, the partners have compensated each other for unequal distributions. The balance in the appropriation account represents the remaining profit available to share between the partners in the agreed profit-sharing ratio.

Since the essence of a partnership is mutual agreement, it is desirable for the partners to agree, before entering into a partnership, to the terms and conditions for operating the business and to their respective rights and powers. Where the agreement is silent with regard to a particular aspect, common law requirements are applied. For example, where the profit-sharing ratio has not been agreed upon, partners share profits and losses in proportion to their capital contributions to the partnership. Where such contributions cannot be determined, it is assumed that partners share equally in the profits. It is important to remember that the partnership agreement must be studied before the financial statements for the partnership are prepared.

In our example, the balance of C184 900 in the appropriation account is the amount available for allocation to the partners in their profit-sharing ratio. The share allocated to each partner is transferred to the partners' current accounts with the following closing entry:

	Dr	*Cr*
Appropriation (T)	184 900	
Current: Simon (OE)		110 940
Current: Gary (OE)		73 960

The final closing entry that is required is to transfer the drawings account of each partner to their respective current accounts:

	Dr	Cr
Current: Simon (OE)	24 000	
Current: Gary (OE)	30 000	
Drawings: Simon (OE)		24 000
Drawings: Gary (OE)		30 000

The relevant ledger accounts of Intense Sports after the closing entries have been taken into account appear as follows:

Profit or loss

Details	C	*Details*	C
Administration	60 000	Trading	990 000
Marketing	59 000		
Rent	12 000		
Telephone	18 000		
Salaries	340 000		
Lights and water	25 000		
Depreciation	20 000		
Interest	4 000		
Appropriation	452 000		
	990 000		990 000

Trading

Details	C	*Details*	C
Cost of sales	990 000	Sales	1 980 000
Profit or loss	990 000		
	1 980 000		1 980 000

Interest expense

Details	C	*Details*	C
Interest payable	4 000	Profit or loss	4 000
	4 000		4 000

Interest on drawings

Details	C	*Details*	C
Appropriation	5 400	Current – Simon	2 400
		Current – Gary	3 000
	5 400		5 400

Interest on capital

Details	C	*Details*	C
Current – Simon	28 000	Appropriation	60 500
Current – Gary	32 500		
	60 500		60 500

Partners' salaries

Details	C	*Details*	C
Current – Simon	132 000	Appropriation	212 000
Current – Gary	80 000		
	212 000		212 000

Appropriation

Details	C	*Details*	C
Interest on capital	60 500	Profit or loss	452 000
Partners' salaries	212 000	Interest on drawings	5 400
Current – Simon	110 940		
Current – Gary	73 960		
	457 400		457 400

Current – Simon

Details	*C*	*Details*	*C*
Interest on drawings	2 400	Interest on capital	28 000
Drawings	24 000	Salary	132 000
		Appropriation	110 940
Balance c/d	244 540		
	270 940		270 940
		Balance b/d	244 540

Current – Gary

Details	*C*	*Details*	*C*
Interest on drawings	3 000	Interest on capital	32 500
Drawings	30 000	Salary	80 000
		Appropriation	73 960
Balance c/d	153 460		
	186 460		186 460
		Balance b/d	153 460

Drawings – Simon

Details	*C*	*Details*	*C*
Cash	24 000	Current – Simon	24 000
	24 000		24 000

Drawings – Gary

Details	*C*	*Details*	*C*
Cash	30 000	Current – Gary	30 000
	30 000		30 000

16.5 Admission of a partner

We will examine here the issues that relate to the admission of a partner to a partnership. The law requires that a change in the members of the partnership ends the existing partnership, and a new one comes into existence.

A change in composition of a partnership results in a change in the profit-sharing ratio. In addition, it is necessary to ensure that the equity of the existing partners is fairly stated. This involves restating the assets and liabilities of the partnership at fair value. Once this has been done and the equity adjusted, a value for goodwill (if any) needs to be determined. Lastly, the capital contribution of the new partner is recorded. The procedure to follow on admission of a partner is summarised as follows:

- adjustment to the profit-sharing ratio;
- restating the assets and liabilities of the partnership to fair value;
- accounting for goodwill;
- recording the new partner's contribution.

At this stage, and as mentioned above, the existing partnership would technically be dissolved and a new partnership formed. However, from a practical perspective, the new partnership normally takes over the assets and liabilities of the existing partnership and uses the same accounting records as used by the existing partnership, after processing the necessary accounting entries required following the procedure set out above. Each step will be discussed in detail, continuing with the Intense Sports example.

Example: Admission of a partner

Simon and Gary had been negotiating with Mark Main for some time for him to join their partnership. The date for Mark's admission was agreed to be 1 January 20X8.

As described in Section 16.4.5 above, Simon and Gary have prepared financial statements for the 20X7 financial year. This has been done to enable Simon and Gary to assess the performance for the period as well as the financial position at the end of the period. (It has also enabled you to learn how to prepare financial statements of a partnership before considering the accounting entries required on admission of a partner.)

We now need to process the accounting entries for the admission of Mark and prepare revised financial statements to reflect these transactions.

- The following are the fair values of the assets:
  - Land C700 000
  - Machinery C 90 000
  - Inventory C 65 000
  - Accounts receivable C144 000
- The useful life of the machinery was reassessed and it was estimated to have a *remaining* useful life of five years from 1 January 20X8. The residual value of zero remained unchanged.
- All other assets and liabilities are considered to be fairly valued.
- Mark contributed C440 000 in cash via an EFT deposit into the partnership bank account for a one-third share of the business, which the remaining partners are to relinquish so that each partner will have one-third of the future profits.

You are required to:

a) Prepare an extract from the statement of changes in equity that will be prepared for the year ended 31 December 20X8, showing the *owner changes in equity* relating to the admission of Mark on 1 January 20X8.
b) Prepare the statement of financial position of Intense Sports at 1 January 20X8, immediately after the admission of Mark.

The information from this example will now be used to illustrate the procedure relating to the admission of a partner to a partnership, before preparing the solution, as required.

16.5.1 Adjustment to the profit-sharing ratio

The profit-sharing ratio is an important aspect of a partnership agreement, because it determines how the profit or loss remaining after appropriations is shared amongst the partners. The existing partners must agree on the basis of relinquishing profit share, and all the partners must agree on the profit share to be allocated to the new partner. Three possible agreements could be reached:

a) The share that the new partner will acquire is relinquished by the existing partners according to their *existing* ratio. As a result, future profits accruing to the partnership will be shared between the original partners in their original profit-sharing ratio.
b) The share that the new partner will acquire is relinquished by the *existing* partners *equally*. As a result, future profits accruing to the partnership will be shared between the original partners in a *different* profit-sharing ratio.
c) The share that the new partner will acquire is relinquished by the existing partners according to an agreed ratio.

Simon and Gary are sharing profits and losses in the ratio of 3:2. For illustration purposes, we will consider all three possible agreements and then continue the example with the agreement as decided.

a) If Simon and Gary relinquish the one-third share of profits given to Mark according to their **existing ratio**, Simon will relinquish 3/15 (3/5 × 1/3) and Gary will relinquish 2/15 (2/5 × 1/3). The new profit-sharing ratio of 6:4:5 is calculated as follows:

	Existing ratio		*Change*		*New ratio*
Simon	3/5	–	3/15	=	6/15
Gary	2/5	–	2/15		4/15
	1				10/15
Mark	(1/3)				5/15
	2/3	=			1

According to this agreement, Simon has given up 3/15 (his share has decreased from 9/15 to 6/15), Gary has given up 2/15 (from 6/15 to 4/15) and Mark has gained 5/15 (3/15 from Simon and 2/15 from Gary). Note that we have expressed the ratios with a common denominator of 15 for ease of calculation.

b) If Simon and Gary relinquish the one-third share of profits given to Mark **equally**, both Simon and Gary will relinquish one-sixth (1/2 × 1/3). The new profit-sharing ratio of 13:7:10 is calculated as follows:

	Existing ratio		*Change*		*New ratio*
Simon	3/5	–	1/6	=	13/30
Gary	2/5	–	1/6	=	7/30
	1				20/30
Mark	(1/3)				10/30
	2/3				1

According to this agreement, Simon has given up 5/30 (his share has decreased from 18/30 to 13/30), and Gary has also given up 5/30 (from 12/30 to 7/30) while Mark has gained 10/30 (5/30 from Simon and 5/30 from Gary). Here the ratios have been expressed with a common denominator of 30 for ease of calculation.

c) If Simon and Gary **agree** to relinquish profits according to an agreement (in this case, each partner will have one-third of future profits) Simon and Gary will relinquish 4/15 and 1/15 respectively of the one-third share of profits given to Mark. The new profit-sharing ratio of 5:5:5 or 1/3:1/3:1/3 is calculated as follows:

	Existing ratio		*Change*		*New ratio*
Simon	3/5	–	4/15	=	5/15
Gary	2/5	–	1/15	=	5/15
	1				10/15
Mark	(1/3)				5/15
	2/3				1

This is the new profit-sharing ratio that the partners in our example agreed upon, and it will be used when recording the change in partnership composition in the accounting records. Note that according to this agreement, Simon has given up 4/15 (his share has decreased from 9/15 to 5/15), Gary has given up 1/15 (from 6/15 to 5/15) while Mark has gained 5/15 (4/15 from Simon and 1/15 from Gary). This analysis of the profit share relinquished by the existing partners and taken over by the new partner is important as it impacts your understanding of the treatment of goodwill prior to the admission of a partner.

Pause and reflect...

In admitting a new partner, the existing partners can relinquish the new partner's share of the partnership's profits according to their existing ratio, equally or in terms of a specific agreement. What is the effect of the method selected on the profit-sharing relationship between the existing partners after the new partner has been admitted, compared to the profit-sharing relationship before the new partner was admitted?

Response

When relinquishing profits according to the *existing ratio*, the relationship between the existing partners is the same after as it was before the admission of the new partner (before: Simon 3/5 and Gary 2/5; after: Simon 6/10 and Gary 4/10).

When the new partner's share of profits is relinquished *equally*, the relationship between the existing partners changes after admission (before: Simon 3/5 or 12/20, and Gary 2/5 or 8/20; after, Simon 13/20 and Gary 7/20).

When the profit is relinquished in terms of a *specific arrangement*, the relationship between the existing partners may or may not be the same after as it was before the admission of the new partner. In this example, it is not the same (before: Simon 3/5 or 6/10, and Gary 2/5 or 4/10; after: Simon 5/10 and Gary 5/10).

16.5.2 Restating the assets and liabilities of the partnership to fair value

As a new partnership comes into existence on the admission of another partner, it is important to determine the ***fair value*** of the partnership equity at the date of admission of the new partner. The fair values of the underlying assets and liabilities need to be determined and any changes processed in the accounting records.

Pause and reflect...

Can you remember what is meant by 'fair value'?

Response

Fair value is the price that would be received to sell an asset or paid to transfer a liability in an orderly transaction between independent buyers and sellers.

As mentioned in Section 16.5, from a legal perspective a change in the members of a partnership ends the existing partnership and a new partnership comes into existence. In other words, the partnership with Simon and Gary as partners will cease to exist and a new partnership with Simon, Gary and Mark as partners will be formed. From a practical accounting perspective, however, the accounting records of the existing partnership are used with adjustments being made to ensure that the equity of the existing partners is fairly stated before the new partner is admitted.

It is important to consider how the change in equity resulting from the revaluation is reported in the financial statements. You will recall from Chapter 1, *The accounting environment*, that IAS 1 requires the statement of changes in equity to present changes in equity separated into, first, contributions by and distributions to owners showing each separately (*owner* changes in equity), and second, profit or loss for the period (*non-owner* changes in equity). Owner changes in equity are changes in equity arising from ***transactions with owners in their capacity as owners***. This incorporates contributions to capital by owners and distributions to owners. Non-owner changes in equity are changes in equity arising from ***income and expense transactions***.

The revaluation process on admission of a partner does not generate components of income or expense to be included in profit or loss, or in other comprehensive income as a *non-owner change* in equity. Rather, the gain or loss on revaluation represents an *owner change* in equity. As such, it will not appear on the statement of profit or loss or the statement of comprehensive income, but will appear on the statement of changes in equity as an adjustment to the partners' capital accounts on the admission of a new partner.

A ***revaluation*** account is used to record movements in the values of assets and liabilities, as agreed by the partners. The balance on the revaluation account is referred to as a gain or loss on revaluation and is allocated to the *existing* partners in the existing profit-sharing ratio. This is because the existing partners must benefit or lose from changes in the value of equity while they control the business. The consequence of the revaluation procedure is that the new firm begins with its assets recorded at their agreed values, and the partners' equity is adjusted to reflect the interest of the partners in the assets of the business.

Pause and reflect...

Is the revaluation account described above the same as the revaluation surplus account used on revaluation of property, plant and equipment?

Response

The accounts are not the same. The adjustments to both current and non-current assets on admission of a partner to a partnership are recorded in the revaluation account and not in profit or loss or other comprehensive income, and are recognised as an *owner change in equity*. The revaluation surplus on the revaluation of property, plant and equipment is recorded as an item of other comprehensive income as a *non-owner change in equity*.

Accounting entries

The accounting entries to record the revaluation of **non-current assets** were described in Chapter 10, *Property, plant and equipment*. The entries that you will see here are similar, except, as described in the preceding paragraphs, the revaluation is recognised as an owner change in equity.

The fair value of the land is C700 000 – an increase of C130 000 over the cost as reported on the statement of financial position. As the land is not depreciated, the entry to record the revaluation is as follows:

	Dr	*Cr*
Land (A)	130 000	
Revaluation (OE)		130 000

The machinery has a fair value of C90 000, compared to its *carrying amount* of C80 000. As the machinery is a depreciable asset, the balance in the accumulated depreciation account must be reversed and then the increase recorded in the asset account. The effect is to record the asset at fair value, with only the depreciation subsequent to the valuation recorded as accumulated depreciation. There are a number of bookkeeping entries which could be processed, all of which achieve the same result. We suggest the following entries:

	Dr	*Cr*
Accumulated depreciation (–A)	20 000	
Machinery (A)		20 000
Machinery (A)	10 000	
Revaluation (OE)		10 000

The effect of these two entries on the machinery account is to record the machinery at its fair value of C90 000 (C100 000 – C20 000 + C10 000). The increase of C10 000 (C90 000 – C80 000) is credited to the revaluation account.

Turning to the **current assets**, the inventory is valued at C65 000 – a decrease of C5 000 compared to the cost on the statement of financial position. The accounts receivable are valued at C144 000; in other words, C10 000 is considered to be uncollectable. The journal entries are as follows:

	Dr	*Cr*
Revaluation (OE)	5 000	
Inventory (A)		5 000
Revaluation (OE)	10 000	
Allowance for doubtful debts (–A)		10 000

The entry to adjust the value of the inventory credits the inventory account to reduce the balance. The entry to adjust the accounts receivable credits the allowance for doubtful debts. This is in line with the treatment of inventory write-downs and the allowance for doubtful debts described in earlier chapters.

The balance on the revaluation account after processing all the changes in asset values as agreed by the partners (except goodwill) is C125 000. (The recognition of goodwill will be dealt with separately in the next section.) This balance represents an increase in the net assets of the partnership. As any change in the net assets changes the interest of the owners in the business, the balance on the revaluation account must be allocated to the capital accounts of the *existing* partners in the *existing profit-sharing ratio*. The accounting entry is as follows:

	Dr	*Cr*
Revaluation (OE)	125 000	
Capital – Simon (OE)		75 000
Capital – Gary (OE)		50 000

The revaluation account is shown below:

Revaluation

Details	C	*Details*	C
Inventory	5 000	Land	130 000
Allowance for doubtful debts	10 000	Machinery	10 000
Capital – Simon	75 000		
Capital – Gary	50 000		
	140 000		140 000

 **Pause and reflect...**

Think about the C125 000 credit balance in the revaluation account that is transferred to the partners' capital accounts.

a) What does this balance represent?
b) How will this be incorporated into the financial statements?

Response

a) The balance in the revaluation account represents the difference between the *carrying amount* of the assets and their *fair value* on the date of admission of the new partner.
b) It will be reported on the statement of changes in equity as an owner change in equity, allocated to the *existing* partners' capital accounts in the existing profit-sharing ratio.

16.5.3 Identification of goodwill

Nature of goodwill

The revaluation of the partnership's tangible assets results in the net assets being stated at their fair value. However, the value of the business as a whole could be greater than the sum of the individual net assets. The excess of the value of a business as a whole (as indicated by the purchase consideration) over the fair value of its identifiable net assets is known as goodwill.

Goodwill is an ***intangible asset***.

An intangible asset is something that is unable to be touched. IAS 38 *Intangible Assets* defines it as an identifiable, non-monetary asset without physical substance.

A more detailed discussion of intangible assets is beyond the scope of this text. Our discussion is limited to goodwill as it impacts upon partnership admission and dissolution.

Goodwill represents anticipated future economic benefits from assets that are not capable of being individually identified and separately recognised. Goodwill arises through factors such as sound management, ongoing advertising, a well-trained workforce and loyal customers.

Accounting practice distinguishes between ***internally generated goodwill*** and ***goodwill arising on a business combination,*** often called ***purchased goodwill***. IAS 38 *Intangible Assets* states that internally generated goodwill is not recognised as an asset because it is not an *identifiable* resource controlled by the entity and its *cost cannot be measured reliably*. This is because internally generated goodwill could be valued differently by different parties and could fluctuate in value as various factors which affect the business change on a daily basis. On the other hand, the value of purchased goodwill is based on an arm's-length transaction between the seller and the purchaser of a business. As a result, where we have the purchase of a business, which is more than just a collection of assets and liabilities and includes an integrated set of activities and assets capable of being managed to provide a return, IFRS requires us to account for the difference between the fair value of the consideration paid for the business *and* the fair value of the identifiable assets acquired and liabilities assumed as goodwill.

This can be represented as shown in Diagram 16.3.

Goodwill arising on acquisition represents a payment made by the acquirer in anticipation of future economic benefits. With the passage of time, goodwill diminishes, reflecting that its service potential is decreasing. However, in some cases the value of goodwill may appear not to decrease over time. This is because the potential for economic benefits that was purchased initially is being replaced by internally generated goodwill.

Turning our attention again to partnerships, any difference between the capital contribution of the incoming partner and the fair value of the net assets is recorded as goodwill. It must be taken into account so that the equity of the existing partners correctly reflects their share of the business at the date of admission of the new partner.

Fair value of consideration paid

Less

Fair value of identifiable net assets acquired

= Goodwill

Diagram 16.3 Goodwill

We will now apply the concepts discussed in the above paragraphs to Intense Sports, as shown in the following calculations. Remember that Mark is being admitted to the partnership on 1 January 20X8.

		Mark 1/3 share	*Total for partnership*
Purchase consideration (A)	*(Total = 440 000 × 3)*	440 000	1 320 000
Fair value of identifiable net assets (B)	*(Mark 1/3 share = 1 128 000 × 1/3)*	376 000	1 128 000
Owner's equity per statement of financial position at 31/12/X7			1 003 000
Adjustment to fair value of assets			125 000
Goodwill (A – B)	*(Total = 64 000 × 3)*	64 000	192 000

It is important to note that the purchase consideration paid by Mark of C440 000 for a one-third share of the partnership results in an *implied* purchase consideration for the partnership as a whole of C1 320 000. The fair value of the identifiable net assets of C1 128 000 (the total for the partnership) is calculated by taking the owners' equity per the statement of financial position at 31 December 20X7 of C1 003 000 and adjusting for the fair value of the assets of C125 000. The amount of goodwill raised on the formation of the new partnership arrangement is C192 000, being the difference between C1 320 000 and C1 128 000.

The recognition of goodwill is an *owner change in equity*, and as such will appear on the statement of changes in equity as an adjustment to the partners' capital accounts on the admission of a new partner. The accounting entries for goodwill will be described in the following section.

Accounting for goodwill

IFRS 3 *Business Combinations* states that goodwill should be recognised as an asset on the statement of financial position and carried at cost less accumulated impairment losses. Since goodwill represents part of the net assets of the entity, the amount of goodwill raised will need to be allocated to the existing partners in the existing profit-sharing ratio. This means that the goodwill raised of C192 000 is recorded in the capital accounts of Gary and Simon, ensuring that the capital accounts reflect a fair value measure.

The accounting entry is as follows:

	Dr	*Cr*
Goodwill (A)	192 000	
Capital – Simon (OE)		115 200
Capital – Gary (OE)		76 800

The goodwill account, after initial recognition, is shown below.

Goodwill			
Details	*C*	*Details*	*C*
Capital – Simon	115 200	Balance c/d	192 000
Capital – Gary	76 800		
	192 000		192 000
Balance b/d	192 000		

 **Pause and reflect...**

Can you think of how the equity of the partnership has been adjusted from the balance of C1 003 000 at 31 December 20X7, taking into account the revaluation of assets and the recognition of goodwill?

Response

	C
Balance per statement of financial position at 31/12/X7	1 003 000
Fair value adjustment of non-current and current assets	125 000
Fair value of identifiable net assets	1 128 000
Goodwill	192 000
Fair value of partnership as a whole	1 320 000

According to IFRS 3, an impairment test should be performed on the amount of goodwill annually, or more frequently if events or changes in circumstances indicate that it might be impaired. Such an impairment test should be performed in accordance with the impairment principles outlined in Chapter 10, *Property, plant and equipment*. Any impairment loss relating to goodwill should be recognised as an expense, therefore an impairment test will be performed at least annually on the goodwill of C192 000 raised in our example, assuming that the partnership's accounting policies conform to IFRS.

On a final note, while IFRS 3 does not permit the amortisation of goodwill, IFRS for SMEs does provide for the amortisation of intangible assets (including goodwill) over their useful lives or, if that cannot be determined without undue cost and effort, over an assumed period of ten years. A detailed discussion on the divergence between IFRS and IFRS for SMEs on this matter is beyond the scope of this book. What is important for our purposes is simply that a partnership is probably not compelled to comply with IFRS or IFRS for SMEs, and would therefore have an accounting policy choice when it comes to the amortisation of goodwill.

16.5.4 Contribution to capital

The new partner's contribution to the equity of the partnership needs to be recorded. The total amount paid by Mark amounts to C440 000. The accounting entry is as follows:

	Dr	*Cr*
Bank (A)	440 000	
Capital – Mark (OE)		440 000

Having now examined in detail all the aspects relating to the admission of a partner to a partnership, we can now prepare a solution to the example: 'Admission of a partner'. The capital accounts of the partners are shown as well for illustrative purposes.

Solution: Admission of a partner

a) Extract from statement of changes in equity (showing owner changes in equity relating to admission of Mark)

INTENSE SPORTS PARTNERSHIP
(EXTRACT FROM) STATEMENT OF CHANGES IN EQUITY
FOR THE YEAR ENDED 31 DECEMBER 20X8

	Capital			*Current*		*Appropriation*	*Total*
	Simon	*Gary*	*Mark*	*Simon*	*Gary*		
	C	C		C	C	C	C
Balance at 01/01/X8	280 000	325 000	—	244 540	153 460	—	1 003 000
Revaluation on admission of partner	75 000	50 000					125 000
Recognition of goodwill	115 200	76 800					192 000
Contributions and distributions							
Contribution to capital			440 000				440 000
Preliminary balance at 01/01/X8	470 200	451 800	440 000	244 540	153 460	—	1 760 000

This shows an extract from the statement of changes in equity as it will appear for the year ended 31 December 20X8, but only including the *owner changes in equity* transactions relating to the admission of the new partner on 1 January 20X8. *Non-owner changes in equity* transactions such as the profit for the period can only be incorporated at the end of the year.

b) Statement of financial position immediately after the admission of Mark

INTENSE SPORTS PARTNERSHIP
STATEMENT OF FINANCIAL POSITION
AT 1 JANUARY 20X8

		Note	*C*
ASSETS			
Non-current assets			982 000
Property, plant and equipment		1	790 000
Goodwill			192 000
Current assets			1 003 000
Inventory	*(70 000 – 5 000)*		65 000
Accounts receivable	*(154 000 – 10 000)*		144 000
Bank	*(354 000 + 440 000)*		794 000
			1 985 000

	Note	*C*
EQUITY AND LIABILITIES		
Equity		1 760 000
Capital accounts		1 362 000
Simon		470 200
Gary		451 800
Mark		440 000
Current accounts		398 000
Simon		244 540
Gary		153 460
Mark		—
Non-current liabilities		
Borrowing – Mega Bank		80 000
Current liabilities		145 000
Accounts payable		141 000
Interest payable		4 000
		1 985 000

INTENSE SPORTS PARTNERSHIP
NOTES TO THE FINANCIAL STATEMENTS
AT 1 JANUARY 20X8

1 Property, plant and equipment

	Land	*Machinery*	*Total*
	C	*C*	*C*
Carrying amount at 01/01/X8	700 000	90 000	790 000
Cost	700 000	90 000	790 000
Accumulated depreciation	—	—	—

 Remember that we are using the same accounting records for the newly formed entity (the Intense Sports Partnership with Simon, Gary and Mark as partners) that was used for the previous entity (the Intense Sports Partnership with Simon and Gary as partners). Both the land and the machinery are thus shown 'at cost' as the fair value to the previous entity is the cost to the new entity.

Pause and reflect...

Are you able to identify the components that make up the fair value of the partnership equity of C1 760 000?

Response

Identifiable net assets before change in partnership arrangement	1 003 000
Fair value adjustment	125 000
Identifiable net assets at fair value	1 128 000
Goodwill	192 000
Additional cash contribution	440 000
Total net asset value after change in partnership arrangement	1 760 000

The capital and current accounts of the partners incorporating the admission of Mark appear as follows:

Capital – Simon

Details	*C*	*Details*	*C*
		Balance b/d	280 000
		Revaluation	75 000
		Goodwill	115 200
Balance c/d	470 200		
	470 200		470 200
		Balance b/d	470 200

Capital – Gary

Details	*C*	*Details*	*C*
		Balance b/d	325 000
		Revaluation	50 000
		Goodwill	76 800
Balance c/d	451 800		
	451 800		451 800
		Balance b/d	451 800

Capital – Mark

Details	*C*	*Details*	*C*
		Bank	440 000
Balance c/d			
	440 000		440 000
		Balance c/d	440 000

Current – Simon

Details	*C*	*Details*	*C*
		Balance b/d	244 540
Balance c/d	244 540		
	244 540		244 540
		Balance b/d	244 540

Current – Gary

Details	*C*	*Details*	*C*
		Balance b/d	153 460
Balance c/d	153 460		
	153 460		153 460
		Balance b/d	153 460

16.6 Partnership dissolution

The dissolution of a partnership can take two forms:

- retirement or death of a partner where the interests of a retired/deceased partner are taken over by either:
  - a new partner, or
  - the remaining partners.
- liquidation of a partnership where the activities are terminated.

16.6.1 Retirement or death of a partner

A partner who retires from a partnership or the estate of a deceased partner is entitled to the settlement of his or her interest in the partnership. The interest of a partner is determined by the partner's share of the equity of the partnership. A partner's share of equity will include the following:

- the balance on the partner's capital account;
- the balance on the partner's current account;
- the partner's share of any gains or losses on the restatement of the assets and liabilities to fair value at date of retirement or death;
- the partner's share of any movement in the value of goodwill, as agreed between the partners;
- a charge against the retiring partner for any assets taken over;
- the partner's share of any costs incurred in the change in partnership composition.

Example: Retirement of a partner

Gary decided to retire at 31 December 20X8. Simon and Mark continued the partnership, sharing profits and losses equally.

On 2 January 20X8, the entity purchased three identical motor vehicles at a cost of C100 000 each. Each motor vehicle has an estimated useful life of four years and an estimated residual value of C20 000. The straight-line basis of depreciation is used.

The statement of financial position of Intense Sports at 31 December 20X8, *before the retirement* of Gary, is as shown below:

INTENSE SPORTS PARTNERSHIP
STATEMENT OF FINANCIAL POSITION
AT 31 DECEMBER 20X8

		Note	C
ASSETS			
Non-current assets			1 184 800
Property, plant and equipment		1	1 012 000
Goodwill			172 800
Cost			192 000
Accumulated amortisation			(19 200)
Current assets			962 000
Inventory			87 000
Accounts receivable	*(175 000 − 10 000)*		165 000
Expenses paid in advance			20 000
Bank			690 000
			2 146 800
EQUITY AND LIABILITIES			
Equity			1 921 800
Capital accounts			1 362 000
Simon			470 200
Gary			451 800
Mark			440 000
Current accounts			559 800
Simon			289 600
Gary			197 600
Mark			72 600

	Note	C
Non-current liabilities		
Borrowings – Mega Bank		80 000
Current liabilities		
Accounts payable		145 000
		2 146 800

INTENSE SPORTS PARTNERSHIP
NOTES TO THE FINANCIAL STATEMENTS
AT 31 DECEMBER 20X8

1) Property, plant and equipment

	Land	*Motor vehicles*	*Machinery*	*Total*
	C	*C*	*C*	*C*
Carrying amount at 31/12/X8	700 000	240 000	72 000	1 012 000
Cost	700 000	300 000	90 000	1 090 000
Accumulated depreciation	—	(60 000)	(18 000)	(78 000)

The fair value of the assets and liabilities at 31 December 20X8 are as follows:

- Land C897 200
- Machinery C80 000
- Motor vehicles C240 000
- Inventory C83 000
- Accounts receivable C160 000

The estimated useful lives and residual values of the machinery and motor vehicles remained unchanged.

An impairment test was performed on the goodwill at 31 December 20X8. It was estimated that the goodwill had a recoverable amount of C172 800. An impairment loss of C19 200 has been recognised and correctly recorded.

It was agreed that Gary would take over (at the carrying amount) one of the three motor vehicles, and the balance would be paid to him in cash.

You are required to:

a) Draw up the revaluation account.
b) Draw up the capital accounts and current accounts in columnar format, beginning with the balances at 31 December 20X8 and recording the entries relating to the retirement of Gary.
c) Prepare the statement of financial position of the Intense Sports Partnership at 31 December 20X8 after Gary's retirement.

The information from this example will now be used to illustrate the procedure relating to the retirement of a partner from a partnership, before preparing the solution, as required.

As mentioned above, a partner who retires from a partnership is entitled to the settlement of his or her interest in the partnership. The accounting procedures on retirement of a partner are therefore directed towards establishing the retiring partner's share of the fair value equity of the partnership as well as the share belonging to the remaining partners. The discussion that follows will consider each of the components of equity and the adjustments required to equity as described in Section 16.6.1.

The starting point is to ensure that we have the latest **balances on the capital accounts and current accounts** of the partners. We do have these balances, as reported on the statement of financial position at 31 December 20X8. The effects on equity relating to the retirement of Gary will be posted to the capital accounts, as described below.

The next step is to account for the **restatement of the assets and liabilities to fair value** at the date of retirement or death. The adjustments will not be described in detail as the principles were explained in the section on partnership admission. Note that the revaluation account shown in the solution has been drawn up on the assumption that each adjustment is debited or credited individually to the account.

	Dr	*Cr*
Accumulated depreciation (–A)	18 000	
Machinery (A)		18 000
Land (A)	197 200	
Machinery (A)	8 000	
Inventory (A)		4 000
Allowance for doubtful debts (–A)		5 000
Revaluation (OE)		196 200

The only new concept that needs to be explained is the treatment of a **depreciable asset which is not revalued** on a change in partnership composition. The motor vehicles are considered to be worth their carrying amount of C240 000. As the new partnership constitutes a new entity, the cost of the motor vehicles to the new partnership is taken as the carrying amount of the motor vehicles to the existing partnership. An entry is therefore required to adjust the existing cost and accumulated depreciation in the accounting records in order to record the carrying amount of C240 000 as the initial cost to the new partnership. The entry is as follows:

	Dr	*Cr*
Accumulated depreciation (–A)	60 000	
Motor vehicles (A)		60 000

There is no impact on the equity of the partnership and therefore the capital accounts are unaffected.

The value of **goodwill** must also be taken into account on the retirement of a partner. Goodwill is assessed for impairment on an annual basis, and the impairment at 31 December 20X8 has already been recorded. As goodwill is an asset and the new partnership constitutes a new entity, the existing cost and accumulated impairment losses must be removed from the accounting records.

Remember that in our example, the carrying amount of goodwill on the statement of financial position is C172 800 (cost of C192 000 and accumulated impairment losses of C19 200). As the cost of the goodwill to the new partnership is taken as the carrying amount of the goodwill to the existing partnership, an accounting entry is needed. The entry is as follows:

	Dr	*Cr*
Accumulated impairment (–A)	19 200	
Goodwill (A)		19 200

The carrying amount of any **assets taken over** by a retiring partner needs to be charged against his or her capital account. In this case, Gary is taking over one of the motor vehicles at a carrying amount of C80 000. The accounting entry to record this transaction is as follows:

	Dr	*Cr*
Capital – Gary (OE)	80 000	
Motor vehicle (A)		80 000

Lastly, the **balance on the current account** of the *retiring* partner is transferred to the capital account:

	Dr	*Cr*
Current – Gary (OE)	197 600	
Capital – Gary (OE)		197 600

At this stage, the balance on the retiring partner's capital account represents the share of the equity owing to the retiring partner. The amount owing to Gary is C634 800 and is paid to him from the funds in the bank account.

Having illustrated the procedure relating to the retirement of a partner from a partnership, we can now prepare a solution to the example: 'Retirement of a partner'.

Solution: Retirement of a partner

a) Revaluation account

Revaluation

Details	C	*Details*	C
Inventory	4 000	Land	197 200
Allowance for doubtful debts	5 000	Machinery	8 000
Capital – Simon	65 400		
Capital – Gary	65 400		
Capital – Mark	65 400		
	205 200		205 200

b) Capital and current accounts after the retirement of Gary

Taking into account all of the entries discussed above, the capital and current accounts of the partners appear as follows:

Capital

Details	*Simon*	*Gary*	*Mark*	*Details*	*Simon*	*Gary*	*Mark*
Motor vehicle		80 000		Balance b/d	470 200	451 800	440 000
Bank		***634 800***		Revaluation	65 400	65 400	65 400
Balance c/d	535 600	–	505 400	Current Gary		197 600	
	535 600	714 800	505 400		535 600	714 800	505 400
				Balance b/d	535 600	–	505 400

Current

Details	*Simon*	*Gary*	*Mark*	*Details*	*Simon*	*Gary*	*Mark*
Capital – Gary		197 600		Balance b/d	289 600	197 600	72 600
Balance c/d	289 600	–	72 600				
	289 600	197 600	72 600		289 600	197 600	72 600
				Balance b/d	289 600	–	72 600

The amount of C634 800 paid to Gary is the balance on his capital account after taking into account the revaluation of the assets, the transfer of the balance from his current account and the motor vehicle taken over by him.

c) Statement of financial position of the partnership after the retirement of Gary

INTENSE SPORTS PARTNERSHIP
STATEMENT OF FINANCIAL POSITION
AT 31 DECEMBER 20X8

ASSETS		
Non-current assets		1 310 000
Property, plant and equipment		1 137 200
Goodwill		172 800
Cost		172 800
Accumulated amortisation		—
Current assets		318 200
Inventory	*(87 000 – 4 000)*	83 000
Accounts receivable	*(175 000 – 15 000)*	160 000
Expenses paid in advance		20 000
Bank	*(690 000 – 634 800)*	55 200
		1 628 200
EQUITY AND LIABILITIES		
Equity		1 403 200
Capital accounts		1 041 000
Simon		535 600
Mark		505 400
Current accounts		362 200
Simon		289 600
Mark		72 600
Non-current liabilities		
Borrowings – Mega Bank		80 000
Current liabilities		
Accounts payable		145 000
		1 628 200

INTENSE SPORTS PARTNERSHIP
NOTES TO THE FINANCIAL STATEMENTS
AT 31 DECEMBER 20X8

1) Property, plant and equipment

	Land	*Motor vehicles*	*Machinery*	*Total*
	C	C	C	C
Carrying amount at 31/12/X8	897 200	160 000	80 000	1 137 200
Cost	897 200	160 000	80 000	1 137 200
Accumulated depreciation	—	—	—	—

Finally, and before moving on, it is necessary to compute the change in the profit-sharing ratio. Simon, Gary and Mark were sharing profits equally (1/3:1/3:1/3) and the remaining partners (Simon and Mark) agreed to share profits equally. The change in profit share can be shown as follows:

	Existing ratio		*Change*		*New ratio*
Simon	1/3	+	1/6	=	3/6
Gary	1/3	–	1/3	=	–
Mark	1/3	+	1/6	=	3/6
	1				1

As you can see from the calculation above, Gary is relinquishing one-third (or 2/6) of profits, which is being taken over as 1/6 each by Simon and Mark.

16.6.2 Liquidation of the partnership

The liquidation of a business means the cessation of its activities. The assets of the business are sold and the liabilities settled. Once the liquidation procedure is complete, the only items remaining on the statement of financial position are the cash in the bank and the owners' equity. The balance on each partner's capital account represents the amount to be paid to each partner on liquidation.

The objective of the liquidation procedure is therefore to realise the maximum possible cash from the assets, to settle the liabilities and to ensure that the partners are paid out their share of the equity of the partnership. The procedure is summarised below:

- Transfer the current account balances to the partners' capital accounts.
- Transfer assets at the carrying amount to a ***realisation*** account.
- Record the proceeds on realisation, as well as other profits or losses on liquidation in the realisation account. It is possible for a partner to take over an asset for his or her own account, at a value agreed upon between the partners, instead of selling it. This will result in the partner's capital account being debited and the realisation account being credited with the agreed value of the asset taken over.
- Settle liabilities and record the profit or loss on settlement in the realisation account.
- Pay expenses.
- Determine the profit or loss on realisation and transfer to the partners' capital accounts.
- The remaining cash is paid to the partners to settle the balances on their capital accounts. It may happen that a partner's interest is not sufficient to cover the loss on realisation, and he or she will thus have a shortfall on his or her capital account, shown by a debit balance. The other partners have a claim against that partner for the amount of the shortfall. If the partner can make good the shortfall, he or she is required to pay the amount into the partnership. Any further remaining cash is distributed to the partners in accordance with the credit balances on their capital accounts.

 **Pause and reflect...**

In accounting for the admission of a partner to or the retirement of a partner from a partnership, changes in the fair value of assets were recorded in a *revaluation* account. Why is a *realisation* account used on the liquidation of a partnership?

Response

A revaluation account is used to record *unrealised* movements in the values of the assets. You will recall that such movements are not realised in cash as there has not been a transaction involving a disposal or settlement. On liquidation, however, *all* partnership assets are realised and liabilities settled in cash, therefore a realisation account is used to record the cash realisation of the partnership's equity.

Example: Liquidation of partnership

Another year later, on 31 December 20X9, Simon and Mark decided to dissolve the partnership. The statement of financial position at that date is presented below.

INTENSE SPORTS PARTNERSHIP
STATEMENT OF FINANCIAL POSITION
AT 31 DECEMBER 20X9

		Note	*C*
ASSETS			
Non-current assets			1 250 000
Property, plant and equipment		1	1 077 200
Goodwill			172 800
Cost			172 800
Accumulated amortisation			—
Current assets			199 400
Inventory			74 000
Accounts receivable	*(124 000 – 10 000)*		114 000
Bank			11 400
			1 449 400
EQUITY AND LIABILITIES			
Equity			1 261 400
Capital accounts			1 041 000
Simon			535 600
Mark			505 400
Current accounts			220 400
Simon			86 800
Mark			33 600
Non-current liabilities			
Borrowings – Mega Bank			80 000
Current liabilities			
Accounts payable			108 000
			1 449 400

INTENSE SPORTS PARTNERSHIP
NOTES TO THE FINANCIAL STATEMENTS
AT 31 DECEMBER 20X9

1) Property, plant and equipment

	Land	*Motor vehicles*	*Machinery*	*Total*
	C	C	C	C
Carrying amount at 31/12/X8	897 200	160 000	80 000	1 137 200
Cost	897 200	160 000	80 000	1 137 200
Accumulated depreciation	—	—	—	—
Depreciation	—	(40 000)	20 000	20 000
Carrying amount at 31/12/X9	897 200	120 000	60 000	1 077 200
Cost	897 200	160 000	80 000	1 137 200
Accumulated depreciation	—	(40 000)	(20 000)	(60 000)

The following additional information is available:

- The land was sold for C850 000.
- The machinery was sold for C58 000.
- The inventory was sold for C64 000.
- Accounts receivable collected amounted to C104 000.
- Suppliers were paid C100 000 in full settlement.

Each partner agreed to take over one of the two remaining motor vehicles at carrying amount.

You are required to:

Show the following ledger accounts in the accounting records of Intense Sports: Realisation; Bank; Loan – Simon; Accounts payable; Capital – Simon; Capital – Mark.

Solution: Liquidation of partnership

Realisation

Details	*C*	*Details*	*C*
Land	897 200	Acc dep: MV	40 000
Motor vehicles	160 000	Acc dep: Machinery	20 000
Machinery	80 000		
Goodwill	172 800	Allowance for doubtful debts	10 000
Inventory	74 000		
Accounts receivable	124 000	Bank (L & B)	850 000
		Bank (Machinery)	58 000
		Bank (Inventory)	64 000
		Bank (Accounts receivable)	104 000
		Accounts payable	8 000
		Capital – Simon (MV)	60 000
		Capital – Mark (MV)	60 000
		Balance	234 000
	1 508 000		1 508 000
Balance	234 000	Capital Simon (1/2)	117 000
		Capital Mark (1/2)	117 000

Bank

Details	*C*	*Details*	*C*
Balance b/d	11 400	Accounts payable	100 000
Realisation	850 000	Borrowings – Mega Bank	80 000
		Balance c/d	907 400
Realisation	58 000		
Realisation	64 000		
Realisation	104 000		
	1 087 400		1 087 400
Balance b/d	907 400	Capital – Simon	545 400
		Capital – Mark	362 000
	907 400		907 400

Borrowings – Mega Bank

Details	*C*	*Details*	*C*
Bank	80 000	Balance b/d	80 000
	80 000		80 000

Accounts payable

Details	*C*	*Details*	*C*
Bank	100 000	Balance b/d	108 000
Realisation	8 000		
	108 000		108 000

Capital – Simon				Capital – Mark			
Details	*C*	*Details*	*C*	*Details*	*C*	*Details*	*C*
Realisation (MV)	60 000	Balance b/d	535 600	Realisation (MV)	60 000	Balance b/d	505 400
Realisation	117 000	Current – Simon	186 800	Realisation	117 000	Current – Mark	33 600
Bank	***545 400***			***Bank***	***362 000***		
	722 400		722 400		539 000		539 000

 The realisation account is used to determine the profit or loss on realisation of the net assets of the business. The amount of the profit or loss is the difference between:

- the proceeds on realisation of the assets and income earned as part of the liquidation; and
- the carrying amount of assets and expenses incurred as part of the liquidation.

Note that the realisation account shows a loss on realisation of C234 000. This is divided equally between the partners, and an amount of C117 000 is debited to the capital accounts of both Simon and Mark.

As mentioned in the introduction to this section, when the liquidation procedure is complete, the only items on the statement of financial position are the cash in the bank and the owners' equity. In this case the bank account has a balance of C907 400, and the capital accounts of Simon and Mark have balances of C545 400 and C362 000 respectively. The final transaction is for the remaining cash of C907 400 to be paid to the partners to settle the balances on their capital accounts.

Pause and reflect...

The balance on the goodwill account of C172 800 was transferred to the realisation account together with the other assets. You will notice that no proceeds were recorded in the realisation account in relation to the goodwill. What is the reason for this?

Response

As goodwill represents anticipated future economic benefits, there can be no value placed on goodwill of an entity in liquidation. Remember that the definition and recognition criteria for an asset require that probable future economic benefits will flow to the entity. Another approach could have been to impair the goodwill immediately rather than transferring it to the realisation account.

Pause and reflect...

In this example, the accounts payable balance of C108 000 was settled for C100 000 and the profit of C8 000 recorded in the realisation account. Can you think of any alternative accounting procedure to record the settlement of the accounts payable?

Response

The accounts payable balance of C108 000 could be transferred to the realisation account and the settlement for C100 000 then recorded in the realisation account. The net result of this procedure would be a profit on settlement of C8 000 in the realisation account.

Revision example

Brian and Jacob have been trading as sole proprietorships for a number of years in similar fields. They decided to form a partnership from 1 January 20X1, at which date the net asset value per the accounting records of Brian's business was C14 000 and Jacob's business was C21 000.

The two partners agreed to the following with respect to their new partnership:

- The partners are to share profits and losses in the ratio of 2:3.
- Valuations confirmed that the land of Brian's business was understated by C1 000 and that of Jacob's business was overstated by C3 000.
- Prior to the formation of the partnership, no allowance for doubtful debts was recorded. The fair value of the combined accounts receivable is C1 000 lower than the carrying amount.
- Brian is to get a partner's salary of 10 per cent of net sales, and Jacob a partner's salary of 12 per cent of gross profit. The balance of the profits is to be shared between the partners in their agreed ratio.
- The business is to use the perpetual method of accounting for inventory.

The summarised trading results of the partnership for the half year to 30 June 20X1 were as follows:

	C
Sales	38 400
Returns inward	2 400
Cost of sales	13 500
Returns outward	900
Operating expenses	12 200

On 1 July 20X1, it was decided to admit Freyja to the partnership. At a meeting of the three partners it was agreed:

- that Freyja was to introduce cash of C19 720;
- that Freyja was to get a 40 per cent share of the profits while Brian and Jacob would share between themselves as they did prior to the admission of Freyja;
  and
- that Brian and Jacob would no longer be entitled to any partner's salaries.

On 30 September 20X1, after the partnership of Brian, Jacob and Freyja had been in existence for three months, Jacob passed away. Brian and Freyja decided to continue in partnership, sharing profits and losses in the ratio of 3:5.

Upon drawing up a profit and loss account for the period 1 July 20X1 to 30 September 20X1, a profit of C2 500 was transferred to the appropriation account.

On 30 September 20X1, the recoverable amount of goodwill was estimated to be C6 650. This has not been taken into account in the determination of the profit.

During the three months between 1 July and 30 September, Brian and Jacob had withdrawn C3 000 each and Freyja had withdrawn C600.

You are required to:

Prepare, in columnar form, the partners' combined capital and current accounts to record the formation of the partnership, the admission of Freyja, and the change caused by the death of Jacob.

 **Solution: Revision example**

			Capital/ current	*Capital/ current*	*Capital/ current*
		Total	*Brian*	*Jacob*	*Freyja*
		C	C	C	C
	Net assets introduced	35 000	14 000	21 000	—
	Land	(2 000)	1 000	(3 000)	—
	Provision for doubtful debts	(1 000)	(400)	(600)	—
01/01/X1	Opening balance	32 000	14 600	17 400	—
	Partners' salaries	6 300	3 600	2 700	—
01/01/X1 – 30/06/X1	Appropriation (share of profit)	4 000	1 600	2 400	—
30/06/X1	Balance on equity before Freyja's admission	42 300	19 800	22 500	—
	Bank	19 720	—	—	19 720
	Goodwill (write-up)	7 000	2 800	4 200	—
		69 020	22 600	26 700	19 720
01/07/X1 – 30/09/X1	Appropriation (share of profit)	2 500	600	900	1 000
	Goodwill (impairment)	(350)	(84)	(126)	(140)
		71 170	23 116	27 474	20 580
	Distributions	(6 600)	(3 000)	(3 000)	(600)
		64 570	20 116	24 474	19 980
	Bank (amount due to Jacob's estate)	(24 474)	—	(24 474)	—
30/09/X1	Balance on equity	40 096	20 116	—	19 980

The main purpose of this question was to focus your attention on equity and on the transactions that affect equity.

The partners' salaries and share of profits is normally credited to the partners' *current* accounts, but to establish the equity of the partnership of Brian and Jacob at 30 June 20X1 (prior to the admission of Freyja), the *capital* and *current* account balances would need to be combined to arrive at the equity of C42 300 as shown in the solution.

Similarly, to calculate Jacob's share of equity at the date of his death, it is necessary to take into account entries to the *current* accounts for share of profit and distributions. In this solution, these transactions have all been posted to the combined capital/current accounts.

Workings

Profit for first half year

Sales	*(38 400 – 2 400)*	36 000
Cost of sales		(13 500)
	Gross profit	22 500
Operating expenses		(12 200)
Profit		10 300
Appropriations:		(6 300)
Commission: Brian	*(10% of 36 000)*	3 600
Commission: Jacob	*(12% of 22 500)*	2 700
Balance of profits		4 000
Brian		(1 600)
Jacob		(2 400)

New profit-sharing ratios

Brian	2/5	×	3/5	=	6/25
Jacob	3/5	×	3/5	=	9/25
	1				
Freyja	2/5			=	10/25
Balance	3/5				1
or					
Brian	10/25	–	*4/25	=	6/25
Jacob	15/25	–	*6/25	=	9/25
Freyja					10/25
					1
* Brian gives up	2/5	×	2/5	=	4/25
* Jacob gives up	3/5	×	2/5	=	6/25

	C
Purchase consideration (19 720/0.40)	49 300
Owner's equity at 30/06/X1	42 300
Total goodwill	7 000

Goodwill on winding up Jacob's estate

	C
Value on admission of Freyja	7 000
Recoverable amount	6 650
Impairment	350

Bibliography

International Accounting Standards Board. 2011. IFRS 11 *Joint Arrangements*.
International Accounting Standards Board. 2013. IFRS 3 *Business Combinations*.
International Accounting Standards Board. 2014. IAS 38 *Intangible Assets*.
Henning, JJ & Delport, HJ. 1984. *Partnership*. Durban, South Africa: Butterworths.
Partnership Act, 1890. www.google.co.uk/webhp?sourceid=chrome-instant&ion=1&espv=2&ie=UTF-8#q=partnership+act+1890 (Accessed 4 September 2015).
Whitlock, R. 2013. Iberdrola awarded contract for PV development in South Africa. www.renewableenergymagazine.com/article/iberdrola-awarded-contract-for-pv-development-in-20130516 (Accessed 20 May 2013).

17 Companies

Business focus

During 2009, the International Accounting Standards Board (IASB) released the *IFRS for Small and Medium-Sized Entities* (*IFRS for SMEs*), which is a self-contained standard of less than 250 pages. A completely revised version of the *IFRS for SMEs* was issued in December 2015. It is designed to meet the needs and capabilities of smaller concerns, many of which were finding the costs of compliance with full IFRS unduly high.

The *IFRS for SMEs* is less complex than full IFRS in a number of ways. For example, it dispenses with many of the accounting policy choices found in the full IFRS in favour of the simpler alternatives. It also requires considerably less disclosure. The IASB is of the opinion that *IFRS for SMEs* will probably provide a suitable basis for accounting for up to 95 per cent of companies. The United Kingdom and many countries around the world may be no exception.

The UK's Financial Reporting Council (FRC) has published FRS 102 *The Financial Reporting Standard applicable in the UK and Republic of Ireland*, which replaces current UK GAAP with effect for periods beginning on or after 1 January 2015. FRS 102 is derived from the IASB's *IFRS for SMEs*, but incorporates changes made by the FRC. One of the important changes widens the scope of the standard significantly compared to the *IFRS for SMEs*, allowing any entity not required to apply full IFRS to apply FRS 102.

In this chapter

A company is a separate legal entity from its owner or owners. This has a number of implications, including the legal form of the entity, the sources of finance and how profit is appropriated. These and other issues are explored in this chapter.

Dashboard

- Look at the *Learning outcomes* so that you know what you should be able to do after studying this chapter.
- Read the *Business focus* to place this chapter's contents in a real-world context.
- Preview *In this chapter* to focus your mind on the contents of the chapter.
- Read the *text* in detail.

- Apply your mind to the *Pause and reflect* scenarios.
- Section 17.5 briefly introduces the concepts of share capital and debentures, and then Sections 17.8 and 17.9 respectively describe the accounting issues in detail.
- Take careful note of the concepts of taxation and dividends in Section 17.7 and the accounting entries for these items.
- Ensure you are aware that the accounting for debentures in Section 17.9 requires some basic knowledge of the mathematical concepts of present value (PV) and internal rate of return (IRR).

- Prepare solutions to the examples as you read through the chapter.
- Prepare a solution to the *Revision example* at the end of the chapter without reference to the suggested one. Compare your solution to the suggested solution provided.

Learning outcomes

After studying this chapter, you should be able to do the following:

1 Identify the types of companies that can be formed in terms of the Companies Act.
2 Recall the specific characteristics of a company.
3 Describe the sources of finance available to a company, the identification of profits retained and the composition of a company's equity.
4 Describe the formation process.
5 Prepare financial information for a company.
6 Prepare accounting entries relating to share issues.
7 Prepare accounting entries relating to debenture issues.

Companies

17.1 Introduction

All UK limited companies must be legally registered with Companies House, the official Registrar of Companies.

A company is formed by submitting certain documents to the Registrar of Companies, the most important of these being the Memorandum of Association and the Articles of Association.

17.2 Types of companies

There are three main types of companies that can be formed in the UK – companies limited by shares, companies limited by guarantee and companies with unlimited liability. The latter are very rare and will not be discussed further.

17.2.1 Companies limited by shares

There are two classes of company limited by shares, known as a *private* company and a *public* company. Before examining the differences between these two types of companies, it is worth reviewing some of the attributes of a company limited by shares.

A company limited by shares is owned by shareholders, managed by directors and formed with the intention of making a profit. These profits can then be reinvested in the company or distributed to the owners in the form of dividend payments. Should the business entity encounter any financial difficulty, the shareholders' liability is limited to the amount of the shares they hold in the company. Recall, however, as mentioned in Chapter 1,

The accounting environment, that shareholders and directors are likely to be the same group of persons in a private company but a different group of persons in a public company.

Private company

Do you remember that the feature story at the beginning of this chapter said the most common type of company limited by shares is the private company? Although large public companies (such as Nestle, Marks & Spencer and Next, to name but a few) are more well known, there are substantially more private companies, many of which are SMEs.

For private companies, the **ability to issue shares is restricted.** A private company is prohibited from issuing any of its shares to the public. This means that a private company wishing to increase its equity by issuing shares will not be able to offer them to the general public. Offers of shares in a private company are normally made to potential investors who are known to the directors or existing shareholders and who have expressed an interest in investing in the company.

Related to this, a private company also has **restrictions on the transferability of its shares**. Although this constrains existing shareholders in terms of their ability to sell their shareholding, it does enable shareholders to maintain control over the ownership of the company.

A private company must have a **minimum of one shareholder and at least one director**. This means that an entrepreneur trading as a sole proprietor could form a private company and conduct his/her business operations using a company as the form of business entity.

The **minimum share capital** is £1 and the **company name** must end with either 'Limited' or 'Ltd'.

Public company

A public company is able to **offer shares to the general public**, which is done by means of a prospectus. A prospectus is a document advertising the sale of the shares and is normally sent to all existing shareholders as well as prospective shareholders who might read about the share issue in the newspaper.

The shares in a public company are also **easily transferable**. As such, a public company has the potential for large growth as it has access to unlimited investors' funds, particularly if it is listed on a stock exchange.

A public company must have a **minimum of one shareholder and at least two directors.**

The **minimum share capital** is £50 000 and the **company name** must end with either 'Public limited company' or 'Plc'.

17.2.2 Companies limited by guarantee

A company limited by guarantee is a private company, but it does not have a share capital. It is commonly used for charities, clubs and community enterprises. Most of such companies are formed as non-profit entities. A company limited by guarantee is registered at Companies House and is subject to all the requirements of the Companies Act, except those relating to shares.

There are no shares and thus no shareholders, but such a company does have members, who meet and control the company through general meetings. The directors are often called a management committee, but in law are still company directors and subject to all the rules that affect other directors.

A company limited by guarantee confers limited liability in the same way as a company limited by shares. Members guarantee to pay its debts, but only up to a fixed amount each, such as £1, and no member can be liable for more than that amount if the entity fails.

Chapter 20 addresses some issues relevant to this type of entity.

17.3 Characteristics of a company

A company is a legal entity distinct from its owners, who are known as the ***shareholders***, who, as a group, own the company through ownership of its shares. A share simply represents ownership of part of the equity of the company.

The Companies Act recognises that the owners and management may be separate and distinct groups of persons and provides for shareholders to appoint a board of directors to manage the company. The directors do not necessarily have to be shareholders themselves, but might be appointed because of their expertise in certain areas. The directors are appointed at a general meeting of shareholders. The company acts through its board of directors, who report periodically to the shareholders. The financial statements comprise one part of the annual report to shareholders.

As mentioned above, the shareholders and the company are separate legal entities. This has two important consequences. First, as a general rule, there is **limitation of liability**. The lenders can usually recover only from the company and not from its shareholders. As a trade-off for the benefit of limited liability and in order to protect lenders, legislation provides that the issue and repurchase of share capital be subject to certain formalities. (Note, however, that the buying and selling of a company's shares on the stock exchange does not constitute the repayment of capital). Second, and related to the above, the company has an **indefinite life** and a shareholder may transfer his or her shares in the company to another party without affecting its existence or continuation.

The role of the auditor is to express an opinion on the fair presentation of the financial statements and whether or not they have been prepared in accordance with the requirements of company law and relevant financial reporting standards.

The Companies Act 2006 requires all companies, both public and private, to appoint an auditor. However, in an attempt to avoid imposing undue cost or burden on smaller entities (also known as small and medium enterprises, or SMEs), an audit exemption is available to private companies only, if certain criteria are met.

Pause and reflect...

Are you aware of the criteria for a private company to be exempt from an audit?

Response

Currently, a private company qualifies for an audit exemption if it meets at least two of the following criteria:

- an annual turnover of no more than £6.5 million;
- assets worth no more than £3.26 million;
- on average, it has 50 or fewer employees.

Lastly, as a separate legal entity, a company is a taxpayer and pays tax on its taxable profits, currently at a rate of 20 per cent.

17.4 Listing of a public company

A public company can be ***listed*** on a stock exchange, which in the UK is known as the London Stock Exchange. When a company's shares are listed on the London Stock Exchange, the company is referred to as a ***listed public company***. Not all public companies are listed, and are referred to as ***unlisted public companies***.

There are a number of specific requirements that have to be met before a public company can apply for a listing on the main board, which are beyond the scope of this book.

Directors considering listing need to consider seriously all the implications, both financial and other, that are associated with a listing. The following factors require careful attention:

- **A clear vision and plan.** Directors of a listed company are selling both the company and their vision of what it could be. The presentation of that vision in a clear and thoughtful manner will greatly enhance the potential investor's decision-making process. A comprehensive business plan is required, supported by market information that identifies the market the company is in, its future potential and the competition.
- **A strong board of executive and non-executive directors.** Investors will want to know the composition of the board of directors and what strengths each member brings to the company. Executive directors need to be capable of implementing the company vision and plans, while non-executive directors need to represent a varied business background and also understand the industry in which the company operates.
- **Good tangible asset backing.** The company's tangible assets need to support earnings growth. If the company's statement of financial position has a number of intangible assets such as goodwill, these may need to be discounted when the company is valued for sale in a public market.
- **Suitable accounting and information systems.** Listed companies are required to report on a timely basis, which requires appropriate accounting and information systems.
- **Proven product.** The company needs a product that has a proven market and can form the basis of future plans for the company.
- **Financial costs.** Substantial costs are involved in a listing. This includes expenses such as legal, accounting and auditing fees, printing costs as well as listing costs that may range between 1.5 per cent and 4 per cent of the total issue value. Underwriting fees may vary between 5 per cent and 15 per cent of the issue value.
- **Hidden costs.** Extensive management time is involved in preparing for a listing. This can result in lost opportunities in other areas while management is focused on the listing. The cost of lost opportunities is hard to quantify.
- **Loss of privacy.** Listing a company results in a loss of the privacy that a private company enjoys. The financial statements are public information and disclose potentially sensitive information such as salaries paid to directors.
- **Potential loss of control.** The initial issue may not include more than 50 per cent of the shares of the company. However, subsequent offers of shares to the public may affect the ability of the founding owners to maintain a controlling interest.

17.5 Sources of finance for a company

Like a sole proprietorship and a partnership, a company can be financed from two sources: investors' funds and borrowed funds.

Cash invested by shareholders in a company is known as the ***share capital***. A company may borrow funds by, for example, taking out ***loans*** or by issuing ***debentures***. Finance obtained by a company by taking out a loan is no different from a loan taken out by any other form of business entity. We will therefore focus our attention in the following paragraphs on the issue of share capital and debentures, as these financial instruments are unique to companies. You should recall from Chapter 15, *Owner's equity and non-current liabilities*, that a financial instrument is any contract that gives rise to both a financial asset of one enterprise (or individual) and a ***financial liability*** or ***equity instrument*** of another enterprise (or individual).

17.5.1 Share capital

A share is an **equity instrument**, which is defined in IAS 32 *Financial Instruments: Presentation*.

An equity instrument is any contract that evidences a residual interest in the assets of an enterprise after deducting its liabilities.

Pause and reflect...

Can you relate the definition of an equity instrument to the *Conceptual Framework*?

Response

The *Conceptual Framework* defines equity as the *residual interest* in the assets of an enterprise after deducting all its liabilities. When a company issues shares, bank increases (increase in assets) and since there is no obligation to return the funds to shareholders (no increase in liabilities), the equity increases, thus making it an equity instrument.

The application of this definition is complex and beyond the scope of this book. It is important for you to appreciate, however, that a share, as an equity instrument, does not establish a contractual obligation of the entity.

Corporate law in some countries may permit companies to issue shares of two different **types**, par value and no par value shares.

Par value shares are those shares that have a specified par or nominal value per share. The par value thus represents the minimum amount which must be paid to the company in respect of each share issued. For example, a company may issue 500 000 shares of

C2 par value in order to raise C1 000 000. Once the share is issued and it is traded on the stock exchange, the par value ceases to be an indication of what the share is actually worth.

Par value shares may be issued at a premium. A premium is an excess issue price over the par value of the share and is described in detail in Section 17.8 dealing with share issues later in this chapter.

Dividends on par value shares are usually stated as a specified number of cents/pence per share, but are sometimes calculated as a percentage of the par value.

No par value shares do not have a specified nominal value per share. They may be issued at any price considered appropriate by the directors at the date of issue. Dividends on no par value shares must therefore be expressed as a specified number of cents/pence per share.

In the UK, all shares have a fixed par value. Shares may be issued in different **classes**, namely ordinary shares and preference shares.

Ordinary shares

Ordinary shares are typically the main risk-bearing shares of the company. If the company succeeds, the ordinary shareholders benefit through growth in the value of their investment as the share price increases and also from ***dividends*** received. Dividends are profits authorised for payment to shareholders. It is important to appreciate that shareholders have no legal right to the profit of the company until the directors have authorised the distribution of the profit in the form of a dividend. If the company fails and the share price drops, the ordinary shareholders bear all the losses of the company, limited, however, to the amount of their initial investment.

Preference shares

Preference shares are shares which receive a dividend prior to dividends paid to ordinary shareholders. The amount of the dividend and the rights attaching to the shares are set out in the terms of issue. Whether the shareholders have preference on winding-up of the company depends upon the terms of issue.

The dividend is normally expressed as a percentage of the issue price of the shares. For example, a 6 per cent preference share with an issue price of C2 will entitle the holder to an annual dividend of 12c per share if profits are available for distribution.

The Articles of Association can also specify if the dividends on preference shares are **cumulative** or **non-cumulative**. If the preference dividend is cumulative and profits are insufficient to pay part or all of the dividend, such shortfall is carried forward until such time as sufficient profits are available to pay arrears and current preference dividends. This right does not apply when the preference dividend is non-cumulative.

Preference shares may also have a further right to participate pro rata with the ordinary shares above a specified preference rate. These shares are known as **participating preference shares**.

A company may also choose to issue **redeemable preference shares**, which will be repaid to shareholders according to the terms of the issue. The classification of these instruments as equity or liability can become complex, but essentially the focus is on the substance of a financial instrument rather than its legal form. If the preference shares are compulsorily redeemable, or are redeemable at the option of the shareholder, they will be classified as a liability and not as equity. Where the redeemable preference shares are classified as a liability, it follows that dividends on such shares should be included with the interest expense on the statement of profit or loss, and not with dividends on the statement of changes in equity.

Pause and reflect...

If the preference shares of a company are compulsorily redeemable, or are redeemable at the option of the shareholder, what is the conceptual reason for these preference shares to be classified as a financial liability?

Response

By issuing such shares, the company creates a present obligation, the settlement of which will probably result in an outflow of future economic benefits. This results in a liability – in this case, a financial one.

17.5.2 Debentures

A debenture is a financial liability. It is a type of loan that enables the company to borrow funds from members of the public or other entities as the total loan is divided up into smaller units as specified in the issuing documents. Such a loan is usually secured by a mortgage over the company's property or by a general notarial bond over other assets. A company wishing to borrow, for example, C5 000 000, could issue 50 000 debentures of C100 each. A debenture generally bears a fixed rate of interest and its terms of repayment are specified.

A trust deed will normally be drawn up between the company and trustees on behalf of debenture holders. The company is required to keep a register of all debenture holders in the prescribed form.

Debentures are negotiable documents and may be sold to a third party. Debentures may be issued and redeemed at par, at a premium or at a discount.

The accounting for the issue of debentures will be described in detail further on in this chapter.

17.5.3 Identification of profits retained

The share capital is usually the primary source of financing for a company. As the business entity trades, profits are earned. However, the shareholders of a company do not have an automatic claim to the profits.

As a separate legal entity, a company pays tax on its profits and it is only the after-tax profits which are available for distribution to shareholders. It is the duty of the directors to decide how much of the after-tax profit to ***declare*** to shareholders as a ***dividend***. Amounts not allocated to shareholders as a dividend, in other words the profits retained, are referred to as ***reserves***. The reserves therefore form part of the equity of a company and are to be regarded as ***distributable*** or ***non-distributable***.

Distributable reserves

Distributable reserves are retained profits which, at the discretion of the directors, may be declared as a dividend to shareholders. However, they are retained to finance future growth of the company. All of the distributable reserves of a company are known as the ***retained earnings***.

When the directors declare a dividend to shareholders, a ***dividends payable*** or ***shareholders for dividends*** account is used to record the liability to shareholders. As management and owners of a public company are, to a large extent, different persons, the payment of a dividend to shareholders is initiated and carried out by the company.

Most large companies, typically listed public companies, declare and pay both interim and final dividends. An interim dividend is declared and paid when the profit for the first six months is known, normally just after halfway through the year. In the UK, the final dividend needs to be approved by shareholders at the Annual General Meeting (AGM) and is thus normally declared, approved and paid only *after* the year end. In this situation, the final dividend of a listed company is not recognised as a liability on the statement of financial position at the end of the reporting period. However, it is disclosed in the notes to the financial statements.

Pause and reflect...

Why is a dividend declared after the end of the reporting period not recognised as a liability?

Response

A liability is defined in the *Conceptual Framework* as a present obligation of the enterprise arising from past events, the settlement of which is expected to result in an outflow from the enterprise of resources embodying economic benefits.

If the reporting period ends, for example, on 31 December 20X3 and a dividend is declared *after* that date, say on 10 January 20X4, there is no present obligation arising from a past event at 31 December 20X3 and thus no liability is recognised on the statement of financial position at that date. (However, a note to the financial statements would be included providing details of the dividend).

Diagram 17.1 shows the difference between profits retained and profits authorised for distribution.

Non-distributable reserves

A non-distributable reserve is one which is not available to be declared as a dividend to shareholders.

You are familiar with the *unrealised surplus* on **revaluation of a non-current asset**. The asset account is debited and the revaluation surplus account is credited with the

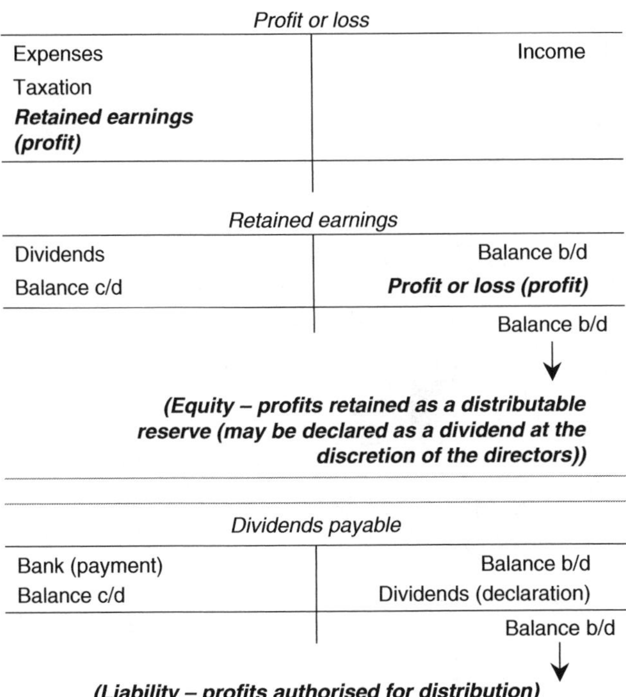

Diagram 17.1 Difference between profits retained and profits authorised for distribution

upward movement in the value of the asset. This revaluation surplus is regarded as a non-distributable reserve.

You are also familiar with the *realised surplus* on **disposal of a non-current asset**. The gain on disposal is accounted for by debiting the asset disposal account and crediting the gain/profit on disposal account. The gain/profit on disposal account is, in turn, transferred to the profit or loss account by a closing entry and therefore appears as an income item on the statement of profit or loss. As an income item, the gain/profit will be included in the profit for the period and will ultimately be included in the retained earnings as a distributable reserve.

It is important to compare the accounting entries on the creation of a non-distributable reserve when a non-current asset is *revalued* with the entries that are processed when a non-current asset is *sold*. When a non-current asset is revalued, and the surplus is therefore unrealised, the unrealised surplus is not recorded as income in the determination of profit or loss. Rather, it is recorded as other comprehensive *income* in the determination of the *total comprehensive income*. On disposal of a non-current asset, however, the realised surplus is reported as an *income* item. This principle is illustrated in Diagram 17.2.

Remember that, as the non-distributable reserve is part of equity, all movements in the non-distributable reserve need to be reported on the statement of changes in equity.

Revaluation of non-current asset

Asset

Balance b/d ***Revaluation surplus***	Balance c/d
Balance b/d	

Revaluation surplus

Balance c/d	**Asset *(surplus)***
	Balance b/d ↓ ***(NDR)***

Disposal of non-current asset

Asset

Balance b/d	Asset disposal

Asset disposal

Asset **Profit on disposal *(gain)***	Bank (proceeds)

Profit on disposal

Profit or loss	**Asset disposal *(gain)***

Profit or loss

Expenses Retained earnings (profit)	Other income **Profit on disposal *(gain)***

Diagram 17.2 Comparison of unrealised surplus on revaluation and realised surplus on disposal

Pause and reflect...

Examine the two scenarios below and consider how each scenario will be reported on both the statement of profit or loss and other comprehensive income *and* on the statement of changes in equity.

a) A company has a profit for the period of C1 200 000 and has revalued land by an amount of C100 000.
b) A company has a profit for the period of C1 300 000, including a profit on sale of land of C100 000.

The company has C5 000 000 of ordinary share capital and an opening balance in retained earnings of C3 500 000.

Response

a) Revaluation of land

EXTRACT FROM STATEMENT OF PROFIT OR LOSS AND OTHER COMPREHENSIVE INCOME	
	C
Profit for the period	1 200 000
Other comprehensive income	
Revaluation of land	100 000
Total comprehensive income	1 300 000

EXTRACT FROM STATEMENT OF CHANGES IN EQUITY

	Share capital	*Revaluation surplus (Non-distributable reserve)*	*Retained earnings (Distributable reserve)*	*Total*
	C	C	C	C
Balance	5 000 000	—	3 500 000	8 500 000
Total comprehensive income	—	100 000	1 200 000	1 300 000
	5 000 000	100 000	4 700 000	9 800 000

b) Sale of land

EXTRACT FROM STATEMENT OF PROFIT OR LOSS AND OTHER COMPREHENSIVE INCOME

	C
Operating profit	1 200 000
Profit on sale of land	100 000
Profit for the period	1 300 000
Other comprehensive income	—
Total comprehensive income	1 300 000

EXTRACT FROM STATEMENT OF CHANGES IN EQUITY

	Share capital	*Retained earnings (Distributable reserve)*	*Total*
	C	C	C
Balance	5 000 000	3 500 000	8 500 000
Total comprehensive income		1 300 000	1 300 000
	5 000 000	4 800 000	9 800 000

17.5.4 Equity of a company

The components of the equity of a company were discussed in the previous sections. In summary, the equity comprises the share capital and the reserves of the company, both distributable and non-distributable.

17.6 Formation of a company

The Companies Act provides for two documents to regulate the activities of a company:

- The Memorandum of Association (the constitution of the company), which sets out its objectives, the powers of the company, its name and main business activity and details of share capital.

- The Articles of Association, which are the set of rules of the company. The Articles of Association define the rights of members and specify the powers and duties of directors.

You will recall from Chapter 16, *Partnerships*, that Simon Smart and Gary Good formed Intense Sports, a partnership retailing endurance running and cycling equipment. The examples in this chapter examine the activities of Simon and Gary, assuming they choose to operate their business as a company, Intense Sports Plc.

We begin with an example dealing with the formation of a company, followed by examples that illustrate the appropriation of profit for a company and finally examples that look at the issue of shares to the public. It is important to note that, on formation, the initial issue of shares is made to the ***incorporators*** of the company – in our examples, Simon and Gary.

Example: Formation of a company

On 2 January 20X7, Simon Smart and Gary Good incorporated Intense Sports Plc with an authorised share capital of 30 000 shares of £1 each. Simon and Gary paid C5 000 for 5 000 shares issued to them.

You are required to:

a) Journalise the above transactions.
b) Prepare the statements of financial position immediately after formation.

Solution: Formation of a company

a) Journal entries

Asset				=	*Liabilities*	+	*Owner's equity*	
Incorporators		Bank					Share capital	
+/L/Dr	−/R/Cr	+/L/Dr	−/R/Cr				−/L/Dr	+/R/Cr
5 000								5 000
	5 000	5 000						

The amount owing by the incorporators is a receivable and is thus recorded as an asset. This represents the amount owing by the incorporators for shares issued to them. The share capital is credited with the issue price of the shares allotted to them.

b) Statement of financial position

GENERAL JOURNAL OF INTENSE SPORTS PLC

Date	*Description*	*Fol*	*Dr*	*Cr*
02/01/X7	Incorporators (A)		5 000	
	Share capital (OE)			5 000
	5 000 shares allotted to the incorporators of the company			
	Bank (A)		5 000	
	Incorporators (A)			5 000
	Cash received for the 5 000 shares			

INTENSE SPORTS PLC
STATEMENT OF FINANCIAL POSITION
AT 2 JANUARY 20X7

	C
ASSETS	
Current assets	
Bank	5 000
EQUITY	
Capital and reserves	
Share capital	5 000

17.7 Producing financial information for a company

Remember that the objective of general purpose financial reporting is to provide financial information about the reporting entity that is *useful* to *existing and potential investors, lenders and other creditors* in making decisions about providing resources to the entity.

Related to this is the concept of ***stewardship***, which refers to the flow of information between management and investors. The board of directors is accountable for the resources entrusted to it and reports back to investors through means of the annual report. Shareholders assess the stewardship of management (see Diagram 17.3) in order to decide, for example, whether to hold or sell their investment in the enterprise and whether to reappoint or replace the management.

17.7.1 Determination of the profit for the period

The profit for the period of a company is determined in the same way as that of a sole proprietorship or partnership, except for an additional line item – the ***income tax expense***. As you will see in the examples that follow, the statement of profit or loss has a subtotal referred to as '***profit before tax***', followed by the '***income tax expense***' resulting in the '***profit for the period***'.

Income tax

Owing to its legal status as a separate legal entity distinct from its shareholders, a company is usually subject to corporation tax (at a rate of 20 per cent in UK) on its taxable income. In the UK, the amount of taxation paid is governed by the provisions of Corporation Tax

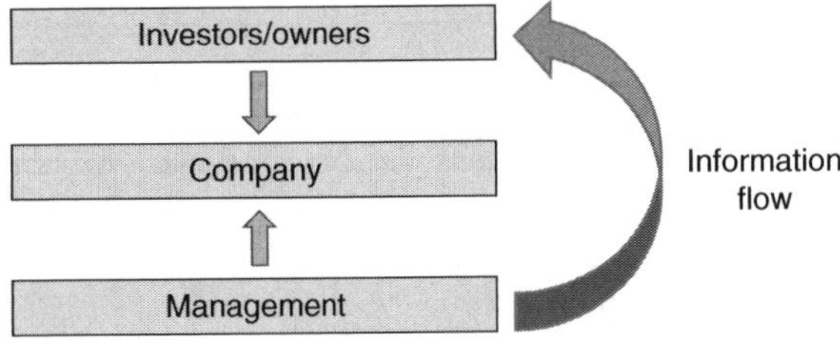

Diagram 17.3 Stewardship of management

Scenario	*Current tax payable: income tax*	
Income tax expense > debit balance in 'Current tax payable: income tax'	Credit balance	Current liability on statement of financial position
Income tax expense < debit balance in 'Current tax payable: income tax'	Debit balance	Current asset on statement of financial position

Diagram 17.4 Current tax payable: income tax

Act 2010 and applicable case law. Taxation is paid to the relevant tax authority, known in the UK as Her Majesty's Revenue and Customs (HMRC).

In the UK, companies are required to use a system of self-assessment for their tax computation. This means that a company is required to perform its own tax computation and pay over the tax due on pre-determined dates. Smaller companies usually pay their corporation tax liability nine months and one day after the end of the accounting period. However, large companies are required to pay quarterly instalments of their corporation tax liability. The four instalments are due on the 14th day of the 7th, 10th, 13th and 16th months after the beginning of the accounting period.

The actual computation of the instalments is beyond the scope of this book; however, the accounting for the instalment payments is summarised below.

The journal entry to record the payment of the instalments is as follows:

Dr	Current tax payable: income tax (A/L)
Cr	Bank (A)

At the end of the financial year, the tax charge for the year is computed and is recorded with the following entry:

Dr	Income tax expense (E)
Cr	Current tax payable: income tax (A/L)

The 'Current tax payable: income tax' account will usually have a *debit* balance when the provisional tax has been paid. When the income tax expense for the current year is recognised, the 'Current tax payable: income tax' is credited with the following outcomes possible (see Diagram 17.4):

The accounting entries for the current tax are illustrated in the example at the end of Section 17.7.2.

17.7.2 Appropriation of profit

Dividends

Shareholders, both ordinary and preference, do not have an automatic claim to the retained profit of the company. A liability to shareholders is only established when the directors declare a dividend. Remember that before the directors declare a dividend, the solvency and liquidity requirements must be considered.

Dividends to shareholders are an appropriation of profits and are not recorded as an expense on the statement of profit or loss. Rather, dividends are recorded in the statement of changes in equity. Remember that the definition of an expense in the *Conceptual Framework* specifically excludes distributions to equity participants, namely the shareholders.

Most companies declare dividends to their shareholders twice during the year. An ***interim*** dividend is declared halfway through the financial year and a ***final*** dividend is declared at the end of the year. As mentioned in Section 17.5.3 above, the final dividend of a large listed company is only declared and approved *after* the year end and therefore the amount is not recognised as a liability on the statement of financial position at the end of the reporting period. However, the final dividend of a small company with one or two shareholders, who are also the directors, may possibly be declared and approved *before* the year end and then only paid *after* the year end. In this situation, the liability for the dividend is reported on the statement of financial position as a current liability.

The journal entries to record the declaration of a dividend are as follows:

Dr	Dividends (OE)
Cr	Dividends payable (L)
	Amount of dividend declared

When the dividend is paid, it is recorded with the following entry:

Dr	Dividends payable (L)
Cr	Bank (A)
	Dividend paid to shareholders

These accounting entries are explained in the example at the end of this section.

A listed public company will normally pay the dividend to a handful of financial services providers who will then be responsible for the transfer of the dividends to the individual shareholders. Most of the major retail banks offer this service. For smaller private companies, it is a relatively straightforward task to process and keep track of dividend payments to individual shareholders.

Capitalisation issue

Many listed companies offer their shareholders a choice of receiving a cash dividend as described above, or of receiving further shares in the company in place of a cash dividend. This is referred to as a ***capitalisation issue***.

A company may have substantial distributable reserves but may not have sufficient cash to be able to distribute them to shareholders. By offering shareholders a capitalisation issue, the shareholders can benefit from the distributable reserves without affecting the cash flow of the company. A capitalisation issue is also known as a ***bonus issue*** as no payment is received from shareholders for the shares issued.

A capitalisation issue is provided from retained earnings and is recorded as follows:

Dr	Retained earnings (OE)
Cr	Share capital (OE)

You should realise that the same effect is achieved by processing two separate entries:

Dr	Dividends (OE)
Cr	Share capital (OE)
and	
Dr	Retained earnings (OE)
Cr	Dividends (OE)

In certain circumstances, a capitalisation issue can be provided from an account known as the share premium. This is discussed in more detail in Section 17.8.2.

The dividend account (for cash dividends or a capitalisation issue processed in this manner) is closed off to the retained earnings account, as will be shown in Section 17.7.3 below.

Effectively, a capitalisation issue results in the capitalisation of part of the retained earnings of the company. In other words, equity that was previously classified as retained earnings (and distributable) is now classified as share capital (and becomes non-distributable).

You should note that in addition to there being *no cash payment from shareholders* associated with a capitalisation issue, there is *no cash payment to shareholders* with a capitalisation issue.

Example: Producing financial information for a company

Simon Smart and Gary Good incorporated Intense Sports Ltd on 2 January 20X7. It is a small company with Simon and Gary as the sole shareholders and directors. The following information is available for Intense Sports Ltd for the year ended 31 December 20X8:

INTENSE SPORTS LTD
TRIAL BALANCE AT 31 DECEMBER 20X8

Description	*Fol*	*Dr*	*Cr*
Ordinary share capital			100 000
Preference share capital (6%)			100 000
Retained earnings			105 000
Loan from bank (5%)			240 000
Debentures (6%)			100 000
Land: cost		510 000	
Furniture and fittings: cost		100 000	
Furniture and fittings: accumulated depreciation			40 000
Inventory		70 000	
Accounts receivable		154 000	
Bank		156 800	
Accounts payable			161 000
Current tax payable		37 200	
Sales			1 860 000
Cost of sales		930 000	
Administration expense		82 000	
Marketing expense		63 000	
Directors' salaries expense		180 000	
Telephone expense		18 000	
Employees' salaries expense		334 000	
Light and water expense		25 000	
Depreciation expense		20 000	
Preference dividends		6 000	
Ordinary dividends		20 000	
		2 706 000	2 706 000

The following information is relevant:

- The preference shares are non-redeemable.
- The debentures were issued on 2 January 20X8 at par.

- Intense Sports Plc borrowed C240 000 from the bank on 2 November 20X8 at an interest rate of 5 per cent per annum.
- The directors' salaries for the year are C200 000.
- The land was purchased with the intention of building the company's retail outlet. Owing to the opening of a new railway station nearby, property prices have increased and the fair value of the land at 31 December 20X8 was estimated at C570 000.
- The current income tax for the year is C50 400.
- An interim dividend of C20 000 was declared at the end of June 20X8 and paid during July 20X8. The final dividend of C50 000 is declared and approved by the directors/shareholders on 24 December 20X8, to be paid by 15 January 20X9.
- The preference dividend for the year ended 31 December 20X8 was declared and paid during December 20X8.

You are required to:

a) Prepare the statement of profit or loss of Intense Sports Ltd for the year ended 31 December 20X8.
b) Prepare the statement of changes in equity of Intense Sports Ltd for the year ended 31 December 20X8.
c) Prepare the statement of financial position of Intense Sports Ltd at 31 December 20X8.

Solution: Producing information for a company

a) Statement of profit or loss

INTENSE SPORTS LTD
STATEMENT OF PROFIT OR LOSS
FOR THE YEAR ENDED 31 DECEMBER 20X8

		C
Revenue from sales		1 860 000
Cost of sales		(930 000)
Gross profit		930 000
Operating expenses		(742 000)
Administration		82 000
Marketing		63 000
Directors' salaries	*(180 000 + 20 000)*	200 000
Telephone		18 000
Employees' salaries		334 000
Lights and water		25 000
Depreciation		20 000
Operating profit		188 000
Finance cost		
Interest	*((100 000 × 0.06) + (240 000 × 0.05 × 2/12))*	(8 000)
Profit before tax		180 000
Income tax expense		(50 400)
Profit for the period		129 600
Other comprehensive income		
Revaluation surplus		60 000
Total comprehensive income		189 600

b) Statement of changes in equity

INTENSE SPORTS LTD
STATEMENT OF CHANGES IN EQUITY
FOR THE YEAR ENDED 31 DECEMBER 20X8

	Share capital		*Revaluation surplus*	*Retained earnings*	*Total*
	Ordinary	*Preference*			
	C	*C*		*C*	*C*
Balance at 01/01/X8	100 000	100 000		105 000	305 000
Total comprehensive income			60 000	129 600	189 600
Dividends					
Preference				(6 000)	(6 000)
Ordinary				(70 000)	(70 000)
Balance at 31/12/X8	100 000	100 000	60 000	158 600	418 600

c) Statement of financial position

INTENSE SPORTS LTD
STATEMENT OF FINANCIAL POSITION
AT 31 DECEMBER 20X8

		Note	*C*
ASSETS			
Non-current assets			
Property, plant and equipment		1	630 000
Current assets			380 800
Inventory			70 000
Accounts receivable			154 000
Bank			156 800
			1 010 800
EQUITY AND LIABILITIES			
Equity			418 600
Ordinary share capital			100 000
Preference share capital			100 000
Revaluation surplus			60 000
Retained earnings			158 600
Non-current liabilities			340 000
Loan from bank			240 000
6% debentures			100 000
Current liabilities			252 200
Trade and other payables			189 000
Accounts payable			161 000
Directors' salaries payable			20 000
Interest payable			8 000
Dividends payable			50 000
Current tax payable	*(50 400 − 37 200)*		13 200
			1 010 800

INTENSE SPORTS LTD
NOTES TO THE FINANCIAL STATEMENTS
AT 31 DECEMBER 20X8

1) Property, plant and equipment

	Land	*Furniture and fittings*	*Total*
	C	C	C
Carrying amount at 31/12/X7	510 000	80 000	590 000
Cost	510 000	100 000	610 000
Accumulated depreciation	—	(20 000)	(20 000)
Depreciation	—	20 000	20 000
Revaluation	60 000	—	60 000
Carrying amount at 31/12/X8	570 000	60 000	630 000
Cost/valuation	570 000	100 000	670 000
Accumulated depreciation	—	(40 000)	(40 000)

17.7.3 Accounting for taxation and dividends

The accounting entries for taxation and dividends will now be expanded upon, using the amounts from the above example.

Income tax expense

At the end of the year, a taxation calculation is performed to determine the amount of the current tax charge for the year. The amount owing could be higher or lower than the total instalment payments, resulting in either a debit or a credit balance on the tax authority account (shown as either current tax receivable or payable).

The trial balance in the example shows a debit balance on the current tax payable account of C37 200. The entry to record the instalment tax payment would have been processed during the year as follows:

	Dr	*Cr*
Current tax payable (A/L)	37 200	
Bank (A)		37 200

At the end of the year, the current tax charge for the year is computed and the following entry is recorded:

	Dr	*Cr*
Income tax expense (E)	50 400	
Current tax payable (A/L)		50 400

	Assets		=	*Liabilities*		+	*Owner's equity*	
	Bank			Current tax payable			Income tax expense	
	+/L/Dr	*−/R/Cr*		*+/L/Dr*	*−/R/Cr*		*+/L/Dr*	*−/R/Cr*
Payment of instalment		37 200		37 200				
Recognition of income tax expense					50 400		50 400	
Balance					13 200		50 400	

For illustrative purposes, it is assumed that Intense Sports Ltd, as a small company, has paid an instalment of C37 200 during the year. After recognising the income tax expense at the end of the year, the current tax payable account reflects a credit balance of C13 200, representing the amount owing to HMRC for current tax at the end of the year, and is reported on the statement of financial position as a current liability. The income tax expense account shows a debit balance of C50 400, representing the income tax expense for the period and is shown on the statement of profit or loss.

Dividends to shareholders

PREFERENCE DIVIDENDS

Preference shareholders must be allocated their dividends before the ordinary shareholders are entitled to share in the profits if the Articles of Association so specifies. In our example, Intense Sports Ltd has issued preference shares with a fixed dividend rate of 6 per cent. The accounting entries to record the declaration and payment of the preference dividends are as follows:

	Dr	*Cr*
Preference dividends (OE)	6 000	
Dividend payable (L)		6 000
Declaration of preference dividend		
Dividend payable (L)	6 000	
Bank (A)		6 000
Payment of preference dividend		

	Assets		=	*Liabilities*		+	*Owner's equity*	
	Bank			Dividends payable			Preference dividends	
	+/L/Dr	−/R/Cr		−/L/Dr	+/R/Cr		+/L/Dr	−/R/Cr
Declaration of preference dividend					6 000		6 000	
Payment of preference dividend		6 000		6 000				
Balance							6 000	

ORDINARY DIVIDENDS

The trial balance shows an ordinary dividend account with a debit balance of C20 000. This represents the interim dividend, which was processed as follows:

	Dr	*Cr*
Ordinary dividends (OE)	20 000	
Dividend payable (L)		20 000
Declaration of interim dividend		
Dividend payable (L)	20 000	
Bank (A)		20 000
Payment of interim dividend		

Note that a company does not have a separate liability account for each shareholder, compared to a partnership where there is a current account for each partner. There are two reasons for this. First, it is impractical because of the large number of shareholders in a public company. Second, it is not necessary because a company *initiates the payment* of dividends to shareholders, whereas partners in a partnership *withdraw* cash as they need it.

The entry to process the declaration of the *final* dividend is the same as for the interim dividend. The entry is as follows:

	Dr	*Cr*
Ordinary dividends (OE)	50 000	
Dividend payable (L)		50 000
Declaration of final dividend		

	Assets		=	*Liabilities*		+	*Owner's equity*	
	Bank			Dividends payable			Ordinary dividends	
	+/L/Dr	−/R/Cr		−/L/Dr	+/R/Cr		+/L/Dr	−/R/Cr
Declaration of interim dividend					20 000		20 000	
Payment of interim dividend		20 000		20 000				
Declaration of final dividend					50 000		50 000	
Balance					50 000		70 000	

 The statement of changes in equity will show ordinary dividends of C70 000, comprising the interim dividend of C20 000 (declared and paid) and the final dividend (declared and approved but not paid) of C50 000. The statement of financial position will reflect a dividend liability of C50 000, representing the obligation of the company to the shareholders for the final dividend.

Pause and reflect...

Can you explain why the amount for income tax expense of C50 400 differs from the amount for current tax payable of C13 200 and why the amount for dividends of C70 000 differs from the amount for dividends payable of C50 000?

Response

- The income tax expense of C50 400 represents the current income tax for the year whereas the current tax payable of C13 200 represents the amount owing to the tax authority after taking into account the instalment payments.
- The dividends of C70 000 represents the total dividends declared during the year (interim and final) whereas the dividends payable of C50 000 represents the final dividend declared and authorised, but not paid at the end of the year.

17.7.4 Closing entries for a company

The closing entries to transfer the trading activities to the trading account, as well as the other income and expense items to the profit and loss account, are identical for all entity forms.

For a company, an additional closing entry is required to close off the taxation expense to profit or loss:

	Dr	*Cr*
Profit or loss (T)	50 400	
Taxation expense (E)		50 400

The profit is then transferred from the profit or loss account to the ***retained earnings*** account, with the following closing entry:

	Dr	*Cr*
Profit or loss (T)	129 600	
Retained earnings (OE)		129 600

A further closing entry for a company is required to transfer the balances on the dividend accounts to the retained earnings account. This entry is as follows:

	Dr	*Cr*
Retained earnings (OE)	76 000	
Preference dividend (OE)		6 000
Ordinary dividend (OE)		70 000

Pause and reflect...

Can you relate the information reported in the retained earnings column of the statement of changes in equity to the closing entries described above affecting retained earnings?

Response

Each line item in the retained earnings column relates to one of the closing entries to retained earnings.

	Retained earnings	*Closing entries*
	C	
Balance at 01/01/X8	105 000	
Total comprehensive income	129 600	Closing entry transferring the profit for the period from the profit or loss account to the retained earnings account
Dividends		
Preference	(6 000)	Closing entry transferring the preference dividend to the retained earnings account
Ordinary	(70 000)	Closing entry transferring the ordinary dividend to the retained earnings account
Balance at 31/12/X8	158 600	

17.8 Share issues

It is important to understand the process that is involved when issuing shares before examining the relevant accounting entries. A description of the process is as follows:

A public company may apply for a listing on the stock exchange once the criteria for listing have been complied with (as set out in Section 17.4 above). There are three methods of obtaining a listing:

- **An introduction.** This is suitable where the company does not need to raise capital and has a sufficiently wide public spread of shareholdings. It is the quickest and cheapest means of listing, as there is no offer to the public and minimal formalities are required.
- **A private placing.** This has proved to be the most common method of obtaining a listing. In this instance, shares in the company are placed or offered to prospective shareholders through private negotiation. Usually this will be done through a sponsor or a merchant bank.
- **A public offer.** A public offer may be an offer for subscription or an offer for sale. In an offer for subscription, members of the public are invited to subscribe for unissued shares and the proceeds accrue to the company, while in an offer for sale, existing shareholders invite subscribers to purchase their shares and therefore the proceeds accrue to the shareholders.

If the public offer is for a subscription, there are further factors to consider and steps to follow:

- **The appointment of an underwriter.** Although it is not a requirement that an offer be underwritten, the appointment of an underwriter has a number of advantages. The company is assured of raising the desired amount of capital, and it creates a good impression if a prominent institution is prepared to underwrite the offer.
- **The issuing of a prospectus.** The public has a certain period of time within which to submit applications and payment.
- **The allotting of shares to applicants.** If the offer is oversubscribed, the company will have to decide on a basis of allocation. The company also earns interest on the payments received until the date of refund, which may be used to offset the costs of the offer.

The shareholding needs to be recorded and this can be done either in a traditional register with paper certificates being issued or in a dematerialised form. Recent EU regulations however, require all shares that are traded on regulated markets to be dematerialised.

Pause and reflect...

How is the equity of a company affected when a company issues shares as opposed to a shareholder selling shares?

Response

When a company issues shares, cash is received by the company and the share capital of the company is increased. On the other hand, when a shareholder sells shares, the transaction is between two shareholders and the equity of the company remains unchanged.

The examples that follow examine the different share issue transactions that could occur, relating to Intense Sports Plc.

17.8.1 Recording an issue of shares

The same procedure is followed on the issue of both ordinary and preference shares. The proceeds on an issue of shares are recorded in a share capital account. The examples that follow deal with the issue of ordinary shares and are all unrelated.

Example: Recording an issue of shares at par

On 2 January 20X7, Simon Smart and Gary Good incorporated Intense Sports Plc with an authorised capital of 30 000 ordinary shares of £1 each. Simon and Gary paid C5 000 for 5 000 shares issued to them.

On 5 January 20X9, after two years of successful trading, the company lists on a regulated stock exchange by means of a public offer of 25 000 shares of £1 each. Applications for 40 000 shares are received. On 1 March 20X9, 25 000 shares are allotted.

You are required to:

a) Journalise the above transactions.
b) Prepare the equity section of the statement of financial position at 1 March 20X9.

Solution: Recording an issue of shares at par

a) Journal entries

GENERAL JOURNAL OF INTENSE SPORTS PLC

Date	*Description*	*Fol*	*Dr*	*Cr*
02/01/X7	Incorporators (A)		5 000	
	Share capital (OE)			5 000
	5 000 shares allotted to the incorporators of the company			
	Bank (A)		5 000	
	Incorporators (A)			5 000
	Cash received for the 5 000 shares			
05/01/X9	Bank (A)		40 000	
	Application account (T)			40 000
	Amount received on application for 40 000 shares			
01/03/X9	Application account (T)		25 000	
	Share capital (OE)			25 000
	25 000 shares allotted as per directors' resolution			
	Application account (T)		15 000	
	Bank (A)			15 000
	Refund to unsuccessful applicants			

b) Equity section

INTENSE SPORTS PLC
(EXTRACT FROM) STATEMENT OF FINANCIAL POSITION
AT 1 MARCH 20X9

EQUITY AND LIABILITIES		
Equity		*C*
Share capital	*(5 000 + 25 000)*	30 000

17.8.2 Recording an issue of par value shares at a premium

A share premium arises when the issue price of par value shares exceeds their par value. The proceeds on issue are recorded in both the share capital account and a ***share premium account***. The *nominal value* of the shares issued is recorded in the share capital account, and the *premium* is recorded in the share premium account. For example, if 100 000 shares of C1 par value are issued at C1.10, then an amount of C100 000 (100 000 × C1.00) is credited to the share capital account and C10 000 (100 000 × 0.10) is credited to the share premium account.

The share premium account is part of the equity of a company and, as part of the permanent capital, may not be distributed as a dividend to shareholders. However, in certain jurisdictions, a company may use the share premium account for specific purposes.

In terms of section 610 of the UK Companies Act, the share premium account may be used by the company for the following purposes:

- writing off share issue expenses (including underwriting commission);
- issuing unissued shares of the company as bonus shares (a capitalisation or bonus issue).

Preliminary costs

The preliminary costs, also known as start-up costs, relate to establishing a company or raising capital and include costs such as legal and secretarial costs incurred.

Such expenditure does provide future economic benefits, but no asset is acquired or created that can be recognised. The preliminary expenses are therefore allocated to profit or loss. The journal entries are summarised as follows:

Dr	Preliminary costs (E)
Cr	Bank (A)

The preliminary costs are closed off to profit or loss as part of the closing entry process:

Dr	Profit or loss (T)
Cr	Preliminary costs (E)

Share issue costs

Share issue costs, also referred to as transaction costs, include all amounts paid relating to the issue of shares by a company, such as the fees of a sponsoring broker, accounting and legal fees, advertising and marketing fees, and underwriting commission (explained in Section 17.8.3). The amount of the share issue expenses can be significant.

Share issue costs are set off against equity, specifically share premium, or if there is no share premium, against retained earnings. The journal entries are summarised as follows:

Dr	Share issue costs (OE)
Cr	Bank (A)

The share issue costs are then set off against share premium or retained earnings:

Dr	Share premium (OE) or Retained earnings (OE)
Cr	Share issue costs (OE)

Note that the share issue costs have been described as an owner's equity (OE) item and not as an expense. This is because they are set off against equity.

Example: Recording an issue of shares at a premium with transaction costs

On 2 January 20X7, Simon Smart and Gary Good form Intense Sports Plc with an authorised share capital of 100 000 ordinary shares of C2 each. The company issued 50 000 shares at C2 per share to the founders. On 01 June 20X9, the company met the requirements for listing on a regulated stock exchange. The directors issued the remaining shares by means of a private placing at C2.50 per share. All the shares were allotted on 30 June 20X9. Share issue costs of C5 000 were incurred and paid. The balance on retained earnings at 30 June 20X9 was C30 000.

You are required to:

a) Journalise the transactions that take place on 30 June 20X9.
b) Prepare the equity section of the statement of financial position at 30 June 20X9.

Solution: Recording an issue of shares at a premium with transaction costs

a) Journal entries

GENERAL JOURNAL OF INTENSE SPORTS PLC

Date	*Description*	*Fol*	*Dr*	*Cr*
30/06/X9	Bank (A)		125 000	
	Share application account (T)			125 000
	Application received for 50 000 shares			
	Share application account (T)		125 000	
	Share capital (OE)			100 000
	Share premium (OE)			25 000
	50 000 shares issued at a premium of C0.50 per share			

GENERAL JOURNAL OF INTENSE SPORTS PLC				
Date	*Description*	*Fol*	*Dr*	*Cr*
30/06/X9	Share issue costs (OE) Bank (A) *Share issue expenses paid*		5 000	 5 000
30/06/X9	Share premium (OE) Share issue costs (OE) *Share issue costs set off against equity*		5 000	 5 000

b) Extract from equity section

INTENSE SPORTS PLC (EXTRACT FROM) STATEMENT OF FINANCIAL POSITION AT 30 JUNE 20X9		
		C
EQUITY AND LIABILITIES		
Equity		250 000
Share capital	*(100 000 + 100 000)*	200 000
Share premium	*(25 000 − 5 000)*	20 000
Retained earnings		30 000

17.8.3 Underwriting an issue of shares

A company may, if it wishes, have the offer of its shares underwritten by a merchant bank or some other financial institution. The underwriter is paid a commission for underwriting the issue and in return undertakes to subscribe for any shares not taken up by the public. The underwriting institution is taking a risk, as it may have to purchase a large number of shares if the offer is undersubscribed. The commission is usually calculated on the issue price.

Example: Preliminary and share issue costs and underwriting commission

On 2 January 20X7, Simon Smart and Gary Good form Intense Sports Plc with an authorised capital of 102 000 ordinary shares of C1 each. The founders (Simon and Gary) subscribe for 2 000 shares of C1 each, and pay for them in full.

On 1 June 20X9, the company applies for a listing on a regulated stock exchange, and the remaining shares are offered to the public at an issue price of C1.25 each. The issue is underwritten by Underwriters Plc for 1 per cent underwriting commission. The public applies for 80 000 shares, and C1.25 is received with each application. The underwriter took up the remaining shares for C25 000. Preliminary costs amounting to C3 000 and share issue costs of C2 000 are paid. The above transactions are finalised on 30 June 20X9.

The balance on retained earnings at 30 June 20X8 amounted to C148 000, and the profit for the period (before accounting for any costs associated with the share issue) amounted to C74 000.

You are required to:

a) Journalise all of the above transactions.
b) Prepare the statement of changes in equity for the year ended 30 June 20X9.

 ***Solution: Preliminary and share issue costs and underwriting commission***

a) Journal entries

GENERAL JOURNAL OF INTENSE SPORTS PLC

Date	*Description*	*Fol*	*Dr*	*Cr*
02/01/X7	Incorporators (A)		2 000	
	Share capital (OE)			2 000
	2 000 shares allotted to the incorporators			
	Bank (A)		2 000	
	Incorporators (A)			2 000
	Cash received from the incorporators			
30/06/X9	Bank (A)		100 000	
	Application account (T)			100 000
	Cash received in respect of application for 80 000 shares			
	Application account (T)		100 000	
	Share capital (OE)			80 000
	Share premium			20 000
	80 000 shares allotted			
	Underwriters Ltd (A*)		25 000	
	Share capital (OE)			20 000
	Share premium			5 000
	20 000 shares allotted to Underwriters Ltd			
	Underwriting commission(OE^)		1 250	
	Underwriters Ltd (A)			1 250
	1 per cent underwriting commission on C125 000			
	Bank (A)		23 750	
	Underwriters Ltd (A)			23 750
	Balance due			
	Share issue costs (OE^)		2 000	
	Preliminary costs (E)		3 000	
	Bank (A)			5 000
	Share issue and preliminary expenses paid			
	Share premium (OE)		3 250	
	Underwriter's commission (OE)			1 250
	Share issue costs (OE)			2 000
	Underwriters commission and share issue costs set off against equity			
	Profit or loss (T)		3 000	
	Preliminary costs (E)			3 000
	Preliminary costs closed off			

*The underwriter (Underwriters Ltd) is treated here as an asset as the consideration for the shares taken up is receivable from them.

^ The share issue costs have been described as an owner's equity (OE) item and not as an expense. This is because they are set off against equity.

b) Statement of changes in equity

INTENSE SPORTS PLC
STATEMENT OF CHANGES IN EQUITY
FOR THE YEAR ENDED 31 DECEMBER 20X8

		Share capital	*Share premium*	*Retained earnings*	*Total*
		C	C	C	C
Balance at 01/7/X9		2 000	—	148 000	150 000
Profit for the period	*(74 000 − 3 000)*			71 000	71 000
Issue of shares		100 000	25 000		125 000
Transaction costs	*(1 250 + 2 000)*		(3 250)		(3 250)
Balance at 31/12/X8		102 000	21 750	219 000	342 750

17.9 Debenture issues

The debenture trust deed (or equivalent document) specifies the par or redemption or face value of the debentures as well as the ***nominal rate*** of interest payable on them, often called the coupon rate as the rate is used to compute the interest paid on the instrument. As with other financial liabilities, the nominal rate determines the amount of interest paid each year and is calculated by multiplying the par value of the debentures by the nominal rate.

The ***market rate*** of interest, on the other hand, is the rate determined by the supply and demand for funds on the money market.

In terms of both IFRS and IFRS for SMEs, debentures need to be carried at amortised cost using an effective interest rate method. The effective rate is the rate that discounts the redemption value and interest payments to the PV of the debenture at the date of issue (being its fair value).

If a company issues debentures at par value, this means that the effective rate is equal to the current market interest rate. If a company issues a debenture with an interest rate lower than the current market rates, the debenture holder is, in effect, compensated by taking up the debentures at below their par or face value. This is effectively the same as issuing the debentures at a discount. On the other hand, if the nominal rate is higher than the current market interest rates, the debentures can be issued at a premium compared to their par value.

These relationships can be summarised as shown in Table 17.1:

17.9.1 Issue of debentures at par

As mentioned above, debentures are issued at par when the nominal rate is equal to the market rate.

Table 17.1 Issue of debentures at par, discount or premium

Debenture issued at	*Circumstance*	*Relationship between effective rate and nominal rate*
Par value	Nominal rate = market rate	Effective rate = nominal rate
A discount	Nominal rate < market rate	Effective rate > nominal rate
A premium	Nominal rate > market rate	Effective rate < nominal rate

Example: Issue of debentures at par

Assume that, on 2 January 20X7, Simon Smart and Gary Good form Intense Sports Plc. After trading for a few years, the company offers 10 000 10% debentures of C100 each to the public *at par*, payable in full on application. Applications are received for 12 000 debentures, which are secured over land and buildings with a carrying amount of C1 500 000. The debentures are issued on 2 January 20Y0 and are repayable on 31 December 20Y4.

You are required to:

a) Journalise the above transactions for the year ended 31 December 20Y0.
b) Show how the interest expense is reported on the statement of profit or loss for the year ended 31 December 20Y0.
c) Show how the debentures are reported on the statement of financial position at 31 December 20Y0.

Solution: Issue of debentures at par

a) Journal entries for year ended 31 December 20Y0

GENERAL JOURNAL OF INTENSE SPORTS PLC

Date	*Description*	*Fol*	*Dr*	*Cr*
02/01/Y0	Bank (A)		1 200 000	
	Debenture application account (T)			1 200 000
	Amount received on application for 12 000 debentures			
	Debenture application account (T)		1 000 000	
	10% debentures (L)			1 000 000
	10 000 debentures allotted			
	Debenture application account (T)		200 000	
	Bank (A)			200 000
	Cash refunded to unsuccessful applicants			
31/12/Y0	Interest (E)		100 000	
	Bank (A)			100 000
	Interest paid for the year			

As the debentures are issued at par, the coupon and effective rate are the same, and the interest expense is C100 000 (C1 000 000 × 0.10).

b) Interest expense on the statement of profit or loss

INTENSE SPORTS PLC
(EXTRACT FROM) STATEMENT OF PROFIT OR LOSS
FOR THE YEAR ENDED 31 DECEMBER 20Y0

	C
Finance cost	
Interest	100 000

c) Debentures on the statement of financial position

INTENSE SPORTS PLC
(EXTRACT FROM) STATEMENT OF FINANCIAL POSITION
AT 31 DECEMBER 20Y0

	C
Non-current liability	
10% debentures	1 000 000

The interest paid is based on the nominal value of the debentures, and the amount paid is therefore C100 000 (C1 000 000 × 0.10). The debenture liability is reported at par value, irrespective of the issue price.

17.9.2 Issue of debentures at a discount

When the nominal rate of interest offered on a debenture issue is lower than the market rate, the debentures are issued to the public at a discount on par value. As mentioned previously, this will result in the effective interest rate being greater than the nominal interest rate.

Example: Issue of debentures at a discount

Assume that, on 2 January 20X7, Simon Smart and Gary Good form Intense Sports Plc. After trading for a few years, the company offers 10 000 10% debentures of C100 each to the public at a discount of 4 per cent, payable in full on application. All the debentures are applied for and allotted on 2 January 20Y0. The debentures are repayable on 31 December 20Y4.

You are required to:

a) Journalise the transaction relating to the debentures for the year ended 31 December 20Y0.
b) Show how the interest expense is reported on the statement of profit or loss for the year ended 31 December 20Y0.
c) Show how the debentures are reported on the statement of financial position at 31 December 20Y0.

Solution: Issue of debentures at a discount

First, it is necessary to set up a schedule of cash flows relating to the debentures in order to calculate the effective interest rate.

02/01/Y0	*31/12/Y0*	*31/12/Y1*	*31/12/Y2*	*31/12/Y3*	*31/12/Y4*
960 000	(100 000)	(100 000)	(100 000)	(100 000)	(1 100 000)

The IRR that equates the initial cash inflow of C960 000 with cash outflows of C100 000 per year for four years and a final cash outflow of C1 100 000 is 11.0845 per cent. This is the effective interest rate.

Pause and reflect...

Are you able to use your financial calculator to compute the effective interest rate? How is this done?

Response

Press the **CASH** button.
Enter the nominal rate of interest as the **i%** = 10% and press **EXE.**
Press **EXE** again on the **Cash=D.Editor x.**
Enter the cash flows from the schedule of cash flows, pressing **EXE** after each one.
Note that the first cash flow of C960 000 is positive while the other cash flows are negative.
Press **ESC** after entering all the cash flows.
Scroll down to **IRR: Solve** and press **EXE.**
The IRR is 11.0845%.

Second, an amortisation table is prepared to calculate the interest expense as well as the carrying amount of the liability on the statement of financial position.

Date	*Effective interest (a)*	*Nominal interest (b)*	*Discount = (a) − (b)*	*Discount balance*	*PV*
02/01/Y0				40 000	960 000
31/12/Y0	106 411	100 000	6 411	33 589	966 411
31/12/Y1	107 122	100 000	7 122	26 467	973 533
31/12/Y2	107 912	100 000	7 912	18 555	981 445
31/12/Y3	108 789	100 000	8 789	9 766	990 234
31/12/Y4	109 766*	100 000	9 766	—	1 000 000

* Rounded.

The nominal or coupon rate is used to determine the interest payments (cash flows) on the instrument, and the effective interest rate is used to account for the unwinding of the instrument. The interest expense is therefore recorded in profit or loss.

a) Journal entries

GENERAL JOURNAL OF INTENSE SPORTS PLC

Date	*Description*	*Fol*	*Dr*	*Cr*
02/01/Y0	Bank (A)		960 000	
	10% debentures (L)			960 000
	Receipt of cash for debentures			
31/12/Y0	Interest (E)		106 411	
	10% debentures (L)			6 411
	Bank (A)			100 000
	Interest paid and unwinding of debenture discount			

The debentures are recorded as a liability at the amount received (C960 000) after deducting the discount (C40 000). At the end of each year, the interest expense comprises the amount of interest paid (C100 000) plus the unwinding of the discount for the year (C6 411). Each year, part of the discount is credited to the debenture liability account so that at the end of the five years the debenture liability account will have a balance of C1 000 000, which is the amount to repay to the debenture holders.

b) Interest expense on the statement of profit or loss

INTENSE SPORTS PLC
(EXTRACT FROM) STATEMENT OF PROFIT OR LOSS
FOR THE YEAR ENDED 31 DECEMBER 20Y0

	C
Finance costs	
Interest on debentures	106 411

The interest expense reported on the statement of profit or loss is the effective interest for the year. This comprises the nominal interest paid of C100 000 plus the amortisation of the discount of C6 411.

c) Debentures on the statement of financial position

INTENSE SPORTS PLC
(EXTRACT FROM) STATEMENT OF FINANCIAL POSITION
AT 31 DECEMBER 20Y0

	C
Non-current liabilities	
10% debentures	966 411

The carrying amount of the debentures on the statement of financial position at 31 December 20Y0 is C966 411 (C960 000 + C6 411). This amount equates to the PV of future cash flows associated with the debentures. This can be proved as follows:

Date of cash flow	*Amount of cash flow*	*PV at 11.0845%*
	C	C
31/12/Y1	100 000	90 021
31/12/Y2	100 000	81 038
31/12/Y3	100 000	72 951
31/12/Y4	1 000 000	722 401
		966 411

The carrying amount can also be proved by taking the par value of the debentures and subtracting the *unamortised* discount (C1 000 000 − C33 589).

17.9.3 Issue of debentures at a premium

When the nominal rate of interest offered on a debenture issue is higher than the market rate, the debentures are issued to the public at a premium on par value. As mentioned previously, this will result in the effective interest rate being lower than the nominal interest rate.

Example: Issue of debentures at a premium

Assume that, on 2 January 20X7, Simon Smart and Gary Good form Intense Sports Plc. After trading for a few years, the company offers 10 000 10% debentures of C100 each to the public *at a premium* of 3 per cent, payable in full on application. All the debentures are applied for and allotted on 2 January 20Y0. The debentures are repayable on 31 December 20Y4.

You are required to:

a) Journalise the transactions relating to the debentures for the year ended 31 December 20Y0.
b) Show how the interest expense is reported on the statement of profit or loss for the year ended 31 December 20Y0.
c) Show how the debentures are reported on the statement of financial position at 31 December 20Y0.

Solution: Issue of debentures at a premium

Again, it is necessary to set up a schedule of cash flows relating to the debentures in order to calculate the effective interest rate.

02/01/Y0	*31/12/Y0*	*31/12/Y1*	*31/12/Y2*	*31/12/Y3*	*31/12/Y4*
1 030 000	(100 000)	(100 000)	(100 000)	(100 000)	(1 100 000)

The IRR that equates the initial cash inflow of C1 030 000 with cash outflows of C100 000 per year for four years and a final cash outflow of C1 100 000 is 9.2242 per cent. This is the effective interest rate.

Pause and reflect...

Are you able to use your financial calculator to compute the effective interest rate? How is this done?

Response

Press the **CASH** button.
Enter the nominal rate of interest as the **i%** = 10% and press **EXE.**
Press **EXE** again on the **Cash=D.Editor x.**
Enter the cash flows from the schedule of cash flows, pressing **EXE** after each one.
Note that the first cash flow of C1 030 000 is positive while the other cash flows are negative.
Press **ESC** after entering all the cash flows.
Scroll down to **IRR: Solve** and press **EXE.**
The IRR is 9.2242%.

As shown previously, an amortisation table is prepared to calculate the interest expense as well as the carrying amount of the liability on the statement of financial position.

Date	*Effective interest (a)*	*Nominal interest (b)*	*Premium = (a) − (b)*	*Premium balance*	*PV*
02/01/Y0				30 000	1 030 000
31/12/Y0	95 010	100 000	4 990	25 010	1 025 010
31/12/Y1	94 549	100 000	5 451	19 559	1 019 559
31/12/Y2	94 047	100 000	5 953	13 606	1 013 606
31/12/Y3	93 498	100 000	6 502	7 104	1 007 104
31/12/Y4	92 896*	100 000	7 104	—	1 000 000

*Rounded.

a) Journal entries

GENERAL JOURNAL OF INTENSE SPORTS PLC

Date	*Description*	*Fol*	*Dr*	*Cr*
02/01/Y0	Bank (A)		1 030 000	
	10% debentures (L)			1 030 000
	Receipt of cash for debentures			
31/12/Y0	Interest (E)		95 010	
	10% debentures (L)		4 990	
	Bank (A)			100 000
	Interest paid and unwinding of premium			

The debentures are recorded as a liability at the amount received (C1 030 000) after adding the premium (C30 000). At the end of each year, the interest expense comprises the amount of interest paid (C100 000) *less* the unwinding of the premium for the year (C4 990). Each year, part of the discount is debited to the debenture liability account so that at the end of the five years, the debenture liability account will have a balance of C1 000 000, which is the amount to repay to the debenture holders.

b) Interest expense on the statement of profit or loss

INTENSE SPORTS PLC
(EXTRACT FROM) STATEMENT OF PROFIT OR LOSS
FOR THE YEAR ENDED 31 DECEMBER 20Y0

	C
Finance costs	
Interest on debentures	95 010

The interest expense reported on the statement of profit or loss is the effective interest for the year. This comprises the nominal interest paid of C100 000 less the amortisation of the premium of C4 990.

c) Debentures on the statement of financial position

INTENSE SPORTS PLC
(EXTRACT FROM) STATEMENT OF FINANCIAL POSITION
AT 31 DECEMBER 20Y0

	C
Non-current liabilities	
10% debentures	1 025 010

The carrying amount of the debentures on the statement of financial position at 31 December 20Y0 is C1 025 010 (C1 030 000 − C4 990). This amount equates to the PV of future cash flows associated with the debentures. This can be proved as follows:

Date of cash flow	*Amount of cash flow*	*PV at 9.2242%*
	C	C
31/12/Y1	100 000	91 555
31/12/Y2	100 000	83 823
31/12/Y3	100 000	76 743
31/12/Y4	1 100 000	772 889
		1 025 010

The carrying amount can also be proved by taking the par value of the debentures and adding the unamortised premium (C1 000 000 + C25 010).

Revision example

Skimbleshanks Plc is a company listed on the London Stock Exchange and is involved in distributing components for the railways. The trial balance of the company at 30 September 20X2 appears as follows:

SKIMBLESHANKS PLC
TRIAL BALANCE AT 30 SEPTEMBER 20X2

Description	*Fol*	*Dr*	*Cr*
Land: cost		250 000	
Buildings: cost		3 000 000	
Buildings: accumulated depreciation (01/10/X1)			375 000
Plant and equipment: cost		1 100 000	
Plant and equipment: accumulated depreciation (01/10/X1)			120 000
Inventory		810 000	
Trade accounts receivable		536 000	
Bank		487 724	
Trade accounts payable			425 000
Current tax payable		90 000	
Ordinary share capital			2 000 000
Share premium			500 000
Retained earnings			667 000
Preference dividends		12 500	
Ordinary dividend		90 000	
12% debentures			1 425 000

Description	*Fol*	*Dr*	*Cr*
10% redeemable preference shares			250 000
Sales			3 002 872
Cost of sales		1 201 148	
Administration expenses		550 000	
Distribution expenses		397 500	
Other operating expenses		240 000	
		8 764 872	8 764 872

The following information is relevant for the preparation of the financial statements:

1 The buildings are depreciated at 2.5% per annum on the straight line method. The buildings were valued on 30 September 20X2 by an independent valuer at an amount of C2 700 000.

2 The plant and equipment is depreciated on the sum of units method. The total estimated output of the plant and equipment is 20 million units. During the current period, a total of 1 750 000 units were produced. All of the plant and equipment was purchased on the same date during the previous financial year.

3 The ordinary share capital at 30 September 20X1 consists of 1 000 000 shares, all issued at the par value of C1 per share. On 1 July 20X2, 1 000 000 ordinary shares were issued to the public at an issue price of C1.50 each. Share issue expenses of C40 000 were incurred and paid, and are included in the 'other operating expenses' on the trial balance.

4 The preference share capital at 30 September 20X2 consists of 100 000 10% redeemable preference shares of C2.50 par value. The shares were placed privately at a large financial institution on 1 April 20X2 at par value each and are subject to compulsory redemption by the company after a period of three years. Share issue expenses of C15 000 were incurred and paid and are included in the 'other operating expenses' on the trial balance.

5 On 1 October 20X1, the company issued 10 000 debentures of C150 par value at a discount of 5 per cent. The debentures are to be redeemed on 30 September 20X6 at par. The interest rate is 12 per cent per annum and is payable annually in arrears on 1 October each year.

The debenture discount is to be amortised over the life of the debentures using the effective interest rate method. The effective interest rate is 13.43675 per cent and the accountant has correctly prepared the following amortisation schedule:

	Par value	*Effective interest*	*Actual interest*	*Debenture discount*	*PV*
01/10/X1	1 500 000			75 000	1 425 000
30/09/X2		191 474	180 000	(11 474)	1 436 474
31/09/X3		193 015	180 000	(13 015)	1 449 489
31/09/X4		194 764	180 000	(14 764)	1 464 253
31/09/X5		196 748	180 000	(16 748)	1 481 001
31/09/X6		198 999	180 000	(18 999)	1 500 000

6 Current income tax must still be accounted for at the correctly calculated amount of C110 320.
7 Dividend transactions are as follows:

   i) The preference dividend for the year was paid on 30 September to all shareholders registered on that date. This has been correctly recorded.
   ii) A capitalisation issue was declared and authorised of one ordinary share for every 25 shares held at the par value of C1 per share to all shareholders registered on 30 September 20X2. This has not yet been recorded and is to be provided from retained earnings.

You are required to:

a) Prepare the statement of comprehensive income of Skimbleshanks Plc for the year ended 30 September 20X2.
b) Prepare the statement of changes in equity of Skimbleshanks Plc for the year ended 30 September 20X2.
c) Prepare the *assets* and *liabilities* sections only of the statement of financial position of Skimbleshanks Plc at 30 September 20X2.

Solution: Revision example

a) Statement of comprehensive income

SKIMBLESHANKS PLC
STATEMENT OF COMPREHENSIVE INCOME
FOR THE YEAR ENDED 30 SEPTEMBER 20X2

			C
Sales			3 002 872
Cost of sales			(1 201 148)
Gross profit			1 801 724
Administrative expenses			(550 000)
Distribution expenses			(397 500)
Other operating expenses	*(240 000 – 40 000 – 15 000)*		(185 000)
Depreciation expenses	*(((1 750 000/20 000 000) × 1 100 000) + 75 000)*		(171 250)
Operating profit			497 974
Finance costs			(203 974)
Debenture interest expense		191 474	
Preference dividend	*(250 000 × 0.10 × 6/12)*	12 500	
Profit before tax			294 000
Taxation			(110 320)
Profit for the period			183 680
Other comprehensive income			
Revaluation	*(2 700 000 – (3 000 000 – 450 000))*		150 000
Total comprehensive income			333 680

b) Statement of changes in equity

SKIMBLESHANKS PLC
STATEMENT OF CHANGES IN EQUITY
FOR THE YEAR ENDED 30 SEPTEMBER 20X2

		Ordinary share capital	*Share premium*	*Revaluation surplus*	*Retained earnings*	*Total*
		C		C	C	C
Balance at 01/10/X1		1 000 000	—		667 000	1 667 000
Issue of ordinary shares		1 000 000	500 000			1 500 000
Transaction costs	*(40 000 + 15 000)*		(55 000)			(55 000)
Total comprehensive income				150 000	183 680	333 680
Ordinary dividend					(90 000)	(90 000)
Capitalisation issue	*(2 000 000/25 × C1)*	80 000			(80 000)	
Balance at 30/09/X2		2 080 000	445 000	150 000	680 680	3 355 680

c) Statement of financial position

SKIMBLESHANKS PLC
STATEMENT OF FINANCIAL POSITION
AT 30 SEPTEMBER 20X2

		Note	*C*
ASSETS			
Non-current assets			
Property, plant and equipment		1	3 833 750
Current assets			1 833 724
Inventory			810 000
Accounts receivable			536 000
Bank			487 724
			5 667 474
EQUITY AND LIABILITIES			
Equity			3 355 680
Ordinary share capital			2 080 000
Share premium			445 000
Revaluation surplus			150 000
Retained earnings			680 680
Non-current liabilities			1 686 474
12% debentures	*(1 500 000 – (75 000 – 11 474))*		1 436 474
10% redeemable preference shares			250 000
Current liabilities			625 320
Trade accounts payable			425 000
Current tax payable	*(110 320 – 90 000)*		20 320
Debenture interest payable	*(1 500 000 × 0.12)*		180 000
			5 667 474

As the preference shares are subject to compulsory redemption by the company, they are reported as a *liability* on the statement of financial position, and the dividends are reported as a *finance cost* on the statement of comprehensive income.

SKIMBLESHANKS PLC
NOTES TO THE FINANCIAL STATEMENTS
AT 30 SEPTEMBER 20X2

1 Property, plant and equipment

	Land	*Buildings*	*Plant and equipment*	*Total*
	C	*C*	*C*	*C*
Carrying amount at 30/09/X1	250 000	2 625 000	980 000	3 855 000
Cost	250 000	3 000 000	1 100 000	4 350 000
Accumulated depreciation	—	(375 000)	(120 000)	(495 000)
Depreciation		(75 000)	(96 250)	
Revaluation		150 000		
Carrying amount at 30/09/X2	250 000	2 700 000	883 750	3 833 750
Cost/valuation	250 000	2 700 000	1 100 000	4 050 000
Accumulated depreciation	—	—	(216 250)	(216 250)

Bibliography

Companies and Intellectual Property Commission. 2013. *Company Statistics.* www.cipc.co.za/Stats_files/April2013.pdf (Accessed 27 May 2013).

Edward Nathan Sonnenbergs. 2013. *General Corporate Information for Foreign Clients: Establishing a Business in South Africa.* http://mandarin.ensafrica.com/Doing%20Business%20in%20SA.pdf (Accessed 26 October 2014).

Grant Thornton. 2008. *Consider Going Public? The Bottom Line.* www.gt.co.za/files/publications/bottomline0808_03_public.pdf (Accessed 26 October 2014).

www.jse.co.za (Accessed on 21 January 2014).

www.strate.co.za (Accessed on 21 January 2014).

The International Accounting Standards Board. 2007. IAS 10 *Events after the Reporting Period.*

The International Accounting Standards Board. 2012. IAS 32 *Financial Instruments: Presentation.*

The International Accounting Standards Board. 2013. *About the IFRS for SMEs.* www.ifrs.org/IFRS-for-SMEs/Pages/IFRS-for-SMEs.aspx (Accessed 27 May 2013).

PART VI

Sundry topics

18 Statement of cash flows

Business focus

Cash flow is of vital importance to the financial health of all business entities. There is a well known saying that 'revenue is vanity, cash flow is sanity, but cash is king'. This suggests that while a large amount of revenue from sales looks good on the statement of profit or loss, the most important focus for a business is cash flow.

It is possible for a business to continue trading in the short to medium term even if expenses exceed income, resulting in a loss. This can be managed, for example, by negotiating a longer period to pay suppliers. However, no business can survive in the long term without enough cash to meet its needs.

Cash inflows are generated mainly from the sale of goods or services whereas cash outflows are used to pay for goods purchased for resale and other operating costs. For a retail business such as a supermarket, the main cash inflows will be from sales and the main cash outflows will be for goods purchased and overheads such as rent, rates, wages, electricity and transport. The difference between the two is called the net cash flow and can be either positive or negative. A negative cash flow means the business is receiving less cash than it is spending resulting in it struggling to pay immediate short-term debts such as amounts owing to suppliers. It may also need to borrow cash to cover the shortfall.

Managing cash flow is important to both the existence of a business and to its long-term well-being. For example, a retailer would expect to sell more just before Christmas and in the January sales. Careful management of cash flows will ensure that the business is aware of potential shortfalls so that it has these planned into its business strategy. This will ensure that there is always enough cash to pay creditors.

In this chapter

We have emphasised the importance of the accrual basis in measuring an entity's financial performance, and the statement of profit or loss and statement of financial position are prepared on this basis. We also mentioned in Chapter 2, *Fundamental accounting concepts*, the relevance of cash flows in measuring financial performance.

This chapter examines the statement of cash flows, one of the components of a complete set of financial statements (along with the statement of profit or loss, the statement of changes in equity and the statement of financial position). We will discuss the importance of cash flows to a user of financial statements and look at how an entity generates cash flows and how they are utilised.

Dashboard

- Look at the *Learning outcomes* so that you know what you should be able to do after studying this chapter.
- Read the *Business focus* to place this chapter's contents in a real-world context.
- Preview *In this chapter* to focus your mind on the contents of the chapter.
- Read the *text* in detail.
    - Apply your mind to the *Pause and reflect* scenarios.
    - Key to understanding the statement of cash flows and to preparing one is the classification of cash flows into *operating*, *investing* and *financing* activities, described in Section 18.3.
    - Pay attention also to the two methods of preparing a statement of cash flows – the *direct* method and *indirect* method, described in detail in Section 18.4.
- Prepare solutions to the examples as you read through the chapter.
- Prepare a solution to the *Revision example* at the end of the chapter without reference to the suggested one. Compare your solution to the suggested solution provided.

Learning outcomes

After studying this chapter, you should be able to do the following:

1 Describe the relevance of cash flow information.
2 Define 'cash flows'.
3 Classify cash flows by operating, investing and financing activities.
4 Prepare a statement of cash flows.

Statement of cash flows

18.1 Importance of cash flow information

The *Conceptual Framework* indicates that the objective of financial reporting is to provide financial information about the reporting entity that is useful to existing and potential investors, lenders and other creditors in making decisions about providing resources to an entity. Information about the cash flows of an entity provides the users of financial statements with details of how the entity *generates* its cash flows and how it *utilises* those cash flows. To make economic decisions, users require information about an entity's ability to generate cash flows and the timing and certainty of their generation.

An entity needs cash to conduct its operations, pay its obligations and provide a return to investors. Cash flow information is useful in assisting users to develop their own models to assess and compare the present value of future cash flows of different entities. It also enhances comparability of the financial information of different entities as it is unaffected by different accounting treatments for the same transactions and events.

It is important, however, that the statement of cash flows is used in conjunction with the accrual basis statement of profit or loss and statement of financial position. The statement of cash flows includes cash flows from transactions that took place in an earlier period as well as those which are expected to result in transactions in future periods. Disclosure of both cash flow information and accrual-based performance as well as financial position information provides users with a better understanding of the factors affecting cash flows. This enables users to assess the timing and certainty of future cash flows.

The IFRS dealing with cash flow information is IAS 7 *Statement of Cash Flows*.

18.2 Meaning of cash flows

We have already briefly covered the meaning of cash and cash flows in Chapter 13, *Cash and bank,* and will briefly review this here before considering the classification of cash flows. Remember that IAS 7 refers to cash flows as inflows and outflows of ***cash*** and ***cash equivalents***.

Cash includes cash on hand and demand deposits.

Cash equivalents are short-term, highly liquid investments that are readily convertible to known amounts of cash and are subject to an insignificant risk of changes in value.

This definition is summarised and explained in Diagram 18.1.

Cash on hand refers to currency notes and coins, and demand deposits normally refer to an account held at a bank that may be withdrawn at any time by the account holder, such as current and savings accounts. The majority of demand deposit accounts are current (cheque) and savings accounts. Cash equivalents include short-term government bonds, money-market investments and other short-term bank deposits.

For the remainder of this chapter, we will refer only to 'cash' and 'cash flows' in the interests of brevity.

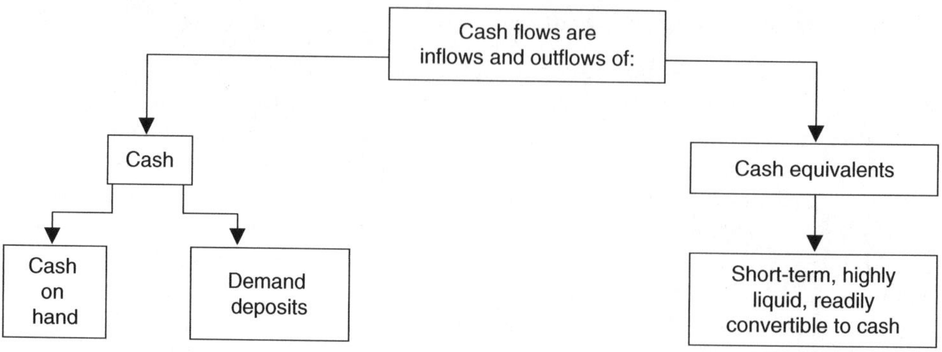

Diagram 18.1 Cash flows and cash equivalents

18.3 Classification of cash flows

The statement of cash flows classifies cash inflows and outflows into the three main areas of a business – ***operating***, ***investing*** and ***financing*** activities.

Classification by activity allows users to assess the impact of those activities on the financial position of the entity. For example, it is relevant for an investor to know whether the cash flow from operating activities is sufficient for the entity to function or whether non-current assets may have to be sold to finance operations. Suppliers and lenders need to know whether there will be enough cash for the entity to pay its obligations as they become due.

It is important for you to know and understand what activities are regarded as operating, investing or financing. IAS 7 defines and describes each activity. We will examine this classification in detail before moving on to the computation and presentation of the statement of cash flows.

18.3.1 Operating activities

Cash flows from operating activities are primarily derived from the *principal revenue-producing activities* of the entity, therefore they generally result from transactions that are taken into account in the determination of profit or loss for a period. There are exceptions, however, such as a profit on sale of plant which, although included in the calculation of profit or loss, is not considered to be an operating activity but rather as an investing activity (this is because the intention of the original cash outflow was to invest in plant and not to immediately generate revenue).

The amount of cash flows arising from operating activities is an important indicator of the extent to which the operations of the entity have generated sufficient cash flows to repay loans, maintain the operating capability of the entity, pay dividends and make new investments without the need to obtain external sources of finance. IAS 7 lists some examples of cash flows from operating activities:

- cash receipts from the sale of goods, the rendering of services and other income;
- cash payments to suppliers for goods and services;
- cash payments to and on behalf of employees;
- cash payments or income tax refunds.

The figure reported as cash flow from operating activities is one of the most important figures for the user. It is often regarded as a key indicator of corporate success since cash flow from operating activities is usually the most important long-term source of cash to an entity. As mentioned previously, however, cash generated from operating activities must not be considered in isolation. For example, it may be that a profitable entity has cash temporarily tied up in inventory and accounts receivable, resulting in a poor cash flow from operating activities in the current period, but that the realisation of working capital in subsequent periods will result in material cash flows from operating activities.

18.3.2 Investing activities

Investing activities relate to the *acquisition and disposal of non-current assets*. Cash flows from investing activities represent the extent to which cash has been utilised for resources intended to generate future profits and cash flows. IAS 7 lists some examples of cash flows from investing activities:

- cash payments to acquire property, plant and equipment, intangibles and other long-term assets;
- cash receipts from sales of property, plant and equipment, intangibles and other long-term assets;
- cash payments to acquire shares or debentures of other entities;
- cash receipts from sales of shares or debentures of other entities;
- cash advances or loans made to other parties;
- cash receipts from the repayment of cash advances or loans made to other parties.

In a period of expansion, it is likely that the investing activities will result in a net cash outflow, referred to as cash utilised. The relationship between cash *generated* from operating activities and cash *utilised* in investing activities is useful information for the investor. The investor can assess whether the entity generates enough cash from operating activities to finance its investment in property, plant and equipment.

18.3.3 Financing activities

Cash flows from financing activities are those that involve the entity's *equity and borrowings*. Information about cash flows from financing activities is useful in predicting claims on future cash flows by the providers of finance. IAS 7 lists some examples of cash flows from financing activities:

- cash proceeds from increases in equity, which, in relation to the three entity forms, implies the following:
  - for a sole proprietorship, cash invested as the sole proprietor's capital;
  - for a partnership, cash invested as the partners' capital;
  - for a company, cash proceeds from issuing shares to shareholders.
- cash paid to owners on repayment or redemption of the equity;
- cash proceeds from long-term borrowings;
- cash repayments of amounts borrowed.

Pause and reflect...

How would you classify the cash outflow relating to the purchase of plant compared to the cash outflow relating to maintaining the plant?

Response

The cash outflow to purchase plant is classified as an *investing* activity since the outflow is recognised as an asset. The outflow relating to maintaining the plant, however, is expensed and would be classified as an *operating* activity.

18.3.4 Classification of specific items

There are a few issues arising from the discussion of operating, investing and financing activities that need clarification.

Gain or loss on sale of property, plant and equipment

The sale of an item of plant, for example, may give rise to a gain or loss, which is included in the determination of profit or loss for the period. The cash receipt from the sale of the plant is, however, included in cash flows from *investing* activities.

Pause and reflect...

An item of plant with a carrying amount of C1 000 is sold for C1 200, resulting in a gain of C200. What amount is reported as a cash inflow from investing activities?

Response

The cash inflow from investing activities is C1 200. The gain of C200 is a non-cash flow item, representing the profit on sale.

Interest and dividends

Interest paid may be included as an *operating cash flow* as it enters into the determination of profit or loss. On the other hand, it may be argued that interest paid is a *financing cash flow* as it is a cost of obtaining borrowed funds.

Interest received can also be included as an *operating cash flow* as it enters into the determination of profit or loss. Conversely, interest received could be classified as an *investing cash flow* as it is the return from investments. The same arguments apply to **dividends received**.

Dividends paid may be classified as a component of cash flows from *operating activities* to assist users in determining the ability of an entity to pay dividends out of operating cash flows.

The other alternative is to classify dividends paid as a *financing cash flow* because it is a cost of obtaining equity financing.

In this text, all of the above items are classified as cash flows from operating activities.

Taxation

Cash flows relating to taxation paid should be classified as cash flows from operating activities. You should bear in mind that the *taxation expense* on the statement of profit or loss is unlikely to equal the cash paid in respect of taxation during a particular period. This is because of the estimates inherent in the calculation of the provisional tax payments and the time lag between submission of a corporate tax return and assessment of taxes payable by the tax authority.

18.4 Preparation of a statement of cash flows

The data that you need to prepare a statement of cash flows is taken from the current and previous years' statements of financial position as well as the current year's statement of profit or loss and statement of changes in equity. You need to examine the *movement* in each non-cash item on the statement of financial position using relevant figures from the statement of profit or loss and statement of changes in equity where necessary. Look at Diagram 18.2.

If you examine Diagram 18.2, you will notice that, by a simple rearrangement of the components of the accounting equation, cash can be isolated from the rest of the statement of financial position items. It then follows that, if you take into account the movement in all the non-cash statement of financial position items, you must be left with the movement in cash. To prepare a statement of cash flows, you need to do the following:

- understand the procedure of examining the comparative statements of financial position to establish the movement in the non-cash items;
- know the format of the statement of cash flows.

IAS 7 mentions two methods for presenting a statement of cash flows – the ***direct*** method and the ***indirect*** method – and encourages entities to use the direct method. It is only the *operating activities* section of the statement of cash flows that is affected by the choice of method. Irrespective of which method is used, the investing and financing sections of the statement of cash flows remain the same. The example that follows will illustrate the preparation of the statement of cash flows using both the direct and

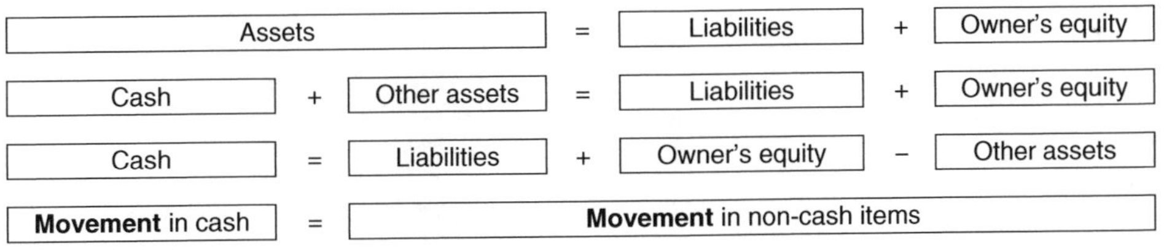

Diagram 18.2 Why an analysis of the non-cash items explains the movement in cash

indirect methods. Each section of the statement of cash flows will be explained separately, and then the complete statement of cash flows using both methods will be shown for comparison.

Example: Preparation of a statement of cash flows

You will recall from previous chapters that Computer World Limited supplies computers to Smart Concepts. Owing to the tremendous popularity of its brand, Computer World Limited has experienced significant growth over the last few years. The statement of profit or loss, statement of changes in equity and statement of financial position of Computer World Limited for the year ended 31 December 20X8 are presented below.

COMPUTER WORLD LIMITED
STATEMENT OF PROFIT OR LOSS
FOR THE YEAR ENDED 31 DECEMBER 20X8

	C000
Sales	30 650
Cost of sales	(26 000)
Gross profit	4 650
Other income	
Investment income	500
Operating expenses	(1 400)
Administration	410
Depreciation	450
Insurance	500
Loss on disposal of equipment	40
Finance cost	
Interest on loan	(250)
Profit before taxation	3 500
Taxation	(300)
Profit for the period	3 200

COMPUTER WORLD LIMITED
STATEMENT OF CHANGES IN EQUITY
FOR THE YEAR ENDED 31 DECEMBER 20X8

	Share capital	*Retained earnings*	*Total*
	C000	*C000*	*C000*
Balance at 1 January 20X8	1 250	1 380	2 630
Issue of share capital	1 150	—	1 150
Profit for the period	—	3 200	3 200
Dividends	—	(1 200)	(1 200)
Balance at 31 December 20X8	2 400	3 380	5 780

COMPUTER WORLD LIMITED
STATEMENT OF FINANCIAL POSITION
AT 31 DECEMBER 20X8

	20X8	20X7
	C000	C000
ASSETS		
Non-current assets	2 430	850
Equipment at cost	3 880	1 910
Accumulated depreciation	(1 450)	(1 060)
Investments	3 440	2 500
Current assets	2 905	3 315
Inventory	900	1 950
Accounts receivable	1 700	1 200
Investment income receivable	100	—
Insurance paid in advance	15	5
Bank	190	160
	8 775	6 665
EQUITY AND LIABILITIES		
Equity	5 780	2 630
Share capital	2 400	1 250
Retained earnings	3 380	1 380
Non-current liabilities		
Loan from bank	1 800	1 040
Current liabilities	1 195	2 995
Accounts payable	130	1 880
Administration expenses payable	35	15
Interest payable	230	100
Taxation payable	400	800
Dividends payable	400	200
	8 775	6 665

Additional information

- Equipment which originally cost C200 000 was sold during the period.
- No loans were repaid during the period.
- No investments were sold during the period.

18.4.1 Preparation of the operating activities section

As mentioned above, there are two methods of reporting cash flows from operating activities. We will first explain and prepare the operating activities section using the direct method and then do the same for the indirect method. All amounts in the following explanation are in C000s.

Direct method

When using the direct method, the starting point is the cash receipts from customers. The cash payments made to suppliers and employees are deducted from the cash receipts from customers in order to arrive at the ***cash generated from operations.*** Payments to suppliers include suppliers of goods for resale as well as all suppliers relating to operating activities. Amounts paid for all distribution, administrative and other operating expenses are therefore included. Note that amounts paid to employees for salaries and wages are often included in distribution or administrative expenses, and are not shown separately.

The cash effects of non-operating items, dividends, interest and taxation are then taken into account in order to arrive at the **net cash from operating activities**. Table 18.1 sets out the calculation to arrive at the net cash from operating activities using the direct method.

CASH RECEIPTS FROM CUSTOMERS

In order to calculate the cash receipts from customers, you need to examine the movement in the accounts receivable account together with sales for the year on the statement of profit or loss. You can reconstruct the accounts receivable account as follows:

Accounts receivable

Details	*C*	*Details*	*C*
Balance b/d	1 200	***Bank***	***30 150***
Sales	30 650	Balance c/d	1 700
	31 850		31 850
Balance b/d	1 700		

The accrual basis sales for the year amounted to C30 650. The cash of C30 150 received from customers is calculated by starting with the opening balance of C1 200, adding the sales of C30 650 and subtracting the closing balance of C1 700. You can therefore calculate the cash received from customers as shown in Diagram 18.3.

Table 18.1 Direct method of presenting cash flows from operating activities

	Cash receipts from customers
–	(Cash payments to suppliers and employees)
=	*Cash generated from operations*
±	Cash effects of non-operating items, dividends, interest and taxation
=	Net cash from operating activities

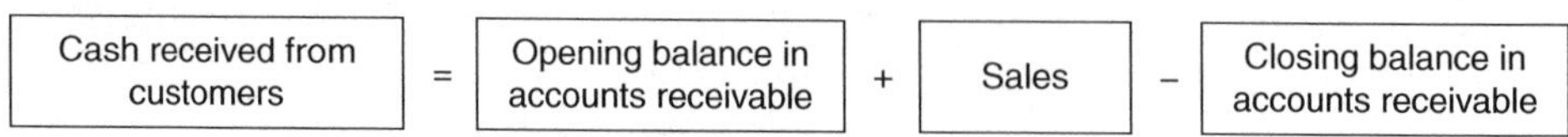

Diagram 18.3 Cash received from customers

Pause and reflect . . .

The calculation of cash received from customers in this example has taken the total sales of C30 650 all to be on credit. Would the amount of cash received from customers of C30 150 change if the total sales of C30 650 comprised credit sales of C25 000 and cash sales of C5 650?

Response

Following the logic of starting with the opening balance in accounts receivable, adding the credit sales and subtracting the closing balance in accounts receivable, the cash received from customers in relation to *credit sales* amounts to C24 500 (1 200 + 25 000 − 1 700). If we then add on the *cash sales* of C5 650, the total cash received from customers (in respect of both credit and cash sales) amounts to C30 150, therefore the cash received from customers does not change.

CASH PAYMENTS TO SUPPLIERS AND EMPLOYEES

IAS 7 requires the cash payments to suppliers and employees to be reported as one figure. Before examining the details of calculating this figure, it is important for you to understand what it comprises. The cash payments to suppliers and employees comprise cash paid to *suppliers of goods for resale* as well as cash paid for *operating expenses* (including salaries). This implies that the cash paid to suppliers includes all types of suppliers including suppliers of inventory (goods for resale) and suppliers of services (operating expenses). Salaries and wages paid to employees are also part of operating expenses and need to be taken into account.

In order to calculate the cash payments to suppliers and employees, you need to examine a number of accounts. First, you need to calculate the purchases for the year by inspecting the movement in the inventory account. Second, you need to combine the purchases figure with the movement in the accounts payable account to calculate the *cash payments to suppliers*. Third, you need to examine the statement of profit or loss and extract all the operating expenses other than non-cash items such as depreciation. These expenses will include cash paid for all operating expenses as well as for salaries. If any of the operating expenses have a corresponding statement of financial position item, you will then also need to combine the statement of profit or loss expense with the movement in the relevant statement of financial position account in order to calculate the cash payment.

To calculate the **cash paid to suppliers of goods for resale**, we begin with the movement in the inventory account, which you reconstruct as follows:

Inventory

Details	*C*	*Details*	*C*
Balance b/d	1 950	Cost of sales	26 000
Accounts payable	***24 950***	Balance c/d	900
	26 900		26 900
Balance b/d	900		

The purchases on credit of C24 950 are calculated by combining the cost of sales for the year of C26 000 with the opening inventory of C1 950 and the closing inventory of C900. In general terms, you can calculate the purchases on credit as shown in Diagram 18.4.

We then take the purchases figure and reconstruct an accounts payable account in order to calculate the cash paid to suppliers:

Accounts payable

Details	*C*	*Details*	*C*
Bank	***26 700***	Balance b/d	1 880
Balance c/d	130	Inventory	24 950
	26 830		26 830
		Balance b/d	130

The cash of C26 700 paid to suppliers is calculated by starting with the opening balance of C1 880, adding the purchases of C24 950 and subtracting the closing balance of C130. The principle used here is shown in Diagram 18.5.

We now need to compute the **cash paid for operating expenses**, including salaries to employees. If you look at the statement of profit or loss, you will notice that there are administration expenses of C410 as well as an insurance expense of C500. If there were no corresponding statement of financial position amounts for the administration expenses or for the insurance expense, we would simply add the C910 (C410 + C500) from the statement of profit or loss to the cash paid to suppliers of C26 700 to arrive at the amount of cash payments to suppliers and employees. In this situation, however, there is a current

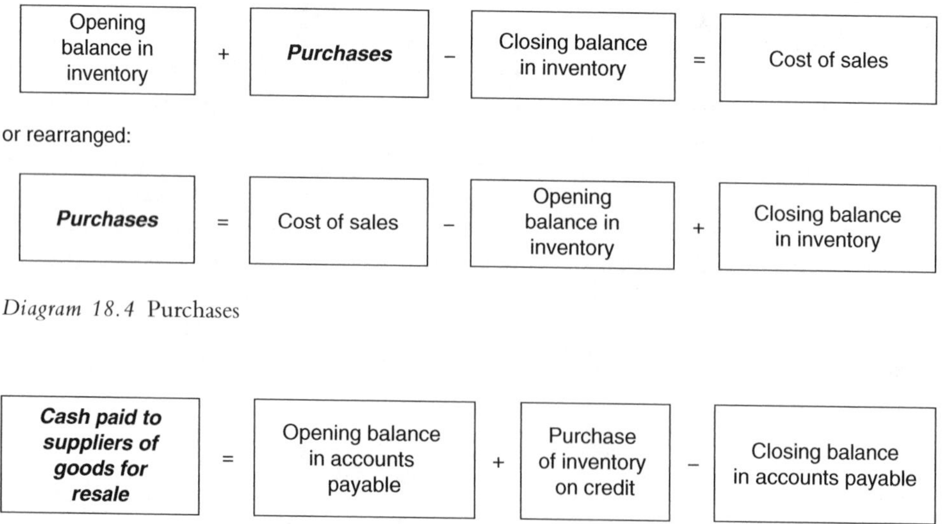

Diagram 18.4 Purchases

Diagram 18.5 Cash paid to suppliers

liability on the statement of financial position for administration as well as a current asset for insurance. The cash paid for administration expenses can therefore be calculated as follows:

Administration expenses payable

Details	*C*	*Details*	*C*
Administration expenses[1]	15	Balance b/d	**15**
Balance c/d	35	Administration expenses[2]	35
	50		50
		Balance b/d	**35**

Administration expenses

Details	*C*	*Details*	*C*
Bank	***390***	Administration expenses payable[1]	15
Administration expenses payable[2]	35	Profit or loss	**410**
	425		425

[1]Reversal of prior year accrual.
[2]Recording of current year accrual.

The cash paid for administration expenses of C390 is calculated by starting with the opening liability of C15, adding the expense transferred to the statement of profit or loss of C410 and subtracting the closing liability of C35. The cash paid for the insurance expense is calculated as follows:

Insurance paid in advance

Details	*C*	*Details*	*C*
Balance b/d	**5**	Insurance expense[1]	500
Bank	***510***	Balance c/d	15
	515		515
Balance b/d	**15**		

Insurance expense

Details	*C*	*Details*	*C*
Insurance paid in advance[1]	500	Profit or loss	**500**
	500		500

[1]Recording of current year expense.

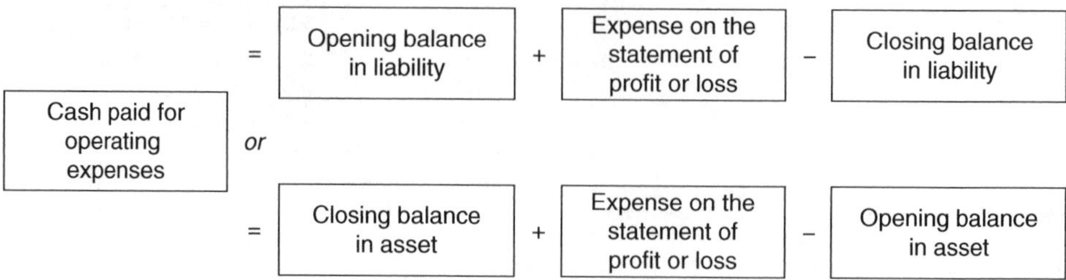

Diagram 18.6 Cash paid for operating expenses

The cash paid for insurance expense of C510 is calculated by starting with the closing asset of C15, adding the expense transferred to the statement of profit or loss of C500 and subtracting the opening asset of C5.

The above principles are summarised in Diagram 18.6.

In summary, the amount that appears on the statement of cash flows as cash paid to suppliers and employees is C27 600 (C26 700 + C390 + C510).

Pause and reflect . . .

What can you say about the operating expenses on the statement of profit or loss and the cash paid for operating expenses if there are no accrued or prepaid expenses on the statement of financial position?

Response

If there are no accrued or prepaid expenses on the statement of financial position, then the operating expenses on the statement of profit or loss must have all been paid for in cash.

CASH EFFECTS OF NON-OPERATING ITEMS, TAXATION, INTEREST AND DIVIDENDS

The non-operating items that typically need to be taken into account are the investment income and interest paid. It is again necessary to examine both the statement of profit or loss item and the relevant statement of financial position amount, if applicable.

Looking at **investment income** first, the investment income receivable account is reconstructed as follows:

Investment income receivable

Details	*C*	*Details*	*C*
Balance b/d	**0**		
Investment income[1]	100	Balance c/d	100
	100		100
Balance b/d	**100**		

Investment income

Details	C	*Details*	C
Profit or loss	**500**	***Bank***	***400***
		Investment income receivable[1]	100
	500		500

[1]Recording of current year accrual.

The cash of C400 received from investment income is calculated by starting with the opening balance of zero, adding the investment income of C500 and subtracting the closing balance of C100.

Turning our attention to the **interest expense**, the interest payable account is shown as follows:

Interest payable

Details	C	*Details*	C
Interest expense[1]	100	Balance b/d	**100**
Balance c/d	230	Interest expense[2]	230
	330		330
		Balance b/d	**230**

Interest expense

Details	C	*Details*	C
Bank	***120***	Interest payable[1]	100
Interest payable[2]	230	Profit or loss	**250**
	350		350

[1]Reversal of prior year accrual.
[2]Recording of current year accrual.

The cash of C120 paid for interest is computed by starting with the opening balance of C100, adding the interest expense of C250 and subtracting the closing balance of C230.

The cash paid for **taxation** and **dividends** (appearing on the statement of profit or loss and statement of charges in equity respectively, with corresponding liabilities on the statement of financial position) is calculated in the same way as the cash paid to suppliers, the cash paid for operating expenses or the interest paid. The statement of financial position accounts are shown below for completeness:

Taxation payable

Details	C	*Details*	C
Bank	***700***	Balance b/d	800
Balance c/d	400	Taxation	300
	1 100		1 100
		Balance b/d	400

Dividends payable

Details	*C*	*Details*	*C*
Bank	***1 000***	Balance b/d	200
Balance c/d	400	Dividends	1 200
	1 400		1 400
		Balance b/d	400

Note that the cash of C700 paid for income tax during the year is different from the taxation expense of C300 on the statement of profit or loss, and the cash of C1 000 paid for dividends is different to the dividend of C1 200 appearing on the statement of changes in equity.

 **Pause and reflect . . .**

Can you answer the following questions by examining the dividends payable account?

a) What is the amount of the interim dividend declared in respect of the current year?
b) What is the amount of the final dividend declared and has this been paid?

Response

a) The C1 000 cash paid in respect of dividends during the current year comprises the cash paid in respect of the final dividend owing from the previous year of C200 as well as an interim dividend declared during the current year of C800.
b) The balance on the dividend payable account at the end of the current year of C400 must represent the final dividend declared for the current year. It has not yet been paid.

We have now considered each item in the *operating activities* section of the statement of cash flows using the **direct method**. This section of the statement of cash flows is presented below. The workings to arrive at each figure are shown in brackets.

		C
Cash flows from operating activities		
Cash receipts from customers	*(1 200 + 30 650 – 1 700)*	30 150
Cash paid to suppliers and employees	*(1 880 + 24 950* – 130) +* *(15 + 410 – 35) + (15 + 500 – 5)* *(*Purchases = 26 000 – 1 950 + 900)*	(27 600)
Cash generated from operations		2 550
Investment income received	*(0 + 500 – 100)*	400
Interest paid	*(100 + 250 – 230)*	(120)
Taxation paid	*(800 + 300 – 400)*	(700)
Dividends paid	*(200 + 1 200 – 400)*	(1 000)
Net cash from operating activities		***1 130***

Indirect method

When using the indirect method, the starting point is the profit before tax on the statement of profit or loss. As this is an accrual basis figure, it is first adjusted for the *effect of non-cash items* included in the determination of profit – for example, depreciation expense or the gain on disposal of a non-current asset. It is then adjusted for the effect of *non-operating items* also included in the determination of profit, for example investment income, interest expense and dividends. Although these items do involve the flow of cash, we reverse the effect of the accrual income or expense at this point and then take into account the cash inflow or outflow after *cash generated from operations*. This brings us to a subtotal, *operating cash flow before working capital changes*.

The next adjustment relates to the effects of working capital movements – that is, movements in accounts receivable, accounts payable and inventory – to give the *cash generated from operations*.

Finally, the cash effects of non-operating items, dividends and taxation are taken into account to arrive at the **net cash from operating activities**. The indirect method of calculating cash flows from operating activities is shown in Table 18.2.

NON-CASH ITEMS

There are some income and expense items included in the determination of profit that do not involve the receipt or payment of cash. Examples are the profit or loss on the sale of non-current assets, depreciation and impairment of assets. Bearing in mind all the time that the starting point for the indirect method is the profit before tax on the statement of profit or loss, income items need to be *subtracted* from the profit before tax, and expense items need to be *added*. This is to reverse the effect of income items which have not resulted in the receipt of cash, and the expense items which have not resulted in the payment of cash. This is summarised in Diagram 18.7.

Table 18.2 Indirect method of presenting cash flows from operating activities

	Profit before tax
±	Non-cash items
±	Non-operating items
=	Operating cash flow before working capital changes
±	Working capital changes
=	*Cash generated from operations*
±	Cash effects of non-operating items, dividends and taxation
=	Net cash from operating activities

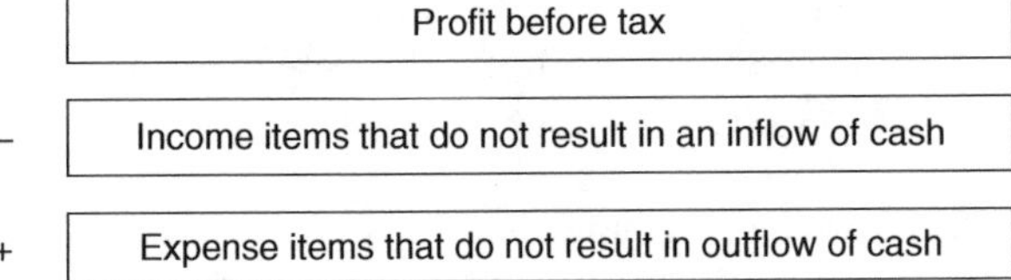

Diagram 18.7 Adjustments for non-cash items

The non-cash items on the statement of profit or loss of Computer World Limited are the depreciation expense of C450 and the loss on disposal of non-current assets of C40.

NON-OPERATING ITEMS

As mentioned above, non-operating items of income and expense, included in the determination of profit before tax, need to be reversed in calculating the operating cash flow. This is a simple matter of subtracting the non-operating income items and adding the non-operating expense items. In this example, we need to subtract the investment income of C500 and add the interest expense of C250.

WORKING CAPITAL CHANGES

When calculating the working capital changes, it is again important for you to remember that the starting point for the indirect method is the profit before tax on the statement of profit or loss. It is only the non-cash components of working capital that are adjusted as the movement in cash is the end result of the statement of cash flows.

Looking at **accounts receivable**, the balance increased from C1 200 to C1 700. This resulted from the *accrual basis sales of C30 650 being greater than the cash receipts from customers of C30 150*. As the accrual basis sales have been taken into account in the determination of the profit, the increase in accounts receivable of C500 (which is the excess of accrual basis sales over cash receipts) must be subtracted from the profit on the statement of cash flows.

Conversely, if the balance on accounts receivable decreased, it would result from *cash receipts from customers being greater than the accrual basis sales*. The decrease in accounts receivable is then added to the profit on the statement of cash flows.

Regarding **accounts payable**, the balance decreased from C1 880 to C130. This resulted from the *cash paid to suppliers of C26 700 being greater than the accrual basis purchases of C24 950* (which is part of cost of sales). As the cost of sales has been taken into account in the determination of the profit, the decrease in accounts payable of C1 750 (which is the excess of cash payments over accrual basis purchases) must be subtracted from the profit on the statement of cash flows.

Conversely, if the balance on accounts payable increased, this would result from the *accrual basis purchases being greater than cash payments to suppliers*. As the accrual basis purchases affect cost of sales, the increase in accounts payable is then added to the profit on the statement of cash flows.

Inventory will appear on the statement of financial position of all trading concerns. Any change in the closing inventory will have a direct effect on the cost of sales and therefore the gross profit and profit for the period. Increases in closing inventory increase profit, and decreases in closing inventory decrease profit. There is no cash effect in the inventory account, and therefore the decrease in inventory of C1 050 must be added to the profit. Conversely, an increase in inventory must be subtracted from the profit.

All changes in the non-cash working capital items must be taken into account. However, the non-operating items as well as taxation and dividends are excluded as they are reported separately. In the case of Computer World Limited, the only other non-cash working capital movements to take into account are the administration payable and the insurance paid in advance.

As **administration payable** is a liability, the principle is similar to the adjustment for accounts payable. The balance on the administration payable increased from C15 to C35.

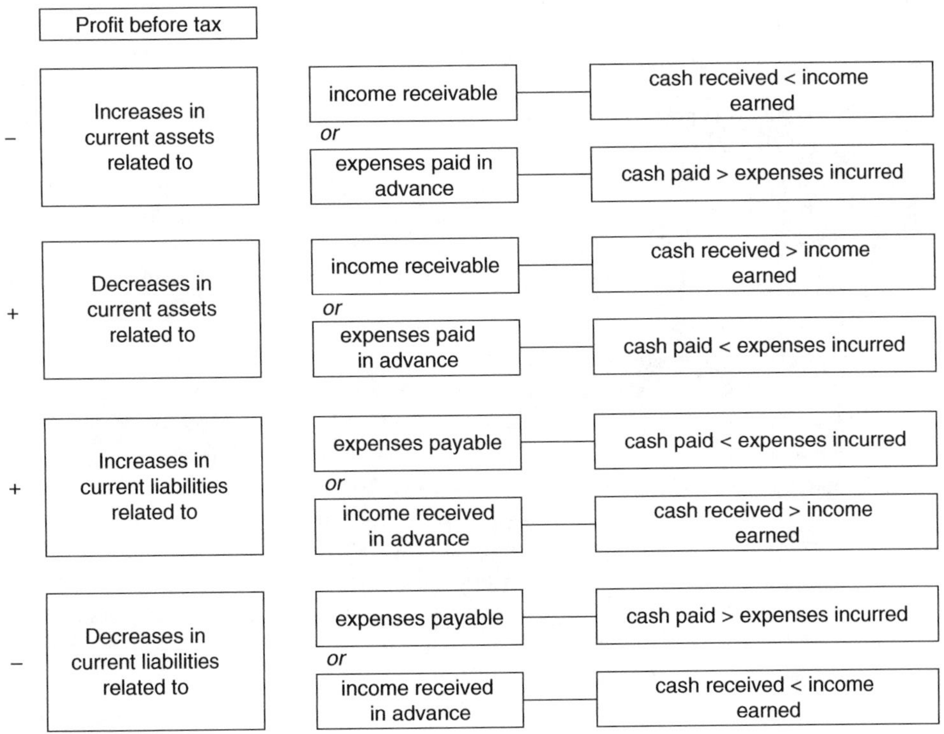

Diagram 18.8 Adjustments to non-cash components of working capital

This resulted from the *cash paid of C390 being less than the accrual basis expense of C410*, therefore the movement of C20 must be added to the profit on the statement of cash flows. Conversely, if the balance on a current liability account decreased, this would result from the *cash paid being greater than the accrual basis expense*, and the movement would have to be subtracted on the statement of cash flows.

The **insurance paid in advance** is an asset and therefore the principle is similar to the adjustment for accounts receivable. The balance on the insurance paid in advance increased from C5 to C15. This resulted from the cash paid of C510 being greater than the accrual basis expense of C500, therefore the movement of C10 must be subtracted from the profit on the statement of cash flows. Conversely, if the balance on a current asset decreased, this would result from the cash paid being less than the accrual basis expense, and the movement would have to be added on the statement of cash flows.

The adjustments relating to the movement in the non-cash components of working capital are summarised in Diagram 18.8. It is important for you to understand the reason for the adjustment, not only the mechanics of it.

CASH EFFECTS OF NON-OPERATING ITEMS, TAXATION AND DIVIDENDS

The treatment of these items is identical for both the direct and indirect methods. With regard to the non-operating items, the investment income and interest expense were reversed in arriving at operating cash flow before the working capital changes, therefore the cash effect is taken into account at this stage, as for the direct method.

Pause and reflect . . .

We have evaluated changes in working capital by comparing the amounts recorded in the statement of profit or loss under the accrual basis to the actual receipts and payments. This comparison enabled us to calculate the appropriate adjustments to the profit before tax amount used in the indirect method. Can you think of an explanation for the accounts receivable and accounts payable working capital changes that is based only on the movements in the statement of financial position?

Response

The accounts receivable balance increased by C500. Notwithstanding the sales recorded in the statement of profit or loss, the C500 increase in accounts receivable indicates that the accrual-based sales are greater than the cash received from customers by an amount of C500; therefore the accrual-based profit is reduced by this amount in reconciling to the cash from operating activities.

The C1 750 decrease in accounts payable indicates that the amount paid to suppliers is greater than the accrual-based purchases by an amount of C1 750. This amount is not included in the cost of sales amount used to determine profit before tax, therefore the accrual-based profit is reduced by this amount in reconciling to the cash from operating activities.

The taxation is reported on the statement of profit or loss *after* the profit before tax and the dividends are reported on the statement of changes in equity. There is thus no adjustment for these items, but rather the cash outflow relating to taxation and dividend is shown, again as for the direct method.

The *operating activities* section of the statement of cash flows using the **indirect** method is shown below.

	Workings	*C*
Cash flows from operating activities		
Profit before tax	*(from S/PL)*	3 500
Adjusted for non-cash and non-operating items		
Depreciation	*(from S/PL)*	450
Loss on the disposal of equipment		40
Investment income	*(from S/PL)*	(500)
Interest expense	*(from S/PL)*	250
Operating cash flow before working capital changes		***3 740***
Working capital changes		
Increase in accounts receivable	*(1 700 − 1 200)*	(500)
Decrease in accounts payable	*(130 − 1 880)*	(1 750)
Decrease in inventory	*(900 − 1 950)*	1 050
Increase in admin and selling payable	*(35 − 15)*	20
Increase in insurance paid in advance	*(15 − 5)*	(10)
Cash generated from operations		***2 550***

Investment income received	*(0 + 500 − 100)*	400
Interest paid	*(100 + 250 − 230)*	(120)
Taxation paid	*(800 + 300 − 400)*	(700)
Dividends paid	*(200 + 1 200 − 400)*	(1 000)
Net cash from operating activities		***1 130***

Note that the cash of C2 550 generated from operations and the net cash inflow from operating activities of C1 130 are the same for both the direct and indirect methods.

18.4.2 Preparation of the investing activities section

The investing and financing activities sections of the statement of cash flows are identical for both the direct and indirect methods. This is because no accrual basis income or expenses are adjusted in these sections. Each section reports cash inflows and outflows that are not on the statement of profit or loss.

Recall that the investing activities relate to the acquisition and disposal of non-current assets. You need to reconstruct the relevant statement of financial position accounts and establish the cash flows. Looking first at the **non-current assets**, the accounts are as follows:

Equipment: Cost

Details	C	*Details*	C
Balance b/d	1 910	Disposal	200
Bank (additions)	***2 170***	Balance c/d	3 880
	4 080		4 080
Balance b/d	3 880		

You were told in the example that equipment which originally cost C200 was sold during the period. By entering the cost of the equipment disposed on the credit side of the equipment account, we can establish that the cash paid for equipment purchased during the period was C2 170.

Equipment: Accumulated depreciation

Details	C	*Details*	C
Disposal	***60***	Balance b/d	1 060
Balance c/d	1 450	Depreciation	450
	1 510		1 510
		Balance b/d	1 450

The depreciation expense of C450, which is reported on the statement of profit or loss, is entered on the credit side of the accumulated depreciation account. We can then deduce that the accumulated depreciation relating to the equipment sold amounts to C60.

There is no cash flow implication in this number, but it is used to reconstruct the disposal account, as follows:

Disposal

Details	*C*	*Details*	*C*
Equipment at cost	200	Accumulated depreciation	60
		Cash (proceeds)	***100***
		Loss on disposal	40
	200		200

The cost and the accumulated depreciation of the equipment sold have been transferred from their respective accounts to the disposal account. The loss on disposal of equipment of C40 is known from the statement of profit or loss, and therefore the cash inflow from the disposal of the equipment is C100.

 **Pause and reflect . . .**

Does the loss on disposal represent an outflow of cash?

Response

The loss on disposal is an accrual-based amount and does not represent any cash flow. The proceeds of C100 represent an inflow of cash.

Turning our attention to the investments, the balance increased from C2 500 to C3 440. As no investments were sold during the period, it is apparent that the cash paid to acquire new investments is C940.

The *investing activities* section of the statement of cash flows is shown below.

		C
Cash flows from investing activities		
Purchase of equipment		(2 170)
Proceeds on disposal of equipment		100
Acquisition of investments	*(3 440 – 2 500)*	(940)
Net cash used in investing activities		***(3 010)***

18.4.3 Preparation of the financing activities section

As the financing activities section relates to the cash flows arising from changes in equity and borrowings, we need to examine the movements in the equity and non-current liabilities sections of the statement of financial position.

The share capital increased from C1 250 to C2 400. This means that there is a cash inflow of C1 150 from the issue of shares. The long-term loan from the bank increased from C1 040 to C1 800, implying a further cash inflow from long-term borrowings of C760. The financing activities section of the statement of cash flows is shown below.

		C
Cash flows from financing activities		
Proceeds from issue of shares	*(2 400 − 1 250)*	1 150
Proceeds from long-term borrowings	*(1 800 − 1 040)*	760
Net cash used in financing activities		***1 910***

Solution: Preparation of a statement of cash flows

For completeness, the full statements of cash flows prepared, using the direct and indirect methods, are shown on the following pages. The only section that is different between the two is the operating activities section. When the direct method is used, it is recommended that a reconciliation between the profit before tax as reported on the statement of profit or loss and the cash generated from operations as reported on the statement of cash flows be presented. This reconciliation, although not required by IAS 7, is shown as a note to the statement of cash flows on the direct method as it provides information that is useful in understanding the statement of cash flows.

Although not required by IAS 7, a note reconciling the taxation and dividends paid with their respective statement of profit or loss amounts is also recommended. This provides users with additional decision-relevant information.

Direct method

COMPUTER WORLD LIMITED
STATEMENT OF CASH FLOWS
FOR THE YEAR ENDED 31 DECEMBER 20X8

	Workings	*C000*
Cash flows from operating activities		
Cash receipts from customers	*(1 200 + 30 650 − 1 700)*	30 150
Cash paid to suppliers and for operating expenses	*(1 880 + 24 950* − 130) + (15 + 410 − 35) + (15 + 500 − 5) (*Purchases = 26 000 − 1 950 + 900)*	(27 600)
Cash generated from operations		2 550
Investment income received	*(0 + 500 − 100)*	400
Interest paid	*(100 + 250 − 230)*	(120)
Taxation paid	*(800 + 300 − 400)*	(700)
Dividends paid	*(200 + 1 200 − 400)*	(1 000)
Net cash from operating activities		***1 130***
Cash flows from investing activities		
Purchase of equipment		(2 170)
Proceeds on disposal of equipment		100
Acquisition of investments	*(3 440 − 2 500)*	(940)
Net cash used in investing activities		***(3 010)***

Cash flows from financing activities		
Proceeds from issue of shares	*(2 400 − 1 250)*	1 150
Proceeds from long-term borrowings	*(1 800 − 1 040)*	760
Net cash used in financing activities		***1 910***
Net increase in cash and cash equivalents	*(1 130 − 3 010 + 1 910)*	**30**
Cash and cash equivalents at beginning of period		**160**
Cash and cash equivalents at end of period		**190**

Reconciliation of profit before tax to cash from operations		
Profit before tax	*(from S/PL)*	3 500
Adjusted for non-cash and non-operating items		
Depreciation	*(from S/PL)*	450
Loss on the disposal of non-current assets	*(from S/PL)*	40
Investment income	*(from S/PL)*	(500)
Interest expense	*(from S/PL)*	250
Operating cash flow before working capital changes		3 740
Working capital changes		
Increase in accounts receivable	*(1 700 − 1 200)*	(500)
Decrease in accounts payable	*(130 − 1 880)*	(1 750)
Decrease in inventory	*(900 − 1 950)*	1 050
Increase in administration payable	*(35 − 15)*	20
Increase in insurance paid in advance	*(15 − 5)*	(10)
Cash generated from operations		2 550

Reconciliation of taxation and dividends paid	*Taxation*	*Dividends*
Liability at beginning of the year	800	200
Amount accrued	300	1 200
Liability at end of the year	(400)	(400)
Amount paid in cash	700	1 000

Indirect method

COMPUTER WORLD LIMITED
STATEMENT OF CASH FLOWS
FOR THE YEAR ENDED 31 DECEMBER 20X8

	Workings	*C000*
Cash flows from operating activities		
Profit before tax	*(From S/PL)*	3 500
Adjusted for non-cash and non-operating items		
Depreciation	*(From S/PL)*	450
Loss on the disposal of non-current assets	*(From S/PL)*	40
Investment income	*(From S/PL)*	(500)
Interest expense	*(From S/PL)*	250
Operating cash flow before working capital changes		***3 740***
Working capital changes		
Increase in accounts receivable		(500)
Decrease in accounts payable		(1 750)
Decrease in inventory		1 050
Increase in administration payable		20
Increase in insurance paid in advance		(10)
Cash generated from operations		***2 550***

Investment income received	*(0 + 500 – 100)*	400
Interest paid	*(100 + 250 – 230)*	(120)
Taxation paid	*(800 + 300 – 400)*	(700)
Dividends paid	*(200 + 1 200 – 4 00)*	(1 000)
Net cash from operating activities		***1 130***
Cash flows from investing activities		
Purchase of equipment		(2 170)
Proceeds on disposal of equipment		100
Acquisition of investments	*(3 440 – 2 500)*	(940)
Net cash used in investing activities		***(3 010)***
Cash flows from financing activities		
Proceeds from issue of shares	*(2 400 – 1 250)*	1 150
Proceeds from long-term borrowings	*(1 800 – 1 040)*	760
Net cash used in financing activities		***1 910***
Net increase in cash and cash equivalents	*(1 130 – 3 010 + 1 910)*	**30**
Cash and cash equivalents at beginning of period		**160**
Cash and cash equivalents at end of period		**190**

Reconciliation of taxation and dividends paid	*Taxation*	*Dividends*
Liability at beginning of the year	800	200
Amount accrued	300	1 200
Liability at end of the year	(400)	(400)
Amount paid in cash	700	1 000

Concepts in context

Flight Centre Limited
Statement of cash flows
For the year ended 30/06/2013

	AU$000
Receipts from customers	1 914 125
Payments to suppliers and employees	(1 446 170)
Dividends received	550
Royalties received	492
Interest received	39 464
Interest paid	(31 575)
Income taxes paid	(106 563)
Net cash flow from operating activities	370 323

Cash flows from investing activities	
Acquisition of subsidiary, net of cash acquired	5 412
Payments for property, plant and equipment	(40 781)
Payments for intangibles	(10 615)
Proceeds from sale of investments	28 217
Loans advanced to related parties	(2 799)
Loans repaid by related parties	3 726
Net cash (outflow) from investing activities	(16 840)
Cash flows from financing activities	
Proceeds from borrowings	11 428
Repayment of borrowings	(68 272)
Proceeds from issue of shares	4 795
Dividends paid to company's shareholders	(117 295)
Net cash outflow from financing activities	(169 344)
Net increase in cash held	184 139
Cash and cash equivalents at the beginning of the financial year	1 027 617
Effects of exchange rate changes on cash and cash equivalents	15 263
Cash and cash equivalents at the end of the year	1 227 019

What concepts in context do you see here?

Can you recognise which method Flight Centre has used for its statement of cash flows? If you look at the top of the statement of cash flows, you will see that it begins with 'receipts from customers' followed by 'payments to suppliers and employees'. This indicates that the direct method has been used, following the format that you have learnt in this chapter.

You should be able to identify many familiar items on Flight Centre's statement of cash flows. In the investing activities section, you have learnt about payments for property, plant and equipment as well as loans advanced and repaid. In the financing activities section, you have learnt about proceeds and repayments of borrowings as well as proceeds on the issue of shares. Note that Flight Centre has chosen to disclose its dividend payments as a financing activity as opposed to an operating activity, as discussed in this chapter.

It is also interesting to note that the cash generated from operating activities of AU$370 323 000 is sufficient to cover both the cash outflow from investing activities of AU$16 840 000 and the cash outflow from financing activities of AU$169 344 000.

Flight Centre is one of the world's largest travel agencies, operating in 10 countries.

Source: admin.flightcentrelimited.com/sites/fctgl.com/files/1.%20FLT%202013%20Annual%20Report_0.pdf (Accessed 24 July 2014).

Revision example

The post-adjustment trial balances of Panchenko Limited at 30 June 20X3 and 20X4 are shown below:

PANCHENKO LIMITED
TRIAL BALANCE
AT 30 JUNE

	20X4	*20X3*
	C000	*C000*
Plant and equipment: Cost	11 000	8 000
Investments	3 000	—
Inventory	5 000	3 600
Accounts receivable	3 600	3 400
Investment income receivable	400	—
Bank	1 200	800
Administration expenses	24 200	—
Loss on disposal of investments	400	—
Interest expense	1 000	800
Taxation expense	2 000	1 400
Dividends	800	800
	52 600	18 800
Share capital	3 800	2 000
Retained earnings	2 800	2 000
Gross profit	30 000	3 800
Investment income	400	—
Plant and equipment: Accumulated depreciation	4 000	2 000
Long-term loan	8 000	6 000
Accounts payable	2 400	1 200
Interest payable	200	800
Taxation payable	600	200
Dividends payable	400	800
	52 600	18 800

Additional information

- Depreciation on plant and equipment of C2 400 000 was provided during 20X4.
- Plant and equipment with a cost of C1 000 000 were sold during the year and a loss of C200 000 was incurred.
- The depreciation and loss on sale of the plant and equipment are both included in administration expenses.
- An investment acquired for C600 000 during the year was disposed of before the year-end.
- Long-term loans of C2 000 000 were repaid during the year.
- Panchenko Limited marks up its goods for resale by 50 per cent on cost to calculate its selling price.

You are required to:

Prepare the statement of cash flows for Panchenko Limited for the period ended 30 June 20X4, using the direct method. Notes to the cash flow are required.

 **Solution: Revision example**

PANCHENKO LIMITED
STATEMENT OF CASH FLOWS
FOR THE YEAR ENDED 30 JUNE 20X4

	Workings	C000
Cash flows from operating activities		
Cash receipts from customers	*(3 400 + 90 000* – 3 600) (*W14)*	89 800
Cash paid to suppliers and employees	*(See W16)*	(81 800)
Cash generated from operations		8 000
Investment income received	*(0 + 400 – 400) (W10)*	–
Interest paid	*(800 + 1 000 – 200) (W9)*	(1 600)
Taxation paid	*(200 + 2 000 – 600) (W12)*	(1 600)
Dividends paid	*(800 + 800 – 400) (W11)*	(1 200)
Net cash from operating activities		***3 600***
Cash flows from investing activities		
Proceeds on disposal of non-current assets (W3)		400
Proceeds on disposal of investments (W8)		200
Acquisition of non-current assets (W1)		(4 000)
Acquisition of investments (W7)		(3 600)
Net cash used in investing activities		***(7 000)***
Cash flows from financing activities		
Proceeds from share issue	*(3 800 – 2 000)*	1 800
Repayment of long-term loan	*(W13)*	(2 000)
Proceeds from long-term loan	*(See W13)*	4 000
Net cash used in financing activities		***3 800***
Net increase in cash and cash equivalents		**400**
Cash and cash equivalents at beginning of period		**800**
Cash and cash equivalents at end of period		**1 200**
Reconciliation of profit before tax to cash from operations		
Profit before tax	*(W14)*	4 800
Adjusted for non-cash and non-operating items		
Depreciation	*(W2)*	2 400
Loss on disposal of fixed asset	*(W3)*	200
Investment income	*(Given)*	(400)
Loss on disposal of investments	*(Given)*	400
Interest expense	*(Given)*	1 000
Operating cash flow before working capital changes		8 400
Working capital changes	*(W15)*	
Increase in inventory		(1 400)
Increase in accounts receivable		(200)
Increase in accounts payable		1 200
Cash generated from operations		8 000

Workings

Plant and equipment: (1)

Details	*C*	*Details*	*C*
Balance b/d	8 000	Disposal	1 000
Cash – addition	***4 000***	Balance c/d	11 000
	12 000		12 000
Balance b/d	11 000		

Accumulated depreciation (2)

Details	*C*	*Details*	*C*
Disposal	***400***	Balance b/d	2 000
Balance c/d	4 000	Depreciation	2 400
	4 400		4 400
		Balance b/d	4 000

Disposal of plant and equipment (3)

Details	*C*	*Details*	*C*
Plant and equipment – cost	1 000	Accumulated depreciation	400
		Bank	***400***
		Profit & loss	200
	1 000		1 000

Inventory (4)

Details	*C*	*Details*	*C*
Balance b/d	3 600	Cost of sales (W14)	60 000
Accounts payable	***61 400***	Balance c/d	5 000
	65 000		65 000
Balance b/d	5 000		

Accounts receivable (5)

Details	*C*	*Details*	*C*
Balance b/d	3 400	***Bank***	***89 800***
Sales (W14)	90 000	Balance c/d	3 600
	93 400		93 400
Balance b/d	3 600		

Accounts payable (6)

Details	*C*	*Details*	*C*
Bank	***60 200***	Balance b/d	1 200
Balance c/d	2 400	Inventory	61 400
	62 600		62 600
		Balance b/d	2 400

Investments (7)

Details	*C*	*Details*	*C*
Bank	***3 600***	Disposal	600
		Balance c/d	3 000
	3 600		3 600
Balance b/d	3 000		

Disposal of investments (8)

Details	*C*	*Details*	*C*
Investment	600	***Bank***	***200***
		Profit & loss	400
	600		600

Interest payable (9)

Details	*C*	*Details*	*C*
Bank	***1 600***	Balance b/d	800
Balance c/d	200	Interest	1 000
	1 800		1 800
		Balance b/d	200

Investment income receivable (10)

Details	*C*	*Details*	*C*
Balance b/d	0	***Bank***	***0***
Investment income	400	Balance c/d	400
	400		400
Balance b/d	400		

Dividends payable (11)

Details	*C*	*Details*	*C*
Bank	***1 200***	Balance b/d	800
Balance c/d	400	Dividends	800
	1 600		1 600
		Balance b/d	400

Taxation payable (12)

Details	*C*	*Details*	*C*
Bank	***1 600***	Balance b/d	200
Balance c/d	600	Taxation	2 000
	2 200		2 200
		Balance b/d	600

Long-term loan (13)

Details	*C*	*Details*	*C*
Bank – repayment	2 000	Balance b/d	6 000
		Bank – raised	***4 000***
Balance c/d	8 000		
	10 000		10 000
		Balance b/d	8 000

PANCHENKO LIMITED (14)
STATEMENT OF PROFIT OR LOSS
FOR THE YEAR ENDED 30 JUNE 20X4

		C000
Sales	*(C30 000 × 150/50)*	90 000
Cost of sales	*(C30 000 × 100/50) or (C90 000 – C30 000)*	(60 000)
Gross profit		30 000
Other income		
Investment income		400
Operating expenses		(24 600)
Administration expenses		24 200
Loss on disposal of investments		400
Finance cost		
Interest expense		(1 000)
Profit before taxation		***4 800***
Taxation		(2 000)
Profit for the period		2 800

Working capital (15)

Increase in inventory (3 600 – 5 000)	(1 400)
Increase in accounts receivable (3 400 – 3 600)	(200)
Increase in accounts payable (3 600 – 5 000)	1 200
	(400)

Cash paid to suppliers and employees (16)

Cash paid to suppliers (W6)	60 200
Administration expenses (W14)	24 200
Loss on disposal of plant and equipment	(200)
Depreciation	(2 400)
	81 800

The statement of cash flows is prepared by reconstructing the relevant ledger accounts. The opening and closing balances are obtained from the trial balance and each ledger account is completed by using the information provided in the question. This enables you to identify all the cash flows as well as the non-cash items.

For the plant and equipment, we need to first establish the C400 accumulated depreciation relating to the item sold by reconstructing the accumulated depreciation account. The proceeds on disposal can then be computed by reconstructing the disposal of plant and equipment account. The account shows that there is a carrying amount of C600 and as a loss of C200 was incurred, the proceeds of sale must have been C400.

The accounts receivable account is used to calculate the cash received from customers of C89 800 and the inventory and accounts payable accounts are used to calculate the cash paid to suppliers for goods purchased of C60 200. Note that sales and cost of sales amounts need to be computed from the gross profit, using the mark up of 50 per cent on cost. In addition, we will need to take into account the cash paid for operating expenses to determine the total of the line item 'cash paid to suppliers and employees'.

The cash paid for investments is determined from the investments account. As there is no opening balance and a closing balance of C3 000 and investments costing C600 were disposed of, the cash paid for investment is calculated as C3 600.

The cash paid for interest, taxation and dividends are all calculated following a similar logic of taking into account the opening and closing balances as well as the accrual movement for the year.

The proceeds raised from the long-term loan need to be separated from the amount repaid. The liability increased by C2 000 from C6 000 to C8 000 and as C2 000 was repaid, an amount of C4 000 must have been raised.

Bibliography

SAICA. 2013. *The Financial Reporting Investigations Panel.* www.saica.co.za/Technical/Financial Reporting/FinancialReportingInvestigationPanelPanel/tabid/529/language/en-ZA/Default.aspx (Accessed 17 May 2013).

The International Accounting Standards Board. 2010. *The Conceptual Framework.*

The International Accounting Standards Board. 2009. IAS 7 *Statement of Cash Flows.*

19 Analysis of financial statements

Business focus

Warren Buffett is an American entrepreneur, investor and philanthropist. He is the chairman, chief executive officer and largest shareholder of Berkshire Hathaway, a company headquartered in Omaha, Nebraska, in the United States. Berkshire Hathaway is a multinational holding company with investments in numerous companies including Heinz, American Express, Coca-Cola and IBM.

Buffet is consistently ranked amongst the world's wealthiest people and is known for his personal frugality despite his enormous wealth, as well as for being a notable philanthropist.

Over the past 40 years, Warren Buffett has emerged as possibly the greatest investor of his time. Many people refer to him as a 'value' investor, finding overlooked shares, buying them at below intrinsic value and holding them for long periods. However, while value is important to Buffett, quality is more so. If you had invested $10 000 in Berkshire Hathaway when he took control in 1965, your holdings would be worth more than $50 million today.

In this chapter

This book has focused on preparers of financial statements. We now turn our attention to their users – the investors and creditors who need to analyse financial statements and examine the tools and techniques of analysis of financial statements.

Dashboard

- Look at the *Learning outcomes* so that you know what you should be able to do after studying this chapter.
- Read the *Business focus* to place this chapter's contents in a real-world context.
- Preview *In this chapter* to focus your mind on the contents of the chapter.
- Read the *text* in detail.
    - Pay attention to the *definitions of the ratios,* and apply your mind to the *Pause and reflect* scenarios.
    - The ratios are easier to remember if you focus on understanding the relationship the ratio is portraying. Pay attention to this when studying the ratio analysis in Section 19.4.

  - As you read the chapter, go online and look at ratios that most listed companies provide as part of their annual report. You will most often find the annual report within the 'investor relations' section of the website. Relate the ratios and definitions that you see in annual reports to what you learn in this chapter.

- Prepare solutions to the examples as you read through the chapter.
- Prepare a solution to the *Revision example* at the end of the chapter without reference to the suggested one. Compare your solution to the suggested solution provided.

Learning outcomes

After studying this chapter, you should be able to do the following:

1 Explain the objectives of financial statement analysis.
2 Identify the external influences affecting a business entity.
3 Prepare common-size and comparative financial statements as tools of financial statement analysis.
4 Recall ratios appropriate to analyse a set of financial statements and apply ratios as tools of financial statement analysis.

Analysis of financial statements

19.1 Objectives of financial statement analysis

Financial reporting provides information about the financial position, performance and cash flows of a business entity. All the information is useful to a wide range of users in making economic decisions. The users need to evaluate the financial position of a business entity and the results of its business operations when making economic decisions. This evaluation is the overall objective of financial statement analysis.

The analysis of financial statements may be used to predict future events, based on the past performance of the business and its financial position at a particular time.

Different users of the financial statements have different needs for information, and the specific objectives of the users will therefore depend on the use to which the user wishes to put the information.

The user may be a potential investor in the business entity who is concerned about the future performance of the business, such as the rate of return the business will achieve and its ability to make distributions to its owners.

The user may be a potential lender to the business entity. Such a user will be concerned that the business entity will have sufficient cash resources to be able to service its interest payments and repay its debt when it falls due for repayment.

Management, in addition to wanting to assess past performance and financial position and to predict future performance and financial position of the business entity, will want to be able to identify potential problem areas, such as a shortage of cash resources, in order to take timeous corrective action.

19.2 External influences

A business entity is affected by many outside factors.

The state of the economy in which it operates has a major influence on the entity. If the economy is in recession, this is likely to have an adverse effect on the financial position and performance of the business enterprise.

Changes in the particular industry in which the entity operates also impact on its financial position and results. A switch in demand from an existing product, such as a traditional mobile phone, to a new product, such as a smartphone, can have a disastrous impact on entities which do not predict such changes.

When analysing the financial position and results of a business entity, it is important to be aware of these external influences and to incorporate their effects in the evaluation.

19.3 Tools of financial statement analysis

We will now consider the various tools which are commonly used in analysing financial statements.

Depending on the needs of the user, the analysis of the financial statements will focus on one or more of the following areas:

- short-term liquidity;
- capital structure and long-term solvency;
- operational efficiency and profitability.

Let us consider particular interests of three typical user groups of financial statements. Potential lenders or suppliers to a business entity are interested in the short-term liquidity of the entity as assurance that it will be able to repay the amounts owing when these fall due.

Potential investors in a business entity are interested in the long-term solvency of the entity. The potential investors seek a return on the investment, on an ongoing basis, as well as growth in the value of the investment. In order to achieve this, long-term solvency is vital.

Management as well as investors are interested in measuring the performance of the business entity and seek to measure both operational efficiency and profitability.

As well as looking at ratio analysis, which is a widely used tool of financial statement analysis, we will also look at other tools of financial statement analysis, which provide valuable insight into the composition of the financial statements and of trends over time.

It is always important when interpreting the ratios or the results of the other tools of financial statement analysis to 'look behind' the numbers. As we consider the various measures of performance and financial position, we shall see that a result, which might be expected to be a warning of a problem or potential problem, may be able to be explained satisfactorily, in a way that indicates that no problem exists.

We shall use the example which follows to explore the various tools of financial statement analysis.

We must always remember that an outside user of financial statements, such as a potential investor, is limited to published information regarding business entities and has to work with that information when analysing financial statements. This limitation can reduce the meaningfulness and effectiveness of the analysis.

Example: Ratio analysis

Home Build plc is a retailer of home improvement products with stores situated close to main urban areas. The financial statements for the year ended 30 September 20X6 (together with comparative information for 20X5 and 20X4) are provided below.

HOME BUILD PLC
STATEMENT OF PROFIT OR LOSS
FOR THE YEAR ENDED 30 SEPTEMBER 20X6

	20X6	*20X5*	*20X4*
	C000	*C000*	*C000*
Sales	10 920	8 730	8 050
Cost of sales	(7 280)	(5 580)	(5 367)
Gross profit	3 640	3 150	2 683
Other income			
Investment income	135	122	120
Operating expenses	(2 906)	(2 907)	(2 189)
Selling and distribution	1 751	2 307	1 439
Administration	1 155	600	750
Finance cost			
Interest expense	(204)	(170)	(140)
Profit before taxation	665	195	474
Taxation	(245)	(75)	(174)
Profit for the period	420	120	300

HOME BUILD PLC
STATEMENT OF CHANGES IN EQUITY
FOR THE YEAR ENDED 30 SEPTEMBER 20X6

	Ordinary share capital	*Preference share capital*	*Retained earnings*	*Total*
	C000	*C000*	*C000*	*C000*
Balance at 30 September 20X3	3 000	500	310	3 810
Profit for the period			300	300
Preference dividends			(30)	(30)
Ordinary dividends			(130)	(130)
Balance at 30 September 20X4	3 000	500	450	3 950
Profit for the period			120	120
Preference dividends			(30)	(30)
Ordinary dividends			(50)	(50)
Balance at 30 September 20X5	3 000	500	490	3 990
Profit for the period			420	420
Preference dividends			(30)	(30)
Ordinary dividends			(180)	(180)
Issue of ordinary share capital	2 000			2 000
Balance at 30 September 20X6	5 000	500	700	6 200

HOME BUILD PLC
STATEMENT OF FINANCIAL POSITION
AT 30 SEPTEMBER 20X6

	20X6	*20X5*	*20X4*
	C000	*C000*	*C000*
ASSETS			
Non-current assets	6 120	3 400	4 000
Property, plant and equipment	4 620	2 400	3 000
Investments	1 500	1 000	1 000
Current assets	3 450	4 130	2 470
Inventory	1 630	2 360	1 170
Accounts receivable	1 150	1 770	850
Bank	670	—	450
	9 570	**7 530**	**6 470**
EQUITY AND LIABILITIES			
Equity	6 200	3 990	3 950
Ordinary share capital	5 000	3 000	3 000
Retained earnings	700	490	450
Ordinary shareholders' interest	5 700	3 490	3 450
6% non-redeemable preference share capital	500	500	500
Non-current liabilities	2 550	1 750	1 750
8% debentures	1 750	750	750
Long-term borrowings	800	1 000	1 000

	820	1 790	770
Current liabilities			
Accounts payable	550	1 460	720
Taxation payable	70	20	50
Current portion of borrowings	200	—	—
Bank overdraft	—	310	—
	9 570	**7 530**	**6 470**

Additional information

- 500 000 ordinary shares were issued at C3 per share on 1 October 20X5.
- The company purchased a new administration building on 1 October 20X5.
- The market price of the ordinary shares at the end of each financial year was:
    - 20X4 – C4.50
    - 20X5 – C3.90
    - 20X6 – C5.50
- 20X3 financial information available:
    - Sales C7 245 000
    - Cost of sales C4 830 000
    - Gross profit C2 415 000
    - Inventory C735 000
    - Accounts receivable C760 000
    - Accounts payable C612 000
    - Total assets C5 850 000
- Ordinary shareholders' interest C3 310 000
- Tax rate for the company is 28 per cent.

19.3.1 Common-size financial statements

Common-size financial statements are prepared using percentages for each item on the financial statements instead of showing the actual amounts. This technique is also referred to as ***vertical analysis***.

In the case of the statement of profit or loss, the sales are shown as 100 per cent, with all other items shown as a percentage of sales.

In the case of the statement of financial position, the totals of both the assets section and the equity and liabilities section are shown as 100 per cent. Individual items are shown as a percentage of the total assets or of the total equity and liabilities. Interest-bearing and interest-free debt are often shown separately in a common-size statement of financial position.

The common-size financial statements reveal relationships between the various components of the financial statements. For example, the common-size statement of profit or loss indicates the percentage of sales absorbed by each expense item, while the common-size statement of financial position indicates relationships, such as the percentage of the entity's financing which comes from debt and the percentage which comes from equity, or what proportion of total assets comprises cash.

Common-size financial statements are useful when users wish to compare different business entities. They can also be used to perform a trend analysis for the same business entity over a period of time.

The common-size financial statements of Home Build plc follow.

COMMON-SIZE ANALYSIS STATEMENT OF PROFIT OR LOSS FOR THE YEAR ENDED 30 SEPTEMBER 20X6

	20X6	*20X5*	*20X4*
	%	%	%
Sales	100	100	100
Cost of sales	(67)	(64)	(67)
Gross profit	33	36	33
Investment income	1	1	2
Operating expenses	(26)	(33)	(27)
Selling and distribution	16	26	18
Administration	10	7	9
Interest expense	(2)	(2)	(2)
Profit before taxation	6	2	6
Taxation	(2)	(1)	(2)
Profit for the period	4	1	4

 The common-size statement of profit or loss shows the following:

- The 20X5 year is problematic. There is a slightly higher percentage of gross profit to sales in 20X5 (36 per cent) compared to 20X4 and 20X6 (both 33 per cent), but a much lower percentage of profit to sales (1 per cent compared to 4 per cent) in both other years.
- This indicates a problem in the area of operating expenses – the percentage of selling and distribution expenses to sales in 20X5 (26 per cent), was significantly higher than in 20X4 (18 per cent) or 20X6 (16 per cent).
- The higher expenses in 20X5 led to the percentage of profit to sales dropping to 1 per cent compared to the 4 per cent in 20X4 and in 20X6.

COMMON-SIZE ANALYSIS STATEMENT OF FINANCIAL POSITION AT 30 SEPTEMBER 20X6

	20X6	*20X5*	*20X4*
	%	%	%
ASSETS			
Non-current assets	64	45	62
Property, plant and equipment	48	32	46
Investments	16	13	16
Current assets	36	55	38
Inventory	17	31	18
Accounts receivable	12	24	13
Bank	7	0	7
	100	100	100

EQUITY AND LIABILITIES			
Equity	65	53	61
Ordinary share capital	53	39	46
Retained earnings	7	7	7
6% non-redeemable preference share capital	5	7	8
Non-current liabilities	26	23	27
8% debentures	18	10	12
Long-term borrowings	8	13	15
Current liabilities	9	24	12
Accounts payable	6	19	11
Taxation payable	1	1	1
Current portion of borrowings	2	0	0
Bank overdraft	0	4	0
	100	100	100

 The common-size statement of financial position shows the following:

- Confirmation that the 20X5 year is problematic. The percentage of inventory (31 per cent) to total assets is significantly higher than in 20X4 (18 per cent) and 20X6 (17 per cent). In addition, the percentage of accounts receivable (24 per cent) to total assets is significantly higher than in 20X4 (13 per cent) and 20X6 (12 per cent). This indicates a combination of slow-moving inventory and difficulties in the collection of amounts owing by customers.
- Accounts payable comprise a much higher percentage of equity and liabilities in 20X5 (31 per cent) compared to 20X4 (18 per cent) and 20X6 (17 per cent), indicating difficulties in paying suppliers.

19.3.2 Comparative statements

Comparative financial statements show the financial statements for each of the required number of years, side by side, thereby highlighting changes in individual items from year to year. This technique is also referred to as ***horizontal analysis***.

The percentage increase or decrease in an individual item is calculated as follows:

$$\frac{\text{Current year amount} - \text{prior year amount}}{\text{Prior year amount}} \times \frac{100}{1}$$

The usefulness of comparative statements is limited in that meaningful percentages cannot be computed when there is a movement from a positive to a negative, or vice versa, or if the amount for the previous year was zero. If an item has a positive value for a previous year and is zero in the current year, the decrease is 100 per cent.

The comparative statement of profit or loss and selected items from the statement of financial position for Home Build plc follow.

COMPARATIVE ANALYSIS STATEMENT OF PROFIT OR LOSS FOR THE YEAR ENDED 30 SEPTEMBER 20X6

	20X6 *C000*	*20X5–20X6* *change %*	*20X5* *C000*	*20X4–20X5* *change %*	*20X4* *C000*
Sales	10 920	*25*	8 730	*8*	8 050
Cost of sales	(7 280)	*30*	(5 580)	*4*	(5 367)
Gross profit	3 640	*16*	3 150	*17*	2 683
Investment income	135	*11*	122	*2*	120
Operating expenses	(2 906)	—	(2 907)	*33*	(2 189)
Selling and distribution	1 751	*(24)*	2 307	*60*	1 439
Administration	1 155	*93*	600	*(20)*	750
Interest expense	(204)	*20*	(170)	*21*	(140)
Profit before taxation	665	*241*	195	*(59)*	474
Taxation	(245)	*227*	(75)	*(57)*	(174)
Profit for the period	420	*250*	120	*(60)*	300

 The comparative analysis statement of profit or loss shows the following:

- The increase in gross profit between 20X4 and 20X5 (17 per cent) and 20X5 and 20X6 (16 per cent) is effectively the same.
- There is, however, a 60 per cent increase in selling and distribution expenses between 20X4 and 20X5 leading to a 59 per cent decrease in profit before tax between those two years.
- This confirms the issues highlighted by the common-size analysis.
- The increase in administration expense between 20X5 and 20X6 (90 per cent) needs to be investigated but can be attributed in part to an expected increase in depreciation resulting from the purchase of the new administration building.

COMPARATIVE ANALYSIS STATEMENT OF FINANCIAL POSITION AT 30 SEPTEMBER 20X6

	20X6 *C000*	*20X5–20X6* *change %*	*20X5* *C000*	*20X4–20X5* *change %*	*20X4* *C000*
ASSETS					
Non-current assets	6 120	*80*	3 400	*(15)*	4 000
Current assets	3 450	*(16)*	4 130	*67*	2 470
Inventory	1 630	*(31)*	2 360	*102*	1 170
Accounts receivable	1 150	*(35)*	1 770	*108*	850
Bank	670	^	—	*(100)*	450
	9 570		**7 530**		**6 470**
EQUITY AND LIABILITIES					
Capital and reserves	6 200	*55*	3 990	*1*	3 950
Non-current liabilities	2 550	*46*	1 750	—	1 750

Current liabilities	820	*(54)*	1 790	*132*	770
Accounts payable	550	*(62)*	1 460	*103*	720
Taxation payable	70	*250*	20	*(60)*	50
Current borrowings	200	^	—	—	—
Bank overdraft	—	*(100)*	310	^	—
	9 570		7 530		6 470

^ Cannot compute a meaningful percentage.

 The comparative analysis statement of financial position shows the following:

- The non-current assets increased by 80 per cent from 20X5 to 20X6, caused mainly by the purchase of the new administration building.
- Inventory increased by 102 per cent from 20X4 to 20X5, and accounts receivable increased 108 per cent over the same period. This confirms the build-up of inventory and accounts receivable.
- Accounts payable increased by 103 per cent from 20X4 to 20X5, and bank decreased by 100 per cent (going into overdraft), further confirming the pressure on short-term liquidity.

19.4 Ratio analysis

Think back to the objective of general purpose financial reporting as discussed in Chapter 2, *Fundamental accounting concepts*, to provide information about the entity that is useful to existing and potential investors, lenders and other creditors in making financial decisions. The information is used to evaluate the performance and financial position of the business entity and the efficiency of management. Individual items in financial statements do not provide meaningful information when viewed in isolation. Ratios are therefore used to summarise financial data and to monitor trends in performance and deviations from past trends. Ratios can also be used to evaluate the results of a business entity against the results of others in the same industry.

You will notice that where the ratio incorporates a statement of profit or loss amount in the numerator and a statement of financial position amount in the denominator, an average is often used for the statement of financial position amount. Averages are used in an attempt to smooth out fluctuations between the current year and the prior one. However, it is important to note that the ratios can be satisfactorily calculated without the use of averages if prior year information is not available. The user then needs to take this into account when interpreting the ratios.

 **Pause and reflect...**

A commonly used ratio (which you will learn about in Section 19.4.3) is the profit-to-sales ratio. It is calculated as follows, using the 20X6 and 20X5 amounts:

	20X6	*20X5*
$\frac{\text{Profit for the period}}{\text{Sales}} \times 100$	$\frac{420}{10920} \times 100$	$\frac{120}{8730} \times 100$

When analysing this ratio, is it more useful and appropriate to comment that the ratio was 1.4 per cent in 20X5 and increased to 3.8 per cent in 20X6, or that it was 1.37457 per cent in 20X5 and increased to 3.84615 per cent in 20X6?

Response

When using ratios in financial analysis, we are looking for broad trends. What is important here is that the profit-to-sales ratio increased (almost two and a half times) and this is indicative of an improved performance, although off a low base. If the ratio had increased from, say, 1.5 per cent to, say, 3.7 per cent, our conclusion would not change.

Calculating ratios to one or two decimal places is therefore sufficient for the purposes of ratio analysis.

For some ratios, there is more than one accepted formula, and one definition is as valid as the next. This is why it is important always to know and understand the underlying definition before interpreting any ratio.

It is useful when analysing financial statements to group ratios into categories according to the area of analysis. Table 19.1 shows the classification used in this book, although there are other acceptable classifications.

We shall use the information in the Home Build plc example to illustrate the calculation of each ratio we discuss.

19.4.1 Short-term liquidity

There are several ratios which are used to measure whether a business entity has sufficient liquid resources to enable it to meet its short-term liabilities. This is an issue which is important to a variety of users, including the following: suppliers who seek assurance that they will be paid within agreed time limits; lenders who seek assurance that they will receive interest and loan repayments when due to them; employees who seek assurance that they will receive their remuneration regularly; and investors who do not wish to see their investment jeopardised by the business entity experiencing a cash crisis, which could ring the death knell for the entity.

Table 19.1 Categories of ratios

Category of ratios	*Purpose of ratios*
Short-term liquidity	Effectiveness in the management of working capital
Capital structure and long-term solvency	Analysis of the financial structure or gearing
Operating efficiency and profitability	Effectiveness in generating profits
Market measures	Analysis of the returns to investors

Current ratio

The current ratio measures the ability of the current assets to meet existing current liabilities and is calculated as follows:

$$\frac{\text{Current assets}}{\text{Current liabilities}}$$

A business needs to balance its ability to meet its short-term liabilities with its need to minimise those current assets that generate a low return. A current ratio of 2:1 is generally regarded as acceptable, but this assumption can be challenged. The adequacy of the current ratio depends on the nature of the business, and the composition and turnover rate of its current assets. Retail entities such as supermarkets sell most of their goods for cash and therefore do not have large accounts receivable. This normally results in a current ratio much lower than 2:1, but they are able to meet their short-term liabilities effectively.

If the current assets comprise mostly cash and accounts receivable, the business will be in a stronger position to meet its short-term liabilities than if its current assets comprise mostly inventories, which may take some time to realise in cash.

The current ratio for Home Build plc for the 20X6, 20X5 and 20X4 years is calculated as follows:

20X6	*20X5*	*20X4*
$\frac{3\,450}{820}$	$\frac{4\,130}{1\,790}$	$\frac{2\,470}{770}$
= 4.21:1	= 2.31:1	= 3.21:1

The current ratio decreased in 20X5, although it is still above the generally accepted level of 2:1.

Acid test or quick ratio

The acid test or quick ratio is a refinement of the current ratio in that the inventory and prepayments are excluded from the current assets. Inventory is excluded from the calculation as it is the least liquid component of current assets and may take some time to be realised in cash. Prepayments are excluded as they represent expenditure paid in advance and cannot be realised in cash. An acid test ratio of 1:1 is normally regarded as acceptable, although many enterprises operate with a ratio of less than this. A business where the majority of sales are for cash and which, as a result, has a low level of accounts receivable, will normally have an acid test ratio of less than 1:1. The ratio is calculated as follows:

$$\frac{\text{Current assets} - \text{inventory} - \text{prepayments}}{\text{Current liabilities}}$$

The acid test ratio for Home Build plc for the 20X6, 20X5 and 20X4 years is calculated as follows:

20X6	*20X5*	*20X4*
$\frac{3\,450 - 1\,630}{820}$	$\frac{4\,130 - 2\,360}{1\,790}$	$\frac{2\,470 - 1\,170}{770}$
= 2.22:1	= 0.99:1	= 1.69:1

The acid test ratio also decreased in 20X5. It is just below the generally accepted level of 1:1 and therefore the absolute amount of the ratio is not of concern. The more important issue is the decrease in the ratio from 1.7 in 20X4.

Inventory turnover ratio

The inventory turnover ratio is used to measure the rate at which inventories move through and out of the entity and is an indication of the efficiency with which the business manages its inventory levels and its sales of inventory. The ratio is calculated as follows:

$$\frac{\text{Cost of goods sold}}{\text{Average inventory}}$$

The average inventory is the average of the opening and closing inventory.

The inventory turnover ratio for a business entity needs to be compared over a period of time in order for the ratio to convey meaningful information. It can also be useful to compare the inventory turnover ratio of a business entity with those of other entities in the same industry.

A high inventory turnover ratio can indicate efficient inventory management, but a ratio that is too high can also be indicative of inventory holdings which are too low. Low levels of inventory could lead to the business entity losing sales if particular inventory items are not available to meet customer demand. An inventory turnover ratio that is low could be indicative of the entity holding excessive levels of inventory as a result of poor sales, or purchases of inventory for which there is little customer demand. However, it could also result from increasing levels of inventory in anticipation of increased customer demand or in anticipation of interruptions in normal supplies of inventory. It is therefore important for the analyst to explore the underlying causes of an inventory turnover ratio that is out of line.

The inventory turnover ratio for Home Build plc for the 20X6, 20X5 and 20X4 years is calculated as follows:

20X6	*20X5*	*20X4*
$\frac{7\,280}{(1\,630 + 2\,360)/2}$	$\frac{5\,580}{(2\,360 + 1\,170)/2}$	$\frac{5\,367}{(1\,170 + 735)/2}$
= 3.65	= 3.16	= 5.63

The inventory turnover ratio indicates that the average inventory holding 'turned over' – that is, moved through and out of the entity – 5.6 times in 20X4 and only 3.2 times in 20X5. This highlights that slow-moving inventory was part of the problem in 20X5.

Inventory-holding period

The inventory-holding period measures the number of days it will take to sell the *average* inventory in a given year. Looked at differently, it measures the average age of the inventory. The inventory-holding period is calculated as follows:

$$\frac{365}{\text{Inventory turnover ratio}}$$

The inventory-holding period for Home Build plc for the 20X6, 20X5 and 20X4 years is calculated as follows:

20X6	*20X5*	*20X4*
$\frac{365}{3.65}$	$\frac{365}{3.16}$	$\frac{365}{5.63}$
= 100 days	= 116 days	= 65 days

The inventory-holding period provides much the same information as the inventory turnover ratio, but expressed in terms of numbers of days. Here we can see that inventory was held, on average, for 65 days before being sold in 20X4 and for 116 days in 20X5.

A related measure is the number of days it will take to sell the closing inventory. This ratio is calculated as follows:

$$\frac{365}{\text{Cost of goods sold/closing inventory}} = 365 \times \frac{\text{Closing inventory}}{\text{Cost of goods sold}}$$

The number of days it will take for Home Build plc to sell its closing inventory for the 20X6, 20X5 and 20X4 years is calculated as follows:

20X6	*20X5*	*20X4*
$\frac{365 \times 1\,630}{7\,280}$	$\frac{365 \times 2\,360}{5\,580}$	$\frac{365 \times 1\,170}{5\,367}$
= 82 days	= 154 days	= 80 days

This ratio focuses on the number of days to sell the closing inventory. The results mirror those of the previous ratio.

Accounts receivable turnover ratio

The accounts receivable turnover ratio is used to indicate how many times the average accounts receivable is generated or collected during the year. The ratio is calculated as follows:

$$\frac{\text{Net sales on credit}}{\text{Average accounts receivable}}$$

A high accounts receivable turnover ratio indicates that the collection of accounts receivable is being handled efficiently. On the other hand, it may be indicative of a credit policy which is too restrictive and which could be costing the business entity lost sales opportunities.

Most entities do not provide a breakdown between cash and credit sales on the statement of profit or loss. It is therefore necessary to use the total sales amount and, depending on the estimated level of credit sales, appreciate that the ratio will be overstated.

The accounts receivable turnover ratio for Home Build plc for the 20X6, 20X5 and 20X4 years is calculated as follows:

20X6	*20X5*	*20X4*
$\frac{10\ 920}{(1\ 150 + 1\ 770)/2}$	$\frac{8\ 730}{(1\ 770 + 850)/2}$	$\frac{8\ 050}{(850 + 760)/2}$
= 7.48	= 6.66	= 10.00

The accounts receivable turnover ratio shows that efficiency of collection of accounts receivable deteriorated in 20X5.

Collection period for accounts receivable

The collection period for accounts receivable is used to measure the number of days it takes, on average, to collect the accounts receivable. It is therefore a measure of the efficiency of the business enterprise in assessing credit risk when granting credit and in collecting its accounts receivable. The ratio is calculated as follows:

$$\frac{365}{\text{Accounts receivable turnover ratio}}$$

The collection period calculated should be compared with the terms of the credit policy of the business entity. If the collection period is higher than the policy allows, there may be problems with the collection process or there may be potential bad debts, which may prove to be irrecoverable. On the other hand, a low collection period may indicate a credit policy which is too restrictive and which is costing the business entity lost sales opportunities.

The collection period for accounts receivable for Home Build plc for the 20X6, 20X5 and 20X4 years is calculated as follows:

20X6	*20X5*	*20X4*
$\frac{365}{7.48}$	$\frac{365}{6.66}$	$\frac{365}{10.00}$
= 49 days	= 55 days	= 37 days

 The collection period for accounts receivable provides much the same information as the accounts receivable turnover ratio, but it is expressed in terms of numbers of days. Here we can see that it took the entity, on average, 37 days to collect outstanding receivables in 20X4 and 55 days in 20X5.

Valuable information regarding the accounts receivable of the business entity can also be gained from an age analysis of the accounts receivable, in which outstanding amounts are aged and shown as current, 30 days, 60 days, 90 days, and 120 days and over. Such age analyses are extensively used by credit controllers.

Accounts payable turnover ratio

The accounts payable turnover ratio is used to indicate how many times the average accounts payable is generated and paid during the year. Often, the amount for credit purchases (or total purchases) is not available from the financial statements, in which case the cost of sales can be used in its place.

Pause and reflect...

Can you think of a way to estimate an amount for purchases?

Response

We can take the concept of:

- 'opening inventory + purchases − closing inventory = cost of sales' and re-arrange it as
- 'purchases = cost of sales + closing inventory − opening inventory'.

We can then use this to estimate an amount for purchases.

The ratio is calculated as follows:

$$\frac{\text{Net purchases on credit}}{\text{Average accounts payable}}$$

The accounts payable turnover ratio for Home Build plc for the 20X6, 20X5 and 20X4 years is calculated as follows:

20X6	*20X5*	*20X4*
$\frac{7\,280 + 1\,630 - 2\,360}{(550 + 1\,460)/2}$	$\frac{5\,580 + 2\,360 - 1\,170}{(1\,460 + 720)/2}$	$\frac{5\,367 + 1\,170 - 735}{(720 + 612)/2}$
= 6.52	= 6.21	= 8.71

The accounts payable turnover ratio has decreased from 8.7 in 20X4 to 6.2 in 20X5, emphasising the difficulties experienced in 20X5.

Payment period for accounts payable

The payment period for accounts payable is used to measure the number of days it takes, on average, to pay the accounts payable. It is calculated as follows:

$$\frac{365}{\text{Accounts payable turnover ratio}}$$

It may seem beneficial if this ratio is high, indicating that the business entity is not paying out its cash resources too hastily. However, this must be balanced against the cost of losing early settlement discounts or even of having suppliers withdraw credit facilities to the business entity if normal settlement terms are not complied with.

The period it takes for Home Build plc to pay its accounts payable for the 20X6, 20X5 and 20X4 years is calculated as follows:

20X6	*20X5*	*20X4*
$\frac{365}{6.52}$	$\frac{365}{6.21}$	$\frac{365}{8.71}$
= 56 days	= 59 days	= 42 days

The payment period for accounts payable provides much the same information as the accounts payable turnover ratio, but is expressed in terms of numbers of days. Here we can see that it took the entity, on average, 42 days to pay suppliers in 20X4, and 59 days in 20X5.

19.4.2 Capital structure and long-term solvency

When assessing the capital structure and prospects for the long-term solvency of a business entity, we need to consider the level of debt in relation to the equity invested by the owners of the business entity, and also the ability of the business entity to service its debt. If the rate of return on the assets of the business is greater than the cost of debt, it is an advantage for the business entity to be funded by as much debt as possible in order to maximise returns to investors. This must, however, be balanced with the inherent risk of being funded by debt rather than by equity. If a business entity is unable to service its debt or to repay amounts when due, it runs a real risk of being placed into liquidation.

A greater proportion of debt funding than equity funding can also be regarded by potential suppliers and lenders as a lack of commitment on the part of the owners of the business entity. It must be remembered that the equity funding provided by the owners of a business entity provides a margin of safety for the suppliers of, and lenders to, the business entity.

The terms 'gearing' and 'leverage' refer to the use of debt in the capital structure of the business entity.

Debt and equity ratios

These ratios measure the relative contributions of equity and debt to the total funding of the entity and are measured in the following ways:

$$\text{Debt ratio} = \frac{\text{Total liabilities}}{\text{Total assets}}$$

$$\text{Equity rate} = \frac{\text{Total equity}}{\text{Total assets}}$$

$$\text{Debt equity ratio} = \frac{\text{Total debt}}{\text{Total equity}}$$

The sum of the first two ratios must equal 1.

The debt ratio measures the extent of debt financing. If this is too high, the business entity is at risk of not being able to meet its commitments. If it is too low, the business entity may be losing opportunities to increase the return to the owners (through gearing or leverage) by taking advantage of a cost of debt that is less than the rate of return earned on the assets of the business entity.

As with other ratios, there are a number of alternative definitions. Considering the debt ratio, the 'debt' in the numerator may be replaced by interest-bearing debt only or net debt (which reduces debt by any positive cash balances). Similar adjustments can then be made to the denominator in place of total assets.

The debt ratio for Home Build plc for the 20X6, 20X5 and 20X4 years is calculated as follows:

20X6	*20X5*	*20X4*
$\frac{2\,550 + 820}{6\,120 + 3\,450}$	$\frac{1\,750 + 1\,790}{3\,400 + 4\,130}$	$\frac{1\,750 + 770}{4\,000 + 2\,470}$
= 0.35	= 0.47	= 0.39

The equity ratio for Home Build plc for the 20X6, 20X5 and 20X4 years is calculated as follows:

20X6	*20X5*	*20X4*
$\frac{6\ 200}{6\ 120 + 3\ 450}$	$\frac{3\ 990}{3\ 400 + 4\ 130}$	$\frac{3\ 950}{4\ 000 + 2\ 470}$
= 0.65	= 0.53	= 0.61

The debt equity ratio for Home Build plc for the 20X6, 20X5 and 20X4 years is calculated as follows:

20X6	*20X5*	*20X4*
$\frac{2\ 550 + 820}{6\ 200}$	$\frac{1\ 750 + 1\ 790}{3\ 990}$	$\frac{1\ 750 + 770}{3\ 950}$
= 0.54	= 0.89	= 0.64

The debt and equity ratios show that the company was more highly geared in 20X5 compared to 20X4 and 20X6. Referring back to the common-size statement of financial position, you will notice that short-term debt comprised a more significant amount of the debt at the end of 20X5 compared to either 20X4 or 20X6.

Interest cover ratio

The interest cover ratio measures the ability of the business entity to meet its interest charges. It is calculated as follows:

$$\frac{\text{Profit before tax and interest expense}}{\text{Interest expense}}$$

The higher the interest cover ratio, the better it is for investors in the business entity. This is because the business entity is at less risk of being unable to make its interest payments when due.

The interest cover ratio for Home Build plc for the 20X6, 20X5 and 20X4 years is calculated as follows:

20X6	*20X5*	*20X4*
$\frac{665 + 204}{204}$	$\frac{195 + 170}{170}$	$\frac{474 + 140}{140}$
= 4.26	= 2.15	= 4.39

The lower interest cover ratio in 20X5 relates to the difficulties the company experienced in that year.

19.4.3 Operating efficiency and profitability

We are now going to consider several ratios which measure operating efficiency and profitability. These ratios can be based on either sales or investment.

Profit margin ratios

MARK-UP PERCENTAGE

The mark-up percentage is used to compare the gross profit margin earned on goods sold with the mark-up used by the business entity. It is calculated as follows:

$$\frac{\text{Gross profit}}{\text{Cost of goods sold}} \times \frac{100}{1}$$

The mark-up percentage for Home Build plc for the 20X6, 20X5 and 20X4 years is calculated as follows:

20X6	*20X5*	*20X4*
$\frac{3\,640 \times 100}{7\,280}$	$\frac{3\,150 \times 100}{5\,580}$	$\frac{2\,683 \times 100}{5\,367}$
= 50.00%	= 56.45%	= 50.00%

GROSS PROFIT PERCENTAGE

The gross profit percentage measures the ability of the business entity to earn a gross profit from sales. It also represents how much of each sales pound, euro or rand is left over after paying for the cost of the goods sold. The gross profit percentage is an indication of the efficiency of the management of the business entity in controlling the costs of its inventory (which may be either purchased or manufactured inventory) and also in recovering increased costs through its sales. The gross profit percentage is calculated as follows:

$$\frac{\text{Gross profit}}{\text{Sales}} \times \frac{100}{1}$$

The gross profit percentage for Home Build plc for the 20X6, 20X5 and 20X4 years is calculated as follows:

20X6	*20X5*	*20X4*
$\frac{3\,640 \times 100}{10\,920}$	$\frac{3\,150 \times 100}{8\,730}$	$\frac{2\,683 \times 100}{8\,050}$
= 33.33%	= 36.08%	= 33.33%

PROFIT PERCENTAGE

The profit percentage measures the ability of the business entity to earn a profit from sales. It represents how much of each sales pound, euro or rand is left over after accounting for all expenses incurred in earning the profit during the year, and after accounting for the taxes due on the profit for the year. The ratio is calculated as follows:

$$\frac{\text{Profit for the period}}{\text{Sales}} \times \frac{100}{1}$$

The profit percentage for Home Build plc for the 20X6, 20X5 and 20X4 years is calculated as follows:

20X6	*20X5*	*20X4*
$\frac{420 \times 100}{10\ 920}$	$\frac{120 \times 100}{8\ 730}$	$\frac{300 \times 100}{8\ 050}$
= 3.85%	= 1.37%	= 3.73%

In ratio analysis, we are looking for trends. Although the mark-up percentage and the gross profit percentage both showed a small increase in 20X5, the trend is more or less constant. The profit percentage, however, decreased by more than half in the problematic 20X5 year.

Total asset turnover ratio

The relationship of sales to total assets is a measure of asset utilisation and is a means of determining how effectively the assets are utilised in terms of sales generated. The ratio is calculated as follows:

$$\frac{\text{Sales}}{\text{Average total assets}}$$

Generally, a high asset turnover ratio is an indication of effective asset utilisation. A low ratio may be indicative of an excessive investment in assets or of poor sales, but there may be an acceptable reason for the low ratio, for example a major new investment in assets just before the end of the year. In such a situation, it is preferable to base the ratio on the weighted average of the total assets if this information is available to the user preparing the analysis.

The total asset turnover ratio for Home Build plc for the 20X6, 20X5 and 20X4 years is calculated as follows:

20X6	*20X5*	*20X4*
$\frac{10\ 920}{(9\ 570 + 7\ 530)/2}$	$\frac{8\ 730}{(7\ 530 + 6\ 470)/2}$	$\frac{8\ 050}{(6\ 470 + 5\ 850)/2}$
= 1.28	= 1.25	= 1.31

Focusing on the trend of the total asset turnover ratio, this ratio has remained more or less constant over the three years. The small changes – from 1.31 in 20X4 to 1.25 in 20X5 and to 1.28 in 20X6 – are not significant. The results of this ratio also confirm that the problems in 20X5 were related to working capital and operating expenses.

Return on total assets ratio

The return on total assets ratio (often referred to as the return on investment or ROI ratio), is used to assess the relationship between profit after tax and the resources invested in the business entity to generate that profit. The profit is adjusted to a 'before interest amount' in order to assess the return, irrespective of the source of finance. The calculated return can then be compared by the user with the returns available on alternate investments. The ratio is calculated as follows:

$$\frac{\text{Profit after tax} + \text{interest expense } (1 - \text{tax rate})}{\text{Average total assets}} \times \frac{100}{1}$$

The return on total assets ratio measures the efficiency with which the assets of the business entity are managed in order to generate a return on those assets.

The return on total assets ratio for Home Build plc for the 20X6, 20X5 and 20X4 years is calculated as follows:

20X6	*20X5*	*20X4*
$\frac{420 + (204 \times 0.72) \times 100}{8\,550}$	$\frac{120 + (170 \times 0.72) \times 100}{7\,000}$	$\frac{300 + (140 \times 0.72) \times 100}{6\,160}$
= 6.63%	3.46%	= 6.51%

The return on total assets has decreased in 20X5 because of the lower profit in that year.

Return on ordinary shareholders' equity ratio

The return on ordinary shareholders' equity ratio, or ROE ratio, measures the percentage of profit after tax and preference dividends which are available to ordinary shareholders; in other words, the return to ordinary shareholders. The profit after tax (which, by implication, is after interest) is used, as the return to ordinary shareholders can only be assessed after taking into account interest on debt. The ratio is calculated as follows:

$$\frac{\text{Profit after tax} - \text{preference dividend}}{\text{Average ordinary shareholders' equity}} \times \frac{100}{1}$$

The return on ordinary shareholders' equity for Home Build plc for the 20X6, 20X5 and 20X4 years is calculated as follows:

20X6	*20X5*	*20X4*
$\frac{(420 - 30) \times 100}{(5\ 700 + 3\ 490)/2}$	$\frac{(120 - 30) \times 100}{(3\ 490 + 3\ 450)/2}$	$\frac{(300 - 30) \times 100}{(3\ 450 + 3\ 310)/2}$
= 8.49%	= 2.59%	= 7.99%

 The return on equity has decreased in 20X5 because of the lower profit in that year.

Earnings per share

The earnings per share (commonly known as EPS) ratio measures the amount of profit after tax and preference dividends attributable to each ordinary share issued by a company. It is calculated as follows:

$$\frac{\text{Profit after tax} - \text{preference dividend}}{\text{Number of ordinary shares issued}}$$

The earnings per share ratio enables a user to compare the earnings of different-sized companies. A comparison of the profit after tax and preference dividends of different companies will be less meaningful than a comparison of the earnings per share, as the number of shares issued by each company may differ substantially. The earnings per share ratios provide a common denominator by which the investment returns on different investments can be measured.

The earnings per share for Home Build plc for the 20X6, 20X5 and 20X4 years are calculated as follows:

20X6	*20X5*	*20X4*
$\frac{420 - 30}{1\ 500}$	$\frac{120 - 30}{1\ 000}$	$\frac{300 - 30}{1\ 000}$
= 26c	= 9c	= 27c

 The earnings per share also decreased in 20X5 because of the lower profit in that year.

Dividends per share

The dividends per share (commonly known as DPS) ratio measures the amount of dividends attributable to each ordinary share issued by a company. It is calculated as follows:

$$\frac{\text{Ordinary dividend}}{\text{Number of ordinary shares issued}}$$

The dividends per share for Home Build plc for the 20X6, 20X5 and 20X4 years are calculated as follows:

20X6	*20X5*	*20X4*
$\frac{180}{1\ 500}$	$\frac{50}{1\ 000}$	$\frac{130}{1\ 000}$
= 12c	= 5c	= 13c

The reduced dividends per share in 20X5 are clearly attributable to the shortage of cash in that year, but this recovers to previous levels in the following year.

19.4.4 Market measures

None of the operating efficiency or profitability ratios which we have considered is based on the amount which an investor pays for shares in a company. When making investment decisions, it is important to measure performance against the cost or the value of the investment. In the case of shares that are listed on a stock exchange, the investor needs to measure performance against the market value of the shares. We shall now look at various ratios which relate profitability to the market price of listed shares. As the market price fluctuates, so does the value of these ratios, which are often reported in the financial press alongside share prices.

Earnings yield

The earnings yield measures the earnings of the company in relation to its market value. It is calculated as follows:

$$\frac{\text{Earnings per share}}{\text{Current market price per share}} \times \frac{100}{1}$$

The earnings yield for Home Build plc, calculated using the market price at the end of the 20X6, 20X5 and 20X4 years, is as follows:

20X6	*20X5*	*20X4*
$\frac{26c \times 100}{550c}$	$\frac{9c \times 100}{390c}$	$\frac{27c \times 100}{450c}$
= 4.73%	= 2.31%	= 6.00%

The earnings yield decreases in 20X5 in line with the decrease in profits.

Price earnings ratio

The price earnings or P/E ratio compares the market price of the share with the earnings per share, and is the reciprocal of the earnings yield. It is calculated as follows:

$$\frac{\text{Current market price per share}}{\text{Earnings per share}}$$

The P/E ratio can be interpreted as being an indication of the number of years of earnings investors are buying. It provides a common point of reference for comparing one share with another, with the section in which that share is listed, and with the stock market as a whole. In addition, the P/E ratio serves as a yardstick, since it enables direct comparisons to be made between companies with high share prices and those with low share prices, and between shares with high earnings and low earnings.

By comparing the P/E ratios of different companies, investors are able to compare the performance of companies of different sizes, with substantially different numbers of shares issued. A high P/E ratio indicates that investors are willing to pay a high multiple of expected earnings because of underlying profitability and growth potential, whereas a low ratio is an indication of less potential for profitability and growth.

It is, however, important to investigate the underlying reasons for any change in the P/E ratio. An increase in the P/E ratio could be caused by the market price rising more rapidly than earnings or the earnings falling in relation to the market price.

The P/E ratio is more useful as an indication of performance than the dividend yield, as it considers the total earnings of the company rather than just the amount which the directors have decided to distribute as dividends.

The P/E ratio for Home Build plc, calculated using the market price at the end of the 20X6, 20X5 and 20X4 years is as follows:

20X6	*20X5*	*20X4*
$\frac{550c}{26c}$	$\frac{390c}{9c}$	$\frac{450c}{27c}$
= 21.15	= 43.33	= 16.67

The high P/E ratio in 20X5 may appear out of place considering the poor performance in that year. However, it is caused by the large decrease in earnings during that year. This again emphasises the importance of examining trends, and the P/E ratio of 21.15 in 20X6 is more in line with that of 16.67 in 20X4.

Dividend yield

The dividend yield measures the return in cash, by way of dividends, that investors can expect to receive on their investment. It is calculated as follows:

$$\frac{\text{Dividends per share}}{\text{Current market price per share at the end of the year}} \times \frac{100}{1}$$

While it does indicate to investors the return on their shares (which they receive in cash), it ignores earnings which have been retained in the company. This information could have a major impact on future earnings if returns were wisely reinvested to fund future expansion and replacement of assets.

The dividend yield for Home Build plc, calculated using the market price at the end of 20X6, 20X5 and 20X4 years is calculated as follows:

20X6	20X5	20X4
$\frac{12c \times 100}{550c}$	$\frac{5c \times 100}{390c}$	$\frac{13c \times 100}{450c}$
= 2.18%	= 1.28%	= 2.89%

The dividend yield decreased in 20X5 but shows signs of recovery towards previous levels in the following year.

Summary of ratios for Home Build plc

	20X6	*20X5*	*20X4*
Short-term liquidity			
Current ratio	4.21	2.31	3.21
Acid test (quick ratio)	2.22	0.99	1.69
Inventory turnover	3.65	3.16	5.63
Inventory-holding period (days)	100	116	65
Days to sell closing inventory	82	154	80
Accounts receivable turnover	7.48	6.66	10.00
Collection period for accounts receivable (days)	49	55	37
Accounts payable turnover	6.52	6.21	8.71
Payment period for accounts payable (days)	56	59	42

	20X6	*20X5*	*20X4*
Capital structure and long-term solvency			
Debt ratio	0.35	0.47	0.39
Equity ratio	0.65	0.53	0.61
Debt equity ratio	0.54	0.89	0.64
Interest cover	4.26	2.15	4.39

	20X6	*20X5*	*20X4*
Operating efficiency and profitability			
Mark-up %	50.00%	56.45%	50.00%
Gross profit %	33.33%	36.08%	33.33%
Net profit %	3.85%	1.37%	3.73%
Total asset turnover	1.28	1.25	1.31
Return on total assets	6.63%	3.46%	6.51%
Return on ordinary shareholders' equity	8.49%	2.59%	7.99%
Earnings per share	26c	9c	27c
Dividends per share	12c	5c	13c

	20X6	*20X5*	*20X4*
Market measures			
Earnings yield	4.73%	2.31%	6.00%
P/E ratio	21.15	43.33	16.67
Dividend yield	2.18%	1.28%	2.89%

19.5 Headline earnings

The concept of headline earnings originates from the Institute of Investment Management Research (IIMR), a forerunner of the UK Society of Investment Professionals (UKSIP). It is used by the *Financial Times* for the P/E ratios in its London Share Service.

A detailed explanation of headline earnings is beyond the scope of this book. In short, the concept of headline earnings is designed to provide a profit number (referred to as ***headline earnings***) that investors can use to assess a company's ongoing profitability.

Earning figures are complex and are affected by many factors such as a loss on sale of property, plant and equipment. This will impact on the profit of the company but as it is not a recurring event, the profit figure may not really reflect its ongoing profitability.

Headline earnings therefore exclude items that do not relate to the trading and operating activities of an entity, such as the gain or loss on disposal of non-current assets and the impairment of non-current assets and goodwill.

You will see references to headline earnings in the financial reports of listed companies.

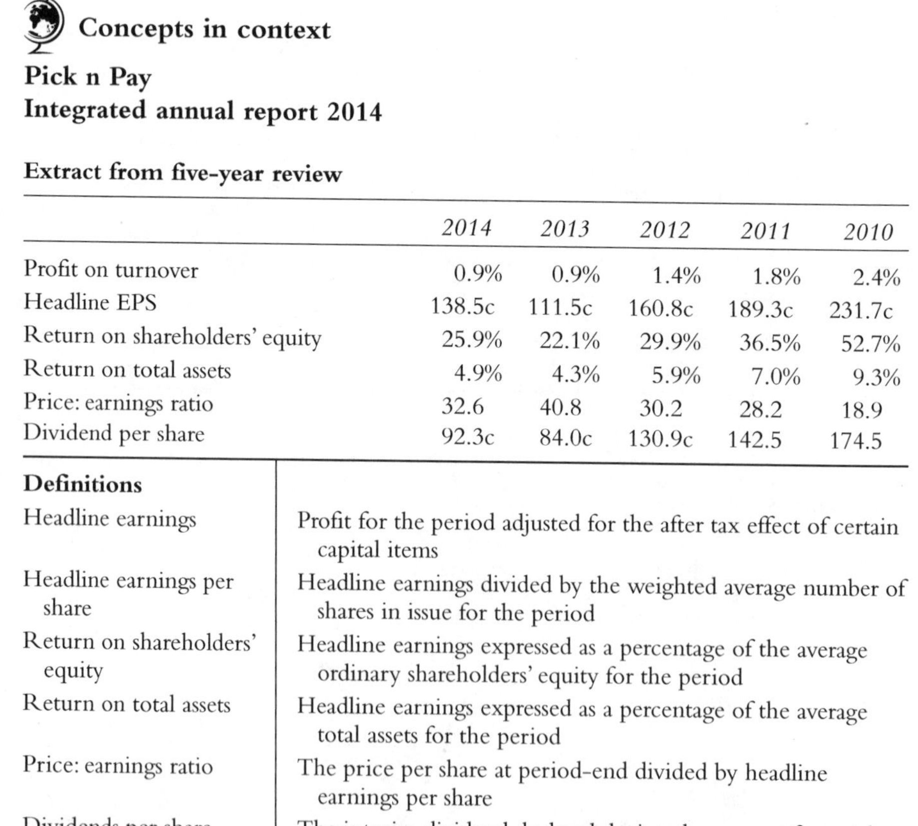

Concepts in context

Pick n Pay
Integrated annual report 2014

Extract from five-year review

	2014	*2013*	*2012*	*2011*	*2010*
Profit on turnover	0.9%	0.9%	1.4%	1.8%	2.4%
Headline EPS	138.5c	111.5c	160.8c	189.3c	231.7c
Return on shareholders' equity	25.9%	22.1%	29.9%	36.5%	52.7%
Return on total assets	4.9%	4.3%	5.9%	7.0%	9.3%
Price: earnings ratio	32.6	40.8	30.2	28.2	18.9
Dividend per share	92.3c	84.0c	130.9c	142.5	174.5

Definitions	
Headline earnings	Profit for the period adjusted for the after tax effect of certain capital items
Headline earnings per share	Headline earnings divided by the weighted average number of shares in issue for the period
Return on shareholders' equity	Headline earnings expressed as a percentage of the average ordinary shareholders' equity for the period
Return on total assets	Headline earnings expressed as a percentage of the average total assets for the period
Price: earnings ratio	The price per share at period-end divided by headline earnings per share
Dividends per share	The interim dividend declared during the current financial period and the final dividend declared after period-end, in respect of the current period

What concepts in context do you see here?

Almost all listed companies provide multi-year reviews including selected ratios for analysis purposes. Having read this chapter, you should recognise all of the information reported here by Pick n Pay.

Note the low profit percentage ratio (referred to by Pick n Pay as profit on turnover). This is typical in the supermarket industry.

Pick n Pay is the second largest supermarket chain store in South Africa, established in 1967. It can also be found in other regions of southern Africa.

Source: www.picknpayinvestor.co.za/financials/annual_reports/2014/2_five_year_review.php (Accessed 27 September 2014).

Revision example

Investors Bank is evaluating an application for a short-term loan from Bread Ahead plc, a company with artisan bakeries in small towns and villages across the country. The company supplies bread to hotels and restaurants, as well as selling to the public. Selected financial statement items for Bread Ahead plc and the corresponding industry average are as follows:

	Bread Ahead plc *31/12/X5*	*Industry average* *31/12/X5*
	C000s	*C000s*
Bank	4 000	12 000
Short-term investments	5 000	8 000
Accounts receivable	58 000	72 000
Expenses paid in advance	9 000	7 000
Closing inventory	72 000	96 000
Opening inventory	64 000	92 000
Accounts payable	36 000	50 000
Expenses payable	22 000	30 000
Sales (all credit)	420 000	660 000
Cost of sales	320 000	500 000

You are required to:

a) Calculate the following ratios for both Bread Ahead plc and for the industry average:

   i) Current ratio
   ii) Quick ratio
   iii) Average number of days to collect accounts receivable
   iv) Inventory-holding period
   v) Average number of days taken to pay accounts payable.

b) Consider the information provided and your calculations in part (a), and prepare a report to assist Investors Bank in making a decision.

c) State what limitations you see in your analysis and what additional information might be helpful to the loan officer in making her decision.

Solution: Revision example

a) Calculation of ratios

		Calculation	Ratio
i)	***Current ratio*** Bread Ahead plc	$\frac{4\,000 + 5\,000 + 58\,000 + 9\,000 + 72\,000}{36\,000 + 22\,000}$	2.56
	Industry average	$\frac{12\,000 + 8\,000 + 72\,000 + 7\,000 + 96\,000}{50\,000 + 30\,000}$	2.44
ii)	***Quick ratio*** Bread Ahead plc	$\frac{4\,000 + 5\,000 + 58\,000}{36\,000 + 22\,000}$	1.16
	Industry average	$\frac{12\,000 + 8\,000 + 72\,000}{50\,000 + 30\,000}$	1.15
iii)	***Days outstanding in accounts receivable*** Bread Ahead plc	$\frac{58\,000 \times 365}{420\,000}$	50 days
	Industry average	$\frac{72\,000 \times 365}{660\,000}$	40 days
iv)	***Inventory-holding period*** Bread Ahead plc	$\frac{(72\,000 + 64\,000)/2 \times 365}{320\,000}$	78 days
	Industry average	$\frac{(96\,000 + 92\,000)/2 \times 365}{500\,000}$	69 days
v)	***Days outstanding in accounts payable*** Bread Ahead plc	$\frac{36\,000 \times 365}{320\,000}$	41 days
	Industry average	$\frac{50\,000 \times 365}{500\,000}$	37 days

b) Report on the short-term loan application of Bread Ahead plc

Based on the information provided, Bread Ahead plc has been analysed on the following ratios in relation to the industry average:

i) Current ratio
ii) Quick ratio
iii) Average number of days to collect accounts receivable
iv) Inventory-holding period
v) Average number of days taken to pay accounts payable

i) Current ratio

The current ratio measures the company's ability to meet existing current liabilities. Bread Ahead plc has a ratio of 2.55 in comparison to the industry average of 2.44. This indicates that Bread Ahead plc is more liquid than the industry average.

ii) Quick ratio

The quick ratio measures the company's ability to meet existing current liabilities by excluding inventory from the current ratio in its calculation, as this is the least liquid current asset. Bread Ahead plc has a ratio of 1.16 in comparison to the industry average of 1.15.

The industry average for this ratio is similar to that of Bread Ahead plc, which indicates that Bread Ahead plc is not as liquid once inventory is excluded.

iii) Average number of days to collect accounts receivable

This ratio measures the number of days it takes to collect the accounts receivable.

Bread Ahead Ltd takes 50 days to collect their accounts receivable in comparison to the industry average of 40 days, suggesting a higher risk to the collectability of accounts receivable. It would be wise to question whether the provision for doubtful debts is sufficient in this instance.

iv) Inventory-holding period

This ratio measures the number of days it takes to sell the average inventory in a given year. Bread Ahead plc takes 78 days to sell their inventory in comparison to the industry average of 69 days.

Bread Ahead plc is taking longer to sell their inventory. This indicates that they are holding more inventory than the industry average. Bread Ahead plc's inventory-holding policy is more risky than the industry average since there is a greater chance of inventory becoming obsolete and unsaleable.

v) Average number of days taken to pay accounts payable

This ratio measures the number of days it takes to pay the accounts payable. Bread Ahead plc takes 41 days to pay their accounts payable in comparison to the industry average of 37 days.

Bread Ahead plc is taking longer to pay their accounts payable. This indicates that they are not as liquid as the industry average since they have to extend their repayments to 41 days.

General

Even though Bread Ahead plc has a better current ratio than the industry average, the other ratios indicate that the company is not as liquid as the rest of the companies in the industry.

The current assets do not appear to be as liquid as the industry average. There is a greater risk that the accounts receivable will not be collected and that inventory is not saleable. As a result, Bread Ahead plc does not have the cash available to pay suppliers on time.

c) Limitations

Bread Ahead plc's results need to be compared to those of previous periods. Ratios are calculated from historic cost, and therefore are not a good predictor of future performance.

The industry accounting policies may not be the same as those applied by Bread Ahead plc (e.g. inventory costing — FIFO vs weighted average).

Additional information

- detailed statement of profit or loss, statement of financial position and statement of cash flows;
- profitability ratios, for example GP %, return on total assets, return on equity, earnings per share;
- gearing ratios (long-term solvency), for example debt and equity ratios, interest cover;
- knowledge of the industry in which Bread Ahead operates;
- knowledge of Bread Ahead plc's operations, for example terms granted to customers, terms negotiated with suppliers, inventory-holding policies – in order to understand why the ratios differ from those of the industry;
- changes in the business over the past period in comparison to prior periods;
- plans for the future;
- length of time in operation.

Bibliography

Bradshaw, J and Brooks, M. 1996. *Business Accounting & Finance for Managers and Business Students*. Cape Town, South Africa: Juta.

Buffet, M and Clark, D. 2008. *Warren Buffet and the Interpretation of Financial Statements: The Search for the Company with Durable Competitive Advantage*. London: Simon & Schuster.

Fraser, LM. 1995. *Understanding Financial Statements*. Englewood Cliffs, NJ: Prentice Hall.

Maynard, J. 2013. *Financial Accounting, Reporting & Analysis*. Oxford, UK: Oxford University Press.

20 Non-business entities

Business focus

Johannesburg, South Africa, attracted the highest levels of society from around the world in the early twentieth century. The Country Club became the epicentre of this vibrant social scene. One of the best-known mining engineers of his time, John Hays Hammond, even remarked that he and his wife experienced a better social life in Johannesburg than they had in London, Paris or New York.

Surprisingly, the original motivation to form The Country Club was not a social one but a shrewd business move by Auckland Park Real Estate Limited. The company's manager, Herbert Moss, called together five of Johannesburg's most prominent citizens and proposed that they be part of the club's very first committee.

The Country Club Johannesburg was officially formed on 17 November 1906 and the Auckland Park Clubhouse opened on 22 December that same year. William Kidger Tucker (the mayor of Johannesburg at the time) was not exaggerating when he said that the official opening had 'great social significance for Johannesburg, the Transvaal colony and South Africa'. A reporter for the *Rand Daily Mail* waxed lyrical about the club's grounds, saying, 'To state that the grounds are picturesque very inadequately describes the real beauty of their situation'.

In this chapter

The primary focus of this text has been on the accounting and reporting requirements of business entities whose main objective is to earn profits. However, organisations exist whose primary objective is to provide services to their members and/or to society in general. Examples of such organisations are sports and social clubs, welfare organisations and religious organisations. These are known as non-profit or non-business entities and are the subject of this chapter.

Dashboard

- Look at the *Learning outcomes* so that you know what you should be able to do after studying this chapter.
- Read the *Business focus* to place this chapter's contents in a real-world context.
- Preview *In this chapter* to focus your mind on the contents of the chapter.
- Read the *text* in detail.

- Apply your mind to the *Pause and reflect* scenarios.
  - Take note of the accounting for funds in Section 20.2.2 as there are some specific accounting entries that are unique to non-business entities.
  - Pay attention to the subscriptions account in Section 20.3.1 and note that there will often be two adjustments to the account at the end of a period – for subscriptions *in arrear* and for subscriptions *in advance*.
  - Prepare solutions to the examples as you read through the chapter.
- Prepare a solution to the *Revision example* at the end of the chapter without reference to the suggested one. Compare your solution to the suggested solution provided.

Learning outcomes

After studying this chapter, you should be able to do the following:

1 Describe the characteristics of a non-business entity.
2 Recall the sources of finance available to a non-business entity.
3 Produce financial information for a non-business entity.

Non-business entities

20.1 Characteristics of a non-business entity

The primary objective of a non-business entity is to provide a service to its members, such as sports or social clubs, and to ensure that income earned is greater than expenditure incurred so that the entity can continue in existence.

The members of a non-business entity are not owners of the entity and therefore do not expect to receive any distribution, either on an annual basis or on termination of the entity's activities.

A non-business entity does not exist to make a profit. However, in order to provide the service to members for which it was established, it needs to generate sufficient income to cover expenditure incurred. Income earned in excess of expenditure is regarded as a ***surplus*** and not as a profit. Similarly, expenditure incurred in excess of income earned is described as a ***deficit*** and not a loss. Accordingly, the profit or loss account is referred to as an income and expenditure account, and the statement of profit or loss as an ***income and expenditure statement***.

The accounting records of a non-business entity are the same as those maintained by a business entity, except for specific requirements relating to the accounting for funds. Fund accounting is an important aspect of the reporting for a non-business entity, because it provides control over the resources of the entity entrusted to management. It will be described in the following section.

Management of a non-business entity is entrusted to persons appointed by the members. For smaller entities such as a suburban tennis or bowls club, management is normally the responsibility of a committee comprising members of the club who provide their services on a voluntary basis. Larger clubs, such as the country clubs which provide a range of sporting activities including golf, cricket, tennis and bowls and have facilities such as a restaurant, bar and a swimming pool, operate with full-time managers and staff who are paid employees of the entity.

Non-business entities are not constrained by the requirements of International Financial Reporting Standards (IFRS). We will therefore refer, in this chapter, to a balance sheet and, as seen above, to an income and expenditure statement and not to the terminology of the IASB.

20.2 Sources of finance for a non-business entity

To understand the accounting implications relating to the sources of finance for a non-business entity, it is necessary to examine the accounting equation in a non-business entity.

A non-business entity does not have capital contributed by owners in the same way as a business entity does. Instead, it has an ***accumulated fund*** represented by entrance fees paid by members, the surplus retained from the entity's activities and discretionary donations or legacies. In addition to the accumulated fund, a non-business entity may also have a number of ***special funds***, established from non-discretionary legacies or donations. The accounting for the accumulated fund and the special funds will be described in the paragraphs that follow. A non-business entity may also borrow funds from a financial institution. We can therefore restate the accounting equation for a non-business entity as shown in Diagram 20.1.

20.2.1 Funds

As mentioned above, a non-business entity can have two types of funds – accumulated funds and special funds.

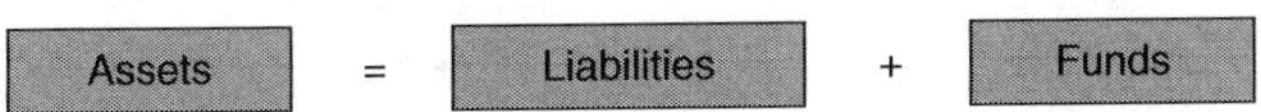

Diagram 20.1 Accounting equation for a non-business entity

Accumulated funds

The accumulated fund is equivalent to the capital of a business entity and comprises the entrance fees paid by members, the surplus retained from activities as well as discretionary donations. These aspects are discussed below.

Members of a non-business entity pay **entrance/joining fees** when joining a club or association. As this is a single amount paid when joining and is non-recurring, entrance/joining fees received are credited directly to the accumulated fund and do not comprise income earned during a period. This is similar in concept to the capital invested by owners of a business entity, which is credited to owner's equity.

The **surplus retained** in a non-business entity is similar in concept to the profits retained in a business entity. However, a non-business entity is exempt from the payment of tax and does not distribute any amounts to members. The cumulative excess of income over expenditure therefore represents the surplus retained in a non-business entity and it is used to maintain and expand the services and facilities offered to members.

Discretionary donations refer to legacies or donations received where there is *no stipulation* on the use of the funds. These amounts are not regular sources of income and therefore should also be credited directly to the accumulated fund rather than included as part of income for the period.

Special funds

Special funds are accounted for separately from the accumulated fund. They arise from **non-discretionary** legacies or donations to a club or institution. These legacies or donations *stipulate* the use of the capital amount and any income earned from the possible investment of this amount. The terms of the legacy or donation could stipulate the following:

- The capital amount is to be used to purchase or construct a specific asset.
- The capital sum is to remain intact and the income from the fund used either for:
  - a specific expense, for example coaching fees for the first team of a football club or a bursary to a student of an educational institution; or
  - for general expenses.

We can summarise the funds of a non-business entity as shown in Diagram 20.2.

Example: Funds

During 20X5, Simon Smart joined the Misty Mountain Country Club with the intention of socialising with potential customers. The Misty Mountain Country Club received the following legacies and donation during the 20X5 year:

1 C150 000 from the estate of P Fost on 2 January 20X5. The terms of the legacy stipulated that the capital sum should remain intact and be invested. The interest earned could be used to pay for coaching fees. On 2 January 20X5 the funds were invested in a fixed deposit at 6 per cent per annum. During the sports club's financial year ended 31 December 20X5, the club paid coaching fees of C35 000.

2 C100 000 from the estate of J Daniels on 4 April 20X5. The terms of the legacy stipulated that the amount should be used to build new tennis courts. The tennis courts were completed and paid for on 15 September 20X5 at a cost of C100 000.

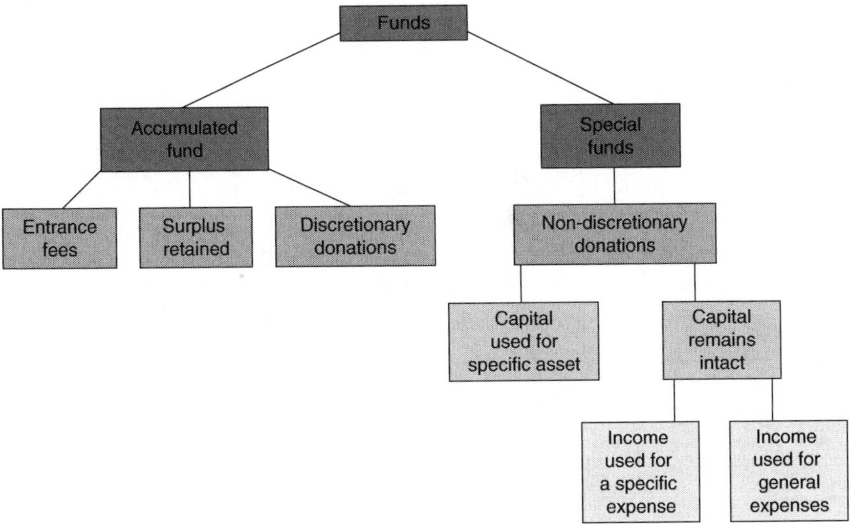

Diagram 20.2 Funds in a non-business entity

3 A C200 000 donation from D Simpson, a well-known philanthropist, on 1 January 20X5. The terms of the donation stipulated that the capital sum should remain intact and be invested. The interest earned is to be used to pay for general expenses to run the club. On 2 January 20X5 the funds were invested in a fixed deposit at 6 per cent per annum.

Additional information

- Subscriptions earned and received, C250 000
- Operating expenses incurred and paid, C258 000
- Accumulated fund balance at beginning of year, C14 000
- Bank balance at beginning of year, C14 000.

You are required to:

a) Record the above transactions in the ledger of the Misty Mountain Country Club.
b) Indicate how the legacies and the fund investments will be reported on the balance sheet of the Misty Mountain Country Club at 31 December 20X5.

 **Solution: funds**

a) Ledger accounts

Fost fund

Details	*C*	*Details*	*C*
Coaching fees	9 000	Bank	150 000
Balance c/d	150 000	Bank	9 000
	159 000		159 000
		Balance b/d	150 000

Fost investment

Details	*C*	*Details*	*C*
Bank	150 000		
		Balance c/d	150 000
	150 000		150 000
Balance b/d	150 000		

Daniels fund

Details	*C*	*Details*	*C*
		Bank	100 000
Balance c/d	100 000		
	100 000		100 000
		Balance b/d	100 000

Tennis courts

Details	*C*	*Details*	*C*
Bank	100 000		
		Balance c/d	100 000
	100 000		100 000
Balance b/d	100 000		

Simpson fund

Details	*C*	*Details*	*C*
		Bank	200 000
Balance c/d	200 000		
	200 000		200 000
		Balance b/d	200 000

Simpson investment

Details	*C*	*Details*	*C*
Bank	200 000		
		Balance c/d	200 000
	200 000		200 000
Balance b/d	200 000		

Bank

Details	*C*	*Details*	*C*
Balance b/d	14 000	Fost investment	150 000
Fost fund	150 000	Tennis courts	100 000
Daniels fund	100 000	Simpson investment	200 000
Simpson fund	200 000	Coaching fees	35 000
Fost fund	9 000	Operating expenses	200 000
Interest income	12 000	Balance c/d	50 000
Subscriptions	250 000		
	735 000		735 000
Balance b/d	50 000		

Interest income

Details	*C*	*Details*	*C*
Income and expenditure	12 000	Bank	12 000
	12 000		12 000

Income and expenditure

Details	*C*	*Details*	*C*
Operating expenses	200 000	Subscriptions	250 000
Coaching fees	26 000	Interest income (Simpson)	12 000
Accumulated fund	36 000		
	262 000		262 000

Coaching fees

Details	*C*	*Details*	*C*
Bank	35 000	Fost fund	9 000
		Income and expenditure	26 000
	35 000		35 000

Accumulated fund

Details	*C*	*Details*	*C*
		Balance b/d	14 000
		Income and expenditure	36 000
Balance b/d	50 000		
	50 000		50 000
		Balance b/d	50 000

The Fost fund is a non-discretionary legacy for which the capital must remain intact and the income can be used for coaching fees. The cash received is deposited into the bank account and the fund account is increased. The cash is then invested into an income-earning account. The income earned from the investment is added to the fund, and the specific expense up to the amount of the income earned is set off against it. This process is summarised in the following entries:

Fost fund	*Dr*	*Cr*
Bank (A)	150 000	
Fost fund (F*)		150 000
Receipt from estate of P Fost		
Fost investment (A)	150 000	
Bank (A)		150 000
Investment of funds		
Coaching fees (E)	35 000	
Bank (A)		35 000
Payment of coaching fees		
Bank (A)	9 000	
Fost fund (F)		9 000
Interest earned (C150 000 × 0.06)		
Fost fund (F)	9 000	
Coaching fees (E)		9 000
Set off of interest against coaching fees		

* F = Funds (as explained in Section 20.2, a non-business entity does not have equity contributed by owners).

The Daniels fund is a non-discretionary legacy used to purchase a specific asset. The cash received is deposited into the bank account and the fund account is increased. The available cash is then used to construct the tennis courts. The entries are as follows:

Daniels fund	*Dr*	*Cr*
Bank (A)	100 000	
Daniels fund (F)		100 000
Receipt from estate of J Daniels		
Tennis courts (A)	100 000	
Bank (A)		100 000
Payment for tennis courts		

The Simpson fund is a non-discretionary donation for which the capital must remain intact and the income can be used for the general expenses of the club. Again, the cash received is deposited into the bank account, the fund account is increased and the cash is invested into an income-earning account. The income earned from the funds invested is treated as income in the income and expenditure statement and is not added to the Simpson fund. The entries are summarised as follows:

Simpson fund	*Dr*	*Cr*
Bank (A) Simpson fund (F) *Receipt of donation from D Simpson*	200 000	200 000
Simpson investment (A) Bank (A) *Investment of funds*	200 000	200 000
Bank (A) Interest income (I) *Interest earned (C200 000 × 0.06)*	12 000	12 000

b) Balance sheet

MISTY MOUNTAIN COUNTRY CLUB BALANCE SHEET AT 31 DECEMBER 20X5		
		C
ASSETS		
Non-current assets		450 000
Tennis courts		100 000
6% fixed deposit investments		350 000
Current assets		
Bank		50 000
		500 000
FUNDS AND LIABILITIES		
Funds		500 000
Accumulated fund	50 000	
Balance at begining of year	14 000	
Surplus	36 000	
Fost fund	150 000	
Introduced	150 000	
Interest	27 000	
Coaching fees	(27 000)	
Daniels fund	100 000	
Introduced	100 000	
Simpson fund	200 000	
Introduced	200 000	
		500 000

20.2.2 Loans

All entities, business and non-business, may finance part of their operations or activities by borrowing from a financial institution.

20.3 Income from subscriptions and trading activities

Before considering the preparation of financial statements for a non-business entity, there are two important items on the income and expenditure statement which need explanation. These are the members' subscriptions and the results of trading activities.

20.3.1 Members' subscriptions

Subscriptions received from members represent income earned, and for some non-business entities this is the largest single source of income. Subscriptions must not be confused with entrance/joining fees, which, as previously described, are allocated directly to the accumulated fund.

In accounting for subscriptions, the following aspects need to be considered:

- subscriptions owing by members at the end of the *previous* period (an asset on the balance sheet, often referred to as *subscriptions receivable* or *subscriptions in arrear*);
- subscriptions received in advance from members at the end of the *previous* period (a *liability* on the balance sheet, often referred to as *subscriptions in advance*);
- subscriptions received from members during the current period in respect of:
    - amounts owing from the previous period;
    - amounts for the current period;
    - amounts received in advance for the following period.
- the membership of some members may be terminated for non-payment of their subscriptions;
- subscriptions owing by members at the end of the *current* period;
- subscriptions received in advance from members at the end of the *current* period;
- the subscription income earned during the current period and transferred to the income and expenditure account.

The following example illustrates the application of these items.

Example: Subscriptions

Simon Smart enjoys the finer pleasures in life and has a substantial wine collection. Simon joined the Chelsea Wine Tasters Club so as to indulge in his favourite pastime. At 1 January 20X7, the Chelsea Wine Tasters Club had 500 members. The annual subscription per member is C30. At 1 January 20X7, 50 members owed subscriptions for 20X6, and 31 members had paid their 20X7 subscriptions in advance. Of the members who owed 20X6 subscriptions, 10 cannot be traced and their membership of the club has been terminated. During the year ended 31 December 20X7, C14 400 was received in respect of subscriptions. Included in this amount is C330 in respect of 20X8.

You are required to:

Prepare the subscriptions account in the ledger of the club.

Solution: Subscriptions

Subscriptions

Details	*C*	*Details*	*C*
Subscriptions in arrears	1 500	Subscriptions in advance	930
		Bank	14 400
Income and expenditure	14 700	Bad debts	300
Subscriptions in advance	330	***Subscriptions in arrears***	***900***
	16 530		16 530

Workings

	C
Opening members	500
Less bad debts	(10)
Total members for the year	490
Membership fees earned (490 × C30)	14 700

Subscriptions in advance

Details	*C*	*Details*	*C*
Subscriptions	930	Balance b/d	930
Balance c/d	330	Subscriptions	330
	1 260		1 260
		Balance b/d	330

Subscriptions in arrears

Details	*C*	*Details*	*C*
Balance b/d	1 500	Subscriptions	1 500
Subscriptions	***900***	Balance c/d	900
	2 400		2 400
Balance b/d	900		

The balances in the subscriptions in arrears account and the subscriptions in advance account are transferred to the subscriptions account at the beginning of the period. These are typical reversing entries, previously explained in Chapter 5, *Recording internal transactions*. The cash received during the year of C14 400 is entered in the subscriptions account as well as the bad debts. (Note that the entry to account for the bad debts is to debit bad debts expense and to credit subscriptions.) This is because the opening balance in the subscriptions in arrears account was transferred to the subscriptions account as one of the reversing entries. The subscriptions in advance at the end of the year is given at C330 and the income earned is calculated at C14 700. The subscriptions in arrears of C900 is a balancing figure.

20.3.2 Trading activities

Most clubs trade with their members by providing food and beverage facilities. In larger clubs, this often includes a full restaurant and a bar. As these trading activities are not the main reason for the existence of the club, the gross profit or loss from such activities is included as a line item on the income and expenditure statement, along with subscription income, investment income and any other income earned during the period.

The concept of gross profit is the same as for a trading entity. The details of the gross profit computation for the specific trading activity can be shown on the face of the income and expenditure statement or as a note.

Example: Trading activities in a non-business entity

The Chelsea Wine Tasters Club caters for its members in the club canteen. The following is an extract of the canteen trading information of the Chelsea Wine Tasters Club for the year ended 31 December 20X8.

CHELSEA WINE TASTERS CLUB
(EXTRACT FROM) TRIAL
BALANCE AT 1 JANUARY 20X8

Description	*Dr*	*Cr*
Canteen inventory	7 550	
Canteen accounts payable		3 500

Additional information

- Receipts from canteen sales were C24 900.
- Payments to canteen suppliers were C6 800.

- Canteen inventory at 31 December 20X8 was C4 800.
- Canteen accounts payable at 31 December 20X8 was C2 200.

You are required to:

Prepare the canteen trading account for the year ended 31 December 20X8. (Include the canteen accounts payable, canteen inventory and canteen sales accounts in support of your answer.)

Example: Trading activities in a non-business entity

Canteen accounts payable

Details	C	*Details*	C
Bank	6 800	Balance b/d	3 500
Balance c/d	2 200	*Purchases*	*5 500*
	9 000		9 000
		Balance b/d	2 200

Canteen inventory

Details	C	*Details*	C
Balance b/d	7 550	Trading	7 550
Trading	4 800	Balance c/d	4 800
	12 350		12 350
Balance b/d	4 800		

Canteen sales

Details	C	*Details*	C
Trading a/c	24 900	Bank	24 900
	24 900		24 900

Canteen trading account

Details	C	*Details*	C
Canteen inventory (opening balance)	7 550	Canteen sales	24 900
Purchases	5 500	Canteen inventory (closing balance)	4 800
Income and expenditure	16 650		
	29 700		29 700

In a non-business entity, trading activities are disclosed as income if a profit is made from the activity, or an expense if a loss is incurred.

20.4 Producing information for a non-business entity

There are no statutory requirements relating to the financial statements prepared for a non-business entity. The information produced should meet the needs of members and be appropriate to the size and type of club, society or institution.

A ***receipts and payments statement***, prepared on the cash basis of accounting, or an ***income and expenditure statement***, prepared on the accrual basis of accounting, can be prepared, depending on the nature of the non-business entity.

20.4.1 Receipts and payments statement

A receipts and payments statement is used for smaller non-business entities which have no significant assets other than cash resources. It reports all the cash received and paid by a non-business entity over a specific period of time. All receipts and payments, whether of an income or capital nature, are included.

The receipts and payments statement is simply a summary of the cash journals of the entity and can be compared to a cash flow statement. As such, this statement will not disclose gains or losses on the disposal of assets, neither will the effect of consumable stores on hand be recognised. Internal transactions are not taken into account.

20.4.2 Income and expenditure statement

An income and expenditure statement is normally prepared by larger non-business entities which require more detailed reporting because of the more complex nature of their activities. The income and expenditure statement is prepared on the accrual basis of accounting and thus performs the same function and is prepared on the same principles as the statement of profit or loss of a business entity.

Example: Producing information for a non-business entity

Gary Good (Simon Smart's partner in Intense Sports) is a keen outdoor person. He has a dog that he trains at the German Shepherd Dog Training Club. The following information relates to the German Shepherd Dog Training Club.

The balance in the bank at 1 January 20X7 is C15 570. During the year ended 31 December 20X7, the club received the following:

	C
Subscriptions	30 600
Donations	3 200
Sale of raffle tickets	10 010
Proceeds of dog walk	3 250
Loan from W Katrigrah to pay for the new floodlights	15 000

The following amounts were paid:

	C
Rent for clubhouse	12 000
Lights and water	4 000
Expenses for dog walk	2 080
Secretarial expenses	5 200
Stationery	2 200
Wages	3 000
Refreshments	4 000
Socials	3 525
Prizes	3 900
Dog-training equipment (expected life five years)	5 000
Trailer (expected life four years)	7 000
Floodlights (expected life 20 years)	15 000

In addition to the above, C700 was owing to the club in respect of subscriptions at 31 December 20X7. Expenses in respect of the wages incurred but not yet paid totalled C220. The loan was taken out on 1 April 20X7, and interest is payable annually in arrears at 8 per cent per annum.

You are required to:

a) Prepare a receipts and payments statement for the German Shepherd Dog Club for the year ended 31 December 20X7.
b) Prepare an income and expenditure statement for the German Shepherd Dog Club for the year ended 31 December 20X7.

Solution: Producing information for a non-business entity

a) Receipts and payments statement

GERMAN SHEPHERD DOG TRAINING CLUB
RECEIPTS AND PAYMENTS STATEMENT
FOR THE YEAR ENDED 31 DECEMBER 20X7

	C
Cash received from	62 060
Subscriptions	30 600
Donations	3 200
Sale of raffle tickets	10 010
Proceeds from dog walk	3 250
Loan from W Katrigrah	15 000
Cash paid for	66 905
Rent for clubhouse	12 000
Lights and water	4 000
Expenses for dog walk	2 080
Secretarial expenses	5 200
Stationery	2 200
Wages	3 000
Refreshments	4 000
Socials	3 525
Prizes	3 900
Dog-training equipment	5 000
Trailer	7 000
Floodlights	15 000
Net decrease in cash	(4 845)
Cash at beginning of period	15 570
Cash at end of period	10 725

The statement simply reflects the cash received and paid. This is consistent with Chapter 2 where the difference between the cash basis and accrual basis of accounting was explained.

b) Income and expenditure statement

GERMAN SHEPHERD DOG TRAINING CLUB
INCOME AND EXPENDITURE STATEMENT
FOR THE YEAR ENDED 31 DECEMBER 20X7

	Workings	*C*
Income:		45 680
Subscriptions	*(30 600 + 700)*	31 300
Donations		3 200
Sale of raffle tickets		10 010
Dog walk	*(3 250 − 2 080)*	1 170
Expenses:		(42 445)
Rent for clubhouse		12 000
Lights and water		4 000
Secretarial expenses		5 200
Stationery		2 200
Wages		3 220
Refreshments		4 000
Socials		3 525
Prizes		3 900
Interest	*(15 000 × 0.08 × 9/12)*	900
Depreciation – dog-training equipment	*(5 000/5 years)*	1 000
Depreciation – trailer	*(7 000/4 years)*	1 750
Depreciation – floodlights	*(15 000/20 years)*	750
Surplus		3 235

Revision example

The following receipts and payments statement of the Greenfingers Gardening Club for the year ended 31 December 20X2 has been prepared by the club's treasurer.

GREENFINGERS GARDENING CLUB
RECEIPTS AND PAYMENTS STATEMENT
FOR THE YEAR ENDED 31 DECEMBER 20X2

	C
Cash received from	130 840
Seed sales	16 840
Sale of tickets to non-members for national flower show	4 000
Lawnmower sales	38 000
Subscriptions received	
– 20X1	800
– 20X2	67 200
– 20X3	4 000

	(142 200)
Cash paid for	
Purchase of tickets and brochures for national flower show	36 000
Seed purchases	19 000
Lawnmower purchases	54 000
Transport to national flower show	4 900
Rent of clubhouse	5 000
Gardening magazines for members' use	3 900
Secretarial expenses	9 400
Architect's fees for proposed new clubhouse	10 000
Net decrease in cash	(11 360)
Cash at beginning of period	8 760
Cash at end of period	(2 600)

The club's executive committee has decided that members should receive an income and expenditure statement for the year ended 31 December 20X2 and a balance sheet as at that date. The treasurer has extracted the following additional information from his records:

1 The assets and liabilities of the club (other than bank balances or overdrafts) are as follows:

	1 Jan 20X2	*31 Dec 20X2*
Plot of land for proposed new club building	20 000	20 000
Seed inventory, at cost	2 500	5 600
Accounts receivable – lawnmower sales	4 000	13 700
Members' subscriptions		
– in advance	2 400	4 000
– in arrears	1 200	1 600
Accounts payable		
– lawnmower supplier	8 000	1 700
– seed growers	1 100	3 400

2 The club obtains lawnmowers from a supplier and sells them at cost price to members. The club never holds any stock of lawnmowers.

3 Any member who had not settled his or her 20X1 arrear subscriptions by the end of 20X2 had his or her membership terminated on that date. Membership fees are C400 per year.

You are required to:

a) Prepare a trial balance for the club at 1 January 20X2.

b) Prepare an income and expenditure statement for the club for the year ended 31 December 20X2.

c) Prepare a balance sheet for the club at 31 December 20X2.

Solution: Revision example

a) Trial balance

TRIAL BALANCE AT 1 JANUARY 20X2

Description	*Dr*	*Cr*
Land	20 000	
Inventory of seeds	2 500	
Accounts receivable – lawnmowers	4 000	
Membership subscriptions in arrears	1 200	
Membership subscriptions in advance		2 400
Accounts payable – lawnmowers		8 000
Accounts payable – seed growers		1 100
Bank	8 760	
Accumulated fund		24 960
	36 460	36 460

b) Income and expenditure statement

GREENFINGERS GARDENING CLUB
INCOME AND EXPENDITURE STATEMENT
FOR THE YEAR ENDED 31 DECEMBER 20X2

		C	
Income			
Subscriptions			71 200
Expenses			(56 960)
Loss on sale of seeds		1 360	
Cost of flower show		36 900	
Rent		5 000	
Magazines		3 900	
Secretarial expenses		9 400	
Bad debts	*(1 200 – 800)*	400	
Surplus			14 240

c) Balance sheet

GREENFINGERS GARDENING CLUB
BALANCE SHEET
AT 31 DECEMBER 20X2

	C	
Assets		
Non-current assets		30 000
Land at cost	20 000	
Architect's fees	10 000	

	20 900
Current assets	
Inventory of seeds	5 600
Accounts receivable – lawnmowers	13 700
Members' subscriptions in arrears	1 600
	50 900

FUNDS AND LIABILITIES	
Funds	
Accumulated fund	39 200
Balance at beginning of year	24 960
Surplus	14 240
Current liabilities	11 700
Accounts payable – lawnmowers	1 700
Accounts payable – seed growers	3 400
Member subscriptions in advance	4 000
Bank overdraft	2 600
	50 900

Workings

Subscriptions

Details	C	*Details*	C
Subscriptions in arrears	1 200	Subscriptions in advance	2 400
Subscriptions in advance	4 000	Cash	72 000
		Bad debt	400
Income and expenditure	***71 200***	Subscriptions in arrears	1 600
	76 400		76 400

Flower show trading

Details	C	*Details*	C
Cost of tickets	36 000	Sale of tickets	4 000
Transport	4 900	Income and expenditure	36 900
	40 900		40 900

Accounts payable – seed growers

Details	C	*Details*	C
Cash	19 000	Balance b/d	1 100
Balance c/d	3 400	***Purchase***	**21 300**
	22 400		22 400
		Balance b/d	3 400

Seed trading

Details	C	*Details*	C
Inventory	2 500	Sales	16 840
Purchases	21 300	Inventory	5 600
		Income and expenditure	1 360
	23 800		23 800

Accounts receivable – lawnmowers

Details	C	*Details*	C
Balance b/d	4 000	Cash	38 000
Sales	***47 700***	Balance c/d	13 700
	51 700		51 700
Balance b/d	13 700		

Accounts payable – lawnmowers

Details	C	*Details*	C
Cash	54 000	Balance b/d	8 000
Balance c/d	1 700	***Purchases***	***47 700***
	55 700		55 700

Lawnmower trading

Details	*C*	*Details*	*C*
Inventory	—	Sales	47 700
Purchases	47 700	Inventory	—
	47 700		47 700

Bibliography

The Country Club Johannesburg. www.thecountryclub.co.za/About_the_Country_Club_ Johannesburg/CCJ_History.aspx (Accessed 12 July 2016).

21 Incomplete records

Business focus

In a survey conducted by the website Accounting WEB, 32 per cent of respondents said they were interested in finding a better system for dealing with clients' incomplete records.

Shoeboxes, black bin bags and other containers of documentation are still brought in by small clients to the offices of accountancy firms. For most accountants (or their patient bookkeepers), it is a very time-consuming task to take bundles of bank statements, invoices and receipts, and turn them into a set of financial statements. This requires a lot of data entry work – and then there is usually a follow-up task to spot any incorrect entries. The receipts and payments are then analysed in order to allocate them to the correct asset, liability, income or expense code.

Software does exist that can extract data from bank statements. This saves a considerable amount of time in data entry and has a much higher accuracy rate than human input. The data can then be analysed and exported to a system to produce the financial statements.

In this chapter

Ask any accountant about the shoebox or black bin bag clients (referred to in the Business focus) and they will relate to it! At some point in your training as an accountant, you will probably be required to prepare financial statements for such a client, which involves preparing financial statements from incomplete records. This chapter shows you how to do it.

Dashboard

- Look at the *Learning outcomes* so that you know what you should be able to do after studying this chapter.
- Read the *Business focus* to place this chapter's contents in a real-world context.
- Preview *In this chapter* to focus your mind on the contents of the chapter.
- Read the *text* in detail.
    - There is one comprehensive example that forms the basis of the chapter, which is in Section 21.3. You are advised to allocate a few hours to properly attempt this example without reference to the suggested solution. It incorporates revision of many of the concepts that you have learnt in earlier chapters. Once you have completed it, compare your solution to the suggested solution provided.

Learning outcomes

After studying this chapter, you should be able to do the following:

1 Describe the situations giving rise to incomplete records.
2 Prepare financial statements from incomplete records.

Incomplete records

21.1 Circumstances giving rise to incomplete records

No new concepts are taught in this chapter. An understanding of all the concepts taught in this book is required, however, to solve a problem where the accounting records are incomplete.

There are varying degrees of incompleteness in accounting records. The procedures to be adopted when preparing financial statements will depend upon the nature of the records or data available.

There are various reasons for the records of a business entity being incomplete, for example:

- The person compiling the records has inadequate accounting knowledge.
- Financial data is not available because it has been lost, destroyed or stolen.
- The information is incomplete due to fraud.
- Transactions are not recorded on a double-entry basis and therefore the records may not directly provide the information necessary to determine:
    - the financial performance of the entity;
    - the financial position of the entity.

It is often not feasible or practical for a small business to maintain accounting records using a full double-entry system of book keeping. Many small business entities are satisfied with the information they obtain from keeping a record of receipts and payments, and of their accounts receivable and accounts payable. A large number of owners of such entities may not know how to correctly record transactions. They may record the details of a transaction once only, if at all! Many transactions may not be recorded, leading to incomplete information. It is, however, necessary for such business entities to maintain some form of accounting records for the following reasons:

- The owners need to know if the business entity is profitable.
- It is necessary to determine the profits in order to submit information required by the tax authorities.

- In the case of a partnership, it is essential to know what profits have been made in order to allocate the profits to the partners.

Every set of circumstances that you will encounter, both in practice and in an exam, will be different. However, if the assignment is approached with the conceptual understanding that has been taught in this book, you should be able to reconstruct the information to produce a set of financial statements. A typical set of procedures to follow when preparing financial statements from incomplete records is given in the following section.

21.2 Preparation of financial statements from incomplete records

As mentioned above, the procedure for the preparation of financial statements from incomplete records will vary depending upon the circumstances. However, the following guidelines can be adapted to most situations:

- Establish or reconstruct the financial position at the end of the previous period.
- Reconstruct information relating to the key areas of performance measurement:
  - cash and credit sales;
  - cash and credit purchases;
  - other income and expenses.
- Identify any capital contributions from owners and any distributions to owners.
- Determine any relevant adjustments at the end of the period.
- Prepare the financial statements.

21.3 Practical application

Donald (a university friend of Simon's) assisted Michael and Minnie to form a private company called Euro Products Limited in October 20X5. They sell cuddly toys that are imported from France. Donald, who was an accountancy student, helped Michael and Minnie prepare the financial statements for the 20X6, 20X7 and 20X8 year ends. He, however, graduated from university at the end of 20X8 with honours and left the country to work in Paris. This put Michael and Minnie in a predicament and as a result, no accounting records have been kept for the 20X9 year. They have now come to you to ask for assistance in preparing the financial statements for the year ended 30 September 20X9. They have given you several boxes of papers from which you are able to ascertain the following:

 1 The opening balances per the trial balance at 1 October 20X8:

	C
Ordinary share capital	350 000
Retained earnings	74 525
Loans from shareholders	100 000
Land	400 000
Motor vehicles: cost	200 000

Furniture and fittings: cost	65 000
Computer equipment: cost	34 000
Motor vehicles: accumulated depreciation	97 600
Furniture and fittings: accumulated depreciation	15 400
Computer equipment: accumulated depreciation	17 000
Inventory	84 256
Accounts receivable	25 022
Insurance paid in advance	3 546
Cash on hand	547
Accounts payable	55 262
Lights and water payable	3 217
Telephone payable	654
Bank overdraft	98 713

2 They banked their takings periodically after paying the following amounts in cash:

Salaries	C1 000 per week (each, to Michael and Minnie)
Staff wages	C456 per week (each, to six employees)
Repairs and maintenance	C14 262

The cash on hand at 30 September 20X9 amounted to C963.

3 A loan was taken out on 1 March 20X9 from Scrooge Bank in order to purchase a new motor vehicle. The loan bears interest at 8 per cent pa, which is payable on 28 February each year in arrears. The loan is repayable in five years' time.

4 The land was revalued on 30 September 20X9 to C450 000. Euro Products had acquired the land two years ago with the intention of building its own premises.

5 Depreciation is provided as follows:

Motor vehicles – 20 per cent per annum on the reducing balance method
Furniture & fittings – 10 per cent per annum on cost
Computer equipment – 25 per cent per annum on cost

All the items have a nil residual value.

6 Bank account

6.1 Michael and Minnie were not able to record any transactions in a journal and ledger, and thus do not have a general ledger bank account. They were, however, able to work through the bank statements of Euro Products Limited and summarise the deposits and payments as follows:

	C
Balance per bank statement at 30/09/X8 (overdraft)	(76 616)
Deposits	
Deposits from sales	2 280 559
Deposit – loan	150 000
Payments	
Acquisition of motor vehicle	(150 000)
Delivery charges outwards	(134 876)

Insurance	(14 940)
Advertising	(52 548)
Lights and water	(40 817)
Rent	(54 000)
Repairs and maintenance	(46 874)
Salaries	(232 994)
Telephone	(7 806)
Payments to suppliers	(1 532 964)
Balance per bank statement at 30/09/X9	86 124

6.2 The bank statement balance at 30 September 20X8 did not agree with the balance in the 20X8 financial statements. There was an outstanding cheque for C22 097 (payable to Pop Importers Limited, which only cleared the bank on 7 October 20X8. There were no outstanding deposits at 30 September 20X8.

6.3 The last three cheques made out on 28 September 20X9 did not clear the bank account until 5 October 20X9:

Cheque no 1128	Accounts payable (Pop Importers)	C100 800
Cheque no 1129	Advertising	C3 981
Cheque no 1130	Repairs and maintenance	C2 121

6.4 An amount of C26 874 was deposited into the bank account on 30 September 20X9. This amount was processed by the bank on 1 October 20X9.

7 An inventory count was conducted at 30 September 20X9. The cost price of this inventory was C78 425. Included in the total inventory of C78 425 were items at a cost price of C26 896, which, according to Minnie, will only be able to be sold for C24 218. In addition to the inventory counted above, there was C12 658 of goods on consignment from Quick Quack Merchandise.

8 In September 20X9, for the first time Michael decided to import goods directly from an overseas supplier, Mars Distributors Plc. Goods to the value of C24 213 were ordered from the supplier in Paris on 15 September 20X9. The goods were transported by road from Paris to Rotterdam, where they were loaded onto a ship. The terms of the contract were FOB Rotterdam. The ship left Rotterdam on 29 September 20X9.

9 Michael and Minnie mark up their goods at 66.67 per cent above cost.

10 An accounts receivable listing was maintained on a monthly basis.

10.1 The list of accounts receivable at 30 September 20X9 was as follows:

Customer	*Amount*
	C
Floppy Dog Toy Shop	17 623
Goof's Toy Bar	35 241
The Little Cabin	4 213
Beautiful Animals	3 122
Daisy Toy World	24 125
Dark Wing Distributors	22 525
White Soft Toys	12 165
Total	119 014

10.2 At the year end, Dark Wing Distributors had become insolvent and no cash was expected to be received from them.

10.3 Beautiful Animals, on the other hand, had not paid their account for five months as they were experiencing financial difficulties.

11 Apart from the goods purchased from Mars Distributors Plc (see 8. above), Euro Products had only purchased their goods from one supplier, Pop Importers Limited.

11.1 The statement received from Pop Importers Limited at 30 September 20X9 showed the following:

Date	*Description*	*Doc*	*Debit*	*Credit*
31/08/X9	Balance		252 400	
04/09/X9	Payment	R254		151 200
10/09/X9	Invoice	I4785	21 222	
12/09/X9	Credit note	C478		4 252
25/09/X9	Invoice	I4821	20 712	
30/09/X9	Balance			138 882
			294 334	294 334

11.2 On scrutinising the statement you discover the following:

- The payment made on 28 September 20X9 had not been credited on the statement.
- The credit note C478 should have been for C4 225.
- The August statement balance was overstated by C400. This had still not been corrected on the September statement.

12 Michael informs you that they had failed to keep a record of inventory that they had taken as gifts for customers at Christmas. They are happy for you to determine the figure.

13 The telephone account and lights and water account for September 20X9 were only received in October:

Lights and water	C3 536
Telephone	C732

14 The amount paid for insurance was for a contract taken out on 1 January 20X9 in respect of insurance cover for the period ending 31 December 20X9.

15 The taxation expense for the year is C39 170.

You are required to:

a) Prepare a statement of comprehensive income for Euro Products Limited for the year ended 30 September 20X9.

b) Prepare a statement of changes in equity of Euro Products Limited for the period ended 30 September 20X9.

c) Prepare a statement of financial position of Euro Products Limited at 30 September 20X9.

Solution: Practical application

a) Statement of comprehensive income

EURO PRODUCTS LIMITED
STATEMENT OF COMPREHENSIVE INCOME
FOR THE YEAR ENDED 30 SEPTEMBER 20X9

			C
Sales	*(W1)*		2 662 375
Cost of sales	*(W4)*		(1 600 103)
Opening inventory 01/10/X8		84 256	
Purchases	*(1 594 114 − 2 520) (W3/4)*	1 591 594	
Goods available for sale		1 675 850	
Closing inventory 30/09/X9	*(W5)*	(75 747)	
Gross profit			1 062 272
Operating expenses			(932 846)
Advertising	*(52 548 + 3 981)*	56 529	
Bad debts	*(22 525 + 3 122)*	25 647	
Delivery expenses	*(Q6 given)*	134 876	
Depreciation	*(W6)*	52 980	
Gifts	*(W5)*	2 520	
Insurance	*(W7)*	14 751	
Lights and water	*(W8)*	41 136	
Rent	*(Q6 given)*	54 000	
Repairs and maintenance	*(46 874 + 14 262 + 2 121)*	63 257	
Salaries	*(232 994 + (2 × 1 000 × 52))*	336 994	
Telephone	*(W8)*	7 884	
Wages	*(456 × 6 × 52) (W2)*	142 272	
Finance cost			
Interest on loan	*(W8)*		(7 000)
Profit before taxation			122 426
Taxation	*(Note 15 given)*		(39 170)
Profit for the period			83 256
Other comprehensive income			
Revaluation			50 000
Total comprehensive income			133 256

b) Statement of changes in equity

EURO PRODUCTS LIMITED
STATEMENT OF CHANGES IN EQUITY
FOR THE YEAR ENDED 30 SEPTEMBER 20X9

	Ordinary share capital	*Revaluation surplus*	*Retained earnings*	*Total*
	C	C	C	C
Balance at 1 October 20X8	350 000	—	74 525	424 525
Total comprehensive income	—	50 000	83 256	133 256
Balance at 30 September 20X9	350 000	50 000	157 781	557 781

c) Statement of financial position

EURO PRODUCTS LIMITED
STATEMENT OF FINANCIAL POSITION
AT 30 SEPTEMBER 20X9

		Note	C
ASSETS			
Non-current assets	*(Q1, 3, 4 and W6)*	1	716 020
Land and buildings			450 000
Motor vehicles			214 420
Furniture and fittings			43 100
Computer equipment			8 500
Current assets			204 121
Inventory (W5)			75 747
Goods in transit	*(Q8 given)*		24 213
Accounts receivable	*(Q10: 119 014 − 22 525 − 3 122)*	2	93 367
Insurance paid in advance	*(W7)*		3 735
Cash and cash equivalents	*(W9: Bank) + (Q2: Cash – given)*	3	7 059
			920 141
EQUITY AND LIABILITIES			
Share capital and reserves			557 781
Ordinary share capital	*(Q1 given)*		350 000
Revaluation surplus	*(Q4 given: 450 000 – 400 000)*		50 000
Retained earnings			157 781
Non-current liabilities			250 000
Loans from shareholders			100 000
Loan from Scrooge Bank			150 000
Current liabilities			112 360
Accounts payable	*(W3: Pop Importers: 37 709) + (Q8: Mars: 24 213)*		61 922
Expenses payable		4	11 268
Taxation payable	*(Q15)*		39 170
			920 141

EURO PRODUCTS LIMITED
NOTES TO THE FINANCIAL STATEMENTS
AT 30 SEPTEMBER 20X9

1) Non-current assets

	Land	*Motor vehicles*	*Furniture and fittings*	*Computer equipment*	*Total*
	C	*C*	*C*	*C*	*C*
Cost					
30/09/X8	400 000	200 000	65 000	34 000	699 000
Acquisitions		150 000			150 000
Revaluation	50 000				50 000
30/09/X9	450 000	350 000	65 000	34 000	899 000

Accumulated depreciation					
30/09/X8	—	97 600	15 400	17 000	130 000
Depreciation	—	37 980	6 500	8 500	52 980
30/09/X9	—	135 580	21 900	25 500	182 980
Carrying amount	450 000	214 420	43 100	8 500	716 020

2) Accounts receivable

		C
Accounts receivable	*(Q10: 119 014 – 22 525)*	96 489
Allowance for doubtful debts	*(Q10)*	(3 122)
		93 367

3) Cash and cash equivalents

		C
Bank	*(W9)*	6 096
Cash	*(Q2 given)*	963
		7 059

4) Expenses payable

		C
Lights and water payable	*(W8)*	3 536
Telephone payable	*(W8)*	732
Interest payable		7 000
		11 268

Workings

1) Sales

Accounts receivable

Details	C	*Details*	C
Balance	25 022	Cash (W2)	2 568 383
Sales	***2 662 375***	Bad debts	22 525
		Balance*	96 489
	2 687 397		2 687 397
Balance	96 489		
Accounts receivable listing	119 014		
	(22 525)		
	*96 489		

The accounts receivable amount for the statement of financial position is calculated from the information in point 10 of the example. The listing shows that, at the year end, accounts receivable totalled C119 014. However, in 10.2, the information indicates that the amount owing by Dark Wing Distributors needs to be written off as a bad debt. By reconstructing the accounts receivable account, the sales figure is calculated.

2) Cash receipts

Cash

Details	*C*	*Details*	*C*
Balance	547	Bank (actual deposits)	2 280 559
Accounts receivable (cash received)	***2 568 383***	Bank (outstanding deposit)	26 874
		Wages (52 × 6 × 456)	142 272
		Repairs and maintenance	14 262
		Salary (1 000 × 2 × 52)	104 000
		Balance	963
	2 568 930		2 568 930

In order to reconstruct the accounts receivable account, the total cash received from customers is required. To calculate this, you need to reconstruct the cash account. The example gives the opening and closing balance of the cash account, the amount of cash banked, an outstanding deposit and amounts paid for in cash. The difference in the cash account is therefore the cash received from customers.

3) Purchases

Accounts payable: Pop Importers

Details	*C*	*Details*	*C*
Bank*	1 510 867	Balance	55 262
Bank (cheques in transit)	100 800	***Purchases*** (including inventory for gifts)	***1 594 114***
Balance**	37 709		
	1 649 376		1 649 376

	C
* Payments – from bank	1 532 964
X8 outstanding cheque	(22 097)
Current year's payments	1 510 867

** **Supplier's reconciliation**	*C*
Balance per supplier's statement	138 882
Adjusted for:	
Payment not on statement	(98 280)
Mistake on credit note	27
Gifts	(2 520)
Cast error from August not adjusted	(400)
Balance per accounting records	37 709

To determine the purchases figure, you need to reconstruct the accounts payable account. The example gives an opening balance but not a closing one, therefore the only way to determine the closing balance is to do a suppliers' reconciliation with the information from point 11 in the example. The rest of the information is supplied in the example – that is, payments made.

4) Gifts

Cost	*100.00*	
GP/MU	66.67	GP % = 66.67/166.67 = 40%
SP	166.67	

Therefore:

		C	
Cost	100.00	1 597 425*	
GP/MU	66.67		
SP	166.67	2 662 375	(W1)

	C
Cost of sales* (1 597 425 + 2 678)	1 600 103
Inventory 30 September 20X8 (opening)	84 256
Purchases (W3)	1 594 114
Inventory 30 September 20X9 (closing)	(75 747)
Gifts	(2 520)

Using sales and the GP %, cost of sales (before the inventory write-down) is first calculated. The cost of sales is then adjusted to the amount of the inventory write-down of C2 678, then by using the opening inventory, purchases and closing inventory, the cost of gifts is calculated.

5) Inventory

		C
Inventory at cost		78 425
Inventory write-down	(26 896 – 24 218)	(2 678)
Final inventory balance		75 747

6) Depreciation

				C
Motor vehicles – old	20%	C102 400	(1 year)	20 480
Motor vehicles – new	20%	C150 000	(7 months)	17 500
Furniture and fittings	10%	C65 000	(1 year)	6 500
Computer equipment	25%	C34 000	(1 year)	8 500
				52 980

7) Insurance paid in advance

Insurance paid in advance

Details	C	*Details*	C
Balance b/d	3 546	**Insurance expense**	***14 751***
Bank	14 940	Balance c/d*	3 735
	18 486		18 486
Balance b/d	3 735		

*14 940 × 3/12 = 3 735

By reconstructing the insurance paid in advance account and using the information in point 14 of the example, you can determine the insurance expense for the statement of comprehensive income and the insurance paid in advance for the statement of financial position.

8) Expenses payable

Telephone payable

Details	C	*Details*	C
Bank	7 806	Balance b/d	654
Balance c/d	732	***Telephone expense***	***7 884***
	8 538		8 538
		Balance b/d	732

Lights and water payable

Details	C	*Details*	C
Bank	40 817	Balance b/d	3 217
Balance c/d	3 536	***Lights and water expense***	***41 136***
	44 353		44 353
		Balance b/d	3 536

Interest on loan

C150 000 (0.08 × 7/12 months)	C7 000

Total expenses payable	C
Telephone	732
Lights and water	3 536
Interest	7 000
	11 268

The telephone and lights and water expenses are calculated by reconstructing the respective liability accounts. Interest is calculated from the date that the loan was taken out.

9) Bank reconciliation

				C
Balance per bank statement				86 124
Less outstanding cheques	1128	Supplier	100 800	
	1129	Advertising	3 981	
	1130	Repairs and maintenance	2 121	(106 902)
Add outstanding deposit				26 874
Balance per Euro Products' records				6 096

To determine the bank balance for the statement of financial position, a bank reconciliation needs to be performed using the information in point 6 of the example.

Bibliography

Incomplete records: New approaches to an old problem. www.accountingweb.co.uk/article/incomplete-records-new-approaches-old-problem/546379 (Accessed 19 September 2014).

Index

The page numbers in **bold** are the primary reference for the entry.